MARTIN HENGEL is Professor of New
Testament and Early Christianity at the
University of Tübingen. His many academic
awards and distinctions include the Fellowship
of the British Academy, the Fellowship of
Heidelberg Academy of Science and an
Honorary Doctorate of Divinity from Durham
University. He is the author of many
publications including *Acts and the History of
Earliest Christianity*; *Jews, Greeks and Barbarians*;
Judaism and Hellenism and *The Charismatic Leader
and His Followers*.

THE ZEALOTS

THE ZEALOTS

INVESTIGATIONS INTO THE JEWISH FREEDOM
MOVEMENT IN THE PERIOD FROM HEROD I UNTIL
70 A.D.

BY

MARTIN HENGEL

Institutum Judaicum, Tübingen

TRANSLATED BY

DAVID SMITH

T. & T. CLARK

EDINBURGH

Authorised English Translation © T. & T. Clark Ltd, 1989.
Originally published under the title *Die Zeloten: Untersuchungen zur Jüdischen Freiheitsbewegung in der Zeit von Herodes I. bis 70 n. Chr.* © E. J. Brill, Leiden/Cologne, 1961; second improved and enlarged edition 1976.

Typeset by C. R. Barber and Partners, Fort William,
printed and bound in the U.K. by Billing & Sons Ltd., Worcester

for

T. & T. CLARK LTD,
59 George Street, Edinburgh EH2 2LQ

Authorised English Translation first printed 1989

British Library Cataloguing in Publication Data

Hengel, Martin
The Zealots : investigations into
the Jewish freedom movement in the
period from Herod I until 70 A.D.
1. Zealots (Jewish party)—History
I. Title   II. Die Zeloten. *English*
296.8' 1   BM175.Z4

ISBN 0-567-09372-7 (CASED)

ISBN 0-567-29372-6 (PAPERBACK)

TO MY PARENTS

FOREWORD

I submitted the present work as a dissertation to the Evangelisch-theol. Fakultät of the University of Tübingen. My immediate stimulus was the translation of Josephus that had been made by Professors O. Michel and O. Bauernfeind, a task in which I had been permitted to collaborate as a research assistant. I am especially indebted to my supervisor of studies, Professor Michel, for his constant and lively interest in my work and for the understanding and patience he has continued to show in its progress, despite the many interruptions and adversities that occurred in the course of it. I have also to thank him for the many stimuli that he provided and the valuable suggestions that he made. I also owe a debt of gratitude to Professor Bauernfeind, my old friend Dr Betz, Dr Gese and Rabbi Dr Geis in Karlsruhe for the many helpful conversations I had with them. I finished the book away from the University, while I was doing a very different type of work in industry. There are certain gaps in the bibliography and these were caused by difficulties in obtaining the necessary books and articles. However, I am deeply indebted to the staff of the Württemberg Library in Stuttgart, who were quite tireless and did everything possible to supply me with the books I needed. I have also to thank the Institutum Judaicum of Tübingen and Dr Betz and Herrn Schmidt in particular for reading and correcting my text. Finally, my debt to my dear wife simply cannot be expressed in mere words.

AALEN, 1 March 1961   Martin Hengel

FOREWORD TO THE SECOND EDITION

Various printing and other errors have been corrected, new sources have been added, the bibliography has been extended and several smaller changes and additions have been made to the text in this second edition. I have also provided an answer to my critics in a supplement at the end of the book. I have, however, made no substantial alterations to the text. This seemed unnecessary, as I would still defend the results of my original dissertation submitted to the University of Tübingen fourteen years after first publishing it.

I have unfortunately not had time to consider the results of David M. Rhoads' very interesting dissertation presented to Duke University in 1973, *Some Jewish Revolutionaries in Palestine from 6 A.D. to 73 A.D. According to Josephus*, but I hope that it will be possible for me to make up for this omission as soon as the book which is announced by Fortress Press appears. I must confess, however, that I remain unconvinced by the author's attempt to play down the importance of the Jewish freedom movement *prior* to the outbreak of the Jewish War in 66 A.D. on the basis of the evidence in Josephus. As an apologist for Judaism, Josephus was vitally concerned to minimize as far as possible the influence of the Jewish revolutionaries who were opposed to Rome before the Jewish War broke out and to present its effects on the people as unimportant. This applies particularly to the period between Quirinius' census or the appearance of Judas of Galilee in 6 A.D. and the death of King Agrippa I in 44 A.D., a period reported only fragmentarily or in the form of anecdotes by Josephus. The latter's failure to say anything about the Jewish freedom movement of that period can only be seen in the same light as his silence about the Christians. He also tells us very little about the Jewish parties and their leaders and there is no reference of any kind in any of his writings to the existence of a Teacher of Righteousness in the Qumran Community, Simeon b. Shetach, the schools of Hillel and Shammai, the early Christian Church and its mission or even to the names of the leading contemporary Pharisaical teachers up to and including Johanan b. Zakkai. Is this, however, sufficient reason for causing us to doubt that they existed and were active in history? Josephus was a thoroughly tendentious writer and we have to weigh what he says and what he omits in the light of his own interests. This, of course, makes him a very important model for the student of polemics in the ancient world. Each one of his statements must be critically examined for its tendency.

I have to thank my colleague Helmut Merkel, Dr G.O. Neuhaus and Herrn Dr Fritz Herrenbrück for reading through this book and the last named especially for his careful compilation of the lengthy index and his corrections to the text.

TÜBINGEN, January 1975   Martin Hengel

FOREWORD TO THE ENGLISH TRANSLATION OF
THE ZEALOTS

I decided in September 1955, thirty-two years ago, that the Jewish freedom movement during the period between Herod and the Jewish War should be the theme of my dissertation. After spending one university year in the Evangelical *Stift* at Tübingen as a 'coach' (*Repetent*), I had become a research assistant, working under Professor Otto Michel. One of my tasks was to help him in the preparation of his translation of Josephus' *Jewish War*, which had by that time reached the end of Book I. I was struck by the fact that the problems of the Jewish freedom movement, which had brought about the Jewish insurrection in 66 A.D., had so far never been dealt with in a fundamental way in the form of a monograph. The theme attracted me also because, at that time, that is, in the mid-nineteen-fifties, there was no special interest in Germany in the Jewish environment in which early Christianity had come about and in the social and political questions connected with that environment. There was clearly a great need for this gap to be filled — a need that was strengthened by the recent finds that had been made at that time at Qumran. The emphasis in New Testament research in those days was on hermeneutical problems; the demythologization debate was particularly prominent and the question of the influence of a 'pre-Christian gnosis' was being widely discussed.

Even when I was teaching in the Evangelical *Stift* I had disliked this exegetical euphoria with its one-sided orientation towards Marburg University and its speculative tendency to dismiss too lightly the true relationships between the sources. I therefore decided to begin my own first work at a completely different point of departure, to let the Jewish sources speak for themselves and at the same time to throw light on an area to which very little attention had hitherto been given, at least in German scholarship. In that respect, I was part of an established Tübingen tradition. Adolf Schlatter, the founder of my present chair at Tübingen University, had not only made essential progress in our theological understanding of the Jewish historian — he had also stressed the importance of the rabbinic sources for our understanding of early Christianity and its roots. He had achieved this in his numerous publications and in particular in his great commentaries.

The task that I had set myself provided me with the opportunity to immerse myself in both these fields, which had been complemented by the recently discovered Qumran texts and the Pseudepigrapha. As I proceeded with the work, it also became clear to me that research into ancient Judaism and the early period of Christianity was inseparable from and essentially dependent on a knowledge of the surrounding history of the Hellenistic and Roman period. It was the work of a largely self-taught man. I had completed my studies relatively quickly in four university years, from 1947 to 1951, that is, in the difficult time following the end of the Second World War. Afterwards, the circumstances prevailing at the time had obliged me to spend some time first in Church work (1951/52) — the resulting experience was very valuable — and then, though not by choice, in the textile industry and in sales management (1945/6 and 1953/4). At the Evangelical *Stift*, I had to teach first philosophy and then introduction to the New Testament. Josephus and the rabbinic sources were still completely unknown territory for me. There were no grants available then for intensive specialized studies and I had to make my own way almost unaided in the field of rabbinic literature. There was at that time too little help and encouragement for specialization, whereas now there is sometimes perhaps too much.

During this all too brief novitiate in critical study at Tübingen, which only lasted for two and a half years, the sword of Damocles was always hanging over me: the threat that I would have to go back to industry. With a heavy heart, I left Tübingen in March 1957 and thought it would be for ever. I had written up about twenty per cent of the material and had made excerpts of the most important sources — there were no photocopies at that time! I took my manuscript and materials with me when I returned of necessity to the completely different environment of industry and management, firmly — I might almost say, desperately — resolved, whatever happened, to finish the work I had begun. That I succeeded in doing this — in spite of inexpressible difficulties, far from the university with its many stimuli to study and its abundant library resources and following a totally different and very exhausting profession — I owe to a very great extent to the understanding, encouragement and patience of my wife.

The work that I submitted as my dissertation in 1959 appeared in print in 1961. A second, improved and enlarged edition appeared in 1976. I have placed this little autobiographical look at the past at the beginning of the English translation because this work is for me personally very much more than simply a first book that was followed by others in a relatively straight line. What I learned from it was an intimate association with ancient Jewish and Graeco-Roman sources and it was perhaps good that, for reasons of time and because many books were not available to me, I had to concentrate principally on those sources. At the same time, quite contrary to all human expectations, it also determined my future way of life and made it possible for me to return at the end of 1964 to the historical and theological study that I loved so much.

I was surprised by the positive reception of my dissertation by the 'scholarly world' when it was published. I responded to a few scholars who criticized my work from the beginning of the nineteen-seventies onwards in an Appendix (p. 380), which was published in a shorter form in the Festschrift written in honour of O. Michel (p. 380, n. 1). I was not very convinced by the objections that were made at that time and since then, although several younger authors have dealt assiduously with the theme, there have been hardly any fresh criticisms. One has the impression that the controversy is basically going round in a circle. Were I therefore to write the book again today, I would not make any far-reaching change in the fundamental theses of the work, although I have in details come to some new points of view. The reader can find information about the contributions made to the debate in the past twelve years in the Supplementary Bibliography (p. 430).

I would like to deal with a couple of fundamental points in the following paragraphs.

(1) When I was writing *The Zealots*, works with a strongly historico-political and socio-historical flavour were not particularly highly regarded. That did not trouble me very much at the time and I also tried to express the social problems of first-century Judaea in my work. In this respect, research has advanced in a particularly intensive way and my work could certainly be amplified and extended here. In the meantime, a radical change has taken place in the situation in research — to say nothing of the intellectual fashion. The main, indeed the overwhelming emphasis in any self-respecting work, whether it is published in East Germany or in the United States, will be now on the social reasons for the preparation for and the outbreak of the Jewish War. It can — at least partly — base itself on Josephus, who was not interested in tracing the catastrophe back to movements motivated by religion. He was far more concerned, for apologetic reasons, to make a minority of criminals, 'bandits' who were striving for possessions and power and who belonged to the dregs of society, and at the same time inefficient and corrupt procurators responsible for the fall of the Holy City. The insurrectionary groups appear then principally as relatively diffuse social revolutionaries who were bound together only by hatred of the exploitative system of an unjust social order sanctioned by the Romans. This failure to understand the fundamental significance of religious

views and hopes in Judaism during the early Roman imperial period,
which also determined the political activity of radical groups, must
inevitably lead to an erroneous judgement of that fascinating and tragic
epoch in Jewish history in which Christianity emerged from Jewish
roots and at the same time Jewish civilization nearly destroyed itself in
three revolts in Judaea (and Egypt).

Life was certainly no better socially for the non-Jewish peasant in
Syria, Egypt and Asia Minor than for the Jewish peasant in the
motherland. They would probably both have profited much more from
the imperial *Pax Romana*, which brought an end to the unending wars
and civil wars of the late Hellenistic period and introduced an —
undoubtedly relative — legal certainty, which did not completely
exclude the *peregrini*. No insurrections took place there between
Augustus and Hadrian of a violence comparable to that of the three
Jewish revolts. Leo Mildenberg has shown in a very convincing way in
his great monograph, *The Coinage of the Bar Kokhba War*, (*Typos.
Monographien zur antiken Numismatik* 4), Aarau, Frankfurt a.M. and
Salzburg 1984, see Gnomon 58, 1986, 326–331, that the economic
relationships of the Jewish peasants were by no means so bad on the eve
of the revolt of Bar Koseba that their uprising could be based on social
distress. This applies particularly to Judaea in the first century A.D.,
where considerable wealth had accumulated in Jerusalem, which had
been developed by Herod as a world-wide place of pilgrimage of unique
importance.

Social distress certainly *also* played at times an essential part in the
prehistory of the first revolt and especially in its further course, but it was
not the dominant and main reason. It was not a revolt of the rural
proletariat fighting for its survival. The Jewish uprisings can also hardly
be compared with the uprisings that took place in other parts of the
Roman Empire in the first century: the seven-year war of the Numidian
Tacfarinas (17–24 A.D.) and the revolt of the Batavian Julius Civilis and
Julius Classicus of the Treveri in 69 A.D., all of whom had first been
Roman officers, the disturbances caused by the predatory Isaurians in
Asia Minor or the Bucolics in the marshes of the Nile Delta and so on.
The ultimate cause of all three suicidal wars is in the end undoubtedly to
be found in the Jewish religion, which was unique in the ancient world
with its theocratic ideal and its especially pronounced eschatological
expectation around the turn of the millennium. It is not purely by
chance that the only occurrence of the word θεοκρατία in antiquity is in
Josephus (*Ap* 2,165; see also p. 376, n. 315) to name the special form of
the Jewish state, whereas Philo speaks of God's μοναρχία in connection

with the first commandment. If these terms are used in a politically coarser sense under the rubric 'rule of God', it is surely only a step to Judas the Galilaean, with whom — even in the opinion of Josephus himself— that religious and political ideology that led to the catastrophe of 70 A.D. had its beginning. T. Mommsen described this state of affairs both concisely and precisely in his very impressively written chapter on 'Judaea and the Jews' in the fifth volume of his work on Roman History and quite correctly referred at the beginning of the same chapter to the 'Mosaic theocracy' and the controversial new form that it assumed after the Maccabaean uprising.

Another outstanding historian, Jacob Burkhardt, not only named the Jews, in the chapter on 'the state as conditioned by religion' ('Der Staat in seiner Bedingtheit durch die Religion') in his *Weltgeschichtliche Betrachtungen*, as occupying the first place among 'the greatest, the historically most important and the most powerful theocracies', but also regarded this as an essential characteristic of their history: 'One sees the *Jews* again and again striving towards theocracy throughout all the changes that took place in their history' (Kröner, ed. R. Merx, 1935, 108). He also calls the Jewish revolts both briefly and pertinently 'outbursts of *religious* anger' (*ibid.*, 166; my italics), which can, for this reason, be distinguished from the revolts in the other provinces that were socially conditioned. Anyone who fails to recognize this special religious character of the Jewish revolts against Rome — all of which had an eschatological and messianic aspect — and at the same time their uniqueness, will not be able to judge the events in Judaea between 6 and 70 A.D. in accordance with the facts. The power of fanatical Islamic fundamentalism that is so frightening for enlightened Europeans and Americans today may well serve as an example to enable us to understand the feelings that the Greeks and Romans experienced when confronted with the *furor Iudaicus*. Tacitus' statements in his *Hist* 5,5.1–3; 13.3 (see p. 384) speak for themselves.

(2) For this reason, we are bound to go further and examine the religious ideology that determined the Jewish freedom movement, despite its fragmentation from the beginning of the Jewish Revolt itself. A fundamental denial of the existence of such an ideology would certainly lead to a wrong assessment of the situation. A fundamental importance has undoubtedly to be attributed to the figure of Judas the Galilaean. Zeal for God and his law, which led to the honorary title of 'Zealot', must also have played an essential part. Josephus, it is true, gives the name 'Zealot' from the outbreak of the revolt — *almost* — only to one group in Jerusalem, that is, to the overwhelmingly priestly ζηλωταί.

There are, however, exceptions to this and in particular the first mention
of them in *Bell* 2,444, where the name is applied to the followers of
Judas' son, Menahem, a group of men whom Josephus as a rule describes
as *Sicarii* (a word derived from the Latin *sicarius*, assassin). This was
certainly not a name that the members of this earliest insurrectionary
group originally gave themselves.

I have gone into all these questions so exhaustively that I am bound to
ask whether individual critics have really read what I have said about the
matter. I am for this reason particularly grateful for this English
translation, because it may possibly make it easier for certain scholars to
take cognizance of arguments. If, for example, it is asserted that the use
of the term λῃσταί, which is so striking in Josephus' work, should be
applied for social reasons, not to insurgents who were motivated by
religion, but to ordinary robbers, then it is easy to show, by referring to
Rengstorf's concordance, that, with only one exception (*Ant* 9,183 = 4
Reg 13,20f.), these 'robbers' only appeared at the beginning of the
Roman rule and, more precisely, with the victory of the young Herod
over the 'Robber Captain' Hezekiah, who was quite certainly not an
ordinary robber captain (*Bell* 1,204 = *Ant* 14,159). As in the case of his
entire presentation of Herod in his *Jewish War* and in *Antiquities*, 14–17
Josephus has here taken over the linguistic usage of his notoriously pro-
Roman and anti-Jewish source Nicolaus of Damascus, who was
influenced by the Roman linguistic rule, that is, to describe all irregular
insurgents acting against the power of Rome as *latrones* and not as *hostes*
(see p. 382). Josephus generally uses this defamatory way of speaking for
his own work, including the *Vita*. Even today, in the official jargon of
the government of Afghanistan and its 'protecting power', the
Mujahedin who are fighting for their Islamic faith and for the freedom
of their homeland are called 'bandits'. How often events repeat
themselves in the history of man!

As for the problem of 'party names', it is possible to show by means of
numerous examples in the modern world how variable and
interchangeable they are. The same also applies to ancient Judaism: 'We
are confronted ... by a cardinal problem when we compare between
Josephus' description of the aristocratic non-strict Sadducees and the
Halakhoth ascribed to the Sadducees in the Talmud, for they do not
tally'. In the as yet unpublished Halakhic letter that was presumably
written by the Teacher of Righteousness to the 'godless high-priest', the
author pleads in favour of the Halakhoth, as attributed in the Talmudic
sources to the Sadducees. Who, then, were the true 'Sadducees'? Was the
Talmudic tradition or was Josephus right? Or were both right? In the

same letter, the author stresses: 'We have separated ourselves from the multitude of the peo(ple) (*pršnw* mrwb h'[m])'. Who, then, were the true 'Pharisees'? (see E. Qimron and J. Strugnell, 'An Unpublished Halakhic Letter from Qumran', *The Israel Museum Journal* 14 (1985), 9–12, especially 10).

In a word, then, I believe that it is highly likely that the followers of Judas the Galilaean thought of themselves as the true 'Zealots' — for God and his law — and regarded later groups that took over this name and may perhaps have broken away from them as apostates. The fact that Josephus — who, together with several rabbinic and patristic references which confirm my supposition (see p. 74), is our only (and unfortunately very tendentious and indeed unreliable) source — withholds this *religious honorary title*, the origin of which he of course knew very well (*Bell* 7,269ff.; 4,106f.), from them, the main culprits, may well be connected with its being too positive a title for these criminals. In his opinion, they were only common 'murderers', in other words, *Sicarii*.

I hope, then, that this English translation of my book may give a few new impulses to the debate about the Jewish freedom movement up to the first war, a debate that seems to have reached a dead-end.

I have to thank the publishers and the translator for undertaking a difficult task. I would also like to thank my students, Ulrich Heckel and Anna Maria Schwemer, Institutum Judaicum, Tübingen, for proofreading, and especially Paul Cathey, Institutum Judaicum Delitzschianum, Münster, for proofreading and editing the translation.

TÜBINGEN, July 1988   Martin Hengel

CONTENTS

INTRODUCTION

1. The History of Research

The history of Palestinian Judaism from the time of Pompey's conquest of Jerusalem until the Revolt of Bar Koseba about two hundred years later is deeply marked by the Jews' struggle for religious and political freedom. It was during the middle period of those two centuries — from the time when Judaea became a Roman province until the destruction of Jerusalem - that the so-called 'Zealots' appeared as exponents of that struggle for freedom.

Other late Jewish parties and sects such as the Pharisees, the Sadducees, the Essenes and even the early Palestinian Christians have been studied, often in great detail, on numerous occasions, but there have been relatively few exhaustive studies of the freedom movement of the Zealots. The old masters of Jewish historiography, Graetz[1] and Derenbourg,[2] devoted special attention, it is true, to the development of the Jewish struggle for independence and added a great deal of information to the data provided by Josephus by examining the rabbinic sources. Nonetheless, it cannot be denied that the essence and the solidarity of the Zealot freedom movement could never be fully elaborated in these general treatments of the subject. K. Kohler attempted to do this in his article 'Zealots' in *The Jewish Encyclopaedia* and later in an essay in the *Festschrift* in honour of A. Harkavy.[3] He was, however, so limited by space that all that he was really able to do was to assemble the material, although he carried out this task in a masterly way. Schürer gave very little consideration in his great historical work

---

[1] H. Graetz, *Geschichte der Juden*, III, 1/2, *Geschichte der Judäer von dem Tode Makkabis bis zum Untergang des jüdischen Staates*, 5th. ed., rev. M. Braun, Leipzig 1905, see Index under 'Zeloten' and nn. 24,26 and 29.

[2] J. Derenbourg, *Essai sur l'histoire et la géographie de la Palestine d'après les Thalmuds et les autres sources rabbiniques. Première Partie: Histoire de la Palestine depuis Cyrus jusqu'à Adrien*, Paris 1867, 237ff.

[3] See *JE* 12 (1906), 639-643 and the article 'Wer waren die Zeloten oder Kannaim?', *Festschrift in Ehren des Dr A. Harkavy*, Petersburg 1909, 6-18. In his *Jewish Sects and Parties in the Time of Jesus*, London 1925, J.W. Lightley also provides a portrait of the Zealots, but confines himself almost exclusively to the data supplied by Josephus. His work is therefore clearly retrograde in comparison with that of the Jewish scholars.

to the Zealot movement,[4] but Adolf Schlatter discussed the theological aspects of the movement in particular in several of his works. He also clearly recognized the importance of the Zealots for our understanding of the New Testament and the gospels especially.[5] Robert Eisler's constant theme was Zealotism and the New Testament,[6] but, despite his 'speculative genius',[7] the breadth of his learning and the wealth of striking individual observations, his results can hardly be regarded as valid. Joseph Klausner approached the question of the Zealots from the distinctive point of view of Jewish nationalism. The two final volumes of his 'History of the Second Temple' contain what is probably the most detailed summary of the historical material concerning the Zealots, but again this is presented within the framework of a general treatment of late Jewish history.[8]

In addition to the authors whose work I have mentioned so far, there are many others who have expressed opinions more briefly about the Zealots. The very diversity of these views points to the fact that there has been little agreement about the form and development of this movement. Zealotism has, for example, been regarded by some scholars partly at least as no more than a general tendency within late Judaism.[9] On the other hand, the Zealot party has also been seen as no more than a single group within the Jewish War.[10] There has always been a temptation to misinterpret Zealotism in a nationalistic political sense.[11] More recently, W.R. Farmer has pointed to the close connection between the Zealots and the tradition of the Maccabaean period, but he too has left many important questions open in his specialized study. What he failed above all to emphasize sufficiently was the problem of the

---

[4] *History of the Jewish People in the Age of Jesus Christ*, Edinburgh 1973-86, 1, 382, 462ff.

[5] *Geschichte Israels von Alexander dem Grossen bis Hadrian*, 3rd. ed., Stuttgart 1925, 259ff. and *passim*, see Index; 'Die Theologie des Judentums nach dem Bericht des Josephus', *BFChTh.M*, 2nd. Series 11, 3rd. and 4th. eds. (1926), see Index; *Die Geschichte des Christus*, Stuttgart 1921, 304ff. In his article , ζῆλος, *TD* 2, 884ff., A. Stumpff for the most part uses Schlatter's results.

[6] Ἰησοῦς βασιλεὺς οὐ βασιλεύσας, *die messianische Unabhängigkeitsbewegung vom Aufreten Johannes des Täufers* ..., 2 Vols., Heidelberg 1929/30.

[7] 'Kombinatorische Magie'; M. Dibelius described R. Eisler's method in this way; see *ThBl* 6 (1927), 219.

[8] היסטוריה של הבית השני, 4th. ed., Jerusalem 5714 + 1954, see Index 5, 317, under קנאים. See also J. Klausner, *Jesus of Nazareth*, 1925, 168, 203ff.

[9] See, for example, C. Guignebert and Bo Reicke; see below, p. 82, n. 33.

[10] See especially F.J. Foakes Jackson and K. Lake, the editors of *The Beginnings of Christianity*, 1, *The Acts of the Apostles*, London 1920, 1, 421ff.

[11] See, for example, S. Dubnow and H. Preisker; see below, 141.

possible eschatological character of both movements.[12]

The manuscript discoveries of the Dead Sea led several scholars to suppose that the authors of the scrolls should be identified with the Zealots.[13] This view could not, however, be sustained, since there were powerful archaeological, comparative and historical reasons against it.[14] It is therefore hardly necessary for me to discuss here the often very forced connections that were at one time made between Qumran and the Zealots.

2. The Structure and Aim of the Presentation

In this book I have tried to find a way from the sources to an understanding of the particular religious nature and the historical growth of the Zealot movement during the more restricted period between Herod I and the Jewish War. Throughout, I have also attempted to interpret the sources in the light of the corresponding religious views in late Judaism and rabbinism generally. The sources are, however, so diverse and fragmentary that frequently no more than simply a degree of probability can be reached in the case of individual results and we very often have to be satisfied with hypotheses that can be substantiated only to a very limited extent. Despite these very real difficulties, I have sought to achieve as complete a picture of the Zealot movement as possible.

The structure of my study can be summarized as follows: (1) I begin with a critical examination of the sources and in particular of the principal source, the works of Josephus. (2) I then consider from the philological and historical points of view the names given by various

---

[12] W.R. Farmer, *Maccabees, Zealots and Josephus, An Inquiry into Jewish Nationalism in the Greco-Roman Period*, New York 1956; see also the same author's article, 'Judas, Simon and Athronges', *NTS* 4 (1957/58), 147ff.

[13] The first to express this view was H.E. del Medico, *Deux manuscrits de la Mer Morte* (1951) and *The Riddle of the Scrolls* (1958). J. Klausner, *Hist* 5, 324ff., also suspected that there was a connection between the Scrolls and the Zealots. C. Roth, *The Historical Background of the Dead Sea Scrolls*, Oxford 1958, and G.R. Driver, *The Judaean Scrolls*, Oxford 1965, are prominent among those who have supported this thesis more recently.

[14] H.H. Rowley, 'Qumran, the Essenes and the Zealots', *Von Ugarit nach Qumran, Beiträge zur alttestamentlichen und altorientalischen Forschung, O. Eissfeldt dargebracht*, Berlin 1958, 184-192, has been especially prominent in showing how untenable these suppositions are. See also the number of theories quoted by M. Burrows, *The Dead Sea Scrolls*, 1956, 123-186. For the refutation of the hypothesis that the Zealots were the authors of the Scrolls, see the same author's *More Light on the Dead Sea Scrolls*, 1958, 232-245, 271-274, and R. de Vaux, 'Essenes or Zealots?', *NTS* 13 (1966/67), 89-104.

sides to the Jewish freedom movement. (3) This leads on to a consideration of the sect of the 'fourth philosophy' founded by Judas of Galilee. I begin by attempting to bring out as clearly as possible the independent character and the organization of the party that originated with Judas and then go on to discuss the distinctive features of this new sect: its demand for the exclusive rule of God, co-operation with God in the struggle for freedom and a rejection of the census. What emerges from this investigation is the primarily religious character of this new movement.

(4) The following chapter is devoted to an examination of the concept of 'zeal'. My point of departure is the understanding of Phinehas in the Jewish tradition. The meaning of zeal in contemporary Judaism generally is then considered and this is followed by an analysis of 'zeal' in connection with the Zealot movement, divided into its two aspects of zeal for the law and zeal for the sanctuary. This fourth chapter concludes by showing that this zeal has to be seen as an eschatological intensification of the law.

(5) The various eschatological aspects of the Zealot movement are examined next and related to the wider context of Jewish eschatology. The essential features here are prophetic enthusiasm and the idea of a pre-messianic time of suffering. It is in the light of these features that such concrete factors as the renunciation of possessions, flight into the desert and an unconditional readiness to die as a martyr can be explained. The way to the rule of the Messiah lies via a Holy War. The ultimate aim is Israel's government of the world.

(6) The final chapter provides a survey of the historical development of the Jewish freedom movement, beginning with a consideration of the murder of Hezekiah, the leader of the band of 'robbers', by the young King Herod I. The latter's rule thus prepared the way for the disturbances that broke out immediately after his death. The rebels were, however, initially without organization or ideological cohesion. These were only achieved by Judas. From his time onwards, the 'Zealots' formed a party that, though quite close to Pharisaism, was nonetheless independent. Josephus' very fragmentary reporting, however, enables us to follow their development only partially, although traces of them can also be found in the New Testament and the rabbinic tradition. The Zealots achieved their aim when the Jewish War broke out, but the party was divided at the crucial moment when Menahem, Judas' son, was murdered. From then onwards, there were several different groups in conflict with each other. They perpetuated

the spiritual heritage of the Zealots, but were themselves incapable of decisive, united action.

The fundamental thesis should now be apparent from this summary of the structure of the book. It is that the 'Zealots' formed a relatively exclusive and unified movement with its own distinctive religious views and that they had a crucial influence on the history of Palestinian Judaism in the decisive period between 6 and 70 A.D.

CHAPTER I

THE SOURCES

The question of the essential nature of the Zealot movement can only be answered by examining the nature and tendency of the sources. This is the fundamental difficulty confronting any scholar who tries to arrive at a more precise understanding of the subject.

A. JOSEPHUS AS THE PRINCIPAL SOURCE

The fullest account of the Jewish freedom movement during the period with which we are concerned here is provided by the Jewish author Flavius Josephus. Almost everything that we know comes from his *Jewish War* and Books XIII-XX of his *Antiquities of the Jews* and, for one very definite period, the time at the beginning of the Jewish War, his so-called *Life*. Josephus' works, however, confront us with two problems. On the one hand, the author uses sources of different tendencies and from various origins and, on the other, he reveals in the selection and evaluation of his material a very distinctive position that, moreover, varies somewhat in the individual writings.

His political attitude was determined above all by his own background and life-style. He was a member of the priestly nobility of Jerusalem, the distinguished class of Jehoiarib, to which the Hasmonaeans, with whom he was directly related, also belonged.[1] He therefore moved in circles, the overwhelming majority of whose members were hostile to the Jewish freedom movement, at least from the time of Herod I onwards. Later, he described himself as a follower of the Pharisees,[2] but he and his family also had close bonds of friendship with the leading Sadducees.[3] His activities in Galilee brought him into opposition with the leaders of the radical wing of the rebels[4] and he broke definitively with their party when he eventually went over to the

---

[1] *Vita* 2,198; *Bell* 1,3; 3,352; *Ap* 1,54; see also 1 Chron 24.7-18; 1 Macc 2.1,14. His great-great-grandfather married one of the daughters of the high-priest Jonathan.

[2] *Vita* 12. This statement has to be accepted with some caution; see below, p. 371, n. 286.

[3] *Vita* 204 describes Josephus as a φίλος ...καὶ συνήθης of the high-priest Jeshua b. Gamala.

[4] *Bell* 2,585ff.593f.598; *Vita* 43ff.134ff. etc.

Romans. He received a substantial reward for his services to the victorious Romans after the end of the War.[5] He was also granted Roman citizenship and a pension after having been released from prison by the Emperor and he lived in the palace that had previously belonged to Vespasian.[6]

Because he was indebted in this way to the Flavian imperial house, Josephus dedicated the whole of his written work to the Emperor. Even the title of his first work, *On the Jewish War*, shows that it was written from the Roman point of view.[7] The Greek version that has come down to us was preceded by an Aramaic text, which aimed above all to draw the attention of the non-Roman East to the power of Rome's weapons and the futility of a rebellion.[8] The later Greek text was a free and extended adaptation of the Aramaic original. It is written in brilliant, classical Greek,[9] but Josephus was on his own admission not particularly gifted in the Greek language. Greek stylists must therefore have played a part in its final composition,[10] which also explains why this historical work by the son of a priest from Jerusalem was clothed in such a completely Hellenistic garment. The final version of The Jewish War was produced between 75 and 79 A.D.[11] It was dedicated to Vespasian and Titus,[12] who provided it with a signature in his own hand.[13]

Josephus' main source for the details of the early history of the Maccabaean period, until Archelaus became ethnarch, was the historical

---

[5] *Vita* 422.425.429. His reward consisted of quite extensive estates and during the reign of Domitian he was exempted from paying taxes.

[6] *Vita* 423.

[7] Josephus himself uses this title in his later writings; *Ant* 20,258 (*Vita* 412): περὶ τοῦ Ἰουδαϊκοῦ πολέμου. The first scholar to point this out was R. Laqueur, *Der jüdische Historiker Flavius Josephus*, 1920, 98. In the manuscripts taken into account by Niese in his edition, the title (with the exception of the first two books of *Codex Parisianus*) is περὶ ἁλώσεως; see his introduction to 6, iii. R. Eisler, 1, 264ff., assumed that this was the title of the original Aramaic version.

[8] *Bell* 1,3.6. It is not possible to determine the relationship between this version and the Greek *Polemos*. R. Eisler, 1,135f., has correctly assumed that this tendentious political document was intended not only for the Jews, but also for all Aramaic speaking people in the East.

[9] According to H. St. J. Thackeray, *Josephus, the Man and Historian*, 1929, 104, Josephus' work was 'an excellent specimen of Atticistic Greek'.

[10] *Ant* 20,263; *Ap* 1,50. For the great number of Greek stylists engaged in this work, see W. Weber, *Josephus and Vespasian*, 1921, 13 and H. St. J. Thackeray, *op. cit.*, 103ff.

[11] The earliest date was the dedication of the Temple to the goddess of peace (*Bell* 7,158), according to Dio Cassius, 66,15.1, 75 A.D. and the latest date was the death of Vespasian in July 79; see Schürer 1, 47; *CAH* 10, 884.

[12] *Vita* 361; *Ap* 1,50.

[13] *Vita* 363; see also H. St. J. Thackeray, *op. cit.*, 27.

work written by Herod's friend Nicolaus of Damascus.[14] A direct result
of this was a one-sided and partisan attitude towards this part of the
history of the Jews. Josephus criticizes the Jewish people, for example,
for their unruliness and praises the Hellenistic Syrians for their loyalty.[15]
He condemns the Hasmonaeans' attempts to regain power and judges
Herod I relatively favourably.[16] What is also noticeably absent from this
part of Josephus' work is the characteristically Jewish religious
motivation for the course of history and the emphasis on divine
intervention, an element that occurs frequently in the later part of his
work.[17] All the attempts made by the Jews to regain their independence
have almost as a matter of course to be interpreted negatively. The
continuous narrative thread, however, is abruptly broken off as soon as
this source ceases and the tradition becomes extremely scanty in its
presentation.[18] Josephus confines himself for the most part to reporting
Jewish disturbances under Pilate, the Emperor Caligula and the later
procurators, Cumanus and Felix.[19] It is only when he is dealing with the
period immediately prior to the Jewish War that his reports become
more detailed again.[20] He was particularly well suited, as he himself
points out, to provide an account of the further course of the history of
the period. He had taken part personally in the crucial events as an eye-
witness and was familiar with the situation in both camps.[21] All the same,

---

[14] A friend of Herod who is frequently mentioned in *The Jewish War* and the
Antiquities and who dealt in detail with the history of the Jews, writing a Universal
History consisting of one hundred and forty-four books; see G. Hölscher, 'Josephus',
PW 9 (1916), 1945ff.; Schürer, 1, 51; *CAH* 10, 885. For the general tendency of
Nicolaus of Damascus' thought, see A. Schlatter, GI, 241-245. Josephus' entire text in
Bell 1,31—2,110 may be simply a detailed excerpt from Nicolaus' work. See B.Z.
Wacholder, *Nicolaus of Damascus*, Berkeley 1963, 60ff. and *passim*.
[15] *Bell* 1,88.90.94; 2,92; see Hölscher, *op. cit.*, 1945.
[16] *Bell* 1,171ff.357. Even in his assessment of Herod's family difficulties, Nicolaus was
usually on Herod's side; see 1,432.436f. Despite his occasional criticisms of the ruler, see
1,493.533.543, Nicolaus presented his government in a very positive light; see
1,429f.665.
[17] See, for example, *Bell* 3,404; 4,323.622; 5,2; 6,288,310.
[18] It ends with the imposter Alexander; see 2,110. G. Hölscher, *op. cit.*, 1949, thought
that the source did not end until the banishment of Archelaus, 2,116.
[19] *Bell* 2,169ff.184ff.247ff.
[20] *Bell* 2,277ff., from Florus' being appointed to office.
[21] According to *Bell* 1,3 and *Vita* 5, Josephus was born in the first year of Caligula's
reign (13 August 37 to 16 March 38 A.D.); see Hölscher, *op. cit.*, 1934. He was therefore
twenty-eight years old at the beginning of the war. He stresses the fact that he was an
eye-witness most emphatically in his debate with Justus of Tiberias; see *Vita* 357-367 and
Ap 1,46-56 and also his criticism of previous expositions of the Jewish War, *Bell*
1,3ff.6.18; *Ap* 1,55. According to *Ap* 1,49, he also had to interrogate those who went
over to the other side and was therefore well informed about events in the city.

there are certain differences in the reports of the course of the war that give rise to the suspicion that Josephus also at least partly had recourse to written sources.[22] W. Weber may well have gone too far in his hypothesis that Josephus may have made use of an already existing Flavian historical work,[23] but we are fully justified in supposing that he might have resorted to hitherto unpublished war reports made by Roman *imperatores*, since these were, on his own admission, known to him.[24] Even Agrippa II seems to have contributed material.[25]

A special problem is raised by the great differences between Josephus' reports about his activity in Galilee in the second book of *The Jewish War* and in his *Life*.[26] Very divergent opinions have been expressed about the value as a source of this *Vita*, which was, to judge from its style, written by Josephus himself.[27] Since the appearance of R. Laqueur's study, however, there has been a growing conviction that Josephus comes closer to the historical truth in his *Vita* than he does in the parallel account in *The Jewish War*.[28] The *Vita* presumably goes back to notes

---

[22] Schürer, 1, 47, believed that Josephus obtained most of his material in note form during the war. W. Weber, *op. cit.*, 68ff., 79ff. etc., and H. Drexler, 'Untersuchungen zu Josephus und zur Geschichte des jüdischen Aufstandes', *Klio* 19 (1925), 277ff., have, however, both pointed to the difference between Josephus' usual style and that of the 'Roman passages, which, in contrast to the usual style, are 'terse, matter-of-fact and translucent'; see Drexler, *op. cit.*, 292, n. 2; see also 304. A striking feature is the presence of precise times and places.

[23] *op. cit.*, 78ff. etc. This work included, according to Weber, almost all the material contained in 3,1-7,162. For a criticism of Weber's hypothesis, see R. Laqueur, *Philologische Wochenschrift* 41 (1921), 1105ff., and Thackeray, *op. cit.*, 37. Josephus' negative judgement of his predecessors' work, *Bell* 1,1ff., and the difficulty in establishing a time — the Flavian work, the Aramaic and the Greek *Polemos* must have been written between 75 and 79 A.D. — make Weber's supposition very unlikely. Titus' interest in Josephus' work would also be incomprehensible in the case of mere plagiarism; see *Vita* 363.

[24] *Vita* 342,358; *Ap* 1,56.

[25] He points out in a letter cited in *Vita* 366 that he had hitherto unknown facts to communicate to him.

[26] The date of the composition of the *Vita* is disputed and is dependent on the date of the death of Agrippa II, that is, 93/94 or 100 A.D. G. Hölscher, *op. cit.*, 1941f., supposed, on the basis of *Ant* 20,265, that the earlier date was more likely, but at the same time assumed that the *Vita* was directly linked, in an earlier version, to the *Antiquities* and was not extended to form an apology against Justus of Tiberias until later. See R. Laqueur. *Der jüdische Historiker Flavius Josephus*, 1920, 2ff.; A. Schlatter, GI, 342f.; M. Gelzer, 'Die Vita des Josephus', *Hermes* 80 (1952), 67ff.; T. Frankfort, *RBPH* 39 (1961), 52ff., favours the dates: 92/4 the death of Agrippa II; 93-4 *Antiquities*; 93/6 *Vita*.

[27] Schürer, 1, 58: 'his weakest achievement is the 'Life''; G. Hölscher, *op. cit.*. 1994; N. Bentwich, *Josephus*, 1926, 74; H. Drexler, *op. cit.*, 303.

[28] R. Laqueur, *op. cit.*, Foreword and Part 1. Laqueur's thesis, that the *Vita* is basically a report by Josephus about his activities in Galilee in opposition to the Synhedrium, goes

made earlier and used later by the author as a basis for his criticism of the attacks made by Justus of Tiberias.[29] The most striking difference, however, between the *Vita* and *The Jewish War* is to be found in the author's report of his mission to Galilee. In the *Vita*, he describes himself simply as a member of a legation, whereas in *The Jewish War* he presents himself as a man with all the powers of a supreme commander. It is all too obvious that he wanted to attribute military rank and glory to himself.[30] The *Vita* is moreover particularly important because of the insight that it provides into the structure of rural and small town life in Galilee at the beginning of the Jewish War and the relatively clear picture that it gives of the social relationships and complicated party struggles outside Jerusalem.

The fundamental orientation of Josephus' work should by now be apparent from what I have said about the author's personality and *The Jewish War*. He wrote the work under the protection of the Emperors Vespasian and Titus and he may even have been commissioned by them to write it with a specific intention, that of convincing readers that the defeat of the Jews was justified and that the power of Rome was invincible.[31] This intention had a religious significance for Josephus,[32] who was convinced that God himself had ordained the downfall of Jerusalem and the Temple, because of the sins that had been committed in it — particularly by the Zealots.[33] This is clear from his admonition of his compatriots:

---

too far; see R. Helm's detailed criticism in the *Philologische Wochenschrift* 41 (1921), 481-493 and 505-516. Only R. Eisler, 1, xxxviiif.,233 and *passim*, accepted Laqueur's hypothesis uncritically, finding in it confirmation of his own even more imaginative combinations.

[29] See W. Weber, *op. cit.*, 99; M. Gelzer, *op. cit.*, 87f. These notes are probably older than *The Jewish War* and may have been taken during the siege of Jerusalem or while Josephus was in prison.

[30] M. Gelzer, *op. cit.*, 90: 'It was more advantageous for him personally to disseminate a heroic image of himself and so the leader of the partisans reluctantly exaggerated his status to that of regular army commander.'

[31] *Bell* 3,108: 'I have not described this event in order to praise the Romans, but rather to comfort those who have been subjected and to restrain those who are seeking rebellion'. This text follows a detailed description of the Roman military apparatus. This applied, of course, first and foremost to the Aramaic-speaking East, which was always in a state of unrest, and also to the Greek-speaking Jewish diaspora in the Empire itself, which was also in a state of ferment after the war; see *Bell* 7,407-453.

[32] This was emphasized by Weber, *op cit.*, 66 and 77: 'As a historian, Josephus clothed himself in the garment of a prophet' and he did so, what is more, in conscious contrast to the image of the Jewish Zealot prophet; see below, p. 241f. He made speeches admonishing those whose hearts were hardened (*Bell* 5,393): ἐμὲ τὸν παρακαλοῦντα πρὸς σωτηρίαν ὑμᾶς βλασφημεῖτε, see 6,96; and lamented the state of the city (5,19f.; see also 1,12).

[33] *Bell* 2,539; 5,60.368ff.; 6,4.39f.299.

'I believe therefore that the Deity has fled from his Sanctuary and is on the side of those against whom you are fighting!'[34]

Vespasian and Titus, on the other hand, had been chosen by God to chastise his people and to announce the future kingdom of peace.[35] At the same time, however, Josephus also defended his people, with whose religious faith and destiny he was so intimately linked, by attributing the great misfortune to no more than a small minority of fanatical reprobates and by exonerating the great mass of the people as their passive victims.[36] On the one hand, then, his literary work was an accusation of the criminal authors of a war, namely the members of the Jewish freedom movement, who were in his opinion entirely responsible for the downfall of the city and the sanctuary. On the other hand, it was a defence of the noble Roman Titus, who had made every attempt to prevent the terrible work of destruction. Josephus outlined his entire programme in the Introduction to *The Jewish War*:

'The fact that internal disorders destroyed it and that the tyrants of the Jews forced the Romans to hurl the firebrand against the Temple — its destroyer, the Emperor Titus, bears witness to this. Throughout the whole of the war he was moved by sympathy for the people terrorized by the rebels and again and again he decided to postpone taking the city by storm in order to give the guilty men time to be converted during the siege. If, however, anyone should criticize us for the accusation that I have brought against the pack of robbers while bemoaning the misfortune that has befallen the fatherland, then he should take my pain into account as an apology for this offence against the law of historiography'.[37]

The hated opponents of the Roman rule became the dark background against which the young hero, Titus, shone even brighter.[38] Josephus could certainly be sure of winning his imperial patron's favour with this unambiguous political emphasis with its religious overtones; Titus' signature, which I have already mentioned, the consent of Agrippa II and Josephus' own material success all confirm that this was in fact the case.[39]

---

[34] *Bell* 5,412; see also 6,300 and Ezek 10.18f.; 11.22f.

[35] *Bell* 3,6.401; 4,622; 5,2.367. Josephus draws a clear parallel in his great admonitory address, *Bell* 5,362-419, with Jeremiah and Nebuchadnezzar (390ff.411).

[36] *Bell* 2,445.449.525.529.538.540; 5,28.53.265.333f.; see also *Ant* 20,166.172.

[37] *Bell* 1,10f.; see also 5,15-20.

[38] W. Weber, *op. cit.*, 215: 'It is reasonable to suppose that Josephus, hating his enemies and courting Titus, painted dark portraits of those opponents in order that the shining hero might radiate all the more'.

[39] *Vita* 363-366; *Ap* 1,50f.; see also above, nn. 5 and 6.

His *Antiquities of the Jews* ('Ιουδαϊκὴ ἀρχαιολογία) are also a particularly important source of information about the early history of the Zealot movement during the reign of Herod I and its development under the procurators. This is above all because the work is even more detailed in its presentation of Jewish history until the outbreak of the Jewish War. It was completed in 93/94 A.D.[40] and was dedicated not to the Emperor, but, like the *Vita* and *Contra Apionem*, to Epaphroditus, one of Josephus' patrons.[41]. Josephus was at that time no longer so closely associated with the imperial house as he had been during the time of Vespasian and Titus. The *Antiquities* are therefore less politically orientated and have a stronger religious and ethical intention. Josephus clearly wanted to enlighten cultured Roman and Hellenistic readers about the history and faith of the Jews and to obtain recognition for the despised Jewish people.[42] This meant that the emphasis in the *Antiquities* was fundamentally different from that in *The Jewish War*. In its outward form, the work is patterned after a Hellenistic model.[43] With the aim of making what he says more credible, the author frequently mentions the sources on which he has drawn and cites a large number of early authors.[44]

The problem of the sources on which the *Antiquities* are based is much more complex than it is in *The Jewish War*. In addition to Nicolaus of Damascus, Josephus certainly also draws on the first book of the Maccabees and probably also on Strabo.[45] He also makes use of certain individual Jewish legends, some of which can be found in the Talmudic literature.[46] One striking characteristic of his treatment of the history of

---

[40] *Ant* 20,267: in the thirteenth year of Domitian's reign.

[41] *Ant* 1,84; see R. Laqueur, *op. cit.*, 23-36; H. St J. Thackeray, *op. cit.*, 53.

[42] *Ant* 1,5 and 15: 'I exhort the one into whose hands these books come to turn his mind to God and to verify whether our lawgiver has correctly grasped the nature of God and has ascribed to him only those deeds that are worthy of his power'; 16,175: 'I mention these things again and again in order to make foreign people acquainted with our institutions and to eradicate from the minds of unreasonable men the deep causes of hatred against us and our veneration of God'.

[43] Josephus followed the 'Ρωμαϊκὴ ἀρχαιολογία of Dionysius of Halicarnassus, which, like Josephus' own *Antiquities*, is also divided into twenty books; see Schürer 1, 48f.

[44] See the arrangement in G. Hölscher, *op. cit.*, 1964f. Josephus only read a fairly small number of authors in the original languages, of course, and took the other quotations from his own sources.

[45] Strabo is cited most frequently — as many as twelve times in Books 12-15. His historical work, which can be regarded as friendly towards the Jews, goes back to about 30 B.C. Nicolaus of Damascus, on the other hand, is only quoted seven times in Books 12-16.

[46] *Ant* 13,282f. = Sot 33a parr.; 13,288-298 = Kidd 66a; 14,22ff. = Taan 3,9ff.; 15,245 = Taan 23a etc. See Derenbourg, 74-150; G. Hölscher, *op. cit.*, 1973f.

Herod is that he frequently incorporates sharp criticism into the text —
something that he did not do in *The Jewish War*. It is of course possible
that he had a particular source of Jewish origin that was hostile to Herod
at his disposal in the case of the *Antiquities*.[47] In addition there were also
documents from Roman archives, which above all drew attention to the
Jews' free practice of their religion in earlier times.[48] Finally, as the son of
a priest, Josephus laid great emphasis on the history of the high priests
and here too he probably relied on written evidence.[49]

Because of the number of sources, the *Antiquities* make a less unified
and homogeneous impression than the *Bellum* and stylistically the work
cannot be compared with *The Jewish War*, especially as far as the last
books are concerned.[50] A certain negligence in the style and content led
Laqueur to suspect that much of the text of the *Antiquities* was simply
copied or paraphrased from *The Jewish War*, and also that the former
had been rewritten and extensively revised by the author.[51] Josephus had
a far greater number of anecdotal reports at his disposal for the period of
the procurators than he had when he was compiling *The Jewish War*.
They were for the most part reports of disturbances in Judaea, the fate of

---

[47] Schürer, 1, 51; *CAH* 10, 886. G. Hölscher, *op. cit.*, 1971ff., suspected that 'a
tendentious corrector or out-and-out falsifier' combined Nicolaus' work and a
biography of Herod, which may have been derived from Ptolemaeus of Ascalon (see
1981) and adapted it in a Jewish and anti-Herodian sense; see also W. Otto, *Herodes I*,
11f. This construction is, however, very unlikely. The term 'falsifier' can most fittingly
be applied to Josephus himself. R. Laqueur, *op. cit.*, 218, and H. St. J. Thackeray, *op. cit.*,
67, attribute the anti-Herodian passages (16,150ff,183ff,395 etc.) to Josephus himself.
Laqueur rightly assumes that Josephus was at this time coming close to the Jewish
national point of view.

[48] Schürer, 1, 51f.; H. St. J. Thackeray, *op. cit.*, 70ff.; R. Laqueur, *op. cit.*, 221-230.

[49] *Ap* 1,31; see also Schürer, 1, 51f. G. Hölscher, *op. cit.*, thought that both the
documents and the list of high-priests went back to the conjectural Jewish historical
work; see also G. Hölscher, 'Die Hohenpriesterliste bei Josephus und die evangelische
Chronologie', *SAH* 30 (1939/40), 1ff.

[50] For this, see especially H. St. J. Thackeray, *op. cit.*, 105-124. According to *Ant* 1,7ff.,
Josephus wanted to abandon the work. He frequently changed his Greek stylists. As in
the *Vita*, Book XX was written by the author himself.

[51] *op. cit.*, 128-215 and especially 198ff. R. Eisler, 1, 108f., has shown that parts of the
Antiquities can be compressed to half the length without any loss of meaning. See,
however, G. Hölscher, *op. cit.*, 1988, and Schürer's answer, 1, 52, n. 19, to a similar
suggestion made by B. Niese, *HZ* 76 (1896), 218ff.: 'One of the sources more liberally
used in the Archaeology (presumably Nicolaus of Damascus) is also at the basis of the
shorter version of the *Bellum Judaicum*'. The hypothesis that Josephus reworked the
Antiquities is closely connected with the problem of "the events of my life", mentioned
by him at the end of his work (*Ant* 20,266). It is however very questionable whether this
theory holds to the extent assumed by R. Laqueur, *op. cit.*, Foreword, 79,91, n. 3,234ff.
and *passim* and R. Eisler, 1, 97f.,233f.,526, n. 4 and *passim*.

the Herodians and events concerning the Temple and its cult. E.
Norden[52] pointed out that Josephus made use of a fixed plan of
composition in his enumeration of the disturbances and that similar
plans were used by the Roman annalists. It is not at all easy to determine
the origin of these anecdotes individually. It is possible that Josephus had
procurators' reports and similar documentary material at his disposal in
Rome.[53] It is also possible that Agrippa II and the whole Herodian
family connection may have been a source of information.[54] Finally, we
may also assume that personal recollections and oral reports served as
sources for the events in the period following Felix.[55]

A distinctive aspect of the *Antiquities* is that, because of the author's
greater distance from the imperial house and the pro-Jewish apologetical
tendency of the later work, the question of fidelity to the law is more
strongly emphasized in it than in *The Jewish War*.[56] Despite this,
however, the author's judgement of the Jewish freedom movement, the
origin and development of which he describes in even greater detail in
the *Antiquities*,[57] remained unchanged. He judges it just as harshly as
before and declares just as firmly that the terrible disaster that caused
confusion, distress, misery and rebellion in the whole of Judaea and
ultimately led to the complete destruction of the Jewish state was caused
by the founders of the 'fourth philosophy'.[58] On the other hand,
however, he also stresses more strongly in this later work that the
Roman administration and the procurators Felix, Albinus and Florus in
particular were partly responsible for the general disorder.[59] He even

---

[52] 'Josephus und Tacitus über Jesus Christus', *NJKA* 31 (1913), 643.

[53] This was Eisler's opinion, 1, xxxixf.,26f. etc. E. Norden, *op. cit.*, 642, n. 2, assumed
the mediation of a Roman annalist such as Cluvius Rufus; see also G. Hölscher, *op. cit.*,
1985.

[54] *Vita* 362ff.; *Ap* 1,51.

[55] G. Hölscher, *op. cit.*, 1971-1993, attributed the reports about the period of the
procurators to his 'anonymous Jewish author'; see 1974 and above, n. 47. This unknown
author was, Hölscher believed, essentially responsible for the last three books of the
Antiquities. He supported the moderate Jewish point of view, was faithful to the law and
was critical of renegades and of the Zealots alike. According to Hölscher, 1992f., he was
liberal in his attitude towards Hellenistic culture, the theatre and gladiatoral combats.
Hölscher describes him as an 'aristocratic priest, full of enthusiasm for the Hasmonaeans
and distinguished people in general, opposed to the plebs and full of hatred for the
upstart Herod'; see 1982f. But surely his description can best be applied to Josephus
himself!

[56] See *Ant* 16,186f.; 19,329ff.; 20,100.143f.218 and *passim*; see also, however, the
positive assessment of the apostate Tiberius Alexander, *Bell* 5,45ff.

[57] See *Ant* 18,4-9.23ff. and *Bell* 2,118; see also *Ant* 20,5.102.160ff. etc.

[58] *Ant* 18,25; 20,252-258.

[59] *Ant* 20,162ff., which should be compared, however, with *Bell* 2,256; 20,215.252ff.

attributes part of the blame for the later catastrophe to the Roman occupying forces.[60]

Too high a value should not be placed on Josephus as a reliable writer of history. His reliability is above all dependent on the quality of his sources. He also often wrote hastily and this led him simply to overlook wrong or contradictory statements in his sources.[61] Despite the great stress that he placed on his love of truth and his ability as a historian, he was basically not so much a historiographer as a tendentious writer and apologist. His different writings are all characterized by firm political or religious views.[62]

For my purpose, which is to investigate the Zealot movement within the period delineated above,[63] three very important conclusions emerge from the description that I have just given of the principal sources and their author, Flavius Josephus. These are:

(1) Josephus' source material on the Zealots was very fragmentary and varied in its origins. This applies in particular to the early period of the Zealot movement.[64]

(2) Josephus himself was not at all interested in making the history of the movement, its teachings and the fate of its leaders tally with the facts. His selection of his material was very arbitrary and tendentious. In other words, whenever it suited his purpose, he exaggerated, altered or suppressed facts and events.[65]

---

[60] *Ant* 19,366; 20,175.

[61] A small collection of obvious contradictions is supplied by R. Eisler, 1, 99ff.; see also below, p. 331, n. 102.

[62] For his description of himself, see *Bell* 1,16; 7,455; *Ant* 16,187; 20,157: 'We have the firm intention of telling only the truth'. N. Bentwich, *Josephus*, 1926, 106, commented pointedly: 'He was a sophist rather than a sage and circumstances compelled him to be a court chronicler rather than a national historian'.

[63] See above, p. 1.

[64] See above, pp. 7ff. and 12f.; see also below, p. 76ff.

[65] See, for example, the contradictory description of John of Gischala, *Bell* 2,585ff. and *Vita* 43ff. Examples of typical exaggerations are: *Bell* 4,382ff.559-565; 5,429ff.562ff.; 6,201ff. W. Weber, *op. cit.*, 35,43ff., pointed to the suppression of the Zealots' messianic expectation or its re-interpretation by Josephus in favour of Vespasian; see also below, p. 237f., 241; only a few traces of this can be detected in the *Antiquities* (4,125; 10,210; 17,45). The author's re-interpretation of the name 'Zealots', *Bell* 4,160f., is also very significant. This situation was very obvious to H. Drexler, *Klio* 19 (1925), 287: '... we learn nothing essential about the ideas and the underlying motivating forces of this radical national and religious movement or the differences beween the individual groups. Josephus saw them simply as criminals and responsible for the downfall of the people'. W. Weber, *op. cit.*, 215, was also aware of it: 'Josephus' tirades about the recklessness of the 'robbers' and 'tyrants' blur the outlines of the whole picture ... It is only now and then that he mentions the strength of the party or the names of the junior

(3) This came about as the result of his bitter hostility towards the Jewish freedom movement.[66] His entire interest was directed towards the task of presenting the Zealots as lawless men (ἄνομοι), criminals for whom no punishment was too severe, or as madmen.[67]

We are therefore confronted with two difficulties. The image of the Zealots that we have from Josephus is not only fragmentary — it is also blurred and distorted. I see it as my task, then, not only to complete Josephus' image of the Zealots by drawing attention to other source material, but also to present, at least in certain points, the true features of that controversial movement.

Excursus I: The Slavonic Josephus

The Old Russian version of *The Jewish War*[68] contains, among other things, several remarkable passages concerned with John the Baptist, Jesus and the early Christian community and connecting these with the Jewish freedom movement.[69] R. Eisler attempted to prove that the Old Russian translator worked from a Greek version of *The Jewish War* that went back to the Aramaic original.[70] He added 'sources recently disclosed by him' to this foundation.[71] and built up a fantastic picture of the time of Jesus, in which the Baptist, Jesus himself and the early Church were all entirely absorbed into the Zealot movement. Most scholars who examined Eisler's work were very critical of it,[72] but some were prepared to believe in the possible authenticity

---

leaders . . .; these, like the leaders themselves, remain mere sketches, when one disregards Josephus' effusions'.

[66] See below, p. 41. See also the description in *Bell* 1,11; see also above, p. 11, n. 37 and the summary in conclusion, *Bell* 7,253-274: 'We may even say that they suffered too little for what they did, since there is no just punishment for them' (7,273; see also *Bell* 4,185).

[67] In his descriptions of them, Josephus preferred such words as ἀπόνοια, ἄνοια and μανία; see *Bell* 2,265.651; 3,454.479; 4,362; 5,34.121.424.436; 6.20; 7,213.267.412 and *passim*; *Ant* 17,263.271; 18,25; *Vita* 19.

[68] The text is *La prise de Jérusalem de Josèphe le Juif, Texte vieux-russe*, edited by V. Istrin, A. Vaillant and P. Pascal, Paris, 1, 1934, 2, 1938 (cited below as Istrin). Books 1-4 are available in a German translation: *Flavius Josephus, Vom jüdischen Kriege, I-IV, nach der Slavischen Übersetzung deutsch herausgegeben und mit dem griechischen Text verglichen*, edited by A. Berendts and K. Grass, Dorpat 1924.

[69] These additions had already been considered by A, Berendts, 'Die Zeugnisse vom Christentum im slawischen de bello judaico', *TU*, New Series 4 (1906). Their value as a source had already been rejected in an important article by E. Schürer, *ThLZ* 31 (1906), 262-266.

[70] See above, n. 8.

[71] Among other texts, the Hebrew Josippon, the Acts of Pilate and the Toledoth Jeshu; see Index, Vol. 2.

[72] See the critical discussions of his work by W. Bauer, *ThLZ* 55 (1930), 557-563; H. Levy, *DLZ* 50 (1930), 491-494; W. Windfuhr, *Philologische Wochenschrift* 50 (1930), 1421-27; M. Goguel, 'Les théories de M. Robert Eisler', *RHPhR* 10 (1930), 177-190;

of these strange additions in the Slavonic version.[73] As far as my own study is concerned, these additional passages have a value as source material in that I am also bound to take the Baptist movement and early Christianity at least partly into account as having Zealot tendencies with political and religious aims.

Several scholars have, however, demonstrated quite clearly that Eisler's hypothesis is extremely improbable.[74] Analysis has shown the text to be a relatively late hybrid form.[75] An examination of the omissions and abbreviations has also revealed that these are probably the result of quite arbitrary decisions on the part of the translator.[76] Finally, the text is in many places expanded, but, apart from certain Christian insertions, these extensions are purely literary and stylistic and have no historical validity.

The Christian interpolations contain nothing that cannot be traced back to apocryphal themes, the Fathers of the Church, Christian polemics against the Jews or the gospels themselves.[77] The writer simply wanted to entertain his readers in an edifying way. The aim of his presentation as a whole was the glorification of Jesus and his disciples.[78] He may perhaps be the same as the

---

H. Windisch, 'Unser Wissen um Jesus', *Neue Jahrbücher für Wissenschaft und Jugendbildung* 7 (1931), 289-307.

[73] S. Reinach, *REJ* 87 (1929), 113-131, and, with certain reservations, R. Laqueur, *HZ* 148 (1933), 326-328, were of this opinion. Thackeray, who published the additions as an appendix to his edition of *The Jewish War*, was also inclined to accept Eisler's thesis; see his *Josephus, the Man and Historian*, 1929, 33f.,152. More recently, several other scholars have attempted to justify the historical value of the interpolations as sources. They include S.G.F. Brandon, *The Fall of Jerusalem and the Christian Church*, 1951, 110-118; F. Scheidweiler, 'Sind die Interpolationen im altrussischen Josephus wertlos?', *ZNW* 43 (1950/51), 155-178, and O. Cullmann, *The State in the New Testament*, 51f.

[74] The most important are: S. Zeitlin, *Josephus on Jesus with Particular Reference to the Slavonic Josephus and the Hebrew Josippon*, 1931; J.M. Creed, 'The Slavonic Version of Josephus' History of the Jewish War', *HThR* 25 (1932), 276-319; J.W. Jack, *The Historic Christ*, 1933, and E. Bickermann's outstanding study, 'Sur la version vieux-russe de Flavius-Josèphe', *Mélanges Franz Cumont*, 1936, 53-84. N.A. Mescerkij, who was the last Russian to study this question in detail, rejected Eisler's thesis completely; see the discussion of his work by S. Szyszman in *RdQ* 1 (1959), 451-458.

[75] The text corresponds most closely to Niese's group VR, but often reveals influences of PA and L; see Levy, *op. cit.*, 487f.; Creed, 290ff., and Bickermann, 59f.

[76] Creed, 293ff.; Bickermann, 61ff., and others pointed out that the whole important episode of Menahem is omitted, a fact that Eisler was hardly able to explain; see 1, 319f. and 2, 556.

[77] Bickermann, 69f.,77ff.; Zeitlin, 36-50,106ff. There are, among other things, also connections with the apocryphal Gospel of Nicodemus. The question of the Messiahship of Herod (Istrin, 1, 55) originated with the discussion about the Church Fathers; see Bickermann, 74; Eisler, 1, 348. The sharp attack against the Latins (Istrin, 1, 107f.) was caused by the Fourth Crusade and the establishment of the Latin Empire.

[78] J.W. Jack's conjecture, *op. cit.*, 77ff., is not to be taken seriously; he suggested that a Judaizing Russian sect falsified the text. The so-called Hegesippus, a Latin translation of *The Jewish War*, made in the fourth or fifth century A.D. with Christian adaptations, also contains a number of interpolations concerning Jesus and the apostles; see Zeitlin, 52.

translator into Old Russian (in the twelfth or thirteenth century A.D.) and it is also possible that he was a Byzantine chronicler.[79]

The most recent Russian investigation into the Slavonic text of Josephus also rejects the historical authenticity of the controversial additions. It is significant that, in his concern to safeguard his hypothesis, Eisler dismissed as Christian interpolations all the elements in the Old Russian work that contradicted his own construction. The insertions were able to cause such a sensation because of a strategem, clearly exposed by E. Bickermann, on the part of the Byzantine interpolator, who

'gave the Gospel figures an appearance that seemed new and struck people of our own time as attractive. John the Baptist, Jesus and the apostles were all presented as revolutionaries'.[80]

B. The Secondary Sources

The other source material that can be usefully considered in this context in addition to the works of Josephus is very varied in origin. It is only possible to understand its significance and to classify it if its relationship with the data provided by Josephus is borne in mind. I therefore propose to make a distinction between the contemporary Jewish sources other than the works of Josephus, the rabbinic material, the Christian sources and the material provided by other ancient authors.

1. Contemporary Jewish Sources

The great history of the Jews of Justus of Tiberias, which was so bitterly attacked by Josephus and whose author Josephus — certainly wrongly — described as the leader of the rebellious party in Tiberias,[81] — is lost. This is very unfortunate, since, if it were still in existence, we would probably learn more from it about the Jewish freedom movement than from the extremely tendentious Josephus. After their defeat by the Romans, the Zealots were not able, as the victorious Maccabees had been in the past, to develop a historiography of their own, which might have presented the spirit and the actions of the Jewish

---

[79] Bickermann, 81f.; Zeitlin, 36,60; Levy, *op. cit.*, 489ff.; see also H. Fuchs, *Der geistige Widerstand gegen Rom*, 1938, 73. M. Dibelius, *ThBl* 6 (1927), 221, had already expressed this opinion.

[80] *op. cit.*, 79.

[81] See *Vita* 34ff.88 etc.; see also Schürer, 1, 59f. and H. Luther, *Josephus und Justus von Tiberias*, Halle 1910, 41ff.

fight for freedom according to their understanding of it. The only text which can be ascribed with some degree of probability to the Jewish rebels and which has come down to us is a brief collection of Jewish days of remembrance and commemorations of victories known as the Megillath Taanith or 'Scroll of Fasting'[82]. It is, however, so short and its meaning has been so disputed that very little information can be gained from it. The Assumption of Moses, which presumably dates back to the beginning of the first century A.D.[83] and has been regarded by certain scholars as a Zealot text,[84] does not contain any specifically Zealot aspects, at least in the form in which it has been handed down to us. We cannot therefore be at all certain that it was produced within the Jewish freedom movement.[85] It is equally possible to describe it as quietistic and ascribe it to the Pharisees or the Essenes.[86]

It is, then — with one exception — not possible to attribute individual works in the rich body of late Jewish Palestinian literature directly to the Zealot movement. There are, however, many concepts contained in that literature that are in a special way of significance to the 'Zealots'. Above all, there is the concept of 'zeal' for the law and the Sanctuary, which includes an unconditional readiness to suffer, prophetic enthusiasm, a hatred of pagan oppression, the idea of a 'Holy War' and the expectation of a warrior Messiah and Israel's eventual supremacy over the people of the world. Many late Jewish writings have been

---

[82] For the text of the Megillath Taanith, see G. Dalman, *Aramäische Dialektproben*, 1896, 1-3 and 32-34. See also H. Lichtenstein, 'Die Fastenrolle', *HUCA* 8/9 (1931/32), 268ff. For the dating, see Schürer, 1, 114f.; S. Zeitlin, *Megillat Taanit as a Source for Jewish Chronology and History in the Hellenistic and Roman Period*, 1922, 3f.; Lichtenstein, *op. cit.*, 257f., and W.R. Farmer, *Maccabees, Zealots and Josephus*, 1956, 208f. The fact that dates of the Bar Koseba rebellion may also possibly be mentioned does not seriously call this assumption into question, since the later events were simply appended. For this problem, see Farmer, *op. cit.*, 6,151ff.,158: 'The purpose of the Megillath Taanith was to inspire the Jews in their resistance to Rome by reminding them of the Maccabaean victories...'. See also J.Z. Lauterbach, 'Megillat Taanit', *JE* 8, 427, and S. Zeitlin, *op. cit.*, 4. See also below, p. 203.

[83] For the dating, see Schürer, 3, 281f., and O. Eissfeldt, *The Old Testament: an Introduction*, 1965, 624.

[84] For the advocates of the hypothesis that the Assumption of Moses was a Zealot text, see J.W. Lightly, *Jewish Sects and Parties in the Time of Jesus*, 1925, 349. In the second German edition of his work, 3, 219, Schürer agreed with this hypothesis, but he opposed it in the third German edition, 3, 300 (cf. English tr. 3, 283f.).

[85] Schürer was of this opinion in the third German edition of his work, 3, 300. See also C. Clemen, in Kautzsch, *APAT* 2, 315; *B.-Gr.Rel.* 87/88, n. 3.

[86] S.P. Riessler, *Altjüdisches Schrifttum ausserhalb der Bibel*, 1928, 1301; J. Klausner, *The Messianic Idea in Israel*, translated into English by W.F. Stinespring, 1955, 325; O. Eissfeldt, *op. cit.*

brought forward in evidence in the elaboration of this theory of 'Zealot' concepts. They include, for example, both books of the Maccabees, the Ethiopic Enoch, the Book of Jubilees, the Testaments of the Twelve Patriarchs, the Psalms of Solomon, the Third and Fourth Books of the Maccabees, the Assumption of Moses itself, certain parts of the Sybilline Books, the Apocalypses of Esdras and Baruch and the pseudo–Philonic *Liber Antiquitatum Biblicarum*. Philo's historical and apologetical document, On the Embassy to Gaius, must also be taken into consideration here. It completes the picture painted by Josephus and provides an interesting insight into the confrontation between Palestinian Judaism and the claims of the worship of the emperor.

Valuable information can also be found in the Essene literature that has come to light as a result of the discoveries in the region of the Dead Sea. One of these scrolls in particular, 'The War of the Sons of Light against the Sons of Darkness', contains a description of the Holy War at the end of time that is, as far as its content is concerned, in many respects close to the spirit of the Zealot movement.[87] Some of the ideas contained in the eschatological and messianic fragments found in Caves I and IV and certain passages from the Community Rule and the hymns are also not unlike the concepts and themes of the Zealots.

Another source of a very special kind is found in the coins of the first Jewish rebellion of 66–70 A.D.[88] Their inscriptions and illustrations provide us with some of the relatively rare extant pieces of evidence of the Jewish freedom movement of the first century A.D.

Josephus provided a very one-sided and fragmentary picture of the Zealots' religious convictions. It is therefore only by investigating the comparative religious material found in Hellenistic and Roman Jewish sources that we can usefully complete the religious picture of the movement. An examination of these sources also reveals a concentration of views in Zealotism that were at the same time quite widespread in Palestinian Judaism as a whole.

2. The Rabbinic Sources

The rabbinic tradition first began to be committed to writing towards the end of the second century A.D. and the whole process covered a very long period.[89] By that time, the Jewish freedom movement had finally

---

[87] See below for a detailed analysis, p. 277ff.
[88] L. Kadman, *The Coins of the Jewish War of 66-73*, Jerusalem 1960.
[89] S.H. Strack, *Introduction to the Talmud and Midrash*, 3rd. ed. 1963, 20ff.; G.F. Moore, *Judaism*, 1, 93ff.

collapsed. Despite this, however, the rabbinic contribution to our knowledge of the Zealot movement is undoubtedly our most important source of information apart from the work of Josephus himself. Following the usual forms in the rabbinic tradition, there are no lengthy connected reports, but only scattered individual statements or anecdotes in which the 'Zealots' or the *Sicarii* are mentioned.[90] The names of the leaders of this movement are also noted.[91] The tradition concerning the 'Zealot' Phinehas is especially interesting, since this is a case of a Zealot Midrash having been preserved in that tradition and criticized and changed in a later tradition.[92] This state of affairs is typical of the attitude of later rabbinism with regard to the Jewish freedom movement, which finally collapsed with the defeat of Bar Koseba's revolt. The attempt to 'hasten' the coming of the kingdom of God by violent means in a struggle against the worldly power of the pagans was condemned as acting purely on the basis of human authority.[93] This negative attitude towards the struggle of the Jewish people for independence explains why there are relatively few historically valuable data about the Zealot movement in the first century A.D. among the abundance of rabbinic writings on other themes. The events of the recent past were seen from the point of view of suffering rather than as 'history' that had to be judged positively.[94]

The question of the historical value of the rabbinic traditions, several of which were concerned in one way or another with the Zealot movement, can therefore only be answered in individual cases on the basis of the age of each tradition and its relationship with other source material.

Historical information about the Zealots and their theological views, then, were assimilated into the rabbinic tradition and discussed within it. This would certainly seem to indicate that there was still an active spirit of revolt against Roman rule among the individual teachers of the earlier Tannaitic period.[95] It is even possible that this conflict with

---

[90] See below, pp. 50f. and 66f.

[91] See below, pp. 50, n. 212; 349f. and 360f.

[92] See Chap. IV B 3, p. 156ff.

[93] See below, p. 124.

[94] See N.N. Glatzer, *Geschichte der talmudischen Zeit*, 1937, 11: 'Jewish history writing did not cease because of flagging energy, but because it was recognized that there was no longer any Jewish "history" in the real sense of the word. . . . The Jews were no longer creating history. They were suffering it'.

[95] It is hardly possible to overestimate the effect of the catastrophes that occurred between 70 and 134/35 A.D. on the inner development of Judaism. The image provided by the later rabbinic authors of the period before the political collapse is one-sided and should be regarded critically.

Zealotism and its transformation or exclusion was one of the essential elements in the development of rabbinism following the destruction of Jerusalem in 70 A.D.

3. The Christian Sources

There are traces of the Zealot movement in the gospels,[96] the Acts of the Apostles[97] and the Pauline letters. Paul had a more positive attitude towards 'zeal' in Pharisaism before the destruction of Jerusalem than the later rabbinic authors. This fact emerges quite clearly from a number of places in his epistles.[98] The later writers of Church history such as Eusebius, however, saw the Zealots only as Josephus had seen them and therefore contributed nothing new to the fund of our knowledge of the movement.[99] Several valuable pieces of information about Zealotism are contained, on the other hand, in Hippolytus' description of various Jewish sects in his 'Refutation of all Heresies'. He obviously regarded the Zealots as a sub-group of the Essene movement.[100]

The New Testament references to the Jewish freedom movement are, of course, particularly interesting because of their closeness in time to the events. Hippolytus' brief account is, however, particularly impressive because of his description of the zeal of the Zealot movement, which is, moreover, confirmed by related Talmudic descriptions.[101]

4. Other Ancient Authors

It is obvious that disturbances in a remote country such as Palestine would have had no more than a marginal effect on the ancient world and the aims of the anti-Roman movement with rebellion in mind were no doubt regarded as hardly worth mentioning. It was only when the Jewish War itself broke out that attention was drawn to the Zealots at least in the eastern part of the Roman Empire, since there had not been an uprising of an oppressed people in the Empire for several decades. It is also probable that Roman historians became interested in this war because Vespasian, the commander of the army that had been sent to suppress the Jewish rebellion, was surprisingly made emperor and his

---

[96] See below, p. 337ff.
[97] See below, pp. 47 and 78f.
[98] See below, pp. 177 and 180ff.
[99] *HistEcc* 2,20; 3,6f.
[100] See below, p. 70ff.
[101] See below, pp. 190ff and 197ff.

son Titus, who later succeeded him as emperor, led the army to ultimate victory in the Jewish War. This, then, is why Tacitus, Suetonius and Dio Cassius barely mention the disturbances in Judaea before the outbreak of war,[102] but deal with the war itself in some detail, thus supplementing Josephus' account in a very valuable way.[103] It is possible that at least part of their source material was derived from the *De Judaeis* of Antonius Julianus, who was, according to Josephus, the procurator of Judaea during the siege of Jerusalem.[104] We also have a note by Pliny the Elder, but we may assume that the author himself did not in fact take part in the siege.[105] Epictetus mentions the martyrdom of the 'Galilaeans' and it is likely that this is a reference to the fact that the rebels were condemned to death at the end of the Jewish War.[106] We may therefore conclude that the contribution made by ancient authors who were not Jews is relatively insignificant.

---

[102] Only Tacitus provides a few data; see *Ann* 12,54; see also below, p. 348, n. 183. See also his terse statement: 'Duravit tamen patientia Iudaeis usque ad Gessium Florum procuratorem', *Hist* 5,10.

[103] See Tacitus, *Hist* 5,10-13; Suetonius, *Vesp* 6; *Tit* 3f.; Dio Cassius, 66,1.4-7.

[104] *Bell* 6,238; his work is mentioned by Minucius Felix, *Oct* 33,4; see Schürer, 1, 33, and especially E. Norden, *Neue Jahrbücher für das klassische Altertum* 31 (1913), 664ff.

[105] See below, p. 335, n. 116. See, for a view that was opposed to earlier opinions, Sir R. Syme, *Tacitus*, Oxford 1958, 1, 20f., and especially n. 5; see also M. Stern, *JRS* 52 (1962), 258.

[106] See below, p. 58f.

CHAPTER II

THE VARIOUS NAMES GIVEN TO THE JEWISH FREEDOM MOVEMENT

The members of the Jewish freedom movement have various names in Josephus' work and these also occur at least to some extent in other sources. Each of these names has a definite content and a clear historical background and each characterizes the freedom movement in a different way.

A. THE 'ROBBERS' (λῃσταί)

The commonest term in Josephus for the members of the movement is λῃστής, although λῃστικοί also occurs.[1] The word λῃστής is usually translated as 'robber', but, as I shall show further on, the concept has a wider meaning in Josephus' work than our word 'robber'. The author did not simply happen to use it by chance. If we are to understand its meaning, we have first of all to examine the general significance of what lies behind the term.

1. The Ancient Linguistic Usage

λῃστής is a classical Greek word derived from λῃΐς, booty, or λῃΐζομαι, to seize as booty.[2] It is synonymous with ἅρπαξ, although this has the meaning more of a robber of another's property, while λῃστής is rather a criminal, often armed and violent.[3] It frequently occurs with the meaning of 'pirate', especially in the context of the Hellenistic eastern Mediterranean.[4] In addition, it is also used of irregular soldiers working in bands in search of booty.[5] The Latin word *latro* corresponds exactly

---

[1] For Josephus' linguistic usage, see below, p. 41ff.

[2] See H.G. Liddell and R. Scott, *Greek-English Lexicon*, 9th. ed. Oxford 1940, 1046. (Cited below as Liddell-Scott.)

[3] There is a similar relationship between the corresponding terms *latro* and *rapax* in Latin and ליסטים and גַּזְלָן in Talmudic Hebrew; see below, p. 34ff.

[4] See Liddell-Scott, *op. cit.*

[5] F. Passow, *Handwörterbuch der griechischen Sprache*, 5th. ed. 1841ff., II,1, 54: 'Also bands that are not waging regular war, but are making incursions into enemy territory and then withdrawing according to circumstance'. See, for example, Sir 36.31 (=LXX/Vs 26).

to the Greek λῃστής.[6] Both words were used by ancient authors, together with the related abstract nouns λῃστεία and *latrocinium*, for the most part when they were discussing the widespread phenomenon of disorder caused by robbers. The words were also legal technical terms.

Excursus II: The Scourge of Robbers in the Ancient World

(a) In the Roman Empire[7]

The parts of the Empire that suffered most from robbers were the frontier provinces and territories. These provided favourable hiding-places for robbers because of their geographical situation. There were also individual tribes and groups within the Empire that were particularly inclined to robbery or λῃστεία. In Egypt, for example, the Bucoli, who were cowherds in the swamps of the Nile Delta, had been feared for centuries.[8] They had been mentioned as early as the third century B.C. by Erastosthenes, but they were not annihilated until after their dangerous revolt under Marcus Aurelius.[9] According to the various papyri of the second and third centuries A.D., inhabitants of Egyptian villages were obliged to support the police as so-called λῃστοπιασταί. If they refused to do so, they could expect to be punished severely.[10]

The scourge of robbers was also never completely eliminated in Asia Minor. The Pamphylians had a bad reputation as robbers[11] and Augustus had to wage regular war against the neighbouring Isaurians, who had

---

[6] Varro, *LinglLat* 7,52, derives it from the Greek λάτρις, a hired servant or mercenary; see Forcellinus, *Lexicon totius Latinitatis*, 1831ff., 2, 673f., and T. Mommsen, *Römisches Strafrecht*, 1899, 629, n. 4. In contrast to the term *latro*, there is also a word *grassator*, which means an individual unarmed footpad. The two meanings, however, overlap. See I. Opelt, *Die lateinischen Schimpfwörter*, Heidelberg 1965, Index, under the word *grassator*.

[7] See L. Friedländer, *Roman Life and Manners in the Early Empire*, 1928, 1, 294-299; Daremberg and Saglio, *Dictionnaire des antiquités grecques et romaines*, III, 2, 991f., article *latrocinium*, written by G. Humbert (C. Lécrivain); O. Hirschfeld, *Kleine Schriften*, 1913, *Die Sicherheitspolizei im römischen Kaiserreich*, 576-612, especially 593ff.; R. MacMullen, *Enemies of the Roman Order*, 1966, 60ff.

[8] Strabo 17,1.6 (792); 17,1.19 (802).

[9] The revolt began with the murder of two Roman tax-collectors, one of whom seems to have been sacrificed and eaten. Some sections of the population of Egypt joined the rebels and these threatened Alexandria. Avidius Orosius, the emperor's commissioner for the East, did not venture to engage in pitched battle with them 'because of their desperate anger and ferocity'. He was eventually victorious, but only because of their own disunity; see Dio Cassius 71,4; *ScriptHistAugMarcAurel* 21. See also Heliodorus, *Aethiopica, passim*, but especially 6,2-12. There are obvious parallels with the Jewish freedom movement.

[10] See O. Hirschfeld, *op. cit.*, 613f., and T. Mommsen, *op. cit.*, 307, n. 1. A similar situation seems to have existed, at least according to *Bell* 2,229 (= *Ant* 20,114), in Palestine.

[11] Strabo 12,7.2 (570).

terrified Asia Minor for centuries and continued to do so until the Byzantine period, in an attempt to check their banditry.[12]

Apuleius paints a vivid picture in his *Metamorphoses* of the uncertainty in Greece generally and Thessaly in particular, where the main reason for the bad situation was the presence of too few troops. There was also a continuous change of governors in these senatorial provinces.[13] Paul's κινδύνοις λῃστῶν may have been due to his experiences while travelling in Asia Minor and Greece.[14]

The interminable difficulties involved in combatting robbers are clear from the example of Sardinia, where they caused such extensive public nuisance that great areas of fertile land remained uncultivated.[15] Cicero speaks of 'robbers clothed in sheepskins' with whom the *propraetor* there, supported by a cohort of the *Auxilia*, had to struggle.[16] During the reign of Augustus, the disorders became a formal rebellion and, from 6 A.D. onwards, a regular war had to be waged against the rebels.[17] In 19 A.D., Tiberius sent four thousand released men, who had been contaminated by Jewish and Egyptian 'superstitions' and had been pressed into armed service, to Sardinia 'in order to fight the robbers there'.[18] There are obvious parallels here with the situation in Palestine.

Similar situations must also have existed in certain parts of Spain.[19] At the time of the republic, the Roman authorities were constantly waging 'robber wars' there, although it is difficult to distinguish between half-subjected tribes revolting and real robbers. According to Appian, a 'band of robbers' consisting of ten thousand men gave the Romans a great deal of trouble. Both leaders had Roman names and may have been soldiers at one time.[20] Appian says of the Spanish robbers that

'the robbers were in such good spirits that none of the prisoners would endure slavery. Some of them committed suicide, while others killed those who sold them. Some sank the ships that took them away'.[21]

---

[12] Dio Cassius 55,28.3: Ἴσαυροί τε γὰρ ἐκ λῃστείας ἀρξάμενοι καὶ εἰς πολέμου δεινότητα προσήχθησαν. The same could have been said of the Jews at the beginning of the Jewish War. See *CAH* 10, 261,270ff. During the reign of Claudius, the Cilician hill people, the Cieti, overran the fertile coastal regions of the province; see Tacitus, *Ann* 12,55; see also *CAH* 10, 682.

[13] See Hirschfeld, *op. cit.* 594; see also Apuleius, *Met* 2,18.3: 'Passim trucidatos per medias plateas videbis iacere, nec praesidis auxilia longinqua levare civitatem tanta clade possunt'. For the inadequate military occupation of this province, see *Bell* 2,366,368.

[14] 2 Cor 11.26.

[15] Varro, *ReRust* 1,16.2: 'Multos enim agros egregios colere non expedit propter latrocinia vicinorum: ut in Sardinia quosdam ...' See also Josephus, *Bell* 2,279 and *Ant* 20,256.

[16] *ProvCons* 7: 'Res in Sardinia cum mastrucatis latrunculis a propraetore una cohorta auxiliaria gesta'.

[17] Dio Cassius 55,28.1.

[18] Tacitus, *Ann* 2,85: 'Coercendis illic latrociniis'; cf. Suetonius, *Tib* 36.

[19] Varro, *op. cit.*: 'ut in Hispania prope Lusitaniam'.

[20] *HistRom* (*Hispania*) 6,68.

[21] *op. cit.*, 6,77; see also the heroic suicide of Jewish rebels, below p. 262.

Augustus placed on the head of the Spanish robber Korokotta a reward of 250 000 drachmae, but when the latter submitted voluntarily, he went unpunished and received the reward himself.[22] Impressive evidence of the activity of these robber bands is found in the inscriptions on the tombs of their victims.[23] Robbers also caused considerable public nuisance even in Italy, where they seem to have been very widespread.[24] There is general agreement among many Roman authors writing between Augustus and Domitian that travelling in Italy itself was extremely dangerous.[25] The situation there was particularly bad at the end of the civil war, at the beginning of Octavian's reign.[26] Octavian was energetic in his attempts to control the disorder caused by robbers[27] and Tiberius and Claudius continued the work that he had begun.[28]

(b) In Syria and Palestine

The position with regard to 'robbers' was no better in Syria and Palestine than in the Roman provinces discussed above. Even in the Old Testament, there are signs that social deprivation led to soldiers of fortune recruiting dissatisfied men without possessions into their bands and waging private wars with them.[29] The best example of this kind of leadership is provided by David. After he had been rejected by the king, he assembled a group of volunteers without roots in society around him[30] and retired with them into the Judaean desert, where they lived in caves. What is particularly striking,

---

[22] Dio Cassius 56,43.3. Josephus refers to a similar case of self-surrender against a promise of life or freedom; see *Bell* 2,64 (*Ant* 17,284) and *Bell* 2,253 (*Ant* 20,161). See also below, p. 328, n. 91; p. 350, n. 193.

[23] In Spain: *CIL* II, 2968 '. . . eques f(ilius) annorum XX a latronibus occisus'; 3479 '. . . caeditu)r infesto concursu forte latronum'; in Dacia: *CIL* III,1, 1559,1585; in Dalmatia: *CIL* III,1, 2399,2544.

[24] See the detailed survey of the situation there in Friedländer, *op. cit.*, 1, 294–299.

[25] Horace, *Epist* 1,2.32; Seneca, *Dial* 3,16.1; 5,43.3; 6,20.5: 'locata publice latrocinia'; *Benef* 1,10.5; 2,18.6, etc.; *Epist* 14,9: only the poor man could be safe, 'nudum latro transmittit'; Juvenal, *Sat* 10,22: 'cantabit vacuus coram latrone viator'. Epictetus, *Diss* 3,13.3, is similar. See also Juvenal's impressive descriptions, *Sat* 3,305–307, and those by Martial, *Epigr* 14,20, and Pliny the Younger, *Epist* 6,25.

[26] Appian, *BellCiv* 5,132.

[27] Suetonius, *Aug* 32,1: 'Igitur grassaturas dispositis per opportuna loca stationibus inhibuit'.

[28] Suetonius, *Tib* 37,1: 'Imprimis tuendae pacis a grassaturis ac latrociniis seditionumque licentia curam habuit'. The three words *grassatura*, *latrocinium* and *seditio* clearly represent three stages in intensity; see *Claudius* 25,2; see also Seneca, *Clem* 2,1.1. At a later period, the unsuccessful struggle conducted by the emperor, Septimius Severus, against the robber captain Felix Bulla is particularly relevant; see Dio Cassius, 71,10.6: 'Severus was furious because he won wars in Britain, but was defeated by a robber in Italy'.

[29] See Judges 9.4 (Abimelech); 11.3 (Jephthah) and 1 Kings 11.24 (Eliada).

[30] David's troops went out, according to 2 Sam 3.22, on expeditions (as robbers). For the composition of this troop, see 1 Sam 22.2 and, for the territory where it operated, 1 Sam 27.1ff.; 23.14; 24.1 etc.

however, is that this very 'worldly' phenomenon could be given a religious interpretation by the Old Testament author, according to whom Abigail said to David: 'My lord is fighting the battles of the Lord'.[31]

During the later period of the monarchy, peasant farmers were empoverished by debt because the land became increasingly the property of a few rich owners.[32] This led to a sharp decline in society and the formation of many bands of robbers.[33] The revolt of the Maccabees also took the form, at least in its initial stages and after Judas' death, of a war waged by bandits. It also, however, in its first part at least, bore the imprint of a war of faith and I shall be discussing this aspect of it later.[34] With the collapse of the Seleucid Empire towards the end of the first century B.C., the country fell to a great extent into the hands of Arabian and Iturean tribes.[35] These had since time immemorial regarded it as their special privilege to plunder caravans.[36]

Pompey's troops occupied Syria partly at least with the aim of putting an end to this activity.[37] Jews had also taken part in the formation of small 'robber states'. Their Mediterranean port of Joppa became a pirates' den, making the whole of the eastern Mediterranean unsafe.[38] The tranquillity that the Romans had hoped to bring about with their occupation did not materialize. Even if the 'robber captain' Hezekiah and his followers were really members of the Jewish freedom movement and should therefore not be regarded as 'robbers',[39] such men were undoubtedly present in Trachonitis and Josephus called them also λῃσταί, although they hardly had anything to do with the later Zealots. The rugged territory of Trachonitis was quite unsuitable for agriculture, but its network of caves provided many safe hiding-places. The inhabitants were for the most part shepherds,[40] but

---

[31] 1 Sam 25.28.

[32] See Amos 2.6ff.; 4. 1f.; 5.11f.; 6.3ff.; 8.4-6; Is 3.14f.; 5.8 etc.

[33] See Hos 7.5 and 6.9.

[34] See below, p. 149.

[35] T, Mommsen, *Römische Geschichte*, 14th. ed. 1933, 3, 139ff.; M. Rostovtzeff, *Social and Economic History of the Hellenistic World* 1941, 2, 841f.,868; see also Strabo 16,2,18.20 (755f.).28 (759).

[36] See Gen 16.12; 1 Sam 30.1ff.; 2 Chron 22.1; Job 1.15ff. Individual tribes of Israel seem also to have plundered caravans during the early period; see Gen 49.17,19,27; Deut 33.22.

[37] See Justinus (Pompeius Trogus) 40,2.4: 'ne rursus Syriam Iudaeorum et Arabum latrociniis infestam reddat'. See also the Prologue to Book 39. The 'petty tyrants' mentioned in *Ant* 14,38-40 and Strabo 16,2,10.18 (752.755) are no more than leaders of such robber bands who were able to acquire a degree of power because of the general state of anarchy. Pompeius had some of them condemned to death; see *Ant* 14,39; Strabo 16,2.18 (755).

[38] See *Ant* 14,43; see also Strabo 16,2.28 (759). A tomb in Jerusalem during the reign of Alexander Jannaeus shows a naval galley pursuing a ship. Her captain is standing at the prow with his bow drawn; see *IEJ* 6 (1956), 127f.; L.Y. Rahmani and others, 'The Tomb of Jason', *Atiqot* 4 (1964). At the beginning of the Jewish War, the Jews in Joppa became pirates once again; see *Bell* 3,415f.

[39] See below, p. 313ff.

[40] *Ant* 15,346; 16,272. In Jerusalem, shepherds were always suspected of being robbers; see Bill. 3, 114.

most of their income came from the raids that they made on caravans on their way to Damascus. The rulers of this part of Syria left them undisturbed on condition that they made over part of their gains. Herod, who was given this territory by Augustus, found it difficult to control these bands of robbers, since they were protected and supported by the king of the Nabataeans. The disorder that they caused did not come to an end until three thousand Idumaeans and five hundred Jewish cavalrymen from Babylonia cleared out the robbers' dens and settled in the district.[41] Despite this, however, there is a later inscription which probably refers to the expulsion of robbers living 'like animals' in caves in the district either by Agrippa I or by Agrippa II.[42]

People of rank travelling in eastern Jordania had to be given a military escort.[43] Even the Essenes were armed against possible attacks when they travelled[44] and there is confirmation in the New Testament of this general lack of safety.

It is, however, often difficult to decide whether those who are called λῃσταί in the texts were Zealots or whether they were simply ordinary robbers or highwaymen. The robbers in Jesus' parable of the good Samaritan are certainly ordinary highwaymen and there is no reason to go further in search of a more subtle interpretation of the text.[45] The two words used in the image of the good shepherd in the fourth gospel, λῃσταί καί κλέπταί would suggest that there is no direct relationship here with Josephus' λῃσταί. The robber was also a favourite figure in parables in the rabbinic literature.[46] The occurrence of the λῃσταί in the gospel accounts of Christ's passion seems, on the other hand, to point to a connection with the Zealots.[47]

Even after the collapse of the Jewish struggle for freedom, the country continued to be troubled by robbers. Achilles Tatius, for example, speaks of robbers at large in the coastal zone between Gaza and Pelusium.[48] One Claudius caused great trouble with his mounted band of robbers in the

---

[41] *Bell* 1,399; *Ant* 15,343-348; 16,281-285; 17,23-28; see also Strabo 16,2.20 (756). According to an inscription, Dittenberger, *OGIS* 1, 628, No. 415, one of the Idumaean soldiers stationed in Trachonitis dedicated a column to Herod.

[42] R. Cognat-Lafaye, *Inscriptiones graecae ad res Romanas pertinentes*, 1223 = Dittenberger, *OGIS* 1, 634f., No. 424. This inscription is an edict promulgated by Agrippa I or Agrippa II: [Βασιλεὺς Ἀγ]ρίππας φιλοκαῖσαρ [καὶ φιλορω]μαῖος λέγει [...] θηριώδους καταστάσεω[ς ...] οὐκ οἶδ' ὅπως μέχρι νῦν λαθόντες καὶ ἐν πολλοῖς τῆς χώ]ρας μέρεσιν ἐμφωλεύσ[αντες ... ε]ἶχεν ἢ μηδ' ὅλως πότε ... For the interpretation of this inscription, see M.P. Charlesworth, *Trade Routes and Commerce of the Roman Empire*, 1924, 250.

[43] *Ant* 18,112.

[44] *Bell* 2,125.

[45] Lk 10.30-37. According to Rengstorf, *TD* 4, 261, the interpretation attributes a meaning to the parable that was not originally intended.

[46] Jn 10.1,8, as opposed to Rengstorf, *op. cit.*. For the 'robbers' in the rabbinic literature, see below, p. 36ff.

[47] Mk 15.27 parr. and Jn 18.40; see also below, p. 34ff.

[48] 'Leucippe and Cleitophon' 3,5.

whole of Syria and Judaea during the reign of Septimus Severus.[49] Finally, it is interesting to note how often ancient authors criticized the Jews for being a nation of robbers.[50] This judgement was, understandably enough, firmly rejected by Josephus in his apology of Judaism.[51] There are even references in the rabbinic literature to defamatory remarks made against the Jews.[52]

(c) The Judgement and Punishment of 'Robbers'

The governor of each province was responsible for taking steps to combat robbers and all those who supported them.[53] These governors' powers were, however, so different from province to province and the men holding this office changed so frequently that great uncertainty prevailed in most places and this indirectly strengthened brigandry. This is clear from the situation in Palestine before the outbreak of the Jewish War. Although several attempts had been made to create a special security police force, there was at the time still no body of that kind.[54] In places where there were no regular troops, a militia had to be established. The Samaritan militia set up by the procurator Cumanus to combat the attacks of the Jews led by the 'robber captain' Eleazar b. Dinai is an example of this.[55] The Temple guard in Jerusalem may also have been regarded by the Romans as a militia that was permanently stationed in one place.[56]

---

[49] Dio Cassius 75,2.4. J. Juster, Les Juifs dans l'Empire Romain, 1914, 2, 202, n. 4, suspected that he was a Jew.
[50] See Strabo 16,2.37 (761); see also 28 (759); Justinus 40,2.4. See also below, p. 162.
[51] Ap 1,62.
[52] R. Joshua of Siknin in the name of R. Levi (third/fourth century A.D.); see Bill., Introduction, 140, GenRab 1,2: 'so that the nations may not speak abusively to Israel and say: Are you not a people of robbers?' For anti-Jewish polemics in this context, see W. Bacher, 'The Supposed Inscription upon 'Joshua the Robber'', JQR 3 (1891), 354-357.
[53] Dig 1,18,13 Prol (from Ulpianus, Lib VII De officio proconsulis): '(praeses) sacrilegos latrones plagiarios fures conquirere debet et prout quisque deliquerit in eum animadvertere, receptoresque eorum coercere, sine quibus latro diutius latere non potest'. Marcianus, Dig 48,13,4.2; see Hirschfeld, op. cit., 593, is very similar. According to Dio Cassius, 54,12.1, governors who caught robbers or disciplined rebellious towns demanded a triumphal procession.
[54] See Mommsen, Römisches Strafrecht, 1899, 318ff., and J. Juster, 2, 253. For the situation in Egypt, see above, p. 25, n. 10.
[55] See Ant 20,122. The office of εἰρηνάρχαι had existed in Asia Minor since the second century A.D. and the local militia of the διωγμῖται were subject to these men; see Hirschfeld, op. cit., 594ff.; Mommsen, op. cit., 308. According to the 'Martyrdom of Polycarp', 6 and 7, they were involved in persecuting Christians, since the latter were regarded as rebels and disturbers of the peace. For the use of this concept against robbers, see Marcianus, Dig 48,3,6.1 (from one of Antoninus Pius' edicts while he was a governor in Asia Minor, 133-136 A.D.).
[56] See Lk 22.52; see also Acts 4.1; 5.24,26. Luke's ὡς ἐπὶ λῃστήν can be understood if this function of the Temple guard, as a municipal militia, to proceed against λῃσταί is borne in mind. According to Bell 2,263, it may also have been involved in warding off the Egyptian prophet. What Josephus has to say about the population of Jerusalem is only general. What is very important is that the revolt in Jerusalem in 66 A.D. was initiated by their commanding officer; see below, p. 358ff.

There were various stages of severity in the judgement of a ληστής or *latro* in Roman law.[57] The simplest definition was concerned with the armed criminal who attacked others with the purpose of robbing them, but did not murder them.[58] As such, he was subject to the *lex Cornelia de sicariis et veneficiis* passed by Sulla.[59] It was in principle forbidden in the Empire, at least at a later stage, to possess weapons without the necessary authority.[60] Vagabonds (*grassatores*) who were armed could be treated as robbers (*proxime latrones habentur*).[61] The penalty was increased when robbers worked together in a band (*factio*).[62] Anyone supporting robbers in any way could be simply identified with them.[63] *Latrocinium* was distinguished from lesser crimes such as theft or manslaughter, but there was a clear political demarcation in Roman law:

'Hostes sunt, quibus bellum publice populus Romanus decrevit vel ipsi populo Romano: ceteri latrunculi aut praedones appellantur. Et ideo qui a latronibus captus est, servus latronum non est, nec postliminium illi necessarium est: ab hostibus autem captus, ut puta aut Germanis et Parthis, et servus est hostium et postliminio statum primum recuperat'.[64]

'Hostes hi sunt, qui nobis aut quibus nos publice bellum decrevimus; ceteri latrones aut praedones'.[65]

Robbers, then, were placed outside the law of the state. The fact that they had considerable military strength or other forms of power at their disposal did not make them enemies (*hostes*) of the state with equal rights. They only became *hostes* by virtue of a legally valid declaration of war. Both in the linguistic usage of the ancient authors and in legal language, the concept of ληστής or *latro* was applied to the individual armed highwayman at the one extreme and the well organized army of a rebellious province at the other.[66]

---

[57] For what follows, see Mommsen, *op. cit.*, p. 629f. and Pfaff, article on *latrocinium*, PW 12, 978-980.

[58] See Cicero, *Pro Tull* 21 (50); Seneca, *Benef* 5,14.2: 'Sic latro est, etiam antequam manus inquinet: quia ad occidendum iam armatus est, et habet spoliandi atque interficiendi voluntatem'.

[59] Julius Paulus, *Sent* 5,23.1: 'Lex Cornelia poenam deportationis infligit ei qui hominem occiderit eiusve rei causa furtiue faciendi cum telo fuerit'. See also *Inst* 4,18.5.

[60] See Mommsen, *op. cit.*, 564, n. 2, and J. Juster, 2, 219, n. 6. Juster, following Dio Cassius, 69,12.2, believed that carrying arms was permitted in Palestine and that in this case it was simply a question of an obligatory handing over of arms to the Romans before the revolt of Bar Koseba; see R. Eisler's detailed discussion of this matter in 2, 268f., n. 6.

[61] Callistratus, *Dig* 48,19,28.10.

[62] Marcianus, *Dig* 48,19,11.2.

[63] Julius Paulus, *Sent* 5,3.4: 'receptores adgressorum itemque latronum eadem poena adficiuntur qua ipsi latrones'; see Mommsen, *op. cit.*, 775, n. 2. This basic principle also applied to Palestine; see *Bell* 2,253. See also above, p. 30, n. 53 and below, p. 349.

[64] Ulpianus, *Dig* 49,15,24. For the *postliminium*, see Weller's article, PW 22, 863-873.

[65] Pomponius (mid-second century A.D.), *Dig* 50,16,118; see also Julius Paulus, *AdSabDig* 49,15,19.2.

[66] See Forcellinus, *op. cit.*, 2, 637, under *latrocinium*: 'Milites qui illegitimum bellum

This explains why the Romans were only able to call the members of the Jewish freedom movement, even after the outbreak of the Jewish War, λῃσταί and were only able to regard them as lawless disturbers of the peace[67] and give them the same status as they gave to common criminals, even when they were confronted with them in open battle.

Insofar as they were Roman citizens, these 'robbers' were punished in accordance with the *lex Cornelia* by banishment, a relatively lenient penalty that was tightened up considerably in the course of time.[68] It was from banishment that *deportatio*[69] and later, in the case of the *humiliores* at least, the death penalty by *bestiae* or the *crux*[70] were developed. What probably happened here was that the preferential treatment of Roman citizens was adapted to the more severe penalties imposed on slaves and inhabitants of the provinces. The most severe punishment was, of course, awarded to members of large bands who were found guilty of causing an insurrection (*seditio*) or of endangering the state (*crimen majestatis*).[71] Even in the earliest days of the Empire, *famosi latrones* were sentenced to death by crucifixion.[72] Crucifixion was one of the *summa supplicia*[73] and, although it was initially mainly slaves and non-Romans who had been condemned to death who were crucified,

---

privata auctoritate collecta manu, nullo duce publico dato movent . . .' This idea seems to have been at the root of Caesar's thinking, *BellCiv* 3,109f., where the Egyptian enemies are described in the following way: 'ut potius privatorum paucorum et latronum consilio quam regio susceptum bellum videtur'.

[67] In the legal sense, everyone who disturbed the peace was a λῃστής . This is why λῃστής and στασιαστής could be used with the same meaning by Josephus; see below, p. 42f.

[68] See Mommsen, *op. cit.*, 631f.

[69] Julius Paulus, *Sent* 5,23.1; Marcianus, *Dig* 48,8,5.1 etc.

[70] Julius Paulus, *op. cit.*: 'Humiliores vero in crucem tolluntur aut bestiis obiciuntur'. See also a similar statement in Marcianus, *op. cit.* The famous robber Felix Bulla was condemned to be thrown to the beasts; see Dio Cassius 76,10.7. As a punishment for the Zealots, see *Bell* 6,418; 7,24.37ff.

[71] See Mommsen, *op. cit.*, 562ff. and 657ff.; see also Julius Paulus, *Sent* 5,22.1 = *Dig* 48,19,38.2: 'Auctores seditionis et tumultus vel concitatores populi pro qualitate dignitatis aut in crucem (furcam; *Dig*) tolluntur aut bestiis obiciuntur aut in insulam deportantur'.

[72] Under Hadrian, *Dig* 48,19,28.15: 'Famosos latrones in his locis, ubi grassati sunt, furca (= cruce; see Mommsen, *op. cit.*, 921, n. 2) figendos compluribus placuit, ut et conspectu deterreantur alii ab iisdem facinoribus . . .' A similar regulation seems to have existed in the first century A.D.; see Petronius 111,5: 'cum interim imperator provinciae latrones iussit crucibus adfigi'; Seneca, *Epist* 7,5: 'Sed latrocinium fecit aliquis: quid ergo meruit ut suspendatur'. According to Galen, ed. Kuhn, 2,385, it was quite possible to carry out studies of human anatomy using the bodies of robbers crucified on the hills.

[73] Callistratus, *Dig* 48,19,28 Prol and 15; Julius Paulus, *Sent* 5,17.2: 'Summa supplicia sunt crux, crematio, decollatio'; 5,23.17: 'bestiis obici aut cruci suffigi'. For the crucifixion of rebels in Palestine, see below, p. 259f. etc. Like Callistratus, the rabbinic authors were also acquainted with crucifixion and burning as the supreme penalties; in *ExRab* 9,4, Pharaoh says: 'If the son of Amram (that is, Moses) comes to me again, I will kill him; I will crucify him, I will burn him'. This statement presupposes a knowledge of the principles of Roman law.

criminals of lower standing were later, subject to the patronage of the *honestiores*, put to death in this way.[74] It was not a special punishment for political crimes. The judge could to a great extent use his own discretion with regard to the way in which the death penalty was carried out.[75]

(d) The Social Causes

There are several different reasons for the presence of robbers in the ancient world. In the case of the tribes living in the Taurus Mountains in Asia Minor and the inhabitants of Sardinia and Lusitania, for example, there had since time immemorial been restless, discontented groups among the population. In almost all other cases, however, those who became robbers were above all slaves who had run away,[76] soldiers who had deserted[77] and impoverished peasants whose land had been taken from them by great landowners or who had been driven from their homes and land by merciless tax-officials. In districts where the scourge of banditry had gained a firmer foothold because the inhabitants had insufficient protection against robbers, the collapse of small peasant farming was undoubtedly hastened by the hindrance of a well organized agricultural system.[78] The famous robber chief Felix Bulla, for example, sent a captured centurion back to his unit with the message: 'Tell your masters to feed their slaves, so that they will not become robbers'. He had many slaves in his band who had been emancipated by the emperor, but who had received no reward.[79]

In Egypt, becoming a robber corresponded to *anachoresis* and in Palestine flight into the mountains of the wilderness. A longing for adventure may also have led many men to become robbers.[80] The free, adventurous life of the robber attracted the attention of the ancient world. Not only ghost stories and love stories, but also adventures featuring robbers and bandits were among the most popular forms of literature at the time.[81] J. Juster also pointed to another very important aspect of this question: 'In the ancient

---

[74] Mommsen, *op. cit.*, 918-921; Hitzig, article on *crux*, *PW* 4, 1728-31; J. Blinzler, *The Trial of Jesus*, 1959, 246ff.

[75] The *auctores seditionis* were threatened with this form of the death penalty; see Julius Paulus, *Sent* 5,22.1, but it was also applied to ordinary murderers or to everyone affected by the *lex Cornelia*; see *op. cit.*, 5,23.1.

[76] See the great uprisings of slaves during the period of the Republic in Sicily, 135-132 B.C. and 104-102 B.C., and in Italy in 73-71 B.C. (Spartacus' revolt). According to *Bell* 2,57 = *Ant* 17,253, a group of rebels had a royal slave as their leader; see also *Bell* 4,510.

[77] See Spartianus, *HistAug, PescNiger* 3,4: 'ad comprehendendos desertores qui innumeri Gallias tunc vexabant'; see also below, p. 38, n. 121: NumRab 20,19.

[78] For examples from Egypt, see M. Rostovtzeff, *Social and Economic History of the Hellenistic World*, 1941, 2, 877.

[79] Dio Cassius, 76,10.5f.

[80] Dio Cassius, 74,2.5: by ceasing to recruit the praetorians from Italy, Septimius Severus led young men who were longing for adventure and combat to become gladiators and robbers; see also *Ant* 18,10.315.

[81] See Friedländer, *op. cit.*, 1, 297f.. The authors include Apuleius, Heliodorus, Achilles Tatius, Petronius and Longus.

world, pirates and brigands were not thought by the population as a whole to be following a discreditable profession. Therefore, although they committed murders, they should not be regarded as mere murderers'.[82]

Piracy and highway robbery could therefore be seen at least partly as chivalrous activity and particularly daring leaders of robbers' bands sometimes became popular figures.[83] Under such circumstances, the authorities might impose quite brutal penalties, but were only to a very limited degree able to control the public nuisance of robbery that was a constantly recurring feature of life in the ancient world. 'It is probable that, in districts where it proved impossible to eradicate the scourge of robbers, the government often preferred to leave the brigands in peace or even to try to establish good relationships with them.'[84] Sometimes an attempt was made to solve the problem by transforming the robbers into soldiers. Josephus, for example, tried to make allies of the 'robbers' of Galilee by awarding them pay.[85] The last procurators in Palestine seem to have been to some extent resigned to the constant disturbances in the country.[86] The same attitude can be discerned in the way in which Dio Cassius described the scourge of robbers which could never be fully overcome. It had always been there, he maintained, and it would not cease to exist as long as human nature remained the same.[87]

2. The לִיסְטִים in the Rabbinic Literature

The rabbinic authors used the term לִיסְטֵיס (in the plural לִיסְטִים) as a loan-word together with a number of derivations.[88] They also used it

---

[82] J. Juster, *Les Juifs dans l'Empire Romain*, 1914, 2, 208.

[83] See Thucydides 1,5ff.; Justinus 43,3; W. Kroll, *PW* 2, 1037, for the popularity of such robbers as Korokotta (see above, p. 27) or Felix Bulla in Italy under Septimius Severus (Dio Cassius 76,10). Arrian, a pupil of Epictetus, wrote a biography of the robber Tilliboras, who was active in Asia Minor; see Lucian, *Alexander* 2. The old theme of the noble robber makes its appearance here. See the legend of John in Clement of Alexandria, *Quis dives salv* 42 = Eusebius, *HistEcc* 3,23.6-19, and the slave Drimakos on Chios: *Athen* 6,265d/266e. Individual robbers seem also to have been popular figures in the rabbinic literature; see, for example, Eleazar b. Dinai, below, p. 349f.

[84] Hirschfeld, *op. cit.*, 594.

[85] According to *ScriptHistAugMarcAurel* 21, the latter enlisted into his army the robbers of Dalmatia whom he could not bring under his control. Caesar also criticized his opponents in Egypt for similar behaviour; see *BellCiv* 3,110, in which he claims that they recruited their troops 'ex praedonibus latronibusque Syriae Ciliciaeque provinciae finitimarumque regionum'. For Josephus, see *Vita* 77.

[86] Both Albinus and Florus were corrupted by 'robbers' and allowed them to move about relatively freely subject to the payment of money; see *Bell* 2,273.278 = *Ant* 20,215.255; see also below, p. 355ff.

[87] 36,20.1. He wrote of pirates and highwaymen: οὐ γὰρ ἔστιν ὅτε ταῦτ' οὐκ ἐγένετο, οὐδ' ἂν παύσαιτό ποτε ἕως δἂν ἡ αὐτὴ φύσις ἀνθρώπων ᾖ.

[88] Aramaic לִיסְטָא; as an abstract, 'robbery' לִיסְטוּת and Aramaic לִיסְטָיוּתָא; other derivations: לִיסְטֵירִין from ληστήριον; לִיסְטָיָא from ληστεία; אַרְכִילִיסְטֵיס from ἀρχιληστής. There is also the verbal form לִיסְטֵם, piel. See S. Krauss, *Griechische und*

relatively frequently. The closest Mishnaic equivalent to this group of Hebrew words is גֵּזֶל. The difference between these two groups of words is more or less the same as that between the Greek terms ληστής and ἅρπαξ.[89]

The principal meaning of לִיסְטִים is an armed and violent criminal who may also work in bands.[90] K.H. Rengstorf tried to prove that ληστής and לִיסְטִים were used similarly by Josephus and the rabbinic writers and that the לִיסְטִים of the rabbinic literature went back to Josephus' 'robbers'.[91] He also claimed that the Zealots 'made honourable a name that their opponents had used to abuse them'.[92] This is, however, an opinion that can hardly be upheld when it is remembered that the linguistic usage of the rabbinic literature cannot be directly related to the Jewish freedom movement, as Rengstorf himself admits.[93] The texts that he cites prove, on closer inspection, to be no exception to this general rule. If, for example, non-Jews (גּוֹיִים), robbers (לִיסְטִים) and a demon are listed together as causes of fear, this can only mean at the most that they all endanger man at night.[94] Even the crucifixion of captured לִיסְטִים may have no greater importance in view of the fact that it was not a specifically political penalty and could be imposed, in the provinces at least, in the case of any serious offence.[95] The rule that robbers had to be punished in the place where they had committed their crimes[96] can, it

---

Lateinische Lehnwörter in Talmud, Midrasch und Targum, 1898f., 2, 131,315f.; M. Jastrow, *A Dictionary of the Talmudim,* 1950, 2, 708f.,713 and 1, 122. Vocalization according to Jastrow. G. Dalman, *Aramäisch-Neuhebräisches Handwörterbuch,* 3rd. ed. 1938, 218, vocalized throughout as לִיסְטִים etc.

[89] For גֵּזֶל, see Jastrow, *A Dictionary, op. cit.,* 1, 231. The term refers above all to offences against property carried out with violence.

[90] The word גַּיִּס frequently appears with the meaning of 'band'; see J. Levy, *Neuhebräisches und Chaldäisches Wörterbuch über die Talmudim und Midraschim,* 2nd. ed. 1876ff., 1, 318; see also Jastrow, *op. cit.* 1, 237.

[91] Article ληστής, *TD* 4, 59f.; see also 261: 'The interpretation is suggested by the homogeneity of the use of ληστής in Palestine (Josephus and the rabbinic authors)'. Elsewhere, this writer's judgement is less decisive; see 260: 'It is even possible to say that, despite a different use later, לִיסְטִים originally meant the Zealots in the rabbinic literature'.

[92] *op. cit.* 260 (italicized by Rengstorf).

[93] *op. cit.* 259: 'The rabbinic usage is, in my opinion, by no means so clear in this case as Josephus'.

[94] Shab 2,5, cf. tTaan 2,12 (l. 218).

[95] The rabbinic authors reported several cases of crucifixion of robbers; see Sanh 46b bar (following a parable of R. Meir's); EccRab 7,26; EsthRab 3,14 on 1.12 etc. Crucifixion, however, was in no sense simply a political punishment; see above, p. 32, n. 72. For the special evaluation of crucifixion as martyrdom, see below, p. 260.

[96] EsthRab 3,14 on 1.12 (Bill. 3, 182).

is true, be inferred from Roman law,[97] but all that it really indicates at
the most is that Jews had no legal authority of their own in capital
offences.[98]

The two principles, 'the robber's wife is like the robber himself'[99] and
'the robber's companion is like the robber himself'[100] cannot be
explained in the light of martial law, but can either be traced back to
Roman law[101] or be understood as proverbial sayings with the meaning
of 'the receiver of stolen goods is like the thief'. When a לִיסְטִיס takes his
victim's garment[102] and gives him his own in exchange, he does not do
this with Deut 24.13 in mind, but simply because he wants to exchange a
bad garment for a good one. This is also clear from the parallel case of the
tax-collector who takes a good animal and leaves an old worn out beast
behind.

In addition to those cited by Rengstorf, there are many other
examples showing that the word does not point in the rabbinic texts
specifically to the religious and political 'Zealots' of the first century
A.D. In all these examples, it is clear that robbers were responsible for
making highways unsafe and that they preferred to wait at crossroads,
watching out for travellers.[103] They tended to frequent the caravan
routes through the desert,[104] thus making travelling extremely
dangerous.[105] Travellers protected themselves against these highway
robbers by carrying weapons.[106] They also helped each other in various
ways and set up look-out posts,[107] wore amulets and said special

---

[97] See above, p. 32, n. 72.

[98] For the legal situation in Palestine, see *Bell* 2,117; Mommsen, *op. cit.*, 243f.; see also
Jn 18.31 and J. Blinzler, *The Trial of Jesus*, 1959, 160ff.

[99] jKet 26d,38.

[100] jSanh 19b (l. 18): according to a conversation between the אנגטוס הזמון (Quietus at
the time of Trajan?) and Johanan b. Zakkai; see S. Krauss, *Monumenta Talmudica* V,
Geschichte 1, *Griechen und Römer*, 1914, No. 168, n. 5 (cited below as *MonTal* V1):
'Probably a proverbial way of speaking'.

[101] Julius Paulus, *Sent* 5,3.4; Ulpianus, *Dig* 1,18,13 Prol; see Mommsen, *op. cit.*, 775, n.
2; see also above, p. 31, n. 63, as opposed to Rengstorf, *op. cit.*, 265, 7.

[102] BK 10,2; see Rengstorf, *op. cit.*, 266, n. 23.

[103] Sanh 72a = jSanh 26b,75f. bar; GenRab 75,3 on 32.2; 92,6 on 44.1ff.; LevRab
30,6 etc. Even Nazirites could not be safe from them: Naz 6,3a.

[104] For the desert as a place of refuge for robbers, see SifDeut on 32.10, ed. Friedmann,
313. See also below, n. 107.

[105] Ber 1,3; MekEx 14,19 and 19,4; AZ 25b/26a: a distinction is made here between
robbers in Palestine and those in Babylonia; the former respected the teacher. See also
AZ 43a; Yeb 16,7 and BK 116b.

[106] RSh 1,9; see also Josephus *Bell* 2,125.

[107] RSh 2,5; Pes 3,7: it was permitted to help others attacked by robbers even on the
Sabbath. For the setting up of look-out posts against robbers, see LevRab 35,5;

prayers.[108] Country people and shepherds also lived in constant danger of attack by robbers operating in bands.[109]

There are also texts of a very distinctive kind that consist of a confrontation between robbers and the authorities. They are for the most part *mashal* texts rather than anecdotes based on an originally historical event. They form part of the royal parables that are so typical a feature of the later Midrashim.[110] They are all based on the presupposition that a deadly hostility existed between the king and the robber, who very frequently threatens to kill the king's son.[111] The prince is captured, but rescued by his father, who puts the bandits to death.[112] Sometimes it is the king's daughter whose life is threatened by robbers.[113] In some stories of this kind, the robbers destroy the king's vineyard and are in turn killed by the owner.[114] Very often the bandits are taken prisoner[115] and punished[116] by the state. The theme of an attack against the king's official representatives is the one that can most easily be applied to the activities of the Zealot :[117]

> 'The blessing is accompanied by protection. A king of flesh and blood has a servant in Syria while he remains in Rome. The king gave him a hundred *litrai* of gold. The servant took these and went on his way. But he was

---

NumRab 20,2; SongRab 6,11; MTeh 10,2 (see *MonTal* V1, No. 360b) mentions *burganin* or look-out stations in the desert. Caravans were required to halt there because of the danger of robbers. Such *burgi* in North Africa are frequently mentioned in inscriptions; see *CIL* II, 2494,2495; see also Daremberg-Saglio III, 2, 992.

[108] Ber 4,4 and 29b; LevRab 25,1.

[109] BM 7,9; BK 6,1; Peah 2,7f.; SifLev on 19.5.

[110] *MonTal* V1, 161ff., No. 383–390, and I. Ziegler, *Die Königsgleichnisse des Midrasch*, 1903, 93–100, have assembled at least part of the material.

[111] YalShim 2,620 from Mek (*MonTal* V1, No. 389); see also MekEx on 14.19 and SongRab on 3.6,3: 'He (the angel) was like a robber (ארכיליסטיס) struggling with a king's son (Jacob)'; see also GenRab 77,2 on 32.24.

[112] ExRab 20,12; see Ziegler, *op. cit.*, 94.

[113] ExRab 21,5; see Ziegler, *op. cit.*, 95.

[114] ExRab 30,17; see Ziegler, *op. cit.*, 93.

[115] GenRab 48,6 on 48.1 = *MonTal* V1, No. 386; LevRab 30,6 = *MonTal* V1, No. 390.

[116] EcclRab on 3.17: R. Hanina b. Papa (end of the third century A.D.): 'God will judge both the righteous and the evil man; the robber will go up to the place of judgement and Rabbi Akiba will go up the place of judgement'. See also tYeb 4,5 (Z. 244) = bYeb 25b and YalShim 1,76; see Ziegler, *op. cit.*, 97, for the execution of a robber in Cappadocia. For the crucifixion of robbers, see above, p. 32f, nn. 73 and 74. Released prisoners are also reported; see Ziegler, *op. cit.*, 99f.

[117] NumRab 11,5 = *MonTal* V1, No. 384 and Ziegler, *op. cit.*. 93. For another example of this kind, see LevRab 30,6 = *MonTal* V1, No. 387: a robber's attack on a royal tax-collector.

attacked by robbers who took from him everything that he had been given and that he had with him. Could he (the king) have protected him from the robbers? Therefore: 'the Lord bless you' — with wealth — and 'the Lord will protect you' — from robbers'.

It should, however, be borne in mind that these parables are generally expressions of relatively late traditions and that similar events are also mentioned elsewhere in early texts.[118] It is also important to note that robbers are not given any religious motivation or glorified in any way in these parables. On the contrary, they are usually strongly condemned and given the same status as the *goyim* or wild animals.[119] The ancient authors are often interested in the courage and the adventurous way of life of robbers, but this is, of course, fully in accordance with the attitude that generally prevailed in antiquity.[120] It is probably also the reason why robbers featured so frequently in the popular didactic form of the parable. The popular fairy-tale theme of the deceived robber also recurs with many variations.[121]

It is also interesting to note that foreign oppressors are often depicted as robbers. Tax-collectors are placed alongside robbers in a text already mentioned - both deprive travellers of their possessions.[122] A foreign army of occupation is also equated with a band of robbers by the

---

[118] A concrete case of this kind is mentioned by Josephus, *Bell* 2,228 = *Ant* 20,113, and, outside Palestine, by Pliny the Younger, *Epist* 6,25. Dio Cassius, 76,10.2, said of Felix Bulla, see above, p. 9f., n. 28, that he knew who all those who left Rome on a journey or who landed in Brundisium were and what they had with them.

[119] Shab 2,5; BM 7,9; tTaan 2,12 (Z. 218); see Bill. 4, 99; Ber 29b bar; MTeh 10,2.47a; see *MonTal* V1, No. 360b. For other examples of the condemnation of robbers, see EcclRab on 3.17 and 7.26; Sanh 72a bar; DeutRab 4,5 on 10.1. See also Lk 18.11 for the Pharisee's boastful prayer that he is not a robber (ἅρπαξ), which can also be included within this context.

[120] For this, see above, p. 34, n. 83. The aspect of popularity is particularly clear in the case of an important third century author, Simeon b. Lakish, known as Resh Lakish, who is reputed to have been a robber himself in his youth and who was condemned by R. Johanan b. Nappacha when they happened to be bathing together in the Jordan; see BM 84a. W. Bacher, *Aggada der Palästinensischen Amoräer*, 1892ff., 1, 342, believed, however, that Resh Lakish sold himself, according to Gitt 47a, as a gladiator. The two facts are not mutually exclusive, since gladiators and robbers are placed side by side in *Shab* 10a and gladiators who had run away frequently became members of bands of robbers in the ancient world; see Dio Cassius 74,2.5.

[121] GenRab 92,6 on 44.1f.; ExRab 30,24; LevRab 30,6; NumRab 20,19: A soldier leaves his king and becomes a robber; when he wants to return, the king refuses to take him back; see Ziegler, *op. cit.*, 96.

[122] BK 10,1.2; see also Bill. 1, 378f.; Shebu 39a bar: R. Simeon b. Jochai, ca. 150: 'There is no family in which a tax-collector is and none in which a robber is unless they are all robbers (לִיסְטִים)'.

inhabitants of the occupied country.[123] The following parable can be understood in this light:

'Like a ruler entering a country and with him many bands of robbers. One said to the other: 'How terrible this lord is'.[124]

It is probable that such comparisons express a bitter experience of the cruelty of the Roman occupation troops, whose predatory raids are vividly portrayed in various anecdotes.[125] Senior officials are rated no higher:

'Governors, duces and eparchs go out into the villages to rob and plunder (גּוֹזְלִים וּבוֹזְזִים)'.[126]

Pilate is included as a 'plunderer' in a list of procurators, governors and other odious persons as Haman's ancestors.[127] Not only the representatives of Roman domination, however, but also the power of the world itself appears in this light:

'R. Jose b. Hanina referred the verse to Esau (Eccles 5.7): If you see Esau oppressing and robbing the needy in the great city of Rome'.[128]
'The government of Edom boasts, while it violates and robs, but gives the appearance of setting up the judgement-seat'.[129]
'... and for whom does he (that is, the evil-doer = Rome) amass so much money? For Israel, as it is said: ... They will rob their robbers and plunder their plunderers (Ezek 39.10)'.[130]

The Mekilta compares the Romans, who destroyed the Temple, to a band of robbers, who plundered and burned down a king's palace and killed his servants. The king sits in judgement over the robbers, has some of them held captive and others put to death. Some he has crucified. Then his rule is recognized in the whole world.[131]

---

[123] jKet 26d,44.

[124] LevRab 9,8.

[125] See the description of the attack on Timnah in Judaea by a troop of plundering soldiers: YomTob 21a bar = Tosit. 2,6 (Z. 203). There were also similar reports from Galilee; see Shab 145b. According to Gitt 57a bar, a revolt on the part of the Jews was caused by an attack by Roman soldiers on a wedding procession. See Josephus' judgement of the Roman occupation troops, *Ant* 19,366 and *Bell* 2,268. These complaints also have parallels in other ancient traditions; see L. Friedländer, *Roman Life and Manners in the Early Empire*, 1928, 1, 192f; Philo, *Flacc* 5 (M 2, 518); Apuleius, *Met* 9,39-42; Juvenal, *Sat* 5,16,7-34. For Palestine, see also Lk 3.14.

[126] ExRab 31,17; *MonTal* V1, No. 335.

[127] *MonTal* V1, No. 165: בֶּן בּוֹזֶה בֶּן אִיפְלוֹטָס according to the second Targum on Esther, Soferim 13,6 etc.; see also H.L. Strack, *Jesus, die Häretiker und die Christen nach den ältesten jüdischen Angaben*, 1910, 45f.

[128] EcclRab on 5.7; *MonTal* V1, No. 335.

[129] LevRab 13,5; *MonTal* V1, No. 76; see also GenRab 65,1 on 26.34.

[130] ExRab 31,11; Bill. 4, 937.

[131] MekEx on 15.18 (L 2, 79f.); the individual details in the parable would lead one to assume that the conquest of Jerusalem was still remembered at the time.

This judgement of Rome, presumably founded on the polemics conducted by Israel's prophets against Assyria and Edom,[132] is clearly the antithesis to the attacks made by the ancient world against the Jews as a nation of robbers. In the Hellenistic East during the period of the Republic at least, Rome's predatory policy caused great offence and certain questionable aspects of its early history also gave rise to similar attacks.[133] These criticisms, however, gradually ceased and Jews, followed by Christians, were eventually the only people who continued to view the Empire in a critical light.[134] The Roman Empire, in which everyone who rebelled against the yoke of its rule was persecuted as a lawless 'robber', had to put up with the criticism that it was itself a robber state.

There is considerable agreement between the description of the scourge of robbers in the Roman Empire and the rabbinic statements about the לִיסְטִים. This applies, on the one hand, to the various levels of meaning contained in the term 'robber', including, for example, the individual highwayman, robber bands of different sizes and the hostile private army that was not recognized legally as an opponent of equal rank by the Romans. It also applies, on the other hand, to the protective measures taken by the state to deal with this always troublesome and often dangerous opponent. Any special nuances that might possibly have pointed to the Zealot movement in the first century A.D. cannot be found in the rabbinic use of the word לִיסְטִים.

It is important to add that, unlike the term σικάριος, which I shall be considering later, very many words were derived from ληστής, several of them taken over from the Greek.[135] It is also significant that ληστής, occurs as a loan-word in Syriac.[136] There is no justification for the assumption that the term לִיסְטִים was derived from Josephus' λησταί and may therefore perhaps have been a name that the Zealots gave to themselves. It is quite possible that this loan-word was incorporated at an earlier stage into the everyday language of Palestinian Judaism.

The only possible conclusion to which we can come on the basis of the rabbinic linguistic usage — a conclusion which is also borne out by other

---

[132] See Ezek 39.10 (see n. 130 above); Is 17.14 and 33.1.

[133] See H. Fuchs, *Der geistige Widerstand gegen Rom*, 1938, 15f.,40,46ff.

[134] See Augustine: 'remota itaque iustitia quid sunt regna nisi magna latrocinia?' (*CivDei* 4,4). For the judgement of the Zealots, see below, p. 305f. Part of the background to this is to be found in the crisis of the Empire in the third century; see M. Avi-Yonah, *Geschichte der Juden im Zeitalter des Talmud*, Berlin 1962, 85-134.

[135] See above, p. 34f., n. 88.

[136] S.C. Brockelmann, *Lexicon Syriacum*, 2nd. ed. 1928, 368.

ancient sources — is that the scourge of robbers in Syria and Palestine —
a scourge which was undoubtedly conditioned by the geographical and
sociological structure — was particularly widespread and also that Jews
played a significant part in it. This applies both to the period preceding
the Roman rule and to that following the revolt of Bar Koseba. There
are also several parallels to be found in other parts of the Roman Empire.

3. The λῃσταί in Josephus

Jewish λῃσταί are mentioned for the first time by Josephus in the
context of the annihilation of the ἀρχιλῃστής Hezekiah and his band by
the young Herod.[137] The next time that they occur is during the war
between Herod and the last Hasmonaean, Antigonus, in the Galilaean
highlands of Arbela.[138] Josephus mentions several times robbers and their
defeat in Trachonitis.[139] After the death of Herod, the λῃσταί were
particularly prominent and caused disturbances that shattered the peace
of the whole of Judaea.[140] These reports of robbers probably go back to
the work of Nicolaus of Damascus, Herod's friend,[141] although it is only
the bands of men operating in Trachonitis that we would, in our own
linguistic usage, describe as 'robbers'. In most other cases, these 'robbers'
were in fact men who were in revolt for political and possibly even more
for religious reasons.[142]

It is probable that Josephus took this use of the concept 'robber', as
applied to political and religious partisans, from Nicolaus of Damascus.
All that he says of the founding of the fourth sect of philosophy by Judas
the Galilaean is that it led to a great increase in the scourge of robbers[143]

He mentions the activity of the λῃσταί again in connection with the
procurators after the death of Agrippa I.[144] holding them more

---

[137] *Ant* 14,159 = *Bell* 1,204, cf. *AntAnt* 17,271 = *Bell* 2,56. For what follows, see
G.W. Buchanan, *HUCA* 30 (1959), 169-177; 31 (1960), 103-105.

[138] *Ant* 14,415ff. = *Bell* 1,304.

[139] See above, p. 28.

[140] *Ant* 17,285; *Bell* 2,65: τότε λῃστρικοῦ πολέμου τὴν Ἰουδαίαν πᾶσαν ἐνεπίμπλασαν.
It is possible to ask whether an *illegitimum bellum*, see above, p. 31f., n. 66, or an external
form of 'guerilla war', see below, p. 43, n. 160, is meant here. The term probably
includes both.

[141] See above, pp. 8 and 12; see also K. Kohler, *Harkavy Festschrift*, 1909, 7.

[142] See below, p. 144f.

[143] *Ant* 18,7f.

[144] *Bell* 2,228.235.238: ἐτράποντο δὲ πολλοὶ πρὸς λῃστείαν; 253f.264 etc.; *Ant*
20,5.113.121.124.160.165 etc.

responsible than anyone else for the outbreak of the Jewish War.[145] He also mentions the names of individual leaders of bands,[146] but in most cases the activity of the ληϲταί is described in general terms.[147] In his account of the beginning of the war, he makes a clear distinction between the extreme group, which he also describes as ληϲταί, and a moderate party, to which he probably belonged himself. The latter group he usually calls οἱ Ἰουδαῖοι.[148] Another name that he uses, mostly in the negative sense, for the rebels is οἱ ϲταϲιαϲταί .[149]

After the murder of the Zealot leader Menahem,[150] the ληϲταί recede almost completely into the background as a group engaged in warfare and Josephus only mentions the annihilation of their Galilaean forces by a Roman division on Mount Asamon.[151] This 'honorary title' is given only to John of Gischala, Josephus' bitter opponent,[152] and to the splinter group in Masada, the members of which are usually called ϲικάριοι .[153] Josephus had to give an important place in his *Vita* to the 'robbers', since they constituted the really powerful group.[154] He begins to use the term more frequently after the overthrow of Galilee, that is, after his own crossing over to the Roman camp. In this context, he calls the radical war party that plunged Jerusalem into ruin 'robbers'.[155] He also employs the words ζηλωταί and ληϲταί side by side, although the first appears more commonly in his work as the name of the party.[156] The more general terms οἱ Ἰουδαῖοι and ϲταϲιαϲταί occur quite often in addition to this. He speaks of ληϲταί especially whenever he intends to express his

---

[145] *Bell* 2,417; see also 425.431.434.441; *Vita* 21.28.77ff.

[146] The ἀρχιληϲτής Tholomaeus, *Ant* 20,5; Eleazar b. Dinai, *Bell* 2,253; *Vita* 105: one Jesus with a band near Ptolemais; *Bell* 2,587: John of Gischala; 2,652: Simon bar Giora; 3,450: Jeshua bar Tupha. See also *Bell* 2,275.

[147] See *Bell* 2,264ff.; *Ant* 20,160f.167.185. As a rule, Josephus speaks only in general terms about robbery, murder and plundering and mentions individual events only in very few cases, as, for example, in *Ant* 20,208ff.

[148] See *Bell* 2,517ff.523.536.543-554: the victory over Cestius; 3,9.17f.22.130.-136.149f. etc.: the defence of Jotapata.

[149] See *Bell* 2.452.484.525.534.538.557.651 etc. In addition, Josephus also speaks about νεωτερίζοντεϲ, *Bell* 2,417 etc. or about τὸ νεωτερίζον, 3,463 etc.

[150] *Bell* 2,443ff.; see below, pp. 293ff. and 366.

[151] *Bell* 2,511: τὸ δὲ ϲταϲιῶδεϲ καὶ ληϲτρικόν; in his account of the struggles to defend Jerusalem, *Bell* 2,541, Josephus speaks again of ληϲταί, possibly with the tactics of a surprise attack in mind. Otherwise, the term recedes completely into the background.

[152] *Bell* 2,587ff.593; 4,84.97; see below, p. 374.

[153] *Bell* 2,653; 4,406ff.; see below, p. 365f.

[154] *Vita* 28,77ff.105–11. Josephus' relationships with them were good and he made sure of their allegiance by awarding them fixed, regular pay.

[155] *Bell* 4,134f.138.242.244.555.

[156] *Bell* 4,199.202.

moral condemnation of the opponent, with the result that the word occurs more frequently as the horror increases in the besieged city.[157] It is also possible that the names οἱ Ἰουδαῖοι and στασιασταί go back to Josephus' Roman sources, while λησταί is his own contribution.[158]

He also used the term to describe a special tactic in warfare — a rapid movement forward in small groups to surprise the opponent and an equally rapid withdrawal. He even employs the word in this sense in speaking of his own method of fighting in the defence of Jotapata: ἐκτρέχοντες γὰρ λῃστρικώτερον κατὰ λόχους,[159] but he certainly does not intend, in this use of the concept, to describe himself and his fellow-combatants as λησταί . It would be quite justifiable to use the modern term 'guerrilla warfare' in this context.[160] This form of warfare was certainly known in the ancient world.[161]

If we compare the concept λῃστής in Josephus' writings with the data that we have considered so far, it at once becomes apparent that the same range of meanings exists in his use of the word, that is, it includes the individual robber,[162] bands of robbers and the rebellious army.[163] In the same way, the tactics of the λησταί, their sociological basis and the punishment that they received at the hands of the Roman authorities are all in accordance with parallel phenomena in other parts of the Roman Empire.[164] It is very likely that Josephus consciously stressed those aspects that his λησταί had in common with robbers in the rest of the ancient world. His intention was clearly to destroy the image that the Zealots may have had as occupying an exceptional political and religious position. 'They are slaves,' he declared, 'a rebellious rabble, the dregs of the population'.[165]

---

[157] Bell 5,30: στασιάζοντες οἱ ἀρχιλῃσταί; 5,448.515.524.546; 6,129.195.277.324.-363.370.417 etc.

[158] See above, p. 8f. It is, however, not possible to separate the terms completely.

[159] Bell 3,169, cf. 177.

[160] Bell 2,65: λῃστρικοῦ πολέμου was translated by H. St. J. Thackeray, Josephus, 2, 347, as 'guerilla warfare'.

[161] See Appianus, HistRom (Hispania) 6,73; Pausanias, GraecDescr 7,7.6; Sallust, Jug 97,5: 'pugna latrocinio magis quam proelio similis'. See also above, p. 25f.

[162] Bell 2,587, John of Gischala.

[163] στασιασταί and λησταί are to some extent used synonymously: Bell 2,441f.511; 5,448; 6,417 etc.

[164] See above, p. 30ff.

[165] Bell 5,443. The tension is made clear by Josephus' contradictory statement that the army of Simon bar Giora consisted not only of slaves and robbers, but also of citizens, who obeyed him as they would have obeyed a king; see Bell 4,510.

He was, of course, fully aware of the difference between a band of robbers and a regular army,[166] but he shared completely the Roman legal view, according to which anyone who rebelled against Roman rule was regarded as a lawless criminal, whether an individual robber or a whole army of insurgents. This view was closely connected with a moral condemnation of the Jewish freedom fighters. Josephus saw their actions as no more than raids made by robbers in search of booty[167] and their whole activity therefore as outside the law.[168] It is interesting to note that this judgement is much less prominent in the *Vita*, in which Josephus had to admit that he collaborated with the λῃσταί . Finally, he points out emphatically that the Zealots' ideal of freedom, which they valued so highly, was not their real reason for acting as they did:

> 'Great bands of robbers made continuous attacks and the most important men were killed, ostensibly with the aim of re-establishing the common state, but in reality in the hope of personal gain'.[169]

This theme recurs in his final diatribe against the Zealots:

> 'This (their demand for freedom) was only a cloak which they used to conceal their cruelty and greed, as their actions so clearly showed'.[170]

There could, in other words, be no doubt that such men fully deserved to be called λῃσταί.

It is, of course, very difficult to discern the true features of the Zealot movement behind this caricature. In individual cases, it is often hardly possible to determine whether Josephus is referring to the Zealots or only to ordinary highwaymen when he speaks of λῃσταί.[171] It may also be true, as at least one scholar has pointed out, that this term indicated a split in the movement.[172] If that was the case, it would apply above all to the period of the Jewish War itself, during which the freedom movement divided into several mutually hostile groups as the result of a breakdown in the central leadership.[173]

It is also important to bear in mind the sociological components of the

---

[166] *Bell* 4,408, the *Sicarii* in Masada.
[167] *Bell* 2,265: ... κατὰ λόχους διήρπαζον ...; 2,275.652f.; 4,134.405; 6,202f.358 etc.; *Ant* 20,185.187.210.256.
[168] See above, p. 16, n. 67; see also below, p. 183ff.
[169] *Ant* 18.7.
[170] *Bell* 7,256, cf. 264.
[171] See, for example, *Ant* 20,5.113.
[172] This is the opinion of K.H. Rengstorf, *TD* 4, 258f.
[173] See below, p. 369f.

term. The ληϛταί consisted to a very great extent of members of socially disadvantaged groups fighting, among other things, for a new system of ownership, which they regarded as God's will. This aspect of the concept also has parallels in the ancient world.[174] It is reasonable to assume that Josephus' criticism of greed on the part of the 'robbers' was based on this.

It is, however, essential to remember that Josephus used the word ληϛταί in order to brand the Zealots as lawless rebels and criminals in the Roman sense and as men who in the end received the punishment that they deserved.[175] Seen from this point of view, then, it is extremely unlikely that ληϛταί was ever a word that the Zealots used in its Aramaic form to describe themselves.[176] The most that we can ask in this context is whether it was not those members of the Jewish population who were hostile towards the Zealots, that is, the property-owning upper class, who in fact called the freedom fighters 'robbers'. This is certainly a possibility. In any case, ληϛταί was clearly not just a special term applied only to the Zealots, but, as we have seen from our examination above of the rabbinic usage in this respect, it simply meant 'armed robbers'. Identifying the Zealots with armed robbers, then, at once lowered their status.

We do not, moreover, know when the word ληϛτής entered Palestine as a loan-word. It occurs quite frequently in the Mishnah,[177] which means that it must have been known at the latest until the end of the first century A.D. It was possibly assimilated under the Ptolemies or the Seleucids, when the people were experiencing a strong wave of Hellenization. It hardly needs to be said that the Hellenistic inhabitants of Palestine, the neighbouring Syrians and the Roman officials in Palestine described the Zealots as ληϛταί. An example of this can be found in the linguistic usage of Nicolaus of Damascus.[178] There are also possible examples of the evangelists calling the Zealots ληϛταί.[179] Josephus, then, took the word over in the sense in which it was employed by members of the Jewish upper class and by the Hellenistic neighbours and gave it a sharp polemical emphasis, strongly influenced

---

[174] See *Bell* 2,265.427: the burning of the archives; see below, pp. 335. 361f. H. Kreissig, *Die sozialen Zusammenhänge des jüdischen Krieges*, Berlin 1970, does not, unfortunately, go deeply into the meaning of the concept.

[175] *Bell* 7,272–274; see also above, p. 11, n. 37.

[176] See above, p. 35f.

[177] See above, p. 34f.; cf. Schürer 2, 73, n. 246.

[178] See above, p. 41, n. 141.

[179] See below, p. 339.

by his own political attitude.[180] We can gain no information about the inner nature and meaning of the Zealot movement or its principles and aims from the term. The most that it can do is to throw some light on the external form of the movement and the way in which it conducted its campaigns. Neither of these aspects are typical of the Zealot movement as such, but they have parallels in other parts of the Roman Empire.

B. THE *SICARII*

1. The Basic Latin Meaning

A second name for the Jewish freedom party or a definite group within the movement is the term σικάριοι, which is closely related to the concept λησταί.

This word was originally Latin: *sicarius*, assassin. The term is derived from the name of the weapon used in the act of assassination: *sica*, dagger. Even at the beginning of the imperial era, however, its meaning had become much wider, so that it meant a murderer or a violent criminal who intended to commit murder:[181]

> 'Nam per abusionem sicarios etiam omnis vocamus, qui caedem telo quocumque commiserunt'.[182]

The *lex Cornelia de sicariis*, passed by Sulla, was directed against

> 'homicidas . . . vel eos, qui hominis occidendi causa cum telo ambulant'.[183]

This law was concerned above all with robbers and for this reason *latro* and *sicarius* came to have the same meaning in legal language.[184]

2. The Sicarii in Josephus

The term *sicarius* = σικάριος occurs as a loan-word[185] only in the writings of Josephus, where it appears quite suddenly. After describing

---

[180] See above, pp. 11 and 15f.

[181] S. Kleinfeller, article on *Sicarius, PW* 2, Series 2, 2185f. and Forcellinus, *Lexicon totius Latinitatis*, 1831ff., 4, 105; O. Betz, article on σικάριος, *TD* 7, 278ff.; I. Opelt, *Die lateinischen Schimpfwörter*, Heidelberg 1965, 133ff.,209; see also R. Till, *Historia* 11 (1962), 322, n. 14.

[182] Quintilianus, *Inst* 10,1.12.

[183] *Inst* 4,18.5; see also Mommsen, *Römisches Strafrecht*, 1899, 627ff.: 'condemnare aliquem lege de sicariis' (Tacitus, *Ann* 13,44). In Roman law, *inter sicarios* or *de sicariis* were fixed formulae for a case of murder that had to be dealt with in court; see Cicero, *MarcAntPhil* 2,4(8): 'quo modo sis eos inter sicarios defensurus'.

[184] See above, p. 31f.; see also Mommsen, *op. cit.*, 613,629f.

[185] *Thesaurus graecae linguae a H. Stephano*, ed. E.B. Hase, G. Dinsdorf and L. Dinsdorf,

Felix' vigorous and successful proceedings against the λησταί in the country in the *Bellum*, Josephus reports the appearance of a 'new kind of robber in Jerusalem'.[186] These 'robbers' were applying new tactics and murdering their opponents in broad daylight and especially on feast-days, when there were great crowds of people. For this purpose. they carried small swords hidden in their garments. According to Josephus, their first victim was the high-priest, Jonathan b. Ananus.[187] Josephus changes this report, however, in his *Antiquities*, claiming that the procurator, Felix, himself took the initiative to have Jonathan murdered. This information is not reported in the *Bellum*. Josephus also notes that, when the murderers received no punishment for their action afterwards, they used this mode of killing more frequently.[188]

Josephus does not speak of *Sicarii* until a little later, in the context of Festus' appointment to the office of procurator, and then he describes their new tactics in greater detail than he had in the *Bellum*.[189] Their first appearance during the procuratorship of Felix is confirmed by Luke.[190] In this text of the Acts of the Apostles, the Chiliarch and commander of the Fortress of Antonia, Claudius Lysias, confuses Paul with the Egyptian who led four thousand *Sicarii* into the desert. Luke was probably combining several events in this one text.[191] There is no evidence of an earlier occurrence of the term.[192]

Paris 1842–46, 5, 265. It is only in a later papyrus (Oxyrhynchus, 1294,8 = 10, 248; second or third century A.D.) that σικάριον appears as a loan-word from Latin with the meaning of 'dagger'; see Liddell-Scott, 2104.

[186] *Bell* 2,254; cf. 425. G. Baumbach, *ThLZ* 90 (1965), 731, transferred, completely without foundation, 'the social subject of the party of the *Sicarii*' to Galilee.

[187] *Bell* 2,256.

[188] *Ant* 20,162–165.

[189] *Ant* 20,186(f.): οἱ δὲ σικάριοι καλούμενοι ληταί. Their weapon was similar in size to the Persian short sword or *akinake*, but it was curved like the Roman *sica*. The method of perfidious assassination for political and religious reasons seems to have been practised previously in 'Zealot' circles and also by their predecessors. In *Ant* 15,282ff., there is reference to a conspiracy of ten men against Herod; the plan was for these men, with daggers hidden under their garments, to kill the king. A similar procedure is described in Acts 23.12-15. The model was Ehud's assassination of Eglon, Judges 3.11-30.

[190] Acts 21.38.

[191] S.F.J. Foakes Jackson and Kirsopp Lake, *The Beginnings of Christianity*, I *The Acts of the Apostles*, 1920, 1, 422; E. Haenchen, *The Acts of the Apostles*, 1971, 61ff. It is, however, very doubtful whether Luke took these passages over from Josephus. A parallel tradition like that in Acts 5.37 is more probable; see below, p. 78.

[192] O. Cullmann, *The State in the New Testament*, 15, tried to make a connection between the name given to the traitor Judas, Ἰσκαριώτης, and the *Sicarii*, following F. Schulthess in this, but his argument is not convincing. The form assumed by Schulthess, σικαριώτης, cannot be proved in any way to be authentic and the interpretation of the

This fact, taken together with the Latin origin of the word, would seem to suggest that σικάριοι, as a name for the λῃσταί, can be traced back directly to the Roman authorities and soldiers in Palestine. They presumably gave the Jewish freedom fighters this name when the latter had been compelled by the successes achieved by the Roman procurator Felix in combatting them in the open country[193] to turn their attention to Jerusalem and make the city the theatre of their small-scale war, using new methods of fighting. It has until now been assumed that the *Sicarii* formed an independent party.[194] This is, however, not the case. They were a particularly active group within the λῃσταί, employing a new method of fighting. They took the struggle into the city itself and in this way came substantially closer to achieving the aim that they had been hoping to achieve, that of a general uprising against Rome. The ultimate decision about this could, after all, only be taken in Jerusalem itself.[195]

Josephus at first used the two concepts unhesitatingly side by side when speaking of the most active and at the same time leading group of insurgents who were pressing for war.[196] It was not until there was a division in the ranks of the Jewish freedom movement at the beginning of the revolt that parties emerged.[197] One of these parties, consisting of the followers of the murdered Menahem, was from that time onwards called by Josephus σικάριοι.[198] These men had established themselves under the command of Eleazar b. Ari, a close relative of Menahem, in the mountain fortress of Masada in the region of the Dead Sea.[199] They did not play an important part in the further course of the war, in the end preferring collective suicide to subjection by the Romans.[200] Josephus called the Jewish rebels who fled to Egypt after the end of the war in Judaea σικάριοι.[201] These men could hardly, at least according to Josephus' account, have been refugees from Masada, since the entire

---

'*Sicarii* as non-Jewish, alien robbers' is completely unfounded; see the author's *Das Problem der Sprache Jesu*, 1917, 41 and 54ff., and his article in *ZNW* 21 (1922), 250ff. See also E. Klostermann, *Das Markusevangelium* (*HNT* 3), 4th. ed. 1950, 35.

[193] *Bell* 2,253f.
[194] See *Beginnings*, 1, 422f.
[195] See below, p. 358ff.
[196] See, for example, *Ant* 20,164f. and *Bell* 2,254f.; see also *Ant* 20,210; *Bell* 2,408: ... τινὲς τῶν μάλιστα κινούντων τὸν πόλεμον and 425.
[197] *Bell* 2,441-448; 2,564f.; 4,138f.; 5,2ff.; see also below, p. 366ff. and 369ff.
[198] *Bell* 2,653: λῃσταί; *Bell* 4,400ff.: οἱ προσαγορευόμενοι σικάριοι; see also 4,504: λῃσταί; 516f.: σικάριοι.
[199] *Bell* 2,447; 7,399. See below, p. 332, n. 106.
[200] *Bell* 7,253.275-406.
[201] *Bell* 7,410ff.437; see also below, p. 260f.

garrison there had committed suicide. The constant distinction made by Josephus between those who defended the city against Titus and the *Sicarii* is evidence that they did not originate in Jerusalem,[202] but it is hardly possible to achieve real clarity in this matter. What is of critical importance, however, is that the *Sicarii* in Egypt were closely associated, through their open confession of the 'sole rule of God', with the organizer and spiritual father of the Jewish freedom movement, Judas the Galilaean.[203]

In another place, in his final settlement of accounts with the rebels, Josephus makes a direct connection between the *Sicarii* and Judas, as the one who had caused the whole 'evil'. The *Sicarii*, he claims, had, according to Cyrenius' census, already risen at that time (τότε γὰρ οἱ σικάριοι συνέστησαν)[204] and had thrown down the gauntlet of battle to all who looked for peace. This link was based on an ideal and at the same time on a dynastic and therefore also an organizational datum, namely that the leaders of the *Sicarii*, Menahem and Eleazar b. Ari, were descendants of Judas the Galilaean.[205] The name *sicarius* was, as we have seen, not introduced until a few years before the outbreak of the Jewish War in Palestine and the native population of that country could hardly have been familiar with the basic meaning of the Latin word. For these reasons, then, it is possible that, unlike the term λῃστής, the word *sicarius*, although it had originally been used as a term of abuse by foreigners, was later taken over by the members of the group concerned as an 'honorary title'.[206] It is obvious, however, that it could never have been a name that they originally gave themselves.

The name is found in Greek texts after Josephus only in a few writings of the Church Fathers.[207] Its use in the rabbinic literature, which I would now like to consider, is much more important.

---

[202] See the list of defenders, *Bell* 5,248ff.358; 6,92.148.

[203] See below, p. 90.

[204] *Bell* 7,254, cf. 262. See also below, pp. 332ff.

[205] *Bell* 2,433.447; 7,253. See also below, p. 78.

[206] This is similar to the names 'Protestants', 'Huguenots', 'water-beggars' and so on.

[207] Hippolytus, *Phil* 9,26, *GCS*, ed. P. Wendland, 1916, 2,260. The *Sicarii* are here, together with the Zealots, derived from the Essenes; see below, p. 70f. Origen, *Contra Celsum* 2,13, *GCS*, ed. P. Koetschau, 1899, 1, 142, reported that the Samaritans were killed as '*Sicarii*' because they kept to the practice of circumcision. In other words, they were, after Hadrian's prohibition of circumcision, made subject to the *lex Cornelia de sicariis*; see Schürer 1, 538, n. 107; 1,539, n. 111. Mommsen, *Strafrecht*, 638, n. 4, is wrong. See G.W.H. Lampe, *A Greek Patristic Lexicon*, 1233, and below, p. 52, n. 223.

3. The Sicarii *in the Rabbinic Literature*

The סִיקָרִין are mentioned only in one text in the Mishnah:[208]

'The people from Jerusalem once hid fig-cakes in water because of the *Sicarii* and the wise men declared them to be pure'.

It is very probable that this anecdote refers to the famine brought about by the siege of Jerusalem. Josephus vividly describes how the 'robbers' deprived the inhabitants of the city of their remaining provisions.[209] According to another later tradition, the *Sicarii* destroyed the water-pipe that supplied Jerusalem with water from Etham.[210] Again, according to the second version of the Aboth D'R. Nathan, they set fire to the city's supplies of corn before the siege[211] and, according to a parallel tradition, this destruction by fire was caused by Ben Battiach, R. Johanan b. Zakkai's nephew and the leader of the *Sicarii* (ראש סיקרין)[212] This leader of the rebels is called 'Abba Sikera, the bandit leader in Jerusalem' (אבא סיקרא ריש בריוני דירושלם) in another parallel text.[213] Here the name *sicarius* has almost become a proper name. What we have here, then, is presumably a further development of earlier traditions. One text refers to the moderation of the *Sicarii*. This is the only text where it is possible to question whether the reference is to the same *Sicarii* who took part in the Jewish War.[214]

What is surprising. however, is that, with the exception of this last text, the rabbinic authors always apply the name *Sicarii* to the rebels in Jerusalem. They therefore to some extent contradict Josephus.[215] What

---

[208] Maksh 1,6: מעשה באנשי ירושלים שטמנו דבילתן במים מפני הסיקרין . See also Derenbourg, 279ff., n. 3.

[209] *Bell* 6,193–213 and *passim*.

[210] LamentRab on 4.4,7; the tradition goes back to Abba b. Kahana (second half of the third century A.D.; see Bill. *Introduction*, 142. The usual manuscripts have the reading החניות for the place and מציקים for the author (for this, see below, p. 53), but the corrected texts by S. Buber, Vilna 1899, have מְעַיטָם and סוקרים; see S.A. Büchler, 'On the Provisioning of Jerusalem in the Year 69-70 c.e.', *Studies in Jewish History*, 1956, 102, and G. Dalman, *Jerusalem und sein Gelände*, 1930, 279. This event was really an act of terror committed before the outbreak of the Jewish War or by Simon bar Giora. This water-pipe had been extended by Pilate, who financed the work with money from the Temple treasure; see *Bell* 2,175 = *Ant* 18,60. See also G. Dalman, *op. cit.*, 279.

[211] c. 7, ed. Schechter (1887), 20. According to the first version, c. 6,8, they were the קנאים, the Zealots. For this, see *Bell* 5,24 and Tacitus, *Hist* 5,12.

[212] EcclRab on 7.12. Here סְקָרִין should be read instead of קסרין.

[213] Gitt 56a; cf. LamentRab on 1.5,31: here the leader is called Ben Battiach. For a senseless criticism of a wrong translation by S. Zeitlin, *JBL* 81 (1962), 398, see J. Klausner, *Hist* 5, 230, and Jastrow, *Dictionary*, 2, 986.

[214] jSot 20b,69, according to R. Oshaia, ca. 200; see Bill. *Introduction*, 135.

[215] See above, p. 49.

we have here, then, may be a fundamentally earlier form of linguistic usage, since we are bound to assume that the Roman authorities at least must have extended the use of the name *sicarii* to all Jewish freedom fighters since its introduction under the procuratorship of Felix. In the two traditions of the Aboth D'R. Nathan, the *Sicarii* of the second version are contrasted with the 'Zealots' (קנאים) of the first version.[216] It would seem that both terms were used without distinction for the rebels in Jerusalem. Josephus, on the other hand, usually confined his use of the two names to definite groups. This can possibly be explained by the fact that the different parties appropriated the terms as names for themselves after the split in the Jewish freedom movement.[217] We cannot really learn anything, however, about the real nature of the movement from the name σικάριοι since, like the related term λῃσταί, it was given to the Jewish rebel party by their opponents and pointed fundamentally only to the perfidious tactics that they used in fighting.

Excursus III: The Sikarikon Law

For a long time it was thought that the rabbinic term סִיקָרִיקוֹן was connected with Josephus' σικάριοι, since it was always concerned with the acquisition and possession of land or of slaves which or who had changed owners under the pressure of foreign hegemony. The word could apply to these possessions or the new owners as well as to the law that regulated the change of ownership and the acquisition of the property in question.[218] The view was widely held that the *Sicarii* had obtained others' property even before the Jewish War by means of threats or extortion and that the sikarikon law was there to protect owners who had been robbed in this way.[219] It was then pointed out by Elbogen that the term had nothing

---

[216] See below, p. 66.

[217] See above, p. 49, n. 206, and below, p. 366.

[218] The texts in question are: Gitt 5,6; Tos 5,1 (Z. 328); j 47b,18ff.; b 44a and 58b; Bikk 1,2; tAZ 3,16 (Z. 464); tTer 1,6 (Z. 25): although the term 'sikarikon' does not appear here - only the matter is discussed; MekEx 23,19 (L 3, 187); SifDeut 26,2.297, ed. Friedmann; BB 47b.

[219] This view was held by H. Graetz, 'Das Sikarikongesetz', *Jahrbuch des jüdischen theologischen Seminars*, Breslau 1892; F. Rosenthal, *MGWJ* 37 (1893), 1ff.57ff.105ff.; S. Krauss, 'Zur griechischen und lateinischen Lexicographie', *Byzantinische Zeitschrift* 2 (1893), 511ff.; J. Levy, *Neuhebräisches und Chaldäisches Wörterbuch*, 1896ff., 3, 518f.; Schürer, 1, 463, n. 33, who follows him. Graetz and Rosenthal assumed that the sikarikon law was passed by the Synhedrium before the destruction of Jerusalem. Rosenthal also presupposed a second stage, in which extortion was practised not by the *Sicarii*, but by the Roman fiscus, which received, by expropriation, large portions of land after the war. S. Krauss, *Griechische und lateinische Lehnwörter im Talmud, Midrasch und Targum*, 1899, 2, 392f., thought that סיקריקון should be read in many cases instead of סיקריך, insisting that סיקריקון was itself derived from σικαρικόν, which was a parallel formation from λῃστρικόν, so that the meaning was ultimately the same, that is, 'robbery and everything connected with it'.

directly to do with the *Sicarii* before and during the Jewish War, but that it only applied to property and especially land that was expropriated during and after the War by the Roman state. He came to no conclusions regarding the origin of the concept.[220] Various attempts, most of them based on Greek legal terminology, were then made to interpret the meaning of the term. These interpretations were, however, unsatisfactory from the linguistic point of view.[221] Following Elbogen, Jastrow, for example, suspected that it was a 'disguise of καισαρίκιον',[222] in other words, land confiscated by the imperial fiscus, but even this otherwise very plausible attempt at interpretation did not do justice to the corresponding linguistic parallels.

A further investigation into the origin and meaning of the word showed that, according to certain Church Fathers and Roman legal sources from the time of Hadrian onwards, circumcision had been equated with castration and had been punished according to the *lex de sicariis*.[223] סיקריקון would therefore refer to the expropriation of property as a punishment for circumcision.

This derivation from the *lex de sicariis* undoubtedly comes closer to the reality of the situation than the other interpretations, but its application should not be seen simply as the result of Hadrian's prohibition of circumcision. The *Sicarii* could also be prosecuted during the Jewish War under this law and be deprived of their possessions.[224] The number of confiscations increased enormously especially after the War — so much so that the rabbis tried to check the wasteful disposal of Jewish land and property by means of the 'sikarikon provisions'. A situation similar to that which existed after 70 A.D. once again arose after the revolt of Bar Koseba, with consequences lasting until the rabbinic period.[225] The 'sikarikon provisions' may have been in force throughout the whole of this time.

---

[220] 'סיקריקון eine Studie', *MGWJ* 69 (1925), 249-257. For the expropriation of land after the war, see *Bell* 7,216f. See also S. Klein, 'Neue Beiträge zur Geschichte und Geographie Galiläas', *Pal. Studien* 1 (1923), 15ff. Elbogen's view is supported above all by jGitt 47b,11ff., in which there is unequivocal evidence that the initiative to expropriate land was taken by Rome and that it began during the war and continued after it. In several places in the text, the new, illegal owners — among whom Josephus himself can also be included (see above, p. 7, n. 5) — are identified with robbers, thieves or men of violence; see Bikk 1,2; tTer 1,6 (Z. 25) etc.

[221] S. Feist, 'Zur Etymologie von סיקריקון', *MGWJ* (1927), 138-141, believed that the word was derived from the Greek legal term νόμος συνκρίνων. A. Gulak, *Tarb* 5 (1933/34), 23-27, was of the opinion that the Hellenistic legal practice of compulsory sale was at the basis of the term, that is, ὑπὸ κήρυκι or συνκήρυκι. He was followed in this by N.N. Glatzer, *Geschichte der talmudischen Zeit*, 1937, 29.

[222] *Dictionary*, 2, 986. Only the adjective καισάρειος, meaning belonging to Caesar or his property, appears in the *PapyOxy* 477,5. See Liddell-Scott, 860.

[223] S. Safrai, 'Sikarikon', *Zion* 17 (1952), 56-64. See also the comment by Origen cited above, p. 49, n. 207.

[224] For the dating, see above, n. 220. It is remarkable that the Gemara of the two Talmuds on the Mishnah Gitt 5,6, in which the question of the sikarikon is treated in greatest detail, discusses the war under Vespasian and Titus exhaustively.

[225] See Gitt 5,6; see also S. Safrai, *op. cit.*; see also M. Avi-Yonah, *op. cit.*, 29f. (see above, p. 40, n. 134).

Despite the work of Elbogen and others, Klausner[226] continued to insist that the term סיקריקון referred to members of the Jewish freedom movement. To support his view, he linked together two rabbinic statements about Galilee:

'In Galilee, it is always necessary to take the possibility of 'sikarikon' into consideration'.[227]

'Oh Galilee, Galilee! You have despised the Torah! You will soon have to deal with extortioners'.[228]

By these 'extortioners',[229] Klausner understands 'Zealots flocking together in bands'.

S. Klein's interpretation is preferable to Klausner's. He was of the opinion that the 'extortioners' (מְצִיקִים) were the new landowners appointed by the Romans.[230] סיקריקון and מציקים may well have been the same men. They are not, however, the *Sicarii* of the period before and during the war. They are in fact those favoured by Rome after the end of the war.[231]

C. *BARJONE* AND *GALILAEANS*

1. *The* Barjone (בַּרְיוֹנֵי)

In a text that has already been mentioned, the Babylonian Talmud calls the rebels in Jerusalem by a special name:

'Among them were *barjone* and, when the rabbis advised going out and making peace with those men (the Romans), they did not permit it'.[232]

There are also two references in the same passage to a certain 'Abba Sikera, the leader of the *barjone* in Jerusalem'. The reply given by R. Johanan b. Zakkai to Vespasian is also recorded:

'... and to your reproach concerning why I have not come until now, (I reply:) the *barjone* among us have not let me'.[233]

It might be possible to conclude from this that *barjone* (בַּרְיוֹנֵי, the plural of בַּרְיוֹנָא or בִּירְיוֹנָא; Hebrew בַּרְיוֹן, plural בַּרְיוֹנִים)[234] was an established and original name for the Zealots. R. Eisler was particularly

---

[226] *Jesus of Nazareth*, 1925, 173, n. 103.

[227] jGitt 47b,20 bar.

[228] jShab 15d,50 bar, attributed to Johanan b. Zakkai.

[229] מְצִיקִים = מסיקים; see *BK* 116b.

[230] *op. cit.*, 16ff.

[231] BK 5,1: 'If someone has robbed (גזל) his neighbour of a field and "extortioners" (מְצִיקִים) have taken it away from him ...'

[232] Gitt 56a; this translation follows L. Goldschmidt, 6, 364.

[233] Gitt 56b; this translation also follows Goldschmidt, 6, 365; see above, p. 50, n. 212.

[234] G. Dalman, *Aramäisches-Neuhebräisches Wörterbuch*, 3rd. ed. 1938; J. Levy, *op. cit.*, 1, 266; S. Krauss, *op. cit.*, 2, 165f., reviews the texts in question. See also J. Nevada, *JQR* 63 (1973), 317ff.

in favour of this interpretation[235] and justified his decision by appealing to the derivation of the word. That suggested derivation can already be found in Levy.[236] The word was, he claimed, formed from the root בַּר; בָּרָא.[237] According to this interpretation, the English terms 'outcast' or 'outlaw' reproduce the meaning of the term most closely. It is not difficult to imagine that the rebels, living in inaccessible parts of the country in deserts and caves, may have been given this name by their compatriots.[238]

There is, however, a very powerful argument against this attempt to link the term so closely to the Jewish λῃσταί of the period prior to 70 A.D. It is that the account of the Babylonian Talmud of the siege of Jerusalem and the fate of R. Johanan b. Zakkai is seen, when compared .with the rabbinic parallels, to be a legendary, extended and later form.[239] What is more, even the occurrence of the concept elsewhere does not point with any certainty to a connection between the *barjone* and the Zealots.[240]

S. Krauss therefore looked for a completely different explanation.[241] He took as his point of departure the parables of the king in the Midrashim:

'A parable of a king whom his *barjonim* insulted in the purple that he was wearing ...'[242]

'A parable about a *barjon* who threw stones at the statue of the king; then they all flocked together ...'[243]

'A parable about a *barjon* who was drunk, broke open the gaol, let the prisoners out, threw stones at the statue of the king, cursed the governor and said: 'Show me where the king is and I will teach him the law'.[244]

---

[235] 2,67f.; see also L. Goldschmidt, 1, 38, n. 392: '*Barjone* was originally the name of a warring party in Jerusalem ... Later it came to mean rowdies or hooligans'.

[236] *op. cit.*, 1, 266; see Jastrow, *Dictionary*, 1, 193.

[237] 'Outside', but also 'uncultivated land, forest, wilderness'; as an adjective, 'living in the wilderness'. See also the corresponding Syriac word ܒܪܝܐ = *agrestis, externus, profanus*; see C. Brockelmann, *Lexicon Syriacum*, 2nd. ed. 1928, 88.

[238] S. Baron, *A Social and Religious History of the Jews*, 1937, 1, 220, saw in them 'social outcasts', seeking their fortune in armed resistance to Rome.

[239] EcclRab on 7.12; LamentRab on 1.5,31; AbRN 4,6, ed. Schechter, 23. In no case does the concept appear here. The name 'Ben Battiach' (EcclRab on 7.12 and LamentRab on 1.5; see also Kel 17,12) is more original than the imaginary name 'Abba Sikera' in Gitt 56a.

[240] Ber 10a; Taan 23b and Sanh 37a; *Barjone* means simply bad, undisicplined people in these related traditions, which are connected partly with R. Meir, partly with Abba Hilkia, the son of Honi, who prayed for rain, and partly with R. Zera.

[241] See especially *Mon Tal* V1, No. 343b, n. 7. In *Griechische und Lateinische Lehnwörter*, 2, 165, Krauss suggested that it was derived from φρούριον = soldier, officer.

[242] ExRab 30,18.

[243] YalShim(Esther) 2,1056 (2MonTal V1, No. 202).

[244] ExRab 30,11 (translation based on Wünsche, 228).

In S. Krauss' opinion, these *barjonim* were in fact the Praetorian Guard (*praetoriani* = יוני — טור — בר), who rose several times in the course of Roman history against the imperial masters. In the text quoted above from Gitt 56b, Krauss therefore translated בַּרְיוֹנֵי as 'watchmen'.[245] But only the Zealots could have been meant here and it is very unlikely that a name for the Zealots should have been derived from the *praetoriani*, quite apart from the fact that the linguistic derivation also seems to be rather forced.

Jastrow[246] therefore made a distinction between the two words, suggesting that בַּרְיוֹנָא, plural בַּרְיוֹנֵי, meant 'rebel, outlaw' and that בִּרְיוֹן, plural בִּרְיוֹנִים (the change in vocalization should be noted), meant 'palace-soldier, castle-guard' and was derived from בִּירָה, residence, fortress or temple. This interpretation has the highest degree of probability, but it is still not entirely satisfactory. On the one hand, the terms בַּרְיוֹנָא and בִּרְיוֹן are simply placed side by side as the Aramaic and the Hebrew forms of the same word and, on the other, no attempt is made to reject the conjecture that the parables describing the destruction of the images of the king by *barjonim* may have a background of bitter hostility on the part of Jewish rebels to worship of the emperor.[247] Finally, there is no certainty regarding which of the two meanings the word should have.[248]

R. Eisler placed such emphasis on the need to interpret the word *barjona*, the singular form of the Aramaic plural *barjone*, in the sense of 'Zealot' because he believed that Simon Peter, called Βαριωνᾶ in Mt 16.17, was originally a Zealot.[249] O. Cullmann quite recently accepted this supposition.[250] Quite apart from the problem raised by the name Bar-Jona - a problem that has still not been resolved — there are very serious misgivings arising from the context in which it occurs in the gospel. It is probable that the correct state of affairs is reflected in the Greek translation of the Βαριωνᾶ of Mt 16.17 into 'son of John' in Jn 1.42 and 21.15.[251]

---

[245] *MonTal* V1, No. 128.

[246] *op. cit.*, 1, 193. J. Nedava, *JQR* 63 (1973), 321, has a similar solution to the problem.

[247] See Philo, *LegGai* 200f. (M 2,575), the destruction of the imperial altar by the Jews in Jamnia.

[248] See MekEx 17,8 (L 2,138); jKidd 61a,45 and Tan ארא 8, ed. Buber, 23f.

[249] *op. cit.*, 2, 67.

[250] The State in the New Testament, 1963, 16f.; *Jesus und die Revolutionären seiner Zeit*. 1970, 22f.

[251] Σίμων ὁ υἱὸς Ἰωάννου. See also the Gospel of the Nazarenes, Hennecke–Schneemelcher, *New Testament Apocrypha*, 1963, 1, 148, No. 14. According to Mk 1.30 and 1 Cor 9.5, Simon was married, owned a house in Capernaum (Mk 1.29)

It is therefore very uncertain as to whether the Jewish rebels of the period preceding 70 A.D. were ever called בִּרְיוֹנֵי in the sense of 'outlaws' by their compatriots. With a few exceptions, the term was used at a relatively late period and it is too slight a point of departure on which to base wider conclusions, particularly where the gospels are concerned.

2. The Galilaeans

Judas, the organizer of the Jewish freedom movement, is given the name (ὁ) Γαλιλαῖος in Acts 5.37 and usually in the works of Josephus.[252] It is clear from the stubborn resistance to Herod and the revolt in Sepphoris, when the throne changed hands after the death of the king, that Galilee was the centre of resistance to foreign rule from the very beginning.[253] This attitude of fierce opposition is explained by the Galilaeans' bravery and love of freedom, so praised by Josephus,[254] as well as their pride and zeal for the law.[255] He describes them in the Vita as zealous protagonists of revolt against Rome.[256] Later, in Jerusalem, the men of the σύνταγμα τῶν Γαλιλαίων who came to the city with John of Gischala were more impetuous and cruel than any others.[257]

If, then, the Zealot movement was founded by a Galilaean and was given special support in that part of the country, it would be quite understandable for the followers of Judas also to be called 'Galilaeans'. There are several data which indicate that this was in fact the case. There is in the Mishnah, for example, the following remarkable controversy between a 'Galilaean heretic' (מִין גְּלִילִי) and some Pharisees:[258]

---

and followed his brother Andrew as a fisherman (Mk 1.16). This does not tally with the idea of an outlaw in the desert. See also J.W. Jack, The Historic Christ, 1933, 187ff.; G. Dalman, Grammatik des jüdisch-palästinischen Aramäisch, 2nd. ed. 1905, 179, n. 5, and W. Bauer, Wörterbuch zum Neuen Testament, 7th. ed. 1971, 265.

[252] Bell 2,118, ἀνὴρ Γαλιλαῖος; 2,433; Ant 18,23; 20,102. See also CIJ 1285,5.14; 1286,10.

[253] Bell 1,204ff. = Ant 14,158ff.; Bell 1,303ff. = Ant 14,413ff.; Bell 2,56 = Ant 17,271.

[254] Bell 3,41f.

[255] jKet 29b,37f.; MK 23a; Pes 55a, see E.G. Hirsch, 'Galilee', JE 5, 554. See also G. Dalman, Sacred Sites and Ways, 1935, 6ff. The radical Galilaean Eleazar forced Izates of Adiabene to be circumcised, Ant 20,43. The Galilaean 'robber' in the caves of Arbela killed himself and his whole family rather than yield to Herod: Ant 14,429f.

[256] Vita 39, from the address given by Justus of Tiberias: νῦν εἶναι καιρὸν ἀραμένους ὅπλα καὶ Γαλιλαίους συμμάχους προσλαβόντας. See also 99,102.143.177.262.306.311. It is noteworthy that it was only in Galilaean Jotapata and part of Gamala bordering on Galilee that there was serious resistance to the Romans.

[257] Bell 4,558.

[258] Yad 4,8. The revised editions have צדוקי. J. Levy, Wörterbuch 4, 174b, believed

'I accuse you, Pharisees, of writing the name of the ruler (מוֹשֵׁל) with the name of Moses in the bills of divorce. The Pharisees replied: "We accuse you, Galilaean heretic, of writing (the name of) the ruler and the name (of God) in (a) column (בְּדַף). And what is more, you write the name of the ruler above and the name (of God) below, for it is said: And Pharaoh said: Who is YHWH, whose voice I should heed, and let Israel go?"'.

Both A. Geiger[259] and H. Graetz[260] suspected that this מִין גְּלִילִי was a follower of Judas of Galilee, who was the first to demand that a Jew should recognize no other Lord than God alone.[261] The Galilaean in this dialogue attacks the Pharisees for writing the name of the ruler of the time on bills of divorce in such a way that it appears on the document alongside the name of Moses.[262] The Pharisees ironically reverse the accusation and accuse the Galilaean — or rather, the Galilaeans — of writing the names of the sovereign ruler and of God in a column (in the Torah) and doing so in such a way that, as Ex 5.2 shows, the name of the ruler appears first. The point is, then, that what is possible in the Torah is permitted on a bill of divorce. At the same time, the main argument of the Jewish freedom movement, that all secular rulers lose all claim to legitimate authority because God is the only ruler, is refuted.[263] It is, of course, quite possible to dispute the correctness of this interpretation of the 'Galilaean heretic' as a follower of Judas of Galilee,[264] but it does seem to be the best possible explanation of this difficult text.[265]

---

that the co-founder of the Zealot Party, Zadok the Pharisee, was involved here; see *Ant* 18,4. The anecdote is contained in a mutilated form in the Tosefta; see tYad 2,20 (Z. 684). Here it is a Jewish baptist sect, the טובלי שחרין, who are criticizing the Pharisees.

[259] *Urschrift und Übersetzungen der Bibel*, 1857; 2nd. ed. 1928, 35. The author is mistaken in speaking about a 'Galilaean called Theudas', the confusion arising no doubt because of Acts 5.36. See, however, Bill. 4, 351, n. 1.

[260] H. Graetz, *Geschichte der Juden*, 2nd. ed. 1863, 3, 209f.

[261] See below, p. 90.

[262] See *Gitt* 8,5; see also G. Lisowsky, *Die Mischna, Text, Übersetzung und ausführliche Erklärung*, ed. G. Beer et al., VI, 11, Jadajim 1956, 80.

[263] G. Lisowsky's interpretation, *op. cit.*, 81, is not convincing. If these heretics had used the name of God, the sovereign ruler, on bills of divorce, their criticism of the Pharisees would have been without foundation. 'On (a) sheet or column' refers to the Torah.

[264] Bill. 4,351; L. Goldschmidt, 12, 853, n. 31: 'It was obviously a Judaeo-Christian who was involved, since he recognized no ruler other than God'. S. Lieberman, *JBL* 71 (1952), 205, thought that the Galilaean heretic might possibly have been an Essene. According to *Bell* 2,145, the 'name of the lawgiver' was especially protected among them. The tYad parallels can also be understood in this light; see above, n. 258. The question, is, however, once again raised as to a possible correspondence between Essenes and Zealots; see below, p. 281f.

[265] Apart from Geiger and Graetz, see J. Derenbourg, 161; K. Kohler, 'Zealots', *JE* 12, 641; J. Klausner, *Hist* 4, 201; A. Schlatter, *GI*, 434; J. Finkelstein, *The Pharisees*, 3rd. ed. 1962, 2, 819.

Both Justin[266] and Hegesippus[267] provide lists of Jewish sects and
'Galilaeans' are included in both authors' lists.[268] Most scholars who have
ventured to identify these 'Galilaeans' have assumed that they were
Judas' followers.[269] Justin and Hegesippus were, because of their own
origins, familiar with the Judaeo–Palestinian tradition and their data
were no doubt based in a historical situation.

The 'Galilaeans' are also mentioned by Epictetus, one of the ancient
philosophers:[270]

'. . . how is it that a tyrant, armed men or their swords should frighten him? If
a man can be so changed by madness (ὑπὸ μανίας) or by habit (ὑπὸ ἔθους), as the
Galilaeans have been, that he develops such a (philosophical) attitude
towards these things, then no man would be able to learn by reflection and
evidence that God has made everything . . .'

This passage is usally applied to Christians[271] and their attitude in the
persecutions. As one scholar has said: 'There can be no doubt that the
Galilaeans mentioned here can only be Christians . . . How is it possible
that Epictetus should, in the lectures that he gave about 110 A.D., have
mentioned the Zealots of Judas the Galilaean, who had been eradicated
many decades before his time and of whom he had hardly heard?'[272]

There are, however, quite convincing arguments against this. In the
first place, Epictetus was in Rome in the years following the Jewish War
and it is very likely that he heard of the events in Palestine when he was

---

[266] *DialTryph* 80,2.

[267] Eusebius, *HistEcc* 4,22.7.

[268] Justin: Sadducees, Genists, Merists, Galilaeans, Hellenians, Pharisees and Baptists;
Hegesippus: Essenes, Galilaeans, Hemero–Baptists (the Jewish baptist sect),
Masbotheans, Samaritans, Sadducees and Pharisees. A. von Harnack, 'Judentum und
Judenchristentum in Justins Dialog', *TU* 39 (3,9) (1913), 58, stressed that the two lists
were independent of each other. See also his *Geschichte der altchristlichen Literatur*, 1893, 1,
149; J.T. Milik, *RB* 60 (11953), 288, n. 2, and M. Black, 'The Patristic Accounts of
Jewish Sectarians', *BJRL* 41 (1958), 287f.

[269] This view was held by A. Hilgenfeld, *Ketzergeschichte des Urchristentums*, 1884, 31;
G. Hoennicke, *Das Judenchristentum*, 1908, 36, n. 1; E. Meyer, *Ursprünge und Anfänge des
Christentums*,4th. ed. 1925, 2, 407; B.-Gr. Rel. 88; H. Karpp, 'Christennamen', *RAC* 2,
1131. Harnack, on the other hand, rejected this interpretation, *TU* 39, 59: 'It is best to
abstain from every hypothesis'.

[270] Arrian, *Diss* 4,7.6.

[271] A. von Harnack, *Mission and Expansion of Christianity*, 1908, 1,401f. The name for
Christians appeared at a late stage and was rarely used, apart from during the period of
Julian the Apostate; see *op. cit.*, 413 and 187. Other examples can be found in H. Karpp,
op. cit. In Acts 1.11 and 2.7, it is merely a case of using names to indicate a geographical
origin. The same also applies to the 'Galilaeans' in the Bar Koseba letter from the Wadi
el-Murabba'at; see J.T. Milik, *RB* 60 (1953), 276ff.

[272] E. Meyer, *op. cit.*, 3, 530, n. 1.

in the city.[273] What is more, Josephus explicitly emphasizes that the *Sicarii* were resolute in martyrdom and that this steadfast attitude was widely known:

'Their steadfastness, their madness (ἀπόνοια) or their strength of mind, whatever one chooses to call it, aroused universal astonishment'.[274]

Finally, the name 'Galilaean' was only very rarely applied to Christians before the time of Julian the Apostate.[275] This fact at least to some extent justifies the application of Epictetus' text to the Zealots rather than to Christians.[276]

The 'Galilaeans whose blood Pilate had mingled with their sacrifices', that is, of course, with the blood of their sacrifices (Lk 13.1) have also quite often been interpreted as Zealots.[277] Even if a revolt within the context of a passover feast is presupposed here, however, it may still be a case of using a name indicating a geographical origin.

There is, then, relatively little information about the possible name 'Galilaeans' for the Zealots and what exists is very scattered. We may assume with some degree of probability, however, that they were at least to some extent called that. They formed an independent sect alongside other Jewish religious groups and their origins have, simply on the basis of that name, to be sought in the activity of the Galilaean Judas.

D. The 'Zealots'

1. Greek Linguistic Usage

The name for the members of the Jewish freedom movement with the most substantial content that occurs in Josephus' works is ζηλωτής. In its original meaning, this word, which is derived from ζηλοῦν,[278] was used

---

[273] Epictetus was born about 55 A.D. in Hierapolis in Phrygia and went as a young slave to Rome, where he lived with his master and patron Epaphroditus, Nero's freedman; see the *Oxford Classical Dictionary*, 1970, 390.

[274] *Bell* 7,417; cf. *Ant* 18,23f.: 'Since their stubbornness (in martyrdom) has become generally known as a result of observation, I think that I can refrain from further comments about them'. Josephus was still able to write in this way in about 93/94 A.D.

[275] See above, p. 58, n. 271.

[276] See also J. Klausner, *Hist* 4, 201 and A. Schlatter, *GI* 443 and 'Die Märtyrer in den Anfängen der Kirche', *BFChTh* 19 (1915), 66 (290), n. 35.

[277] This was the opinion of R. Eisler, 2, 516–525; see also S.G.F. Brandon, *The Fall of Jerusalem and the Christian Church*, 1951, 106; H.G. Wood, *NTS* 4 (1956), 236; O. Cullmann, *The State in the New Testament*, (1963), 14. For an interpretation, see below, p. 337f. See also S. Zeitlin, *JQR* 64 (1974), 189-203.

[278] To enthuse about something, to admire something, to make something the aim of one's striving, to try vigorously to imitate, to envy; see A. Stumpff, ζῆλος, *TD* 2, 77f.

to denote a man who committed himself entirely to a cause that he wanted to make his own. It therefore meant an emulator, an imitator or an adorer. It appeared relatively late for the first time in the fourth century B.C.[279] Plato, for example, speaks of ζηλωταί, ἐρασταί and μαθηταί of the Spartan methods of education.[280] In this sense, the ζηλωτής may also directly indicate the learner.[281] The word was also frequently used in the context of the virtues[282] or care for the well-being of the Polis.[283] Philo's use of the term is similarly strictly related to the virtue or cause with which he is concerned and, because of its too strong affective emphasis, he employs it in a negative sense[284] more often than positively.[285] Even Josephus frequently applies ζηλωτής in this way to a virtue or a good cause[286] and the same usage also occurs in the New Testament and the works of the early Christian authors.[287]

The application of the word to persons, that is, its use in the sense of 'adorer', 'disciple' or 'follower', was later,[288] although it was employed in this way with increasing frequency from about the beginning of the Christian era onwards. Plutarch employed the concept almost

---

[279] For the following, see the various dictionaries: F. Passow, *Handwörterbuch der griechischen Sprache*, 5th. ed. 1841ff., 1, 1309; Liddell-Scott, 775; W. Bauer, *Wörterbuch zum Neuen Testament*, 7th. ed. 1971, 668f.

[280] Protagoras 343a; similarly Diodorus Siculus, *BibHist* 1,73 and Herodian, *ExcDiviMarc* 6,8.2.

[281] Philodemus, *Reth* 2,262 (first century B.C.); Diogenes Laertius 9,38; Thrasyllus (first century A.D.) on Democritus: ζ.τῶν Πυθαγορικῶν, that is, of the doctrines of the Pythagoreans. See also Iamblichus, *VitaPyth* (XXVIII) 151, third century A.D.: ζ.τῆς Ὀρφέως ἑρμηνείας.

[282] Isocrates, *Dem* 1,11: ζ.τῆς πατρῴας ἀρετῆς: Epictetus, Arrian, *Diss* 2,12.25.

[283] Aeschines, *Orat* 2,171; W. Dittenberger, *SIG*, 3rd. ed. 1915ff., 675,27f. and 756,32; Plutarch 2 (*Moralia*) 6D: Demosthenes for Athens.

[284] *VitaMos* 2,55.161: ζ.τῶν Αἰγυπτιακῶν πλασμάτων; similarly 2,196; *Abr* 22; *MutNom* 93; *SpecLeg* 1,333; 4,89.91.199 etc.

[285] *Abr* 33: ζ.τῆς δικαιοσύνης; 60: εὐσεβείας and ἀρετῆς; similarly *SpecLeg* 1,30; *Virt* 175 etc.

[286] *Bell* 6,59: the first Roman soldiers to climb the walls of the fortress Antonia were ζ.τῆς ἀνδρείας; *Ap* 1,162, where Pythagoras is called a ζ. of σοφία and εὐσέβεια. Those places in which Josephus follows the Jewish tradition and speaks of zeal for the Law and faith (*Ant* 12,271 and *Ant* 20,47) could be understood by a Hellenistic reader in the pedagogical and philosophical sense. For a typical interpretation of the name of the party by Josephus as ζηλωταί, see *Bell* 4,160. See also below, p. 65f.

[287] 1 Cor 14.12; 1 Pet 3.13; Tit 2.14; 1 Clem 45,1; *EpPol* 6,3.

[288] The earliest examples of this are found on inscriptions; Dittenberger, *op. cit.*, 717,33: τῶν καλλίστων (that is, of the Attic *epheboi*, 100/99 B.C.); see also Strabo 10,5.6 (486) and the historian Memnon (first century B.C. — first century A.D.?) in *FGrHist* F 1,35: ζ.τῆς Λαμάχου προαιρέσεως (of the activities of Lamachus).

exclusively in relation to persons[289] and Epictetus, for example, speaks of a ζηλωτὴς τῆς ἀληθείας καὶ Σωκράτους καὶ Διογένους.[290] In the later period of classical antiquity, the term was predominantly applied to human examples.[291] When Josephus calls himself a ζηλωτής of the hermit Bannus in his *Vita*, it is entirely in accordance with Hellenistic linguistic usage.[292]

The word was also used in the religious and ethical sense by the Stoic moral philosophers of the first century A.D. and applied to God. Musonius, for example, required the king to behave ethically and to be a ζηλωτὴς τοῦ Διός.[293] This demand was repeated by his pupil Epictetus, who applied it to the philosopher:[294]

'If the deity is faithful, he (the philosopher) must also be faithful. If the former is free, he must also be free. If the former is benevolent, he must also be benevolent. If the former is magnanimous, he must also be magnanimous. In all that he says and does, he must behave as an imitator of God (ὡς θεοῦ ... ζηλωτήν)'.

In both cases, the words should be interpreted in the sense of the *imitatio Dei*, since the Jewish idea of 'zeal for God' would have been impossible for the Stoic philosopher.[295]

The word ζηλωτής was very rarely used in the absolute sense. The earliest evidence, in a fragment of Epicurus, has obscure meaning that cannot be interpreted in any of the customary ways.[296] It occurs once in the Didache in the negative sense alongside ἐριστικός and θυμικός.[297] Apart from this, it occurs with an absolute meaning only in the writings of much later authors such as Iamblichus and Marinus, where it means

---

[289] S.D. Wyttenbach, *Lex Plutarcheum*, 1843, 1, 393: 1 (*Vitae*) 357B.504A.718C. 781F etc.; 2 (*Moralia*) 154C.741D.975C.

[290] Arrian, *Diss* 3,24.40.

[291] Dio Cocceianus (Chrysostomus), *Orat* 38 (55),6; Lucian, *Herm* 14; *HistQuomConscr* 15; *Demon* 48.

[292] *Vita* 11.

[293] *Fragm* 8, 87, ed. O. Hense, 1905. The badly preserved fragment of the otherwise unknown Pythagorean Sthenidas, Stobaeus 4,7.63, would seem to call for a similar meaning.

[294] Arrian, *Diss* 2,14.13.

[295] See A. Heitmann, *Imitatio Dei*, Rome 1940, 40f.,44, for Musonius; H.D. Betz, *Nachfolge und Nachahmung*, 123, n. 3. Paul, in calling himself a θεοῦ ζ. in Acts 22.3, was speaking in accordance with the Old Testament and Jewish tradition; cf. Rom 10.2. See also below, pp. 177f., 179f., 392.

[296] See T. Gompertz, 'Die Überreste eines Buches von Epikur περὶ φύσεως', *WSt* 1 (1879), 30; see also Liddell-Scott, 775.

[297] 3,2; in addition there is also the significant concluding sentence: ἐκ γὰρ τούτων ἀπάντων φόνοι γεννῶνται. Does this indicate a recollection of the Zealots? See Bo Reicke, 'Diakonie, Festfreude und Zelos', *UUA* (1951), 383.

'disciple' or 'follower'.[298] A special case is the translation of אֵל קַנָּא[299] in the Septuagint as θεὸς ζηλωτής. An apposition is formed here from the attributive adjective, thus giving special emphasis to zeal as an essential aspect of God. What is particularly striking is that the article is not used in all the examples in which the concept is employed with an absolute meaning.

We may summarize the content of this section by saying that ζηλωτής is used predominantly in Greek literature in the pedagogical and moral sense. Hellenized Jewish authors are no exception to this general rule. The affective emphasis is no less in the employment of the concept. As we shall see later, when we come to examine this question more closely,[300] this emphasis is the distinctive characteristic of the specifically Jewish use of the term. There is no equivalent in the Greek world and it can only be fully understood in the religious perspective.

2. The 'Zealots' as a Party in Josephus' Jewish War

The word is found in certain places in *The Jewish War* in the plural, in the absolute sense and with the article: οἱ ζηλωταί. This would certainly seem to point to a permanent name for a party and, what is more, in the light of what I have said above, a name that could hardly have come from the Hellenistic world. As we shall see later on, it is much more likely that this name was based on a Hebrew or Aramaic form.[301]

What is remarkable, however, is that Josephus only used this party within a relatively limited framework and at the same time quite often within that framework. It occurs almost exclusively in the fourth and fifth books in the author's description of the civil war in Jerusalem and the first part of the siege. He never applies the name οἱ ζηλωταί to all the rebels, whom he calls στασιασταί or οἱ Ἰουδαῖοι.[302] He in fact uses it only when speaking of a special group confined to the followers of John of Gischala, Simon bar Giora and the Idumaeans.[303] Their leader was the priest Eleazar b. Simon, who began to play a distinctive part as the head of the radical wing after the victory over Cestius Gallus in Jerusalem.[304]

---

[298] *VitaPyth* VI (29), end of the third century A.D.; *VitaProcli* c. 38, ed. Boissonade, 1814.

[299] Ex 20.5; 34.14; Deut 4.24; 5.9; 6.15. See also Nah 1.2 and below, pp. 146 and 177ff.

[300] See below, pp. 140ff. and 177ff.

[301] *Bell* 2,444.564.651; 4,160ff. etc.; 5,5ff.99ff.250.358.527; 6,92.148; 7,268f.: τὸ τῶν ζηλωτῶν κληθέντων γένος.

[303] See the list of the four parties that defended Jerusalem: *Bell* 5,248ff.358; 6,92.148.

[304] *Bell* 2,564; 5,5–21.99ff. In *Bell* 4,225, the priests Eleazar (with *MVRC* υἱὸς Σίμωνος instead of Γίωνος) and Zechariah of Amphikallei are named as the ἡγεμόνες τῶν ζηλωτῶν. See below, p. 115f.

The moderate party led by the high-priest Ananus b. Ananus, which was numerically superior, directed its attack against the tyrannical regime of these 'Zealots'.[305] The latter were able to assert themselves when they were driven back into the Temple building itself; the betrayal of John of Gischala and the occupation of the city by the Idumaeans ultimately helped them to secure a victory.[306] Together with the Idumaeans, they were, according to Josephus, able to establish a new reign of terror,[307] although they were powerless to achieve any kind of success in the countryside, where Simon bar Giora dominated.[308]

John of Gischala set himself up as leader of the 'Zealots' in the city, helped by his Galilaean followers.[309] In order to break their tyranny, however, the people of the city eventually brought in Simon bar Giora and the 'Zealots' were forced to retreat to the Temple hill.[310] There was then a rift between John and his Galilaean followers on the one hand and the 'Zealots' proper, who consisted overwhelmingly of priests.[311] This was because the 'Zealots' were no longer able to submit to the rule of the Galilaeans. For a second time, they concentrated on the Temple building, from which they defended themselves against John, who was in control of the Temple hill.[312] By this time, Titus was already outside the city. John succeeded by a ruse in gaining control of the Temple and many of the 'Zealots' fled into the underground vaulting of the Temple. Others were executed.[313]

Because they were all threatened by the Roman siege, however, all the opposing parties soon made peace with each other and it was not long before the 'Zealots' again formed their own group in the Temple. From the beginning of the siege onwards, they fought together with their previous opponents, the followers of John of Gischala. Their initial strength was two thousand four hundred men. They were certainly numerically the weakest of the four groups defending Jerusalem.[314]

---

[305] *Bell* 4,160-162.193.197.201.

[306] *Bell* 4,208ff.216.288ff.305ff.

[307] *Bell* 4,326ff.

[308] *Bell* 4,514.538ff.556.

[309] *Bell* 4,389ff.558f.

[310] *Bell* 4,574ff.

[311] Their leaders were priests (see above, p. 62,.n. 304, and below, p. 360ff.). and the Temple was their main base; see *Bell* 4,152.196ff.578ff.; 5,5ff.98ff. This points clearly to a majority of priests in this group. See also below, p. 372f.

[312] *Bell* 5,5-10.

[313] *Bell* 5,100ff.103.

[314] *Bell* 5,104; 6,92.148. For the various strengths, see 5,248-250: the other militant groups were much stronger, Simon bar Giora having 10000 men, John of Gischala 6000 and the Idumaeans 5000.

It is not difficult to understand, on the basis of this distinctive and apparently very definite use of the party name οἱ ζηλωταί in the writings of Josephus, why it has proved possible to claim that it did not become a permanent name for a party until after 66 A.D.[315] Neither the 'fourth sect of philosophy' of Judas the Galilaean[316] nor the *Sicarii*, it has been claimed, can be identified with them, since 'it is the name arrogated to themselves by the followers of the famous John of Gischala'.[317]

This view, namely that the party of the 'Zealots' did not come into existence until after John of Gischala arrived in Jerusalem, is, however, untenable. Josephus mentions the Zealots as an established group towards the end of the second book of his *Jewish War*.[318]

An assembly of the people in Jerusalem, then, refused immediately after the victory over Cestius Gallus to appoint Eleazar b. Simon as leader of the state, since

> 'they knew his tyrannical nature and the Zealots, who were devoted to him, behaved like bodyguards towards him'.[319]

Eleazar does seem, however, to have been the first leader of this party.[320] Menahem, the son of Judas the Galilaean and one of the men who initiated the revolt, was also a leader of the Zealots. Writing about his murder, Josephus said:

> 'Following this arrangement, they attacked him in the Temple, where he had gone up in pomp, adorned with a royal garment and followed by armed Zealots'.[321]

A comparison with the Greek linguistic usage in other contexts shows that τοὺς ζηλωτάς should not be translated as 'his followers'. The word is definite in form with no further modification, as in other cases in which Josephus uses it specially as a party name.[322] The obvious conclusion to be drawn from this, then, is that Menahem's followers were also called οἱ

---

[315] *Beginnings* 1, 421-425.

[316] See below, p. 76ff.

[317] *op. cit.*, 1, 423.

[318] See, for example, *Bell* 2,651.

[319] *Bell*, 2,564.

[320] This opinion was held by S. Zeitlin. This is clear, for example, from his correction of the view held by the authors of *The Beginnings of Christianity* in *JQR* 34 (1943/44), 381, n. 364: 'The party of Zealots came into existence in the year 66 and was organized by Eleazar ben Simon'.

[321] *Bell* 2,444: καὶ τοὺς ζηλωτὰς ἐνόπλους ἐφελκόμενος.

[322] See H. Drexler, *Klio* 19 (1925), 286. See also above, p. 62 and below, p. 390ff. For the most recent discussion of this question, see M. Smith, *HThR* 64 (1971), 1ff. and J.-A. Morin, *RB* 80 (1973), 334f.

ζηλωταί. The fact that this name was later applied only to one very definite group may be connected with the special theological interest that the radical wing in question had, as we shall see later on,[323] in being called 'Zealots'. It is, however, in no way necessary to confine this name to these men alone. This is clear from the fact that John of Gischala applied it to himself and his followers after gaining power in Jerusalem.[324] It is quite possible that several competing groups claimed this title for themselves after the split had occurred in the Zealot movement[325] and that the priestly party was able to stand up most emphatically for what it represented, with the result that the name was given to its members.

In his final diatribe against the Jewish rebels in the seventh book of his *Jewish War*,[326] Josephus begins with Judas the Galilaean, then goes on to speak about the *Sicarii*, John of Gischala and the Idumaeans and only at the end deals with the 'Zealots', thus going against the historical order. This gives them a special importance that they did not have in the political situation of the period. This may be because Josephus knew that the 'Zealots' were not in fact the smallest group defending Jerusalem at the time, but that they had a much greater share in shaping the events leading up to the Jewish War than we would at first suppose from his limitation of the name itself.[327]

In Book VII, Josephus also provides an explanation of the name that is quite in accordance with his own understanding of Zealotism:

'They affirmed the correctness of their name by their actions, because they imitated every crime (πᾶν γὰρ κακίας ἔργον ἐξεμιμήσαντο) and, if tradition reported anything wrong that had happened in the past, they did not neglect to emulate that as well (μηδ' ... αὐτοὶ παραλιπόντες ἀζήλωτον). They gave themselves their name on the basis of their professed zeal for what is good, but (in reality) they either wanted to deride their unfortunate victims in

---

[323] See below, p. 174f.

[324] See *Bell* 4,389ff.566; 5,5ff.93ff. In many places, Josephus calls those whom John of Gischala named radicals, 'Zealots'. At the same time, however, he sometimes confines this name strictly to the followers of Eleazar b. Simon; see, for example, 5,103. The mistake made by Lake and Foakes Jackson (see above, p. 64, nn. 315 and 317) has its origin at least partly in the fact that Josephus' use of this term was not consistent.

[325] See below, p. 372f.

[326] *Bell* 7,259-274.

[327] In *Bell* 5,3f., Josephus speaks of the 'attack made by the Zealots against the people', which led to the defeat of the city. One might think at first that this is a reference to the outbreak of civil war in Jerusalem under Ananus b. Ananus, but one is bound then to ask whether Josephus was not in fact going back as well to the period of disturbance before the outbreak of war against Rome; see, for example, 2,264f.

accordance with their inhuman nature or else they regarded the greatest crimes as good works'.[328]

It is clear from this that ὁ ζηλωτής, or rather its original Hebrew or Aramaic form, was the title of honour that these men gave themselves and, what is more, the only original one that has been handed down to us from the Jewish freedom movement of the first century A.D.[329] Josephus himself was not able to suppress the positive fundamental meaning of this name, although he interpreted it in a Hellenistic manner and very vaguely. He does not tell us, for example, what this alleged 'zeal for what is good' (ἐπ' ἀγαθῷ ζηλουμένων) was, but, in accordance with his general tendency, twisted it round to mean the opposite.[330] This is possibly why Josephus imposed such a limitation on his use of this name, which, as he well knew, had a very positive meaning for Jews, and why he employed it only when he required it to make a distinction between the various parties in Jerusalem. By contemptuously calling the Jewish freedom fighters 'robbers' both before and during the war, and thus degrading them, he was able to avoid using the name that they had proudly given themselves: 'Zealots'.

If we are to throw further light on the meaning of the name 'Zealots', we have to see whether it is used to name a party in sources other than Josephus' works.

3. The 'Zealots' as a Party in the Jewish Tradition

The 'Zealots' are only mentioned twice — by their Hebrew name קַנָּאִים[331] — as a party in the Talmudic literature. I have already referred to the first version of the Aboth D'R. Nathan:[332]

'When the Emperor Vespasian advanced to fight against Jerusalem, the 'Zealots' tried to burn all the supplies with fire'.

If this version of the text is compared with the second version, it becomes apparent that the difference between the *Sicarii* and the 'Zealots', which was, with one exception, made clear by Josephus, was not recognized in the rabbinic tradition.

---

[328] *Bell* 7,269ff. See also *Bell* 4,160f.: τοῦτο (that is, ζηλωταί) γὰρ αὐτοὺς ἐκάλεσαν ὡς ἐπ' ἀγαθοῖς ἐπιτηδεύμασιν ἀλλ' οὐχὶ ζηλώσαντες τὰ κάκιστα τῶν ἔργων ... (Text according to Lu Lat) ὑπερβαλλόμενοι.

[329] See above, pp. 40f. and 49; see also below, 159f.

[330] See above, p. 15f. and below, p. 183f.

[331] Singular קַנַּאי; see M. Jastrow, *Dictionary*, 2, 1388.

[332] c. 6, ed. Schechter (1887), 32; see above, p. 50, n. 211, and below, p. 394, n. 44.

The 'Zealots' are also mentioned once in the Mishnah:

'Whoever steals the sacrificial bowl and whoever curses with Kosēm and whoever cohabits with an Aramaean woman — Zealots may descend on him'.[333]

(הגונב את הקסוה והמקלל בקוסם והבועל ארמית (ה)קנאין פוגעין בו:)

The קְסְוָה in this text is a vessel that was used in the Temple worship.[334] The word בְּקוֹסֵם is more difficult to explain. It presumably points to a description or a distortion of the divine name for the purpose of magical practice.[335] The 'Aramaean' may well be simply 'pagan woman' in general.[336] The punishment of this crime is exemplified in the action of Phinehas in Num 25.7ff. This example led to Phinehas being regarded in the rabbinic tradition as the first 'Zealot'. Phinehas and his zealous execution of punishment are similarly discussed in detail in the Gemara of the Jerusalem and the Babylonian Talmud referring to our text.[337]

This may provide us with a key to our understanding of the name 'Zealot' both in our text in the Mishnah and in Josephus' linguistic usage. According to one manuscript of the Mishnah and the Jerusalem Talmud, the term קַנָּאִין is definite[338] and has therefore to be seen as a party name, just as it has in Josephus' writings. These 'Zealots' presumably aimed to restore the purity of Israel, the people's faith and the Temple.[339] Their biblical example was the priest Phinehas, who, at the most critical juncture, circumvented the standard justice process and killed a public sinner in the midst of the assembly of the people.[340]

---

[333] Sanh 9,6; for what follows, see the detailed explanation of this text by S. Krauss, *Die Mischna, Text, Übersetzung und ausführliche Erklärung*, ed. G. Beer et al., IV, 4 and 5, Sanhedrin-Makkot, 1933, 261ff.

[334] See M. Jastrow, *op. cit.*, 2, 1395; J. Levy, *Wörterbuch*, 4, 345. The term is also found in the Old Testament: Num 4.7 etc. It is possible that the vessel was also used for the libation of water and wine at Sukkoth. According to Sukk 4,9 (Babylonian Talmud 48b) and *Ant* 13,372, the Sadducaean priests were opposed to water libations. It was for this reason that A. Geiger, *JZWL* 5 (1867), 106ff., regarded this text as anti-Sadducaean; see also I. Epstein, *The Babylonian Talmud, Seder Nezikin VI. Sanhedrin* II, 547, n. 7. It may possibly be this vessel that is represented on the coins of the first and second revolts; see A. Reifenberg, *Ancient Jewish Coins*, 2nd. ed. 1947, 58.

[335] S. Krauss, *op. cit.*, 261f. H. Danby, *Tractate Sanhedrin*, 1919, 119, n. 2, assumed that it was an abbreviation of a non-orthodox name of God like κοσμοπλάστης or else a corrupt form of the tetragrammaton. See the Jerusalem Talmud, 27b,29f. See also M. Jastrow, *op. cit.*, 2, 1396; G. Driver, *JTS*, 14 (1963), 133: 'in (the manner of) one casting spells', like Balaam, Num 22.7; 23.23; cf. Deut 18.10.

[336] I. Epstein, *op. cit.*.

[337] See Num 25.5-13; jSanh 27b,28ff.; bSanh 82a and b.

[338] See S. Krauss, *op. cit.*, 262: the Munich manuscript of the Mishnah and the Jerusalem Talmud 27b,31. Presumably what we have here is the original reading.

[339] See below, pp. 146f., 186ff.

[340] See below, pp. 146–177.

Any investigation into the religious foundations of the Zealot movement would have to begin here. The dating of the above Halacha presents us with great difficulties. Certain Jewish scholars believe that it should be dated early[341] and appeal to a legal enactment dating back to the time of the Hasmonaeans and relating to sexual intercourse with a non-Jewess.[342] There are no references, however, to the activity of a party of 'Zealots' at such an early period. In addition, the קַנָּאִים were faithful to their model Phinehas and held a kind of unofficial Vehmic court, executing criminals on the spot if they were not punished officially for breaking the law. The Hasmonaean enactment, on the other hand, should be regarded as an indication that intercourse with a pagan woman was in fact officially punishable under the law. The Halacha, then, applied in the period between 7 and 66 A.D., when, apart from a short interlude during the reign of Agrippa I, the Jews were deprived of the *ius gladii*.[343] It seems to have been used as a threat against offenders who could no longer be prosecuted by the Synhedrium under the normal processes of penal law because of foreign rule.[344]

There are two other references to the 'Zealots' in later Jewish literature which are very much more ambiguous. Both are cases of names or even nicknames which may have been applied to a member of the Zealot party. A. Geiger[345] believed that the rabbinic teacher Nechonia b. Hakkana was, by virtue of his family name, the son of a Zealot. Instead of the inexplicable הקנה , he suggested, the word הקנא should be read here.[346] This teacher could then be seen as adopting a critical position in his way of life with regard to his father's attitude:

---

[341] K. Kohler, *JE*, 639: 'A statute evidently of the Maccabean time'; similarly in the *Harkavy Festschrift* 13. Kohler equates the 'Zealots' with the Hasidim. See also J. Klausner, *Hist*, 3, 252; I. Epstein, *op. cit.*, *Seder Nashim* VI. Sota 113, n. 4, identifies the 'Zealots' with the rebellious Pharisees under Alexander Jannaeus.

[342] Sanh 82a: 'The court of the Hasmonaeans laid down that whoever cohabited with a non-Jewess was guilty of (sleeping with) a woman in menstruation, a female slave, a non-Jewess or a married woman'. R. Dimi, fourth century A.D., is regarded as handing down this tradition; see Strack, *Introduction*, 147.

[343] *Bell* 2,117; *Ant* 20,200ff.; Jn 18.31; see also T. Mommsen, *Römisches Strafrecht*, 1899, 240f., n. 2; Schürer. 1, 368f.; Juster, 2, 132ff.

[344] One is reminded here of procedures such as those outlined in Acts 23.12f.; see below, pp. 214f. and 346.

[345] *JZWL* (1863), 38; see also Derenbourg, 239, n. 1; K. Kohler, *JE* 12, 640; T.R. Herford, 'Pirqe Abot zu 3,7', R.H. Charles, *The Apocrypha and Pseudepigrapha of the Old Testament*, 1913, 2, 699, n. 5.

[346] For the person of the teacher, see W. Bacher, *Aggada der Tannaiten*, 2nd. ed., 1, 55-88. See also E. Stauffer, *Jerusalem und Rom*, 64 and 71.

'Everyone who accepts the Torah is set free from the yoke of government (מלכות) and from the yoke of mundane matters (דרך ארץ), but everyone who makes himself free from the yoke of the Torah has the yoke of government and the yoke of mundane matters laid on him'.[347]

Study of the Torah is contrasted here with the apparently militant political ideal of freedom promoted by the Zealots and is put forward as the true way to freedom. If this teacher's surname was really 'the Zealot', then this may be authentic evidence of the existence of the name קַנָּאִים for the Jewish freedom party long before the war. We cannot, however, be absolutely certain of this, since all that we may have in this case is a hitherto unknown name or nickname.

There is a possible parallel in an inscription in the Jewish synagogue on Monteverde in Rome:[348]

ΙΩΝΙΟC Ο ΚΕ ΑΚΟΝΕ CΕΦΩΡΗΝΟC: 'Ionios, who is also (καί) called 'Akone' from Sepphoris'.

Juster believed that 'Akone' may simply have been a translation of הַקַּנָּא, 'the Zealot'.[349] The first scholar to investigate this inscription gave it, with many reservations, a late date.[350] If Juster's supposition is correct, 'Akone' is a nickname of a similar kind to that found in the gospels. But this interpretation is very uncertain because of the problem of dating.

4. The 'Zealots' in Christian Sources

Luke refers twice to one Σίμων ὁ ζηλωτής among Jesus' disciples.[351] The Aramaic equivalent is preserved in Mark and Matthew:[352] ὁ Καναναῖος,

---

[347] Ab 3,5 (see AbRN, c. 32, 2nd. version, ed. Schechter, 68); translation based on K. Marti, G. Beer, 'Abot', Die Mischna, op. cit., IV, 9, 1927, 67ff.

[348] N. Müller and N. Bees, Die Inschriften der jüdischen Katakombe am Monteverde zu Rom, 1919, No. 74; J.B. Frey, CIJ, 1, 1936, No. 362. For other inscriptions of Palestinians, see H.J. Leon, The Jews in Ancient Rome, 1960, 239, who has suggested 'the Cohen?'.

[349] 2, 229. Juster also pointed to the teacher Nechonia b. Hakkana mentioned above.

[350] Müller and Bees, op. cit.: 'third or fourth century A.D.?'; for this, see 175, where the authors say that the dates are 'to a great extent merely hypothetical'. The catacomb contained numerous examples of inscriptions of the first and second centuries A.D.

[351] Acts 1.13; Lk 6.15, which is even clearer: Σίμωνα τὸν καλούμενον ζηλωτήν. See also the Ebionite Gospel according to Epiphanius, AdvHaer 30,13, Hennecke–Schneemelcher, Neutestamentliche Apokryphen, 4th. ed. 1968, 1, 156. A 'Judas Zelotes' is mentioned in both the Coptic and the Ethiopic Epistola Apostolorum, ed. C. Schmidt and Wajnberg, TU 43 (1919), 26, c. 2; see also Hennecke–Schneemelcher, op. cit., 1, 192 and 2, 31f. In the same way, several early Latin texts have 'Judas Zelotes' instead of Θαδδαῖος in Mt 10.3; see the New Testament in Greek, ed. G. D. Kilpatrick, 1958.

[352] Mt 10.4 and Mk 3.18; see also the Acts of Thomas 1, E. Hennecke, op. cit., 258.

derived from קַנְאָנָא, st. abs. קַנְאָן, a parallel form of קַנָּאי, the Zealot.[353] Other attempted interpretations, such as 'the man from Cana' or 'the Canaanite' are unconvincing.[354] The authors of *The Beginnings of Christianity* believed either that Luke made an error in translation or else that the meaning of the nickname is very vague. They suggested that it might mean something like 'Simon the zealous man' and pointed in this connection to Acts 22.3, 2 Macc 4.2 and *Ant* 12,271.[355] In these texts, however, the word ζηλωτής is made more precise by the addition of τοῦ θεοῦ or τῶν νόμων, whereas in the gospels — and in Josephus' *Jewish War* — it is used in the definite form with no further modification. It is therefore legitimate to regard the nickname of 'the Zealot' given to the disciple Simon as an indication that a definite group of men had the name 'the Zealots' at the time of Jesus.[356]

There is a second and very important indication in Hippolytus' *Philosophumena*. Towards the end of a passage on the Essenes that is parallel to Josephus' account, he suddenly reports a distinctive and remarkable tradition:[357]

> 'In the course of time they divided into four parties, each of which had its own code of conduct. The members of one party go so far in following the precepts of the law that they do not touch a coin in the conviction that an image should not be carried, seen or made. They also refuse to enter a city so that they do not go through a gate on which statues are placed, since they regard it as wrong to pass under statues. When a member of the second tendency hears that someone has been speaking about God and his laws, but is not circumcised, he lies in wait for him and when he finds him alone

---

[353] See M. Jastrow, *Dictionary*, 2, 1388; W. Bauer, *Wörterbuch zum Neuen Testament*, 7th. ed. 1971, 795; F.C. Burkitt, *The Syriac Forms of New Testament Proper Names (Proceedings of the British Academy 5)*, 1912, 5; G. Dalman, *Jesus-Jeshua*, 1929, 12; E. Klostermann, *Das Markusevangelium (HNT 3)*, 4th. ed. 1950, 75f.; A. Stumpff, *TD* 2, 886f.; S.G.F. Brandon, *The Fall of Jerusalem and the Christian Church*, 1951, 104; H.P. Rüger, *ZNW* 59 (1968), 118.

[354] Jerome according to E. Klostermann, *op. cit.*: 'de vico Galilaeae ubi aquam dominus vertit in vinum'. This, however, should be καναῖος. Canaanites = כְּנַעֲנִי would be rendered as χαναναῖος. The contention of J. Klausner, *J of N* 206, cf. G. Dalman, *Words of Jesus*, 1902, 50, that the community changed the original word κανναῖος into καναναῖος because it was regarded as incomprehensible for a disciple of Jesus to have been a Zealot is without foundation. The only evidence in favour of this view is the secondary reading καναναίτης in the Codex Sinaiticus, the Koridethi and the *Textus Receptus*.

[355] *op. cit.*, 1, 425. See also O. Holtzmann, *Neutestamentliche Zeitgeschichte*, 2nd. ed. 1906, 207, who believed that the name had 'no political significance'.

[356] See Mt 10.3, where Matthew is called ὁ τελώνης. J.-A. Morin, *RB* 80 (1973), 348f.,355, overlooked the fact that this name occurs only once.

[357] In his *Ref Omn Haer* 9,26, *GCS*, ed. P. Wendland, 1916, 1–3, 260; translation based on K. Preysing, *Des heiligen Hippolytus von Rom Widerlegung aller Häresien (Bibliothek der Kirchenväter)*, Munich 1922, 260. K. Kohler was the first to point to this text in his article 'Zealots', *JE* 12, 639f.

threatens him with death if he does not let himself be circumcised. If he does not obey, he is not spared, but killed. For the sake of this cause, they have assumed the name of Zealots. Many call them *Sicarii*. The members of another tendency call no one Lord other than God, even if they are tortured or killed. The later members have deviated so far from the originally strict code of conduct that those who still follow it will not even touch them. If they happen to touch them, however, they wash themselves at once, as though they had touched a foreigner'.

In his account of the Essenes, Hippolytus is therefore almost completely in agreement with Josephus. May we, then, assume that he obtained his information from the Jewish historian? Several facts — a number of significant deviations[358] and above all the remarkable insertion about the Zealots — indicate, however, that this would be a wrong assumption. The Roman author must at least have had other, unknown sources apart from the works of Josephus.[359] In the introduction to his addition, he deviates in quite a remarkable way from the source that he has used up to this point, the account of the Essenes in *The Jewish War*, and says that 'in the course of time they divided into four parties' (... εἰς τέσσαρα μέρη διαχωρισθέντες). Unlike Hippolytus, Josephus speaks in this context of a division into four classes:

'According to the duration of their discipline (that is, in the sect), they are divided into four classes (Διῄρηνται δὲ ... εἰς μοίρας τέσσαρας), those entering later being subordinate in rank to those who had joined earlier, in such a way that the latter, being touched by the former, wash themselves at once, as though they had been made unclean by a foreigner'.[360]

---

[358] Apart from the addition of 'Zealots' mentioned above, 9,23: they swear not to hate their enemies (as opposed to *Bell* 2,139), which is probably a change to give a Christian emphasis, since 1 QS 9,21 speaks for Josephus against Hippolytus; 9,25: a few do not rise from their beds on the Sabbath (which is absent from *Bell* 2,147); 9,27: resurrection and universal conflagration (as opposed to *Bell* 2,154ff.); both are confirmed in the Qumran texts: for the resurrection, see 1 QH 3,28ff.; 6,18; 1 QS 2,17.

[359] A. Hilgenfeld, *Die Ketzergeschichte des Urchristentums*, 1884, 133f. and W. Bauer, Ἐσσαῖοι, *PW Suppl* 4, 388, both thought that Hippolytus depended directly on Josephus. R. Eisler, 2, 197, n. 1, on the other hand, favoured the existence of a common source. K. Kohler, *Festschrift für Dr A. Harkavy*, 1909, 8, regarded Hippolytus' account as 'earlier and more original'.G. Ricciotti, *Flavio Giuseppe tradotto e commentato*, 1, Introduction, 2nd. ed. 1949, 58, n. 3, thought that it was possible that Josephus' account had already been amended in Hippolytus' original text. He also firmly rejected R. Eisler's view. M. Black, *The Background of New Testament Eschatology. Studies in Honour of C.H. Dodd*, 172-175, who has most recently investigated this theme, has unfortunately not examined this important question. L.E. Toombs' attempt to connect the Zealots and the Essenes of Hippolytus with Bar Koseba in *NTS* 4 (1957/58), 70f. is quite irrelevant. See also the controversy between M. Smith, *HUCA* (1958), 272ff. and S. Zeitlin, *JQR* 49 (1958), 292ff.

[360] *Bell* 2,150, cf. *Ref Omn Haer* 9,26.

Hippolytus also describes an exaggerated striving after purity, but he does it at the end of his insertion about the Zealots, thus taking up Josephus' thread again. It is clear from a comparison with the relevant Qumran texts that the account of the Essenes in *The Jewish War* corresponds to a considerable extent to the situation described in those texts.[361] We may therefore assume that Josephus' version is closer to the historical state of affairs and that Hippolytus misunderstood his source. This wrong interpretation led him to insert his traditions concerning the Zealots here, by dividing the material at his disposal into three groups, each of which he introduced with ἕτεροι. The fourth group was missing and Hippolytus may have identified it with the ἕτερον Ἐσσηνῶν τάγμα, at the end of his report, which was already present in his Josephus source.[362]

If his claim that the Essenes were divided into four groups has to be dismissed as a misunderstanding, then his division of certain characteristic features of the Essenes into three groups — a rejection of images, compulsory circumcision and the exclusiveness of the rule of God — can also not be understood as characteristics of different sects. They have rather to be seen as characteristics of one and the same movement and can all be classified under the one heading of 'zeal for God and his law'. It is interesting to note in this context that Hippolytus himself derives the name of the second group — the only one that he names — from the religious basis of the movement as a whole: 'for the sake of this cause, they have assumed the name of Zealots' (ὅθεν ἐκ τοῦ συμβαίνοντος τὸ ὄνομα προσέλαβον ζηλωταὶ καλούμενοι).

Hippolytus, then, provides us with several interesting details about the religious attitude of the 'Zealots' in his description of them as a party that was rigoristic in its observance of the law. For this reason, his account is a valuable addition to the very incomplete statements made by Jospehus, who was tireless in his revilement of his former allies, but was reluctant to give any clear information about their real intentions or disposition.[363]

He also makes another significant comment: 'Many call them (the

---

[361] See *CD* 14,3ff.: priests, Levites, Israelites and novices; 1 QS 2,19: priests, Levites and laymen; novices are added in 6,13ff., as those who may not yet 'touch the purity of the many'. A similar division is also to be found in 1 QSa 1 and 2, *Qumran Cave* I, ed. D. Barthélemy and J.T. Milik, 1955, 109ff.

[362] *Ref Omn Haer* 9,28 = *Bell* 2,160f. K. Kohler, *op. cit.*, 8, misunderstood Hippolytus' account here.

[363] See above, p. 65f. and below, p. 183f.

'Zealots') *Sicarii*.[364] As is to some extent the case in the rabbinic tradition, the two names refer, as they do not in Josephus' linguistic usage, to the same party.

He also presents the 'third group' in quite a remarkable way, leaving these men, unlike the 'Zealots' or the *Sicarii*, without a name. Their chief characteristic is the only one that is also confirmed by Josephus, who also stresses the demand that only God should be recognized as Lord as the fundamental thesis of this 'fourth philosophy' founded by Judas the Galilaean.[365] It is not easy to decide whether Hippolytus was directly dependent in this passage on Josephus or whether he also had access to an independent tradition here. In the first case, he would have had to go back to the *Antiquities*.[366] Whatever the case may be, his account points to the probability of some inner connection between the 'Zealots' and the radical demands made by Judas of Galilee.

E. SUMMARY

An analysis of the various names for the Jewish freedom movement occurring in very diverse sources has proved to be a very suitable point of departure for an examination at greater depth of the structure and history of that movement. It is worth summarizing the results of this analysis briefly here.

It is hardly fortuitous that the most general name employed by Josephus to describe the Jewish freedom fighters more precisely — that is, the term of abuse, λῃστής — appears in his writings for the first time very soon after Judaea had been subjugated by the Romans. This name then appears again and again in the Jewish historian's work until the outbreak of the Jewish War or the destruction of Jerusalem. This name, 'robbers', certainly indicates that a bitter small-scale war was being fought between the occupying forces and the Jewish francs-tireurs, but Josephus quite consciously lets the dividing line between the defenders of faith and freedom and ordinary highwaymen disappear and equates the former unhesitatingly with criminals. For him, they are lawless rebels. He even tries to suppress the real aim of his opponents and stresses greed as their fundamental motive — a charge motivated by the social aims of the rebels.

No direct relationship can, however, be established in the rabbinic

[364] *Ref Omn Haer* 9,26: ... ζηλωταί καλούμενοι ὑπό τινων δὲ σικάριοι.
[365] See below, p. 90ff.
[366] The wording is most closely in agreement with *Ant* 18,23; see Juster, 2, 343, n. 5.

literature between the loan-word לִיסְטִים and Josephus' λῃσταί, but the image drawn in his work of the 'robber' fits very well into the framework of ideas of the scourge of robbers that was very widespread throughout the ancient world. The concept of λῃστής in Josephus, then, may simply point to the tactics, organization and, in some respects, social background of the Jewish fight for freedom between the time of Herod and the Jewish War.

The name *Sicarii* originally had a very similar meaning. It was given to those who were in revolt by their Roman enemies because of their way of fighting. In Josephus' writings, the name applied above all to a particular group of men — the followers of Menahem who had fled to Masada after his murder. According to rabbinic tradition, this name was also given to the rebels in Jerusalem. We may have the original meaning of the name here, since the Romans were able to call every Jewish freedom fighter a *sicarius*. It is also beyond dispute that the beginnings of the group which Josephus called by this name go back to Judas the Galilaean, who founded the 'fourth philosophy' during Cyrenius' census.

The name 'Galilaean' gives emphasis to the importance of Galilee in the fight against Roman rule. Galilee was a part of the country in which there had been frequent disturbances and Hellenistic influences were to a great extent rejected. It had become a centre of resistance against the occupation forces.

It is not possible to say with any certainty whether the Jewish partisans called themselves *barjone*. The word may perhaps point to their outward way of life in the mountains and the desert.

We come closest to the real intention of the Jewish freedom movement in the name by which its members called themselves: ζηλωταί — קַנָּאִים. The definite and absolute use of this term in Josephus' work, as opposed to the usual Greek linguistic usage, is very distinct and the word clearly points to a definite religious and political party within Jerusalem at the beginning of the Jewish War. In at least one place, this name is not strictly confined to the followers of Eleazar b. Simon. That is where Josephus also calls the members of the retinue of Menahem, the son of Judas the Galilaean, by this name.

The rabbinic and Christian sources supplement Josephus in three respects: (1) the name can to some extent be used with the same meaning as the other party name *Sicarius*; (2) it is probable that the term was also applied before the Jewish War, at the time of Jesus, to members of the Jewish freedom movement; (3) it is an honorary title which goes back to Old Testament models and which members of that movement gave to themselves.[367] A deep religious driving force lies behind this name, which can best be expressed as 'zeal for God and his law'. This zeal was in turn expressed in a rigorous refusal to compromise in carrying out God's commandments and in the use of violence against all who did not obey those commandments, which were interpreted in the most radical way.[368]

On the basis of what I have said so far, two phenomena have clearly to be investigated in the two chapters that follow. The first is the so-called 'fourth philosophy' founded by Judas the Galilaean and the second is the religious phenomenon of 'holy zeal' in late Judaism.

---

[367] See A. Schlatter, *Die Geschichte des Christus*, 1921, 304. The authors of *The Beginnings of Christianity*, 1, 426, regarded ζηλωτής as an honorary title, similar to 'Hasid', but also thought that the name was freely given to individual pious men. There is, however, no clear evidence for this. See also M.J. Lagrange, *Le Judaïsme avant Jésus-Christ*, 3rd. ed. 1931, 214, and M. Smith, *HTR* 64 (1971), 6ff.; see also below, pp. 388, 390f., and 392.

[368] See V. Nikiprowetzky, 'La mort d'Eléazar fils de Jaire', *Hommages à André Dupont-Sommer*, Paris 1971, 469, n.: 'All these messianic movements ... had one thing in common, the doctrine of zeal and synergism, which was the legacy of the 'fourth philosophy'. The name 'Zealots' was therefore a particularly suitable one for all of them, because of the religious teaching in the name of which they acted'. See also below, p. 173f.

CHAPTER III

JUDAS THE GALILAEAN'S 'FOURTH PHILOSOPHY'

A. THE STATEMENTS MADE IN THE SOURCES

Only Josephus provides a more detailed account of Judas the Galilaean and the sect founded by him. All that is found in *The Jewish War* is a brief note, saying that, after Archelaus' territory had been transformed into a Roman province, a 'certain Galilaean named Judas' had incited his people to revolt,

> 'by declaring their tolerance in the payment of taxes to the Romans and in the recognition of mortal men as rulers rather than God to be a disgrace. He himself, however, became the "teacher" of his own sect, which had nothing at all in common with the others. There are three kinds of philosophical schools among the Jews: ... the Pharisees ... the Sadducees ... the Essenes'.[1]

Josephus tells us much more about Judas in his *Antiquities*. As in *The Jewish War*, his point of departure is the transformation of Judaea into a Roman province, but he goes on to report in detail how the census carried out by the governor of Syria, Cyrenius, almost caused a revolt on the part of the Jews and how that revolt was only prevented with some difficulty.[2] At that time, 'Judas the Gaulanite',[3] together with a Pharisee called Saddok, incited the people to rebellion. According to Josephus, this incitement contained two main arguments:

(1) The census would lead to slavery, with the result that the people should fight for their freedom.[4]

(2) God would only help them if they worked actively with him to liberate themselves and did not lose heart.[5]

These arguments met with widespread joyous approval, with the result that the audacious undertaking made great progress.[6] But what

---

[1] *Bell* 2,117-119.

[2] *Ant* 18,2f.

[3] *Ant* 18,4. For the question of Judas' origin, see below, p. 330ff.

[4] τήν τε ἀποτίμησιν οὐδὲν ἄλλο ἢ ἄντικρυς δουλείαν ἐπιφέρειν λέγοντες καὶ τῆς ἐλευθερίας ἐπ' ἀντιλήψει παρακαλοῦντες τὸ ἔθνος (*Ant* 18,4).

[5] *Ant* 18,5: καὶ τὸ θεῖον οὐκ ἄλλως ἢ ἐπὶ συμπράξει τῶν βουλευμάτων εἰς τὸ κατορθοῦν συμπροθυμεῖσθαι μᾶλλον.

[6] *Ant* 18,6.

followed were disturbances and disorder caused by robbers, the best men were murdered and in the end civil war broke out, the land was ravaged by famine and the Temple was destroyed.[7] Josephus names Judas and Saddok explicitly as the authors of this entire catastrophe and says that they 'founded an intrusive fourth school of philosophy'[8] and 'at that time found many fanatical adherents (ἐρασταί) for it'.

Josephus ends his account with a reference to the later effects of their doctrines:

> 'They also established the roots of the evils that occurred at a later period by a doctrine of a kind that had never been heard before'.

After briefly outlining the views of the Pharisees, the Sadducees and the Essenes, Josephus returns to Judas and his sect:[9]

> 'Judas had been appointed leader of the fourth among the schools of philosophy. This is in all its other parts in accordance with the Pharisees. Its love of freedom is, however, insurmountable and it recognizes only God as ruler and Lord.
>
> 'They endured quite unusual forms of death and disregarded the death penalty in the case of their relatives and friends, if only they needed to call no man Lord (δεσπότην). Since their stubbornness is universally known and evident, I shall refrain from reporting it in greater detail. I do not need to fear that what has been said by me about this may not be believed. On the contrary, I have rather to be concerned that the words of this account may be too weak to describe their disregard of the excess of suffering that that they have accepted.
>
> 'The people began to be seized by the madness[10] that originated with this when the procurator Gessius Florus drove them to such despair by abusing the authority of his office that they rebelled against the Romans'.

Josephus closes his excursus on the four Jewish philosophies with the laconic remark: 'To that extent, philosophy is practised among the Jews'.

Judas and the fourth sect are presented in the *Antiquities*, in accordance with the general tendency of the work, in an exaggerated way and in an artificial, inflated and stilted style.[11] The concepts have a thoroughly

---

[7] *Ant* 18,7f.

[8] *Ant* 18,9: τετάρτην φιλοσοφίαν ἐπείσακτον ἡμῖν ἐγείραντες.

[9] *Ant* 18,23-25.

[10] ἄνοια (ἀπόνοια, μανία) is one of those very typical terms that Josephus uses again and again to characterize the ideas and the aspirations of the Jewish freedom movement. See above, p. 16, n. 67.

[11] See above, p. 12ff. See also the description of the Greek stylist employed by Josephus in this part of his *Antiquities* by H. St. J. Thackeray, *Josephus, the Man and the Historian*, 1929, 108: 'Books XVII-XIX betray the idiosyncrasies and pedantic tricks of a hack, an

Hellenistic colouring which is even more pronounced than in *The Jewish War* and which does not make the task of interpreting Josephus' account any easier.

In addition to the principal texts cited above in which Judas and his movement are discussed, there are also several references in *The Jewish War* which confirm the essential points that have already been mentioned. In his first reference to Menahem, Josephus names his father Judas:

> 'the son of Judas, the so-called Galilaean, a violent leader of the people who, under Cyrenius, once reviled the Jews because they were also subject to the Romans'.[12]

There is a similar reference at the beginning of Josephus' concluding criticism of the rebels:

> '... Eleazar, a descendant of Judas, who had persuaded a number of Jews ... not to let themselves be assessed for tax when Cyrenius had been sent to Judaea as censor. The *Sicarii* joined together at that time against those who wanted to obey the Romans ...'[13]

A similar reference with contents of the same kind can also be found in the *Antiquities*.[14]

The only source apart from Josephus that refers to Judas is the address in Acts 5.37 by Gamaliel, who speaks of the uprising of Judas the Galilaean:

> 'After him (Theudas) Judas the Galilaean arose in the days of the census and drew away some of the people after him; he also perished and all who followed him were scattered'.

Judas, then, proclaimed and instigated open revolt. According to the biblical source, which differs from Josephus, it was presumably not long before Judas was killed and an end was put to his movement. We are told nothing about the views held by his followers or about any continuing effect of their revolutionary ideas. It is not easy to answer the question as to where Luke obtained this historical information. A direct dependence on Josephus is unlikely.[16] It is possible that there were common oral

---

imitator of Thukydides'; 111: 'This journalistic hack is verbose and prefers to use two or more words to one'; 112: 'The writer had the faults of the inferior journalist'.

[12] *Bell* 2,433.

[13] *Bell* 7,253. See also above, p. 46ff.

[14] *Ant* 20,102.

[15] E. Haenchen, *The Acts of the Apostles*, 1971, 253, n. 8, has commented: 'Luke combines here the Greek expression "leading people to revolt" with the biblical expression "drawing away people after him"'.

[16] I disagree here with M. Krenkel, *Josephus und Lukas*, 1884, 163ff., and H.H. Wendt,

traditions here and in other places.[17] M. Dibelius' investigations have shown that Gamaliel's address in Luke was very probably a 'free composition'.[18] On the other hand, however, the fact that the tradition was preserved for such a long time shows that the foundation of this new movement must have made a very deep impression on the minds of Jewish people living at the time.[19]

It is clear from the accounts of Judas and his sect provided by Josephus and cited above that there was an inner connection between the new movement and the downfall of Jerusalem. Josephus in fact regards it as directly responsible for the later development.[20] We may therefore conclude from this that the activity of the movement initiated by Judas lasted until the Jewish War.

It is also remarkable that Josephus describes the party founded by Judas and Saddok as a τετάρτη φιλοσοφία within Judaism. One is bound to ask what these rebels could have had in common with a 'school of philosophy'. Any offence caused by this strange expression disappears, however, as soon as the Hellenistic garment in which the *Antiquities* is dressed and to which I have referred above, is recalled. It was Josephus' aim in that work to enable his Greek readers to understand the formation of sects in Judaism by analogy with the Greek schools of philosophy.[21]

The *Antiquities* is different from *The Jewish War*, in which Judas' new

---

Apostelgeschichte (Meyers Kommentar), 9th. ed. 1913, 43f. and 128. This is in no sense an 'imprecise reminiscence of *Ant* 20,5.1 (97f. and 102)'. O. Bauernfeind, *Die Apostelgeschichte (ThHK)*, 1939, 96, and M. Dibelius, *Studies in the Acts of the Apostles*, 1956, 186, were right to oppose this view.

[17] See Acts 5,36; 11,28; 12,20-23; 21,38.

[18] *op. cit.*, 160; see also 130, n. 4.

[19] See W.O.E. Oesterley, *A History of Israel*, 2, 1951 (1932), 386: 'The trouble must have been grave to have been recalled in later days'. See also the author's Note 4: 'See Acts V.37'.

[20] *Bell* 2,433; 7,253f.; *Ant* 18,9f. and 25. See also above, p. 48f.

[21] J.W. Lightley, *Jewish Sects and Parties in the Time of Jesus Christ*, 1925, 330 insisted that it was 'a Jewish party not a philosophical sect', but this is misleading, because, after having committed himself to the use of the Hellenistic collective term 'school of philosophy', Josephus was able to describe the 'fourth sect' just as well with this concept as the other three. This fact is also overlooked in *B.-Gr. Rel.* 87: '... the party of the so-called Zealots, which Josephus ingenuously describes as the 'fourth philosophical sect', but whose members were in fact nothing but nationalistic fanatics ...' and by E. Meyer, *Ursprung und Anfänge des Christentums*. 1921ff., 2, 402, M.J. Lagrange, *Le Judaïsme avant Jésus-Christ*, 3rd. ed. 1931, 214, and S. Baron, *A Social and Religious History of the Jews*, 1937, 1, 220. The state of affairs was correctly interpreted by G. Hölscher, *Geschichte der Israelitisch-Jüdischen Religion*, 1922, 227: 'This covenant was also correctly described by Josephus as a religious association'. H. Rasp, *ZNW* 23 (1924), 28, correctly emphasized the author's 'concern for a foreign, that is, a Greek reading public'. See also G. Ricciotti, *Flavio Giuseppe*, 2, 208, on *Bell* 2,119.

sect is contrasted sharply with the three 'schools of philosophy' (τρία γὰρ παρὰ Ἰουδαίοις εἴδη φιλοσοφεῖται), in that Judas' sect appears in the *Antiquities* as a 'fourth school' with at least to some extent equal status alongside the three traditional Jewish religious parties, the Pharisees, the Sadducees and the Essenes.[22] The independent character of the movement initiated by Judas is also stressed in *The Jewish War* and the author insists that the new sect has nothing in common with the others (οὐδὲν τοῖς ἄλλοις προσεοικώς). The *Antiquities* makes the charge that Judas' sect is alien (ἐπείσακτος) and unusual (ἀσυνήθης) and that its founders even changed the laws (ἡ τῶν πατρίων καίνισις).[23] This would seem to suggest that what was involved in the sect founded by Judas was an independent group existing alongside the other Jewish parties and having its own distinctive ideas.

The assumption is, however, to some extent contradicted by the clear statement made in the *Antiquities* (18,23) that the fourth sect was distinguished from the Pharisees only by its demand for the 'sole rule of God'.[24] This is in accordance with Josephus' assertion that the co-founder of the movement, Saddok, was also a Pharisee. The obvious contrast that is brought to light here cannot really be dismissed by the unlikely hypothesis that Josephus later produced a second, revised version of the *Antiquities*.[25] The only way in which this problem can be

---

[22] See *Bell* 2,118 and *Ant* 18,9.23. The analogy with the Greek schools of philosophy, which Josephus used quite consciously, is very wide-ranging. In *Vita* 12, for example, he compares the Pharisees with the Stoics, whereas, in *Ant* 15,371, he compares the Essenes with the Pythagoreans. It is perhaps possible to find a parallel between the Sadducees and the Epicureans and between the fourth sect and the Cynics, although they certainly did not share the latters' indifference towards political relationships. See M.J. Lagrange. *op. cit.*, and H. Rasp, *op. cit.*, 31: 'Josephus believed that the Jews were outstanding not only in the field of politics, but also in the cultural sphere, since they had schools of philosophy'. G. Ricciotti, *Flavio Giuseppe*, 2, 208 on *Bell* 2,229, expresses a similar view.

[23] *Ant* 18,9. See also above, p. 77, n. 8. According to *Bell* 2,414, the radical priests who wanted to initiate sacrifice to the emperor were criticized for introducing a new and alien religion'. See also below, pp. 106f., 205.

[24] This contradiction was observed by O. Holtzmann, *Neutestamentliche Zeitgeschichte*, 1st. ed. 1895, 161; Seiffert, 'Zeloten', *RE* 12, 656; M.J. Lagrange, *op. cit.* 214; G. Ricciotti, *op. cit.*. W.R.Farmer, 30ff., also deals with the question at length.

[25] W.R.Farmer, 33, n. 23, tries to approach the question along this path. Josephus' account in *Ant* 18,1–27 is, however, quite uniform and, apart from the contrast mentioned above, perfectly consistent. Josephus first speaks of the effectiveness of Judas and Saddok and then mentions that they founded a 'fourth school of philosophy' (18,9). In order to make this intelligible to the Hellenistic reader, he goes on to outline briefly the other three parties — partly by referring to his more detailed presentation of them in *The Jewish War*. Then, following their enumeration, he goes on to discuss the fourth sect (18,11–22). In this context, he speaks in particular about their views and their behaviour (18,23–27). The hypothesis suggested by Laqueur that Josephus later produced a

satisfactorily resolved is by going more deeply into the relationship between Judas' sect and the Pharisees.

One particularly striking aspect of the new movement is its anonymity. Josephus gives us the names of its founders, but he leaves the 'fourth philosophy' that they created, unlike the other parties, without a name. This problem also calls for further investigation.

I propose to leave all discussion of such detailed problems as the historical preparation for the founding of the new sect and the person of the founder and his fate until I come later to provide a historical outline of the movement. At this point, I would like to concentrate on the following questions, which have been raised by the preceding discussion:

(1) Did Judas really found an exclusive and well-defined independent sect and can its further development be traced in Jewish history until the destruction of Jerusalem?

(2) What was the relationship between this movement and the Pharisees?

(3) What was the name of this new sect?

Josephus provides us with some information about several of the views held by the fourth sect:

(1) The most important doctrine is that only God may be called Lord or ruler.[26]

(2) Another essential aspect of the movement is its 'invincible love of freedom'.[27]

(3) In addition to this, Judas also seems to have made the people's co-operation with God for their own liberation a necessary precondition for his intervention and help.[28]

(4) The bitter rejection of the census leads to the supposition that it must have deeply offended the religious sensibilities of pious Jews.[29]

The point of departure for any investigation into the religious ideas that were current in the movement founded by Judas and Saddok must be provided by the four points outlined above. At the same time, they also make it possible for us to define more precisely the religious and historical position of the newly founded movement within late Judaism.

---

completely rewritten version of the *Antiquities* is in itself very improbable (see above, p. 13, n. 51). There is no reason to assume that such a version ever existed in the case of our passage.

[26] *Ant* 18,23f.; *Bell* 2,118,433; see also below, p. 90ff.

[27] *Ant* 18,4.23; see also above, p. 77, n. 9, and below, p. 110ff.

[28] *Ant* 18,5; see also above, p. 76, n. 5, and below, p. 122ff.

[29] *Ant* 18,3f.; *Bell* 2,118; 7,253; *Ant* 20,102; Acts 5.37; see also below, p. 127ff.

A further essential point, the readiness of the members of the movement for martyrdom, will also be investigated later in this book.[30]

B. The 'Fourth Philosophy' as an Independent Party Within Late Judaism

1. The Fourth Philosophy: Exclusive Fraternity and Independent Movement

As I have already pointed out, Josephus contrasts the fourth sect that began with Judas as an ἰδία αἵρεσις or a τετάρτη φιλοσοφία with the three other Jewish groups. The first answer that can be given to the question as to whether this sect was a 'political party' or a 'religious sect' is that all Jewish groups formed in the first century A.D. were always both political and religious at the same time. The Sadducees, who were closest to a political party, also had very definite religious views and the 'religious sect' of the Essenes again and again made themselves conspicuous with their clear attitude towards political events.[31] The decision which directly concerns my theme in this book, that is, whether the new 'haeresis' was, in its views and aims, primarily determined by political and national or by religious motives, can only be made after investigating the ideas that prevailed in it.

One might with apparent justification raise the objection that the new movement that began with Judas should not be compared with the other three 'parties' since it shows none of their clearly delineated unity. For in later accounts, Josephus describes the Jewish freedom movement in the form of individual groups and bands operating without any visible connection between them.[32] Even the radical wing of the rebels split up during the Jewish War into several different groups in violent conflict with each other. Subject to these preconditions, it is possible to call the fourth sect 'a tendency rather than a constituted party'.[33] The names used

---

[30] Ant 18,24; see also above, p. 77, and below, pp. 259ff., 265ff.

[31] For the Sadducees, see Bell 2,164ff.; Ant 13,173.297f.; see also Schürer 2, 404ff.; J. Wellhausen, Pharisäer und Sadducäer, 1874, 52f. For the Essenes, see the sharp disputes with the Hasmonaeans: 1QpHab; TestLev 14-16; Jub 23,22ff. They did not even shrink from controversy with Rome: Bell 2,152f.; see also J.T. Milik, Ten Years of Discovery in the Wilderness of Judaea, 1959, 94–98.

[32] See Bell 2,234ff.: Eleazar b. Dinai; Ant 20,5: Tholomaeus; Ant 20,97ff.: Theudas; Bell 2,261 = Ant 20,169ff.: the Egyptians. This is also borne out by the vagueness of the name λῃσταί; see above, p. 44, n. 172.

[33] This was the opinion of C. Guignebert, The Jewish World in the Time of Jesus, 1939, 170f, who also suspected that Judas the Galilaean hardly merited the importance that Josephus attributed to him: 'I have no great trust in this history, which is in accordance

by Josephus in his presentation of the Jewish War for the members of the Jewish freedom movement — λησταί, σικάριοι and ζηλωταί — would then be understood as an indication of the existence of several groups that were independent from the very beginning, and the influence of the Galilaean Judas could thus be limited exclusively to certain doctrines and views.[34]

What has, however, to be said in opposition to this argument is that Josephus not only explicitly makes the movement that was initiated by Judas responsible, as I have already pointed out, for the later catastrophe, but also that the movement has a clearly recognizable history. This history began with the foundation of the movement during the census conducted under Cyrenius, that is, in 6/7 A.D., reappeared (before 48 A.D.) at the time of the crucifixion of two of Judas' sons by Tiberius Alexander,[35] was continued at the beginning of the Jewish War by Menahem, another of Judas' sons who claimed to be the Messiah, and only ended with the suicide of the occupation forces in Masada or the martyrdom of the *Sicarii* in Egypt in 73 A.D.[36]

The continuity of the new sect as an organization was guaranteed by the continued existence of Judas' dynasty in his sons and grandsons. The unchanged tradition of his doctrine manifested itself in the persistence with which the *Sicarii* clung to the thesis of the 'sole rule of God' even under torture.[37] It is therefore impossible to regard Judas simply as a 'teacher' (σοφιστής).[38] His message was inseparable from active revolt against foreign rule. It presupposed the formation of an organized community.[39]

Josephus must therefore be regarded as correct in his presentation of the party led by Judas as an independent group, even though it is true

---

with the constant need that was felt in the ancient world to relate collective movements to an initiative taken by an individual' (*op. cit.*, 170). See also Bo Reicke, 'Diakonie, Festfreude und Zelos', *UUA* 5 (1951), 199: 'We should not think of zealotism in such a narrow way as Josephus did. It was not confined to one strictly limited party, but was a general movement that was important for the whole of Judaism of that time both inside and outside Palestine ...' J.-A. Morin, *RB* 80 (1973), 332ff., expresses a similar view.

[34] For this, see especially the editors of *The Beginnings of Christianity* (see above, p. 64, n. 317), who were followed in this by R.H. Pfeiffer, *History of New Testament Times*, 1949, 35f.,59. The opposite opinion is held by J. Klausner, *Hist* 4, 201f. and S.G.F. Brandon, *The Fall of Jerusalem*, 1951, 105, n. 1.

[35] *Ant* 20,102.

[36] *Bell* 7,253f.275-419.

[37] *Bell* 7,417ff. See also below, p. 260ff.

[38] This is the title given to Judas in *Bell* 2,118 and 433. For this, see below, pp. 86f., 227, 333.

[39] It is clear from Acts 5.37 that Judas was not simply a teacher of revolutionary ideas, but that he also played a leading part in an attempted revolt.

that other more or less independent bands appeared at the time. The other Jewish 'parties' were also not strictly delimited unities, but were themselves split up into several splinter groups.[40]

It was only in the course of the conflict that fratricidal war began to be waged between the rebels during the Jewish War. They were completely united during the first few weeks of the revolt, when Menahem, who has already been mentioned above, emerged as their leader (ἡγεμὼν τῆς στάσεως). This was a role which could only be assigned to him because he had already been recognized within the Jewish freedom movement — presumably on the basis of his descent from Judas — as a considerable authority. His opponents were therefore not those bands who controlled the open countryside, but a group of priests who had allied themselves with parts of the population of the city.[41] It was only when Menahem had been murdered together with a large number of his followers that the divisions, which had such a fatal effect on the later course of the revolt, began to occur.

Josephus has relatively little to say about the further fate of Judas' sect. This may, on the one hand, be at least partly connected with his reluctance to make any positive pronouncement about those who bore the main guilt.[42] On the other hand, however, it is also certainly determined by the lack of source material. What was involved here was not a movement which willingly exposed its plans and views to everyone. On the contrary, it must, in accordance with its whole being, have represented a kind of secret society:

> 'We do not know how the party was united into a community and what form its meetings, its signs of recognition and so on took. All that can be learnt from the information provided by Josephus is that it emerged in the years leading up to the revolt as something that was quite separate from the other groups within the people'.[43]

According to some of Josephus' statements, such an organization of the fourth sect would seem to have been a 'secret society'. In his view, a precondition of the new sect must certainly have been a permanent head, but he names Judas explicitly as the ἡγεμών of the 'fourth school of philosophy', while Menachem later appears as the ἡγεμών of the whole

---

[40] The Boethusians formed a special group within the Sadducees; see Schürer 2, 406, n. 16. For the Essenes, see *Bell* 2,160. Judas' party could in one respect be seen as a splinter group from the Pharisees and even the division between the schools of Hillel and Shammai amounted in practice to a split between the Pharisees; for this, see below, pp. 200–206.

[41] See *Bell* 2,434.441–448.

[42] See W. Weber, *Josephus und Vespasian*, 1921, 26; see also above, p. 10f.

[43] Schlatter, *GI*, 263.

revolt and Eleazar — who was probably a grandson of Judas — also seems to have been the undisputed authority in Masada.[44]

Another essential aspect of the activity of the Galilaean's new sect was the unhesitating use of violence, which did not stop at the shedding of blood and murder. Its members regarded as opponents not only the Roman oppressors and their accomplices, but also all Jews who were prepared to submit to the Roman rule for the sake of peace[45] and indeed all those who, in their opinion, violated the law. In a certain sense, the following statement undoubtedly applied to such men:

> 'Everyone who sheds the blood of godless men is like one who offers a sacrifice'.[46]

Since rich Jews, who were particularly concerned to safeguard their property, looked for a compromise with the Roman authorities, the activity of the new sect had to some extent the aspect of social revolution.[47] There are several anecdotes dating back to the years before the outbreak of the war and reported by Josephus which show clearly that the activities of the sect were well organized and firmly directed.[48] The best indication of the position of power that the new party was able to achieve even before the outbreak of the Jewish War is the fact that the last two procurators, Albinus and Gessius Florus, were compelled to undertake negotiations with the insurrectionary movement, which had by then grown to the dimensions of a tidal wave. This was a measure of success that individual bands operating independently of each other and without any common plan could never have achieved.[49]

---

[44] *Ant* 18,23; *Bell* 2,434; 7,253.275-410. See Schlatter, *GI*, 262: 'Because the new party not only disseminated a doctrine, but also called for action, it also had a party leader who was in control of all that the members undertook. This was not the case with the Pharisees or the Sadducees, who had no party leader to whom the foundation of a party was ascribed in a similar manner'. It is, however, possible to point, as a parallel case, to the 'teacher of righteousness' and to the leading part played by the relations of the Lord in the Palestinian Christian community.

[45] See *Bell* 7,254: 'At that time (in the days of Judas) the *Sicarii* joined together in opposition to those who wanted to obey the Romans and treated them in every respect as enemies'. Before the outbreak of the Jewish War, the bands of robbers 'threatened those who submitted to the Roman rule with death ...' (see *Bell* 2,264). The *Sicarii* in Egypt killed eminent Jews who opposed them (see *Bell* 7,411).

[46] NumRab 21,3 (on Num 25.13), Bill. 2, 565 parr. See T. Asher, 4; Jn 16.2 and Acts 23.12ff.

[47] See *Bell* 2,265.427.

[48] See *Bell* 2,256 = *Ant* 20,163f.: the murder of the high-priest Jonathan and the murders committed by the *Sicarii* in the Temple; *Ant* 20,208: the abduction of the scribe of the captain of the Temple, Eleazar b. Ananias. For this, see below, pp. 353f. and 398.

[49] *Ant* 20,215 and 255. See also below, p. 355f.

Bearing in mind all these various points, then, we may assume that, in the so-called 'fourth philosophy', Judas the Galilaean founded a real party not only with quite definite opinions — which I shall be examining later on — but also with a firm organization and a single leadership. That party also determined the fate of the Jewish people throughout the two following generations and formed the permanent focal point of the growing Jewish freedom movement.[50]

2. The 'Fourth Philosophy' and the Pharisees

I have already pointed to the strange contradiction in the characterization of the sect founded by Judas contained in Josephus' accounts of it in his *Jewish War* and *Antiquities*. In *The Jewish War*, which was an early work, Josephus understandably made a very clear distinction between the three other Jewish parties and in particular the Pharisees, to whom, he tells us, he himself belonged[51] (and who were also the only party to have survived the catastrophe), and the new party founded by Judas, in order to ensure that suspicions were not aroused that they also took part in criminal machinations.[52] Even in the later *Antiquities*, there is, however, still a certain tension between what Josephus has to say about the newness of the sect and his later statements about its firm dependence on the Pharisees. Since, as I have indicated, the problem cannot be solved by text-critical operations, but only postponed, it must actually reflect the character of the sect itself.

In *Ant* 18,23, Josephus states unequivocally that God is the only Lord of Israel even in the political sphere and that the recognition of a foreign sovereign is therefore equivalent to breaking the first commandment and to reverting to paganism. Taking this clear statement as our point of

---

[50] Mommsen, *RG* 5, 515, expressed the fundamental elements of this state of affairs concisely and clearly: 'Alongside the Pharisees, the Sadducees and the Essenes, he (Judas) and his followers were regarded by the later Jews as the fourth "school". At that time, they were known as Zealots, but later ... as the *Sicarii* ... Their doctrine was very simple: God alone was the Lord, death was a matter of indifference and freedom was everything. This doctrine remained and the children and grandchildren of Judas became leaders of the later insurrections'. See also Klausner, *Hist* 4, 200; J.W. Lightley, *Jewish Sects and Parties in the Time of Jesus*, 1925, 360; Schlatter, *GI*, 259,262ff.

[51] *Vita* 12; see also above, p. 6, nn. 2 and 3.

[52] This was the opinion of O. Holtzmann, *Neutestamentliche Zeitgeschichte*, 1st. ed. 1895, 161. H. Drexler, *Klio* 19 (1925), 285, suspected that the fourth sect was mentioned in the account of the three sects that was available to Josephus, who suppressed it, however, in *The Jewish War* and only made use of it in his *Antiquities*.

departure, it is possible to assert quite simply that these were 'doctrines that had never been heard before' in Judaism before the time of Judas the Galilaean.[53] The same may also apply to the new sect's invincible love of freedom, if the concept of freedom is understood not in the profane political sense, but rather in its eschatological sense, that is, in the sense that the 'love of freedom', with sword in hand, will force the Eschatological Redemption. Seen from these two perspectives, which Josephus explicitly excludes in his comparison between the fourth sect and Pharisaism, his preceding statements about the 'change in the laws' and the 'new' doctrines of Judas and Saddok are fully justified.

On the other hand, however, the fact that a Pharisee co-operated in the foundation of the new movement and that, as the addition of σοφιστής to his name clearly indicates, Judas was also a scribe,[54] also presupposes that the new sect was 'in its other views' closely connected with the Pharisees and may even be regarded as their extreme 'left wing'.[55] The contradiction in Josephus' account is therefore only an apparent one, since the contrast between the new doctrine and dependence on the Pharisees goes back to the two faces of the new party founded by Judas and Saddok which, on the one hand, was firmly rooted in the Jewish and Pharisaical tradition and, on the other, developed new and revolutionary ideas.

It is obvious that the uncompromising rejection of pagan rule by the members of this new 'Pharisaical' group must soon have led to a break with those Pharisees whose attitude towards the question of foreign rule was more realistic and mediatory. This detachment from Pharisaism and the new sect's own inner development was undoubtedly also encouraged by its strict organization under a single head of the party and its activity, which was directed less towards teaching and meditation than towards armed struggle. The schism between the schools of Hillel and Shammai, in the Pharisaism of the first century A.D., presumably

---

[53] For this, see above, p. 80f.; W.R. Farmer, however, says, 14: 'The distinctive features of the sect, said to have originated with Judas of Galilee, are precisely those for which the Maccabees were remembered, as the Maccabean literature, and even Josephus himself, indicates'. See also pp. 33, 35 and elsewhere. Unfortunately, Farmer neglects to provide satisfactory evidence with regard to the 'sole rule of God'.

[54] For this, see below, pp. 227 and 333.

[55] See C. Guignebert, *The Jewish World in the Time of Jesus*, 1939, 169: 'The extreme left wing of the Pharisees . . .'; Klausner, *J of N*, 205: 'The Zealots were basically nothing but extreme Pharisees'; Schürer, 1, 382; G. Hölscher, *Geschichte der jüdischen Religion*, 1922, 220; G. Ricciotti, *The History of Israel*, 1955, 2, 381f. See also R. Meyer, *TD* 9, 26f.

indicates the differences among the Pharisees at the time which, among others, also involved the new movement founded by Judas.[56]

The fundamental Pharisaical attitude of the 'fourth party' has been confirmed by the excavations that have taken place at Masada. The precise delivery of tithes and taxes, the synagogue and the *miqweh* or ritual bath are clear signs of this.[57] Josephus' pointing to the intimate connection between the Jewish freedom movement and Pharisaism should make us take into account the fact that at least some parts of the Pharisaical party were closer to the fourth sect in its hostility towards the Romans than the later rabbinic tradition would have us believe.[58]

3. The Name of the New Movement

There can be no doubt at all that the fourth sect founded by Judas is identical with the group that was later called the *Sicarii* by Josephus.[59] The name *Sicarii* was, however, certainly not an original one — it seems in fact only to have emerged during the Roman occupation under the procurator Felix. The fourth sect founded by Judas therefore at first continued to be without a name in Josephus' works. This is an extremely curious fact, since the author unhesitatingly calls the other three Jewish sects by their names. It is possibly connected with the fact that the new movement did not have its own party name during the time of its founder Judas and was regarded by outsiders as a radical branch of the Pharisees, whereas the members of the sect saw themselves as the true embodiment of Israel.[60] It is quite possible that Josephus did not want to call the new group by its name because he thought that it was inapposite. This might possibly be assumed on the basis of his explanation of the party name ζηλωταί, especially as what was involved in this case was an honorary title based on Old Testament examples.[61] The earliest evidence

---

[56] See below, pp. 200ff., 333f.

[57] Y. Yadin, *Masada*, London 1966, 96f.,164ff. See also E. Güring, *Terumot, Die Mischna*, I,6, 1969, 21f.

[58] See above, p. 21f.; see also below, pp. 118f., 123f., 168f. and elsewhere.

[59] See above, pp. 48f., 82f. etc.

[60] See below, p. 142f. The movement or primitive community initiated by Jesus can be cited here as a parallel, since, to begin with, it also had no real name for itself. At first only the neutral name μαθητής is found; see A. von Harnack, *Mission and Expansion of Christianity*, 2nd. ed. 1908, 399ff. and K.H. Rengstorff, 'μαθητής', *TD* 4, 457f. The opponents of the Christian movement were in fact the first to give it a name.

[61] See above, p. 53f.; see also below, p. 157ff. See also *Bell* 4,161 and 7,268-270.

that we have of the party name 'Zealot' is about 30 A.D., when it was
applied to a disciple of Jesus. In Josephus' writings it appears for the first
time as the name of the followers of Judas' son Menahem.[62] A trace of
this name which the members of the movement gave themselves, can,
however, perhaps be recognized in Josephus' detailed account of the
fourth sect in his *Antiquities* (18,3-9), since he speaks twice in that passage
about ἐρασταί.[63] This is a term that is fairly near to the concept of ζηλωταί,
but belongs much more closely to classical Greek. This transformation
may possibly be attributed to the Greek stylist.

Although it is not possible to achieve absolute certainty in this
question, one assumption appears to be not entirely without foundation.
That is that the name that the members of the new movement gave
themselves, that is, 'Zealots', a name that was honourable, had deep
religious significance and was rooted in the Old Testament tradition,
had been claimed and applied to themselves by the followers of Judas the
Galilaean even before the Jewish War. When I come later to speak about
those who belonged to the Jewish freedom movement, I shall, for this
reason, use the concept 'Zealots'.[64]

We cannot, however, assume that the name 'Zealots' was already
employed before the time of Judas by Jewish groups as a party name or
an honorary title, since there is a total lack of evidence that can be
precisely dated and the Jewish freedom movement was also very
disunited and had no centre to sustain it.[65] The appearance of Judas was
without any doubt a very incisive event in the history of the Jews'
struggle for freedom.

---

[62] *Bell* 2,444. See also above, p. 64.

[63] *Ant* 18,5.9; for the meaning of this word, see Liddell-Scott, 681. See also above, p. 60, n. 280.

[64] Schürer's presentation, 1, 382f., which was, according to him, criticized several times (see above, p. 64, nn. 315 and 320), is therefore fully justified. M. Noth, *History of Israel*, 1958, for example, almost completely suppresses the activity of Judas the Galilaean (422) and suggests that the Zealots did not appear until after the death of Agrippa I (432f.). Seen as a whole, then, the picture that he gives is quite false.

[65] I disagree here with K. Kohler, *Harkavyfestschrift*, 9ff. (*JE* 12, 639f.), and Klausner, *Hist* 3, 251; 4, 201f., and *J of N*, 202f; Kohler and Klausner both derive the 'Zealots' directly from the Hasidim of the Maccabaean period, appealing to Sanh 9,6 and bTal to support their argument, according to which Judas simply gathered into one the 'Zealots' who had until then been scattered. A similar view was expressed by W.O.E Oesterley, *A History of Israel*, 1934, 2, 383, n. 2. As I have already pointed out (see above, p. 67f.), the earliest date for Sanh 9,6 is the first century A.D. What is more, there is nothing in the sources to suggest that the concept 'Zealots' was ever used before as the name of a group.

C. The Message of Judas the Galilaean

1. The Sole Rule of God

(a) The Statement made in the Sources

The fundamental position of the so-called 'fourth school of philosophy' is most clearly visible. It has been handed down to us in the same way in both *The Jewish War* and the *Antiquities*. It is that, alongside God, no other human ruler may be acknowledged or given the corresponding honorary title of κύριος or δεσπότης. The places in Josephus' works that have to be considered here have already been cited and dealt with in some detail above.[66] For this reason, I shall in this section only cite and discuss those that have so far not been mentioned.

In the great death-speech in *The Jewish War*, Josephus places the fundamental dogma of the fourth sect in the mouth of Eleazar b. Ari, the commander of Masada and presumably also Judas' grandson:

'A long time ago, brave comrades, we firmly resolved to be subject neither to the Romans nor to any other person, but only to God, for only he is the true and lawful Lord of men'.[67]

Even after all hope had been abandoned, the *Sicarii* who had fled to Egyptian territory still tried to persuade the Jews who were resident there:

'They ought not to regard the Romans as more powerful than themselves, but rather acknowledge God as the only Lord'.[68]

If they were taken prisoner by the Romans, they allowed themselves be tortured to death rather than 'confess the emperor as their Lord'.[69]

Confessing the sole rule of God therefore became a fundamental article of faith, for which the most gruesome treatment in martyrdom was accepted in preference to a denial.

Judas the Galilaean certainly did not so much defend his thesis as an opinion held by a scribe in the school; rather he upheld it in public and with prophetic conviction. He 'urged his listeners to rebellion' (ἠπείγετο ἐπὶ ἀποστάσει) and his and Saddok's call to action was addressed to the whole people (... παρακαλοῦντες τὸ ἔθνος).[70] According to *The Jewish War*, he reviled his compatriots (κακίζων) because they paid taxes to the

---

[66] *Bell* 2,118, see above, p. 76, n. 1; *Ant* 18,23.24, see above, p. 78, n. 12; *Bell* 2,433, see above, p. 78, n. 12. See also Hippolytus, *Ref Omn Haer* 9,26, see above, p. 70.
[67] *Bell* 7,323.
[68] *Bell* 7,410.
[69] *Bell* 7,418.
[70] *Ant* 18,4.

Romans and tolerated mortal men as rulers apart from God. His insurrectionary sermon should be regarded as having the form of a prophetic denouncement speech of the kind with which we are familiar in the preaching of John the Baptist and Jesus.[71]

Judas' thesis marked a break with a tradition of foreign rule which had lasted for centuries and which the Jews had endured relatively willingly until the rule of Antiochus Epiphanes. Even later, under the Maccabees, subjection to foreign rulers had not been rejected so fundamentally as it was by Judas. Confessing the 'sole rule of God' meant not only a life and death struggle with Rome, but also a break with what had hitherto been the Jewish tradition. We are therefore bound to ask how it was possible for Judas' demand to arouse such a powerful response among his fellow-countrymen who were so conscious of tradition. It is probable that his message had a deeper effect than any other doctrine had ever had on Palestinian Judaism during the first century A.D. At the most, only Paul's proclamation of freedom from the law could have had a comparable effect.

(b) The Different Points of Departure of the New Doctrine

Josephus provides us with no further information as to how Judas arrived at his revolutionary theses, but it is perhaps possible to deduce the presuppositions of his demand for the sole rule of God from various religious components that were current during his own time. It is, after all, only the question of the reasons for this enormous challenge that can enable us to understand its meaning and its effect completely.

(aa) The Kingdom of God

The idea of the kingdom of God has its roots in the Old Testament, in which three groups of meaning can be distinguished:[72] 1. Yahweh is king in the universal sense, in other words, he is the king of the nations and the world as their Creator and Lord.[73] 2. His kingdom is

---

[71] *Bell* 2,118, see also 433; ὀνειδίσας. For the Baptist's call to repentance, see Lk 3.7ff. and Mt 3.7fff.; for Jesus, see Mt 11.20. See also below, p. 104.

[72] 'King' appears some fifty times in the Old Testament as the name of God; see L. Köhler, *Old Testament Theology*, 1957, 31. For what follows, see W. Eichrodt, *Theology of the Old Testament*, 1961, 187ff., and G. von Rad, 'βασιλεύς' B, *TD* 1, 568-570. See also W.H. Schmidt, *Königtum Gottes in Ugarit und Israel*, 2nd. ed. 1966.

[73] See the so-called enthronement psalms, 47; 93; (95); 96-99; see also Jer 10.7,10ff.; Mal 1.14; Ps 22,29. The idea of Yahweh's everlasting kingdom is also found in this context: Ex 15.18; Ps 145.1ff.; 146.10.

concentrated on Israel, where he is the king of his people.[74] This kingdom of Yahweh, his rule over Israel, is made particularly acute in the conflict with the earthly kingdom. The fact that Israel wishes to have a king like the nations surrounding it leads to a rejection of Yahweh, since 'Yahweh your God is your king'. The same idea can be found in Gideon's reply to the request that he should rule over Israel: 'Yahweh will rule over you'.[75]

3. Yahweh's kingdom is understood in the eschatological sense, in other words, that it will only be realized in the future.[76] This understanding means that the people can hope for the future kingdom of God both in the universal sense and in the sense that he will once again establish his rule over Israel. The Book of Daniel, for example, speaks on the one hand of the kingdom in its timeless form[77] and, on the other, in its eschatological form. The latter emerges very forcefully and, what is more, it is presented as God conferring his rule on his people.[78] This idea of the eschatological realization of the kingdom of God by the rule of his people or of his anointed in the world became extremely important in the apocalyptic literature of the ensuing period and remained so in the rabbinic tradition.[79] The establishment of the eschatological kingdom of God and his people in the world of necessity presupposed the elimination of all earthly or secular powers.[80] This immediate expectation of an imminent realization of the eschatological kingdom of God and his people in the world, which was widespread in pious circles in Palestinian Judaism is to some extent in opposition to the idea of a timeless and constantly present divine 'rule' that was proclaimed in the cult of Israel[81] and also obliged individual pious Jews to act in a certain way because of its concrete demands. According to Jub 12,19, for

---

[74] Num 23.21; Deut 33.5; Is 41.21; Jer 8.19 etc. A combination of points (1) and (2) can be found in Is 43.15 and 44.6.

[75] 1 Sam 12.12 and Judg 8.23; see also 1 Sam 8.19.

[76] Is 24.23; 33.22; Zech 14.9,16. These are all very late texts. The concept מְלוּכָה appears for the first time in the eschatological sense in Obad 21.

[77] See Dan 3.33; 4,31,34.

[78] There is no direct reference to this conferring of God's rule in Dan 2.44, but it appears all the more clearly in Dan 7.14,18,27.

[79] See EthEn 84,2; 90,30 etc.; PsSol 5,18f.; 17,3; AssMos 10,1ff. Further examples will be found in B.-Gr. Rel. 215ff.; Volz, Esch, 168f. For the eschatological hope of the kingdom of God in the rabbinate, see Bill. 1, 178ff. and the material assembled in that volume. See also S. Schechter, Some Aspects of Rabbinic Theology, 1908, 99ff.; G.F. Moore, Judaism, 2, 346f.,371-375.

[80] See Dan 2.44 and 7.11,26; see also Bill. 1, 175(g,h),179(b) and Volz, Esch, 310,369f. This was essential for the Zealots (see below, pp. 108f., 305ff.).

[81] See the prayer formula in Yom 4,1e.2f.; 6,2c; Tam 7,4 = Ps 93.

example, Abraham prays: 'I have chosen you and your kingdom' and this is at once followed by God's commandment to him to leave Haran. This idea also occurs above all later in the rabbinic tradition, in which it is expressed in the fixed formula: 'taking on oneself the yoke of the kingdom of God' (קיבל עול מלכות שמים) and applied in that formula to the obligation to say the *Shema* prayer and the confession of monotheism that is connected with it.[82]

It is possible to ask whether this opposition, which is expressed in the rabbinic usage by the מלכות שמים, was not resolved by Judas the Galilaean. In common with the other pious Jews of his own period, he certainly expected the kingdom of God and Israel to be realized as a miraculous eschatological act of God. At the same time, however, he also rejected a purely passive and quietistic kind of hope and believed that God would only bring about his kingdom and with it the kingdom of his people in the world if Israel acknowledged his absolute claim to rule here and now, with no reservations whatever.[83] The fact that the Jews were prepared to obey the godless secular ruler of the world, the Roman emperor, however, detracted from this claim to rule. 'Conversion' under the sign of the imminent kingdom of God and readiness to 'take on oneself the yoke of the kingdom of God' therefore logically consisted in ceasing — here and now — to obey the human and earthly ruler and in placing all one's trust in God, who would not under any circumstances forsake his people in the bloody conflict between the empire and the kingdom of God that would inevitably ensue. We have only to recall the extent to which Palestinian Judaism had been again and again aroused from the time of the Maccabees onwards by an expectation of the imminent end[84] and how bitterly the people had struggled on the one hand outwardly for religious and political independence and, on the other, internally for the right theocratic structure.[85] With this in mind, it is possible to understand that the thesis

---

[82] See Bill. 1, 172f.(i-n),176ff. See also K.G. Kuhn, 'βασιλεύς' C, *TD* 1, 572. For the *Shema* prayer, see especially Bill. 1, 177f.; see also I. Elbogen, *Der jüdische Gottesdienst*, 1924, 554f.; S. Schechter, *op. cit.*, 64ff.; G.F. Moore, *op. cit.*, 1, 465; Schlatter, *GI*, 437, n. 255.

[83] *Ant* 18,5; see also below, p. 122f.

[84] This imminent expectation is found both among the Essenes (1QpHab 2,5; 9,6 etc.; CD 4,4; 6,11) and the Pharisees (PsSol; *Ant* 17,43ff.) on the one hand and in John the Baptist and primitive Christianity on the other.

[85] Parallel with the Jewish people's external struggle for independence was their internal struggle for the right theocratic structure. It is very probable that the acceptance of the title of king (*Ant* 13,301) by Aristobulus or his brother Alexander Jannaeus (see A. Reifenberg, *Jewish Coins*, 41 No. 15ff.) played a part in making the pious Jews rise up

of Judas the Galilaean was eagerly accepted by many Jews as the best solution to the oppressive problem of how to realize the kingdom of God. Josephus himself had, after all, described the inner structure of Judaism as a θεοκρατία[86] and had explicitly stressed the fact that the Jews should regard their laws as their masters and not look for any others, 'for it is sufficient that God should be the leader (of the people)'.[87]

This radical solution of the problem of the kingdom of God was also encouraged by two further components, both of which form the main reason why the rule of the emperor and the kingdom of God came to be regarded by pious Jews as irreconcilably opposed to each other.

(bb) 'I am the Lord your God ...'

The description of God, אָדוֹן, which was originally used above all as an honorary title when addressing God in prayer, represented in the New Testament period, together with its later form אֲדֹנָי, the name of God, Yahweh,[88] which was accordingly translated as κύριος in the Septuagint.[89] The Old Testament words אָדוֹן and אֲדֹנָי were, on the other hand, frequently reproduced in the Septuagint by δεσπότης.[90] This development is the outward sign of a profound change in the use of the divine name, which distinguishes Judaism during the Hellenistic and Roman period from the Israel of the Old Testament. Whereas the early divine names receded more and more into the background and Israel's real name for God, Yahweh, was completely excluded from everyday usage, other names for God, which in fact belonged to the category of

---

against the latter. It is clear from the demands made by the Jews to Pompey (*Ant* 14,41; Diodorus 40,2, see Reinach, 76) that they rejected the — non-Davidic — kingship. The pious Jews similarly rose up in opposition to Herod, since the dignity of king could not be attributed to him as an Idumaean (see *Ant* 14,386.403f.; see also below, p. 316f.). After his death, the Jews approached Augustus with the demand that the monarchy should be abolished (*Bell* 2,53.90f.).

[86] *Ap* 2,164f. For this, see R. Eisler, 2, 81, n. 4, who believes that the Hellenistic scribe employed by Josephus may have derived this concept from the Jewish Malkuth hash-Shamaim.

[87] *Ant* 4,223: καὶ τοὺς νόμους ἔχοντες δεσπότας κατ' αὐτοὺς ἕκαστα πράττετε· ἀρκεῖ γὰρ ὁ θεὸς ἡγεμὼν εἶναι.

[88] See G. Quell, 'κύριος' C, *TD* 3, 1060ff., and W. Eichrodt, *op. cit.*, 1, 164.

[89] G. Quell, *op. cit.*, 1056f. A concise survey of the way in which the name of Yahweh receded into the background and was replaced by κύριος in the Septuagint will be found in *B.-Gr. Rel.* 307, n. 1.

[90] Gen 15.2,8; (Josh 5.14); Is 3.1; 10.33 etc. This use of such concepts as κύριος and δεσπότης as translations of of the Old Testament names for God penetrates to the deepest level of the meaning of the Israelites' understanding of God; see L. Köhler, *op. cit.*, 30: 'The fundamental principle of the theology of the Old Testament is that God is the commanding Lord'; a similar view is held by G. Quell, *op. cit.*, 1060, ln. 21.

secular names and titles for rulers or for indicating status, gradually came to be used. The term, 'king' (מֶלֶךְ — βασιλεύς), with its different variations is the first that has to be mentioned in this context.[91] Two of the most noteworthy of these variations are 'the King of kings',[92] which was taken from language of the oriental court, and the term 'Great King',[93] which is derived from the same sphere. In addition to אֲדֹנָי — אָדוֹן, which I have already mentioned and which are also used to address God in prayer,[94] the Aramaic words (מרא)[95] and רִבּוֹן,[96] also occur, the second especially in the rabbinic literature. In Greek, we find the title κύριος, which, as qere for the tetragrammaton, became the most widely used divine name in the Septuagint.[97] In addition, the word δεσπότης,[98] which was used above all by Philo and Josephus, also occurs as well as the special form δυνάστης,[99] which was originally a distinctively political

---

[91] See B.-Gr. Rel. 376, n. 1 for the Apocrypha and the Pseudepigrapha.

[92] See B.-Gr. Rel. 303, n. 2 and E. Lohmeyer, 'Die Offenbarung des Johannes', HNT, 2nd. ed. 1953, 144. Alongside this, there is also the triadic formula מלך מלכי המלכים, see A. Marmorstein, The Old Rabbinic Doctrine of God, 1: The Names and Attributes of God, 1927, 90f. Further examples will be found in 'Das Alenugebet', Bill. 1, 175; Ab 3,1; 4,22 (29); the words of Johanan b. Zakkai on his death-bed, Ber 28b bar; Sir 51.12 (XIV) = 51.34 Segal; SlavEn 39,8. For the origin of these formulae in the Ancient Near East, see Liddell-Scott, 309.

[93] EthEn 9,4; 84,2.5; 91,13; PsSol 2,32; Tob 13,5; Sib 3,499.560; 2 Macc 13.4; 3 Macc 5.35; for the origin of the concept, see E. Peterson, Der Monotheismus als politisches Problem, 1935, 107, n. 20.

[94] See Schürer. 2, 453; B.-Gr. Rel. 309. The beginnings of the Qumran psalms are typical of this way of addressing God in prayer: 1QH 1,20; 3,19.37 etc.; the concept is not, however, used in everyday speech, see G. Dalman, Words of Jesus, 1902, 179ff. For the rabbinic usage, see A. Marmorstein, op. cit., 62f. and W. Foerster, 'κύριος' D, TD 3, 1084.

[95] For this, see G. Dalman, op. cit., 180ff.; W. Foerster, op. cit., and A. Marmorstein, op. cit., 93f.

[96] See G. Dalman, op. cit., 324f.; Bill. 2, 176 on Lk 10.21 and 3, 671f. on Heb 1.2; A. Marmorstein, op. cit., 98f. and W. Foerster, Op. cit., 1085. The earliest evidence is the prayer of Honi the rain-maker (ca. 100 B.C.), Taan 3,8: רִבּוֹן שֶׁל עוֹלָם; in Ant 14,24, his prayer begins: ὦ θεέ, βασιλεῦ τῶν ὅλων.

[97] See W. Foerster, Herr ist Jesus, 1954, 57-120; see also TD 3, 1081-88. The name even entered the Targum as a name for God, see Jastrow, Dictionary, 2, 1369, a sign that the concept had become widespread even in Palestine.

[98] See K.H. Rengstorf, 'δεσπότης', TD 2, 44f.; W. Foerster, Herr ist Jesus, op. cit., 65; W.W. Graf Baudissin, Kyrios als Gottesname im Judentum und seine Stelle in der Religionsgeschichte, ed. O. Eissfeldt, 1929, 2, 162, sees δεσπότης as the concept of God that bore the strongest impression of Hellenism. For Philo's use of language, see the unfortunately incomplete index in J. Leisegang, Philonis Opera, ed. L. Cohn and P. Wendland, 7, 1928 and W. Foerster, op. cit., 119, n. 3. For Josephus, see H. St. J. Thackeray, A Lexicon to Josephus, 1930ff., 130 and A. Schlatter, 'Wie sprach Josephus von Gott?', BFChTh 14 (1910), 8ff.

[99] See Liddell-Scott, 453. Josephus uses this term for the petty and semi-autonomous

name and referred in Judaism almost exclusively to God. Finally, the name ἡγεμών[100] is also occasionally encountered especially in the works of Josephus.

All these concepts were used for preference in prayer formulae and combinations such as 'Lord of the world'[101] or 'Lord of the universe'[102] were particularly frequent. They were intended to express the unlimited fullness of God's power. The importance of God's power as ruler is shown by the fact that later rabbinic authors insisted that calling God king, especially in the popular formula 'King of the world', ought to become part of every prayer.[103]

This practice of proclaiming God as ruler when addressing him in prayer can best be illustrated by a few examples:

> 'Ruler of heaven and earth, Creator of the water, King of the whole of your creation'.[104]
> 'Blessed are you, Lord, King great and powerful in your greatness, Lord of the whole creation of heaven, King of kings and God of the whole world! Your power, your kingdom and your greatness remain in all eternity . . . For you have created everything and you govern it . . . And now, God, Lord and great King, I implore and ask you . . .'[105]

Here God's lordship and kingship refer especially to creation, but they can also be extended to the political sphere:

---

princes of the East; see Thackeray, *op. cit.*, 195. As a divine name, it appears almost exclusively in Judaism; see W. Grundmann, 'δύναμις', TD 2, 286. A remarkable case is found in 2 Macc 15.3-5, where the earthly Nicanor is contrasted with the heavenly δυνάστης. For other texts, see *B.-Gr. Rel.* 376, n. 3; see also below, p. 97, n. 111.

[100] See *Ap* 2,185: θεὸν ... ἡγεμόνα τῶν ὅλων; *Ant* 4,185: ὁ θεός τε ... ὁ μέχρι νῦν ἡγεμονεύσας ἡμῖν; 4,223; see also above, p. 94, n. 87 and the demand made by Judas the Galilaean in *Ant* 18,23. See also A. Schlatter, *op. cit.*, 11f., and Philo, *SpecLeg* 1,32 (M 2, 216); *VitMos* 1,318 (M 2, 131); 2,168 (160): ἕνα ... ἡγεμόνα τῶν ὅλων.

[101] See EthEn 58,4; 81,10; Jub 25,23; AssMos 1,11; 1Q 20 fr. 2,5, *Qumran Cave* I, ed. Barthélemy and Milik, 87: מרה עלמא. Formulae of this kind occur very frequently in the rabbinate; see A. Marmorstein, *op. cit.*, 62f.,93,98f.

[102] Wis 6.7; 8.3; TestJos 1,5. The formula 'Lord of the universe' can be found in Philo; see *LegGai* 3 (M 2, 546) etc. It also occurs frequently in Josephus (*Ap* 2,185; *Ant* 1,72; 4,46; 14,24 etc.). In *Bell* 4,366, for example, Vespasian can be called κύριος τῶν ὅλων. See also ep. Arist 195.

[103] Ber 12a: 'R. Johanan (+ 279) said: "A prayer of praise in which the name of king (מַלְכוּת) is not found is not a prayer of praise" '. See Bill. 1, 184. See also I. Elbogen, *Der jüdische Gottesdienst*, 2nd. ed. 1924, 5, and G.F. Moore, *Judaism*, 2, 373. V. Aptowitzer, *MGWJ* 73 (1929), 93-118, and C. Roth, 'Melekh ha-'olam: Zealot Influence in the Liturgy', *JJS* 11 (1960), 173-175, suspected that there was a Zealot influence in these 'king' formulae. J. Heinemann, *JJS* 11 (1960), 177, believed that they were a protest against the cult of the emperor.

[104] Jdt 9.12.

[105] EthEn 84,2.3.5; see also 9,4f. and 81,3.

'Blessed are you, highest God, Lord of all worlds. You are the Lord and ruler over everything and over all the kings of the earth you are ruler, in order to pronounce judgement on them'.[106]

Although it is at first hardly audible, a new emphasis is heard when God is addressed in prayer not simply as Lord and ruler, but as the 'sole ruler' or the 'only Lord':

'Lord, Lord, King of heaven and ruler of the whole of creation, ... sole ruler, almighty ...'[107]

Μόναρχος, which was originally a political name for a ruler,[108] can be found in specifically Jewish literature and especially in Philo, who particularly valued the concept as an analogy between the oriental monarchy and God's sovereign power as ruler.[109] It is also found in the Sibylline Oracles: 'A God, who rules alone ...'.[110] It appears, however, again and again in late Jewish literature, whether this is of Hellenistic or of Palestinian origin. In the same description of the Third Sybilline Oracle, in which God is called μόναρχος in connection with the joys of the time of salvation, the demand is made: 'Let us send to the sanctuary, for he is the only God (μόνος ἐστὶ δυνάστης).'[111] In Josephus, King Izates prays for victory over his opponents:

'Ruler, Lord, if I do not share in your goodness in vain, but ... you rightly as the only and first Lord of all things ...'[112]

---

[106] *A Genesis Apocryphon*, ed. N. Avigad and Y. Yadin, 1956, col. 20,12f., from a prayer of Abraham for help against Pharaoh: בריך אנתה אל עליון מרי לכול (see above, pp. 90 and 94, and below, p. 139) עלמים די אנתה מרה ושליט על כולא ובכול רין בכולהון למעבד שליט אנתה ארעא מלכי. In l. 15, God is called 'Lord of all kings of the earth' (מרה לכול מלכי ארעה).

[107] From the prayer of the Simeon the high-priest in 3 Macc 2.2: κύριε κύριε, βασιλεῦ τῶν οὐρανῶν καὶ δέσποτα πάσης κτίσεως ... μόναρχε, παντοκράτωρ ...

[108] Liddell-Scott, 1143.

[109] See, for example, Philo, *SpecLeg* 1,13–65 (M 2, 213ff.): οἱ περὶ μοναρχίας νόμοι; and for the first commandment of the Decalogue, see *Decal* 155 (M 2, 205): ἓν αἴτιον τοῦ κόσμου καὶ ἡγεμὼν καὶ βασιλεὺς εἷς. According to E. Peterson, *Der Monotheismus als politisches Problem*, 1935, 21ff., the concept of μοναρχία was, for Philo, an expression of God's rule over Israel: 'Israel was a theocracy and the one nation was ruled by a divine monarch' (22–23). The monarchy of God also applied to the cosmos (23) and was comparable to that of the Great King (24ff.).

[110] Fragm 1,7 (in Theophilus, *Auto* 2,36): εἷς θεὸς ὃς μόνος ἄρχει ... See also 3,704: At the time of salvation, pious Jews will rejoice in the blessings of peace οἷς δώσει κτίστης ὁ δικαιοκρίτης τε μόναρχος. *Monarchia* formulae also appear with relative frequency in the prayers of the Apostolic Constitutions (tr. J. Donaldson, ANCL, vol. xvii, part 2, 1870) that go back, at least partly, to Jewish origins: 5,15.3; 5,20.11; 6,9.1; 7,35.9; 8,11.2. For this, see W. Bousset, '*Eine jüdische Gebetssammlung im 7. Buch der apostolischen Konstitutionen*' (*NGWG.PH*), 1915, 435ff.

[111] 3,718: πέμπωμεν πρὸς ναόν, ἐπεὶ μόνος ἐστὶ δυνάστης. See also 760 and 1 Tim 6.15.

[112] *Ant* 20,90: ... τῶν πάντων δὲ δικαίως μόνον καὶ πρῶτον ἥγημαι κύριον.

In Azaria's prayer, which presumably goes back to a Hebrew original, the pious implore God to save them from their oppressors:

'Let them know that you alone are Lord, God and famous throughout the whole of the earth'.[113]

A possible objection to the *monos* formula is that too much importance should not be attributed to it in prayer addressed to God, since its use here was relatively widespread.[114] One is, however, bound to ask whether this formula was not inevitably given a deeper meaning within the sphere of Jewish faith, in view of the fact that the relationship between the people of Israel and their God was quite unique among the religions of the ancient world. In the Book of Jubilees this fact is expressed in the following way:

'He has given no angel or spirit power over Israel; he alone is her Lord and he alone protects her'.

The statement of faith which Josephus ascribes to Judas the Galilaean and his followers: μόνον ἡγεμόνα καὶ δεσπότην τὸν θεὸν ὑπειληφόσιν,[116] is no more than an ultimate conclusion drawn from the view which was universally held by Jews and which I have outlined above, namely that God was the sovereign ruler of the world in general and the Lord of Israel in particular. Believing that the earthly ruler of this world was being increasingly deified, Judas and his successors proclaimed the unrestricted rule of God even within the political sphere.

All that Judas did was basically to narrow down and intensify the first commandment. If the name of 'God' is replaced here by the term 'Lord', which had almost exactly the same meaning in late Judaism, we arrive at the Zealots' confession of faith: 'I am Yahweh, your Lord . . . You shall have no other lords except me!' It is perhaps not purely by chance that the Decalogue was still prayed in the first century A.D. every day by pious Jews together with the *Shema*,[117] which also contained a confession of the one Lord[118] and was at the same time also understood as a

---

[113] Dan 3.45 (LXX) γνώτωσαν ὅτι σὺ εἶ μόνος κύριος ὁ θεὸς . . . For the original Semitic form, see O. Eissfeldt, *Old Testament: an Introduction*, 1965, 590. See also 3 (1) Ezra 8,25: εὐλογητὸς μόνος ὁ κύριος; EsthRab 14; 2 Macc 1.24: ὁ μόνος βασιλεύς.

[114] For this, see G. Delling, 'ΜΟΝΟΣ ΘΕΟΣ', *ThLZ* 77 (1952), 468–476.

[115] Jub 15,32; this relationship between God and Israel is also expressed by Josephus: according to *Ant 5,93*, God is the πατὴρ καὶ δεσπότης τοῦ Ἑβραίων γένους; 4,201 is similar: θεὸς γὰρ εἷς καὶ τὸ Ἑβραίων γένος ἕν.

[116] *Ant* 18,23; for this, see G. Delling, *op. cit.*, 476.

[117] Tam 5,1; see I. Elbogen, *op. cit.*, 242. For Philo, *Decal* 155 (M 2, 205), the first commandment is ὁ . . . πρῶτος τῶν περὶ μοναρχίας.

[118] Deut. 6.4: יהוה אֱלֹהֵינוּ יהוה אֶחָד.

proclamation of the 'kingdom' of God.[119] Seen in this perspective, the obvious conclusion to be drawn is that Judas' revolutionary demand that only God should be recognized as Lord had grown out of the heart of Jewish faith itself. An acknowledgement of God as the 'sole ruler' even in the political sphere was for Judas the unconditional presupposition for the fulfilment of Deuterozechariah's promise (Zech 14.9):

> 'And the Lord will become king over all the earth; on that day the Lord will be one and his name one'.

The underlying motive for this would seem to have been the increasing prominence of the worship of the emperor in the East.

(cc) Palestinian Judaism's Encounter with the Cult of the Emperor

The cult of the ruler in Hellenism was a typical product of religious enlightenment and the collapse of traditional religion. After faith in the reality of the old gods and their power had disappeared, it was replaced by veneration of the visible political powers.[120] The conception of the divinity of the ruler, the way towards which had already been prepared by the hero-worship of the classical period, became, under the impression of the outstanding figure of Alexander the Great, common knowledge in the Hellenistic East. This development was encouraged above all in Ptolemaic Egypt by the long established God-king tradition of the Pharaohs. The fact that the Jews — if the legendary Third Book of the Maccabees, which in any case points more to the Roman period, is disregarded — never came seriously into conflict with the cult of the ruler of the Ptolemies[121] can be explained on the basis of the greater

---

[119] See above, p. 92, n. 81. K. Köhler, *Harkavyfestschrift*, 9, has already pointed to the close relationship between Judas' principal demand and the Jewish confession of faith, the *Shema*. See also the martyrdom of Akiba, Ber 61b.

[120] For books and articles on this subject, see especially M.P. Nilsson, *Geschichte der griechischen Religion* 2: *Die hellenistische und römische Zeit* (*HAW*), 2nd. ed. 1961, 132-185: Die Religion im Dienst der Könige; 384-395: Der Kaiserkult. In our context, the essential books and articles are: E. Kornemann, 'Zur Geschichte des antiken Herrscherkultus', *Klio* 1 (1901), 51-146; H. Heinen, 'Zur Begründung des römischen Kaiserkults v. 48 v.-14 n. Chr.', *Klio* 11 (1911), 129-177; G. Herzog-Hauser, 'Kaiserkult', *PW Suppl.* 4, 806-852; H. Dessau, *Geschichte der römischen Kaiserzeit*, 1924ff., I, 353-360; II,1, 121-131; A.D. Nock, *CAH* 10, 481-502; E. Stauffer, *Jerusalem und Rom*, 1957, 20-39; F. Taeger, *Charisma* 2, 1960. For the honorary titles of God, see D. Magie, *De Romanorum iuris publici sacrique vocabulis*, 1905, 62-69. Of fundamental importance for Egypt is P. Bureth, *Les titulatures impériales*, Brussels 1964. For the title of Kyrios, see W. Foerster, *Herr ist Jesus*, 1924, 99-118; see also *TD* 3, 1049 and 1054-58. For the relationship between Judaism and emperor-worship, see J. Juster, 1, 339-354.

[121] Here too the cult of the ruler is only dealt with allusively (2.29,31 and 3.21). This

tolerance shown by pre-Maccabaean Judaism towards Hellenism. On the other hand, the revolt of the Maccabees was at least partly caused by the worship of the ruler required by Antiochus Epiphanes.[122] The Jews living in Palestine were at first spared further encounters because of the independence that they had fought so hard to achieve, but they had become very sensitive and felt that they had to oppose any attempt on the part of a man to appropriate divine dignity.

This did not become a really burning question again until Judaea once more came under the yoke of foreign rule a hundred years later. Pious Jews then directed their hatred against the victorious Pompey, who had accepted divine honours of various kinds in the East. The Psalms of Solomon speak of the 'haughtiness of the dragon' (ὑπερηφανία τοῦ δράκοντος), thus anticipating later descriptions of the Antichrist:

> 'He had not considered that he was a man and had not considered the end,/ had thought: I am the Lord of land and sea,/ not known that God is great,/ strong in his enormous power./ He is King above in heaven/ and judges kings and kingdoms'.[123]

The cult of the ruler that appeared in Rome in the ensuing period had one new aspect distinguishing it from the Hellenistic veneration of the ruler. In the East, it was based on the complete identification of the king with the state. The state did not exist as an independent reality. Everything was dependent on the king and his means of power. The gradual decline of the king's power in the empires of the Diadochi had removed the props supporting the cult of the 'God-king' in each case. The Roman state, on the other hand, was an independent power before, and was independent of, its emperors. This was in accordance with the fact that, under Augustus, the earlier cult of Dea Roma was generally

---

work, which can be dated between the end of the first century B.C. and the destruction of the Temple in 70 A.D. (see O. Eissfeldt, *Old Testament: an Introduction*, 1965, 582), contains some material that is of historical value from the period of the Ptolemies. See V. Tcherikover, *ScrHie* 7 (1961), 1-26.

[122] See E. Kornemann, *op. cit.*, 81, n. 7. 2 Macc 6.7 speaks of the Jews' forced participation in the monthly sacrifice at the celebration of the king's birthday. For this, see F.M. Abel, *Les livres des Maccabées*, 1949, 262f. 2 Macc 11.23 mentions the Seleucid custom of the apotheosis of dead kings; see Abel, *op. cit.*, 428. in Dan 6.8, the cult of the ruler is presupposed; see A. Bentzen, *Daniel* (*HAT*), 1952, 52. In Jdt 3.8, the worship of Nebuchadnezzar is required; see also 2.5; 6.2; M. Hengel, *Judaism and Hellenism*, 1964, 285ff. For the divine name of the ruler in the case of Antiochus IV, see Abel, *op. cit.*, 20. Antiochus III the Great and later his son, Epiphanes, consistently promoted the cult of the ruler; see Nilsson, *op. cit.*, 168 (*OGIS* 224) and Schürer, 1, 147, n. 23.

[123] PsSol 2,25.28f. For the divine veneration of Pompey in the Hellenistic east, see Nilsson, *op. cit.*, 179.

connected with that of his person.[124] He gave emperor-worship such stability and order that it became independent of the personal animus of the individual ruler — especially in the East — and proceeded along certain clearly prescribed paths. The really decisive step in this direction was taken when the dead Caesar was raised to the level of *Divus Iulius*.[125] A little later, Octavian quite consistently called himself *Divi filius*.[126] This was rendered in the East by the term υἱὸς θεοῦ,[127] the simple word θεός appearing alongside it.[128]

These honorary titles must have seemed blasphemous to the Jews and the fact that they were the only subjects who were exempted from using these offensive names did not change the situation for them in any way.[129] They were equally unable to appreciate the personal moderation of the emperor, since this basically only concerned Roman citizens and had hardly any effect in the provinces.[130] On the contrary: though the cult of a given ruler in the hellenistic monarchies was always restricted by time and geographical limits, veneration of the God-emperor spread over the whole of the world insofar as it was ruled by Rome. It did not even stop at the frontiers of the Holy Land. Herod I, who was entirely dependent on the emperor's grace, hastened to introduce the cult of the emperor into the predominantly Hellenistic parts of his country, even though he was — externally at least — a Jew. In 27 B.C., Octavian had assumed the title of 'Augustus' (Σεβαστός)[131] and in the same year Herod

[124] Nilsson, *op. cit.*, 177, E. Kornemann, *op. cit.*, 94.

[125] The decision was made in 1 Jan. 42 B.C. by the people and the Senate; see Kornemann, *op. cit.*, 96; H. Heinen, *op. cit.*, 135f.; H. Bengtson, *Grundriss der römischen Geschichte*, 1967, 239.

[126] 40 B.C; A.D. Nock, *CAH* 10,482: 'A title in itself unique for a Roman and liable to lead to more'. See also H. Heinen, *op. cit.*, 140, nn. 2 and 3.

[127] Evidence of this will be found in A. Deissmann, *Licht vom Osten*, 4th ed. 1923, 294f.

[128] See D. Magie, *op. cit.*, 66; A. Deissmann, *op. cit.*, 292ff.

[129] See Juster, 1, 342, n. 3; in the official documents, which Josephus reproduces, the appellation θεός does not appear anywhere. In *Ant* 19,284, Claudius is critical of Caligula's demand that the Jews should call him 'Theos'. In 19,345 (= Acts 13.22), Agrippa I is called 'Theos' by his flatterers, but punishment follows immediately and the king is himself shaken by his offence (347). On the other hand, Josephus knows about the apotheosis of the emperor. In 19,289, for example, he (or his source) makes Claudius call his grandfather Augustus 'divine' (τοῦ θείου Σεβαστοῦ). See also Josephus' apology directed against Apion, *Ap* 2,73ff. The hymn that Philo reproduces in his *LegGai* 143ff. (M 2, 566f.) shows just how far Judaism of the Diaspora went to meet the claims made by the cult of the emperor. For this, see E. Stauffer, *op. cit.*, 33f.

[130] See H. Dessau, *op. cit.*, 1, 335ff.

[131] See H. Heinen, *op. cit.*, 151. For the title itself, see E. Kornemann, *op. cit.*; 98. H. Dessau, *op. cit.*, 1, 35f.; A.D. Nock, *op. cit.*, 483: 'Between man and god it represents just such a compromise as does princeps between citizen and king'.

changed the name of the city of Samaria, which he had rebuilt, to Sebaste and erected a temple there to the emperor.[132] In 22 B.C., he began to construct the port of Caesarea on the site of the earlier Strato's Tower. Here too he built a temple, containing statues that were larger than life, to Augustus and Rome.[133] When it was dedicated in 9 B.C., games to be played every four years were instituted in honour of the God-emperor.[134] Herod had also already established similar games (in 25 B.C.?) in Jerusalem for the glorification of Augustus. The theatre that had recently been built there was also decorated with inscriptions in honour of the emperor.[135] In 20/19 B.C., Paneas (later known as Caesarea Philippi) also contained a temple dedicated to Augustus.[136] As all these temple buildings were erected on the holy ground of the land that had once been promised by God to Israel, it is not difficult to understand that this active zeal on the part of Herod for the greater honour of his divine sovereign inevitably incurred the displeasure of his Jewish subjects.[137]. He argued in his own defence that he had not done this of his own free will, but had acted in obedience to a higher command. Even Josephus, however, could not believe this assertion[138] and either he or his source, Nicolaus of Damascus, stresses explicitly that there was no place in the entire kingdom in which the king had not erected something in honour of the emperor.[139]

It is possible that Herod even tolerated divine veneration of his own person. This would seem to be a reasonable assumption on the basis of the statue of Herod erected by an Idumaean mercenary that was found in the temple of Canatha in Batanaea.[140] W. Otto even thought that the

---

[132] *Ant* 15,292f.296ff. = *Bell* 1,403. See also Schürer, 1, 290, n. 8,306; 2, 160ff. and especially 162; H. Heinen, *op. cit.*, 152, n. 3 and E. Stauffer, *op. cit.*, 27f.

[133] *Ant* 15,293.331-341 = *Bell* 1,408-414. For the Temple and the colossal statues, see especially *Ant* 15,339 and *Bell* 1,414, where the author says that the statue of the emperor was modelled on that of the Zeus of Olympia. According to *Ant* 17,87 = *Bell* 1,613, the port itself was named 'Sebastos' after Augustus.

[134] *Ant* 15,341; 16,136-141; *Bell* 1,415f. See Suetonius, *Aug* 59; Schürer, 1, 306; 2, 115ff., and for the games, 2, 46f.

[135] *Ant* 15,267-275; *Bell* 1,415. See also Schürer, 1,304, n. 56; E. Stauffer, *op. cit.*, 28.

[136] *Ant* 15,363f. = *Bell* 1,404. See also Schürer 2, 169; E. Heinen, *op. cit.*, 156, n. 4.

[137] For the various attacks against Herod, see below, pp. 258ff. and 320ff.

[138] *Ant* 15,327-330. For this, see Juster, 1, 341, n. 1 and W. Otto, *Herodes*, 1913, 67-69; A. Schalit, *König Herodes*, 1969, 421ff.

[139] *Bell* 1,407.

[140] Dittenberger, *OGIS* 1, 628, No. 415. See also *Ant* 16,158: The Jews did not find favour with him, 'since they were not able to flatter the king or further his ambition by means of columns, temples or similar structures'. W. Otto, *op. cit.*, 106,112; A. Momigliano, *CAH* 10, 332, n. 4; A. Schalit, *König Herodes*, 1969, 457f.

eagle above the entrance to this temple should be understood in this sense.[141] It is hardly likely that Herod would have had this eagle with its very significant content — an image which also appears on his coins[142] — set up on such an exposed site simply in response to a playful whim. It was, after all, both a divine symbol[143] and the sign of the power of the king and the arms of the emperor.[144] The eagle also appears in the Jewish apocalyptic literature of the period as the sign of the imperial rule of Rome[145] and it is therefore quite possible that the zealous pious Jews who destroyed this offensive figure and paid for this act with their lives saw in it the symbol of a hated rule and at the very least the intrusion of Hellenistic symbols and conceptions into the sanctuary.[146]

The revolt which broke out with elemental violence after Herod's death assumed such dimensions because many Jews saw in the claim of

---

[141] *Ant* 17,149-167 = *Bell* 1,648-654. W. Otto, *op. cit.*,112f., says: 'It is perhaps justifiable to connect the placing of the eagle on the Temple and on coins during the king's last years with these longings for deification.' A. Momigliano, *op. cit.*, 335, n. 2, is more cautious.

[142] See A. Reifenberg, *Jewish Coins*, 43 No. 34, and G.F. Hill, *Catalogue of the Greek Coins of Palestine*, 1914, 227 = XXIV, 15. The eagle was used again by Herod Agrippa I, *op. cit.*, 238 = XXVI, 4.

[143] For the symbol of the eagle, see Oder, 'Adler', *PW* 1, 373f.; T. Schneider, 'Adler', *RAC* 1,87ff. and E. Goodenough, *Jewish Symbols in the Greco-Roman Period*, 1958, 8, 121-142. The eagle was the symbol of Jupiter. As such it appeared on the front and the back of the Capitoline temple (see Tacitus, *Hist* 3,71) and on the Roman standards, which were accorded divine worship (*Bell* 6,316). The eagle was also found, as the bird of the Baal Shamin or the sun-god, on Syrian temples; see R. Eisler, 2,169f., and E. Goodenough, *op. cit.*, 125f. It is possible that it is mentioned in this capacity in Dan 9.27; see A. Bentzen, *Daniel (HAT)*, 1952, 68.

[144] See T. Schneider, *op. cit.*, 89: 'A sign of the rulers who belonged, like the eagle, to the generation of the gods and in whose rule the reign of the deity and especially that of Zeus or Jupiter was manifested'. A special part was played by the eagle in the Roman apotheosis of the emperor; see F. Cumont, *Etudes syriennes* 2 (1917), 35ff.; see also E. Bickermann, *ARW* 27 (1929), 1-34; and E. Goodenough, *op. cit.*, 129f.

[145] It was a political metaphor even in the Old Testament; see Deut 28.49; Is 46.11; Jer 48.40;45.21; Hab 1.8. The text in Habakkuk is interpreted in 1QpHab 3,8 as applying to the Kittim (that is, to the Romans). In AssMos 10,8, it is perhaps Israel's victory over the eagle (that is, Rome) that is described. The vision of the eagle in 4 Ezra 11 is more clearly a reference to Rome; see also Sib 3,611; EthEn 90,1ff.

[146] See, for example, H. Graetz, 3,226; also A.H.M. Jones, *The Herods of Judaea*, 1938, 148. E. Goodenough, *op. cit.*, 123ff., believed that the eagle was at that time a symbol that was also widespread in Israel. However, there was in Judaism of that period a marked intensification in the attitude towards the prohibition of images (see below, p. 190ff.); Goodenough has taken his examples from a much later period. Even if the symbol of the eagle did not in any way refer to the Roman or the Herodian rule, it was certainly a pagan symbol of the gods and was therefore firmly rejected by believing Jews. A. Schalit, *op. cit.*, 734, has suggested biblical allusions in this case, connected with the political theology of the king.

the Roman emperor to rule a threat to the purity of Jewish faith. It was feared that the bad times of Antiochus Epiphanes might return.[147] A little later this rejection of imperial rule was given a clear 'theological' foundation by Judas the Galilaean. On the basis of the immediate imminence of the kingdom of God and presumably also in accordance with the confession of faith in the one Lord of Israel, Judas demanded that Israel should recognize only God as Lord and ruler and should no longer obey the emperor. Although Josephus dressed this demand in a philosophical and universally valid garment, Judas' call really had certain charismatic aspects. In stressing the proximity of the kingdom of God, he was in fact calling on Israel to be converted.[148] Just as Elijah had once demanded that Israel should choose between Yahweh and Baal, so too was Judas insisting on a decision between God the Father and the Roman God-emperor. He did not in any sense aim to found an 'anarchistic' movement.[149] On the contrary, he himself became the ἡγεμών of this sect which, according to Josephus, recognized God alone as ἡγεμών, and other clearly messianic leaders also arose in the further course of the movement's history.[150] It is therefore probable that the real emphasis in Judas' message was placed not so much on the prohibition against recognizing 'mortal men as rulers rather than God'[151] as on the prohibition against obeying men who claimed divine dignity for themselves. Recognition of the Roman emperor was for him the same as serving an idol. Josephus could not include this aspect in his presentation of the situation, since, as a believing Jew, he had himself to reject the cult of the ruler. Indirectly, then, he admitted in his outline of this point that Judas was right.

The further development of the movement appeared to confirm the demand made by Judas that a clear choice had to be made between the rule of the emperor and that of God. The handful of anecdotes reported by Josephus in his account of the period of the procurators refer again and again to the Jewish people's clashes with the emperor-cult. At the beginning of his period of office, for example, Pilate had a unit of Roman troops bring the effigies of the emperor on the standards into

---

[147] It is possible that is the explanation of the future image of the eschatological tyrant in AssMos 8,1ff., in which — shortly after the death of Herod (see 6,2-7) — certain aspects of the persecution under Antiochus Epiphanes are applied to a world ruler who was imminently expected.

[148] See above, p. 91, n. 71: the reference to the 'prophetic denouncement speech'.

[149] I do not agree here with M.J. Lagrange, Le Judaïsme avant Jésus Christ, 3rd. ed. 1931, 214.

[150] See above, p. 77, n. 9; see also below, p. 290.

[151] Bell 2,118; see also above, p. 76, n. 1.

Jerusalem, but went against previous practice in having this done by night. Since the soldiers were presumably accommodated in the Antonia quarter, the Sanctuary of the Temple was also violated at the same time.[152] Later, the procurator seems to have set up in front of his official residence, the royal palace, consecrated shields on which only the name of the emperor appeared. It is possible that offence was caused by this inscription, the precise content of which has not been handed down to us.[153] In both cases, Pilate had to give way to pressure on the part of the outraged people. A few years later, Vitellius, the governor of Syria, avoided renewed disturbances only by agreeing to the earnest entreaties of the Jews and having his troops with their standards go around Jewish territory.[154]

The worst fears of the Jews were, however, exceeded by Caligula's illusions of grandeur. The cult of the emperor and consequently conflict with the Jewish population reached an initial climax under him. In Alexandria, for example, their refusal to worship the emperor led to wild riots against the Jews on the part of the mob. After Caligula's death, they took their revenge for this by rising in armed revolt with the help of their Palestinian and Egyptian tribesmen.[155] The pagan minority also provoked the Jewish population in Palestinian Jamnia by building an altar to the emperor there. This altar was regarded by the Jews as so offensive that they destroyed it. Acting on the report made by the imperial official in Jerusalem, Caligula gave the ominous command to have a statue of himself set up in the Temple. The entire Jewish population was aroused to action by this and only the murder of the emperor himself prevented a general revolt.[156]

---

[152] Bell 2,169-174 = Ant 18,55-59. For this, see also C.H. Kraeling, 'The Episode of the Roman Standards at Jerusalem', HTR 35 (1942), 263-289. According to Eusebius, DemEvang, GCS, ed. I. Heikel, 1913, 6, 390, Philo also reported this episode; Pilate is in fact reputed to have set up the standards by night in the Temple, that is, in the Antonia. See also Schürer, 1, 384, n. 135, and R. Eisler, 2,166f.

[153] Philo, LegGai 299-302 (M 2, 589f.). It is doubtful whether the copper coins with the lituus and the simpulum minted by Pilate gave offence in the way assumed by E. Stauffer, op. cit., 17,35. In addition to these coins, there were also the even more offensive silver denarii. See below, p. 193f. According to A. Kindler, IEJ 6 (1956), 55, these lituus coins had already been struck by Valerius Gratus.

[154] Ant 18,120-122. See P.L.Maier, HThR 62 (1962), 109-121.

[155] For the events in Alexandria, see Philo, Flacc 41ff. (M 2, 523f.) and LegGai 132ff. (M 2, 564f.). For this, see also Schürer, 1, 389ff. and V.A. Tcherikover and A. Fuks, CPJ, 1957, 1, 68, n. 2, and 69. For the Jews' revolt, see Ant 19,278f. The Jews received support from Palestine and the Egyptian hinterland; see Claudius' letter, CPJ 2, 36ff., col. V, 96ff.

[156] For the events in Jamnia, see Philo, LegGai 199ff. (M 2, 575); for the further events

This event must have had a shattering effect on the Jews of Palestine. For the first time since the reign of Antiochus Epiphanes, the hand of a pagan tyrant had grasped the vital nerve of the Jewish people — their faith in the one true God.[157] The memory of this was preserved in the rabbinic tradition[158] and probably even went beyond it and entered the New Testament.[159] There could have been no better confirmation of Judas the Galilaean's thesis than Caligula's crazy demand and it is probable that the Zealot movement, which resolutely rejected compromise of any kind with Rome, was essentially reinforced by it. Even the Jew who was loyal in his attitude towards the Romans was after this event bound to recognize that the cult of the emperor contained a latent threat to the Jewish faith in God.[160] It is possible that the government of Herod Agrippa I, which followed immediately, prevented the people from finally and completely breaking with Rome. Even the strict protection of Jewish religious interests — as, for example, in the case of the incident in Dora[161] — could not, however, in the long run check the growth of groups of this kind which regarded obedience to the Roman God-emperor as irreconcilable with obedience to God's commandment.

The sign of the final break with Rome was given by an event that directly concerned the emperor: a refusal to offer sacrifice for him twice

---

in Palestina, see *Bell* 2,184-203 = *Ant* 18,261-309 and Tacitus, *Hist* 5,9; see also Schürer, 1, 141-158; H. Graetz, 3, 332-343; H. Dessau, II,2, 788ff.; M. Charlesworth, *CAH* 10, 662f.

[157] J.W. Lightley, *Jewish Sects and Parties in the Time of Jesus*, 1925, 368: 'Though the danger was over, the episode left an indelible impression on the mind of the people'.

[158] S. Derenbourg, 207ff.; H. Graetz, 5th ed., 3,573,742f.,770. In the Scroll of Fasting 11 (26), the day on which the news of Caligula's death was reported was regarded as a day of rejoicing; according to TSot 13,6 (Z. 319), the high-priest 'Simon the Righteous' heard in the Holy of Holies a resounding voice proclaiming the death of Caligula and the revocation of all orders enforcing the service of idols. For this, see P. Winter, 'Simeon der Gerechte und Caius Caligula', *ZRGG* 6 (1954), 72ff.

[159] Mk 13.14 parr.; for this, see E. Klostermann, 'Das Markusevangelium', *HNT*, 4th. ed. 1950, 135. See also 2 Thess 2.4-12; for this, see M. Dibelius, 'An die Thessalonicher I und II', *HNT*, 3rd. ed. 1937, 45f.

[160] This was the opinion of N. Bentwich, *Josephus*, 1926, 27 and J.W. Lightley, *op. cit.*: 'The wantonness of the affront to the religion must have gone far to convince even the more pacific that there was but one way out of the existing impasse, and that was a way of violence'.

[161] *Ant* 19,300ff.: Hellenistic disturbers of the peace had tried, by setting up a bust of the emperor, to desecrate the synagogue there. That attempt was very sharply criticized in an edict issued by the governor of Syria, who stressed explicitly that he was, 'like his royal friend Agrippa, most anxious that the Jews should not mob together for revolt under the pretext of defence'. See *Ap* 2,73ff.

daily.[162] This has been described as 'a theocratic form of declaration of war'.[163] The *Sicarii*, who had, in Egypt, preferred to be tortured to death rather than give the emperor the title of δεσπότης, were only the latest link in a long and consistent development, in which Judas the Galilaean had a position of critical importance. His deep conviction that there could never be a compromise of any kind between Roman 'emperor-metaphysics' and the imminent kingdom of God even in the profane political sphere enabled him to supply the Jewish freedom movement with its fundamental fighting formula. Because the emperor claimed divine dignity, obedience to him was equivalent to breaking the first commandment and was therefore worshipping an idol. In view of the approaching time of salvation, only God could be regarded as the true ruler of Israel and the whole of the world. 'Whoever sacrifices to any god, save to Yahweh only, shall be utterly destroyed' (Ex 22.19).

(c) The Further Effect of the Idea of the Sole Rule of God

The conflict between the rule of the emperor and the Jewish people continued and can be traced in the Apocalypses of Ezra and Baruch and in the Christian tradition of the Antichrist, in which it appears especially in Rev 13 (see below, p. 303f.).

Even the message of the 'sole rule of God',[164] however, continued to be proclaimed as an expression of eschatological hope, especially in the prayers of the synagogue.[165] Disappointed in their messianic hopes, the Jewish people had sought refuge more in their prayer than in the learned debate of their rabbis. In those prayers, we find not only an affirmation that God alone is the true king of Israel, but also, linked with that affirmation, a petition for the speedy realization of God's rule. The Palestinian version of the *Shemoneh Esreh* or 'Eighteen Benedictions', which goes back to the first century A.D., provides the most notable example of this:

---

[162] *Bell* 2,409: This refusal — obscured by Josephus in the general statement that no non-Jew could henceforth offer sacrifice in the Temple — was given a special emphasis by the fact that it was above all directed against the emperor. Caligula was particularly offended by the fact that, although the Jews sacrificed to another God for him, they would not sacrifice to him directly; see Philo, *LegGai* 356 (M 2, 598). It must also have been impossible for the 'Zealots' to accept the idea of offering a sacrifice to God for a man who described himself as God and to whom non-Jews accorded divine honours.

[163] J. Wellhausen, *Israelitische und Jüdische Geschichte*, 5th. ed. 1904, 367.

[164] For an early form from Qumran, see 4 QDibHam = M. Baillet, *RB* 68 (1961), 208, col. V, 9; cf. Is 45.21.

[165] The first scholar to point to this connection was K. Kohler, *JE* 12, 640 and the *Harkavy Festschrift*, 9.

'Bring back our judges as formerly and our counsellors as in the beginning and be King over us, you alone'.[166]

What is more, the twelfth petition that follows this one implores God to eradicate the 'haughty rule' (מֶמְשֶׁלֶת זָדוֹן), that is, the rule of Rome, while the preceding one, that is, the tenth petition, asks for the coming of freedom (חֵירוּת).

Similar formulae occur in many other old Jewish prayers:

'In truth, you are a Lord to your people and a strong King, to contest their legal action ... and apart from you we have no king!'[167]
'Our Father, our King, apart from you there is no king for us!'[168]
'... let the haughty rule (מַלְכוּת זָדוֹן) disappear from the earth and be, Yahweh, the sole King over all your works on Mount Zion, the dwelling-place of your glory, and in Jerusalem, the city of your holiness!'[169]
'He is our God, we truly have no King apart from him!'[170]

These extracts from early Jewish prayers show clearly enough the extent to which an awareness of God as the only Lord and King of Israel persisted in the life of faith of rabbinic Judaism. The only difference was that no attempt was made in that later period to make the kingdom of God a living reality with holy zeal and with weapons in the political sphere. There was, on the contrary, a withdrawal into research into the Torah, pious works and the practice of prayer. The task of bringing about God's rule was left to God himself and that rule consequently receded into the distant future.

Two texts dating back to the decades immediately following the destruction of the second Temple show that the question of the 'political realization' of God's rule continued to concern Jewish teachers. Eliezer b. Hyrcanus, who could himself be called a 'Zealot' among learned Jews,

---

[166] The eleventh petition: וּמְלוֹךְ אַתָּה לְבַדְּךָ. The text is based on W. Staerk, *Altjüdische liturgische Gebete*, 1930. See also I. Elbogen, *Der jüdische Gottesdienst in seiner geschichtlichen Entwicklung*, 1924, 244f., who gives a very early date to the *Shemoneh Esreh*, but at the same time stresses that paticularly messianic parts of these prayers were included at a later date. As the Palestinian version with the inclusion of the twelfth petition against the heretics was given its definitive form in about 100 A.D., our formula would seem to go back to the period of the Zealots.

[167] From the benedictions pronounced at the morning prayer (after the *Shema*), the so-called *geullah*. See W. Staerk, *op. cit.*, 7.

[168] The second petition from the *Abinu Malkenu*; see W. Staerk, *op. cit.*, 38. According to Taan 25b bar, R. Akiba used this prayer to pray for rain.

[169] From the prayer וּבְכֵן תֵּן פַּחְדְּךָ, one of the *musaph* prayers pronounced at the feast of the New Year. See W. Staerk, *op. cit.*, 23; I. Elbogen, *op. cit.*, 141.

[170] From the *Alenu*; the text is according to the *Siddur sephath emeth*, Edition B, Frankfurt and Rödelheim 1927; see also Bill. 1, 175 and I. Elbogen, *op. cit.*, 143.

was quite convinced that the destruction of Rome was a precondition for the coming of the rule of God:

> 'When will the name of those be rooted out (that is, the name of Amalek = Rome)? At the time when idolatry is eradicated, it together with its worshippers, and God will be in all the earth as the One and his kingdom exists in all eternity — at that time, 'Yahweh will go forth and fight against those nations' (Zech 14.3) . . . 'and Yahweh will become King over all the earth' (Zech 14.9)'.[171]

Eliezer b. Hyrcanus takes the same presuppositions as the Zealots for his point of departure, but the setting up of the rule of God is in his case treated as an event that will take place in the uncertain future. He hopes for it, but he does not try to bring it about by violent means. Instead, he leaves it to God's discretion.

This tension between the present and the future is also clear from a statement made by Jose the Galilaean, a contemporary of Eliezer b. Hyrcanus:

> 'YHWH will be King (יִמְלֹךְ) for ever and ever (Ex 15.18)' . . .
> 'If the Israelites had said at the sea: "YHWH has become King (מָלַךְ)", then no nation and no tongue would have gained power over them. But they said: "YHWH will be King for ever and ever", in other words, for the future'.[172]

For Judas and his followers, that 'future' had already arrived. God had 'become King' and all that they had to do was to translate that fact consistently into a political reality. The words of Jose the Galilaean seem, by contrast, to be almost like an apologetical declaration of the the unnatural state of foreign rule, in which the realization of the rule of God is relegated to the distant future by means of an exegetical play on words.

The contrast between the claims made by the rule of the emperor and those of God's real majesty was also clearly recognized, as Judas had recognized it previously, by the teachers of the Tannaitic period:

> '"Yours, Y(ahweh), are the greatness and the power and the glory and the victory and the majesty" (1 Chron 29.11). "I will sing to Y(ahweh), for he is truly exalted." If a king of flesh and blood enters a city, they all praise him, saying that he is strong, and yet he is not, for he is weak; saying that he is rich, and yet he is not, for he is poor; saying that he is wise, and yet he is not, for he

---

[171] MekEx on 17.14 (1. 2, 158). Eliezer b. Hyrcanus was a pupil of Johanan b. Zakkai, which means that his youth goes back to the period before the destruction of the second Temple. For his personality, see Schürer, 2, 373ff. and W. Bacher, *Aggada der Tannaiten*, 2nd. ed. 1903, 1, 100ff.
[172] MekEx on 15.18 (1. 2, 80); the translation is based on Bill. 1, 179. Jose the Galilaean was a contemporary of R. Akiba; see Bill. Introduction, 126.

is foolish, saying that he is merciful, and yet he is not, for he is cruel; saying that he is just and faithful — but he has none of all these virtues and they all flatter him. But not the one who spoke and the world was ...'[173]

It should be clear from the above examples that the ideas of the Zealots went further than the destruction of Jerusalem and the revolt of Bar Koseba that followed two generations later and entered and had an effect on the rabbinic tradition. They were certainly toned down and given a new interpretation, becoming less radical and acute, but it is quite legitimate to conclude from their continued existence that there was a close connection between the rabbinate and the Jewish freedom movement in the first century A.D.

2. Israel's Freedom

(a) In Josephus

Josephus above all stresses 'freedom' as the aim of the struggle conducted by the fourth sect. According to Judas and Saddok, the tax assessment brought 'obvious enslavement' in its wake, with the result that they summoned the people to the 'salvation of freedom'.[174] In his second summary of their aims and views, Josephus says that Judas and his followers had an 'invincible love of freedom',[175] and freedom also occurs again and again in his *Jewish War* as the fundamental motive of the rebels.

It is also the central theme in the death-speech of Judas' grandson Eleazar b. Ari, the defender of Masada. In Josephus' *Jewish War*, Eleazar, as the representative of the declining insurrectionary movement, expresses remarkably noble thoughts in a speech which forms a striking contrast to Josephus' severe judgement of the Zealots elsewhere in his writings.[176] Eleazar, who can be regarded, on the basis of his blood-relationship with Judas, as a genuine spokesman of the fourth sect founded by Judas,[177] begins his address with a reference to the past: 'From the very beginning, when we were aiming to achieve freedom ...'[178] Later in his speech, he complains that he had been mistaken in

---

[173] MekEx on 15.1 (1. 2, 8f). E. Stauffer, *op. cit.*, 39, believed that this was a 'battle text from the time of Hadrian'.

[174] See G. Baumbach, 'Das Freiheitsverständis in der zelotischen Bewegung', *Das ferne und das nahe Wort. Festschrift für L. Rost (BZAW* 105), 1967, 11-18.

[175] *Ant* 18,4.23: δυσνίκητος δὲ τοῦ ἐλευθέρου ἔρως ἐστὶν αὐτοῖς. See above, p. 76f.

[176] *Bell* 7,323-336 and 341-388; for this speech, see H. St.J. Thackeray, *Josephus. The Man and Historian*, 1929, 45.

[177] *Bell* 7,253; cf. 2,447. See also p. 263f.

[178] *Bell* 7,327.

believing that 'he had found good comrades in the struggles for freedom'.[179] He calls the dead happy, for 'they have fallen in the fight for freedom'.[180] Freedom is in fact emphasized throughout the whole of his speech as the aim of the struggle.[181] Josephus even interprets the mass suicide of the defenders of Masada as an expression of that enormous love of freedom which made them prefer death to slavery.[182]

Josephus says of the insurgents who overran the country during the chaotic period before the beginning of the Jewish War that:

> 'The seducers of the people (γόητες) and robbers (ληστρικοί) joined together, seduced many to rebellion and urged them to achieve freedom'.[183]

The rebels themselves gave their quest for freedom as the reason for their secession from Rome:

> 'We revolted against the Romans because of our longing for freedom ...'[184]

The theme of freedom occurs again and again in important places above all in the speeches which Josephus makes various leading figures deliver in his *Jewish War*. Agrippa II, for example, includes an 'absurd hope of freedom'[185] among the three main causes of the belligerent mood prevailing in Jerusalem:

> 'Many strike up powerful hymns of praise to freedom ...'[186]
> 'But ... why do you so venerate freedom? If you regard servitude as unendurable, your complaints about the government are quite superfluous!'[187]

One might almost think that Josephus was here attributing one of the Zealots' own arguments to Agrippa II, since even a lenient and understanding Roman administration could not justify subjection to Rome in the opinion of the Zealots, who were bound to hate a rule of that kind even more than the reign of terror of a Gessius Florus.

Titus also speaks of freedom as the aim of the Jews in their war[188] and he even believes of the men of Gischala that 'their hope of freedom is

---

[179] *Bell* 7,341.
[180] *Bell* 7,372.
[181] *Bell* 7,324ff.329.334.350.370.386.
[182] See the author's extraordinarily positive judgement in *Bell* 7,406. For the question of 'heroic suicide', see below, p. 262ff.
[183] *Bell* 2,264.
[184] *Bell* 2,443.
[185] *Bell* 2,346.
[186] *Bell* 2,348: πολλοὶ ... τὰ τῆς ἐλευθερίας ἐγκώμια τραγῳδοῦσιν.
[187] *Bell* 2,349: τί σεμνύνετε τὴν ἐλευθερίαν;
[188] *Bell* 3,480.

pardonable'.[189] In the speech and counter-speech between the high-priest Jesus b. Gamalas and the leader of the Idumaeans, Simon b. Caathas, the high-priest was unable to convince the Idumaeans that the moderate party would not betray the cause of freedom.[190] It proved impossible to dissuade Simon that the Zealots were the 'champions of freedom'.[191]

Finally, Josephus himself also, during his Galilaean period, called on others to fight for freedom.[192] Later, however, as an orator speaking for the Romans, he condemned the insurgents' fight for freedom in the same way:

> 'If it is admitted that it is noble to fight for freedom, then they should have done that earlier. Since they have become subjects and have tolerated this for such a long time, an attempt to shake off the yoke would be the work of men who love death and not freedom'.[193]

For Josephus, the conquest of Jerusalem by Pompey was the decisive event in Jewish history and the Jews themselves were, in his opinion, to blame for their fate:

> 'When did our servitude begin? ... Then, when the insanity of an Aristobulus and a Hyrcanus and their quarrelling between themselves caused Pompey to attack the city and God subjected them, unworthy as they were of freedom, to the Romans!'[194]

The Jewish defenders on the walls were admittedly unable to grasp and express for themselves this change of attitude outlined by Josephus. They continued to assure those laying siege to the city that they preferred death to servitude,[195] thus expressing an attitude that is encountered again and again throughout the course of the Jewish War.[196] Even obvious defeat could not shake this 'fanaticism for freedom' and the *Sicarii* who fled to Egypt

> 'persuaded many (of their compatriots) who had received them to gain freedom for themselves, not to regard the Romans as superior to themselves and to recognize God as the only Lord'.[197]

---

[189] *Bell* 4,95: συγγνωστὸν ἐλευθερίας ἐλπίδα.

[190] *Bell* 4,246ff.

[191] *Bell* 4,272.

[192] *Bell* 3,357.

[193] *Bell* 5,365.

[194] *Bell* 5,395f.: ὑπέταξεν ὁ θεὸς τοὺς οὐκ ἀξίους ἐλευθερίας.

[195] *Bell* 5,321; cf. 458.

[196] The Jews frequently preferred to die rather than to be taken prisoner: *Bell* 3,331 nd 355ff. in Jotapata; 4,79f. in Gamala, etc. See also below, p. 263f.

[197] *Bell* 7,410.

In his final and very severe condemnation of the Jewish rebels, Josephus reports that, after Cyrenius' census, the *Sicarii* had joined together against those who wanted to continue to obey the Romans and had treated them as enemies, because

> 'such men could not be distinguished in any way from non-Jews, since they had so ignominiously abandoned the hard fought for freedom (περιμάχητον ... ἐλευθερίαν) of the Jews and had willingly chosen slavery under the Romans'.[198]

It is true that Josephus adds here that this was only an excuse for their greed and cruelty, but this can be regarded as tendentious defamation. It is in any case quite clear that the theme of freedom runs through Josephus' accounts of the fourth sect and the later insurrectionary movement up to the end of the Jewish War like a scarlet thread.[199] His attitude towards the Jewish fight for freedom is, however, itself not completely unambiguous. In the *Antiquities* especially, he takes up a positive position with regard to the desire of the Jewish people for freedom during the earlier period of their history.[200] In *The Jewish War* on the other hand, there is, with the exception of those places in which the Jews' longing for freedom is directed against their own 'tyrants' — in other words, against the leaders of the insurgents[201] — very little sign of this positive understanding of the concept of 'freedom'. The desire for freedom is presented in that work as a completely profane and unjustified longing for purely political freedom.[202]

---

[198] *Bell* 7,255; see also *Bell* 4,146, where respectable Jews were condemned by the Zealots as προδότας ... τῆς κοινῆς ἐλευθερίας.

[199] See *Bell* 4,178.229.273 etc. See also *Ant* 20,120.

[200] Josephus proudly stresses the Jews' love of freedom in *Ant* 2,281; 3,19 etc. He calls freedom God's gift to Israel: *Ant* 2,327; 3,64; cf. 7,95. In *Ant* 6,20, he makes Samuel say: οὐκ ἐπιθυμεῖν ἐλευθερίας δεῖ μόνον, ἀλλὰ καὶ ποιεῖν δι' ὧν ἂν ἔλθοι πρὸς ὑμᾶς. In so doing, his position is clearly similar to that of the Zealots. The Maccabaean wars are also described as wars of Freedom; see *Ant* 12,281.302 for the claims of Mattathias and *Ant* 12,433f. for Josephus' description of Judas Maccabaeus; see also the summary in *Ant* 13,1. W.R. Farmer has pointed out this discrepancy in Josephus' judgement between the Maccabaean and the Zealots' wars of freedom; see 9,14 etc. He is correct in attributing this to 'his dual role as apologist' (20), on the one hand for the Romans and, on the other, for the Jews in confrontation with the Hellenistic world of that time. Unfortunately, however, he gives insufficient emphasis to the difference between Josephus' *Jewish War* and his *Antiquities*. In *The Jewish War*, the apologetical tendency in favour of Rome in general and of the Flavians in particular is so heavily stressed that the Maccabaeans' struggle hardly appears at all as a fight for freedom; the concept of ἐλευθερία, for example, does not occur once in this context.

[201] See *Bell* 2,443.564; the speech of the high-priest Ananus, 4,162-196.389.394 etc.

[202] Josephus consequently has Agrippa II and Titus make comparisons with the failed attempts made by other people to achieve freedom: *Bell* 2,361.365.370.376. etc.

It might therefore be possible to be satisfied with Josephus' presentation of the situation and regard the fight conducted by Judas and his followers and by those who succeeded him up to the time of the *Sicarii* who became dispersed throughout Egypt as a purely secular and political phenomenon with many parallels in the history of the ancient world. Since there is above all no exact equivalent for ἐλευθερία in the Old Testament tradition,[203] it is understandable that this secular ideal of national freedom should have been given prominence in a whole series of historical representations of the Jewish insurrectionary movement. This, however hardly does justice to the aim of Judas and the movement that was initiated by him in the war. We are therefore bound to ask whether more is not contained in the concept of 'freedom', despite Josephus' one-sided representation with its Hellenistic overtones.

There is in *The Jewish War* a remarkable account which is exemplary for the eschatologically overheated atmosphere in Judaea just before the outbreak of the war:

> 'Seducers and deceivers, who have had insurrection and revolution in mind under the cover of divine inspiration, have persuaded the people to such an extent that they have lost their senses and have led them out into the desert[204] (in the belief) that God would show them signs of freedom there. Felix, regarding this as the beginning of a revolt, sent out cavalry and infantry against them and had a great number of them killed'.[205]

More light is thrown on these 'signs of freedom' (σημεῖα ἐλευθερίας), which Josephus defines more precisely in his *Antiquities* as 'signs and wonders which take place in accordance with God's providence', in another passage in the same work:

> 'When Pharaoh's army was approaching, the Israelites 'criticized Moses,

---

[203] ἐλευθερία occurs relatively rarely in the Septuagint. There are only two cases in which a Hebrew equivalent can be specified: Lev 19.20 חֻפְשָׁה and Sir 7.31 חֻפְשָׁה. In both these cases, what is involved is the emancipation of slaves. The only originally Hebrew document in which ἐλευθερία appears in the sense of the political freedom of a people is 1 Macc; see especially 14.26, in which the people say about Simon and his brothers: ἔστησαν αὐτῷ (the people) ἐλευθερίαν. In the purely Greek document of the Septuagint, the concept of freedom occurs more frequently; see 3 Macc 3.28; 3 (1) Ezra 4,49.53. This absence from the Old Testament tradition was unfortunately the reason why the question of a specifically Jewish and Palestinian background to the concept of ἐλευθερία was not considered at all in the *Theological Dictionary of the New Testament*; see H. Schlier, *TD* 2, 487ff., who confines himself simply to the Greek and especially the Stoic prehistory of the term.

[204] For the 'exodus' into the desert, see below, p. 249ff.

[205] *Bell* 2,259.: ὡς ἐκεῖ τοῦ θεοῦ δείξοντος αὐτοῖς σημεῖα ἐλευθερίας. See also *Ant* 20,167f.: δείξειν γὰρ ἔφασαν ἐναργῆ τέρατα καὶ σημεῖα κατὰ τὴν τοῦ θεοῦ πρόνοιαν γινόμενα. For the false prophets, see below, p. 229ff.

because they had forgotten all the signs that had been brought about by God for their freedom.'[206]

According to Mic 7.15f., Yahweh was asked to show the people the same wonders (נִפְלָאוֹת) for the coming of the time of salvation that had taken place in the past in Egypt, so that Israel's enemies would be stricken with fear and terror. In very much the same way, in accordance with the apocalyptic equation that the end of time was the same as the beginning of time, these 'seducers and deceivers' promised that the wonders of punishment and judgement, by which the Egyptian people had been stricken and Israel had been set free, would be repeated during a second exodus into the desert.[207] There can be no doubt that Josephus is describing, in his use of the term ἐλευθερία in these passages, the eschatological redemption of Israel by God's miraculous intervention.

In the light of this, one may legitimately ask whether this eschatologically determined concept of freedom is not very much more in accordance with the aim of the Jewish rebels from the time of Judas the Galilaean onwards than the secular meaning that was derived from Greek political science.[208] One argument in favour of this understanding of the term 'freedom' here is that Josephus connects the theme of freedom closely with the confession of the sole rule of God in many places. It is only when God's kingdom is established over the whole of the earth that Israel will be really free, since the nation would then no longer be prevented on any side from fulfilling God's will in absolute purity and perfection.[209]

---

[206] *Ant* 2,327: πάντων ἐπιλελησμένοι τῶν ἐκ θεοῦ πρὸς τὴν ἐλευθερίαν αὐτοῖς σημείων γεγονότων. See also Eisler, 2,429.

[207] For the parallel between the redemption from Egypt and the eschatological redemptiom, see J. Jeremias, 'Μωϋσῆς', *TD*, 4, 859ff., and G. Kittel, 'ἔρημος', *TD* 2, 658f.; see also P. Volz, *Esch* 2nd ed., 270, and S. Zeitlin, 'Judaism', *JQR* 34 (1943/44), 332. Rabbinic parallels are given in Bill. 1, 86f.; 4, 860f.,939f.,954. A great number of examples of the recurrence at the end of time of the punitive miracles that occurred in Egypt can be found in the Apocalypse of John; see especially Rev 8 and 16. For rabbinic parallels, see Bill. 3, 818.

[208] For the latter, see H. Schlier, 'ἐλευθερία', *TD* 2, 487ff.

[209] See Schlatter, *GI*, 263: 'The community's strict submission to the law was not in any way diminished by the Zealots' praise of freedom as the possession that the holy community could not lose. The Pharisees had taught that the law guaranteed that the people would have freedom from foreign rulers. For this reason, the Zealots believed that freedom would come about as a result of the rule of God, under which man placed himself by fulfilling the law. It was through the holiness of the law that the struggle for freedom acquired the characteristic of a holy duty, before which every other consideration had to take second place. It was, however, equally clear to every Zealot and indeed to the whole people that the fight for freedom could only be justified by the firmness and the greatness of the divine promise'.

(b) On the Jewish Coins of the Revolt

One can look in vain in the Old Testament, in the Book of Ecclesiasticus and in the Qumran documents[210] for an equivalent to the Greek term ἐλευθερία in its purely political meaning.

The first appearance of the Hebrew concept for 'freedom' that can be precisely dated occurs significantly enough at the time of the Jewish War, when we find the word חֵרוּת — originally an Aramaic abstract[211] — for the first time on Jewish coins of the revolt.[212] These are all bronze coins with, on the front, the year (שלוש or שנת שתים = Year 2 or 3 of the revolt) and an amphora with a narrow neck and a lid[213] and, on the back, a vine tendril and leaf[214] and the inscription 'Zion's freedom' (חרות ציון). The term חֵרוּת does not, however, occur so frequently on coins of the first revolt as it does later on Bar Koseba's.[215] The silver shekels of the first uprising, which were much more widespread, have, in addition to the year,[216] the words 'Jerusalem the Holy' (ירושלים הקדושה or simply

---

[210] The formula חק חרות in 1QS 10,6.8.11 should undoubtedly be read as חֹק חָרוּת according to Ex 32.16; see H. Braun, *Spätjüdisch-häretischer und frühchristlicher Radikalismus*, 2 vols., 1957, 1 26f., n. 5. In the rabbinate, this חָרוּת was later reinterpreted as חֵרוּת; see below, p. 118ff.

[211] See M. Jastrow, *Dictionary*, 1, 460; the concept is also found in Syriac; see C. Brockelmann, *Lexicon Syriacum*, 2nd. ed. 1928, 252b ܚܐܪܘܬܐ. The Hebrew חָפְשָׁה of Lev 19.20 was rendered in the Peshitta by this term among others; see above, p. 114, n. 203.

[212] See A. Reifenberg, *Jewish Coins*, 58 Nos. 147-149, see also 32f. Coin 147a, which was struck over an impression of Herod Agrippa I, provides unambiguous evidence that these bronze coins go back to the time of the first revolt. Schürer, 1, 602ff., Appendix IV, came to the same conclusion. Many coins with this inscription have been found in Masada; see L. Kadman, 'A Coin Find at Masada', *IEJ* 7 (1957), 61-65; Y. Yadin, *Masada*, London, 1966, 97,172,206f.

[213] This amphora was probably a vessel used in the Temple, possibly for water and wine libations at the Feast of Tabernacles; see P. Romanoff, 'Jewish Symbols in Coins', *JQR* NS 34 (1943/44), 163ff. See also above, p. 67, n. 334.

[214] The vine may point to the victory symbol of the palm branch; see, among other texts, 1 Macc 13.37; 2 Macc 14.4 and 5 Ezra 2,45. See also P. Romanoff, *op. cit.*, 438 and *JQR* 33 (1942/43), 2nd. ed., 4 and 5. The Hebrew equivalent for the palm branch, חָרוּת, is written in exactly the same way as חֵרוּת. The vine leaf was used on coins as a typical symbol of the first revolt and perhaps as a symbol for fertility (see Joel 2.22; Zech 8.12); it may possibly also have had a messianic significance (Gen 49.11). See C. Roth, *IEJ* 12 (1962), 36f.

[215] See Reifenberg, *op. cit.*, 60ff. No. 164ff. and the explanation, 35ff. Two coin texts are particularly important here: שבלחר ישראל = 'In the second year of Israel's freedom' and לחרות ירושלם = 'For the freedom of Jerusalem'. The second of these two coins was probably struck after the occupation of Jerusalem by the Romans and expressed the inhabitants' longing for the freedom of the holy city.

[216] There is evidence that these silver shekels were current throughout the whole of the revolt from year 1 to 5. A chalice appears on the front of these coins and three

ירושלם קדשה) as a text on the back of the coin.[217] The bronze shekels that were for a long time attributed to Simon the Maccabee with the year 4 and the inscription 'for the redemption of Zion' (לגאלת ציון)[218] also go back, according to the latest finds, to the first revolt. These coins can perhaps be ascribed to Simon bar Giora, who had been admitted into Jerusalem in the fourth year of the revolt (April/May 69 A.D.) in order to liberate the population from the tyranny of John of Gischala. Since the silver treasure in the Temple was in John's hands, Simon could not have any silver shekels struck.

B. Kanael has suggested that the inscription 'for the redemption of Zion' should be understood as an expression of Simon's messianic claims and as pointing to the eschatological liberation of the people, whereas John of Gischala only intended to express political freedom with the word חֵרוּת.[219] This distinction cannot, however, be upheld. Quite apart from the fact that John of Gischala may also have striven for messianic dignity,[220] it is clear from the Bar Koseba coins, on which both concepts frequently appear alongside each other, that חֵרוּת and גְּאֻלָּה are almost identical.[221] The word חֵרוּת can point as well as גְּאֻלָּה[222] to the

---

pomegranates appear on the back. Reifenberg, *op. cit.*, 31f., believed that this chalice, which was probably also a vessel used in the Temple, was the 'cup of salvation' mentioned in Ps 116.13f. This was also the opinion of C. Roth, 'Messianic Symbols in Palestinian Archeology', *PEQ* 87 (1955), 160ff. The pomegranates have also been interpreted in the messianic sense.

[217] Reifenberg, *op. cit.*, 57f. Nos. 137-145; see also Schürer, 1, 605f.

[218] *op. cit.*, 39 Nos. 4-6. Reifenberg admits that the Maccabaean origin of these coins is very questionable, but still insists on it; see 10ff. Schürer, on the other hand, was undecided; see 1, 606. P. Romanoff, *JQR* 33 (1942/43), 6f., and B. Kanael, *BASOR* 129 (1953), 18ff., resolutely date them to the first revolt, because none of these coins have been found at Beth-Zur. This dating has also been confirmed by the latest find of coins at Masada; see L. Kadman, *IEJ* 7 (1957), 61ff.

[219] *BASOR* 129 (1953), 20: 'Redemption in this context means vastly more than freedom, the former being religious and messianic and the latter merely political'.

[220] See below, p. 297f.

[221] See Reifenberg, *op. cit.*, 60ff. Nos. 163,170,181-195; see also 35. All the coins struck during the first year bear the inscription לגאלת ישראל, while those of the later period are inscribed with שבלחר ישראל or לחרות ירושלם.

[222] גְּאֻלָּה has a legal meaning in the Old Testament and refers to the buying back of slaves; see Köhler-Baumgartner, *Lexicon*, 163. The only place in which the term is used in the sense of '(a claim to) liberation' is Ezek 11.15. See, however, the Septuagint and the Latin and Syriac translations. The verb גָּאַל, on the other hand, is often employed with God as the subject in the sense of 'redeem', 'liberate' and so on; see Exod 6.6; 15.13; see also the frequent occurrence of this verb in Deutero- and Trito-Isaiah. It refers to Zion in Is 59.20 and to Jerusalem in 52.9; see also Ps 74.2; 106.10 etc. In the rabbinate, גְּאוּלָּה became a technical term for the messianic liberation of Israel from the rule of the nations; see Bill. 4, 860f.; Jastrow, *Dictionary*, 1, 201f.

eschatological redemption. There are many examples of this in the rabbinic linguistic usage, which will be examined below.

It is a remarkable fact that 'freedom' does not, as it does in the case of the coins of the second revolt, refer predominantly to Israel, but is applied fundamentally to Zion. This points to the supreme significance that the Sanctuary in Jerusalem had for the rebels. The freedom of the whole of Israel depended on the liberation of the Sanctuary. The frequent inscription on coins: 'Jerusalem the Holy' clearly points in this direction: Jerusalem, the city in which God's Sanctuary stood, had been made a truly holy city by the banishment of foreigners and unbelievers.[223] 'Jerusalem the holy city', 'freedom' and the 'redemption of Zion' were concepts in parallel with each other. The fulfilment of the prophetic promise could therefore be expressed in all three texts on the coins of the first revolt:

> 'Awake, awake, put on your strength, O Zion! Put on your beautiful garments, O Jerusalem, the holy city!
> For there shall no more come into you the uncircumcised and the unclean. Shake yourself from the dust and arise, O captive Jerusalem! Loose the bonds from your neck, O captive daughter of Zion!'[224]

It has therefore been suggested, on the basis of inscriptions on the coins of the revolt, that a twofold tradition of the eschatological holiness[225] and freedom[226] of Jerusalem and the Temple was active among the Zealots.

(c) In the Rabbinic Tradition

Because of the fable of the dishonourable origin of the Jewish

---

[223] See below, p. 217ff. This coin text may possibly have been partly influenced by the Tyrean shekel that was so popular in Jerusalem. This shekel bore the inscription τύρον ἱερὸν καὶ ἄσυλον; see I. Abrahams, *Studies in Pharisaism and the Gospels*, 1st. Series, 1917, 84. See also A. Ben-David, *Jerusalem und Tyros*.

[224] Is 52.1f.; see also 9b. A similar promise also appears in Joel 4.17: 'So you shall know that I am Yahweh your God, who dwells in Zion, my holy mountain. And Jerusalem shall be holy and strangers shall never again pass through it'.

[225] The tradition of the future holiness of Jerusalem appears not only in the texts mentioned above, but also in Ezek 44.9; PsSol 17,22.28.30; Rev 21.2,27; see also the most recently published Qumran fragment, J.M. Allegro, *JBL* 77 (1958), 351 = 4Qflor No. 174; see *DJD* 5, 53f.

[226] The idea of a 'free Jerusalem' is found above all in the books of the Maccabees; see the complaint of Mattathias, 1 Macc 2.11: . . . ἀντὶ ἐλευθέρας ἐγένετο εἰς δούλην, which appears to be almost the opposite of Is 52.1f. In 1 Macc 15.7, Antiochus VII Sidetes promises to give Jerusalem freedom and, in 2 Macc 9.14, the penitent and mortally sick Antiochus Epiphanes prays: τὴν μὲν ἁγίαν πόλιν . . . ἐλευθέραν ἀναδεῖξαι. A different Jewish conception of the 'freedom of Jerusalem' may also have been at the basis of the polemical allegory in Gal 4.21ff. (see especially 4.26: ἡ δὲ ἄνω Ἰερουσαλὴμ ἐλευθέρα); see H. Lietzmann, 'An die Galater', *HBzNT* 3rd. ed. 1932, 32.

people,[227] the view was widely held in the ancient world that the Jews were in a special way created for servitude.[228] Seen against this background, it is not difficult to understand why it was so stressed within Judaism that the Jews had always been 'free men'.[229] The Hebrew expression for this concept was בֶּן־חוֹרִין, derived from חֹרִים, which in the Old Testament means free and respected citizens.[230]

On the one hand, the Jews could base their 'freedom' on the fact that God had called their ancestor Abraham.[231] This 'freedom' was not primarily understood in the political or the social sense, but was derived from the high position occupied by the patriarch.[232] As soon as Israel's freedom came to be based, in the Haggadah, on the liberation from Egypt, the political question came to the surface and the Jews were for this reason again and again reminded of the fact that they had, in accordance with their divine destiny, to be a free people.

Moses is said to have called to the Israelites to encourage them during the Exodus: 'From the mouth of power it was said to me that you are free men!'[233]

R. Gamliel II said at the celebration of the Passover: 'We are therefore obliged to thank and to praise . . . in the presence of the One who has brought about this wonder for our fathers and for us all, who has led us out of servitude to freedom (מעבודה לחירות), from mourning to festivity, from

---

[227] According to Manetho, the patriarchs of the Jews were lepers who had been driven out of Egypt, a rebellious mob; see *Ap* 1,227-250. This fable became part of almost all the accounts of the Jews written by ancient historians; see Tacitus, *Hist* 5,2.12; see also Schürer, 3, 151f.

[228] See, for example, Cicero, *ProvCons* 5,10 (Reinach, 241): 'Tradidit (Gabinius) in servitutem Judaeis et Syris, nationibus natis servituti'. Apion criticized the Jews (*Ap* 2,125): δουλεύειν δὲ μᾶλλον ἔθνεσιν καὶ ἄλλοτε ἄλλοις. Titus stressed (*Bell* 6,42) that a defeat would not be shameful for the Jews, since they had learned how to be slaves (μαθοῦσι δουλεύειν). Paradoxically, the Jews were at the same time also accused of being restless and inclined to rebellion.

[229] The Hebrew words כָּל־יֹצֵא צָבָא in the population count in Num 1.3 are rendered by Josephus with the term ἐλεύθεροι in *Ant* 3,196. In *Bell* 7,265, he emphasizes that Simon b. Giora dared to maltreat the Jews as ἐλεύθεροι; see also above, p. 113, n. 200, and H. Guttmann, *Die jüdische Religion bei Josephus*, 1928, 10.

[230] Köhler-Baumgartner, *Lexicon*, 329. See also 1 Kings 21.8,11 etc.; בֶּן־חֹרִין only appears in Eccles 10.17.

[231] Jn 8.33ff., cf. Mt 3.9 parr; BK 8, 6: 'R. Akiba says that even the poorest are regarded in Israel as free men (בני חרין) who have lost their fortunes, for they are sons of Abraham, Isaac and Jacob' (translation based on Goldschmidt, 7, 308). R. Eisler, 2, 665, n. 5, saw in Jesus' discourse in Jn 8 a similarity to, if not identity with, the principles of Judas the Galilaean, but this is rather too fantastic.

[232] See R. Bultmann, *The Gospel of John*, 1971, 437f., n. 6. See also Bill. 1, 117, Shab 128a bar: 'R. Simeon b. Gamaliel and R. Simeon and R. Ishmael and R. Akiba were all of the opinion that all Israelites were kings' sons'.

[233] MekEx on 14.2 (L. 1, 190).

darkness to great light and from slavery to redemption (מִשַׁעְבּוּד לִגְאוּלָה)!'[234]

The evening prayer following the *Shema* reminds us of the liberation from the Egyptian yoke: 'He accomplished wonders for us and dealt retribution to Pharaoh, signs and wonderful acts in the land of the sons of Ham. In his anger, he struck down all the first-born of Egypt and led his people out of their midst to eternal freedom (לְחֵרוּת עוֹלָם) . . . His children saw his power, praised and thanked his name and took his kingdom willingly on themselves . . . And it is said: Y(ahweh) redeemed (פָּדָה) Jacob and liberated (וּגְאָלוֹ) him from the hand of the one who is stronger than he . . .'.[235]

This last example shows particularly clearly how the miraculous liberation from Egypt formed the foundation of the people's hope of their future redemption from the rule of Rome. The hapax legomenon חָרוּת in Ex 32.16 was also cited and accordingly reinterpreted as forming the foundation for Israel's freedom:[236]

'What does חָרוּת mean? (This has been discussed by R. Jehuda, R. Nehemiah and our teachers). R. Jehuda said: Freedom from the governments (חֵירוּת מִן מַלְכוּיוֹת). R. Nehemiah said: Freedom from the angel of death. Our teachers said: Freedom from suffering'.

Since the transformation of חָרוּת into חֵירוּת was taken for granted in rabbinic exegesis of the second century A.D and since the question about the matter to which that freedom referred was still debated, it is possible to assume that this exegetical game had already begun some time before — presumably in circles particularly concerned with the concept of חֵירוּת. It consequently became interpreted in various ways:

According to R. Eleazar, the son of R. Jose the Galilaean (the middle of the second century A.D.), God said to the angel of death: 'I will let you rule over every nation in the world, but not over them (Israel), for I have bestowed freedom on them'.[237]

It is now clear why, after their exodus from Egypt, the Israelites once again came under the rule of foreign nations. If they had waited patiently for Moses and had not made the golden calf for themselves, the first tablets would not have been destroyed and neither oppressors nor the angel of death would have gained power over Israel.[238]

---

[234] Pes 10,5; the text shows, among other things, that חָרוּת and גְּאוּלָה could be used synonymously. The translation is based on Goldschmidt, 2, 665.

[235] W. Staerk, *op. cit.*, 8f.; the benediction comes immediately after the *Shema*, which concludes with a commemoration of Israel's salvation from servitude in Egypt.

[236] TanB כי תישא, 12, ed. Buber, 2, 112; see also Bill. 1, 596, with further parallels. ExRab 41,7 has, instead of 'freedom from the government', מִן גָּלוּת = 'freedom from prison'. What we have here, then, is presumably a late toning down for political reasons. For R. Judah b. Elai and R. Nehemiah (ca. 130-160 A.D.), see Bill. Introduction, 128f.

[237] ExRab 41,7.

[238] This is the conclusion drawn in ExRab 32,1; see also Erub 54a, R. Acha b. Jacob.

It is clear from this and from other examples that the loss of the freedom bestowed on Israel was regarded as a punishment for the people's idolatry. Was there, then, any way of regaining that freedom? For Judas, the only way was to refuse to obey the idolatrous rule of the emperor. For the Jewish teachers of the later period, on the other hand, freedom was to be found in the study of the Torah:

> 'R. Joshua b. Levi said: '. . . and the tablets were God's work and Scripture was God's writing engraved on the tablets. Do not read "engraved" (חָרוּת), but "freedom" (חֵירוּת). For there is for you no free man (בֶּן־חוֹרִין) apart from the one who is employed in the study of the Torah'.[239]

That the Torah brings true freedom is a theme that could have almost polemic overtones as, for example, in the way or rule of life of R. Nechonia b. Hakkana cited in the previous chapter.[240] In a later tradition, this is directly connected with the idea of freedom:

> 'The yoke of the government and of mundane matters is taken from the man who takes on himself the words of the Torah. Just as the desert does not bring forth a festive meal, so too are the sons of the Torah free men (בני תורה בני חורין)'.[241]

This testimony may be regarded as an expression of a different way of looking at the situation after the failure of the fight for freedom. The longing for freedom continued to be felt, but it was seen as a gift of the messianic time:

> 'Proclaim freedom (חֵירוּתָא) for your people, the house of Israel, through the Messiah, as you did through Moses and Aaron on the day of the Passover!'[242]
>
> The call for freedom also appears in the daily prayer of the pious: 'Blow the trumpet to our freedom (לְחֵרוּתֵנוּ) and raise a banner to gather our banished people together. Blessed are you, Y(ahweh), who gather the rejected ones of Israel!'[243]

It is clear, then, from this very brief survey that the understanding of freedom in the rabbinic tradition was closely linked with the theme of the 'kingdom of God'. The point of departure for this understanding was the early history of Israel and especially the liberation of the people from Egyptian servitude and the wilderness. Moreover, the loss of

---

[239] Ab 6,2; R. Joshua b. Levi lived at the beginning of the third century A.D.; see Bill. Introduction, 136. See also ARN 2,3, ed. Schechter, 1887, 10.

[240] Ab 3,5; see above, p. 68f.

[241] TanB חקת, 59, ed. Buber, 4, 576.

[242] Targum on Lam 2.22, quoted by Bill. 4, 576.

[243] Tenth petition of the *Shemoneh Esreh*, W. Staerk, *op. cit.*, 13. Almost exactly the same petition is found in the *Musaph* for the Feast of the New Year; *op. cit.*, 24.

freedom was based on an offence committed during that period.[244]
Finally, it was hoped to regain that freedom in the messianic time.

It is certainly not purely by chance that the earliest fixable date for the
newly-formed concept, חֵ(י)רוּת, is on the coins struck during the period
of the Jewish War. In the rabbinic tradition, it can be established for the
first time at the beginning of the second century A.D., but this tradition
probably goes back to the first century A.D. It is also possible that the
transformation of חָרוּת in Ex 32.16 into חֵירוּת is of Zealot origin.

The rabbinate corrected the Zealots' eschatological hopes of freedom
at the latest shortly after they had been disappointed. This eschatological
awareness diminished and a concern for the Torah came to be seen both
as a recognition of the 'kingdom of God' and as a movement leading to
the freedom that Israel had been promised. The prayer of the synagogue
seems to have been least affected of all by this change — in it, the
eschatological hope of freedom survived almost without a break.

3. Co-operation with God in the Redemption of Israel

(a) The Statements made by Josephus

In his presentation of the arguments used by Judas the Galilaean and
the Pharisee Saddok to win their compatriots over to their cause,
Josephus gives special emphasis to one point:[245]

> 'The deity would only readily contribute to the success of this plan (the
> achievement of freedom) on condition that one actively co-operated in it
> oneself or rather, that those who had, in their convictions, become followers
> of a great cause did not avoid the trouble that would be involved (in its
> carrying out)'.

What Josephus is stressing here in the style of a philosophical treatise is
that Judas and Saddok were not content simply to wait passively for the
coming redemption of Israel with a hope of the kind that was to be
found in certain late Jewish circles.[246] They were, in his opinion, calling
for an active and energetic co-operation of the people with God to bring

---

[244] For the basis of the idea of the kingdom of God in the Exodus from Egypt, see Bill.
1, 172 (d, e).173-175, and Schechter, *Some Aspects of Rabbinic Theology*, 1909, 85f. For
the failure of Israel, see MekEx on 15.18 (L. 2, 80) and the interpretation of the text by
R. Jose the Galilaean.

[245] *Ant 18,5:* καὶ τὸ θεῖον οὐκ ἄλλως ἢ ἐπὶ συμπράξει τῶν βουλευμάτων εἰς τὸ κατορθοῦν
συμπροθυμεῖσθαι μᾶλλον ἂν μεγάλων ἐρασταὶ τῇ διανοίᾳ καθιστάμενοι μὴ ἐξαφίωνται
πόνου τοῦ ἐπ' αὐτοῖς. Conj. πόνου Hudson/Niese; φόνου Codd. Exc.

[246] Traces of this kind of Jewish 'quietism' can be found in AssMos 9,5ff. and possibly

about the coming time of salvation, since they believed that God could only intervene and help if pious Jews ceased to wait and acted.

This emphasis on co-operation with God has a parallel, not, as some scholars have assumed, in the teaching of the Sadducees,[247] but in what Josephus says about the views of the Pharisees:

> 'Doing or not doing justice is to a great extent attributed to men, yet fate is at the side of each one, helping him'.[248]

Unlike this formally philosophical statement about the problem of the will, the argument of the two Zealot teachers, Judas and Saddok, has an eschatological perspective. For them, the course of the eschatological events was determined not only by God, but also by the actions of Israel. In their opinion, the course of events could be either speeded up or slowed down and even stopped altogether. If Israel did not obey God's call, the salvation that had been promised could be changed into judgement. It is clear, then, that, in the message proclaimed by Judas and Saddok — a message that came very close to a prophetic call to decisive action — the synergism of the Pharisees had been transferred to the plane of eschatological hope.[249] It would not be wrong to assume that this reinterpretation only partly met with the approval of the Pharisees who were Saddok's companions. There are many signs that the question as to how much influence human activity might have on the coming of the time of salvation was energetically debated in the later rabbinic tradition.

(b) The Forcing of the Time of Salvation in the Rabbinate

It was by no means unknown in the rabbinic tradition that certain groups within Palestinian Judaism were trying to bring about the

---

also in Lk 2.25f. J. Wellhausen, *Die Pharisäer und Sadducäer*, 1874, 23, believed that these 'quietists' were Pharisees.

[247] See R. Eisler, 2,7; see also H. Rasp, 'Flavius Josephus und die jüdischen Religionsparteien', *ZNW* 23 (1924)m 38f.: 'In praxis there could be no fundamental gulf between Sadducees and followers of Judas and Saddok'.

[248] *Bell* 2,163 (cf. *Ant* 13,172; 18,13): καὶ τὸ μὲν πράττειν τὰ δίκαια καὶ μὴ κατὰ τὸ πλεῖστον ἐπὶ τοῖς ἀνθρώποις κεῖσθαι, βοηθεῖν δὲ εἰς ἕκαστον καὶ τὴν εἱμαρμένην; see also *Ant* 6,20. A. Schlatter, *Theologie des Judentums nach dem Bericht des Josephus*, 1932, 216, thought, on the other hand, that the renunciation of all self-help demanded by Josephus in *Bell* 5,376 was a typically Pharisaical attitude.

[249] Judas and his spiritual followers were certainly not of the opinion that they did not require God's help. In *Vita* 290, the Pharisee Ananias, who belonged to the left wing of the rebels (see also 197 and *Bell* 2,451) explicitly states 'that, if they do not receive that (that is, God's) help, all weapons are useless'.

redemption of Israel by force, by rising up against the 'yoke of the kingdoms of his world':[250]

> 'R. Jose b. Hanina[251] said: Two adjurations are found here (Song 2.7 and 3.5) ... God adjured the Israelites not to rise up against the yoke of the kingdoms of his world and he also adjured the kingdoms of the world not to make the yoke laid on the Jews too heavy, for, if they made the yoke laid on Israel too heavy, they would cause the end-time to come before its appointed hour ...
>
> 'R. Helbo said: Four adjurations are found here. God adjured the Israelites not to rise up against the kingdoms of this world, not to bring about the end-time by force (שלא ידחקו על הקץ) ...
>
> 'R. Huna said: With four oaths God adjured them, according to the four generations who have tried to bring close the appointed time and have therefore come to grief. These are the generation in the days of Amram,[252] that in the days of Dinai,[253] that in the days of Ben Koseba and finally that in the days of Shutelah b. Ephraim'.[254]

It is clear from this that the 'forcing' of the end by revolt against the secular power of Rome could also be found in the rabbinate and, what is more, to such an extent that the memory of their concrete attempts to do this persisted even after more than two centuries. It is obvious that the rabbinate had to reject attempts of this kind after the catastrophes of 70 and 134/135 A.D., but the desire to hasten the coming of the end remained alive, although in a changed form.

Several of the statements made by teachers of the synagogue came very close to the ideas of the Zealots. There is, for example, the clearly formulated argument of R. Eliezer b. Hyrcanus,[255] the pupil and

---

[250] SongRab on 2.7. The parallels provided in Bill. 1, 599 — Ket 111a and TanB דברים, 4, ed. Buber, 2 — are no more than brief summaries. See also Derenbourg, 279f. and H. Graetz, 5th. ed., 3, 431, n. 4.

[251] R. Jose b. Hanina lived in the third century A.D.; see Bill. Introduction, 138. R. Helbo and R. Huna, the teachers who are mentioned later, were contemporaries and lived at the beginning of the fourth century A.D.; see Bill. Introduction, 144.

[252] H. Graetz, op. cit. and 3, 360, K. Kohler, JE 12, 648a, and Klausner, Hist 5, 16f., all identify Amram with this rebel, who, according to Ant 20,4, was banished by Cuspius Fadus. Bill. 1, 599, n. 1, on the basis of a reference to Sot 12a, believes that he was the father of Moses.

[253] This Dinai is the bandit leader mentioned several times in the rabbinic literature (Sot 9,8; Ket 27a; Kel 5,10) and in Josephus. See also below, p. 349f.

[254] See Num 26.35 and 1 Chron 7.20. According to Bill. 1, 599, n. 3, the children of Shutelah anticipated the redemption from Egypt and therefore died on the way to Canaan; see MekEx on 15.14 (L. 2, 72), Sanh 92b etc. According to this legend, the attempt to bring about the time of salvation prematurely by violent means should also be condemned.

[255] For R. Eliezer b. Hyrcanus, see above, p. 108f.; see also below, pp. 202,290f.

contemporary of R. Johanan b. Zakkai, in which the contradiction of
the more lenient R. Joshua (b. Hanania) was immediately brought to
mind:[256]

'R. Eliezer b. Hyrcanus said: If the Israelites do not do penance, they will
not be redeemed in eternity (אם אין ישראל עושין תשובה אין נגלאים לעולם), for it
is said (Is 30.15): "By repenting and remaining peaceful you will be saved".
R. Joshua replied to him: How, if the Israelites rise up and refuse to repent,
will they never be redeemed? R. Eliezer said: The Holy One ... will place
over them a king who is as cruel as Haman. Then they will at once repent and
be redeemed. On what is this founded? "There will be a time of distress for
Jacob, yet he shall be saved out of it" ' (Jer 30.7) ...
    The discussion was taken further. It was only when R. Joshua quoted Dan
12.7, in which the question of the three and a half times between the
desecration of the Temple and the end is discussed, that R. Eliezer withdrew,
presumably because a fixed point in time was established here for the end and
because, according to this text, there had to be a certain period of time
between the destruction of the Temple and the coming of the time of
salvation.[257]

Jose the Galilaean, a contemporary of R. Akiba, held the same
view:[258]

'Repentance is very great because it brings about redemption. It is said:
"There will come to Zion a Redeemer, to those in Jacob who turn from
transgression" (Is 59.20). Why (is it said that): "There will come to Zion a
Redeemer"? Because they "in Jacob turn from transgression" '.

This connection in the rabbinic tradition between repentance and the
time of salvation[259] can be fitted without much difficulty into Judas the
Galilaean's message, since recognition and tolerance of the godless
secular power and its ruler who was venerated as a god were very close
to idolatry. Conversion to the true will of God therefore consisted of a
refusal to obey the emperor and that conversion was the precondition
for God's intervention and help and the coming of the messianic time of
salvation. The exegetical argument of R. Eliezer b. Hyrcanus forms the
foundation for the defeat of the eschatological tyrant, an idea that was

---

[256] jTaan 63d,60ff.; translation based on Bill. 1, 162f.; see also Bill. 1, 600 and 4, 992f.;
Moore, *Judaism* 2, 351; Volz, *Esch*, 103; A. Strobel, *Untersuchungen zum eschatologischen
Verzögungsproblem*, Leiden 1961, 23ff.
[257] See Bill. 1, 163; Eliezer may have expected the end when the Temple was
destroyed and have attributed the delay in the end to the impenitence of Israel.
[258] Yom 86b: גדולה תשובה (שמקרבה) את גאולה. According to Bill. 1, 599 (= W.
Bacher, *Aggada der Tannaiten*, 2nd. ed. 1903, 1, 362), Jose the Galilaean and not R.
Jonathan has to be accepted as the author, since the Yalkuth on Is 59.20 (498) ascribes the
words to Jose. See also Moore, *Judaism*, 2, 351.
[259] See the great number of witnesses: Bill. 1, 162-165 and 599f.

made popular in wide circles of Palestinian Judaism by the example of Herod I and Caligula and was certainly also accepted by the Zealots.[260]

According to the rabbinate, a second possible way of influencing the coming of the messianic time was by perfect obedience to God's commandments. There is, for example, the well-known statement made by R. Simeon b. Jochai, a pupil of R. Akiba, that Israel would be redeemed at once if only the people kept two sabbaths in accordance with the commandments.[261] It was also believed that the rule of God could be brought closer by acts of goodness and the study of the Torah.[262] Even the coming of Elijah as the precursor of the Messiah could be made dependent on the keeping of the commandments.[263]

In the same way, although less frequently, the possibility of delaying the coming of the messianic time of salvation was also discussed in the rabbinic tradition:

> It is said in a Baraita:"The proselytes and those who dally with little girls hold the Messiah back (מעכבין את המשיח)".[264]

It was possible for a combination of these different statements to lead to a theological view of history based on the fact that God could have brought about the time of salvation at any previous stage during the history of Israel and that he had been prevented from doing this only because of the attitude of the Israelites themselves as people who were not ready to repent or to obey the law:

> "Rab said: All times are past. Now the matter is confined to repentance and good works".[265] Just as R. Eliezer was contradicted by R. Joshua, so too was Rab contradicted by Mar Shemuel. With his answer: "It is sufficient for the one who suffers to persist in his sorrow" he showed that he did not want to abandon faith in a fixed time at the end.[266]

This would seem to suggest that the point of departure for this view of the speeding up or the slowing down of the coming of the time of salvation that was so fiercely disputed in the later rabbinic tradition

---

[260] See below, p. 303f.

[261] Shab 118b bar; see also Bill. 1, 600 and Moore, *op. cit.*, 2, 350.

[262] See Bill. and Moore, op. cit.: BB 10a bar and Sanh 99b.

[263] See Deut 11.13, 41 Bill. 4, 789 (q) and Moore, *op. cit.*

[264] Nidd 13b above; translation based on Bill. 1, 600. See also A. Strobel, *op. cit.*, 40ff.

[265] Sanh 97b; translation based on Bill. 1, 164. See also Moore, *op. cit.*, and M. Zobel, *Gottes Gesalbter*, 1938, 80.

[266] Sanh 97b; translation based on M. Zobel, *loc. cit.* For the idea that God wanted to bring about the time of salvation at an earlier period, but that Israel failed here, see above, p. 120f. See also the discussion about Hezekiah, whom God wanted to make the Messiah: M. Zobel, *op. cit.*, 89.

should be sought in the argument of Judas the Galilaean and Saddok that salvation would not come purely automatically, but that pious Jews had to play their part in this and were bound to break definitively with the rule of Rome that was so opposed to God. Although this original idea was later rejected, a variant of it was retained in the rabbinic tradition, in which it persisted as far as the later period, at the same time giving rise to several controversies.

4. The Census

Josephus reports in several places that the first tax assessment to be carried out after Judaea had been changed by the new governor of Syria, P. Sulpicius Quirinius (in the Greek form Κυρίνιος = Cyrenius), into an imperial *territorium* provided the initial impulse for the appearance of Judas the Galilaean and the proclamation of his new teaching.[267] Although the Jews seem 'at first to have accepted the news of the assessment of their possessions very reluctantly',[268] the high-priest Joazar b. Boethus was able to calm them down sufficiently for them to abandon their resistance to the census. Only Judas, Saddok and their followers refused to submit to the demand made by their new rulers. They regarded this measure imposed by a pagan oppressor as a question which called for a decision and which could only be answered with a clear 'no'. Judas therefore also attacked with the greatest asperity those of his own compatriots who were ready to obey the Romans.[269] At the same time,

---

[267] See *Ant* 17,355; 18,2ff.; 20,102; *Bell* 7,253. Acts 5.37 and probably also Lk 2.1ff. refer to this census. The answer to the disputed question as to whether a similar census was carried out under Herod is that it was not. Various attempts have been made to establish the historicity of this: L.R. Taylor, *AJP* 54 (1933), 161ff.; T. Corbishley, *Klio* 29 (1936), 81-93; F.X. Steinleitner, *RAC* 2, 970f.; F.M. Heichelheim, in T. Frank, *An Economic Survey of Ancient Rome*, 1933ff., 4, 160; E. Stauffer, *Jesus*, 1960, 27ff. These can at the most only disprove in part the objections raised by Schürer, 1, 405-427, and they also display insurmountable difficulties; see H. Braunert, 'Der römische Provinzialzensus und der Schätzungsbericht des Lukas-Evangeliums', *Hist* 6 (1957), 192-214. A. Schalit, *König Herodes*, Berlin 1969, 273ff., believed that Herod made several attempts at a comprehensive registration. Fundamental in this question is Schürer 1, 399-427, with a negative conclusion.

[268] *Ant* 18,3: κατ' ἀρχὰς ἐν δεινῷ φέροντες τὴν ἐπὶ ταῖς ἀπογραφαῖς ἀκρόασιν. A. Schlatter, *Die Theologie des Judentums*, 223, n. 2, basing his argument on *Ant* 18,170 and 17,94, interprets ἀκρόασις as 'hearing', but this is certainly too special an interpretation of the text. For the meaning of the word in Josephus, see K.H. Rengstorf, *A Complete Concordance*, 1973, 1, 57.

[269] See *Bell* 2,118 and 2,433. See also A. Schalit, *op. cit.*, 269ff.

'he urged (the people) to insurrection, (asserting that) the assessment would lead to nothing other than obvious slavery ...'[270]

Unfortunately, Josephus, following his usual practice, does not give the deeper reasons why the census caused such unrest among the Jewish people, nor does he tell us how it was able to provide Judas with the incentive to proclaim his revolutionary message.

What was apparently involved in the ἀπογραφή or ἀποτίμησις[271] was a provincial census of the kind of which we also have evidence from other parts of the Roman Empire.[272] There were similarly often disturbances elsewhere when such tax assessments were introduced for the first time.[273] Such events were, however, the exception rather than the rule and they were for the most part confined to the semi-barbarian tribes inhabiting the frontier provinces of the empire. Most of the inhabitants of the provinces submitted to these assessments that were repeated at regular intervals without objecting to them.[274] Judaea's resistance to the census — Galilee, which still formed part of the territory ruled by Herod Antipas, was not yet affected by it[275] — therefore calls for special consideration. At least at the level of the simple, ordinary people of

---

[270] *Ant* 18,4: '... τὴν ἀποτίμησιν οὐδὲν ἄλλο ἢ ἄντικρυς δουλείαν ἐπιφέρειν λέγοντες. See also *Bell* 7,253.

[271] Josephus employs the terms ἀπογραφή (*Ant* 18,3; *Bell* 7,253 in the plural) and ἀποτίμησις (*Ant* 18,4.26). For ἀπογραφή, see Lk 2.2 and Acts 5.37. See also A. Deissmann, *Light from the Ancient East*, London, 1927, 270f. and Arndt and Gingrich, *A Greek–English Lexicon of the N.T.*, 1957, 88f. H.U. Instinsky, *Hochl.* 49 (1956/57), 101,105, makes a distinction between the two terms, but this cannot be accepted as valid. They were used for stylistic reasons.

[272] W. Kubitschek, 'Census', *PW* 3. 1914-1929. See also H. Dessau, 1, 159ff.; G.H. Stevenson, *CAH* 10, 192ff.; T. Corbishley, *op. cit.*, 89f.; H. Braunert, *op. cit.*, 193-202. Augustus wanted to bring together the various monetary sources in the empire and achieve some kind of unity in the taxation system. In this, the provincial census formed the 'basis for direct taxation'; H. Braunert, *op cit.*, 200.

[273] Such difficulties occurred above all in Galilee; see H. Dessau, 1, 157f.; H. Braunert, *op. cit.*, 198. In Dalmatia (Dio Cassius 54,34.36), Lusitania (*CIL* 10, 608), in Germania under Varus (Dio Cassius 56,18.13) there were also difficulties. In Asia Minor under Tiberius, the mountain tribe, Cietae, rose against the authorities when they attempted to carry out a census in the Roman manner (Tacitus, *Ann* 6,41); see H. Braunert, *op. cit.*, 199.

[274] H. Braunert, *op. cit.*, says 'that, according to our literary traditions, the first census in a province always caused the people concerned to revolt'. Nonetheless, it was taken for granted that it was much more common for a census to be carried out without resistance on the part of the people, with the result that historians did not think that it was even worth mentioning. In addition to this, the Jews had been living for more than two generations within the Roman sphere of power and had been heavily taxed by Herod.

[275] See J. Wellhausen, *Israelitische und jüdische Geschichte*, 5th. ed. 1904, 225f. and Schürer, 1, 414.

Judaea who were close to Zealotism, that resistance was long-lasting and persistent.[276] This would certainly seem to suggest that we should look for the causes in the sphere of religion.[277]

(a) The Population Count

Because it was carried out in a territory that had only recently been made accessible to the imperial treasury, the tax assessment took place on the basis of an all-embracing enrolment of persons and their possessions.[278] Resistance was inevitable on the part of the Jewish population even at this point of departure, since an enumeration of this or any kind of the inhabitants was contrary to God's will. Moses had counted the people — with the exception of the tribe of Levi — after the exodus from Egypt, but he had acted on the explicit command of God (Num 1.2ff.). Yet even this census, which had been taken in accordance with God's will, had a sinister aspect. Everyone who had been counted had to redeem himself with half a shekel, so that he would not be killed by a 'plague' sent by God.[279]

As a punishment for the census which David, acting on his own authority, had instituted, God sent a plague down on the people, killing seventy thousand of them (2 Sam 24). The prophetic promise:

'The number of the people of Israel shall be like the sand of the sea, which can neither be measured nor numbered'[280]

must also have made it difficult for pious Jews to agree to take part in the census ordered by the emperor. The numbering of Israel must have

---

[276] This is shown by the increasing influence of the Jewish freedom movement until the outbreak of the Jewish War and the constant emphasis on taxation as the criterion for loyalty to the emperor; see below, p. 138f.

[277] L. Goldschmid, 'Les impôts et droits de Douane en Judée sous less Romains', *REJ* 34 (1897), 209: 'It was undoubtedly religious reasons which predominated among the people and which caused their apathy towards the census'.

[278] For the carrying out of the census, see Schürer, 1, 401ff. and the books and articles cited above, p. 127, n. 267. A graphic — and undoubtedly exaggerated — account of the carrying out of a tax assessment during the period of Diocletian is provided by Lactantius, *MortPersec* 23,1ff. ANCL 22, 184. Lk 2.1-5 may also be taken as a historically faithful portrayal of the carrying out of a census; see H. Braunert, *op. cit.*, 205ff.

[279] Ex 30.12ff. The whole amount of this ransom was used for the building of the sanctuary; see Ex 38.25ff. The half shekel tax for the Temple resulted later from this; see Schürer, 2, 270ff.

[280] Hos 2.1; cf. Gen 15.5; 22.17; 32.12; for this, see Klausner, *Hist* 4, 200. This text is related in NumRab on 20.25 to the end-time and is thereby connected with the idea that the people of Israel were always numbered after they were punished by God. This would not be applicable to the end-time. See also NumRab on 21.7.

seemed to them to be a task that God had reserved for himself —
especially for the end-time.[281]

The sensitivity of the Jews towards a population count can be
discerned from the extreme caution with which one was carried out
shortly before the outbreak of the Jewish War at the request of the
governor of Syria, Cestius Gallus. The number of inhabitants, that is, the
number of Jews present during the Passover feast in Jerusalem — was
obtained not by means of a direct count, but indirectly by counting the
number of paschal lambs.[282]

According to the legendary Third Book of the Maccabees, which
appeared in Alexandria during the first half of the first century A.D., it is
clear that the Jews deeply mistrusted a state registration:

> After that, Ptolemy IV Philopator, who had been forbidden access to the
> Holy of Holies by God's intervention, gave the command: 'All Jews shall be
> subject to a registration (λαογραφία)[283] and to the status of slaves (διάθεσις
> οἰκετική). Those who object to this are to be taken by force and put to death
> and those who are registered (ἀπογραφομένους) are to be branded on their
> bodies by fire with the ivy-leaf symbol of Dionysus and they shall be reduced
> to their former limited status'.[284]
>
> But the majority (of Jews) acted firmly with a courageous spirit and did
> not depart from their religion and 'by paying money in exchange for life
> they attempted to save themselves from the registration (ἐπειρῶντο ἑαυτοὺς
> ῥύσασθαι ἐκ τῶν ἀπογραφῶν)'.[285]

This story shows clearly that the λαογραφία was regarded by Jews
living in Egypt during the early imperial period as a means of depriving

---

[281] ApcAbr 29,17; SyrBar 75,6; see also the counting of the sealed, Rev 7.4 and the
countless number of the redeemed, Rev 7.9. In Judaea, where the people were filled with
tense messianic expectations, such a drastic measure was bound to give rise to
simultaneous eschatological parallels.

[282] Bell 6,422ff., cf. Pes 64b, in which this count is traced back to Agrippa II and not, as
S. Baron, A Social and Religious History of the Jews, 1937, 3, 34, n. 5, would have it, to
Agrippa I. Apparently as many as 255 600 Passover lambs were counted at the time,
which means that there were, if ten is taken as the smallest number of people at each table
fellowship, about 2 700 000 people altogether. This figure, however, bears no
relationship to the historical reality; see J. Jeremias, Jerusalem, 77ff., 84. H. Graetz, 3,
815ff., believed that the Passover, attended by so many people, was a demonstration of
political power; see below, p. 356, n. 221.

[283] λαογραφία is a specifically Egyptian concept; there is evidence of it on the papyri of
the early imperial period; see Liddell-Scott, 1029b; see also Schürer, 3, 538 and V.
Tcherikover, 'The Third Book of Maccabees as a Historical Source of Augustus' Time',
ScrHier 7 (1961), 1-26 and CPJ 1, 60ff.: 'A mark of inferiority imposed on the native
population in Egypt by the Roman authorities'. Of fundamental importance here is
ibid., 'Syntaxis and Laographia', JJP 4 (1950), 179-307.

[284] 3 Macc 2.28-30.

[285] 2.32.

them of their rights and reducing them to slavery[286] or of making them worship idols. In this context, we are confronted with the inevitable question as to whether this kind of suspicion was not bound to arise all the more in Palestine where, as distinct from Egypt, such population counts were new and unfamiliar. Whatever answer may be given to this question, the fact remains that this legendary story can certainly be regarded as illustrating in a particularly valuable way the ideas that were associated in the minds of Jews in the first century A.D. with the concept of ἀπογραφή.

(b) The Registration of Landed Property

In addition to this population count, all the property owned by Jews, including above all landed property as the main source of income in Judaea, which was predominantly rural,[287] had also to be enrolled.[288] It may have been possible to refer back to previous registers in this case, since many details about the tax derived from individual parts of the country must have been already available under Herod.[289] The registration of landed property was carried out by means of a personal declaration of the property made by the owner himself on the site, after which the tax authorities had to verify the details.[290]

Quite apart from the complications and difficulties involved in carrying out this task, this registration of landed property must also have been very difficult for the Jewish population of Palestine to endure because of the political background. According to the Roman conception of land law from the beginning of the imperial period onwards, the land belonging to the conquered people was regarded as

---

[286] See above, p. 76; see also *Ant* 18,4.

[287] Arist 107,112f.; for Galilee, see *Bell* 3,42; see also Juster, 2, 305; S. Baron. *op cit.*, 1, 192ff., and Klausner, *J of N*, 174f. Other books and articles on the subject are cited there.

[288] In *Ant* 5,76-79, Josephus speaks of the survey undertaken by Joshua, in which the value of various classes of estate and land is assessed. There is presumably a connection between this and contemporary events; see E. Stauffer, *op cit.*, 167, n. 23. According to Hegesippus (Eusebius, *HistEcc* 3,20.2), the descendants of Judas the brother of the Lord possessed thirty-nine acres of land, which had a taxable value of 9000 *denarii*. Domitian had these data verified. The whole process presupposes that there was a cadastre or land registration for tax purposes for Palestine. The Roman *agrimensura* is also mentioned in the Talmud: S. Krauss, *MonTal* VI, No. 371 = EstherRab, Introduction, 5. For the general survey of land in the empire under Augustus, see Schürer, 1, 409; see also H. Braunert, *op. cit.*, 204. The latter can, however, hardly be connected with the census.

[289] Archelaus had, however, to provide the emperor with precise data about these: *Bell* 2,24 = *Ant* 17,228; see also W. Otto, *Herodes*, 1913, 97.

[290] For the duty to report on the site, see H. Braunert, *op. cit.*, 195,201f.,; see also Ulpianus, *Dig* 50,15,4.2; Schürer, 1, 403f.; A. Schalit, *König Herodes*, 280ff.

ager publicus and became the property of the Roman people. It was this conception that formed the legal foundation for the provincial taxes.[291] In the case of Judaea, we may also assume that Augustus 'regarded himself as the successor to the deposed sovereign, just as he . . . had put himself in the place of the kings in Egypt'.[292] Even if the distinction between the imperial administration of property (*fiscus Caesaris*) and that of the state (*aerarium Saturni*) did not — contrary to what Schürer has suggested[293] — apply at that time, the registration of landed property certainly gives the impression of a kind of confiscation for inclusion within the imperial property. It was 'as though the head, the land and the wealth belonging to each individual was the property of the Roman ruler and as though the latter could have it as he wished at his disposal. Those who did not understand the constitution and structure of the Roman state can hardly be blamed for regarding the census as a form of slavery'.[294]

These fears were strengthened by the traditional Jewish conviction that the land of Palestine was a sacred inheritance given to Israel by God. The land was and would continue to be God's property and it had only been apportioned to Israel, with the result that no individual had the power to dispose of it as he wished:

> 'The land shall not be sold in perpetuity, for the land is mine; for you are strangers and sojourners with me'.[295]

---

[291] See M.S. Ginsburg, *Rome et la Judée*, Paris, 1928, 128f., who cites a great number of Roman legal sources, among others Gaius (second century A.D.), *Inst* 2,7: 'in eo (sc. provinciali) solo dominium populi Romani est vel Caesaris; nos autem possessionem tantum et usum fructum habere videmur'. See also Mommsen, *RG* 2, 381. T. Frank, *JRS* 17 (1927), 141ff., has pointed out that the claim was not definitively established in the legal sense until the reign of Claudius, although the foundations had been laid much earlier (161). The *opinio* may therefore have already been known in Jewish circles at the beginning of the imperial period.

[292] This is the opinion of H. Dessau, II,2, 778. Archelaus' enormous landed property passed to the emperor's private estate, but a large part of it was sold; see *Ant* 18,2.26. A certain parallel is to be found in the predominantly Jewish cities of Jamnia and Azotus, which had originally belonged to Salome, but which passed after her death to Livia and later to Tiberius. The little territory was governed during the reign of Caligula by one of his own procurators, Herennius Capito; see *Ant* 18,158 and Philo, *LegGai* 199 (M 2, 575). For the emperor's private estate in Palestine, see F.M. Heichelheim in T. Frank, *An Economic Survey of Ancient Rome*, 4, 145, n. 19.

[293] Schürer, 1, 372. For the imperial treasury or *fiscus*, see G.W. Stevenson, *CAH* 10, 194, and the *Oxford Classical Dictionary*. 363.

[294] H.Graetz, 5th ed., 3, 254f. See also L. Goldschmid, *REJ* 34 (1897), 209.

[295] Lev 25.23, in connection with the sabbath year; for this, see also G. von Rad, *Theology of the Old Testament*, 1962, 1, 300, who believed that this statement was 'the theological foundation of the whole land law of ancient Israel'.

The Old Testament accordingly spoke of the land of Canaan not simply as a Israel's inheritance, but as the heritage (נַחֲלָה) and the property or possession (אֲחֻזָּה) of God.[296] Measuring the land — which took place every time after the sabbath year — was almost regarded as a sacral act.[297]

When Jews who were faithful to the Mosaic law and were familiar with this view of the land as God's holy land were suddenly confronted with the registration of that land by the emperor's official representatives — a registration which seemed to them to be almost a taking possession of that land — they were bound to have been to some extent convinced by the message of Judas the Galilaean. Their own fears and longings were, after all, openly proclaimed in that message, namely that the census would lead to obvious slavery, that it was contrary to God's will and that he should be acknowledged as the only Lord of the land and the people. Because of the imperial levy of a tax on landed property, what had been seriously called into question was whether the right to dispose of that property and therefore the keeping of certain legal prescriptions such as the law of the sabbath year[298] and the payment of certain prescribed taxes would not be restricted. The Zealots' later serious concern to set up a land dispensation, valid according to the *law*, is clear from the fact that one of their first acts at the beginning of the revolt was to destroy the archive, presumably because the distribution of the land at that time bore no relationship to the ideal dispensation which was prescribed in Lev 25 and Deut 15 and which was at the same time also in accordance with their own social aims.[299] The original situation which had been given by God would be restored in the time of salvation to which they looked forward. The same concern for the preservation of Israel's inheritance in the Holy Land is also to be found in the rabbinate, although in a very different and much more realistic form.[300]

What can be said with some certainty is that the tax assessment meant

---

[296] For the heritage of God, see 1 Sam 26.19; 2 Sam 14.16; Jer 2.7; 16.18; Ps 68.10; 79.1; for the property of God, see Jos 22.19; also 22.25.

[297] G. von Rad, *loc. cit.*; see also Mic 2.5 and Ps 16.5f.

[298] The sabbath year was also kept during the Hellenistic Roman period; see *Ant* 14,202 and 475; see also Schürer, 1, 19; *B.-Gr. Rel.* 3rd. ed., 131f. and J. Jeremias, 'Sabbatjahr', *ZNW* 27 (1928), 98ff.

[299] *Bell* 2,327; Josephus explains the process on the basis of social reasons. These certainly played a part, but they could not have been the only reasons. Even in the Old Testament, the dispensation governing the land and social reasons were very closely connected; see Lev 25.17f.25ff.35ff.; Deut 15 and Is 5.8ff.; Mic 2.1-5.

[300] tAZ 4,6 (Z. 466) and BB 91b (see H. Graetz, 5th. ed., 3, 716ff.); for the prohibition against emigration and the sale of land to pagans, see AZ 1,8, Bill. 4, 357.

a deep encroachment on the lives and religious ideas of Palestinian Jews. Quite apart from the conflict that it caused with the Old Testament tradition, it seems especially to have given rise, above all among the rural population, to a feeling of deep insecurity.

(c) The Payment of Taxes to the Emperor

It was not primarily the payment of taxes in itself that gave most offence to the population, since the Jews had a long tradition of paying taxes and duties that had continued without interruption for centuries. They had paid them in fact since their return from exile, first to the Persians, then to the Ptolemies[301] and finally to the Seleucids, under whom they must have paid very considerable amounts.[302] After the conquest of Jerusalem, the Romans continued with the existing tax system as they had done elsewhere, for example, in Syria.[303] We hear of a new tax assessment under Caesar, who reduced the taxes paid to a level that was essentially lower than it had been under the Seleucids.[304] Additional burdens were once again imposed during the period of the civil wars.[305]

From the Hellenistic period onwards, it was customary for taxes to be collected by tax-farmers.[306] Herod, whose unbridled profligacy squeezed the people dry, probably assumed personal control over the levying of taxes.[307] When Judaea was changed into an imperial territory, the Jewish population could look back at a long history of oppressive taxation with payments which had, taken as a whole, been at least as

---

[301] See *Ant* 12,155.169ff.175ff. The reception of taxes was made possible by farming out. See M. Rostovtzeff, *Social and Economic History of the Hellenistic World*, 1941, 1, chap. 4, passim; M. Hengel, *Judaism and Hellenism*, 28f.

[302] See 1 Macc 10.29ff. For this, see also M. Rostovtzeff, *op. cit.*, 1, 349ff.

[303] *Bell* 1,154 = *Ant* 14,74; 1QpHab 6,6f/ It is probable that a fixed amount had to be paid to Rome; see M. Rostovtzeff, *op. cit.*, 2, 1000. Gabinius divided the Jewish territory into five toparchies, presumably with the aim of a better payment of taxes. The taxes were probably farmed out to the Roman tax-farmers in Syria; see *Bell* 1,170 = *Ant* 14,91; see also M. Rostovtzeff, *loc. cit.*, Schürer, 1, 268f, and H. Dessau, 1, 153. See also Cicero, *Flacc* 69 (28) for the subjection of the *gens Judaeorum*: 'quod est victa, quod elocata, quod serva facta'.

[304] *Ant* 14,202f.; the amount of land tax payable was calculated at one quarter of the harvest produced each year. The sabbath years were tax-free.

[305] See, among other texts, *Bell* 1,179 = *Ant* 14,105, Crassus; *Bell* 1,220ff. = *Ant* 14,274ff., Cassius; *Bell* 2,85ff. = *Ant* 17,306ff., Herod.

[306] M. Rostovtzeff, *loc. cit.*, believes that a change had already taken place under Caesar; see, on the other hand, S. Baron, *A Social and Religious History of the Jews*, 1937, 1, 204, and H. Dessau, *op. cit.*.

[307] *Ant* 17,308; for Herod's system of taxation, see W. Otto, *Herodes*, 1913, 96; A. Schalit, *König Herodes*, 256-298.

great a burden on the people as those imposed by the new system operating under the rule of the emperor, especially since Augustus had to a great extent withdrawn the task of collecting taxes from the tax-farmers and had handed it over to the recently appointed state financial authorities.[308]

Two direct taxes were levied. The principal one was the land tax (*tributum soli*), which was a levy on the produce of the soil and was, for the most part, paid in natural products.[309] The second was an income tax which was imposed on incomes which were not based on the possession of land (*tributum capitis*) and which was paid in money. Those between the ages of approximately fourteen and sixty were liable to pay this tax.[310] In addition to these and other relatively small and to some extent merely local direct taxes — there was, for example, a tax on buildings in Jerusalem[311] — there were also indirect levies, including especially the custom duties. Because these were collected by tax-farmers, they were correspondingly higher.[312]

Some light is thrown on the question as to how these taxes were regarded by the people by a Haggadic description in Josephus' *Antiquities*. According to Josephus, David is believed to have imposed troops on the subjugated Edomites to occupy their land and to have

---

[308] G.H. Stevenson, *CAH* 10, 191ff.; H. Dessau, 1, 154ff.; J. Jeremias, *Jerusalem*, 125, believes that, under Herod, the tax payable by Judaea came to six hundred talents.

[309] See G.H. Stevenson, *CAH* 10, 196: 'The main tax in every province . . . paid by the occupiers of the land'; see also Schürer, 1, 401f. For the duty on natural produce, see *Ant* 14, 208f.: the delivery of land tax in the form of corn to Sidon (for shipping to Italy). In *Vita* 71ff., there is a reference to the 'imperial corn' that was stored in Upper Galilee; see also the provision of corn for Rome by North Africa: *Bell* 2,382ff.386. For this whole question, see M.S. Ginsburg, *op. cit.*, 128.

[310] See G.H. Stevenson, *loc. cit.*; Schürer, 1, 403; M.S. Ginsburg, *op. cit.*, 129f. and H. Braunert, *op. cit.*, 206f. According to Ulpianus, *Dig* 50,15.3, even women were liable to pay tax from the age of twelve onwards in Syria.

[311] *Ant* 19,299; see also *Bell* 2,383, in which it is said of the population of North Africa that they had to pay tax in many different ways and not only by giving corn; see also L. Goldschmid, *op. cit.*, 203ff., for the levies which passed into Hebrew and Aramaic as loan-words.

[312] For these customs duties, see Schürer, 1, 373-6; L. Goldschmid, *op. cit.*, 199ff.; Bill. 1, 377f. In *Ant* 17,205, there is reference to a customs duty introduced by Herod for trading groups. According to Schürer, 1, 374, n. 100, and L. Goldschmid, *op. cit.*, 201, n. 1, this customs duty is identical with the market duty mentioned in *Ant* 18,90 that was abolished by Vitellius. According to W. Otto, *op. cit.*, 96, n. 2, this was, however, a special tax on all purchases and sales. For the extent of these customs duties, see H. Dessau 1, 164, who thinks that it was about two and a half per cent of the value of the goods. Jewish customs duty collectors in the service of Rome are mentioned in Josephus (*Bell* 2,287) and in the New Testament (Lk 19.2). The tax-collectors in Capernaum were subject to Herod Antipas; see A. Schalit, *König Herodes*, 296ff.

levied a land and head tax on them.[313] Occupation by foreign troops and
the payment of tax were, then, the signs of servitude. The most hated tax
was probably the personal and income tax imposed on the individual. It
is significant that the Greek equivalent (κῆνσος) entered the Hebrew or
Aramaic language as a loan-word with the meaning of 'fine'.[314] When
Jesus was asked: 'Is it lawful to pay taxes to Caesar or not?', this question
referred specifically to this type of tax.[315] It was probably paid with such
great reluctance because it made every adult Jew who worked for
earnings conscious in a very drastic way of the fact that he was not a free
man, but a subject of the Roman emperor.[316]

The displeasure of the population may also have been increased by the
rigorous method of collecting these taxes coupled with a discreditable
network of informers. There is a very revealing account in Philo,the
truthfulness of which is also confirmed in other contemporary
sources.[317]

There are also several examples in the later rabbinic tradition. What is
of particular interest in this context, however, is that — quite apart from
the very widespread complaint that Rome was the 'robber city'[318] — the
right of the 'godless world power' to levy taxes was not rejected, but was
quite often regarded as the instrument of God's punishment of Israel.[319]

---

[313] *Ant* 7,109, where Josephus interprets the וַיְהִי כָל אֱדוֹם עֲבָדִים of 2 Sam 8.14 as
King David's distributing occupation troops thoughout the whole of Idumaea and
levying a land and head tax; see A. Schlatter, *Der Evangelist Matthäus*, 3rd. ed. 1948, 646;
see the land and head tax in Tertullian, *Apol* 13: 'hae sunt notae captivitatis' and Philo,
SpecLeg 1,143. Typical is the discussion in *CPJ* 2, 78 No. 156, col. II, 25ff.: the Jews are
not given the same status as the citizens of Alexandria, but as the Egyptians, who pay tax.
Agrippa I, on the other hand: no one has ever imposed a tax on the Jews. According to
Cicero, *Verr* II, 2,7, the provinces were 'praedia populi Romani' and 3,12, the tax was
'victoriae praemium ac poena belli'.

[314] The term was itself taken over from the Latin *census*. For the Hebrew and Aramaic
equivalent, see J. Klausner, *J of N*, 162; L. Goldschmid, *op. cit.*, 208, and Jastrow,
Dictionary, 2, 1393f. The concept also had a verbal form with the meaning of 'to punish'.

[315] Mk 12.14 parr.; the reading of the Western text interprets ἐπικεφάλαιον.

[316] This was the opinion of A. Schlatter, *Der Evangelist Matthäus*, 3rd. (reprinted) ed.
1948, 648.

[317] *SpecLeg* 3,153-163 (M 2, 325f.): A tax official enforces the payment of the poll tax
on subjects who had run away, because they could no longer pay the tax and he does this
by torturing and killing their neighbours and relatives. The result of this practice is the
devastation of whole districts. See M. Rostovtzeff, *Social and Economic History of the
Roman Empire*, 1926, 300ff. See also Ammianus Marcellinus 22,16.23.

[318] See above, p. 37f., and the examples given there, especially S. Krauss, *MonTal* V,
Nos. 76,165,335; see also SifDeut 32,13, ed. Friedmann, 317 and Bill. 1, 770f., where a
preponderance of traditions from a later period will, however, be found.

[319] MekEx on 19.1 (L. 2, 194), R. Johanan b. Zakkai declared after the destruction of
Jerusalem: 'You did not want to be subject to the control of heaven, so you have become

On the other hand, however, certain very real elements can be found in some of the rabbinic parables. To give only two examples: that of an imperial tax-collector whose task was to collect outstanding debts being pursued or killed by people in the provinces[320] and that of a tax official being attacked by robbers[321]

The resistance on the part of the Jewish people to the payment of taxes was, unlike their rejection of the census, not a single and unrepeated event, which was eventually settled by the intervention of the high-priestly authority, but rather a matter of long duration which remained latent, but increased rather than decreased with the passage of time. Josephus, who had reported the complaints of the Jews about the pressure of taxation under Herod in considerable detail, is understandably silent about this point. There is, however, a brief account in Tacitus, according to whom the Jews pleaded in 17 A.D. for a reduction in the amount of taxes that they had to pay.[322] The New Testament pericope on the tribute money paid to the emperor also shows how deeply the antipathy towards the imperial praxis of levying taxes was rooted in the minds of the people. In his great peace speech, Agrippa II accordingly reproaches the Jews, comparing them with the people of north Africa, who have voluntarily paid enormous sums in taxes,[323]

> 'unlike you, regarding not even a portion of the taxes imposed on them as an unbearable demand!'

This criticism was quite justified, since taxes had been paid only very irregularly — in the open country at least — for some time before the outbreak of the war. The attempt made by Gessius Florus to cover the deficit by taking from the Temple treasury led to the first revolt in Jerusalem.[324] The peace speech by Agrippa II was a final attempt to persuade the Jews to pay their outstanding tax debts[325] and this failed, with the result that the revolt continued. A note in the Scroll of Fasting may possibly point to the fact that the Zealots believed that they had

---

subject to the control of the people (that is, Rome); you did not want to pay one bekah per head to heaven, so you had to pay fifteen shekels to the empire of your enemies . . .'; see also Ket 66b.

[320] See S. Krauss, MonTal V, No. 375; see also Bill. 1, 857.

[321] MonTal V, No. 387.

[322] Tacitus, Ann 2,42: 'Per idem tempus . . . et provinciae Syria atque Iudaea, fessae oneribus deminutionem tributi orabant'.

[323] Bell 2,383.

[324] Bell 2,293; see also below, p. 208.

[325] Bell 2,404ff.

attained the goal towards which Judas the Galilaean was striving:[326]

'On the twenty-fifth day of the month of Siwan the tax-farmers (דִּימוֹסְנָאֵי from δημοσιῶναι) were removed from Judaea and Jerusalem'.

(d) Judas the Galilaean and the Religious Motivation for the Jews' Resistance to the Census and the Payment of Taxes

It is clear from a comment made by Josephus that Judas knew how to make use of the deep antipathy on the part of those Jews who were faithful to the law to the carrying out of the imperial census, which must have seemed to them to be a sacrilege against God's commandments and his Holy Land:

'He persuaded . . ., when Quirinius was sent to Judaea with the task of imposing taxes, a fair number of Jews not to take part in the tax assessment'.[327]

Despite this, the majority of Jews yielded — however reluctantly — to the pressure of the power of Rome. The vote of the High-Priest Joazar seems to have been the decisive factor that tipped the balance in favour of the census, although he did not win the sympathy of either side. Quirinius, for whom he had previously performed a service of such inestimable value, readily handed him over to the disfavour of the people and deposed him.[328]

This action shows clearly how the fronts were firmly established at the very beginning of the Roman rule in Judaea. On the one hand, there were the well-to-do circles of Jews, especially in Jerusalem, who were led by the priestly nobility, while, on the other, there were the radical groups with Judas the Galilaean as their spiritual leader and focal point. In between these two fronts stood the people, who were secretly sympathetic towards the radical party. This was especially so in the case of the rural population, which had suffered much more from the pressure of foreign rule. But reason and a desire for peace were stronger than 'zeal' for God's cause and hatred of the godless foreign rule.

---

[326] MegTaan 9; cf. Sanh 91a; see also H. Lichtenstein, 'Die Fastenrolle', *HUCA* VIII/IX (1931/32), 302ff. The Babylonian Talmud has 24 Nisan instead of 25 Siwan, but the reading in the Megillath Taanith is to be preferred. According to *Bell* 2,403 and 405, the Jews began to pay taxes a short time after the withdrawal of Florus from Jerusalem (*Bell* 2,315: 17/18 Artemisius = *Iyyar*). According to the Scroll of Fasting, this payment of taxes took place ultimately about a month later. See also H. Graetz, 3rd. ed., 3, 573. According to *Bell* 5,405f., the refusal to pay taxes proved to be the main reason for the war.

[327] *Bell* 7,253; cf. *Ant* 18,9.

[328] *Ant* 18,26; the contradiction with 17,339 is based on the difference between the sources.

The motives underlying this conflict were fundamentally religious. The collision with the Old Testament tradition emerged clearly enough in the case of the enrolment of persons and their property. The people's refusal to pay the taxes imposed by the emperor could not, however, be simply traced back to the law. It was only when the first commandment was interpreted in the way in which Judas the Galilaean interpreted it and God was uncompromisingly recognized as the only Lord of Israel that tribute paid to a foreign ruler could be seen as worshipping an idol. This was especially so when that ruler had himself venerated as God. Anyone paying taxes to the emperor ceased to be a true Israelite and could only be regarded as 'a gentile and a tax-collector'.[329]

This formula in the Gospel of Matthew, which can be traced back to a phrase that was customary at the time, can — like the severe judgement of tax-collectors as such, who, as underlings and servants of the godless foreign rule, were simply equated with sinners[330] — be regarded as a norm for the Zealot ideas and arguments that were widely known among the people. Josephus also confirms for us that the *Sicarii*, i.e. followers of Judas, equated appeasers and those willing to pay their taxes with gentiles.[331]

Judas' opposition to the census can probably also be seen in the eschatological perspective. The foreign rule and the consequent suffering of the subjugated people formed the beginning of the 'messianic sorrows' and the census itself pointed to the eschatological testing and separation of Israel. Only those who refused to obey the emperor could be regarded as really belonging to the people of God.

---

[329] Mt 18.17. This equation of the 'pagan' or 'gentile' with the 'tax-collector', with the placing of the 'pagan' first, suggests that this way of speaking was subject to a Zealot influence; cf. the parallelism between τελῶναι and ἐθνικοί in Mt 5.46f.

[330] The concept τελώνης is not simply confined to the 'tax-collector' in the strict sense of the term, but can also be applied to the tax-official in general; see M. Rostovtzeff, *Social and Economic History of the Hellenistic World*, 1941, 1, 328 and 3, 1402, n. 146, with its bibliography. For the rabbinic testimonies, see Bill. 1, 378ff.: The 'tax-collector' was generally equated with the robber; See BK 10, 1f.; Ned 3,4: 'One may vow to robbers, murderers and tax-collectors that something is heave-offering even if it is not or that something belongs to the king's house even if it does not belong to it . . .'; this Mishnah was already being discussed by the schools of Shammai and Hillel. At a later period, that is, from the second century onwards, a restriction was imposed on the permission granted for fraud in the payment of tax; see the discussion in the Gemara on Ned 28a and BK 113a.

[331] *Bell* 7,254f. For the religious motivation underlying the refusal to pay taxes, see E. Stauffer, *Christ and the Caesars*, 1955, 117: '. . . the theological protest of the people of God against the pagan people of the empire and the supreme imperial leader'.

The Galilaean's message also contained a number of prophetic elements.[332] Just as Elijah's zeal had resulted in a remnant of 'seven thousand in Israel, all the knees that have not bowed to Baal',[333] so too had a similarly 'holy remnant' of eschatological Israel gathered around Judas. The members of this new sect founded by Judas, then, had an understanding of themselves as the 'true community of God' which they shared with other late Jewish groups.[334]

Finally, in his struggle against the tax assessment, Judas was also able to appeal to the prophetic promise contained in the Old Testament. God had promised his people that they would cease to pay all tributes to foreign nations:

> 'Yahweh has sworn by his right hand and by his mighty arm: "I will not again give your grain to be food for your enemies and foreigners shall not drink your wine for which you have laboured. But those who garner it shall eat it and praise Yahweh and those who gather it shall drink it in the courts of my Sanctuary" '.[335]

As we have already seen, the realization of God's promise was, according to Judas' teaching, dependent on the co-operation of Israel. For this reason, Israel had to resist the imperial tax assessment and refuse to pay the taxes imposed by the emperor. This was the first precondition for God's fulfilment of his vow.

D. SUMMARY: THE RELIGIOUS CHARACTER OF THE MOVEMENT FOUNDED BY JUDAS

Josephus is very fragmentary in his presentation of the views held by the movement founded by Judas the Galilaean. Nonetheless, it is possible — especially if the comparable material found in the rabbinic sources is also taken into account — to give greater emphasis to the ideas of this new sect, which were, in any case, deeply rooted in Jewish faith. What

---

[332] See above, p. 90f., 104.

[333] 1 Kings 19.10,14,18; for Elijah as a model for the Zealot, see below, p. 162ff.

[334] It is quite clear that the Essenes had this exclusive attitude; see, for example, 1QH 6,8: the idea of the remnant; CD 4,3f. and 1QS 11,16: the elect of the end-time. Among the Pharisees, this eschatological aspect was possibly not quite so prominent. The strict separation of the Haberim of the 'am ha-'aretz, on the other hand, points to an obviously exclusive understanding of themselves. For early Christianity, see Rom 2.28f.; 11.3ff.; Gal 4.28; Phil 3.3. Lk 2.34; Mt 21.42; 1 Pet 2.8 and Rev 2.9 also belong to this context.

[335] Is 62.8f.; see also Is 65.22. These promises point to the removal of the curse pronounced in Deut 28.16-69 (see especially vv. 33 and 49-51).

becomes quite clear in this process is the extent to which the motives underlying the actions of this new group are rooted in the sphere of religion. It is unfortunate that this essential fact has been given too little consideration in many of the presentations of Judas and the Zealot movement.

1. Judas' Sect Considered as a Nationalist Movement

On the basis of their anti-Roman activity and their — in the sense in which Josephus interprets it — profane will to freedom, Judas and his successors have been judged by many scholars as a primarily political movement. Let me give two examples:

> 'The fighters who had recently arisen were not so much zealous for faith as fanatical for political freedom. The religious and the political elements were fused together in them, leading to a passionate urge to liberate the fatherland. The Zealots' love of their fatherland was totally active . . .'[336]

> 'They were driven by a passionate enthusiasm for the political liberation of their country. They were men of action, a band of ardent patriots with thousands of members . . ., agitators for the fight for national freedom, the national kingdom and the national Messiah . . . Wherever there was a strong political will on the part of the people as a whole or even only on the part of a section of the people, every sphere of life was affected and even transformed by it. The religious life of the people could not be untouched by it and remain in a state of undisturbed peace. Everyone had to take up a position with regard to it. That is something that we have witnessed in the present time (!). The situation was no different in Judaism too at the time of Jesus — all the different tendencies were bound to come to terms with the Jewish freedom movement'.[337]

I may have chosen examples of two very extreme positions, but they at least show clearly how easy it was to give way to the temptation to misinterpret the real state of affairs by too hastily applying modern ideas to the first century A.D. The concept 'national', which we use so commonly today together with its various derivations, has frequently been employed to describe the aims of such men as Judas and the movement that he initiated. This has been done despite the fact that the concept has strong overtones of contemporary ideas. It is only in the modern era that the concept 'national' has come fundamentally to presuppose the 'nation' as an independent profane value. This linguistic

---

[336] S. Dubnow, *Weltgeschichte des jüdischen Volkes*, translated by A. Steinberg, 1925ff., 376.

[337] H. Preisker, *Neutestamentliche Zeitgeschichte*, 1937, 227.

usage is found in many leading presentations of late Jewish history and religion:

> 'He (Judas) made Galilee . . . the centre of those who "were zealous for their people", that is, of nationally and idealistically minded revolutionaries'.[338]
>
> 'Opposition to the census led to an important event: the extreme nationalists . . . joined the new party of the Qannaim or Zealots'[339]
>
> 'Their only crime was to follow the prompting of their hearts and be ready to sacrifice their lives for the liberation of the nation . . .'[340]
>
> 'The fire of national enthusiasm continued to smoulder beneath the ashes. And when Herod the Great died . . . it flared up again. The party of the so-called Zealots came into being among the people . . . They were nothing but national fanatics in whom politics and religion were a single reality'.[341]
>
> '. . . they were fierce nationalists who confused the interests of God with those of the Nation'.
>
> '. . . anarchists . . ., who were untamed in their . . . aspirations for national freedom'.[342]
>
> 'The Zealots — fanatical nationalists — had destroyed one another, and the remnants had been exterminated by the Romans'.[343]

I have provided enough examples to show that it has commonly been presupposed that there was a merging of religious and political or national interests in the minds of Judas' followers, the national aspect predominating. But this is a false picture of the Zealots. As in the case of other late Jewish groups such as the Essenes and the Pharisees, there was for Judas and his followers no independent sphere of life which was removed from faith. For them, politics and the nation, for example, did not exist independently of religion. On the contrary, all spheres of life - everyday existence, the law, religion and so on - were regulated by God's will — that is, the law - and the political sphere could not be excluded from this. As I have tried to make clear above, Judas based his attitude both in his teaching and in his corresponding political decisions on certain passages in Scripture,[344] which he interpreted in his own way. If there were, in life in the concrete, certain contradictions in the demands made by the Old Testament,[345] then it was necessary either to

---

[338] Klausner, *J of N*, 1952, 156.

[339] *op. cit.*, 162.

[340] *op. cit.*, 204.

[341] *B.-Gr. Rel.* 87; on the following page (88), the Zealots are called 'chauvinists'.

[342] M.-J. Lagrange, *Le Judaïsme avant Jésus-Christ*, 3rd. ed. 1931, 214.

[343] G.F. Moore, *Judaism*, 3, 22.

[344] The name σοφιστής shows that he was a scribe; see below, p. 333f.; see also pp. 227 and 237f.

[345] See G.F. Moore, *op. cit.*, 1, 259: 'When the exigencies of the time seemed to them to

try, like the Pharisees, to find a *modus vivendi* by means of a compromise or to create, like the Essenes, an ideal form of life by shutting oneself off from the world that was hostile to God.[346] The party founded by Judas chose a third way. Going contrary to reason and against the real interest of the people and taking no account of the existing power structures, the members of Judas' party tried by violent means to establish the order that was in accordance with their conception of the law, in other words, the sole rule of God.

Josephus' presentation again and again makes it quite clear that the new party was guided entirely by its religious conviction and not at all by 'national', in other words, by pragmatic political ideas. Israel was for these men primarily a religious community and only secondarily a *natio*. Those Jews who were disposed towards peace were, in their opinion, ἀλλόφυλοι.[347] The Zealots, on the other hand, were always ready to give life and freedom to those pagans who had themselves circumcised and in this way converted to Judaism.[348] Again, according to Josephus, even their fanaticism, which became more and more pronounced as the Jewish War proceeded, which made the members of the movement ready for any sacrifice and which resulted in the real situation being left completely out of account, should not be interpreted as 'national enthusiasm'. It can only be understood in the light of its religious foundation. It is understandable, then, that Josephus should have emphasized, among his many criticisms of the Zealots, their absolute

---

demand it, the rabbis in council or individually did not hesitate to set aside laws in the Pentateuch on their own authority ...'. The best known example of a compromise of this kind is Hillel's Prozbul regulation, which was concerned with the fifteen year release from debt (Deut 15.1-11); see Shebi 10,3. For other examples, see Moore, *op. cit.*, 1, 260, and A. Schlatter, 'Jochanan b. Zakkai', *BFChTh* 10 (1906), 28f. See also *ibid., Der Evangelist Matthäus*, 3rd. ed. 1948, 648: It was the rule of Pharisaism 'that the law should not become unbearable ...'.

[346] On the basis of their isolation, they were able to create for themselves a pattern of life that they regarded as a preliminary step towards eschatological glory; see J.T. Milik, *Ten Years of Discovery in the Wilderness of Judaea*, 1959, 120: 'Their way of life established them in an intimate relationship with God and the good Spirits'. Apart from the texts on the theme of 'life with the angels' mentioned by this author on the following page (121), two further texts should be included: 1QH 6,13f. and 1QS 11,7. For its stricter Halacha, see A.S. van der Woude, *Die messianischen Vorstellungen der Gemeinde von Qumran*, 1957, 218.

[347] *Bell* 7,255.

[348] See *Bell* 2,454: the commandant of the auxiliary cohorts in the Herodium; *Vita* 112f.149-154: the officers of Agrippa II in Josephus. This struggle was motivated not by national reasons, but exclusively by religious considerations even for the sons of King Izates of Adiabene, who fought in the Jewish ranks (*Bell* 2,520; 5,474; 6,356f.).

refusal to consider the real interests of their own people.[349] Even the fall of the city did not seem to move them:

> 'With happy faces they looked at the burning city and said that they accepted death with glad hearts . . .'[350]

Even banishment from their national home country could not shake their religious zeal in any way. The *Sicarii* who fled to Egypt, for example, did not 'go underground', but continued to enlist support there for the 'sole rule of God'. Even torture and martyrdom could not make them abandon their convictions.[351]

The ideas of the moderate Pharisees, whose leader Johanan b. Zakkai went over to the Romans,[352] were much more 'national' in the 'real political' sense. It was largely because of this group that Palestinian Judaism survived the fall of Jerusalem and the destruction of the Temple and continued as a 'nation'.

2. A Summary of the Events Discussed So Far

The 'Fourth Philosophy' was founded by Judas the Galilaean. Its members were also called *Sicarii* even before the outbreak of the Jewish War, although they gave themselves the name 'Zealots'. It seems to have been a relatively exclusive, well-defined group with a definite leader. After Judas' death, the leadership passed to members of his family.

The census carried out by Quirinius, which must have seemed to those Jews who were faithful to God's law to be contrary to that law, led to the emergence of the new movement. In the message that it proclaimed — probably with prophetic authority — its founders — Judas, who was both eloquent and learned in Scripture, and the Pharisee Saddok, who is only mentioned once — were very close to the radical wing of Pharisaism. They separated themselves, however, from the Pharisaical movement in their unconditional demand for the 'sole rule of God'. Only God merited to be called 'Lord'. All the claims made by the pagan world power, as embodied by the emperor, to lordship and to rule were excluded.

This thesis had its foundation in the conviction that the kingdom and the rule of God had already been initiated. Closely connected with this idea was a new understanding of the decalogue and the *Shema*, both of

---

[349] *Bell* 4,263; 5,4.345.526, etc.
[350] *Bell* 6,364; see also 5,458.
[351] *Bell* 7,410ff.437.
[352] Compare ARN 4 (ed. Schechter, 23); Lam Rab 1,5; Gitt 56a.

which proclaimed God as the 'only Lord'. There was also the underlying and corresponding antithesis against the cult of the emperor, which had by this time penetrated into Palestine.

The proclamation of the 'sole rule of God' was at the same time also seen as the first step towards eschatological 'freedom', a concept which was not interpreted in the profane political sense, but in the light of the very early conception of Israel's redemption. The coming of the time of salvation was not, in the opinion of the members of the new sect, in any way automatic. God had made it dependent on the co-operation of pious Jews, who had to take part themselves in the task of making that redemption a reality by recognizing the need for an unrestricted theocracy and, if necessary, by armed uprising against the pagan oppressors.

The time of redemption was therefore placed in a corresponding relationship with the 'holy zeal' of pious Jews. This radical eschatological message called for an urgent decision and led inevitably to a division in Israel. Jews could only be either for it or against it. Waiting or compromise were in the long run impossible. The attitude that characterized the new movement was, as the name that its members gave themselves — 'Zealots' — indicated, one of zeal for God and his law.

My task in the following chapter will therefore be to examine more closely the origin and the significance of this 'zeal' in late Judaism and in the Zealots themselves.

CHAPTER IV

ZEAL

The honorary title 'Zealot', which the adherents of the movement that began with Judas the Galilaean probably gave themselves, indicates that their own understanding of themselves was determined by Old Testament traditions in which the concept of 'zeal' was central. It is therefore important for us to consider these traditions now.

A. The Old Testament Presuppositions of Zeal for God

We are concerned here with the group of words קנא, pi. to be or to make zealous, with לְ to become zealous, jealously angry about; hiph., causative, to provoke to jealousy; קַנָּא and קַנּוֹא jealous and קִנְאָה zeal, jealousy, passion.[1] These words on the one hand denote jealousy in the sphere of human relationships[2] and are, on the other, an expression of an attitude on God's part, especially towards his people.[3]

1. The Jealous God

What is remarkable is that the adjectives קַנָּא and קַנּוֹא are only applied to God. They always occur in fixed formulae and in places which are especially significant for the Old Testament revelation: the two decalogues Ex 20 (= Deut 5) and Ex 34 and the report of the assembly at Shechem.[4] This points to the fact that zeal was a permanent and essential aspect of Yahweh, who jealously watched to ensure that Israel fulfilled its obligations under the covenant and acknowledged that he was the only God.[5] This zeal was accordingly connected with anger as soon as Yahweh's commandments were broken and especially if alien gods were worshipped.[6]

---

[1] S. Köhler-Baumgartner, *Lexicon in Vet. Test. Libros*, 1953, 852f. For what follows, see also F. Küchler, 'Der Gedanke des Eifers Jahwes im Alten Testament', *ZAW* 28 (1908), 42ff.; A. Stumpff, 'ζῆλος', *TD* 2, 78-80; W. Eichrodt, *Theology of the Old Testament*, 1967, 1, 210f.; G. von Rad, *Old Testament Theology*, 1962, 1, 203ff.

[2] Especially, for example, the verb in Gen 24.14; 37.11; Num 5; Is 11.13.

[3] Predominantly in the case of קִנְאָה, in twenty-five out of forty-three places.

[4] Ex 20.5; 34.14; Deut 4.24; 5.9; 6.15: אֵל קַנָּא. Josh 24.19; Nahum 1.2: אֵל קַנּוֹא. Ex 34.14: יהוה קַנָּא.

[5] See F. Küchler, *op. cit.*, 46; L. Köhler, *Old Testament Theology*, 23 and 67f.

[6] Num 25.11; Deut 29.17ff.; 32.16,21; 1 Kings 14.22f.; Ps 78.58; 79.5; Ezek 5.11ff.;

Yahweh's zeal was, however, similarly aroused if foreign nations oppressed his people. Such foreign oppression resulted in his intervention to help Israel.[7] This saving power could also bring about the beginning of the time of salvation.[8] Fire was a particularly suitable image for the destructive force of Yahweh's zeal.[9] But he also appeared as a 'man of war' and a 'mighty hero' (אִישׁ מִלְחָמָה and גִּבּוֹר) in order to give scope to his zeal.[10] Within the framework of the total image of the Old Testament presentation of God, Yahweh's zeal is probably best understood as an expression of his holiness.[11]

2. Zeal for Yahweh

The counterpart to the image of 'Yahweh's zeal' is to be found in the zeal of the pious for Yahweh's honour and holiness. The first example of this in the Old Testament is Phinehas, the son of Eleazar and the grandson of Aaron. When Israel began to worship the Baal of Peor, God's anger blazed out against the people and he inflicted a plague on them.[12]. Then, in a spontaneous act of intervention, Phinehas killed an adulterous couple who had given particular offence and the plague was lifted from Israel. What is of essential importance in this account is the promise made to Phinehas and his descendants:

> 'Phinehas the son of Eleazar, son of Aaron the priest, has turned back my wrath from the people of Israel, in that he was jealous with my jealousy among them, so that I did not consume the people of Israel in my jealousy. Therefore . . . I give to him my covenant of peace and it shall be to him and to

---

8.3ff.; 16.38ff. etc. In Ezekiel especially, idolatry is seen as adultery and the faithless Israelites incurred Yahweh's jealousy.

[7] Ezek 35.11; 36.5f. (against Edom); Nahum 1.2 (Assyria); Is 37.32 = 2 Kings 19.31.

[8] Is 9.6; 26.11; 42.13; Ezek 39.25; Joel 2.8; Zech 1.14f.; 8.2.

[9] Zeph 1.18; 3.8; Ps 79.5; Is 26.11.

[10] Is 42.13; for this, see J. Hänel, *Die Religion der Heiligkeit*, 1931, 198: 'It cannot be disputed that the warlike nature of the "Yahweh of hosts" is an example of his jealousy'. See Is 9.6; 37.32; 2 Kings 19.31.

[11] See Ezek 39.25: וְקִנֵּאתִי לְשֵׁם קָדְשִׁי; J. Hänel, *op. cit.*, 196f., therefore speaks of the 'jealous holiness of Yahweh'. This formula was taken over by G. von Rad, *op. cit.*, 1, 204, see also 205: 'Jealousy and holiness are no more than concepts with a different shade of meaning for the same characteristic of Yahweh'.

[12] There are certain discrepancies in the overall account in Num 25 and these are traceable to two different sources: J (25.1–6) and P (25.7–18). According to the yahwistic source, God commanded Moses to kill the leaders of the people and Moses passed this order on to the judges of Israel for them to carry out (25.4). According to the priestly tradition, God sent a plague which killed 24 000 people (25.8f.). According to 25.1, the Moabite women were the cause of Israel's defection; in 25.6,15, there is a reference to a Midianite woman, with the result that a war of vengeance is waged later against the Midianites: 25.17; 31.2ff.

his descendants after him, the covenant of perpetual priesthood, because he was jealous for his God and made atonement for the people of Israel'.[13]

Shortly afterwards, Phinehas marched, with the holy vestments, with the army of the Israelites into their war of retribution against the Midianites, which they waged strictly in accordance with the rules of a Holy War.[14]

Elijah was also one of these zealots for Yahweh. After having killed the prophets of Baal at the brook Kishon, he had to flee from Jezebel into the desert.[15]. He complained twice to God on Mount Horeb:

'I have been very jealous for Yahweh, the God of hosts; for the people of Israel have forsaken thy covenant, thrown down thy altars and slain thy prophets with the sword; and I, even only I, am left. And they seek my life, to take it away'.[16]

Like Phinehas, Elijah had been zealous in God's place and had opposed Israel's defection, but God had not confirmed his action. Now Yahweh was to promise him that the faithless Israelites would be punished and his judgement would be carried out by the sword of the Syrian Hazael and the Israelite Jehu, both of whom were later to be anointed king, and by Elijah's successor Elisha and that only a remnant of seven thousand faithful Israelites would be preserved.[17]   Jehu, one of the instruments of this divine judgement, was another zealot for Yahweh. On the way to Samaria, he called Jehonadab, the son of Rechab to him and said: 'Come with me and see my zeal for Yahweh'. This zeal was manifested in the putting to the sword of Ahab's descendents in Samaria. Like Elijah, Jehu had also received a special promise from God for this.[18]

Finally, it is important to mention the tradition of the tribe of Levi in this context. It is true that the concept of 'zeal' does not appear directly in this tradition, but it is materially contained in it. After the people of Israel had gone astray in their worship of the image of the golden calf, the tribe of Levi responded as one man to Moses' call and put everyone to the sword without regard to family or blood relationships. In this case too, a divine promise was given as a reward.[19]

Even though it is not expressed in the special form of 'zeal for Yahweh', zeal for God's cause appears in two post-exilic psalms:

[13] Num 25.11-13.
[14] Num 31.6; cf. Deut 10.9; 20.2; 1 Sam 7.8f. Num 31 is, as a whole, an ideal description of the holy war according to Deut 20.13ff.
[15] 1 Kings 18.40ff.; 19.2ff.
[16] 19.10,14.
[17] 19.17f.
[18] 2 Kings 10.16f. and 10.30.
[19] Ex 32.26-29; the promise appears in the blessing of Moses (Deut 33.8-11).

'Zeal for thy house has consumed me!'[20]

'My zeal consumes me, because my foes forget thy words!'[21]

The first of these two texts refers to the purity or the holiness of the Temple. The second can best be defined with the formula 'zeal for the law'.

This very brief survey of the Old Testament references points clearly to the way in which Yahweh's zeal and zeal for Yahweh on the part of the pious Israelite correspond, subject to certain presuppositions. If he was inspired by 'zeal for Yahweh', the latter could jump into the breach and, as Yahweh's representative, carry out his judgement by putting his faithless fellow-Israelites to the sword whenever they had aroused God's zealous anger by their disobedience and defection. He was also to some extent conscious of the task that Yahweh had given him to carry out God's zeal. To do this could bring about expiation for Israel and avert further punishment. Yahweh's response to this zeal for his honour and holiness took the form of a special promise of salvation.

What is remarkable in this context is that this zeal for Yahweh was always directed exclusively against the faithless people of Israel itself. It is true that — particularly in the later prophetic tradition of salvation — Yahweh was quite able to direct his zeal equally against Israel's enemies, but it is noticeable that the Old Testament never speaks of zeal expressed outwardly in this way on the part of pious Israelites. Finally, at a later period, it would seem that 'zeal for Yahweh' was replaced by zeal for the means of salvation instituted by him, in particular the sanctuary and the law.

B. Zeal for the Law in Connection with the Tradition of Phinehas

1. Zeal at the Time of the Maccabees

The memory of Phinehas' action and the promise that had been given to him by God remained alive in Judaism. He is, for example, recalled and praised in Ps 106.29f.:

'They provoked him[22] to anger with their doings,
and a plague broke out among them.
Then Phinehas stood up and interposed
and the plague was stayed.
And that has been reckoned to him as righteousness
from generation to generation for ever'.

---

[20] Ps 69.9

[21] Ps 119.139.

[22] Read וַיְכַעֲסוּהוּ with the Septuagint, S, Hier. and 6 MSS. Ps 106.29f. corresponds to the P version (Num 25.7-18).

Phinehas is also called 'prince' (נָגִיד) in the first book of Chronicles and a blessing gives emphasis to this reference to him.[23] Jesus Sirach speaks about him in considerable detail in praise of the Father,[24] saying that Phinehas' action achieved expiation for Israel and that the covenant that God consequently made with him could be compared with the covenant he established with David in that it guaranteed the inherited succession of the office of high-priest.

This comparison between God's covenant with Phinehas and that made with David is at the same time also a preliminary stage in the twofold expectation of the Messiah as ruler that was felt in certain circles of Judaism.[25] In addition to this, both in the case of Phinehas and in that of Elijah, the 'fire prophet', Jesus Sirach particularly stresses zeal for God's cause.[26] Farmer's assumption that 'within certain circles of post-exilic Judaism Phineas was regarded as one of the great patriarchs' is probably correct.[27] We may even go further and say that those circles are probably to be found in the ruling priestly dynasty, which was trying to reinforce its legitimacy by appealing to the covenant made with Phinehas. .

The tradition of the zeal of Phinehas was given an importance that was much greater than it had ever had in the past during the period of religious distress experienced under Antiochus Epiphanes. The faith of the patriarchs was very seriously threatened by that king's directives. Many Jews agreed with these and defected.[28] The law was declared invalid, the books of the law were destroyed[29] and the Temple was desecrated.[30] Many Jews who were faithful to the law were put to death.[31] God's anger visited Israel.[32]

What was of essential importance in this situation was that the

---

[23] 1 Chron 9.20.

[24] Sir 45.23-26; cf. 50.24 M. The texts of M, LXX and S are not identical, but the basic idea is the same in each, namely that the hereditary succession will be guaranteed in the high-priesthood as it is in the Davidic kingdom. See J. Klausner, *The Messianic Idea of Israel*, translated by W.F. Stinespring, 1955, 255f.

[25] For the twofold messianic expectation, see K.G. Kuhn, 'Die beiden Messias Aarons und Israels', *NTS* 1 (1954/55), 168-179, and A.S. van der Woude, *Die messianischen Vorstellungen der Gemeinde von Qumran*, 1957, *passim*.

[26] Sir 45.23 and 48.1ff.

[27] W.F. Farmer, 'The Patriarch Phineas', *AThR* 34 (1952), 27.

[28] 1 Macc 1.41ff.52; 2.18; Dan 11.32.

[29] 1 Macc 1.49f.56f.; 2 Macc 6.1ff.

[30] 1 Macc 1.45f.54.59; 2.8f.; 2 Macc 6.4; Dan 9.26f.;11.31.

[31] 1 Macc 1.57.63; 2.29-38; 2 Macc 6.9ff.; see also the legends of the martyrs, 6.18ff. and 7, also Dan 11.33.

[32] 1 Macc 1.64; 2 Macc 5.20; 7.18,33, 38; Dan 9.24ff.; 11.36.

'religious persecution' was based not only on the effects of the king's religious policy, but also equally on a 'movement of reform' undertaken by Jews themselves.[33]

When, for example, an Israelite was prepared to offer sacrifice in Modein in obedience to the king's command, the priest Mattathias was filled with zeal:

'He burned with zeal and his heart was stirred. He gave vent to righteous anger; he ran and killed him upon the altar'.[34]

He also killed the king's official and tore down the altar. The author of the First Book of the Maccabees immediately draws a parallel between Mattathias and Phinehas:

'He burned with zeal for the law, as Phinehas did against Zimri, the son of Salu'.[35]

Finally, Mattathias called on the inhabitants of Modein:

'Let everyone who is zealous for the law and supports the covenant come out with me!'[36]

This call is immediately followed by the flight of Mattathias, his sons and a number of like-minded Israelites into the mountains, leaving their possessions behind. Reinforced by the Hasidim,[37] they translated their 'zeal' into action, turning against the ἁμαρτωλούς and the ἄνδρας ἀνόμους among their compatriots, tearing down the altars and circumcising the male children, if necessary by force.[38]

The address that the author of the book puts into the mouth of Mattathias just before his death, contains another summary of the commitment of these 'Zealots for the law':

---

[33] This aspect of the question was elaborated above all by E. Bickermann, *The God of the Maccabees*, 1979, 83ff., 88ff. and 90ff.: 'The Maccabaean movement was above all a civil war, a religious struggle between orthodoxy and reformers' (90f.). See also M. Hengel, *Judaism and Hellenism*, 1974, 1,277-303. A very non-Greek 'zeal against the law' developed among the Jewish 'reformers' (1,293f.).

[34] 1 Macc 2.24: καὶ εἶδεν ... καὶ ἐζήλωσεν (cf. Num 25.7).

[35] 1 Macc 2.26.

[36] 1 Macc 2.27: πᾶς ὁ ζηλῶν τῷ νόμῳ καὶ ἱστῶν διαθήκην ἐξελθέτω ὀπίσω μου.

[37] 1 Macc 2.42; cf. 7.13 and 2 Macc 14.6. What we have here is a sect which was strictly faithful to the law and which can therefore possibly be identified with the 'wise' of Dan 11.33f. They are probably also mentioned in EthEn 90.6. They shared the same 'zeal for the law', but did not go beyond it, as the Maccabees did, to become politically ambitious; see J. Wellhausen, *Pharisäer und Sadduzäer*, 2nd. ed., 1924, 79ff.; Schürer, 1, 157. The Hasidim formed the common preliminary stage of the Essenes and the Pharisees; see *B.-Gr.Rel.* 457; M. Hengel, *op. cit.*, 1,175f.

[38] 1 Macc 2.44f.

'Arrogance and reproach have now become strong. It is a time of ruin and furious anger. Now, my children, show zeal for the law and give your lives for the covenant of our fathers'.[39]

The speech continues with references to Abraham, Joseph and finally Phinehas:

Phinehas our father, because he was deeply zealous, received the covenant of everlasting priesthood'.[40]

After mentioning Joshua, Caleb and David, Mattathias speaks of Elijah:

'Elijah, because of his great zeal for the law, was taken up into heaven'.[41]

He admonishes his listeners to remain faithful to the law in a statement which may be regarded as summarizing his call to the people:

'My children, be courageous and grow strong in the law, for by it you will gain honour!'[42]

Zeal for God and his law dominated the whole of the early period of the Maccabaean uprising, but the movement was later compelled by circumstances to extend its activities into a Holy War against the oppressor. As the struggle progressed, the aim of the war changed. After freedom had been obtained for the Jewish faith and the Hasidim had been eliminated[43] and above all after the death of Judas,[44] 'zeal for the law' receded more and more into the background in confrontation with other themes — especially that of the struggle for political independence.[45] It is not purely fortuitous that the example of Phinehas and the concepts ζῆλος and ζηλοῦν cease to appear in the latter part of the First Book of the Maccabees.[46]

Two closely related factors emerge at once from a comparison between the early Maccabaean 'zeal for the law' and the Old Testament

---

[39] 1 Macc 2.49f.

[40] 1 Macc 2.54.

[41] 1 Macc 2.58.

[42] 1 Macc 2.64.

[43] For freedom of faith, see 1 Macc 6.58 = 2 Macc 11. 14ff. For the elimination of the Hasidim, see 1 Macc 7.13f. Dan 11.34b may perhaps also indicate that they were not in agreement with the way that the fight for freedom was developing.

[44] 1 Macc 9.18. In the hymn to Judas (1 Macc 3.2ff.), his action against the ἀνόμους, ἐργάτας ἀνομίας, and ἀσεβεῖς is especially praised. In comparison with this, the profane aspects of the mirror of the ruler predominate in the praise of Simon (14.4–15).

[45] See Schürer, 1, 167f.: '... the foundation was no longer questioned'. See also J.C. Dancy, A Commentary on I Maccabees, 1954, 1f.

[46] The term νόμος is a similar case: It appears nineteen times in the first four chapters, whereas, in the twelve that follow, it occurs only seven times altogether.

idea of 'zeal for Yahweh': firstly that the people were in danger of defecting and secondly that God's anger was on them. Mattathias intervened spontaneously and executed judgement on the apostates and those who led them astray, involving others in the adventure in which they were required to risk their lives for God and his law. Although he himself was able to place his trust in the decisive help that would come from God's direct intervention, the apocalyptical observer was able to describe this turning point as 'a little help'.[47]

It is true that idea of expiation is not mentioned explicitly in the reports, but it is expressly stated in the hymn to Judas that:

'He went through the cities of Judah, he destroyed the ungodly out of the land; thus he turned away wrath from Israel'.[48]

The meaning of this text is quite unambiguous and completely in accordance with the Old Testament tradition, namely that, by removing the offence in Israel that was scandalizing God, God's anger would be turned away from his people.[49]

The theme of penance is more prominent than that of zeal in the Second Book of the Maccabees and in Daniel.[50] The Second Book of the Maccabees may perhaps give greater emphasis to the Hasidic view, according to which religious distress is regarded — in striking contrast to the First Book — as God's punishment for the purification of Israel.[51] The promise of salvation which characterizes the Old Testament generally and with which God responded to his people's zeal for his cause, is also missing from the Second Book, although this can be explained by the absence of prophetic inspiration.[52] This was replaced by

---

[47] Dan 11.34; see A. Bentzen, *op. cit.*, 83; M. Noth, *History of Israel*, 1958, 370.

[48] 1 Macc 3.8; cf. 2 Macc 8.5.

[49] See, apart from Num 25, Josh 7; 1 Sam 7.3ff.; 14.37ff.

[50] See 2 Macc 6.12ff.; 7.38; 13.12ff.; Dan 9.3ff.,24; 11.35; see also J.C. Dancy, *op. cit.*, 3; M. Hengel, *Judaism and Hellenism*, 1,179ff.

[51] In contradiction to the historical situation, Judas is described in 2 Macc 14.6 as the leader of the Hasidim. The narrative in 2 Macc breaks off after the victory over Nicanor without dealing with the later fate of the Maccabees and a particular interest is shown in martyrdom and in expressions of personal piety, while the theme of zeal, for example, is absent from the book. It is therefore reasonable to claim that the tendency of both 2 Macc and its model, the historical work of Jason of Cyrene (3.32ff.), deviates markedly from that of 1 Macc; see M. Hengel, *op. cit.*, 1,95ff. For the Hasidim as a penitential movement, see CD 1,7ff.; see also J.T. Milik, *Ten Years*, 80f.; it would, however, be quite wrong to describe them, as Milik does, as 'fiercely nationalistic'.

[52] 1 Macc 4.46; 14.41. The discomfiture over the absence of an authoritative legitimation emerges clearly from the second of these texts. The office of the high-priesthood was 'granted subject to revocation' to the Hasmonaeans and, because of this,

an apologetic use of the Phinehas tradition. In other words, just as Phinehas' zeal legitimated the later high-priesthood of his descendants, so too did the zeal of Mattathias justify the later claims of the Hasmonaeans to the high-priesthood.[53]

What is remarkable in this context is that, in contrast to the Old Testament, this zeal is no longer directly related to God. It is rather related to the law. This change is characteristic of the religious development of Judaism after the exile, when the law came between the individual and God as the norm of man's relationship with God.

In conclusion, it is necessary to mention one essential point that is similarly no longer in the Old Testament tradition. In the early Maccabaean period — at least according to the way in which the theme is presented in the books of the Maccabees — zeal for the law was in no sense eschatologically determined, despite the fact that the religious distress must have given rise in pious circles to a powerful eschatological mood.[54]

2. The Maccabaean 'Zeal for the Law' and the Figure of Phinehas in Josephus' Writings

Josephus, who speaks very proudly of his relationship with the Hasmonaeans,[55] judges the Maccabaean uprising very positively, at least in his *Antiquities*.[56] It is therefore important to ask how he incorporated the concept of 'zeal for the law' into his presentation. The result is disappointing. In all his writings, a clear echo of Mattathias' zeal can be found in only one place:

---

they were later involved in serious complications. See E. Bammel, 'ἀρχιερεὺς προφητεύων', *ThLZ* 79 (1954), 351ff ; H.J. Schoeps, 'Die Opposition gegen die Hasmonäer', *ThLZ* 81 (1956), 664ff., and A.S. van der Woude, *op. cit.*, 223ff., 230ff.

[53] The emphasis in 1 Macc 2.54 on 'Phinehas our father ...' is particularly striking. The priesthood of the Hasmonaeans could be justified in two ways by a reference back to Phinehas: firstly, by its derivation from Phinehas and, secondly, by the zeal that they showed in the same way as he showed it.

[54] This is clear above all from the book of Daniel, which must have originated in the early Maccabaean period between the desecration of the Temple in December 167 B.C. and the march eastwards undertaken by Antiochus IV in the spring of 165 B.C.; see A. Bentzen, *op. cit.*, 8; M. Noth, *op. cit.*, 369f. There is also a reference in CD 1,12, in a review of the past that undoubtedly applies to the Maccabaean period, to the 'last generation'.

[55] *Vita* 4ff.; *Ant* 16,187.

[56] See Book 12 from 265 onwards. In *The Jewish War*, Josephus is much more reserved.

'If anyone is a Zealot for the ancient customs and the veneration of God, let him follow me!'[57]

In this text, 'Zealot' (ζηλωτής) can just as well be understood in the Hellenistic moral philosophical sense of a 'zealous follower of a good cause' as in the Jewish sense of a 'Zealot for the law'.[58] Josephus' presentation, with its completely Hellenistic colouring which emerges in the speech by Mattathias that follows this text, points more in the direction of the first interpretation. Mattathias' speech appears as a call to preserve the traditional structure of the state that is founded on piety towards one's father. Sons will be rewarded by God for their ἀρετή if they behave correctly and will in the end be given freedom.[59] There is no mention of Phinehas or of any other Old Testament figures.

There can be little doubt that the Hellenistic transformation of the original report should be ascribed to Josephus' Greek stylists. Nonetheless, Josephus probably tended to exclude from the source material at his disposal — and the First Book of the Maccabees was one of his sources — everything that might establish a connection between the Maccabees and their fight for freedom on the one hand and the later Zealots on the other.[60]

A further investigation into Josephus' description and judgement of Phinehas' action shows clearly that he omits almost all the elements that were of decisive importance for the later Phinehas tradition. He reports in detail the previous history, even including a dramatic polemical dialogue between Zimri and Moses. This is followed by Phinehas' intervention, which encourages other young men to follow his example. We may look in vain, however, for the key-word 'zeal' or for the promise given by God to Phinehas and his descendants. These are not mentioned at all.

This state of affairs reinforces one's suspicion that Josephus consciously suppressed any elements that may possibly have established a close link between early Jewish history and the principles and aims of the Jewish movement of revolt against Rome.[61]

---

[57] *Ant* 12,271: εἴ τις ζηλωτής ἐστιν τῶν πατρίων ἐθῶν καὶ τῆς τοῦ θεοῦ θρησκείας, ἐπέσθω ... ἐμοί.

[58] See above, p. 59f. The term ζηλωτής appears once in Josephus (*Ant* 20,47) with a very similar meaning; see also Gal 1.14.

[59] *Ant* 12,279.

[60] See W.R. Farmer, 1956, 19ff.

[61] *Ant* 4,131-155. Philo has shown in *Post* 182ff. (M 1, 261) that Phinehas' action could be interpreted in an allegorical and moral philosophical sense without reducing the emphasis on the important points. In *SpecLeg* 1,54ff. (M 2, 220), he even uses this

3. Phinehas (or Elijah) and his Zeal in the Rabbinic Tradition

(a) Sifre Numbers 25 and the Continuation of the Rabbinic Exegesis in Numbers Rabbah and the Talmuds

In complete contrast to Josephus, the figure of Phinehas and his zeal are treated as particularly important in certain parts of the rabbinic literature. The first text that has to be considered in this context is the exegesis of Num 25 in the Tannaitic Midrash Sifre that goes back to the school of R. Ishmael.[62] In this document, the defection of Israel is presented — as it is in Josephus — in considerable detail.[63]   Just as Moses ordered the tribal heads to put the apostates to death, so too did the members of the tribe of Simeon turn to their leader Zimri, who then led Cozbi, the daughter of the Midianite prince, under the protection of his tribe through the assembled people to commit fornication with her. During the session of the great Synhedrium[64] in which Zimri's action was dealt with Phinehas called on the tribes of Judah and Dan to act. Receiving no response from them, he armed himself and acted personally. He managed by subterfuge to gain access to the women's quarters, the guardians consoling themselves with the words: 'The Pharisees have declared this affair to be permitted'. The act itself was regarded as a consequence of six or twelve miracles. The two who had been condemned were publicly displayed by Phinehas. At the same time, the avenging angel killed the Simeonites who were standing outside. After accomplishing the act, Phinehas prayed[65] and there was an end to the dying. The tribe of Simeon now complained to the tribe of Levi about Phinehas' insignificant origin.[66] In addition to this, the desire

---

example to justify the application of lynch-law to apostates. Further examples of 'zeal' in Philo's writings will be found in J.A. Morin, *RB* 80 (1973), 340ff.

[62] See Strack, *Introduction*, 207, and Moore, *Judaism*, 1, 143f. For what follows, see *Tannaitische Midraschim* (*Rabbinische Texte*, Second Series) Vol. 2, *Sifre zu Numeri*, edited and explained by K.G. Kuhn, 1954ff., Chapter 131, 519-527. For the Hebrew text, see the edition by H.S. Horovitz in the *Corpus Tannaiticum* III,3, *Siphre d'be Rab*, Fasc. 1, *Siphre Num*, 1917, 172ff. For the rabbinic parallels, see K.G. Kuhn, *op. cit.*, 519, n. 113: Sanh 82a-b; jSanh 28d,57-29a,2; NumRab 20,25-21,3; TanB בלק, 29 and 30 and פנחס, 1-3, ed. Buber, 74b-76a; Jerusalem Targum on Num 25.4-15. See also C. Colpe, *ZDPV* 85 (1969), 163-196.

[63] See K.G. Kuhn, *op. cit.*, 502-518.

[64] *op. cit.*, 521, n. 126.

[65] On the basis of a re-interpretation of the *yitpallel* of Ps 106.31, the prayer is intended to give emphasis to the religious motivation of the act. The representation of the miracle was taken over by early Christian art from Jewish art; see C. Colpe, *op. cit.*, 170f. and C.-O. Nordström, 'Rabbinica in frühchristlichen und rabbinischen Illustrationen zum 4. Buch Mose', *Idea and Form*, Stockholm 1959, 38-47.

[66] According Ex 6.25, Phinehas' mother was one of the daughters of Putiel, that is, of

to exterminate a whole tribe in Israel was, no doubt wrongly, attributed to him. This was followed by the divine judgement about Phinehas' descent, rank and activity:

'(Phinehas) a priest, the son of a priest, a Zealot, the son of a Zealot, a turner away of wrath, the son of a turner away of wrath, has turned away my wrath from the Israelites' (כהן בן כהן קנאי בן קנאי משיב חימה בן משיב חימה).

The text of Num 25.13: 'because he was jealous (zealous) for his God' was interpreted through Is 53.12: 'because he exposed his life to death',[67] a quotation in which the context must also be borne in mind in this connection. According to the view expressed by the interpreter, Phinehas had put his life in mortal danger and his zeal consisted in his having risked his life for God's honour. It was also stressed that the text should not read: 'he made atonement or expiation (וכפר) then',[68] but 'he is making expiation (ויכפר) now' for the people of Israel. This point was then elucidated in greater detail. According to this interpretation, it meant:

'that he (Phinehas) has never ceased until the present time, but is there eternally making expiation, until the resurrection of the dead.'[69]

Jethro; see MekEx on 18.1 (L. 2, 164). Jethro was an idolatrous priest who later became a proselyte; see SifNum 10.31,80 and Sot 43a. For what follows, see also NumRab on 33.4.

[67] K.G. Kuhn, op. cit., 527, n. 190 (who is followed by J. Jeremias, 'παῖς θεοῦ', TD 5, 686, n. 234), regards the citation only as a more precise interpretation of Phinehas' action and furthermore denies that it intends to refer the prophecy of Is 53 to Phinehas. This is certainly no more than an analogy, although according to rabbinic practice, the following context ('... and was numbered with the transgressors'), which can also be appled to Phinehas, must be taken into consideration. This means that Phinehas was severely condemned by his compatriots, 'yet he bore (= took away) the sin of many and made intercession for the transgressors' (Is 53.12), in other words, he achieved expiation for Israel's sin and prayed to God that the people's punishment should be ended; see Moore, op. cit., 1, 549 and 3, 165, n. 252.

[68] The usual manuscripts of SifNum read here: 'is not said to make expiation' (לכפר). K.G. Kuhn follows a version of the Yalkuth and reads וכפר. See also H.S. Horovitz, op. cit., 173, and l. 17.

[69] K.G. Kuhn, op. cit., 527, n. 196, interprets the text in such a way that, by means of the action that he performed at that time, Phinehas continues to make expiation until the end of the world, to turn aside God's anger and to save Israel from destruction. This interpretation, however, weakens the impact of the אלא עומד ומכפר עד שיחיו המתים. It is possible that, even at that time, more was read into the text on the basis of the בְּרִית כְּהֻנַּת עוֹלָם of Num 25.13 than simply a continuous achievement of expiation; see Moore, op. cit., 1, 549 and 3, 165, n. 253. V. Aptowitzer, Die Parteipolitik der Hasmonäer im rabbinischen und pseudepigraphischen Schrifttum, 247, n. 57, regards this text as the first rabbinic identification of Phinehas and Elijah: 'The same characteristics are attributed

Through the eternal effect of his making expiation, Phinehas himself acquired an importance for Israel that transcended time. This may have been how the tradition of his being carried away and his identification with Elijah, the eschatological high-priest, began.

It is now possible to summarize the essential aspects of the Tannaitic exposition of Num 25 and to complete them with data derived from the later rabbinic tradition:

(1) Phinehas by-passed the usual legal procedures and killed the man who had broken the law. According to the later Midrashim, the session of the great Synhedrium was regarded as a sitting of the supreme court in which the verdict of death was passed on Zimri. The court failed to pass judgement because of cowardice and for this reason Phinehas made a vow to punish the sinner and then left the session.[70] According to a different tradition, Phinehas' decision was based on his recollection of the Mishnah: 'Whoever cohabits with an Aramaean woman, the Zealots will descend on him'.[71] Explanations of this kind were intended to establish a clearer legal foundation for Phinehas' action. An action performed simply and solely on the basis of zeal aroused suspicion at a later period.[72]

(2) Phinehas' action exposed him to extreme danger. He was obviously prepared to die as a martyr. R. Jose (b. Halaphta) attributed this statement to him:

'If the horse risks its life on the day of the battle and is ready to die for its master, ought I too not to do the same for the holiness of the name of God?'[73]

Only the miraculous intervention of the avenging angel was able to prevent the Simeonites from taking a bloodthirsty revenge.[74]

---

here to Phinehas as those that were known to belong to Elijah, namely, eternal life and expiatory activity'.

[70] NumRab 20,25 and TanBalak 30, ed. Buber 74b/75a והוא עמד מתוך העדה ונתנדב, K.G. Kuhn, *op. cit.*, 541, n. 126, is reminiscent of the vow made before the attempt to murder Paul (Acts 23.12ff.), which was preceded by a similarly unsuccessful debate in the presence of the Synhedrium; see Acts 22.30–23.10. See also the oath made by the insurgents, who swore never to give themselves up: *Bell* 6,351.366. For this, see also below, pp. 254, 383f.

[71] jSanh 27b,30f.; Sanh 82a; NumRab 20,25.

[72] Unlike Num 25 and SifNum, the Babylonian Talmud says that Phinehas was given power by Moses (82a towards the end) and suppresses the failure of the Synhedrium. For a direct criticism of Phinehas, see below, p. 168ff.

[73] ExRab 33,5; R. Jose b. Halaphta lived during the second half of the second century A.D. According to NumRab 16,1, Phinehas was one of the spies of Josh 2 and his life was also at risk here.

[74] According to SifNum 25,8, the angel killed more than he had to. In the Babylonian Talmud Sanh 82b (above), the יתפלל of Ps 106.30 is interpreted as 'he judged' rather

(3) Phinehas was condemned because of his zeal. According to Sifre Numbers, he was condemned by the Simeonites. According to the Babylonian Talmud, he was condemned by the whole of Israel and, according to the Jerusalem Talmud, by the members of the Synhedrium.[75]. The quotation from Is 53.12 similarly refers to Phinehas' commitment of his life, to the calumnies pronounced against him and to the expiatory effect of his action.

God, however, confirmed that action:[76]

(4) In complete contrast to the criticisms made of him by those who want to defame him, he was of noble origin and a priest because he was descended from Aaron and Levi.

(5) He was promised that his action would have the effect of eternal expiation. That expiation was in the first place based on Phinehas' having propitiated God's anger by the commitment of his own life and his punishment of the sinner. Numbers Rabbah draws a parallel in this point with the priestly sacrifice: 'The one who sheds the blood of the godless is like one who offers sacrifice'.[77] Sifre Numbers and Numbers Rabbah speak about the expiatory effect of Phinehas' action as a high-priest in a way that points to an effect that transcends time, but this aspect of his action is toned down in both Talmuds.[78]

(6) The name 'Zealot' ((קַנָּאי) for Phinehas is placed in God's mouth and should be regarded as an honorary title. The name 'son of the Zealot' should be seen as referring to Levi, whose zeal with regard to fornication

---

than 'he prayed' (as in SifNum, NumRab and jTal). In other words, Phinehas argued with God about the killing of too many Israelites.

[75] The accusation differs in any case according to the source: in SifNum, Phinehas wanted to exterminate a whole tribe, whereas in bTal and NumRab, he is accused of killing only a leader of a tribe. An attempt is made to tone down Phinehas' action, whereas the accusation itself is given more weight.

[76] A confirmation of this kind is not to be found in jTal; after describing Phinehas' action, the Gemara at once proceeds to speak of the war against the Midianites: jSanh 29a,3ff. In 27b,34f. as well, the promise of salvation is only briefly mentioned. The Babylonian Talmud divides the promises in two parts and makes God speak the words of the one who is zealous and who turns away his anger to the angel who is to prevent Phinehas from accusing God (see above, p. 158, n. 74) rather than to Israel (82b, above). In this way, the whole tradition is altered, making Phinehas as zealous for Israel against God as for God against Israel!

[77] NumRab 21,3; TanPinchas, 3, ed. Buber 76a: שכול שהשופך דם רשעים כאילו המקריב קרבן.

[78] This is completely absent from the Jerusalem Talmud and, in the Babylonian Talmud, it is essentially toned down: 'This expiation is worthy to be an external expiation' (82b). On the other hand, NumRab 22,3 concentrates on the activity of Phinehas that transcends time. Following Num 25.12 and with an appeal to Mal 2.5, the conclusion is drawn 'that he (Phinehas) is still living today'.

is attested in Gen 34 and quoted in the Midrashim. Philo also praises Levi's φιλόθεος σπουδή according to Ex 32.[79] The direct naming of Phinehas as a 'Zealot' has only one parallel in the Jewish Hellenistic sphere. In the Fourth Book of the Maccabees,[80] the mother reminds her sons of their father, who told them of the 'zeal of Phinehas' in the history of Israel: ἔλεγεν δὲ ὑμῖν τὸν ζηλωτὴν Φινεες. As this work was produced at the latest during the first century A.D., it must already have been current at that time to describe Phinehas as 'the Zealot'.[81] It is also very likely that the name of the party — the 'Zealots' — originated here.[82]

A comparison between Sifre Numbers 25 and the later developments of the same traditions reveals an unmistakable toning down of the whole presentation. In the Jerusalem Talmud, this takes the form of hidden criticism, whereas the Bablyonian Talmud attempts to smooth out all sharpness and to tone down the aspects that emphasize the zeal of Phinehas.

(b) Phinehas as a Leader in the Holy War

The second appearance of Phinehas in Num 31.6ff. as a leader in the Holy War against Midian was also described in the Haggadic tradition.[83] This war was not regarded as an act of human vengeance. On the contrary, God had explicitly commanded it:

> 'You will not execute a vengeance of flesh and blood, but the vengeance of the one who spoke and the world was created. For it is said: "The Lord is a jealous God and avenging" (Nah 1.2)'.[84]

Phinehas accompanied the army and his presence 'had as much weight as all of them', that is, as the whole army.[85] He went with the army and

---

[79] See NumRab 21.3 and TanPinchas, 3, ed. Buber 76a: קינא על הזנות תחלה; see K. Kohler, *Harkavy-Festschrift*, 10; Philo, *Spec* 1,79 (M 2, 225).

[80] 4 Macc 18.12.

[81] See Schürer, 3, 589f.; A. Deissmann, in Kautzsch, *Die Apokryphen und Pseudepigraphen*, 2, 150: 'The period may possibly extend from Pompey to Vespasian'. Since the Second Book of the Maccabees has to be presupposed here, however, it cannot have originated before the middle of the first century B.C;. see O. Eissfeldt, *Old Testament, an Introduction*, 1965, 615. E. Bickermann's suggestion, *The Date of IV Maccabees, Louis Ginzberg Jubilee Volume*, 1945, 1, 105ff., that the period lies between 18 and 55 A.D., merits special attention.

[82] See above, p. 88f.

[83] SifNum 31, 157; see K.G. Kuhn, *op. cit.*, 643ff. A summary of the whole Haggadic tradition up to the late period is provided by L. Ginzberg, *Legends of the Jews*, 7 Vols, 1909ff., 3 (1911), 408-411 and 7, nn. 849-853.

[84] SifNum 31,3; K.G. Kuhn, *op. cit.*, 645.

[85] SifNum 31,6; see also Philo, *VitMos* 1,313 (M 2, 130) and Josephus, *Ant* 4,159, where Phinehas is appointed as στρατηγός by Moses.

the ark of the covenant as well as with the insignia and the power of a high-priest.[86]

In another tradition he was regarded as the first anointed for war. The various discussions about this question in rabbinic circles led at a later period to the possibility of reducing Phinehas' rank to the level of an ordinary priest.[87] The overcoming of the arch-seducer Balaam, who was killed by the Israelites in this war, was also partly at least attributed to Phinehas. According to these rabbinic texts, Balaam wanted, with the help of his magic arts, to escape through the air, but Phinehas held his high-priestly phylactery out to him and he fell to the earth.[88] The killing of Balaam was at the same time also an act of revenge for the death of the 24 000 Israelites who had been victims of the seduction that had resulted from following Balaam's counsel.[89]

There is a remarkable discussion between R. Hanina (b. Hama) and a Jewish heretic which ends with the following reply made by the heretic:[90]

> 'You are right. I have read the chronicle of Balaam and in it were the words: The lame Balaam was thirty-three years old when the robber Phinehas (ליסטא פינחס) killed him'.

This enigmatic discussion has been regarded either as anti-Christian polemic on the part of the rabbinate[91] or as an example of anti-Jewish polemic on the part of the gnostics.[92] In neither case, however, is it at all

---

[86] SifNum 31,6; jSanh 29a,12; NumRab 22,3.

[87] tSot 7,17 (Z. 308); Sot 43a; it should, however, be borne in mind that, according to the Tosefta, Phinehas was given the high-priestly vestments, whereas, according to the Babylonian Talmud, he was not. See also Zeb 102a; SongRab 3,5; LevRab 20,2. The Jerusalem Talmud puts Phinehas, at least to some extent, on the same level as ordinary priests; see jYom 38d; jMeg 72a/b; jHor 47d; see also below, p. 170, n. 131. See also V. Aptowitzer, *Die Parteipolitik der Hasmonäer im rabbinischen und pseudepigraphischen Schrifttum*, 1927, 194, n. 10.

[88] jSanh 29a,2, cf. Jerusalem Targum on Num 31.8 and NumRab 20.20, towards the end. In the Targum, Phinehas works the miracle by calling on the name of God. What we may possibly have here is a theme that can also be found in the legend of Peter. For his struggle with Simon Magus in Rome, see H.J. Schoeps, *Aus frühchristlicher Zeit*, 1950, 251f.

[89] SifNum 31,8; jSanh 29a,4f.; Sanh 106a below.

[90] Sanh 106b above, translation based on Goldschmidt, 9, 112. R. Hanina b. Hama, a pupil of Rabbi, lived in the first half of the third century A.D. in Sepphoris; see Bill. Introduction, 135.

[91] See H.L. Strack, *Jesus, die Häretiker und die Christen nach den ältesten jüdischen Angaben*, 1910, 26,42f.; J. Klausner, *J of N*, 1925; K.G. Kuhn, 'Βαλαάμ', *TD* 1, 524, n. 5.

[92] W. Bacher, 'The Supposed Inscription upon "Joshua the Robber" ', *JQR* 3 (1891), 354-357; see also Jastrow, *Dictionary*, 2, 708.

clear why Phinehas is described as a 'robber'. Is it possible that the use of
the word 'robber' is parallel here to the linguistic usage in Josephus and
that ליסטא may have replaced the original קנאי? Whatever the case may
be, 'robber' should certainly be understood in the polemical sense as a
more precise description of Phinehas. What is also quite remarkable in
this context is that, in contrast to the universally negative judgement of
Balaam in both Philo's and the rabbinic writings, Josephus is very
guarded and positive rather than negative in his description of this
figure.[93] Even Balaam's death is suppressed. It is therefore possible to ask
whether Josephus' attitude in this respect, which is completely in
contradiction to the tradition of late Judaism, is not connected with his
similarly fragmentary report about Phinehas. He may perhaps have
wanted to avoid contact with ideas that were current in radical Jewish
circles.[94]

(c) Phinehas' Eternal High-Priesthood and his Identification with Elijah

The 'covenant of salvation (or of peace)' and the 'covenant of an
eternal priesthood' of Num 25.12f., which is not explained at a deeper
level in Sifre Numbers, was later interpreted in a special sense.

In Numbers Rabbah, for example, an appeal is made to Mal 2.5 and
the conclusion is drawn that 'As a result of this, he (Phinehas) is still
living today'.[95] Targum Pseudo-Jonathan goes a step further and
reproduces the divine saying in Num 25.12 in the following way:[96]

> 'Behold, I conclude my covenant of peace with him and I intend to make
> him the angel of my covenant (Mal 3.1) and he will live eternally in order to
> bring the joyous message of redemption át the end of the days'.

The Targum on Ex 6.18 expresses this idea even more clearly:

> '... until he saw Phinehas, that is, the high-priest Elijah, who will be sent
> to the banished people of Israel at the end of the days'.[97]

---

[93] *Ant* 4,103-158; see also K.G. Kuhn, *TD* 1, 524.

[94] It is possible that the opposition between Phinehas and Balaam was interpreted
eschatologically in Zealot circles. Balaam was, on the one hand, the one who led Israel
astray and, on the other, the one who represented the people of the world and the
enemies of Israel; see Bill. 2, 354 (Zeb 116a). The Messiah's struggle against the
eschatological tyrant or the struggle of Elijah and Enoch against the Antichrist features in
the late Jewish apocalyptic; see below, p. 303f.

[95] NumRab 21,3: שעדיין הוא קיים ...

[96] For what follows, see Bill. 4, 463; for the Aramaic text, see *Targum Pseudo-Jonathan*
(*Targum Jonathan b. Uzziel zum Pentateuch*), ed. M. Ginsburger, 1903: ואעידינה
מלאך קיים ויחי לעלם למבשרא גאולתא בסוף ימיא.

[97] עד חמא ית פינחס הוא אליהו כהנא רבא. See also Targum on Ex 4.13, in which

Finally, Phinehas is again identified with Elijah in the later rabbinic tradition:

> 'Simeon b. Lakish said: Phinehas is Elijah. God spoke to him: You have made peace in the world between me and my children; in the (messianic) future too you are to be the one who will make peace between me and my children, as it is said (Mal 3.23f. = 4.5f.): 'Behold, I will send you Elijah the prophet . . .'.[98]

In this case, the link between Phinehas and Elijah was clearly formed by the effectiveness of reconciliation and making peace. In other cases, such as the following one, the connection between the two figures was zeal:

> 'God appeared to Elijah and said to him: "What are you doing here, Elijah?" He said: "I have been very jealous (= zealous)" (1 Kings 19.9f.). God said to him: "You are always zealous; in Shittim because of the fornication (Num 25) and here you are also zealous . . ." '[99]

It is a striking fact that the normative rabbinic tradition eliminated almost all accounts in which Phinehas was identified with Elijah,[100] retaining them at the most as marginal traditions. They must, however, have been fairly widespread, since several of the theologians of the early Church commented on them.[101]

What is essential for us in this context is the age of this tradition. Billerbeck presupposed that Elijah's identification with Phinehas went together with the idea of his high-priesthood and cites, as the earliest tradition in this connection, an anecdote about the appearance of 'Elijah the priest' on the day of Akiba's death to a pupil of that teacher.[102]

The idea of the 'priesthood of Elijah' is, however, essentially older

---

Moses prays: 'I pray to you, Yahweh, to be merciful. Carry out your mission now by means of Phinehas, who has been elected to be sent at the end of time'.

[98] Bill., op. cit., according to YalShim on Num 25.11, 771. See also the Midrash Ma'jan chokhma in A. Jellinek, Beth ha-Midrasch, 1, 61: Phinehas-Elijah as the last link in a tradition originating with Metatron.

[99] Bill. 4, 31 (e) according to Pirke R. Eliezer 29 (end). It should also be noted that Phinehas-Elijah is criticized for his zeal.

[100] See S. Krauss, 'The Jews in the Works of the Church Fathers', JQR 5 (1893), 153: 'The ordinary midrashim seem to have purposely suppressed it, because it smacked of Apocrypha'. In the same way, the identification is also absent from the Talmuds, the early Midrashim and the Targum Onkelos. It is only in certain collected works and in the Targum Ps.-Jonathan that it was preserved.

[101] See S. Krauss, op. cit., 153f.: In Origen, In Johannem 6,14 (7), GCS, ed. Preuschen, 1903, 4, 123: οἱ Ἑβραῖοι παραδιδόασι Φινεὲς τὸν Ἐλεαζάρου υἱόν . . . αὐτὸν εἶναι Ἡλίαν καὶ τὸ ἀθάνατον ἐν τοῖς Ἀριθμοῖς αὐτῷ διὰ τῆς ὀνομαζομένης εἰρήνης. See also Ps. Hieronymus 5, 813, ed. Vallarsi.

[102] Bill. 4, 791 according to MProv 9, 2.

than this. It can already be found at the beginning of the Christian era in the *Vita prophetarum*.[103] Aptowitzer dated it even earlier, suspecting that the figure of Phinehas-Elijah was possibly the Messiah of the Hasmonaean ruler-ideology.[104] Van der Woude tries to make a connection between the high-priest Phinehas-Elijah and the Essenes' expectation of a Messiah from Aaron.[105] In both cases, however, these are mere suppositions that cannot be confirmed in contemporary sources.

There is no reference in any of these hypotheses to the earliest evidence of an identification between Phinehas and Elijah. This evidence is to be found in the so-called *Pseudo-Philonis Liber Antiquitatum Biblicarum*. This is a work with a purely Jewish content which was originally written in Hebrew and preserved in Latin and which originated at the latest at about 100 A.D., but which contains Haggadic material that may well be significantly earlier than this.[106]

In the context of a detailed exposition of Judg 20.28, Phinehas prays aloud after the defeat of the Israelites by the Benjaminites. In this prayer, he refers to his zeal in Shittim:

> 'Et ego zelatus sum anime mee, et ambos suspendi in romphea mea. Et voluerunt insurgere residui adversum me, et mortificare me et misisti angelum tuum et percussisti ex eis viginti quattuor milia virorum'.[107]

---

[103] ed. T. Schermann, *Propheten- und Apostellegenden. TU* 31.3.R.1, 109f. According to this, Elijah was descended from the tribe of Aaron and his father was a priest. According to some manuscripts, he is characterized as a ζηλωτὴς καὶ φύλαξ τῶν θεοῦ ἐντολῶν. The anointing of the Messiah by Elijah according to the Jewish conception in Justin Martyr, *DialTryph* 8,4; 49,1 also presupposes the priesthood of the prophet; see J. Jeremias, "Ἠλ(ε)ίας', *TD* 2, 934f.

[104] V. Aptowitzer, *Die Parteipolitik der Hasmonäer*, 1927. 96ff.

[105] A.S. van der Woude, *Die messianischen Vorstellungen der Gemeinde von Qumran*, 1957, 60,209,228f.

[106] The Latin edition of the text: *Pseudo-Philo's Liber Antiquitatum Biblicarum*, ed. G. Kisch, 1949; see also the English translation with its detailed commentary by M.R. James, *The Biblical Antiquities of Philo*, 1917. For the age of the document, see James, 33: the end of the first century A.D.; see also Schürer, 1, 302. J. Klausner, *The Messianic Idea in Israel*, translated from the 3rd. Hebrew edition by W.F. Stinespring, 1956, 366f., assumed that it originated between 110 and 130 A.D. A later date is hardly possible, since the work could not then have been taken over by Christian circles. A. Spiro, 'Samaritans, Tobiads and Judahites in Pseudo-Philo', *PAAJR* 20 (1951), 281, n. 11, was right to point out that the Haggadic material must have been significantly earlier. For this reason, Phinehas and Elijah cannot be identified with each other with such complete certainty as J. Jeremias has done, *op. cit.*, 2, 933, n. 38, situating this identification in the 'post-New Testament period'.

[107] 47,1, ed. Kisch, 236.

In his reply to this, God says that the defeat was a punishment for the idolatry introduced by Micah (Judg 17), since no Zealot has arisen now:

'Et nullus zelavit et omnes seducti estis'.[108]

The account of the translation of Phinehas appears a little further on.[109] When he had reached the age of one hundred and twenty years, God called on him:

'Et nunc exsurge et vade hinc, et habita in Danaben, in monte, et inhabita ibi annis pluribus, et mandabo ego aquile mee, et nutriet te ibi (1 Kings 17.4ff.), et non descendes ad homines, iam quousque perveniat tempus ut proberis in tempore, et tu claudas celum tunc, et in ore tuo aperietur (1 Kings 17.1 and 18.49). Et postea elevaberis in locum ubi elevati sunt priores tui, et eris ibi, quousque memorabor secule et tunc adducam vos et gustabitis quod est mortis'.

In the first place, attention is drawn in a very positive way in this Haggadic Midrash to Phinehas' zeal. At the same time, the effect of this zeal for God in turning away punishment is presupposed. In addition to this, the account of Phinehas' being translated and his identification with Elijah are fairly abruptly introduced. The conclusion of the passage quoted, which speaks of a third coming of Phinehas-Elijah at the end of time, is obscure. It may perhaps have been curtailed by the Christian adaptors because of its contents.[110] We may certainly assume that the author was acquainted with the tradition of the identification of Phinehas with Elijah.

This combination of the two figures, Phinehas and Elijah, has a meaning which points in two directions. In the first place, it points to the present time and relates to the heavenly priesthood of Phinehas-Elijah referred to in Sifre Numbers which had a permanently expiatory effect for Israel.

'R. Phinehas says in the name of R. Simeon b. Lakish: "Phinehas is Elijah and without him we should have had no existence in Edom (= Rome). That

---

[108] 47,7, ed. Kisch, 238; cf. 45,6, ed. Kisch, 234: God speaks to the adversary: the people of Israel allowed themselves to be led astray by images of the dove, the eagle (!), human beings, calves, the lion and the dragon and so on, 'et qui non sunt tunc zelati, propterea sit eorum consilium in malum . . .' Here and in 38,1-3, one is reminded of the two scribes who destroyed the eagle in the Temple; see below, pp. 257f., 321f.

[109] 48,1, ed. Kisch, 239f. According to the Midrash Ma'jan chokhma, Elijah (Phinehas) is on Mount Horeb; see Jellinek, 1, 60.

[110] The 'priores tui' apparently presupposes that other ancestors of Phinehas were also translated. Nothing is said about his eschatological task at the third coming on the earth — only that he would then taste death with the others who had been translated; see 4 Ezra 6,26; Sukk 52b. Statements about the messianic activity of Phinehas-Elijah may perhaps have been omitted here by Christian adaptors.

is what our teachers said: Since the destruction of the Temple, Elijah offers daily sacrifice in expiation for Israel" '.[111]

This expiatory priestly ministry can perhaps be understood as a reinforcement of Elijah's traditional intercession for Israel.[112]

In addition to this, the combination of the two figures certainly also had an eschatological significance. According to the texts quoted above from the Targums, Phinehas-Elijah was 'to bring the joyous message of redemption (למבשרא גאולתא)' or 'bring the banished people of Israel back'. According to the rabbinate, Elijah had an extraordinary number of different eschatological functions, but what is of essential importance for us is that he could be expected not simply as the precursor of eschatological redemption, but, under certain circumstances, as the eschatological redeemer himself. In the teaching of R. Tanchuma, for example,[113] we find the tradition that two prophets of Levi, namely Moses and Elijah, are to redeem Israel, Moses redeeming the people from Egypt and Elijah redeeming them from the rule of Rome:

'... and when Elijah will redeem them from the fourth kingdom of the world, from Edom, then they will not be enslaved again, since that is an eternal redemption'.

The derivation of Elijah from Levi points clearly to a possible identification with Phinehas. But in other respects too Elijah is often named as Israel's redeemer[114] and even as the people's leader in the battle at the end of time against the nations.[115].

---

[111] See V. Aptowitzer, *op. cit.*, 248, n. 57, according to A. Wertheimer, *Batte Midraschoth*, Jerusalem 1897, 4, 32, from MTeh Shocher Tov on Ps 63 = 2nd. ed. Jerusalem 5728 (1967/8), 1, 396: הוא שאמרו רבותיהן משעה שחרב בהמ"ק ... הוא מקריב שני תמידין בכול יום לכפר על ישראל For the continuous effectiveness of the high-priest Phinehas-Elijah in bringing about reconciliation, see G. Dalman, *Der leidende und strebende Messias der Synagoge im ersten nachchristlichen Jahrtausend*, 1888, 9. Several traditions concerning Phinehas-Elijah have been attributed to R. Simeon b. Lakish; see above, p. 163.

[112] See Bill. 4, 768.

[113] See Bill. 4, 792 according to PesR 4 (13a); see also V. Aptowitzer, *op. cit.*, 104, and M. Zobel, *Gottes Gesalbter*, 1938, 61f. R. Tanchuma (b. Abba) was an important compiler at the beginning of the fourth century A.D., who above all brought together earlier material; see Bill. Introduction, 147 and W. Bacher, *Aggada der palästinischen Amoräer*, 1892ff., 3, 43.

[114] See Bill. 4, 783f. (PesR 33,153a), with other examples on 791f.; see also M. Zobel, *op. cit.*, 42f.,60,62, and V. Aptowitzer, *op. cit.*, 99.

[115] See V. Aptowitzer, *op. cit.*, 103. according to TanMishpatim, 12, ed. Buber 44b: 'At this time of the world, I have sent an angel before you and he has destroyed the people of the world; in the time of the world to come, however, I will send you ... Elijah, as it is said: 'Behold, I am sending you Elijah, the prophet, before the great and terrible day of Yahweh comes'.

How was it possible to identify the two figures? This is a difficult question to answer. Billerbeck and Aptowitzer have shown that the exegetical motivation came about by combining various texts in Malachi with Num 25.12f.,[116] but this scribal argumentation was hardly the first step towards an identification of the two persons.

The first question that has to be answered in this context is whether there was a powerful interest in certain Jewish circles in favour of combining the two figures. Such an interest probably existed not among the Hasmonaeans or the Essenes,[117] but within the Zealot movement. The zeal of Phinehas or Elijah was the great example here for the Zealots and God's covenant of salvation with Phinehas and the promise of eternal priesthood — as a reward for zeal — can also be included within this framework as an example.

The combination of these two examples was made via Mal 2.5 and 7f.,[118] Elijah taking on priestly aspects and Phinehas assuming prophetic features. Even the motive of fire, which is so characteristic of Elijah, was transferred to Phinehas.[119] The whole process was made much easier by the fact that, after Phinehas' extraordinarily long effectivity, the Old Testament has nothing at all to say about his death.[120]

---

[116] Bill. 4, 789f. and V. Aptowitzer, *op. cit.*, 96ff.; see also J. Jeremias, *TD* 2, 933.

[117] See Aptowitzer and van der Woude, see above, p. 164, nn. 104 and 105.

[118] Via Mal 2.5, a combination was made between NumRab 21,3 and TanPinchas, 3, ed. Buber 76a on the one hand and Num 25.12 on the other. Origen (see above, p. 163, n. 101) stressed the importance of the term εἰρήνη (שָׁלוֹם) as the reason for Phinehas' prolonged life; see also S. Krauss, *JQR* 5 (1893), 154.

[119] Josephus attributed prophetic gifts to Phinehas; *Ant* 5,120, see also 159. See also Pseudo-Philo 53,6 (Kisch, 250), Eli to Samuel: 'Finees enim sacerdos precepit nobis dicens: Auris dextra audit Dominum per noctem, sinistra autem angelum . . .' According to Seder Olam Rabbah 20, ed. A.D. Neubauer, *Medieval Jewish Chronicles*, 1895, 2, 52, the prophet is identified in Judg 6.8 with Phinehas; see A. Spiro, 'The Ascension of Phinehas', *PAAJR* 22 (1953), 113. N. Wieder, *JJS* 4 (1953), 164, n. 1, drew attention to the transference of Elijah's prophetic attributes to Phinehas: according to LevRab 1,1, "The Mal'akh of Yahweh (see Mal 3.1 = Elijah) went up from Gilgal to Bochim (Judg 2.1). Was it, then, an angel? Was it not Phinehas? And why does Scripture call him an angel? R. Simon (towards the end of the third century A.D.; see Bill. Introduction, 141) said: 'If the Holy Spirit rested on Phinehas, his face glowed like torches'." See LevRab 21,12 for the reference to Mal 2.7 and similarly NumRab 16,1. N. Wieder refers here to the description of Elijah in Sir 48.1: Ἠλίας προφήτης ὡς πῦρ καὶ ὁ λόγος αὐτοῦ ὡς λαμπὰς ἐκαίετο. In Pseudo-Philo 28,3, it is said of Phinehas the priest: 'exeat de ore eius veritas et de corde eius lumen refulgens.'

[120] He is mentioned for the first time in Ex 6.25 and for the last time in Judg 20.28. In the rabbinate and in Pseudo-Philo, he is therefore the high-priest of the period of the Judges. According to Aphraates, *Patrologia Syriaca*, ed. J. Parisot, 1894, I, 1 Sp. 642, he reached an age of 365 years = the age of Enoch at the time of his ascension; see A. Spiro, *op. cit.*, 102. See also C. Colpe, *ZDPV* 85 (1969), 172f.

As we have seen, the earliest written evidence of an identification between Phinehas and Elijah appeared at about 100 A.D. For this reason, it is more likely that this idea arose in the course of the first century A.D. than at a significantly earlier date. Its elimination in the later orthodox rabbinic tradition can also be most satisfactorily explained if we assume the existence of an originally Zealot tradition here. The entirely positive judgement of Phinehas and Elijah was at least to some extent severely criticized within the rabbinic tradition.

(d) The Rabbinic Criticism of Phinehas and Elijah

The rabbinic criticism of Phinehas is to be found in the judgement of his zealous acts in Shittim:

'It is written: "And Phinehas the son . . ., the priest saw" and so on. What did he see? He saw the act and was reminded of the Halacha: "Whoever cohabits with an Aramaean woman, the Zealots will descend on him" (and carried it out). It is taught that it (the action of the Zealots) was not in accordance with the will of the wise. And Phinehas — did he act against the will of the wise (תני שלא כרצון חכמים ופנחס שלא כרצון חכמים)? R. Judah b. Simon b. Pazzi[121] said: Yes, they wanted to excommunicate him, but it became known that the Holy Spirit had descended on him (שקפצה עליו רה"ק), for it is said: To him and his seed after him the covenant of eternal priesthood is promised'.[122]

It is clear from this exegetical debate that those in rabbinic circles who were concerned with the interpretation of Num 25 were confronted with certain difficulties. The Mishnah Sanh 9,6, which, under certain circumstances, permitted the intervention of 'Zealots',[123] was, it is true, handed on as an ancient tradition, but it was rejected in the Tannaitic period (תני, see above) on the basis of the catastrophes that had occurred in the past.[124] This meant that it became quite difficult to justify Phinehas' action, since it was no longer in accordance with the later principles of the law.[125] These difficulties in the interpretation of Num 25

---

[121] R. Judah b. Simon b. Pazzi from Lydda lived in the first half of the fourth century A.D.

[122] jSanh 27b,33; see the paraphrase in M. Schwab, Le Talmud de Jérusalem, 11 Vols., 1878ff. 11, 38.

[123] See above, p. 67f.; it was included among the early Mishnayoth given by God on Mount Sinai; see Rashi on Sanh 9,6, Bill. 2, 565.

[124] The Pharisees especially were extremely restrained in imposing the death sentence; see, for example, Ant 13,294. Their restraint became even more pronounced in the second century A.D.; see Makk 1.10; see also L. Finkelstein, The Pharisees, 3rd. ed. 1962, 286f.,696f.,699f.

[125] See, for example, the accusation made against the young Herod in Bell 1,209 = Ant 14,167 that even the worst criminals could only be condemned after a regular trial in the

were included in the story and it was stated that Phinehas had not acted in accordance with the will of the 'wise', that is, the members of the 'Synhedrium' of the time, including Moses, with the result that they wanted to excommunicate him.[126] His expulsion was prevented only by the fact that the divine saying pronounced him to be a pneumatic.

After it had become clear that the unambiguously positive statements in the Torah had made impossible a really critical attack against Phinehas' zeal in Num 25 — the Jerusalem Talmud does not, after all, go more deeply into God's promises of salvation for Phinehas[127] — a search was made for other points on which to criticize this model for all Zealots. These were found in sufficient numbers in his behaviour during the period of the judges. He was, for example, held responsible for the death of Jephtah's daughter:

> 'Was (the high-priest) Phinehas not present at that time? He could have cancelled Jephtah's vow! But he thought: He (Jephtah) does not need me, so why should I go to him? ... But both of them, Jephtah and Phinehas, were punished for the blood of the virgin. The former died ... and the Holy Spirit left Phinehas ... (The quotation from 1 Chron 9.20 follows here.) It is not said here: He was the prince over them (נגיד עליהם אין כתיב כאן), but he was a prince previously, when the Eternal One was still with him (אלא נגיד לפנים ה׳ עמו).[128]

The loss of the Holy Spirit is presumably linked with a tradition that originated with the same person or at least at the same period:

> 'Whoever is arrogant[129] — or becomes angry[130] — he is deserted, if he is a wise man, by wisdom and, if he is a prophet, by prophecy'.

---

court of law. A conflict between presumably Pharisaical court rules and the Zealots' conception of due process is described by Josephus in *Bell* 4,341ff.; see below, p. 174. After the Zealots had been defeated, the remaining members of the Pharisaical movement tried to impose a casuistic restraint on the possibility of intervention on the part of the Zealots — which had by then in any case become purely theoretical — and to limit it to cases of flagrante delicto. Unlike that in Sanh 9,6, the description in SifNum tries to do justice to this point.

[126] Whereas in other cases it is the Simeonites or the people who are protesting, this is explicitly a case of protest on the part of scribes.

[127] Silence was one of the most popular polemical means employed by the rabbis.

[128] GenRab 60,3: R. Simeon b. Lakish is named as the one who handed down this tradition; see above, p. 163. LevRab 37,4; EcclRab 10,15 (where the punishment is less severe and Phinehas does penance and once again receives the Spirit) and TanB בחקתי, 5, ed. Buber 57a, are parallels. See also A. Spiro, *op. cit.*, 107, n. 30, and V. Aptowitzer, *op. cit.*, 144 and 277, n. 62.

[129] As was R. Judah in the Name of Rab, 247 + A.D.; see Strack, *Introduction*, 121.

[130] As did Simeon b. Lakish; both traditions can be found in Pes 66b; see Bill. 1, 277; translation based on Goldschmidt, 2, 510.

This strange exposition of 1 Chron 9.20 — a text which aims to emphasize the significance of Phinehas — was also used in a different context against Phinehas:

'In the days of Zimri (Num 25) he protested, in the days (of the violation) of the concubine in Gibeah (Judg 19f.) he no longer protested'.

This change in emphasis was justified by reference to 1 Chron 9.20:

'Previously God had been with him (לפנים ה'עמו), now God had deserted him'.[131]

The tendency of this polemic is quite clear: The hero of all Zealots was criticized in an important passage for being proud and lax and his charismatic gift was at the same time disputed.

It was, however, also possible for zeal itself to be criticized. This is clear from a relatively early tradition of Elijah:

'Elijah looks for the honour of the father, not the honour of the son (= Israel), as it is said: "I have been very jealous (= zealous) for Yahweh, the God of hosts" (1 Kings 19.10) ... And what is said then? And Yahweh said to him: "Go, return on your way ... and Elisha ... you shall anoint to be prophet in your place" In the words "in your place" the prophet is simply told: I am not pleased with your prophecy ...'[132]

It was obviously recognized here that zeal for God could have a destructive effect within Israel itself and it was also pressupposed that God would not be pleased by commitment to a cause that might result in his people being harmed. Seen in this perspective, zeal had to be fundamentally rejected as a form of piety.

The fact that this criticism could also apply to Phinehas emerges clearly from R. Eliezer's collection of sayings,[133] according to which God reproached Elijah on Horeb:

'You are always zealous, in Shittim because of the fornication and here you are also zealous!'

The obvious assumption here is that this criticism of the two figures of zeal in the Old Testament was not based on a playful exercise of rabbinic exegesis, but on much deeper foundations. The rabbinate presumably came at a later period to regard the zeal for God and his law that was

---

[131] jYom 38d,22ff.; jMeg 72a,72ff.; jHor 47d,27ff. The tradition goes back to R. Jose (b. Halaphta); see above, p. 158f. See also V. Aptowitzer, *op. cit.*, 29 and 209, n. 38; A. Spiro, *op. cit.*, 107.

[132] MekEx 12,1 (L. 1, 9); see S. Schechter, *Some Aspects of Rabbinical Theology*, 1909, 205, and Bill. 1, 644 ParSongRab 1,6 (extended and toned down).

[133] See above, p. 163, n. 99.

aroused by the example of Phinehas and Elijah with very mixed feelings and tried to condemn the religious zeal that had prevailed in certain circles in the recent past by cautiously criticizing the Old Testament models.[134]

4. Summary: Phinehas the Zealot as a Model for the Maccabees and the Zealots

Josephus gives us no more precise explanation of the origin of the honorary title 'Zealots' than this text, in which he simply says that the rebels in Jerusalem

'took their name from their professed zeal for what was good',[135]

although this was, in his opinion, a complete distortion of the truth.

Hardly any information about the model of Phinehas can be gained from Josephus, however, since he deprives this figure of his characteristic features and does not employ the word 'zeal' at all in connection with Phinehas. A first step in the direction of an understanding of the name is provided by the early history of the Maccabees, in which such great importance is attributed to the example of Phinehas the Zealot.

(a) The Maccabees and the Zealots

J.M. Jost, the first Jewish historiographer in modern times, pointed to certain connections between the Zealots and the Maccabees.[136] H. Graetz, writing at a later period, was the first to note the importance of Phinehas as a model for the two movements.[137] The comments made by both these authors led K. Kohler[138] to go further and claim that the Zealot movement originated at the time of the Maccabees. Although it cannot be proved that the Zealots existed as an organized movement at that time, it is certain that zeal for God was present as a religious attitude since Mattathias. In his detailed work on the relationship between the Zealots and the Maccabees, W.R. Farmer tried to prove that the Zealots

---

[134] V. Aptowitzer and A. Spiro have also tried to provide the polemic against Phinehas with a historical background. Aptowitzer, *op. cit., passim*, see also Index under Phinehas, believed that they reflected the Pharisaical attacks against the theology of the Hasmonaean court, whereas Spiro thought that what lay behind them was the conflict between the Jews and the Samaritans. Both scholars have, however, dated the historical cause too early.

[135] *Bell* 7,270; see also *Bell* 4,160f.; see above, p. 66, n. 328.

[136] *Geschichte des Judenthums und seiner Secten*, 1857, 1, 327f., n. 1.

[137] *Geschichte der Juden*, 5th. ed. 1905, 3.

[138] *Harkavy-Festschrift*, 9f.

were simply the Maccabees' successors and that their entire movement had been determined by the Maccabees.[139]

It cannot be denied that the two movements had much in common. They both had the same model — Phinehas and the zeal with which he, in a moment of particular distress, acted as the representative of God's anger and killed the law-breaker, thus turning God's punishment away from Israel. Just as Mattathias and his sons executed judgement against transgressors among their own people and at the same time defended themselves against the attacks made by foreign oppressors, so too was the struggle conducted by Judas and his successors directed in the first place against their own compatriots who had, in their view, broken the law of God and had therefore become defectors. Zeal for the law called for unconditional commitment of one's own life, a renunciation of property and flight into the inaccessible desert, a place from which the minor war against both Israel's defectors and the pagan occupying power could be waged. The struggle itself was regarded as a Holy War.[140]

Again, just as religious distress was a sign for the Maccabees that God's anger was on the people, so too was foreign domination a sign of that anger for the Zealots. It could only be turned away and redemption could only come if a zealous action was performed. There was also a parallel with God's covenant with Phinehas: Just as the Hasmonaeans later claimed special rights to rule on the basis of their zeal and that of their father, so too was it possible for the dynasty of Judas to justify certain messianic claims by virtue of their zeal for God's cause. At the same time, both the Maccabees and the Zealots were convinced that they represented the true Israel and were therefore the bearers of God's promise. Finally, the charismatic element that emerged in both Phinehas' and Mattathias' spontaneous action was also reflected later on in the Zealots. The Maccabaean example was revealed, as Farmer has pointed out, among other things even in the naming of Zealot circles.[141]

Although the two movements had many features in common, however, there were also essential differences that cannot be overlooked. During the period of religious persecution, the very foundation of Israel's faith — faith in one God, his law and his sanctuary — was

---

[139] *Maccabees, Zealots, and Josephus,* 1956, *passim.*
[140] For this, see below, p. 282ff.
[141] *NTS* 4 (1957/58), 149. For the name Phinehas among priests, see *CIJ* 1221; 1197f.; 1409.

threatened, although the Romans did not encroach on this at all, but, on the contrary, guaranteed religious freedom for the Jews.[142] The Maccabees had at first to fight for that freedom, but, having achieved it, they to a great extent lost the religious motivation for their struggle, which soon declined to the level of a predominantly political conflict.

For the Zealots, a change of this kind was quite unacceptable. Their call for the sole rule of God gave the whole struggle a fundamentally religious motivation. They regarded any recognition of imperial rule — despite the relatively tolerant attitude of the emperors — as idolatry and apostasy. The Holy War had, for them, to be fought to the bitter end with uncompromising severity. Negotiations with the opponent of the kind that had been conducted again and again by the Maccabees were unthinkable for the Zealots, so long as they continued to include a recognition of a foreign supreme ruler.[143] They responded to all attempts within their own ranks threatening to lead to a peace that involved subjection to Rome by executing the apostate.[144] In comparison with the Maccabees, then, the Zealots displayed a higher degree of intensification.[145]

Finally, the 'Zealots' had a markedly eschatological orientation. It is certainly not just by chance that this element is absent from the First Book of the Maccabees. We may assume that there were essential differences here between the Maccabees and the so-called Hasidim. For the Zealots, however, imminent expectation formed a fundamental part of their struggle.

(b) The Zealots and the Rabbinic Tradition of Phinehas

It is possible to regard the Maccabees in some respects as precursors of

---

[142] The only exception is the attempt made by Caligula to have his image placed in the Temple, when the days of religious persecution threatened to return; see above, p. 105f. and below, p. 341. For what follows, see the review by M. Avi-Yonah, *IEJ* 8 (1958), 202-204.

[143] For the Maccabees' dealings with their opponents, see 1 Macc 6.60ff.; 10.3ff.,15ff.,22ff.,59ff.; 11.23ff.,57ff., etc. The Zealots, on the other hand, refused to surrender even in a hopeless situation. At the most they would only consent to safe-conduct; see *Bell* 6,351ff.; 7,205ff.

[144] For the execution of those who wanted peace and of deserters, see *Bell* 4,378.565; 5,423.534ff.; 6,378ff., etc. The opposition of the Zealots to Ananus b. Ananus, the leader of the moderate wing in Jerusalem, was caused principally by the criticism that he wanted to hand the city over to the Romans; see *Bell* 4,216ff.320f.; see also above, p. 63, n. 305 and below, p. 372, n. 291.

[145] This 'intensification' was unfortunately taken too little into account by W.R. Farmer; see *op. cit.*, 82,87,123f. The Zealots' attitude towards the Torah had clearly become very different from that of the Maccabees; see M. Avi-Yonah, *op. cit.*, 204.

the Zealots. In that case, the rabbinic exegesis of Num 25 can similarly be seen as echoing that movement and as a sign that their influence must have penetrated deeply into Pharisaical circles.[146] In this section, I shall deal briefly with the various points in which the tradition of Num 25 might have been important for the Zealots.

(1) Num 25 to some extent provided them with a theological justification of their activity. Phinehas' zeal and his commitment of his life were the great examples that they followed and the promise that God had made to him legitimated their own actions. Like him, they saw themselves as instruments of God's zealous anger and were consequently prepared to execute judgement on those who broke the law. It is quite probable that the honorary title 'Zealot' was derived directly from 'Phinehas the Zealot'.

(2) They were fully aware of the fact that their 'following of Phinehas' implied circumventing the God-ordained system of justice. Just as Phinehas had in the past acted against the will of the deluded or overawed elders, however, so too were the Zealots convinced that this had to happen everywhere in their own time, wherever God's commandment was ignored and especially where the Synhedrium was entirely dependent on the will of the godless oppressors. Charismatic zealous actions replaced decisions of the court.

A typical example of this contrast between the traditional Pharisaical conception of the law and that of the Zealots can be found in Josephus' account of the murder by 'two particularly audacious Zealots' of Zechariah b. Baris, who had already been acquitted by the court of the seventy in the Temple. Zechariah had been accused of having had treacherous relationships with the Romans. This was a crime that might have been regarded by the Zealots as exchanging worship of God for idolatry. In acquitting the man, the court had, in their view, clearly failed, so they acted like Phinehas and took the law into their own hands.[147]

---

[146] See K.G. Kuhn, *op. cit.*, 519, n. 113, for SifNum 25.5-11: the narrative 'is a glorification of Zealotism, for which Phinehas is the prototype. Conditions in Jerusalem before 70 A.D. therefore form the framework for the representation of the events described in Num 25.5ff'.

[147] *Bell* 4,335-344. Josephus' whole tendency in this account, which represents the Synhedrium of seventy members as a mock court of justice, cannot really be trusted. It is probable that the commitment of the seventy was originally quite serious in its intention (see also the election of the new high-priest), but the 'Zealots' could not tolerate the characteristically Pharisaical leniency of the court. In their view, Zechariah was also subject to the verdict of Deut 13.7-12. The connection made by Wellhausen, *Einleitung zu den drei ersten Evangelien*, 2nd. ed. 1911, 118ff., between this episode and Mt 23.35 is

(3) Phinehas also executed justice against the pagan seducers, the Midianites, and their spiritual leader, Balaam. As a high-priest, and anointed for war, he had led the army against the enemy. The war itself was seen as a war of God's vengeance and it took place strictly according to the rules of a Holy War. It was therefore possible for Phinehas to become the model of a leader in the Holy War against the pagan seducers who were preventing Israel from living according to God's law. The killing of Balaam may therefore possibly have formed the model for the judgement of the 'eschatological tyrant'.[148]

(4) Phinehas' action had the effect of turning away God's anger and of expiation. The Zealots were convinced that the people of Israel had become subject to God's anger because they recognized foreign rule and they believed at the same time that that anger was visible in the form of 'messianic woes'.[149] The people had deserved the oppression that they had suffered under Herod and the Romans, because they had refused to acknowledge God as the only Lord. By taking up arms, as Phinehas had done, and executing judgement not only on the defectors, but also in those who had led them astray, the 'Zealots' believed that they would be able to turn aside God's anger and clear away all the obstacles standing in the way of the beginning of the time of salvation. The killing of the godless became a religious deed, expiatory in its effect and directly comparable to a sacrificial act.[150]

(5) Those who were called to 'follow Phinehas' had to be ready to sacrifice their own lives and to accept the hostility of lawbreakers, who were, of course, in the majority. It is possible that this readiness to accept martyrdom in Zealot circles was based on the reference to Is 53.[151]

(6) This unconditional readiness to sacrifice oneself was rewarded by the promise of the 'covenant of salvation', which was presumably

---

not justified. It is possible, however, that this event is confused in the rabbinate with legendary extensions of 2 Chron 24.19ff.; see Klausner, *Hist* 5, 215.

[148] There may perhaps be a relationship between the tradition of the killing of Balaam by Phinehas and the killing of the Antichrist by Elijah (and Enoch) in CoptApcEl 42; see J. Jeremias, *TD* 2, 939f. See also below, p. 303f.

[149] Judas' proclamation was also a sermon threatening punishment; see above, p. 20f.; for the 'messianic woes', see below, p. 245f.

[150] For the rabbinic thesis: 'The one who sheds the blood of the godless is like one who offers sacrifice', see above, p. 159, n. 77. Jn 16.2: πᾶς ἀποκτείνας ὑμᾶς δόξῃ λατρείαν προσφέρειν τῷ θεῷ suggests that this idea was already operative in New Testament times; see Bill. 2, 565.

[151] See above, p. 157, n. 67; for a movement like that of the Zealots, which again and again produced new martyrs, there was a particularly clear affinity with this glorification of suffering in Is 53.

interpreted in the light of Mal 2.5 as a 'covenant of life and peace' and therefore included, for the Zealots, the certainty of eternal life or of resurrection. The promise of an 'eternal priesthood' was interpreted in a special way by the members of those priestly circles who were close to the Zealot movement. They may perhaps have derived from that promise the claim that the leadership of Israel had to begin with the priesthood.[152]

(7) Elijah must also have been important for the Zealots as the second great figure of 'zeal' in the Old Testament. The strange identification of Phinehas and Elijah, which came about in the course of the first century A.D., can be ascribed to Zealot circles, since it would not be wrong to assume that their interest was greatest in forming a connection between the two figures. This assumption also makes it easier to understand why the official rabbinic tradition was so reluctant to accept this identification and its spread in the popular Haggadah.

(8) This double figure of Phinehas and Elijah may possibly have been expected as the eschatological redeemer in Zealot circles. It was precisely such a predominantly priestly group of men, to whom Josephus as a rule gave the name of ζηλωταί and who had occupied the Temple, who had so vigorously rejected the messianic claims of such men as Menahem and Simon bar Giora.[153] It is possible that it was in that group that the expectation that God would bring redemption about from heaven by a direct intervention in the Sanctuary had its origin. The paucity of statements made in the sources and especially in the works of Josephus, however, do not encourage us to do more with such assumptions than merely formulate a hypothesis.[154]

(9) The widely differing rabbinic judgement of Phinehas and his zeal for God is surely part of the general debate with the ideas of the Zealot movement with which we have already come into contact several times in the works of the rabbinate in the second and third century A.D. A completely positive assessment of Phinehas' action (Sifre Numbers and Numbers Rabbah) can be contrasted with a cautiously negative attitude

---

[152] For the Zealots' hope of resurrection, see below, p. 269f. For the division in the Zealot movement into a group determined by the descendents of Judas the Galilaean and a priestly group, see below, p. 358ff.

[153] For the debates about the Zealots' messianic expectation, see below, p. 293ff.

[154] See below, p. 222f., 242ff. It may perhaps not be purely coincidental that the last high-priest, who was chosen by the Zealots by drawing lots, was also called Phinehas; see, for example, Bell 4,155 and Ant 20,227, Φάννι, Φανάσης. See also K. H. Rengstorf, A Complete Concordance to Flavius Josephus, with Supplement, Leiden 1968 and after, 122. R. Eisler is much too speculative when he identifies this last high-priest Phinehas with the eschatological high-priest Phinehas-Elijah; see 2,159, n. 4 (but cf. also 2, 78, n. 5).

(jer. Sanhedrin) on the one hand and a conciliatory approach (bab. Sanhedrin) on the other. Criticism of the later effectiveness of Phinehas was intended to show that this figure, who was identified above all in the minds of the people with Elijah, had also seriously harmed Israel. It is clear from a number of examples that the zeal of the Old Testament models had become suspect, presumably on the basis of the memory of the terrible distress that the religious ideal of 'zeal for the law' had brought upon Judaism during the first century A.D.

C. 'ZEAL' AS A TYPICAL ELEMENT OF PIETY IN LATE JUDAISM

In the Acts of the Apostles (22.3), Paul begins his address to the people of Jerusalem with these words:

'I am a Jew, born at Tarsus in Cilicia, but brought up in this city at the feet of Gamaliel, educated according to the strict manner of the law of our fathers, being zealous for God[155] as you all are this day'.

Paul's judgement points in the same direction in this text from his letter to the Romans (10.2):

'I bear them witness that they have zeal for God, but it is not enlightened'[156]

This 'zeal for God', then, was not an aspect that was exclusively confined to the Zealots as a clearly defined party. It was something that concerned the whole of Palestinian Judaism at that time. In its most acute form, as revealed in the figures of Phinehas and Elijah, it could be understood as an attitude that led Jews to be zealous for God in the place of God 'with God's zeal'. The Testament of Asher therefore speaks, in a discussion of the punishment of the godless, of an 'imitation of God'.[157] In a more general sense, zeal meant a passionate giving of oneself to God's cause that was associated with a readiness to avenge every form of sacrilege.

---

[155] The ζηλωτὴς ... τοῦ θεοῦ was to some extent undoubtedly experienced as offensive. The Vulgate reads τοῦ νόμου for it and the Harclean version of the Syr. text has with Gal 1.14: τῶν πατρικῶν μου παραδόσεων.

[156] For this, see O. Michel, *Der Brief an die Römer* (*Meyers Kommentar*), 13th ed. 1966, 254, n. 1: 'This zeal for Yahweh was given to Israel as a task and it became the special vocation of Israel. Paul does not call Israel's 'zeal' into question ..., but simply complains of the blindness of the people's zeal ... The struggle for Israel is therefore a debate about the direction taken by Israel's zeal'.

[157] TestAsh 4,3: ὅτι μιμεῖται κύριον ...; cf. 4,5: ... ἐν ζήλῳ κυρίου πορεύονται. See also below, n. 159; p. 180, n. 174; p. 181, n. 183.

The first named radical expression of this appears in the interpretation
of the 'zeal' of Jacob's sons Simeon and Levi in avenging the violation of
their sister (Gen 34). Judith's prayer is relevant here:

> 'O Lord God of my father Simeon, to whom thou gavest a sword to take
> revenge on the strangers ... Thou gavest ... all their booty to be divided
> among thy beloved sons, who were zealous for thee (ἐζήλωσαν τὸν ζῆλόν
> σου), and abhorred the pollution of their blood ...'[158]

The brothers' revenge is expressed in the most emphatic way in the
Book of Jubilees, in which the action performed at Shechem is presented
as a 'pollution of Israel' and the killing of the men of Shechem as decreed
by heaven itself.[159] The circumcision of the Shechemites is suppressed, as
it is in Josephus' *Antiquities*.[160] Levi's zeal is, like Phinehas', rewarded by
God's promise of salvation:

> 'And the seed of Levi was chosen for the priesthood and as Levites, so that
> they would serve God like us every day (that is, the angels in God's sight) and
> so that Levi and his sons would be blessed in eternity, since he was zealous to
> practise justice and judgement and revenge on all those who rise up against
> Israel'.[161]

Finally, in the Testament of Levi,[162] Levi says of himself:

> '... I was zealous because of the atrocity that they had committed against
> my sister'.

Although he had been given the task of taking revenge on Shechem
by the angel of God,[163] he brought God's anger down on himself because
the Shechemites had previously circumcised themselves — against
Levi's will — and had therefore become Israelites *de iure*.

This interpretation of Gen 34, which had already become current at
the time of the Maccabees,[164] is directly opposed to the rabbinic

---

[158] Jdt 9.2ff.

[159] Jub 30,5. For what follows, see K. Kohler, *Harkavy-Festschrift*, 11.

[160] *Ant* 1,337f.: Josephus emphasizes that Shechem wanted to take Dinah as his wife 'in
opposition to the law'.

[161] Jub 30,18, translation based on E. Littmann, Kautzsch, *Apokryphen und
Pseudepigraphen* 2, 91. As in the case of Phinehas in Ps 106.31, it is said in v. 17 that God
'reckoned it to them as righteousness'. The rabbinate also regarded Simeon and Levi as
'zealots' who had been the first to erect a barrier against fornication; see above, p. 160, n.
79.

[162] TestLev 6,3.

[163] TestLev 5,3: The angel gives him the sword and the shield with the task: 'Take
revenge on Shechem for Dinah and I shall be with you ...' A similar view is presented in
the text of Joseph and Asenath 23,14; see P. Riessler, *Altjüdisches Schrifttum*, 1928, 529.

[164] At least the Book of Judith can be dated to this period; see O. Eissfeldt, *Old
Testament: an Introduction*, 1965, 586f.

exposition of Num 25. Whereas in the first case — above all in the later tradition — the aspect of zeal was toned down contrary to the original intent of the text, here — likewise against the actual sense of the text — it was particularly emphasized and even glorified. This fact, taken in conjunction with the emphasis placed on the tradition of Phinehas in the First Book of the Maccabees, which has been discussed above, shows clearly that 'zeal' had already become an influential religious attitude in Palestinian Judaism during the Maccabaean period.

Since the Book of Jubilees and the Testament of Levi are very closely connected with the Essene tradition,[165] it is obvious that we have to look there too for evidence of active religious zeal. Certain statements made by the teacher of the sect are particularly striking:

> 'I became a spirit of zeal (רוח קנאה) against all who are looking for (deceitful) words'.[166]
> 'According to the measure of my closeness (to God), I was zealous against all evil-doers and men of deceit'.[167]

Like his ancestor Levi, who, because of his zeal (Ex 32) was also deemed worthy by the sect of special blessings,[168] the teacher clearly makes himself the instrument of God's zeal. 'Zeal for the law' could also be required, e.g., in the Community Rule where not only 'long-suffering and great sympathy', but also 'zeal for just precepts'[169] were included among the features characterizing the 'way of the spirit of truth'. This demand for 'zeal for the law' reappears later with an eschatological emphasis:

> '(The wise man should preserve) an everlasting hatred against all men of perdition in the spirit of concealment. He should leave the hardship of manual work to them ... He should, however, be a man who is zealous for the commandment and its time until the day of vengeance'.[170]

---

[165] Fragments of the Book of Jubilees and the Testament of Levi were found in the caves at Qumran; see Barthélemy and Milik, *Qumran Cave I*, 1955, 82ff. and 88ff.; see also O. Eissfeldt, *op. cit.*, 670f. and 635. According to the Covenant of Damascus 16,3f., the Book of Jubilees especially is presupposed.

[166] 1QH 2,15; cf. Num 5.14,30; according to CD 1,18, the text should be complemented with דורשי חלקות.

[167] 1QH 14,14; cf. the translation of T. Gaster, *The Scriptures of the Dead Sea Sect*, 1957, 186 and 215, n. 6. What is meant is probably: Since I am close to God, by virtue of membership in the sect, I am zealous (for him).

[168] Cf. the emphasis placed on the blessing of Levi, Deut 33.8-11, in 4QTest (No. 175), 14-20 = 1Q;DJD V, 58.

[169] 1QS 4,3f.

[170] 1QS 9,21-23: להיות איש מקנא לחוק ועתו ליום נקם. Cf. the translation of P. Wernberg-Møller, *The Manual of Discipline*, 1957, 36.

Here, as well, zeal appears as a fundamental religious attitude, but it is confined in the present era to a detailed keeping of the law. Hatred against the 'men of perdition', for example, has to be restrained until the 'day of vengeance', the coming of which is described above all in the War Scroll.[171]

In the New Testament, the concept of zeal is encountered in a particularly striking way in Paul's letters and in references to the Apostle, who had, of course, been a Pharisee. In his own words, he was 'extremely zealous for the traditions of his fathers' (Gal 1.14) and an essential aspect of this attitude was that he was also 'as to zeal, a persecutor of the church' (Phil 3.6).

It should not, however, on any account be assumed that he was a member of the Zealot party.[172] If he had been, he would hardly have been given special and plenary powers by the high-priest to act against Christians (Acts 9.1). No, Paul's 'zeal' is identical with his 'as to righteousness, under the law blameless' (Phil 3.6). Zeal for the law was, after all, an integral part of Pharisaical piety for the law before 70 A.D. The fact that Paul several times used the terms ζῆλος and ζηλοῦν after his conversion can be regarded as an aspect of his Pharisaical inheritance.[173] This applies above all to impressive formulas, e.g., in 2 Cor 11.2:

'I am jealous (= zealous) for you with divine jealousy (= zeal)'[174]

In this text, Paul clearly sees himself as the instrument of God's zeal in the battle for the hearts of the Corinthian community. It cannot be simply a matter of chance that even those Pharisees who had joined the community in Jerusalem are described in Acts 21.20 as being 'zealous for the law'. It would be quite wrong to regard this text as implying that these Pharisees were connected with the Zealot party.[175] All that it indicates is that they took with them into the Judaeo-Christian community their original attitude of piety.

---

[171] For the 'day of vengeance', see T. Gaster, op. cit., 108: The expression is derived from Deut 32.35 (LXX and Sam.). Among the Samaritans, it was understood as the 'day of judgement'. In the Community Rule, this concept occurs in 10,19; see also 1,11; 2,9; 4,12; 5,12. In the War Scroll, see 3,6f.; 4,12, etc.

[172] For this, see H. Schlier, Der Brief an die Galater (Meyers Kommentar), 12th. ed. 1962, 51. For what follows, see also J.-A. Morin, RB 80 (1973), 345ff.

[173] See 1 Cor 12.31; 14.1,12,39; 2 Cor 7.7,11; 9.2.

[174] Concerning the interpretation of this formula, see A. Stumpf, TD 2, 881.

[175] Bo Reicke, 'Der geschichtliche Hintergrund des Apostelkonzils und der Antiochia-Episode Gal 2,1-14', Studia Paulina, Haarlem 1953, 172-187, has attempted to interpret the text in this way. E. Haenchen, Acts of the Apostles, 1971, 608, n. 4, is, on the other hand, correct in his argument that 'Luke took care not to give the impression that Christians were connected with the Jewish Zealots'.

The terms are also used in the New Testament to describe the attitude prevailing in Jewish circles[176] or in such ethical admonitions as ζήλευε ... καὶ μετανόησον in Acts 3.19.[177] A remarkable Johannine use of the word 'zeal' is found in the interpretation of Jesus' cleansing of the Temple, which, with an appeal to Ps 69.10, was understood in the community as an act of zeal. This zeal 'consumed' the one who was seized by it. In other words, it required him to sacrifice his life.[178]

It is not purely fortuitous that the term 'zeal' is not found in the synoptic gospels. Although Jesus — like the Zealots — called for total surrender in obedience to God's will, he did not require his followers to use the violence that formed an essential part of the Jewish concept of zeal. In addition to this, the concept was so emotionally charged in Jewish circles that it easily led to hatred and anger.[179] Jesus rejected 'zeal' as a form of piety in the emphasis that he placed on the commandment to love one's enemies.[180]

Josephus also speaks about the Jews' zeal for the law in several different contexts.[181] This was, in his opinion, a typical feature of Jewish piety. According to him, for example, Agrippa II said, in his great speech to the people of Jerusalem:

> 'You are zealously concerned that not one of the laws that you have inherited from your fathers should be rendered null and void'.[182]

The Apocalypse of Baruch, which dates back to shortly after the destruction of Jerusalem, presents King Josiah as a typical Zealot:

> 'And he not only killed the godless ... He also had the bones of those who had died taken out of the graves (2 Kings 23.16,20) ... He also burned with fire those who had been desecrated (by idolatry). And the people who had obeyed them while they were alive he threw into the Valley of Kidron and piled stones on them. And he was zealous with the whole of his soul with the zeal of the Almighty[183] and he alone clung at that time to the law and

---

[176] The Judaizers: Gal 4.17; the Sadducees: Acts 5.17; the Jews in Pisidian Antioch: 13.45; in Thessalonica: 17.5.

[177] See also Tit 2.14; 1 Pet 3.13. What we have here may be a linguistic usage with Greek overtones.

[178] Jn 2.17; see also R. Bultmann, *Gospel of John, a Commentary*, 1971, 124.

[179] See H. Braun, *Spätjüdischer und frühchristlicher Radikalismus*, 1957, 2, 57ff., n. 1.

[180] See Mt 5.21ff., 38ff.; Lk 6.27ff., etc.

[181] See *Ant* 12,271 (see above, p. 154f.); 20,41.47.

[182] *Bell* 2,393. Even Dio Cassius used the verb ζηλοῦν to describe the proselytes: ὅσοι τὰ νόμιμα αὐτῶν (the Jews) καίπερ ἀλλοεθνεῖς ὄντες ζηλοῦσι 37,17 (Reinach, 182). See also Josephus, *Ap* 2,282.286.

[183] ܘܡܢ ܟܠܗܘܢ ܢܦܫܗ ܛܢ ܒܛܢܢܐ ܕܐܠܗܐ ܕܚܝ cited according to the Syr. text, ed. M. Kmosko, *Patrologia Syriaca*, I,2, 1907, col. 1185f. (= SyrBar 66,5).

admitted no uncircumcised man or evil-doer into the whole of the country
...'[184]

This presentation of Josiah corresponds so closely to the Zealot ideal that we may almost assume that, like Sifre Numbers 25, it includes an element of Zealot scriptural exegesis. At the same time, however, it is important to stress in both cases that neither the Apocalypse of Baruch nor Sifre Numbers were works that were directly connected with the Zealots. The fact that traditions of this kind were included in the wider rabbinic tradition shows clearly that zeal for God and his law was at least to some extent valued as a distinct form of piety in that tradition.

It is in any case strange and cannot in any sense be attributed to mere chance that the high value placed on zeal in the rabbinate only appears in those places where it had already been previously indicated by a tradition — as, for example, in the case of such figures as Phinehas and Elijah[185] — and even there zeal was at least partly judged with surprising criticism. Running parallel to this development was a change of meaning in the concept of 'zeal', which came in the rabbinate to lose its original Hebrew meaning and to be understood more in the sense of 'jealousy' or 'envy'.[186]

In this perspective, it is not difficult to appreciate that even the Old Testament statements about Yahweh in which he was described as a 'zealous (jealous) God' came to be regarded as offensive. Rabbi's interpretation of the אֵל קַנָּא of Ex 20.5, for example, was that God controlled zeal and did not let it rule over him.[187] According to a different interpretation of the same words, this 'zeal of God' was restricted in such a way that it was seen merely as a reaction to idolatry:

> 'In zeal I punish idolatry in them, but in other things I am merciful and gracious ...'[188]

This restrictive change of meaning is all the more remarkable in that it

---

[184] 66,3–5; translation based on Kautzsch, *Apokryphen und Pseudepigraphen*, 2, 437. Death by burning as a punishment for idolators is also to be found quite often in Pseudo-Philo 26,1–5; 27,15; 38,3f.

[185] What is more, the idea of religious zeal occurs very seldom. According to a tradition that goes back to R. Simeon b. Lakish, Abraham appears in GenRab 42,8 to Og, a fugitive from Sodom and the man who brought the news to Abraham of Lot's capture (Gen 14.13), as a קְנִיוֹן, that is, a zealot or avenger. The Yalkuth on 72 reads קַנַּאי = 'zealot'; see Jastrow, *Dictionary*, 2, 1335.

[186] See Jastrow, *Dictionary*. 2, 1387f.,1390; see also A. Stumpff, *TD* 2, 890, n. 12.

[187] MekEx on 20.5 (L 2, 244).

[188] *op. cit.*; following this, there is a dispute between R. Gamliel II and a philosopher about the question of God's zeal with regard to idolatry; see also AZ 54b.

was possible in early Jewish writings to speak of 'God's zeal' in the wider sense.[189] This situation can be explained by the fact that, on the basis of the catastrophes that occurred in 70 and 134/35 A.D., a certain change took place in the rabbinate's way of assessing 'zeal', causing the concept to lose its originally positive meaning.

We may conclude, then, that the history of the Jewish people in Palestine from the time of the Maccabees onwards can provide us with a great number of examples of the representation of zeal as a fundamental religious attitude of Palestinian Judaism at that period. Again and again they showed the same readiness to take the law into their own hands and even to use violent means to preserve the integrity of God's law and his sanctuary, often sacrificing their own lives in the process. Their bitter opposition to Herod, their murderous plot against him and their removal of the eagle from the Temple can all be understood in this light. The same also applies to the revolt in Jerusalem after the tyrant's death and the many disturbances in the city during the rule of the procurators. Whenever the people had the impression that the law of their God or his Temple were threatened by the Roman rulers, they rose up and protested in defence of their religious rights. They did not even shrink from open revolt.[190]

D. ZEAL FOR THE LAW AND THE SANCTUARY IN PALESTINIAN JUDAISM AND AMONG THE ZEALOTS

1. The 'Lawlessness' of the Zealots according to Josephus

It is understandable that Josephus should not have provided us with any direct information about the Zealots' zeal for the law of God and the sanctuary. At the same time, however, it is possible to draw certain

---

[189] See Wis 5.17; TestAsh 4 (see above, p. 177f.); SyrBar 64,3. In Qumran, see 1QH 1,5; 9,3 (cf. Is 42.13: Yahweh as a warrior); 12,14; Fragm 3,17; 1 QS 2,15 in the curse of the priests; 4QDibHam = M. Baillet, *RB* 68 (1961), 202 (III,11); 206 (V,5): God transforms the country into a desert with the fire of his zeal. In the New Testament, see 2 Cor 11.2 and Heb 10.27.

[190] The protests are directed above all against attempts to introduce any form of worship of the emperor into Jewish territory (see above, p. 102ff.) and against attempts to desecrate the Temple (see below, p. 206ff.). The destruction of a scroll of the Torah by soldiers engaged in looting was, for example, a way of devaluing the law which aroused the zeal of the Jews; see *Ant* 20,114ff. = *Bell* 2,228f. According to *Ant*18,84, when the Jews were driven out of Rome during the reign of Tiberius, very many (πλείστους) preferred to be executed rather than act contrary to the law and become soldiers. For the Jews' readiness to sacrifice everything for the law, see Josephus, *Ap* 1,43; 2,219, and Philo, *LegGai* 117 (M 2, 562).

conclusions from the way in which he has presented the attitude of the 'Zealots' towards these two fundamental realities of Jewish faith. For the Zealots' attitude with regard to the law and the Temple, Josephus basically has only two terms: hostility to the law[191] and defilement.

According to Josephus' presentation, it was totally impossible even to enumerate the number of times that the 'Zealots' had broken the law of God, since they had exceeded all bounds.[192] He reports therefore few concrete examples, but brings, rather, a plethora of charges against the Zealots and their accomplices, particularly in various speeches, e.g., of the high-priests, Ananus and Jesus,[193] by Titus[194] or even his own.[195]

Among these charges are accusations that the Zealot leaders had trampled on the laws,[196] that they were prepared to destroy those inherited from the patriarchs,[197], that their senses were blinded by their hostility to the law (παρανομία)[198] and that this hostility was indeed so great that it aroused the abhorrence of the Romans.[199] So great was their crime in fact that they deserved, even more than the Sodomites, to be lost in a second flood.[200]

In the summary that he gives of his position in the seventh book of *The Jewish War*, Josephus declares that the various groups of rebels had each tried to go further than the other in 'evil actions against God' (ἔν τε ταῖς πρὸς θεὸν ἀσεβείαις).[201] He concludes his charge against them with a brief reference to the 'Zealots', saying that these had reached the peak of complete lawlessness (ἀνομία).[202] One criticism above all occurs again and again in *The Jewish War* and this is the same as the one made in the rabbinic tradition of Phinehas by the tribe of Simeon, namely, that the

---

[191] The Zealots were enemies of the law: see *Bell* 4,184; 6,102.

[192] *Bell* 5,393 and 442.

[193] *Bell* 4,163-192 and 238-269.

[194] *Bell* 6,124ff.346ff.

[195] *Bell* 5,362ff.401-419; 6,95.99ff.

[196] *Bell* 4,258: πατήσαντες τοὺς νόμους; cf. *Bell* 4,157: παιζόμενον τὸν νόμον; 4,386: ἐγελᾶτο δὲ τὰ θεῖα.

[197] *Bell* 4,348: A Zealot who had deserted in the presence of the Idumaeans: καταλύουσι τὰ πάτρια.

[198] *Bell* 5,343; the term παρανομία is used especially frequently by Josephus to describe the Zealots: *Bell* 4,144.339.351; 5,393.414.442; 6,122, etc.

[199] *Bell* 6,122f.

[200] *Bell* 5,566.

[201] *Bell* 7,260; cf. *Bell* 5,414: πομπεύετε παρανομοῦντες. For the ἀσέβεια of the Zealots, see *Bell* 4,157; 5,8.15.401ff.411.442; 6,100ff., etc.

[202] *Bell* 7,268: τὴν τελεωτάτην ... ἀνομίαν, ἐν ᾗ τὸ τῶν ζηλωτῶν ... γένος ἤκμασεν.

Zealots had made the blood of their compatriots flow in streams without a judgement of the court.[203]

Josephus accuses the Zealots not only of hostility to the law of God, but also of desecrating his Temple. His detailed criticisms in this respect are very petty[204] and refer, on the one hand, to the Zealots' reputed looting of the Temple[205] and, on the other, to the fact that they had made the Temple a place of battle and bloodshed.[206] These complaints are summarized in the recurring lament that the holy place had been repeatedly defiled by the rebels.[207]

The already existing formula provided by Is 63.18 or in the Maccabaean tradition, that of the 'treading down of the sanctuary', appears twice in The Jewish War:[208]

> 'The place that is venerated by the whole world and is even greatly esteemed, on the basis of hearsay, by foreigners dwelling at the ends of the earth is trodden down by beasts born here'.[209]

It would not be wrong to assume that this very sharp polemic should not be traced back exclusively to a certain rhetorical exaggeration, but that it was used, in accordance with the generally tendentious purpose of The Jewish War, with a definite aim in view. Josephus employed these sharp attacks in an attempt to oppose the view that the Zealots were guided in their struggle against Rome by zeal for the law and the sanctuary. In his opinion, the very opposite was true. The Zealots and their followers had committed inexpressible outrages against God and his commandment and had desecrated the sanctuary in such a way that God had eventually to destroy it. The Romans, on the other hand, had done everything possible to purify it and preserve it.[210]

---

[203] Bell 4,169f.259.266; 5,4.402, etc.

[204] For this, see Schlatter, GI, 340.

[205] Bell 5,36ff.: John uses the wood intended for the building of the Temple to make catapults (ἀσεβείας ὄργανα); 5,562ff.: John has the offerings in the Temple melted down and cares for those defending the Temple with the provisions dedicated to the Temple; see also Bell 7,263f.

[206] Bell 4,201.242; 5,100ff.380f.; 6,121ff., etc.

[207] Bell 2,424; 4,150.201.242f.: δι' ὑπερβολὴν ἀσεβημάτων μιαίνοντες καὶ τὸ ἀβέβηλον ἔδαφος; 4,402; 6,94ff.124ff.

[208] See Seeseman and Bertram, 'πατέω', TD 5, 940ff.; for individual cases, see Dan 8.13 LXX; 1 Macc 3.45; 4.60; also Rev 11.2 and Lk 21.24.

[209] Bell 4,262: . . . παρὰ τῶν γεννηθέντων ἐνθάδε θηρίων καταπατεῖται (text according to P with Thackeray); see also 4,171 and 6,126f.

[210] See Bell 5,411ff.: God has fled from his Temple; similarly Ant 20,266; see also Bell 6,110: God himself brings about the purifying fire that is directed against the Temple and the city. For the Romans' respect for the law and the sanctuary, see Bell 4,180; 5,363.402f.405f.; 6,93ff.101ff.123: 'among the soldiers there was not one who did not

What we have here, is a form of sharpest polemic which can be defined as 'polemical reversal'. The original striving of the opponent is completely reversed and everything that he previously wanted most decisively to reject is imputed to him. Josephus' complete misrepresentation of the name of the Zealots, to which I have already alluded several times, also points to this same 'polemical reversal'.

2. Zeal for Israel's Purity and for her Religious Privileges

(a) The Struggle against Magic and Sexual Intercourse with Pagans

According to the Holiness Code in the Book of Leviticus 19-26, God required Israel to be pure and holy.[211] Among other things, this Holiness Code above all forbade all forms of magic[212] and all sexual offences.[213] In some cases these sins could be punished by the death penalty.[214]

It may perhaps not be purely fortuitous that, included among the three offences mentioned in Sanh 9,6 that justified the "Zealots'" lynch-law, were a case of magic and a sexual offence. Even in other respects, magic and fornication were usually connected with each other in Palestinian Judaism and often traced back to Balaam as the originator of both.[215] Presumably both were seen as tempting the people to practise idolatry. The מְקַלֵּל בְּקוֹסֵם in Sanh 9,6 points to a definite form of magic, presumably in connection with the use of the divine name. This is derived from the root קסם, which in the later period included all forms of magic.[216]

Magic was taken for granted in the Hellenistic world and even in

---

look up to the Temple with respect, treat it with veneration and pray that the robbers would change their minds before an irretrievable disaster occurred'. See also Philo, *VitMos* 1,295 (M 2, 127): Balaam's advice to Balak.

[211] Lev 19.2; 20.7,26.

[212] Lev 19.26ff.,31; 20.6,27.

[213] Lev 18.6-22; 19.29; 20.10-21; 21.9. Not only individuals, but also the whole country was made unclean by sexual crimes: 18.27.

[214] Lev 20.6,10ff.; 21.9. See Mal 3.5: 'Against the sorcerers, against the adulterers'.

[215] See AscIs 2,5; EthEn 8,2f.; TestJud 23; Shammai in Ab 2,7; Sot 9,13: The wise say: Whoring and magic have brought everything to ruin; LamRab 2,2 (Bill. 1, 1047): Sichnin (was destroyed) because of magic and Magdala (was destroyed) because of fornication'; TanNoah, 20, ed. Buber 24b: Balaam made a beginning with the houses of prostitution ... and with magic'. Balaam had already been described in Josh 13.22 as קוֹסֵם.

[216] See Jastrow, *Dictionary*. 2, 1396f.

Judaism it seems to have been very widespread.[217] It is true that Josephus does not report any steps taken by the Zealots against magic practices, rather he himself calls certain rebels γόητες.[218] There is however a rabbinic account concerning R. Simeon b. Shetach, the leading Pharisee at the time of Alexander Jannaeus and Alexandra, according to which this Pharisee had 'with hot hands' as many as eighty women hanged in Ascalon because of magic practices. Even though the individual details of this event have been given a legendary colouring, it is still hardly possible to doubt that it has a historical centre, since it completely contradicted later rabbinic praxis.[219] We are bound to regard this execution as an act of 'zeal', since it took place without reference to the ordinary course of justice.[220]

The second of the two crimes punished by the 'Zealots' was sexual intercourse with a pagan woman. This offence was, of course, what prompted Phinehas to act zealously. During the early period of their history, the Israelites were quite unrestrained in their attitude towards this and the first clear prohibition was formulated in Deut 7.3. From the time of Ezra and Nehemiah onwards, it was condemned with particular severity. The reforming Jews of the Seleucid period were laxer in their approach to this prohibition,[221] whereas the Hasidim, appealing to Gen 34, gave it a much sharper emphasis. This is particularly clear in the Book of Jubilees, in which even the contracting of a marriage with pagans is threatened with the harshest punishments:

'And if there is a man in Israel who wants to give his daughter or his sister to any man from the seed of pagans, (he) shall surely die and is to be stoned, since he has performed a shameful act in Israel. On the other hand, they are to

---

[217] See D. Delling, 'μάγος', TD 4, 356ff.; M.P. Nilsson, Geschichte der griechischen Religion, 2, Die hellenistisch-römische Zeit, 2nd. ed. 1961, 520ff. For Judaism, see B.-Gr.Rel. 339f.; M. Hengel, Judaism and Hellenism, 1,241.

[218] See below, p. 229, n. 4.

[219] Sanh 6,5; SifDeut 21,22.221; jHag 77d, 41-78a, 14 = jSanh 23c,47ff. For the deviation from the rabbinic praxis of the law, see S. Krauss, Sanhedrin/Makkot, Die Mischna, Text, Übersetzung und ausführliche Erklärung, ed. G. Beer et al., IV,4 and 5, 1933, 196.

[220] K. Kohler, Harkavy-Festschrift, 13, has pointed to its relationship with the Zealot spirit; see also E. Stauffer, Jerusalem und Rom, 1957, 63. Both H. Graetz, 5th. ed., 3, 145f. and Schlatter, GI, 157f., are convinced of the historicity of this anecdote, but Schürer, 1, 231, n. 7, is opposed to it, whereas Derenbourg, 69, tries to relate it to Simon the Maccabee.

[221] For what follows, see G. Kittel, Das Konnubium mit den Nichtjuden im antiken Judentum (Forschungen zur Judenfrage 2), 1937. For the period of the Maccabees, see 1 Macc 1.15 and op. cit., 39; M. Hengel, Judaism and Hellenism, 1,279ff.

burn the woman with fire[222] ... And there should be no adulteress and unholiness found in Israel ...; since Israel is sanctified to God and every man who pollutes (it) shall surely die ... And for this law there is no restriction of days and no forgiveness and no pardon ...'

Going beyond the concrete point of departure in Gen 34, marriage with a pagan woman was also strictly forbidden:

'And Israel does not become pure from this impurity if it has a woman from the daughters of the pagans ... (That) brings torment on torment and curse on curse and all kinds of punishment and torment and curse will come both if it does this and if it closes its eyes to those who defile his holy name. (Then) the whole people will be judged ... because of this impurity ... every man and (every) woman (who has done this) are to be desecrators of his sanctuary'.[223]

Since the whole of Israel was polluted, the sanctuary was desecrated and God's judgement was called down on Israel by sexual intercourse with pagans — in the same way as by a sexual offence according to the Holiness Code — the only way in which Israel could achieve expiation from this defilement was by immediately executing the guilty person. In such cases, special importance came to be attached to Old Testament models such as Gen 34 and Num 25.

In the Hasmonaean period, it would seem — at least according to a late account — that sexual intercourse with pagans was prosecuted by law.[224] On the other hand, however, the Hasmonaean rulers were themselves criticized by members of Pharisaical and Essene circles for having intercourse with pagan women and for committing other sexual offences[225] It is even possible that the Psalms of Solomon contain an allusion to this strange contrast between the condemnation of others and at least one Hasmonaean leader's own lifestyle:

'Surpassing everyone in words and conduct, he (= Alexander Jannaeus) is (ready) with harsh words to condemn the guilty in the court. He is prompt to lay his hands on him, as in (pious) zeal (ὡς ἐν ζήλει), while he is himself caught up in a web of sin and impurity. His eyes are directed towards every woman without distinction ... In the night and in secret he sins, because he

---

[222] According to Lev 21.9, this was the punishment for the adulterous daughter of a priest. In the pseudepigraphical tradition, death by burning was the punishment applied to idolators; see above, p. 182, n. 184. What we have here is a typical intensification of the Torah.

[223] Jub 30,7ff.14ff.; translation based on E. Littmann, Kautzsch, *Apokryphen und Pseudepigraphen*, 2, 91.

[224] Sanh 82a; AZ 36b.

[225] TestLev 14,6; see also 9,9f. and TestJud 13,7; 23,2.

thinks that he is not seen. With his eyes he makes sinful arrangements with every woman ...'[226]

The revolt against Alexander Jannaeus can be therefore explained as the result of pious Jews having been aroused to zeal at that time because of this constant disregard of the law and the desecration of the sanctuary. In this respect, then, it is similar to what happened in the Maccabaean period.[227]

It may perhaps have been because he was warned by the example of the Hasmonaeans that Herod, who in other ways frequently overlooked the prescriptions of the Jewish law on a grand scale, was careful to respect it in the question of mixed marriages.[228] Later on, this obligation was observed with considerable laxity in his own family and Josephus, following the Pharisaical tradition quite strictly here, did not hesitate to take up a disapproving attitude.[229]

Josephus' account of the Zealots is, as we have seen, very fragmentary and he tells us nothing about the steps that they may have taken, in accordance with Sanh 9,6, against those who had sexual intercourse with pagans. On the contrary, he accuses them of sexual licentiousness.[230] This criticism can also possibly be regarded as an aspect of the 'polemical reversal' to which I have already referred.

Independently of Sanh 9,6, however, one rabbinic text points to the fact that the prohibition of intercourse with pagan women was given particular attention in Zealot circles. Among the eighteen Halakhoth, which were drawn up some years before the destruction of Jerusalem 'in the upper room of R. Hanania b. Hezekiah b. Garon' and in the drafting

---

[226] PsSol 4,2ff.; see also 2,3.11.13 and 8,9ff. Josephus also refers to the licentious behaviour of Alexander Jannaeus: *Ant* 13,380.

[227] See *Ant* 13,372ff.376.380f. The religious foundation of this civil war is perceptible in the very superficial representation provided by Josephus (which undoubtedly goes back to the account given by Nicolaus of Damascus). See also J. Wellhausen, *Pharisäer und Sadducäer*, 1874, 94–101, especially 96f. For the rabbinic tradition, see Derenbourg, 95-102. The objections raised by Moore, *Judaism*, 1, 64, are not valid.

[228] Herod, for example, required the Arab Syllaeus, who asked for the hand of his sister, to be circumcised: *Ant* 16,225; see also *Ant* 15,320ff.

[229] Herod gave Alexander, his eldest son, a pagan wife (*Ant* 16,11), who first married Juba, the king of Numibia, after her husband's death and then, acting against the law, married her half-brother Archelaus (*Ant* 17,349ff.). According to Josephus, her first husband, Alexander, told her in a dream that she was close to death; see Lev 20.21. Josephus explicitly criticizes the behaviour of Drusilla, who left her husband, who had gone over to Judaism, and married the procurator, Felix: *Ant* 20,142.

[230] *Bell* 4,560ff.: They are reputed to have acted against Deut 22.5 by dressing as women, practising unnatural indecency and transforming the whole of Jerusalem into a brothel; see also 5,402.

of which the Shammaites, who were very close to Zealotism, were able to obtain by force what they wanted in opposition to the minority view held by the Hillelites, there was one precept forbidding Jews to have intercourse with the daughters of the Goyim.[231] We may therefore assume that what was forbidden here is not so much the contracting of marriage — this had already been prohibited by the law proclaimed in Deut 7.1-4 — as every form of extramarital intercourse that, according to Sanh 9,6, led to the intervention of the Zealots. The discussion of the regulation in the Babylonian Talmud,[232] in which Sanh 9,6 is explicitly cited, gives an even sharper emphasis to this point: it is forbidden even to be alone with a non-Jewish woman. It was not so much racial reasons that led to this uncompromising rejection of intercourse with pagans in Palestinian Judaism as presumably the very fact of the Old Testament prohibition itself, the danger of idolatry and the concept of ritual pollution.[233]

The regulation defined in Sanh 9,6 was possibly understood as a *pars pro toto* in the sense that the practice of magic and all cases of a sexual relationship with a non-Jewish woman were handed over to the Zealots for them to carry out punishment. There is no question that both crimes were committed with relative frequency in Judaism during the Hellenistic Roman period.[234] The Zealots, then, appear all the more as the guardians of an 'ideal state' of Israel's perfect purity, a state resting on rigorous demands.

(b) The Struggle for a Strict Observance of the Law Prohibiting Images

In his brief account of the Zealots or *Sicarii*, Hippolytus emphasizes among other things their total rejection of all images of people and animals:

'The members of one party go so far in following the precepts of the law that they do not touch a coin in the conviction that an image should not be

---

[231] jShab 3c,38: ועל בנותיהן ... גזרו על פיתן שלגויים; see Klausner, *Hist* 5, 157. See also below, p. 200ff.

[232] AZ 36b; see Bill. 4, 382f.

[233] This was the opinion of G. Kittel, *op. cit., passim*, as opposed to Moore, *Judaism*, 1, 19f. Very characteristic is the uncompromising position assumed by R. Ishmael (b. Elisha), jMeg 75c,30: 'Whoever marries an Aramaean woman and begets sons from her produces enemies of God'.

[234] For mixed marriages, see G. Kittel, *op. cit.*, 40ff.: It would seem that this regulation was not adhered to so strictly in the diaspora; see Acts 16.1 and Philo, *SpecLeg* 3,29 (M 2, 304); E. Stauffer, *op. cit.*, 95ff.

carried, seen or made. They also refuse to enter a city so that they do not go through a gate on which statues are placed, since they regard it as wrong to pass under statues'.[235]

What we have here is a particularly severe interpretation of the Old Testament prohibition of images.[236] This law was liberally interpreted up to and including the Hasmonaean period,[237] but the interpretation was later narrowed down and this continued until the time of the destruction of Jerusalem.

Josephus' attitude is typical of this very rigorous understanding of the prohibition. He restricted the decoration of the walls of the tabernacle, for example, to ornaments and flowers and excluded all representations of animals.[238] He even sharply criticized Solomon because of the figures of animals in the Temple and the royal palace.[239]

Jewish history of that period provides numerous examples illustrating this uncompromising rejection of all representations of people and animals. Herod the Great scandalized his subjects by placing his trophies in the stadium that had recently been built in Jerusalem and later by the figure of the eagle that he put in the Temple.[240] There were disturbances because of the standards with representations of the emperor erected during the time of Pilate.[241] Vitellius was only able to avoid such disturbances by complying with the Jews' wishes.[242]

---

[235] See above, p. 70, n. 357. K. Kohler, *Harkavy-Festschrift*, 8f.,12, and *JE* 12, 639, has already drawn attention to these connections.

[236] See Ex 20.4ff.; Lev 19.4 and 26.1 (the law of holiness); Deut 4.15ff.; 5.8; 27.25. For books and articles on this subject, see Schürer, 2, 81ff.; Juster, 1, 348, n. 1; S. Krauss, *Talmudische Archäologie*, 3 vols. 1910-12, 2, 295; J.B. Frey, 'La question des images chez les juifs à la lumière des récentes découvertes', *Bib.* 15 (1934), 265-300; E.R. Goodenough, *Jewish Symbols in the Greco-Roman Period.* 1954, 4, 1-24; C. Roth, 'An Ordinance against Images in Jerusalem', *HThR* 49 (1956), 169-177. A concise survey is provided by A. Baumstark, 'Bild I', *RAC* 2, 287-302. See also J. Guttmann and E.R. Goodenough, *HUCA* 32 (1961), 161ff. and 269ff.

[237] Jewish coins of the Persian period, for example, had, with the inscription יהוד, representations of men and animals; see A. Reifenberg, *Ancient Jewish Coins*, 2nd. ed. 1947, 39 Pl. 1. The seven-branched candlestick in the Temple had (according to the representation on the arch of Titus), on its base, an image of a mythical monster and two eagles with garlands in their beaks; see W. Eltester, *NTS* 3 (1957), 102ff. A recently discovered grave of the period of Alexander Jannaeus was found to contain a representation of a ship and its crew and a recumbent stag; see *IEJ* 6 (1956), 127; L.Y. Rahmani et al., 'The Tomb of Jason', *Atiqot* 4 ((1964).

[238] *Ant* 3,113.126; cf. Ex 26.1,31. Unable to remain silent about the cherubim on the ark, Josephus had to admit that they were representations in the form of animals (137).

[239] *Ant* 8,195; cf. ExRab 6,1, R. Simeon b. Jochai.

[240] *Ant* 15,272ff.; 17,151ff. = *Bell* 1,650ff.; see above, p. 100ff.; see also below, p. 321f.

[241] *Ant* 18,55ff. = *Bell* 2,169ff.

[242] *Ant* 18,121f.

In the last two cases and even more particularly in the case of the events during Caligula's reign, it became clear that the question of images was closely connected with that of the worship of the emperor. It is probable that the attitude of strictly believing Jews towards images was intensified by the underlying threat of the emperor-cult.[243] In his apology against Apion (2,75), Josephus was therefore concerned to explain that, in prohibiting images, Judaism did not intend to exclude the honour that was due to the Roman rulers:

> '. . . noster legislator, non quasi prophetans Romanorum potentiam non honorandam, sed tamquam causam neque deo neque hominibus utilem despiciens, . . . interdixit imagines fabricari'.

We may perhaps conclude from this that, in Zealot circles, the prohibition of images in the Pentateuch was used as a 'prophetic' scriptural proof against the cult of the emperor and that this was a view that Apion seized on in his anti-Jewish polemic. Archaeological finds have also confirmed this far-reaching rejection of images between the Maccabaean period and the Jewish War.[244] The only group that formed an exception here was the Hellenized upper stratum of Jewish society and especially the Hasmonaean and Herodian royal house.[245]

The Zealots' attitude in the question of images was quite uncompromising. The destruction of the eagle in the Temple, to which I have referred several times, can be regarded as a typical expression of their hostility to images. This hostility was intensified by the underlying significance of the symbol of the eagle and their own 'zeal for God's house'.[246]

At the beginning of the Jewish War, the revolutionary assembly in Jerusalem decided among other things to destroy the palace built in

---

[243] For this, see C. Roth, *op. cit.* 170, n. 2: 'No doubt, the Jewish opposition was intensified by the "loyal" obligation to show respect to the Imperial symbol'.

[244] Goodenough, *op. cit.*, 7: 'From the days of the Maccabees to the fall of Jerusalem (the Jews) rejected hellenized art, or restricted their borrowings to vine and its variants . . . to the symbolic façade or to rosettes . . .' The Hasmonaean, the Herodian (with the exception of the eagle) and the procuratorian coins also had no images or animals. These are not found until the time of Philippus and Agrippa I, whose territory in the north had an overwhelmingly pagan population; see A. Reifenberg, *op. cit.*, 19ff.

[245] See Aristobulus' gift to Pompey, *Ant* 14,34, and the description in Pliny, *HistNat* 37,2.12. The plinth of a statue of Herod has been preserved; see above, p. 102, n. 140. Portraits of Mariamne and her brother were made and sent to Antonius: *Ant* 15,26f. = *Bell* 1,439f.; see also the statues of the daughters of Agrippa I: *Ant* 19,357. According to tAZ 5,2 (Z. 468), there were already representations of animals, but none of human beings in Jerusalem even before the year 70. The prohibition of images does not seem to have been interpreted so strictly in the Diaspora; see Baumstark, *op. cit.*, 289f.

[246] See above, p. 103; see also below, pp. 258f., 342.

Tiberias by Herod Antipas because this was decorated with images of animals and Josephus was — according to his own statements — given the task of carrying it out. There was, to begin with, strong opposition to this order among the citizens of Tiberias, but eventually the proletariat of the town came under the leadership of one Jesus b. Sapphia, the leader of the radical party in Galilee.[247] This Jesus apparently acted before Josephus and plundered and burned down the palace.[248]

Herod's love of Hellenistic culture was such that his palace in the west of Jerusalem must also have contained statues and wall images.[249] It is therefore understandable that, like the Fortress of Antonia, this palace should have been set on fire by the Zealots, although this action was contrary to all military sense.[250]

No representations of men or animals have been found in Masada. This is perhaps because they were removed by the *Sicarii*. On the other hand, however, graffiti of trees and fortification designs were left behind by the Jewish guards.[251] C. Roth has suggested that there is also a regulation against images in the eighteen Halakoth, but this is very uncertain in view of the fact that he proposes an alteration in the text. Finally, the faces of the gods were filed smooth in the vessels plundered from the revolt of Bar Koseba.[252]

The attitude of the 'members of one party', namely the Zealots, as described by Hippolytus goes much further than most Jews' general hostility to images. In their refusal to accept money and to enter Hellenistic cities, the Zealots excluded themselves to a very great extent from economic life. They were unable, for example, to engage in trading[253] and they had little freedom of movement, being limited to purely Jewish territory. The Essenes are reported to have lived without

---

[247] Jesus b. Sapphia was bitterly hostile to Josephus. He also embodied the spirit of opposition to Rome; see below, p. 371, n. 289.

[248] *Vita* 65ff.

[249] See *Bell* 5,176-182. The term χαλκουργήματα (181) especially can be interpreted as 'bronze statues'. For the Fortress of Antonia, see *Bell* 5,241.

[250] *Bell* 2,430.440; 5,182f. In addition to being furnished with images, they were defiled by the pagan occupation.

[251] See *IEJ* 7 (1957), 27 and Fig. 11. For the arrangement of the Herodian building, see 50ff.

[252] *op. cit.*, 175; jShab 3c,50 צִיּוּר = image, statue, rather than צִיר = fish-broth; see Y. Yadin, *BarKokhba*, London 1971, 99ff.; see also AZ 4,5.

[253] Since the native rulers and the Roman procurators only minted copper coins that were without images, all the silver coins that were in currency in Palestine bore either the image of the emperor — as on the *denarii* — or — as on the Tyrean shekel — the head of Alexander that was stylized in accordance with the ruler at the time. For the circulation of money in Palestine, see Schürer, 2, 62-66 and 270ff.

money, in conformity to an ideal of common ownership.[254] In the case of the Zealots, on the other hand, it was, at least according to Hippolytus, simply a question of strict adherence to the law prohibiting images.[255]

T. Mommsen drew attention to this factor as an 'advance in the theology of opposition' on the Maccabaean period and correctly made a connection between it and the pericope on tribute-money.[256] Not only is the refusal on the part of members of wide circles of Jews to pay taxes to the emperor expressed in it — the images and inscriptions on coins are also given a critical importance. The catch question of the right to pay taxes was put by several politically indifferent Pharisees and the Herodians who were close to the Romans. It is possible that they expected a negative answer from Jesus the Galilaean and the prophetic preacher of the imminent kingdom of God.[257] The fact that they stressed Jesus' love of truth, his fearlessness and his absolute obedience to God's will suggests that they suspected that he was a 'Zealot'. Jesus' counter-question disarmed them completely. The denarius bearing the emperor's head and a description of his dignity,[258] which they showed

---

[254] See Pliny, *HistNat* 5,17.4; Philo, *Omn* 76 (M 2, 457); for the Essenes' common ownership, see *Bell* 2,122.127; 1QS 1,11f.; 5,2 and 6,24f.; CD 13,11f.; 14,20. The discovery of a treasure with 550 coins shows that the Essenes could not, as a community, live without using money. This treasure was presumably their community chest; see J.T. Milik, *Ten Years of Discovery*, 1959, 102, n. 1. It was not unusual to reject the use of money in the ancient world. This practice can be found among the barbarian tribes, the Spartans and in individual philosophers. What lay at the basis of these views was the idea that property held in common and the absence of money was an essential feature of a state of blessedness at the beginning of time; see W. Bauer, 'Essener', *PW Suppl.* 4, 411-413. For the primitive community, see Mk 6.8f. and Acts 2.44f. and 4.32; M. Hengel, *Property and Riches in the Early Church*, London 1974.

[255] This was overlooked by R. Eisler, 2,296ff. The fact that the Zealots minted coins during the Jewish War shows that they did not fundamentally reject money as such.

[256] Mommsen, *RG* 5, 514: 'Although they were few in number, there were saints who believed that they were made unclean when they touched coins bearing the image of the emperor. This was something new and marked an advance in the theology of opposition. The kings Seleucus and Antiochus had not been circumcised and had also received tribute money in silver coins with their own images'.

[257] The representation follows Mk 12.13-17. I do not accept E. Klostermann's suggestion, *Das Markusevangelium*, *HNT*, 4th. ed. 1950, 123, on 12.13, that this is a case of extremist Pharisees acting together with the Herodians, whom they hated, in an attempt to trap Jesus. As a Galilaean prophet, Jesus was from the beginning suspected of extremism and, moreover, the more vulnerable because of the Triumphal Entry and his Cleansing of the Temple; see also Lk 23.2,5 and Jn 11.48f. and 18.19. See also E. Stauffer, *Christ and the Caesars*, 1955, 120: 'Here, in the eyes of his opponents, a new Judas the Galilaean had appeared, a new teacher of the Torah with messianic claims'.

[258] For an illustration of the *denarius* of Tiberius, see E. Stauffer, *Die Theologie des Neuen*

him at his request, proved to them and to all those standing around that they basically recognized the rule of the emperor and were therefore obliged to pay his taxes.[259] Jesus' answer, however, could not be challenged either by the friends of the Romans or by the Zealots, since the use of coins 'with the emperor's image and inscription' implied a positive and open confession of his rule, which was opposed to God, and the payment of taxes was simply the natural consequence of this.

This may explain why the rebels began to put into circulation silver coins bearing representations of the holy objects of cult and festive joy, possibly even including the 'cup of salvation' of Ps 116.13 instead of the offensive image of the emperor and inscriptions proclaiming the redemption of Israel rather than the divinity of the emperor.

Unfortunately Josephus tells us nothing about the Zealots' refusal to touch coins with the the emperor's image. In the rabbinic tradition, however, a few examples of a similarly rigorous hostility to images have been handed down to us. This is in spite of the fact that the rabbinate explicitly declared coins to be free[260] and, under pressure from the community, took a more lenient attitude towards the question of images.[261] The following example illustrates the less rigoristic approach:

'When the house of King Jannaeus was destroyed, non-Jews came and set

---

Testaments, 4th. ed. 1948, Pl. 2 and 5, see also p. 349; see also *Christ and the Caesars*, 1955, 125f. The inscription read: TI(berius) CAESAR DIV(i) AUG(usti) F(ilius) AUGUSTUS; see A. Schlatter, *Der Evangelist Matthäus*, 3rd. unabridged ed. 1948, 648: 'It was no less offensive to give Caesar the title *divus Augustus* than it was to illustrate his head'.

[259] See E. Stauffer, *op. cit.*, 129; *ibid.*, *Die Botschaft Jesu*, 1959, 106; see also G. Bornkamm. *Jesus*, 1960, 121: 'The opponents are referred to a decision which they had already made a long time ago. Gaily they conduct their business, unconcerned about the image and emblem of Caesar on these coins, so long as they can do business with them'. See also R. Eisler, 2,200f., who, however, is too one-sided in his presentation of the state of affairs.

[260] tAZ 5,1 (Z. 468); see also Bill. 4, 393 and A. Schlatter, *loc. cit.*.

[261] In itself, the rabbinic interpretation of the prohibition of images in Ex 20.4 was uncompromisingly strict, see MekEx on 20.4 (L 2, 242ff.), but the strict measures prescribed by the rabbinate were untenable in praxis. This is clear, for example, from the images found in Jewish synagogues from the second century onwards; see S. Goodenough, *op. cit.*, 4, 13ff., and Juster, 1, 348, n. 1. Rabbinic casuistry with regard to the prohibition of images was also fundamentally a toning down of that prohibition; see Bill. 4, 390ff. The members of the family of R. Gamliel II, the great-grandson of Hillel and the first patriarch, who were more open in their attitude towards Hellenistic culture, were especially liberal and broad-minded; see tAZ 5,2 (Z. 468): the seal with human figures in his house; RH 2,8: the figures of the moon for determining the new moon in his upper room; AZ 3,4: his bath in the 'bath of Aphrodite' in Acco, where a statue of the goddess had been erected.

up a Mercurius there. Then other non-Jews, who did not venerate
Mercurius, came and took (the stones) away and paved the roads and streets
with them. Many rabbis avoided these and many ... did not. R. Johanan
said: The child of holy ones walks on these and should we avoid them? —
Who is meant by the son of holy ones? — R. Menahem b. R. Simai. Why is
he called the son of holy ones? — Because he did not look at the figure on a
zuz (= a coin)'.[262]

When this R. Menahem died, the statues were covered with drapery:

'It was said: Just as he did not look at them during his lifetime, so too
should he not see them as one who has fallen asleep'.[263]

The other aspect reported by Hippolytus has a counterpart in the
Mishnah. According to Hippolytus, the Zealot refused to pass through a
gate surmounted by a statue. Similarly, the Mishnah contains a
corresponding prohibition concerning the Asherahs or trees below
which the image of an idol was placed. It was forbidden both to sit in
their shade and to pass underneath them.[264] What we have here is
probably a situation that we have already observed several times before.
It is that the rigorous attitude that prevailed in Zealot circles acted as a
model that worked its way into the rabbinate, even though, broadly
viewed, the precepts had been reshaped and adapted to the
circumstances.

Taken as a whole, C. Roth's view of the question of the prohibition of
images is correct:

'... that the anti-iconic tendency in Judaism reached its climax in the
second half of the first century of the Christian era, at the time of the great
Revolt against Rome'.[265]

---

[262] AZ 50a; translation based on Goldschmidt, 9, 590. The 'house of Jannaeus' may
perhaps be the palace of Herod in Tiberias; see above, p. 192f. R. Johanan (b. Nappacha)
lived in Tiberias and died in 279 A.D; R. Menahem lived towards the end of the second
century A.D. See Strack, Introduction, 117. For parallel traditions, see Bill. 4, 391; see also
K. Kohler, Harkavy-Festschrift, 9.

[263] jAZ 42b,60f.; EcclRab 9,10.2. The prohibition against looking at images can also
be found in another early tradition: tShab 17,1 (Z. 136): 'When passing (on the sabbath),
you should not read the inscriptions under statues and paintings; even on weekdays you
should also not look at paintings, for it is said (Lev 19.4): Do not turn to idols'. This
translation is based on Bill 4, 391, where other parallels will be found.

[264] AZ 3,8; this tradition goes back to the first century A.D. and is interpreted by the
Tannaites R. Simeon (b. Jochai) and R. Jose (b. Halaphta), both of whom lived in the
middle of the second century A.D. The only restriction that is characteristic of the
rabbinate was that it was permitted to pass through if there was no other way available
and the population might therefore be obstructed by the commandment.

[265] op. cit., 177.

(c) Compulsory Circumcision as a Protection of Israel's Privileges

Hippolytus' account continues with the following statement:

'When a member of the second tendency hears that someone has been speaking about God and his laws, but is not circumcised,[266] he lies in wait for him and when he finds him alone threatens him with death if he does not let himself be circumcised. If he does not obey, he is not spared, but killed'.

Two factors emerge from this strange behaviour of the 'Zealots':

(1) They carry out circumcision, in other words, the sign of membership of God's chosen people, on pagans under certain circumstances and also by external force.

(2) They are zealous in seeing to it that Israel's sacred privileges should not be desecrated and usurped by unclean and unauthorized men.

Both these factors were seen as inseparable because of the Old Testament idea that only the circumcised man had a share in the gifts and promises of God's covenant with Israel. Circumcision was the prerequisite for participation in the Passover (Ex 12.44,48) and taking possession of the land (Josh 5.2-11) as well as for admission to the sanctuary (Ezek 44.7). Failure to be circumcised was, on the other hand, threatened with death (Gen 17.4; Ex 4.24ff.) To this can be added the prophetic promise that it would be forbidden in the eschatological age of salvation for anyone who was uncircumcised and impure to enter Jerusalem.[267]

Compulsory circumcision is first mentioned in the case of Mattathias and his sons, who, under certain circumstances, forcibly circumcised Jewish children who had not been circumcised as a result of the religious distress. This was a sign of their 'zeal for the law' that was the dominant characteristic of the early stages of the Maccabaean movement. It was in this way that God's anger about the large-scale defection and the neglect of circumcision that accompanied it was turned aside.[268] Mattathias' grandson Hyrcanus and his son Aristobulus also had the subjected Idumaeans and Ituraeans circumcised by force,[269] but in so doing they went beyond the limits of circumcision defined in the Old Testament.

---

[266] See Aquila's comment, TanMishpatim, 92a = Bill. 3, 489f.: no one can learn the Torah if he has not had himself circumcised.

[267] Is 52.1; Ezek 44.9; for other parallels, see above, p. 118, nn. 224 and 225.

[268] 1 Macc 1.64; 3.8 and 2 Macc 8.5. The Hasidic position, Jub 15,33f., is very illuminating in this context.

[269] *Ant* 13,257.318ff. and 15,264; see also Ptolemy of Ascalon according to Ammonius, *AdfinVocDiff*, ed. Valckenaer, 1822, 73, under Ἰδουμαῖοι.

The Hellenistic conception of the unity of state and religion, with subordination of the latter, can hardly be attributed to the descendants of the Maccabaeans.[270] The real reason for this action, which was incomprehensible to the Hellenistic world, was undoubtedly religious, in that only Israel had the right to inhabit the land of the promise and their conquered neighbours living in the territory that belonged to ancient Israel were therefore confronted with a crucial decision: either they had to become Jews or else they had to leave the country.[271] This demand for the 'purity of the land' also appears in a contemporary ideal image of the messianic kingdom:

> 'He will distribute them according to tribes over the land and no alien (πάροικος) and no foreigner (ἀλλογενής) may live among them'.[272]

The presence of uncircumcised aliens desecrated the Holy Land and encroached on the privilege of Israel, whose inheritance it was.

The same idea is found among the rebels during the Jewish War. When the Herodium had been handed over to the insurgents, the commandant was the only man who was able to save his life because he promised to become a Jew and to accept circumcision.[273] The Galilaean rebels also demanded that two officers of Agrippa II, who had placed themselves under Josephus' protection, should be circumcised. This requirement was rejected by Josephus, who appealed in this case to the principle of religious freedom.[274] He was, however, unable to protect them in the long run from the fanaticism of the Galilaeans and therefore let them escape secretly.[275] According to Dio Cassius, the defenders of Jerusalem accepted Roman deserters, who had found the siege too long,

---

[270] See, for example, S. Baron, *A Social and Religious History*, 63; see also Schürer, 1, 207, as opposed to R. Meyer, 'περιτέμνειν', *TD* 6, 78, n. 39.

[271] See *Ant* 13,257: Hyrcanus: ἔτρεψεν αὐτοῖς (the Idumaeans) μένειν ἐν τῇ χώρᾳ, εἰ περιετέμνοιντο τὰ αἰδοῖα καὶ τοῖς Ἰουδαίων νόμοις χρῆσθαι θέλοιεν. Alexander, on the other hand, destroyed Pella, because the Hellenistic population did not let themselves be circumcised: *Ant* 13,397. Pompey then gave the city back to its earlier inhabitants, who, we may assume, had been expelled. See Schlatter, *GI*, 3rd. ed., 131 and 134, similarly R. Meyer, *op. cit.*; See V. Tcherikover, *Hellenistic Civilization and the Jews*, 1961, 248f. for 1 Macc 15.33f.

[272] PsSol 17,28; for the purity of the land, see also Joel 3.17; Jub 23,30 and 50,5; Sib 5,264 and 4Qflor (No. 174);DJD V, 58.

[273] *Bell* 2,454: καὶ μέχρι περιτομῆς ἰουδαΐσειν ὑποσχόμενον . . .

[274] *Vita* 112f.

[275] *Vita* 149–154; W.R. Farmer, *op. cit.*, 71, n.63, is probably right in his assumption that the accusation made by the Zealot leader Jesus b. Sapphia, who countered Josephus with a scroll of the law and accused him of betraying the law (*Vita* 134f.), was closely connected with this rejection on Josephus' part.

although their supplies were very low[276] and it is very likely that circumcision was also required in this case as well as a condition of acceptance.

The killing of non-Jews in Jewish territory can perhaps be best understood not only as a response to the murder of Jews in the Hellenistic cities,[277] but also as a sign that the demand for purity and the exclusion of all alien people, which had until then applied only to the sanctuary, was now extended to cover the whole country, that is, the inheritance that God had promised his own people only. The ideal of a purified land appears in the above quotation from the Apocalypse of Baruch. In it, Josiah provides evidence of his zeal for the law by 'admitting no uncircumcised man or evil-doer (!) into the whole of the country'.[278]

The second theme, that of zealous vigilance to ensure that Israel's sacred blessings — the people's relationship with God and the law — were not profaned — has several interesting counterparts in the rabbinate:

> 'If a non-Jew celebrates the sabbath, he deserves to die, since it is said: Day and night you shall not rest (Gen 8.22)'[279]

In another text, this statement is further elucidated:

> 'Does the man who, while the king and his spouse are sitting and talking to each other, thrusts between them not, according to practice of the world, deserve to die? In the same way, the sabbath is also between Israel and God, since it is said: Between me and the children of Israel let it be a sign for ever (Ex 3.17)! Therefore every non-Jew who thrusts between them before he has received circumcision deserves to die'.[280]

What applies to the sabbath also applies to the whole of the law:

> 'If a non-Jew concerns himself with the teaching of the law, he deserves to die, since it is said: I handed my law over to Moses as an inheritance (מוֹרָשָׁה, see Deut 33.4). It is an inheritance for Israel, but not for them'.[281]

However strange the tradition concerning the Zealots that was

---

[276] Dio Cassius, 66,5.4.

[277] See Bell 2,457ff. and Vita 67 (Tiberias) and 185f. (Gamala).

[278] See above, 181.

[279] Sanh 58b. See Bill. 1, 362; this statement was made by R. Simeon b. Lakish.

[280] DeutRab 1,21. See Bill. 3, 121; this statement was made by R. Hiyya b. Abba in the name of R. Johanan (+ 279 A.D.).

[281] Sanh 59a. The translation of this statement, which was also made by R. Johanan, is based on Goldschmidt, 8, 697. R. Johanan provides an even more detailed foundation for his argument: the prohibition against a study of the Torah by non-Jews is contained in the prohibition expressed in the Noachian commandments against robbery and fornication; Par. SifDeut 33,4.345.

preserved by Hippolytus may sound, its essentially historical content may be trusted, because it fits surprisingly well, as these parallels in the rabbinic literature show, into the general framework of views that were current in contemporary Judaism. Although he speaks only of a few extreme examples, these may well be typical of the Zealots' radical conception of the law.

(d) The Eighteen Halakhoth and Separation from the Pagans

According to Josephus, the Jews in Caesarea Philippi refused to use pagan oil after the outbreak of the Jewish War and obtained their oil at exorbitant prices from John of Gischala, the Galilaean freedom fighter.[282] Even in the Maccabaean period and to some extent even earlier, there was a demand for ritual purity in food,[283] although this element seems to have been especially emphasized much later in Judaism, that is, in the first century A.D. This is clear from the debates that took place within the early Christian Church, which were sometimes extremely heated.[284] Josephus also speaks of priests who were taken in chains to Rome by Felix and who throughout the whole of the journey ate figs and nuts so that they would not be made unclean. Unfortunately, he tells us nothing about the reason for their captivity. They may have been sent to Rome because of Zealot machinations.[285]

This intensification of the laws of purity with regard to the pagans, however, also had a deeper significance. The above mentioned prohibition of oil from pagan sources can be found in several texts in the rabbinic tradition,[286] in which it is frequently linked with the eighteen Halakhoth of the school of Shammai that I have already mentioned.[287] H. Graetz suspected that this precept, which had already existed for some time, was 'a precedent for the Shammaites, forbidding the

---

[282] *Vita* 74ff.; cf. *Bell* 2,592ff.

[283] Dan 1.8ff.; Jdt 10.5; 12.1ff.19; Tob 1.10f.; 2 Macc 5.27.

[284] See Acts 10.11ff.; Rom 14; 1 Cor 8; 10.25ff.; Col 2.21f. Table-fellowship with pagans was also closely connected with this; see Acts 11.3; Gal 2.12ff. For further examples, see *B.-Gr. Rel.* 93f. and Bill. 4,374ff.

[285] *Vita* 13ff. Josephus made the journey to Rome himself to support them.

[286] AZ 2,6 and tAZ 4,11 (Z. 467); see also Bill. 4, 368. This law probably goes back to the Hasmonaean period. According to *Ant* 12,120, the Jews did not use pagan oil in Antioch and arranged to be paid the equivalent in money when oil was distributed to the citizens.

[287] jShab 3c,37; Shab 17b; AZ 36a/b. The prohibition of oil was later discussed on several occasions. Rab traces it back to Daniel: jShab 3d,16ff.; AZ 35b/36a. Rabbi (or his grandson, the Patriarch Judah II) revoked it: AZ 2,6; tAZ 4,11 (Z. 467); see Bill. 4, 368ff. and S.B. Hoenig, *JQR* 61 (1970/71), 63-75.

enjoyment of other foods and erecting a partition-wall between Jews and pagans'.[288]

According to the earliest writer to deal with the eighteen Halakhoth. R. Simeon b. Jochai, they contained the following precepts: twelve prohibitions of pagan foods[289] and prohibitions against 'their' language, that is, Greek, the 'statements made by them as witnesses',[290] 'their gifts' and their sons, daughters and first-fruits.[291] It is hardly necessary to say that an unbridgeable gulf was created between Jews and non-Jews by these resolutions, which must have had quite radical consequences.

They also came about in quite a unique way in the history of the rabbinate. In the Mishnah, there is only a brief statement to the effect that the eighteen resolutions were drawn up 'in the upper room of R. Hanania b. Hezekiah b. Garon' and the simple report that the school of Shammai outvoted the school of Hillel.[292] The Jerusalem Talmud, on the other hand, tells us a little more about that remarkable session, although in a fragmentary manner:[293]

---

[288] *Geschichte der Juden*, 5th. ed. edited by M. Braun, 1905, 3, 807f.

[289] jShab 3c,49ff.; for what follows, see H. Graetz, 3, 806ff.; Derenbourg, 273; K. Kohler, 'Zealots', *JE* 12, 643; Moore, *Judaism*, 1, 81; A. Edersheim, *The Life and Times of Jesus the Messiah*, reprinted edition 1953, 1, 239f.; Bill. 1, 913 and 4, 368f.; Klausner, *Hist* 5, 156ff. The forbidden foods included: (1) the bread of pagans (פיתן); (2) their cheese (גבינתן); (3) their wine (יינן); (4) their vinegar (חומצן); (5) the juice from their fish (צירן), but see also above, p. 193, n. 252; (6) their fish-broth (מורייסן, from *muria*, salt-liquor, brine); (7) preserved food (כבושיהן); (8) boiled food (שלוקיהן); (9) salted food (מלוחיהן); (10) winnowed spelt (החילקה, from *alica*, spelt grain); (11) ground food (שחיקה); and (12) coarsely ground barley (הטסני, from πτισάνη). The prohibition against individual foods was to some extent also discussed by the Tannaim of the second generation: AZ 2,3-7. Klausner, *Hist* 5, 157 wanted to eliminate most of the dietary commandments from the eighteen so-called Halakhoth because of their insignificance. He assumed that the only prohibitions that were enunciated before the outbreak of the Jewish War were those against the pagans' bread, oil and wine, their language, their validity as witnesses and their sacrificial gifts as well as the prohibitions against their sons and daughters. However, this reduction is not at all necessary. Although the juxtaposition of twelve dietary prohibitions and six other prohibitions gives the eighteen Halakhoth a very harmonious structure, there was, even at quite an early stage, no general agreement about the individual prescriptions. According to Shab 1,4, they were, for example, associated with certain regulations relating to the sabbath. R. Simeon b. Jochai, who handed down the tradition of the Halakhoth in the order listed above, may, however, be regarded as more reliable than Shab 1,4. He was a pupil of R. Akiba and lived in the middle of the second century A.D.

[290] See Graetz, 3, 808, n. 1; According to tGitt 1,4 (Z. 323) and bTal 11a, pagans were permitted as witnesses at the issuing of a bill of divorce. This was no longer possible in this case.

[291] See Bill 4, 369; according to Graetz, *op. cit.*, this was 'quite incomprehensible'.

[292] Shab 1,4; see also tShab 1,16 (Z. 111). Here the eighteen resolutions are related to certain sabbath commandments; for this see above, n. 289.

[293] jShab 3c,34ff. bar according to R. Joshua b. Onias: תלמידי בית שמאי.

'The pupils of the house of Shammai were downstairs (in the house) and brought about a blood-bath among the pupils of the house of Hillel'.

'It is taught (Baraita): Six of them went upstairs (to the upper room) and ranged themselves against the rest with swords and lances'.

The Babylonian Talmud erroneously sets the episode back to the time of Shammai and Hillel themselves and also tones down the harshness of the conflict:[294]

'They put up a sword in the house of learning and called out: Whoever wants to come in, let him enter. No one may go out. On that day, Hillel sat bowed down in front of Shammai like any pupil'.

The conclusion that we may draw from this is that, in opposition to the Hillelites, the Shammaites had their rigorous opinion accepted by force of arms and, to all appearances, even before it came to a vote, several scholars of the school of Hillel who were opposed to the measures were killed. It is therefore not difficult to understand the argument that was used later against the eighteen Halakoth, namely that the scholars had 'for their sake put their lives at risk'.[295]

It is clear that opinion was sharply divided at an early stage concerning these precepts that would bring about a complete break with the pagans:[296]

'R. Eliezer (b. Hyrcanus) said: On that day (of the eighteen Halakhoth), they piled the measure high. R. Joshua (b. Hananiah) said: On that day, they levelled the measure off. R. Eliezer said to him: If there was something lacking in the measure (of the commandments of the Torah) and they filled it up, that is right. It is like a vessel full of nuts — however much sesame you put into it, it will absorb it! R. Joshua said to him: If it was full and they made something lacking, would that be right? It is like a vessel full of oil — however much water you put into it, the same amount of oil will spill out'.

Other Tannaitic teachers were even sharper in their judgement:

'That day was as difficult for Israel as the day on which they made the calf (Ex 32) !'[297]

עמדו להן מלמטה והיו הורגין בתלמידי בית הלל תני ששה מהן עלו והשאר עמדו עליהן בחרבות ורמחים.

[294] Shab 17a; translation based on Goldschmidt, 1, 479: נעצו חרב בבית המדרש.

[295] jShab 3d,60:לפני שעמדה להם בנפשותיהן; see also Derenbourg, 273; H. Graetz, 3, 809 and Klausner, *Hist* 5, 158, all of whom read עמדו.

[296] jShab 3c,39ff.; tShab 1,17 (Z. 111) in an abbreviated form; Shab 153b in an altered form; see also Bill. 1, 913 and Klausner, *op. cit.*, 5, 157f. R. Eliezer b. Hyrcanus and R. Joshua b. Hanania experienced the fall of Jerusalem as young men. For Eliezer, see above, p. 109, n. 171. See tSanh 13,2 and bTal 105a for the controversy about the salvation of the pagans; see also Bill. 1, 360f.

[297] tShab 1,17 (Z. 111):אותו היום היה לישראל כיום שעשו העגל; see also jShab 3c,28 and bTal 17a.

We may safely follow the conclusion drawn by H. Graetz in the matter of the dating of the eighteen Halakhoth:

'Is such a violent and tumultuous synod, the counterpart to the σύνοδος λῃστρική in Ephesus at the time of the controversy in the Byzantine Church, imaginable at any other time than when the Jews were subject to the tremendous impression of the revolt against the Romans and a fanatical hatred of the Romans?'[298]

This assumption is supported by a Baraita, according to which the Scroll of Fasting was also composed by the same R. Hanania, in whose upper room the eighteen Halakhoth were formulated, in conjunction with a circle of scholars.[299] Since this collection of Jewish days of victories and feasts probably originated at the beginning of the Jewish War and can, as far as its contents are concerned, be ascribed to Zealot circles,[300] this datum is of particular importance. H. Graetz even identified this R. Hanania with Eleazar b. Ananias, the captain of the Temple who, according to Josephus, refused to sacrifice for the emperor and thus caused the Jewish War.[301]

Let us look more closely at the individual prohibitions contained in these eighteen precepts and their effects on Jewish life. The prohibition of the twelve foods that were not to be accepted from pagans not only put an end to the already very limited friendly association with non-Jews, but also made it almost impossible for Jews to trade with non-Jews. Fear of levitical impurity thus became an effective means of widening the already existing gulf between Jews and non-Jews still further.

Other prohibitions were no less radical in their effect. The exclusion of the Greek language (לשונן) meant that all attempts to establish a link between Judaism and Hellenistic culture and at the same time the Jews of the Diaspora within the Roman Empire, who were overwhelmingly opposed to the revolt,[302] had to cease. This prohibition seems also to have been confirmed by a Mishnaic text:

---

[298] H. Graetz, 3, 809; see also Klausner, *op. cit.* It would be difficult to date the Halakoth more precisely than Graetz has done. Both he and Klausner assumed that these regulations were enacted because of the persecution of Jews in the Syrian cities. This, however, may already have taken place before the cessation of the practice of offering sacrifices for the emperor; see below, p. 359f. Whatever the case may be, we may certainly date it to the period of the beginning of the Jewish War.

[299] Shab 13b; see also H. Graetz, 3, 810; Derenbourg, 439f.; Klausner, *Hist* 5, 150.

[300] For the Scroll of Fasting, see above, p. 19, n. 82.

[301] 3, 810ff.; see also below, p. 359, n. 235.

[302] See the complaint against the Jews of the Diaspora made by Eleazar b. Ari in his death-speech, *Bell* 7,361ff., and the conduct of the Jews in Antioch, Sidon and Apamea, *Bell* 2, 479, as well as their behaviour in Egypt towards the *Sicarii*, *Bell* 7,412ff.

'In the war of Titus (Quietus?), bridal wreaths were forbidden and it was forbidden to teach one's son Greek'.[303]

According to a Baraita, a curse was pronounced in connection with the conflict between Aristobulus II and Hyrcanus II, in other words, immediately before the beginning of the Roman rule, over the man who had his son instructed in 'Greek wisdom'.[304] This rejection of Hellenistic learning may well have continued into the Hasmonaean period and, under the pressure of the imminent outbreak of war, Jews accepted the ultimate consequence of this rejection and even broke with the Greek language itself.[305] Even after the defeat, an attempt was made to maintain this prohibition and R. Joshua b. Hanania, who had been so sharply critical of the Halakhoth, went so far as to support them:

'R. Joshua was asked: May a man teach his son to read Greek? He answered him: He may teach in an hour that belongs neither to the day nor to the night, since it is said: This book of the law shall not depart from your mouth and you shall meditate on it day and night (Josh 1.8)'.[306]

The prohibition of the Greek language, however, did not simply mean a clear break with Hellenistic culture. It also made new room for the 'Holy Language', Hebrew.[307] Coins of the period provide the best evidence of this aspiration. From the time of Alexander Jannaeus onwards, the Hasmonaeans minted coins with inscriptions in the two languages. Hebrew was completely excluded from coin inscriptions

---

[303] Sot 9,14: בפולמוס של טיטוס גזרו על עטרות הכלה ושלא ילמד את בנו יונית. Since 'Vespasian's war' is mentioned before this, the Codex Kauffmann is followed, in contradiction to all other textual evidence, and קיטוס is read rather than 'Titus' and interpreted as a reference to Lucius Quietus, the governor of Judaea under Trajan in 117 A.D. See Schürer, 2, 80; Bill. 4, 412, H. Bietenhard, Sota, Die Mischna, III,6, 1956, 165 and 196. This reading seems to me to be less certain than has been generally assumed.

[304] Sot 49b; see Bill. 4, 411, who gives other parallels.

[305] Already Aristobulus, Hyrcanus' son, was given the nickname Φιλέλλην, Ant 13,318. Later, Herod was very enamoured of Hellenistic culture and had his sons brought up Hellenistically; see Ant 15,342f.; 16,2.242. S. Lieberman, Hellenism in Jewish Palestine, 1950, 100, claims that the Greek language was not generally prohibited, but that this prohibition was simply confined to Greek wisdom and the teaching of the Greek language to children. Unfortunately, he does not go into the eighteen Halakhoth.

[306] tAZ 1,20 (Z. 461); see Bill. 4, 412, who provides further parallels. A contemporary, R. Ishmael b. Elisha, similarly asked whether it was permissible to study Greek wisdom: Men 99b; see Bill. op. cit.. There was, however, in no sense a consistent attitude towards the prohibition of Greek. Both R. Gamaliel, the great-grandson of Hillel, and his family also held the Greek language in high esteem; see Bill. 4, 412f. For the significance of the Greek language in Palestine generally, see Schürer, 2, 72ff.; G. Kittel, Die Probleme des palästinischen Spätjudentums, 1926, 34ff.; H. Bietenhard, op. cit., 165f.; M. Hengel, Judaism and Hellenism, 1,58ff.

[307] Sot 7,2; see Bill. 2, 443, who gives other examples.

from the time of Herod onwards. Coins struck during the revolt against Rome, on the other hand, once again had purely Hebrew inscriptions, as they had had two hundred years previously, in the days of Hyrcanus.[308]

This fact should be seen in its wider context. Since the Maccabaean period, members of various sects had concerned themselves with the renewal of classical biblical Hebrew, which was regarded as the 'language of creation' that had been revealed to Abraham by an angel.[309] According to the rabbinic tradition, it was the language of the angels and even more - the language of God himself.[310] We may therefore conclude from this primordial and heavenly significance of the Hebrew language that it had an eschatological part to play:

'and there will be one people of God and one language'.[311]

H. Graetz throws a very revealing light on the prohibition against accepting gifts (מתנותיהן) from non-Jews. This prohibition was concerned not only with the private sphere, but also with the greatest of all Jewish institutions, the sanctuary itself. Jews were therefore to refuse to accept consecrated gifts or sacrifices from non-Jews.[312] This very serious break with the earlier Jewish tradition[313] was the external cause of the outbreak of the Jewish War, when the captain of the Temple, Eleazar b. Ananias, had the sacrifice for the emperor discontinued:[314]

'At the same time, Eleazar the son of the high-priest Ananias, who was captain of the Temple at the time and a daring young man, also persuaded the priests who were on duty not to accept a gift or a sacrifice from a foreigner. This was the cause of the war against the Romans, since they had (now) interrupted the sacrifice for them and the emperor'.

The protest made by the peace party, that this was a custom that had been practised since time immemorial, fell on deaf ears. In confrontation with the radical consequences of Zealot theology, the appeal to tradition had no meaning. The assembly of the people, in which, according to

---

[308] See A. Reifenberg, *Jewish Coins*, 41ff.,57ff.

[309] Jub 12,25f.: It had disappeared since the fall of the earth; see also HebrTestNaph 8,6 and Kautzsch, *Apokryphen und Pseudepigraphen*, 2, 491. According to GenRab 18,4, it was not simply that the Torah had been given in the 'Holy Language' — the world had also been created by it.

[310] The serving angels spoke Hebrew: Hag 16a (bar); see Moore, *Judaism*, 1, 451. They only understood Hebrew: Shab 12a and Sot 33a; see Bill. 2, 447, and Moore, *op. cit.*, 3, 136, No. 178. For Hebrew as the language of God: jMeg 71b,44; see Bill. 2, 443.

[311] TestJud 25,3.

[312] 3, 807; A. Edersheim, *op. cit.*, 1, 239; Klausner, *Hist* 5,157: gifts = קורבנות. For this, see tSot 14,10 (Z. 321): צדקה מן הגוים.

[313] See Schürer, 2, 309ff.; Juster, 1, 347f.

[314] *Bell* 2,409ff.: μηδενὸς ἀλλοτρίου δῶρον ἢ θυσίαν προσδέχεσθαι.

Josephus' description of the scene, a dramatic struggle for the will of the people took place, tipped the scales, the majority of the people deciding in favour of Eleazar, while the peace party, represented by the priestly nobility and the moderate Pharisees, suffered a defeat.[315]

The individual precepts of the Halakhoth differ widely from each other in their content and meaning. Some were commandments of secondary importance concerning diet, while others called for radical changes in the life of the people. Some, such as the prohibition of intercourse with non-Jewish 'sons' and 'daughters', had already previously existed in Israel's tradition. Others, like the prohibition of pagan 'gifts', were totally new. What they all had in common, however, was a marked tendency against non-Jews.

This anti-pagan tendency does not mean, on the other hand, that they were directed in a purely negative sense towards separation from the pagans. They also had a positive orientation in their concern for the 'purity of the people'. The dietary laws were intended to preserve levitical purity and those forbidding intercourse with young non-Jewish men and women aimed to maintain moral purity. The prohibition of the Greek language was aimed at keeping the Jewish faith pure.[316] At the same time, it also raised the status of the 'Holy Language'. Finally, the ultimate goal of the prohibition of pagan gifts was the purity of the sanctuary.

We may, then, conclude by saying that the composition of the eighteen Halakhoth can be seen as a sign of the deep inner division within the Pharisaical party, in which the more radical Shammaitic wing was relatively close to the Zealot movement.

3. Zeal for the Purity of the Sanctuary

(a) The Threat to the Temple from the Pagan Rulers

However much Josephus stressed the claims of non-Jewish rulers to be

---

[315] Consequently John of Gischala later had the consecrated gifts of the pagan rulers, including those of Augustus and Julia, melted down. This was an action that Josephus condemned as a 'robbery of the Temple': *Bell* 5,562f. The memory of the discontinuation of the sacrifice as an external cause of the outbreak of the Jewish War was preserved in the rabbinic legend of Bar Qamsa; see Gitt 55b/56a and LamRab 4,2. Whatever the case may be, the historical state of affairs was completely distorted in the interest of apologetics; see below, p. 360f.

[316] That the Jewish faith was threatened by the Greek language and literature is clear from the example of Elisha b. Abuja; see Bill. 4, 399f. The case of Tiberius Alexander, the son of the alabarch Alexander and the nephew of Philo, is very similar; see *Ant*

honoured in the Temple,[317] a much deeper impression must inevitably have been made on Judaism from the time of Antiochus Epiphanes onwards because of their negative experiences of a constant threat to the sanctuary from the pagan rulers.

It began with Antiochus' entry into the Holy of Holies and his plundering of the treasury of the Temple.[318] Another step that he took was to introduce the cult of Zeus Olympios, a 'desolating sacrilege' in the eyes of pious Jews.[319] The extent to which the movement initiated by Mattathias and his sons was related to the Temple is clearly revealed in the emphasis placed on the purification of the Temple and the restoration of the cult of Yahweh in the tradition of the first two books of the Maccabees as well as the institution of the Feast of Hanukkah.[320] The fact that this feast continued to be celebrated in the centuries that followed also shows how firmly rooted the memory both of this 'desolating sacrilege' committed by the pagan ruler and of the Maccabees' fight for freedom were in the minds of the people.

Roman rule had begun with the desecration of the Temple by Pompey in 63 B.C. The treasures that he had left undisturbed were plundered by Crassus in 54 B.C.[321] When he came to power, Herod was able to prevent the Temple from being defiled once again by the Roman conquerors, but he aroused the zeal of pious Jews shortly before his death by placing the emblem of the eagle in the Temple.[322] Immediately afterwards, his son Archelaus caused a blood-bath among the people who had come together for the sacrifice of the Passover lambs in the Temple.[323] Fifty days after this event, Roman legionaries, acting on an order given by Sabinus, the imperial administrator of finances, attacked

---

20,100. R. Johanan (who died in 279 A.D.) therefore based the prohibition of Greek on a reference to the 'traitors': jSot 24c,12; see Bill. 4, 413.

[317] See *Bell* 2,412ff.; 4,262; 5,17.563f., etc.

[318] 1 Macc 1.20ff.; 2 Macc 5.15ff.; *Ap* 2,80.83. See also M. Hengel, *Judaism and Hellenism*, 1,10f.,280f.

[319] 1 Macc 1.54; Dan 9.27; 11.31.

[320] The description of the dedication of the Temple: 1 Macc 4.36-59 and 2 Macc 10.1-8. For the Feast of Hanukkah, see 1 Macc 4.59; 2 Macc 1.9; *Ant* 12,325; see also Jn 10.22 for this feast in New Testament times. For the continued existence of the feast during the period of Roman rule, see W.R. Farmer's detailed justification, 138-145.

[321] For the desecration of the Temple by Pompey, see *Bell* 1,152 (= *Ant* 14,72): 'None of the misfortunes of that time moved the people so powerfully as the uncovering by the pagans of the holy place that had hitherto been hidden from sight'. See also PsSol 2,2f.28f. and Cicero, *Flacc* 67. For Crassus, see *Bell* 1,179 = *Ant* 14,105-109.

[322] *Bell* 1,354f. = *Ant* 14,482ff. For the image of the eagle, see above, p. 103, etc., and below, pp. 258f. and 322.

[323] *Bell* 2,10ff. = *Ant* 17,216ff. See also below, p. 325.

the Sanctuary, set the porticoes on fire and seized at least four hundred talents from the Temple treasury.[324]

The revolt that followed was certainly partly determined by these inroads. Under the first procurator, Coponius (6-9 A.D.), Samaritans apparently desecrated the Temple before the Feast of the Passover with bones of the dead.[325] Pilate (26-36 A.D.) had the standards bearing the emperor's medallions taken into the Fortress of Antonia, which was directly connected with the Temple, and took the liberty of plundering the Temple treasury to build a watercourse.[326] There is even a reference in Luke's Gospel (13.1f.) to a desecration of the Temple by the procurator. The attempt made by the mad Caligula to have his statue set up in the Temple (39/40 A.D.) reawakened the memory of the 'desolating sacrilege' that had taken place at the time of Antiochus. A general catastrophe was averted only by his sudden death.

Under Cumanus (48-52 A.D.), a soldier who was posted on the porticoes of the outer forecourt of the Temple during the Feast of the Passover aroused the people to extreme agitation by making an indecent gesture.[327] The extent to which the Roman rule was regarded as a constant threat to the Sanctuary can be seen from the fact that no further money was deposited in the Temple treasury because of the fear of inroads on the part of procurators. It was preferably spent at once.[328] The action of Florus, the last of the procurators, showed that this mistrust was not without foundation. Presumably in order to make up a tax deficit, he took seventeen talents from the chest in the Temple and this action provoked disturbances that led to the outbreak of the Jewish War.[329]

A particular thorn in the flesh of the Jews was the Antonia Tower. This had been extended by Herod and made into a fortress which was constantly occupied by pagan soldiers and therefore always in a state of cultic impurity.[330] For a long time — until Vitellius handed it over — the

---

[324] *Bell* 2,49f. = *Ant* 17,260ff. See also below, p. 326.

[325] *Ant* 18,29ff.

[326] *Bell* 2,169-177 = *Ant* 18,55-62. According to Shek 4,2, the cost of the water-conduit was covered by a treasury surplus. R. Eisler, 1, 219, n. 2, assumed that Pilate wanted to increase his own wealth in this way.

[327] *Bell* 2,224 = *Ant* 20,106ff. The Jews were very sensitive in this respect; see Ber 61b/62a and the Mishnah relating to it: 9,5b.

[328] *Ant* 20,220.

[329] *Bell* 2,293ff.305ff.325-329. See also below, p. 356f.

[330] For the military significance of the Antonia, see *Ant* 15,403.409.424, *Bell* 5,238-245; see also Acts 21.31ff. During feasts, the roofs of the porticoes surrounding the outside forecourt were usually occupied by the auxiliary cohort stationed in the Fortress: *Bell* 5,245 and 2,224. For the permanent cultic impurity of the Antonia, see Jn 18.28; Ohol 18,7 (Bill. 2, 838ff.).

holy high-priestly vestment was kept in this profaned place.[331] In addition to this, the pagan troops continued to have the opportunity to occupy the forecourt from the Fortress. It was for this reason that the insurgents directed their first attack against the Antonia. Their setting it on fire was probably not so much an expression of popular anger as an act of purification of the Temple. It can best be compared with the cleansing of the Acra during the Maccabaean uprising. It was certainly not simply by chance that a tractate of the Mishnah, the Middoth, has nothing to say about the Antonia and the porticoes of the outer forecourt of the Temple.[332]

The theme of the threat to the Sanctuary appears both in pious legends of the period and in the apocalyptic literature.[333] This is clear evidence of how deeply the feeling that the Sanctuary was permanently threatened had sunk into the minds of the people. This uninterrupted danger of the desecration of the Sanctuary by the pagan occupation of the Fortress of Antonia, combined with the constantly repeated encroachments made by the Roman administration, provided the Zealots with a powerful argument in favour of impossibility of combining the Jewish faith in God with foreign rule. As long as Israel continued to endure the godless tyrants, it would always have to accept a profanation of the sanctuary. In other words, the constant offences against God's sanctuary resulting from pagan encroachments were a direct consequence of Israel's loyalty to the Romans.[334]

This explains Josephus' polemical reversal and the emphasis which he tirelessly placed, on the one hand, on the Romans' care and respect for the Temple and, on the other, on the Zealots' repeated desecration and even destruction of the Sanctuary:

---

[331] See *Ant* 18,90ff. and 20,10ff.

[332] *Bell* 2,430. See also above, p. 193, n. 250. O. Holtzmann, *Middot, Die Mischna*, V,10, 1913, 17.

[333] See Jdt 4.12; 8.21; 9.8; see also the Heliodorus legend, 2 Macc 3, which is also present in 4 Macc 4.1-14. The Third Book of the Maccabees, which was possibly written under the influence of the demands made by Caligula, reports an attempt by Ptolemy Philopator to desecrate the Temple; see 3 Macc 1 and 2. W.R. Farmer, 93ff., assumes that the pattern that is common to all these narratives — the attempt by the enemy of God to desecrate the Sanctuary, prayers of intercession and punishment of the evil-doer by God — also had an effect on Josephus' presentation of the episode involving Caligula. The theme of the violation of the Temple can also be found in the rabbinic tradition: Sukk 56b, a Baraita dating back to the period of the Maccabees and Sot 33a bar concerning Caligula. For the apocalyptic tradition of the violation of the Temple, see Mk 13.14; 2 Thess 2.3; Rev 13.6. See also *B.-Gr.Rel.* 256.

[334] W.R. Farmer, 90: 'So long as Israel was subject to heathen powers, just as long was the holy house of God himself subject to heathen profanation'.

'The Sanctuary has become the reservoir of all (the Zealots' atrocious acts) and unclean hands have defiled the divine domain, which even the Romans themselves have venerated from afar, in so doing disregarding many of their own customs in favour of your law'.[335]

This apologetical and polemical attitude is evident in its most crude form in Josephus' attempt to exonerate Titus from his responsibility for the burning down of the Temple. On the one hand, he several times draws attention to Titus' firm desire to spare the Sanctuary,[336] while, on the other, accusing the Zealots for having been the first to set fire to the Temple.[337] Indeed, it is just this laborious attempt to save the honour of the Romans besieging Jerusalem which shows that, even after the defeat, the overwhelming majority of Jews regarded the Romans themselves as responsible for the desecration and destruction of the Sanctuary.[338]

(b) The Desecration of the Sanctuary from the Jewish Side

After the fall of the Oniads at the time of the Seleucids, many complaints were made in Hasidic circles about the desecration of the Temple by unclean priests.[339] This criticism by the pious continued in the

---

[335] *Bell* 5,402; see also above, p. 184.

[336] See the description of the war council, *Bell* 6,237ff., the attitude of Titus, 241f., and his attempts to have the fire quenched, 254.262.266. This is contradicted by the report of Sulpicius Severus, *Chron* II 30 (*CSEL* I, ed. C. Halm, 84f.), which may possibly go back to Tacitus' Histories: '... At contra alii et Titus ipse euertendum imprimis templum censebant' (see Reinach, 324f., and Schürer, 1, 596, n. 115. According to W. Weber, *Josephus and Vespasian*, 1921, 71ff., Josephus falsified history here for 'political reasons'. G. Ricciotti, *Flavio Giuseppe*, 1 (Introduction), 2nd. ed. 1949, 39, p. 73ff., is, however, opposed to this conclusion. It is hardly possible to make a final decision about this question and we are bound agree with H. Dessau, II,2, 826, who has concluded: 'It looks as though the question of the prince's guilt or innocence when the building was destroyed became at quite an early stage the object of a controversy which was quite tendentious and which is less possible to resolve now than it was at the time'. See also I. Weiler, *Klio* 50 (1968), 139-148.

[337] *Bell* 6,165: ταῖς ἰδίαις χερσὶν ἀρξάμενοι καίειν τὰ ἅγια; Whatever the case may be, all that is involved here are the porticoes touching the Antonia. According to 6,251ff., the Temple building itself was set alight by a torch thrown by a Roman soldier. Nevertheless, Josephus has Titus accusing the Jews (6,347): καὶ τὸν ναὸν ἰδίαις χερσὶν ἐνεπρήσατε.

[338] For views concerning the destruction that were widespread in Judaism, see Bill. 1, 946ff. According to a remarkable tradition expressed in LamRab 1,13.41, the 'accuser' appears to have called on God to let fire fall on his Sanctuary so that the evil-doer (Titus) would not be able to boast that he had caused the Temple to burn down.

[339] See 2Macc 4; AssMs 5,4; Jub 23,21f. See also E. Bickermann, *The God of the Maccabees*, 1979, 38,42f.; J. Jeremias, *Jerusalem in the Time of Jesus*, 3rd. ed. 1969, 181ff.; I. Finkelstein, *The Pharisees*, 3rd. ed. 1962, 635ff.; Moore, *Judaism*, 1, 50f.,76, whose conclusion is not so certain. In certain circles, even the second Temple seems to have been fundamentally rejected: EthEn 89,73f.; 90,28; 91,13; see also *B.-Gr.Rel.* 115.

opposition of the Pharisees and the Essenes to the Hasmonaeans.[340] The complete decline of the high-priesthood under Herod, who put a definitive end to the lifelong and inherited aspect of the office, gave rise to new criticism. Then, when the high-priest Joazar b. Boethus agreed to the census being carried out, the Jewish freedom movement finally broke with priestly nobility. We may assume that his action attracted such hostility on the part of the people that he was removed from office by Cyrenius.

The fact that the high-priests of that time had purchased their office for a high price was the most important aspect of this criticism during the rule of the procurators that followed. This was a major reason why, with few exceptions, the high-priests changed so rapidly at that time, since the procurators and later Agrippa I, his brother and his son[341] had a great interest in continually renewing this source of money. On the one hand, the rabbinic report, and the allusion in Jn 11.49, namely that there was a change of high-priest every twelve months,[342] can be explained in this perspective and, on the other, the fact that the office was, with very few exceptions, limited to four families.[343] Only these families were able

---

[340] See the conflict over the purity of John Hyrcanus I: *Ant* 13,291f. and Kidd 66a. The following probably refer to the situation under Alexander Jannaeus: TestLevi; PsSol 2; 4 and 8; see also above, p. 188f.; CD 4,15ff. and the controversy in 1 QpHab. For further literature on this question, see above, p. 153, n. 52. For the office of high-priest for the period in question, see J. Jeremias, *op. cit.*, 181ff.

[341] After the death of Agrippa I, the right to control the office of high-priest was not given back to the procurators. Instead, it was given first to Agrippa's brother, Herod of Chalcis (*Ant* 20,15), and then handed over to his son Agrippa II.

[342] See SifNum 25,12.131: In the first Temple, there were eighteen high-priests, whereas there were as many as eighty in the second Temple: 'Because they bought it (the high-priestly office) for money, their years were from that time onwards shortened'. For the annual change of office, see Yom 8b: '... since, however, the high-priesthood was bought with money, and they (the high-priests) changed every twelve months, like public officials ...'; cf. tYom 1,7 (Z. 180). It was said of the high-priest Jesus (Joshua) b. Gamala, who was a friend of Josephus, that his bride Martha of the family of Boethus had bought the office of high-priest from Agrippa II (Jannaeus) for three *qab* of gold *denarii*: Yom 18a; Yeb 61a, Derenbourg, 248f., Bill. 2, 569. For the great number of high-priests following Quirinius' levying of taxes, see Schürer, 2, 230ff. and J. Jeremias, *op. cit.*, 194ff. For their great wealth and their practice of buying offices, see *op. cit.*, pp. 96ff., 159.

[343] See Josephus, *Bell* 4,148. These were probably the families of Boethus, Ananus (Hannas; see *Ant* 20,198), Phiabi and Kamithos (Qamchi). They are probably also named in the four 'woes' of Abba Shaul (Pes 57a bar). For the decline of the high-priesthood in the first century A,D., see Schürer, 2, 233ff. and J. Jeremias, *op. cit.*, 49, 96ff., 194ff. E. Bammel, 'Die Bruderfolge im Hohenpriestertum der herodianisch-römischen Zeit', *ZDPV* 70 (1954), unfortunately does not deal with the question of the buying of the high-priestly office. Fraternal succession alone can explain neither the

to provide again and again the necessary means to purchase the office of high-priest.

At the same time, however, these families were able to preserve their wealth, since the office of the high-priesthood provided them with important economic privileges. The trade in the requirements for sacrifice in the Temple forecourt and on the Temple hill took place under their supervision and was partly even subject to their direct control. They were the first who had to be taken into account in the case of priestly incomes from sacrifices.[344] When, after the great famine that took place during Claudius' reign[345] and, as a result of the general uncertainty in the country, the incomes of the priests from the tithes were reduced, it was these high-priestly families who, with the assistance of their private bands, which consisted predominantly of slaves, gathered in the corn-tithes that were generally due to the priests for their own personal use. The result of this was that ordinary priests became increasingly poor.[346]

The general mood with regard to this behaviour on the part of the leading high-priestly families towards increasing their personal wealth is clearly expressed in a Baraita:[347]

> 'The rabbis taught: The Temple forecourt uttered four cries. The first: Leave this place, sons of Eli, you who have made the Temple of the Lord unclean! Then it cried again: Leave this place, Issachar of Kephar Baqai, you who honour yourself and have desecrated the sanctuaries of heaven! ... Then the Temple forecourt cried again: Gates, lift up your heads, so that Johanan b. Nidbai (read נִדְבַּאי instead of נִרְבָּאי), the pupil of the lovers of luxury[348] may enter and fill his belly with the sanctuaries of heaven'.

---

frequency of change of the high priest, nor the unexpectedly long period of office of Caiaphas or Ananias b. Nedebai.

[344] For the trade in sacrificial requirements, see Bill. 1, 850ff.; Klausner, *J of N*, 314; J. Jeremias, *op. cit.*, 99. The family of Hannas probably possessed their own stores: SifDeut 14,22.105; see also Bill. 2, 570f. R. Simeon b. Gamaliel I had to take steps to counter profiteering in sacrificial doves: jTaan 69a,37; see also Bill. 2, 571. For the special claims of the priestly nobility in the question of sacrifices, see tMen 13,18 (Z. 533) and *Ant* 20,181.206. See also below, p. 352.

[345] *Ant* 20,101f.; 3,320; Acts 11.28.

[346] *Ant* 20,179ff.205ff., cf. Pes 57a, Baraita in the name of Abba Shaul; tMen 13,20.21 (Z. 533); see also Bill. 2,570. Josephus provides an account in *Ant* 20,213 of the conflict between the various aristocratic families which resulted in street battles between the bands of the deposed high-priest Jesus b. Damnaeus and those of the newly appointed Jesus b. Gamaliel; see above, p. 211, n. 342.

[347] Pes 57a, Baraita of Abba Shaul (ca. 80–130 A.D.); see also Bill. *op. cit.* Ker 28a (with minor secondary deviations) and jSukk 54d,32f. (abbreviated) are parallels.

[348] פּנְקָאי from פּנק, to revel, live in luxury; see Jastrow, *Dictionary*, 2, 1190, and *B.-Gr.Rel.* 116.

Pious Jews, then, were convinced that the noble high-priests defiled the Sanctuary continually by their pride and avarice. This led to the gulf between the official leaders of the people and the members of circles who were filled with religious zeal becoming unbridgeable.

These noble priestly families were certainly aware of the fact that the people only supported them to a very limited degree and that they owed their wealth, their reputation and their position of power above all to a situation made momentarily secure by Roman rule. They therefore opposed the Zealot movement from the very beginning and placed themselves at the centre of the peace party, which was anxious to have good relationships with Rome.[349]

As the members of the priestly nobility belonged almost without exception to the Sadducean party, they were accused of heterodoxy. Their deviation in faith was not simply confined to such truths mentioned in Josephus and to some extent also in the New Testament as man's freedom of will, the resurrection, the last judgement and the heavenly world.[350] They also rejected the oral tradition,[351] and this resulted in sharp conflicts over the Temple service and the questions of purity that were closely connected with it.[352] This meant that the ruling high-priests could be accused of unlawfulness and impurity in their carrying out of the Temple service.

Wide circles of Jews were therefore embittered not only by the constant threat to the Temple from the power of Rome, but also by the unworthiness of those members of their own people who held the highest office. There was even a rift between members of the priesthood themselves, the ordinary priests (כוהנים הדיוטים) and Levites being sharply opposed for religious and social reasons to the priestly nobility.[353] The ground had therefore been very well prepared during the decades that preceded the outbreak of the Jewish War for the Zealot view that only a violent solution was capable of putting an end to this unworthy state of affairs.

---

[349] This opposition began with Joazar b. Boethus at the time of Judas the Galilaean and ended with the murder of Ananus and Jesus b. Gamala after the battle that was fought in vain against the Zealots in 67 A.D. (Bell 4,314ff.).

[350] Bell 2,162ff.; Ant 13,171ff.; 18,12-17. See also Mk 12.18ff. and Acts 23.8.

[351] Ant 13,297f.; see also Schürer, 2, 487f.

[352] See the many examples in the excursus in Bill. 4, 345ff. According to tPara 3,8 (Z. 632), the burning of the red heifer gave rise to a fierce debate between the Sadducean high-priest and R. Johanan b. Zakkai; see Bill. 4, 347 and Schlatter, GI, 284.

[353] See Ant 20,179ff.205ff.216ff.; see also below, p. 359ff.

(c) Efforts to Preserve the Purity of the Temple

Philo Judaeus has this to say about his compatriots in his *Legatio ad Gaium*:

> 'In the case of all of them, zeal for the sanctuary is exceedingly great and extraordinary.[354] ... Those who cross the barrier of the inner sanctuary and are not members of their own people are destined to die an inexorable death'.

Philo is alluding here to the exclusion of all non-Jews or uncircumcised men from the Sanctuary itself.[355] At the same time, he is also referring to those tables of prohibitions on the barrier separating the outer forecourt from the Sanctuary which are mentioned several times by Josephus and of which two copies have been discovered.[356]

The remarkable threat of punishment that is contained in the inscription does not reveal who is to carry out the punishment.[357] This would suggest that pagans who were encountered in the Sanctuary were not summoned to a regular court, but that they would have to take into account the fact that they might be put to death in an act of 'zeal' carried out by the outraged people or by Jewish fanatics and would not be able to rely on being helped by the Romans.[358]

---

[354] LegGai 212 (M 2, 577): περιττοτέρα δὲ καὶ ἐξαίρετός ἐστιν αὐτοῖς ἅπασιν ἡ περὶ τὸ ἱερόν σπουδή.

[355] See Kel 1,8; *Ap* 2,103f.; Acts 21.28; see also Schürer, 2, 286 and Bill. 2, 761.

[356] For the text of the inscription discovered in 1871 by Clermont-Ganneau, see W. Dittenberger, *OGIS* 2, 295, No. 598: Μηθένα ἀλλογενῆ εἰσπο/ρεύεσθαι ἐντὸς τοῦ πε/ρὶ τὸ ἱερὸν τρυφάκτου καὶ/περιβόλου ὃς δ'ἂν λη/φθῆ ἑαυτῷ αἴτιος ἔσται διὰ τὸ ἐξακολουθεῖν θάνατον. See also Schürer, 2, 285, n. 57. A fragment of a second copy was discovered in 1935; see G.E. Wright, *Biblical Archaeology*, 1957, 224f. The inscriptions undoubtedly go back to the Herodian period; see *Ant* 15,417. See also Josephus, *Bell* 5,193f.402; 6,124ff. See also E. Bickermann, 'The Warning Inscription of Herod's Temple', *JQR* 37 (1946/47), 387-405, and A.N. Sherwin-White, *Roman Society and Roman Law in the New Testament*, 3rd. ed. 1969, 38.

[357] For this, see Schürer. 2, 220ff., who suspected that the punishment was carried out by a regular Jewish court and that this was confirmed by the Romans. E. Bickermann, *op. cit.*, 394f., also mentions the further possibility of punishment by God (Sanh 9,6c) or the lynch-law.

[358] This was the opinion of the discoverer, Clermont-Ganneau, *RAr*, New Series 23 (1872), 232f. A similar opinion was expressed by K. Kohler, *JE* 12, 641b and *Harkavy-Festschrift* 13, n. 1: 'It seems to me to be beyond doubt that the Temple police had the right to cut down the intruder with the sword in accordance with the custom of the Kannaim'. Bickermann, *op. cit.*, 397., was also in favour of this interpretation on the basis of the abundant historical material: 'The trespasser will be executed by the outraged community he had polluted by his act'; cf. 401: 'a sacreligious person would be killed by the multitude'. He also points to 3 Macc 7.10,14, according to which Ptolemy IV allowed the Jews to put all apostates to death without trial by the court. *Bell* 6,125f. is also open to a similar interpretation: Titus criticizes John of Gischala with the words: 'Have we not allowed you to kill those who go beyond the bounds?' The circumstances

It is clear from the Mishnah that certain spontaneous forms of carrying out the lynch-law were tolerated in cases concerning desecration of the Temple:

'If a priest performs the Temple service in a state of impurity, his fellow-priests do not take him to the court of justice. The young priests rather take him outside the Temple and smash his skull with pieces of wood'.[359]

This Mishnah follows immediately after the law which has already been cited several times and which states in advance the spontaneous punishment carried out by the 'Zealots' in the case of certain crimes. The first of the three cases cited there is also concerned with the sanctuary and in particular with the theft of the קְסָוָה, one of the holy vessels of the Temple, which, in this case, may perhaps have represented the holy utensils of the Temple as a whole.[360] E. Bickermann has pointed out that 'zeal', as a spontaneous reaction to the desecration of the sanctuary, can be traced back to the fact that the consequences of such a profanation involved the entire nation and that the way of achieving a reconciliation was by immediately executing those who were guilty of arousing God's anger.[361]

This single example of common Jewish zeal for the integrity of the Sanctuary shows clearly enough how closely connected with the activity of the Zealots the striving of the people was at just this point, in which the 'Zealots' translated the will of the people into action.[362]

This zealous commitment to the integrity of the Sanctuary appears for the first time in Josephus' writings in his account of the two scribes who persuaded their pupils to destroy the eagle on the Temple and died

---

surrounding the imprisonment of Paul, Acts 21.27ff., would also seem to correspond to this. For further examples of this lynch-law, see Jn 8.59; 10.31; *Ant* 14,22. See also Sherwin-White, *op. cit.*, 43, n. 1.

[359] Sanh 9,6; translation based on Goldschmidt, 8, 784; cf. Lev 22.3. The discussion of this Mishnah in the Babylonian Talmud (82b/83a) shows a tendency towards alleviation: the question was asked whether the punishment of this crime ought not to be left to heaven; see, for example, tSanh 14,4f. (Z. 437); see also Bill. 1, 237. For individual cases, see S. Krauss, *Sanhedrin-Makkot, Die Mischna. Text, Übersetzung und ausführliche Erklärung*, ed. by G. Beer et al., IV,4 and 5, 1933, 263.

[360] For קְסָוָה, see S. Krauss, *op. cit.*, 260f.; see also above, p. 67, n. 334.

[361] *op. cit.*, 400: *Bell* 1,229.354; 4,201.215.218; *Ant* 3,318. See also Philo, *SpecLeg* 1,54f. (M 2, 220).

[362] It is quite clear from Acts 23.12ff. that vehmic justice had been officially given a certain latitude precisely when the Jews had begun to lose their supremacy in the matter of justice. The offer made by the forty was accepted without question by the high-priests and elders.

with them at the stake as martyrs. The deep impression that this action
made on the people is clear from Josephus' report of the lamentation for
the dead that began immediately after the death of Herod and the
disturbances that followed. These events, Josephus claims, occurred:

> 'in memory of the men who ... had suffered death from fire for the
> traditional laws and the Temple'.[363]

As the later interpretation by means of Ps 69.10 shows, Jesus'
cleansing of the Temple[364] is also to be understood as a similar act of zeal
for the Sanctuary. It was directed not so much against the money-
changers and dealers — who were presumably gathered in the southern
portico of the outer forecourt[365] — as against those who were
responsible for the whole area of the Temple, the leaders among the
priesthood, who were also, at least indirectly, interested in the business
of money-changing and in the trade in sacrificial animals.[366]

Although this event cannot be reconstructed in detail, it obviously
could not have been too tumultuous or the cohort stationed in the
Antonia would certainly have intervened.[367] The Temple guard and the
priests did not dare to proceed against Jesus because, in his
demonstration, which was comparable to the prophetic parabolic
actions, he was covered by the great mass of pilgrims at the feast.[368] We
may presume that the great number of people present, who had come
together from every part of the country, also shared Jesus' concern that
the Temple should be purified of its desecration by the profane trade in
sacrificial animals, particularly as this was fully in accordance with the
Pharisaical ideas about the holiness of the place.[369]

What is more, this demonstration also had an eschatological

---

[363] *Bell* 2,6; see also below, p. 325f.

[364] Mk 11.15-19; Mt 21.12f.; Lk 19.45f.; Jn 2.13-17. See also S. Mendner, *ZNW* 47
(1956), 93ff.; E. Trocmé, *NTS* 15 (1968/69), 1-22; M. Hengel, 'War Jesus
Revolutionär?', *CH* 110 (1970), 15f.

[365] See I. Abrahams, *Studies in Pharisaism and the Gospels*, 1st. Series 1917, 82ff.; G.
Dalman, *Sacred Sites and Ways*, 1935, 284ff. and E. Klostermann, *Das Markusevangelium*
(*HNT* 4), 4th. ed. 1950, 115f.

[366] This was the opinion of E. Lohmeyer, *Das Evangelium des Markus* (*Meyers
Kommentar*), 12th. ed. 1953, 253. See also J. Jeremias, *Jerusalem*, 3rd. ed. 1969, 49f., 100,
and E. Stauffer, *Jesus*, 1960, 61f; N.Q. Hamilton, *JBL* (1964), 365-72.

[367] I disagree with R. Eisler, 2,476ff., 515, here. It is significant that the consequence
described in Acts 21.31ff. did not in fact take place.

[368] See Klausner, *J of N*, 315. For the consent of the people, see Mk 11.18; Mt 21.15
and Lk 19.48.

[369] Mk 11.16 should be compared with *Ap* 2,106 and the examples given in Bill. 2, 26;
see also Klausner, *op. cit.*, and G. Dalman, *op. cit.*.

significance, in that Jesus was cleansing the sanctuary for the dawn of the kingdom of God.[370] Jesus' 'zeal for God's house' could, however, only arouse in the minds of the Jewish authorities the suspicion that he was a Galilaean revolutionary. This explains the questions about Jesus' authority and paying taxes to Caesar as well as certain essential aspects of Jesus' arrest and trial.[371]

Pilate's encroachments and even more Caligula's insane demand led to certain very impressive proofs of Jewish commitment to the Sanctuary, commitment, according to Josephus, shared by the whole nation. As soon as it became known that Pilate wanted images of the emperor to be admitted into the Fortress of Antonia, representatives from every section of the people followed him to Caesarea and, when he threatened the multitude,

> 'the Jews threw themselves to the ground together as though by pre-arranged signal, bent their necks forward and declared that they would die rather than transgress the law'.[372]

The Jews who were gathered in the presence of Petronius, the governor of Syria, confessed unanimously that, before the statue of the emperor was erected in the Temple, 'he would have to sacrifice the entire Jewish people'.[373] Both Josephus in his *Antiquities* and Philo presuppose that the Jewish people were determined to offer armed resistance — since the Jews were committed to defend the honour of their God, they believed that their cause was not hopeless. The Jewish threat of war is also indicated in Tacitus.[374] This passionate commitment on the part of the people to the Sanctuary and the law — it is hardly possible to separate the two in this case - shows clearly how the strength of the Jewish faith had become consolidated since the time of the Seleucids. The ideology of the Hellenistic Roman state could no longer affect it in any way.

(d) The 'Purification' of the Temple by the Zealots

Josephus tells us nothing about the attitude of the Zealots towards the

---

[370] This was the view held by G. Bornkamm, *Jesus of Nazareth*, 1960, 158f.

[371] For this, see above, p. 194f. It is quite obvious that the event must have taken place towards the end of Jesus' life before the Passover; see S. Mendner, *op. cit.*, 104, nn. 37 and 38. For the eschatological significance of this event, see Zech 14.21b.

[372] *Bell* 2,174; cf. *Ant* 18,58f.

[373] *Bell* 2,197 (cf. *Ant* 18,264): πρότερον αὐτὸν δεῖν ἅπαν τὸ Ἰουδαίων ἔθνος προθύσασθαι.

[374] *Ant* 18,267.270f.; 18,302: Petronius to Caligula: πόλεμον ἄντικρυς Ῥωμαίοις ἀπειλεῖν (cf. Latin); Philo, *LegGai* 213ff.,330 (M 2. 577f.,594). Tacitus, *Hist* 5,9: 'dein iussi a Gaio Caesare effigiem eius in templo locare arma potius sumpsere'.

Sanctuary during the period between the foundation of the new sect and the outbreak of the Jewish War. All that we learn from him is that, when Felix was procurator, they changed their tactics, thus acquiring the name of *Sicarii*, and extended their activities to include Jerusalem and the Temple itself. From the very few concrete data that he provides, we may assume that these *Sicarii* directed their activities above all against the leading high-priestly families who were, in their opinion, defiling the Temple and, by their loyalty to Rome, betraying God and Israel. At the same time, these efforts to obtain a foothold in the city and the Temple also showed how very conscious the Zealots were of the fact that the decision concerning Israel's fate ultimately depended on who was in control of the Sanctuary. For Josephus, on the other hand, this forceful entry of the *Sicarii* into the Temple was a sign

> 'that God, in anger against their godlessness, turned away from our city, no longer regarded the Sanctuary as his pure dwelling-place and led the Romans against us and sent the fire of purification over the city …'[375]

It is even possible to understand this statement as a 'polemical reversal' and to reconstruct the Zealots' attitude towards the Sanctuary:

> 'that God, in anger against the godlessness of the leading priests, has turned away from the Sanctuary and will no longer regard this as his dwelling-place for as long as it is controlled by those men and its constant desecration by sacrifices made for the emperor and the presence of the Romans in the Antonia is tolerated'.

The decision which the Zealots were striving to achieve occurred in the Sanctuary when, with the support of the majority of the priests of lower rank, the captain of the Temple, that is, Eleazar, one of the sons of Ananias b. Nedebai, who was himself a typical representative of the hated priestly nobility, surprisingly refused to accept sacrifices made by non-Jews and in that way also excluded the possibility of further sacrifices for the emperor.[376] That sacrifice, made twice daily, for one individual, who had himself venerated as a god and claimed rights to rule over almost the whole of the known world, must certainly have seemed to the Zealots, ever since the days of Judas the Galilaean, to be blasphemous.

The next steps to be taken in the 'purification of the Temple' followed very quickly. A few days after the battle had already begun in Jerusalem,

---

[375] *Ant* 20,166.
[376] *Bell* 2,409ff.; see also above, p. 205f.

on the 'feast of wood-offering', the minority that wanted peace — in other words, the noble priestly families especially — was excluded from participation in the public services. On the following day, the Fortress of Antonia was stormed and, after two days siege, captured and set on fire. This accomplished — at least externally — the 'purification' of the Temple.

It is certainly not by chance that the revolt in Jerusalem began, even as a military operation, in the Temple.[377] The foundation was in this way laid for the 'freedom of Zion', as the inscriptions on the coins struck for the first revolt postulate it. In the period that followed, the Temple became increasingly the main point of support for the Zealots.[378] This presupposes that the insurrectionary party in the city was supported by the majority of the priesthood.

To begin with, during this early period of the revolt, certain specifically Sadducaean laws concerning worship in the Temple were replaced in such a way that the Pharisaical view predominated.[379] One decisive change that was made concerned the new order of the high-priestly office. The high-priestly families were deprived of their position of pre-eminence and, by drawing lots, one Phinehas b. Samuel from the village of Aphthia was appointed from one of the old high-priestly families, the tribe of Eniachin.[380] The memory of this unique election of a high-priest by drawing lots was even preserved in the rabbinic tradition:[381]

---

[377] *Bell* 2,425.

[378] *Bell* 4,151f.: οἱ δὲ τὸν νεὼν τοῦ θεοῦ φρούριον αὐτοῖς καὶ ... ποιοῦνται καταφυγήν. See also *Bell* 5,21f.

[379] See Bill. 4, 346: MegTaan 8: The offering of a sacrifice of food on the altar on 27 Marheshvan; see H. Lichtenstein, *Die Fastenrolle* (*HUCA* VIII/IX) (1931/32). MegTaan 1 = Men 65a bar: the dispute about the Tamid from the Temple treasure; among the Sadducees, voluntary contributions were made by aristocratic families for this daily offering. The use of the Temple treasure derived its special honour from those who contributed to it, since the practice had some social distinction; see L. Finkelstein, *The Pharisees*, 3rd. ed. 1946, 1, 281f. The law was enacted on 1-8 Nisan; see H. Lichtenstein, *op. cit.*, 290ff.

[380] See *Bell* 4,147-150.153-157. The name varies; see the great edition of the text prepared by B. Niese, 6, 367, l. 11. Whatever the case may be, Phinehas is certainly behind it, at least according to A. Schalit, *Namenwörterbuch zu Flavius Josephus*, 122. The priestly tribe Ἐνιάχιν, which is not known elsewhere, was traced by Lowth back to the tribe of Jakim, 1 Chron 24.12; he reads ἡ Ἰακίμ for it; see B. Niese. *op. cit.*, l. 10.

[381] tYom 1,6 (Z. 180); see Derenbourg, 268f.; J. Jeremias, *Jerusalem*, 155, 165; Par SifLev 21,10, ed. J.H. Weiss, *Siphra d'be Rab*, Vienna 1862, 94c. He was a stone-mason by trade, but he has also been called, with reference to 1 Kings 19.19, a 'ploughman' (חוֹרֵשׁ). In addition to this, he was also related by marriage to R. Hanina b. Gamaliel II;

'They told the story of how Phinehas from Haphta was appointed as high-priest by drawing lots, whereupon the treasurers and leaders (of the priesthood) went to him and found him lifting and arranging stones. But they filled his stone-pit with gold *denarii*'.

This new high-priest had, then, the simplest origins — a fact that is stressed by Josephus. In contrast to the rabbinic tradition, which appears to approve of this action, Josephus attributes it to the madness (ἀπόνοια) of the Zealots and their hostility to the law (παρανομία).[382] As this Phinehas was not directly descended from a high-priest and the hereditary succession within the high-priestly families had been interrupted, the Zealots had, in Josephus' opinion, broken with an ancient Jewish custom. In reality, the families that had been deprived of their power had received their position of pre-eminence in the first place from Herod I and the procurators, whereas the Zealots — as Josephus himself indirectly admits — were trying to restore validity to the legitimate Zadokite line that had been interrupted since the time of the Seleucids.[383] In order to discover the high-priest whom God wanted from among the families under consideration (μίαν τῶν ἀρχιερατικῶν φυλήν), they made use of an Old Testament form of divine judgement and cast lots.[384] This new order of high-priestly office also satisfied a desire that had been felt in circles of strict believers and had already been expressed two generations previously in a demand made by the people:

'... They had the right to elect a more God-fearing and more pure (high-priest)'.[385]

Josephus, on the other hand, especially since he was himself a member of one of those families that had been set aside, makes the leader of 'Korah's band' express this demand:

---

see also Tan אמור, 6, ed. Buber 43a. See Zeitlin, *JQR* 34 (1943/44), 352, who believes, on the basis of tYom 1,7, that the high-priestly office was at the same time also limited to one year. Quite apart from the fact that Josephus may have mentioned this break with tradition, the rabbinic tradition also places this text in a different context; see above, p. 211, n. 342.

[382] *Bell* 4,147.155. The election itself is an ἀσέβημα, 157.

[383] See J. Jeremias, *op. cit.*, 192ff.: '... (it) can only be a family which was descended from the *legitimate* Zadokite high-priestly family, which had provided the high-priests in Jerusalem until 172 BC, and after that in Leontopolis'. Klausner, *Hist* 5, 209, interprets the election in a purely profane and political sense and therefore fails to discern its deeper meaning.

[384] See Schlatter, *GI*, 329: '... since no other means of experiencing God's will were known ...' See Lev 16.8ff.; 1 Chron 24.5ff. and the drawing of lots for the priestly ministry according to the tractates Yoma and Tamid. See also Lk 1.9 and, for early Christianity, see Acts 1.26; Heb 5.4.

[385] *Bell* 2,7; cf. *Ant* 17,207.

'Moses, acting contrary to the law, handed the priesthood over to his brother Aaron, not by means of a shared resolution on the part of the people, but at his own discretion'.[386]

This may also be another case of 'polemical reversal'. In other words, whereas even members of rabbinic circles compared the high-priests with the 'sons of Eli' before the destruction of the Temple, Josephus placed the desires felt in circles that were inspired by religious zeal in the mouths of those who belonged to 'Korah's band'. The execution of several particularly unpopular leaders of the traditional upper stratum of Jewish society[387] was no more than the latest consequence of a controversy for which there had been a long period of preparation.

(e) The Sanctuary as the Central Point and Stronghold in the Final Battle against Titus

The fact that Titus first attacked the Temple, which was protected by the Fortress of Antonia, and that, after his victory, the Jews showed hardly any interest in using the favourable defence installations in the part of the city situated at a higher level[388] shows clearly that the sanctuary was the central point and stronghold of the battle. This complete collapse of the Jewish will to resist after the taking of the Temple can be contrasted with the desperate hope with which they had previously defended it. Even when the Romans had taken the Antonia and were occupying the outer forecourt, so that the Jews had to cease offering the Tamid, John of Gischala was able to call to Josephus in the presence of the assembled people, that he

'... could never fear a conquest, since the city belonged to God'.[389]

---

[386] *Ant* 4,15; see also R. Eisler, 2,78.

[387] See *Bell* 2,428f.441: the murder of the high-priest Ananus b. Nedebai and his brother Hezekiah; *Bell* 4,314: the murder of the high-priest Ananus b. Ananus and Jesus b. Gamala; *Bell* 5,527ff.: the execution of Matthias b. Boethus with his three sons. Josephus was probably exaggerating in his accounts of the murders committed by the Zealots; a very large number of aristocrats and many members of the priestly aristocracy were able to go over to the Romans when the latter had penetrated into the forecourt of the Temple: *Bell* 6,113f.

[388] They were prepared to give up the city and to go into the desert: *Bell* 6,351; see also below p. 254f. Even the strongly fortified Herodium with its towers that were regarded as impregnable was vacated without a battle: *Bell* 6,399f. See also Farmer, *op. cit.,* 111f.

[389] *Bell* 6,98: ... θεοῦ γὰρ ὑπάρχειν τὴν πόλιν. Even during the siege of Jerusalem by Sossius and Herod, the Jews were preoccupied with a similar certainty: *Bell* 1,347 = *Ant* 14,470; see also A. Schlatter, *Die Theologie des Judentums nach dem Bericht des Josephus,* 1932, 221.

This certainty, which did not reflect the truth of the situation, can probably be traced to the activity of Zealot prophets who strengthened the defenders' determination by predicting that God would save his sanctuary by a miraculous intervention:

> '... It would in any case be saved by the one who dwells in it and, since they had him as an ally, they could simply scoff at all the threats that were not supported by actions, because the final result rested with God'.[390]

The result of this hope was that the insurgents fought in the forecourt of the Temple before the walls of the Sanctuary itself with extremely bitter determination:

> '... With an undiminished excess of strength and courage they tried to repel (the Romans), because they believed that, if the Romans entered the Sanctuary, ultimate defeat would follow'.[391]

By their superhuman commitment, they actually did make the Romans yield and withdraw to the Antonia.[392] This utter abandonment and carelessness for their own lives showed itself anew when a Roman soldier threw a blazing torch into the Sanctuary and set it on fire:

> 'When the flames ascended, a cry rose up from the Jews as an expression of their horror. Together they hastened to the assistance. They took no account of their own lives and did not spare themselves, when the place, of which they had been the guardians, threatened to collapse'.[393]

The battle for the Sanctuary is impressively described by Dio Cassius, whose account complements that of Josephus. The Roman troops, he says,

> '... did not penetrate at once (into the Sanctuary) because of a superstitious fear. They only broke into the interior later, when Titus urged them on. The Jews defended themselves against them with extraordinary courage, acting as though it was a gift of fortune to fall near the Temple and in the battle for it'.[394]

Even in the heat of the battle, the defenders treated the Sanctuary with the honour that was due to it. The ordinary people fought in the forecourt and

---

[390] *Bell* 5, 459. According to Dio Cassius, even individual Roman soldiers gave credence to the rumours that the city was invincible and consequently went over to the Jews (66,5).

[391] *Bell* 6,72ff.

[392] *Bell* 6,79f.

[393] *Bell* 6,253. I agree with Destinon and Thackeray that δι' ὄν should be read in the last sentence (Mss: δι' ὅ and δι' οὕ, Latin *cuius gratia*); see B. Niese's edition, 6, 546, in the apparatus, l. 10.

[394] Dio Cassius 66,6 (Reinach, 193).

the nobility (βουλευταί) in the inner courts, while the priests defended the Temple building itself.[395]

Dio Cassius continues his description of the defence of the Temple with these words:

'... and they were not overcome — although there were only a few of them fighting against a great majority — until a part of the Temple went up in flames. Immediately some of them tried to be pierced by the swords of the Romans, others murdered one another, yet others killed themselves and a few threw themselves into the fire. They all believed and the last believed most of all that it meant not ruin, but victory, salvation and blessedness if they perished with the Temple itself'.

This shattering account is also illustrated by a legendary rabbinic anecdote, according to which the young priests standing on the roof of the burning Temple are said to have thrown the key to the Temple up and God is said to have received it,

'... then they jumped down and threw themselves into the fire'.[396]

Dio Cassius, who was not a Jew, saw the desperate battle for the Sanctuary in quite a different light from Josephus and it is quite reasonable to trust his report much more than that written by Josephus, whose account is distorted by his strong anti-Zealot tendency. The non-Jewish author shows us how the Jews observed the laws of purity in the Temple until the end and how their zeal remained undiminished until the Temple was on fire. Presumably they waited until the very end for God's direct intervention, in accordance with the apocalyptic law: the greater the need, the nearer is God's miraculous help.

According to Josephus, immediately before the Sanctuary was taken, a Zealot prophet proclaimed to the people as God's commandment that they should go up to the Temple, where 'they would receive the signs of redemption'.[397] Even in the Apocalypse of Ezra, which was composed under the influence of the destruction of Jerusalem, the Messiah was — while a countless army gathered from all nations came together at one point, that is, probably before Jerusalem — 'to go up to the top of Mount Zion ... (and) punish the nations that had marched against him for their sins'.[398]

---

[395] The distinction between the people and the nobility can probably be traced to the observer who was not acquainted with Jewish relationships. It is possible that the Levites were meant by this second group.

[396] Taan 29a bar; translation based on Goldschmidt, 3, 741; see also SyrBar 10,18 and AbRN, ed. Schechter, 4, 24.

[397] Bell 6,285f.; see also below, pp. 229, 242.

[398] 4 Ezra 13.34-37. According to SyrBar 40,1, the hostile ruler (see below, p. 304)

The final shattering battle for the Temple is certainly the most impressive example of that 'zeal for the Sanctuary' that filled Judaism to such a striking degree prior to 70 A.D. Although the defenders could have saved their lives and preserved their freedom at any time by going over to the Romans, they preferred to fight a lost cause, yet not without hope, to the bitter end.[399] It is clear, then, that this zeal was closely associated with eschatological hope: in response to their unconditional self-offering, they expected God to intervene.

E. Summary: Zeal as an Eschatological Intensification of the Torah

As I have already said above, zeal for God's cause, that is, for the law and the Sanctuary, was a phenomenon that had characterized the whole of Palestinian Judaism in general from the time of the Maccabees and in particular the groups of Essenes and Pharisees who had emerged from the Hasidim. Even early Christianity had been at least to some extent influenced by its Jewish inheritance. This 'zeal' was based on a consciousness of Israel's election and separateness and it was therefore experienced in a completely positive way. It was not until the catastrophes of 70 and 135 A.D. that the rabbinate, influenced by those events, began to develop a more critical attitude towards certain aspects of this zeal.

(1) The ultimate starting point for this zeal was the zeal of God himself for Israel's purity and freedom. It was above all Phinehas who appeared as a human model for this in two respects:

(a) Zeal called — especially in moments of danger — for a total surrender to God's will and a passionate commitment, going as far as a readiness to offer one's own life, to the cause of God's honour or to that of the task of saving the threatened principles of faith. This leads to the still open question of martyrdom in the case of the Zealots.[400]

This zeal was similarly concerned with the law and the Sanctuary.

---

was killed on Mount Zion by the Messiah. See also Rev 14.1: the Lamb on Mount Zion. See also Bill. 1, 151; PesR 36 (162a): the Messiah reveals himself on the pinnacle of the Temple.

[399] See *Bell* 6,229. Even the most guilty leaders of the Zealots were accepted. It was only after the Temple had been burnt down that deserters were rejected. This order was, however, later revoked: *Bell* 6,352.386ff.

[400] The call to be prepared to die as a martyr was already present in the case of Judas the Galilaean; see above, p. 77. Even in the case of Phinehas, it was presupposed in the Haggadah (in contrast to its absence from the Old Testament); see above, p. 158. See also below, p. 257ff.

These two elements were inseparably connected with each other before the destruction of the Temple:

> 'The parts they played were complementary; the Torah mediated God's revelation to his people, while the temple worship mediated the nation's devotion to its God'.[401]

Entire sections of the Torah were, on the one hand, devoted to the Sanctuary with its cult and formed a protective wall around it, while, on the other, the Sanctuary, as the place where God was present with his people, formed the visible central point around which all Jews who were faithful to the Torah assembled.

(b) This 'zeal for God's cause', represented vicariously the anger of God's judgement. The Zealots therefore used violent means when it was necessary either to restore validity to the law when it had been disregarded by their fellow-countrymen or to defend the Sanctuary when it was threatened by pagans. In every case of serious threat to Israel's sacred blessings, either from within Israel or from outside, the use of violence became a sacred duty. This, of course, confronts us with the question of the Holy War, which will be discussed in the following chapter.

A 'passionate surrender to God's will' also formed an essential part of Jesus' activity and that of the early Christian community, but the obligation to use violence was necessarily rejected. Paul, for example, rejected the Jews' ζῆλος θεοῦ as οὐ κατ' ἐπίγνωσιν (Rom 10.2). His clear pronouncement that revenge and retribution are matters for God alone and that the believer should love his enemy can perhaps also be

---

[401] W.R. Farmer, 85. Bousset's thesis (*B.-Gr.Rel.* 113) that popular piety had become 'increasingly separated' from the Temple and its cult can no longer be regarded as valid. The three reasons that he gives for this are quite untenable for the following three reasons: (1) the finds at Qumran have clearly shown how deeply the Essenes were influenced by the priestly and cultic ideal. They did not reject the Temple because it no longer meant anything to them, but because they regarded it as no longer sufficiently pure; see *Ant* 18,8. They traced their origin back to a secession from priestly circles. (2) The way of Jesus inevitably led to Jerusalem and into the Sanctuary. It was there that his fate was decided. (3) The assertion that the Jewish religion was 'hardly shaken' by the destruction of the Temple is quite certainly wrong. Faithful Judaism and rabbinism did not remain 'the same as they had previously been' after the destruction of the Temple. The later rabbinate however had good reasons for trying to efface this break and to conceal the past connection on its left wing with the Zealots (see above, p. 21f., and below, p. 333f.). An impressive example of this serious religious crisis following the destruction of the Temple can be found in the so-called Fourth Ezra apocalypse. For this question, see H.J. Schoeps, *Die Tempelzerstörung im Jahre 70. Aus frühchristlicher Zeit* (1950), 144-183, especially 168; see also C. Thoma, *BZ*, New Series 12 (1968), 30-54, 186-210.

understood as a repudiation of zeal of the wrong kind, as practised by the Zealots.[402] The early Christian community did not therefore use violent means even in the case of grave sinners, but left them to be punished by divine intervention.[403] Since there could be no compromise between Zealotism and the early Church in the question of the employment of external violence, it is extremely unlikely that Christians took part in the revolt against Rome.[404]

For the Zealots, however, this was undoubtedly the most decisive aspect of 'zeal'. Following Old Testament examples, they were quite convinced that God's holy will could only be achieved in this world, dominated as it was by powers that were hostile to God, by the sword. Men like Jesus and Paul must indeed have seemed to them to be dangerous enthusiasts, possibly because they were in many other ways so close to themselves. By their constant readiness to take harsh action against those who transgressed the law, the Zealots in the course of time developed, with the silent toleration of the Jewish authorities, a kind of vehmic jurisdiction, intervening whenever there was a breakdown in the Jewish jurisdiction, which was so restricted by the power of the procurators.

(2) An essential aspect of Zealotism, which also predominated in a very similar way in the Essene community and in the preaching of Jesus, is — as H. Braun has pointed out[405] — that the teaching of the Torah was given a sharper emphasis in a 'radicalization of obedience'. This 'intensification' of God's demand can also be seen as a characteristic of the Zealot movement. The sources, it is true, tell us nothing about the

---

[402] See Rom 12.19ff.; see also Mt 5.39ff.,44ff.; 6.12; Lk 9.54f.; 10.5-37, etc., and, referring to Jesus himself, 1 Pet 2.23.

[403] Acts 5.1-11; see also 1 Cor 5.3ff. The rabbinate was also acquainted with the idea of 'punishment by heaven', but this was, in the rabbinic tradition, restricted to certain sins; see Sanh 9,6c and Rashi on Shab 25a; see also S. Krauss, *op. cit.*, 264.

[404] This thesis has been presented in a very decisive but not very convincing way by S.G.F. Brandon, *The Fall of Jerusalem and the Christian Church*, 1951; see above, pp. 10, 174f. What Brandon has above all failed to perceive is that the Zealots' messianic hope could not be reconciled in any way with faith in Jesus as the Messiah who will come again; see below, p. 300f.

[405] *Spätjüdisch-häretischer und frühchristlicher Radikalismus*, 2 Vols, 1957, 1, 17,32f.,73,99. The author has unfortunately opted in the Pirke Aboth for a one-sided and therefore unfavourable comparative basis for rabbinic ethics. It is no more possible to derive the latter from that tractate than it is to base Old Testament ethics as a whole on the Book of Proverbs. The Pirke Aboth, which was codified at the beginning of the third century A.D., idealizes the preceding period in a one-sided manner. It also provides no more than a selection of individual rules of life and for these reasons cannot be regarded as really reflecting Pharisaical piety of the first century A.D.

significance attributed to the exegesis of the Torah by the Zealots. It is, however, legitimate to conclude from the fact that they originated in Pharisaical circles and that their founder, Judas the Galilaean — like his son Menahem, who later became the leader of the party — was called σοφιστής[406] that, despite the ongoing military struggle and the uncertainty that accompanied that situation, the study of the Torah continued in Zealot circles. This conclusion is especially justified in view of the fact that they always remained in contact with the Shammaites, the radical wing of Jewish scholars.

One particular emphasis given to the original demand made by the law was their fundamental thesis of the struggle for freedom, namely that only the God of Israel could be acknowledged as 'Lord' and that all foreign political rule had therefore to be rejected.[407] The rejection of the census, the refusal to pay taxes and to make sacrifices for the emperor and the call for the unconditional 'freedom of Israel' can all be traced back to this original thesis and can therefore also be seen as a similar 'intensification'. The inevitable consequence of this radicalization of the first commandment was that those who continued to subject themselves to the foreign power were regarded as apostates or pagans and were therefore 'punished' with death.[408]

The strict hostility to images, which was even extended to representations on coins, the demand that pagans should be circumcised if necessary by force, the zealous vigilance over Israel's sacred blessings and the rigorous laws against intercourse with non-Jews — all these can also be regarded as 'intensifications' of the Torah. The same applies to the harsh application of the death penalty, the purpose of which was to achieve the purity that was required by the Torah.

The sources, of course, are very fragmentary and only provide us with small and purely fortuitous excerpts of the Zealots' interpretation of the law. Despite this, what emerges quite clearly from those sources is that the guide-lines for personal action were always polemical. They contained elements of fierce opposition to non-Jews and those who committed outrages against the Jewish faith as well as to those Jews who supported the foreign oppressor and who disregarded the law. The teaching of the Zealots, then, was not a form of legal casuistry or metaphysical speculation, but a militant doctrine of action as the expression of zealous confession.

---

[406] See above, p. 83, n. 38; 86f.; see also below, p. 333.

[407] See above, p. 90ff. What was presumably at the basis of this demand was a new understanding of the first commandment and the *Shema*.

[408] *Bell* 2,264; 7,254f.; see also above, p. 138f.

(3) H. Braun has correctly traced this radical tendency in the Essene community and in the proclamation of Jesus back to an imminent expectation of the Eschaton in Judaism.[409] The radicalization of the law in Zealot circles can similarly be regarded as having its origins in the fundamentally eschatological attitude of the sect.

The insistence on the 'sole rule of God' that was so closely associated with the revolt against Roman rule was for the Zealots the first step towards bringing about the kingdom of God, the coming of which was at least partly dependent on the personal participation of God's people. In the same way, the attempt to achieve by every possible means the 'purity of Israel' was at the same time an attempt to prepare the way for the eschatological coming of God. It is also quite obvious that such radical elements as the renunciation of property and the ethics of martyrdom, to which H. Braun draws attention in his work,[410] fully apply to Zealotism. It is important in this context to stress, however, that neither the Essenes nor the Zealots regarded their understanding of the law as an 'intensification' in the sense of an emphasis that changed or added a new element to the ancient Torah given to Moses. The very opposite is true — they wanted to restore validity to the Torah in its original and unadulterated sense here and now at the end of time. It is significant that Josephus frequently criticizes the Zealots for having introduced new doctrines or for having changed old ones.[411]

Finally, I would like to conclude this chapter with a conjecture that cannot be verified in detail without going beyond the scope of the present work. It is that, by analogy with the Essenes, the proclamation of Jesus and the Zealots, it may also be possible to understand the Pharisaical movement in its original form, before the period of rabbinic ossification, in the light of the theme of an eschatological intensification of the Torah. To do this, it is only necessary to refer on the one hand to their struggle against the Hasmonaeans and Herod and, on the other, to the fact that the founders of the Zealot movement, Saddok and Judas, and, on the other hand, a figure such as Paul had their origins in Pharisaical circles.[412]

---

[409] *op. cit.*, 1, 31f.: 'This zeal and this perfection can only be fully understood if we bear in mind the proximity of the eschaton'; see also 1, 56f.,112; 2, 19ff.,45,53, etc.

[410] See H. Braun, *op. cit.*, in the index to Vols 1 and 2 under the words 'Besitzverzicht' and 'Märtyrerethik'.

[411] See *Ant* 18,9f.; *Bell* 2,410.412.414: with reference to the sacrifice for the emperor: καινοτομεῖν θρησκείαν ξένην, and the election of the high-priest, *Bell* 4,157.

[412] H. Braun, *op. cit.*, 1, 10, n. 3, points to the absence of the term 'zeal' in Aboth I-IV. It would, however, be wrong simply on this basis to draw certain conclusions regarding the Pharisees at the time of Jesus; see above, p. 225, n. 401.

CHAPTER V

THE ZEALOTS AS AN ESCHATOLOGICAL
MOVEMENT

A. ZEALOT PROPHETS

1. The False Prophets according to Josephus

In his account of the destruction of the sanctuary, Josephus mentions false prophets who were appointed by the Zealots for the purpose of propaganda:

'Many (prophets) were suborned by the tyrants at that time for the people. They announced that the people should adhere to God's help so that fewer would desert and those who lived in fear and mistrust would be strengthened in hope'.

The pronouncement made by a false prophet of this kind (ψευδοπροφήτης) resulted in the death of six thousand people who were waiting in one of the halls of the Temple for a 'sign of redemption': either they were killed by the Romans or they died in the flames.[1] We may conclude from this that such prophets had already been active at an earlier period among the Zealots.

Josephus speaks more than once of those who led the people astray and of false prophets who appeared during the rule of the procurators. There was apparently a Samaritan prophet or pseudo-Messiah who caused unrest under Pilate.[2] A second pseudo-Messiah appeared at the time of Cuspius Fadus (who ruled from 44 A.D. onwards) — one Theudas,[3] 'who claimed that he was a prophet',[3] but who was, in Josephus' opinion, no more than an ordinary deceiver.[4] He was followed by a great number of people — according to Acts 5.36, four hundred strong

---

[1] *Bell* 6,286 (cf. 283ff.). For Josephus' linguistic usage, see J. Reiling, *NT* 13 (1971), 147ff.

[2] *Ant* 18,85-87. R. Eisler, 2, 700ff., has connected this with fantastic combinations.

[3] *Ant* 20,97f.; cf. Acts 5.36. This identity is beyond doubt; see Schürer, 1, 456.

[4] γόης. For Josephus, this concept undoubtedly had the meaning of 'deceiver' and 'those who led the people astray' and he applied it above all to false prophets; see *Bell* 2,261; *Ant* 20,160.167.188. See also *Bell* 4,85: John of Gischala; *Bell* 5,317: the trick employed by the Jew Castor; *Vita* 40: Justus from Tiberias.

— who went with him, carrying all that they possessed, to the Jordan, the waters of which he intended to divide by his command so that they could all pass through with him. There is an obvious analogy here with the Exodus from Egypt of the Israelites, who also took all their movable possessions when they left their homes in Goshen and went with him into the desert. Moses divided the Sea of Reeds at the time of their greatest need and they passed through while their pursuers drowned.[5]

In the case of Theudas, those who were pursuing him remained in control of the situation. He was decapitated and his head was brought back to Jerusalem as a trophy of war and a deterrent. According to all the evidence, he was not an ordinary 'prophet'. He may possibly have regarded himself as a *Moses redivivus* in accordance with Deut 18.15f.[6]

An astonishing parallel can be found in the *Vitae Prophetarum*,[7] according to which Ezekiel divided the waters of a river (possibly the Euphrates, according to Is 11.15f.) and led the Israelites to the opposite bank, while their Chaldaean pursuers, who had feared a rebellion (ἀντάρωσις) on the part of the Jews, drowned. Theudas cannot be regarded as a 'Zealot prophet' in the strict sense of the term. He can rather be seen as a prophetic and messianic pretender of unique stamp.[8]

During Felix' period of office (52–60 A.D.), the machinations of the 'tricksters and deceivers' (γόητες καὶ ἀπατεῶνες ἄνθρωποι, *Ant*), who 'caused unrest and disruption under the cloak of divine inspiration' increased more and more. Their enthusiasm had a contagious effect on the people (δαιμονᾶν τὸ πλῆθος). Eventually, they led a great number out into the desert, where God, they claimed, would reveal to them the 'signs of freedom'. They suffered, however, the same fate as Theudas.[9]

---

[5] In analogy with Ex 13.18ff., his followers were presumably also armed.

[6] For the expectation of the eschatological prophet, see TestBenj 9,2; Jn 1.21,25; 6.14. For the problem itself, see J. Jeremias, 'Μωϋσῆς', *ThWAT* 4, 862ff. The narrow basis of sources was enlarged by the discoveries made at Qumran; see 1QS 9,11 and 4QTest (No. 175), 5 with the quotation from Deut 18.18f., see DJD V, 58. Deut 18.15 is also interpreted messianically in Acts 3.22 and 7.37. For the idea of *Moses redivivus*, see Volz, *Esch*., 194f., J. Jeremias, *op. cit.*, 4, 865ff., N. Wieder, *JJS* 4 (1953), 158ff., and A.S. van der Woude, *Die messianischen Vorstellungen der Gemeinde von Qumran*, 1957, 80f. It is unlikely that Theudas would have appeared as Joshua *redivivus*; see R. Meyer, 'προφήτης', *TD* 6, 826, and R. Eisler, 2, 705.

[7] T. Schermann, 'Propheten- und Apostellegenden', *TU* 31.R.3, 3, 1907, 90,1.9ff. The theme of the crossing of the river is possibly connected with Is 11.15 and it also appears in 4 Ezra 13,44.47 and Acts 16.12.

[8] For the messianic interpretation, see J. Jeremias, *op. cit.*, 4, 858.,862. R. Meyer, *Der Prophet aus Galiläa*, 1940, 54, was right to stress that Theudas was regarded in the Palestinian early Christian tradition as in competition with Jesus.

[9] *Bell* 2,259f. = *Ant* 20,167. For the signs of freedom, see above, p. 114f.

At the same time, an 'Egyptian' — presumably an Egyptian Jew — appeared, also claiming to be a prophet. There are discrepancies between Josephus' description of the event and the statements that he makes about the number of his followers[10] in *The Jewish War* on the one hand and the *Antiquities* on the other. The Egyptian presumably led his followers into the desert and from there to the Mount of Olives.[11] There he aimed to make the walls of Jerusalem fall — as the walls of Jericho had done under Joshua — and in this way to gain control of the city. Felix, however, led his troops against him and his band of followers was defeated.

What is very difficult to believe is that the inhabitants of Jerusalem supported the Roman troops in this.[12] The prophet himself also disappeared in an inexplicable way.[13] He also gives the impression of having been not an ordinary prophet, but a messianic pretender. According to *The Jewish War*, he promised:

'... to overcome the Roman occupation troops in Jerusalem and to assume the rule over the people (τοῦ δήμου τυραννεῖν), appointing those who were ready to enter the city with him as bodyguards'.[14]

There is also a corresponding theme in the later Haggadah, according to which the Israelites marched to Rome in obedience to 'a voice from

---

[10] *Ant* 20,169: ; *Bell* 2, 261: , cf. Acts 21.38. According to *Bell* 2,261, there were some thirty thousand of them, whereas four thousand *Sicarii* are mentioned in Acts 21.38. Josephus speaks in *Ant* 20,171 of four hundred dead and two hundred prisoners, but, according to *The Jewish War*, the majority of them were killed or taken prisoner. F.J. Foakes Jackson and K. Lake, *The Beginnings of Christianity*, I, *The Acts*, 1920ff., 4, 277, assumed that there was a reading error of Δ = 4000 in Λ = 30000. The explanation suggested by D. Georgi, *Die Gegner des Paulus*, 1964, 123f., is fantastic.

[11] This is suggested in *Bell* 2,262; see also Acts 21.38. According to the *Antiquities*, he only led the mob from Jerusalem to the Mount of Olives, whereas, according to *The Jewish War*, he assembled his followers in the country and led them first into the desert. In the first case, which is favoured by E. Haenchen, *The Acts of the Apostles* 1971, 618ff. it is difficult to explain why the Egyptian first left the city and then wanted to make its walls fall in order to gain control of it.

[12] This is suggested in *Bell* 2,263; it is possible that the Temple police marched out as a kind of 'municipal militia' against the Egyptian; see above, p. 30, n. 56.

[13] *Ant* 20,171. The people probably believed in a miraculous escape and expected him to return; see Acts 21.38.

[14] *Bell* 2,262. E.Lohmeyer, *Das Evangelium des Markus (Meyers Kommentar)*, 12th. ed. 1953, 229 (on 11.1), assumed that, because of Ezek 11.23 and especially Zech 14.4, the Mount of Olives had a certain significance within the framework of messianic ideas in late Judaism. Despite the objections raised by W. Foerster, 'ὄρος', *TD* 5, 484, n. 102, this assumption is not improbable; see also *The Beginnings of Christianity*, 5, 22, and R. Eisler, 2, 440, n. 1. For examples from the later Haggadah, see Bill. 1, 841 and 2, 298f. (LekTob Num 24.17).

heaven' telling them: 'Do with Rome what Joshua did with Jericho'. They acted accordingly and the walls of Rome fell.[5]

This Egyptian was, like Theudas, in no way a 'Zealot' in the strict sense of the word, that is, one who belonged to the party founded by Judas the Galilaean. On the contrary, he founded his own movement and made claims to rule for his own person.[16] His followers are called *Sicarii* in Acts 21.38. This can be explained by the fact that all armed insurgents could be described, as far as the Romans serving under Felix were concerned, as *sicarii* or murderers.

Another '*goet*' appeared under Festus, predicting 'salvation and an end to all evil' to his victims who followed him into the desert. Festus, however, had him pursued and put to death together with his followers.[17]

What is common to all these 'false prophets' is their going into the desert and their promise that redemption would take place there. This points to a firm prophetic pattern of 'redemption' that is closely connected with the Exodus from Egypt.[18]

There is also an indication of this in Matthew's Gospel. Whereas the synoptics contain several general warnings against pseudo-prophets, Matthew is more precise in his description of this particular warning (24.26).

> 'So, if they say to you, "Lo, he (the pseudo-prophet or pseudo-Messiah) is in the wilderness", do not go out . . .'[19]

We may therefore assume that this warning was formed by the concrete event in the years preceding the outbreak of the Jewish War. It is also characteristic that, both in Josephus and in the gospels, the dividing line between the pseudo-Messiah and the pseudo-prophet is somewhat fluid.[20]

Josephus, however, makes a clear distinction between the 'slaughterers' (σφαγέων), that is, the *Sicarii*, and 'a second band of rascals,

---

[15] For this, see G. Dalman, *Der leidende und sterbende Messias der Synagoge*, 1888, 12.

[16] For the various attempts to identify the person of the Egyptian, see R. Eisler, 1, 177, n. 6 and 2, 708.

[17] *Ant* 20,188; there is possibly a doublet here.

[18] For the analogy with the Exodus, see above, pp. 114f. and 119f.; for the desert, see below, p. 249ff.

[19] For the general warning of false prophets, see Mk 13.6 = Mt 24.5; Mk 13.12f. = Mt 24.23f.; see also Mt 7.15 and 24.11.

[20] See the juxtaposition of ψευδόχριστοι and ψευδοπροφῆται in Mk 13.22 = Mt 24.24, who 'show signs and wonders' without distinction. For Josephus' false prophets, see R. Meyer, *Der Prophet aus Galiläa*, 1940, 84 and *TD* 6, 826f.

whose hands were cleaner, but whose intention was, however, even more depraved . . .' in other words, the false prophets.[21] These men made less use of weapons and more use of visionary insight. They formed in each case short-lived followings that fell apart whenever the procurators intervened.

The Zealots, on the other hand, were well organized and they were scattered throughout the country in their various hiding-places. Despite individual successes on the part of the procurators, they continued to oppose the latter and could not be overcome. There must, however, also have been an active prophetic and enthusiastic element present in the case of these Zealots.

The first example of this is provided by Judas himself, the founder of the sect: he is named in the Gamaliel speech together with the enthusiast Theudas. Some aspects of his preaching and their effects can also best be explained by the fact that he proclaimed his message with prophetic authority. Referring to the period immediately preceding the outbreak of the Jewish War, Josephus explicitly confirms the link between the Zealots and the *goets*:[22]

'Hardly had these (disturbances) been suppressed when an inflammation broke out in another place, as though in a sick body. For the deceivers (γόητες) and robbers (γῃστρικοί) joined forces, led astray many to insurrection and encouraged them to gain freedom . . . .

One last figure who should be mentioned in this context is a certain Jonathan. He had previously been a *sicarius* and had fled to Cyrene, where he had initially worked for a time at his trade as a weaver, but had later led a great number of people of the lower level of society into the desert, 'after having promised to show them miracles and apparitions'. The governor quickly put an end to this unarmed exodus. This example shows, however, that visionary enthusiasm also had an intimate place in the lives of the *Sicarii*.[23]

2. Prophecy in Late Judaism

R. Meyer has shown clearly in his outstanding investigation, 'Prophecy and Prophets in Judaism during the Hellenistic Roman

---

[21] *Bell* 2,258; S. Zeitlin, *Who Crucified Jesus*, 2nd. ed. 1947, 96ff., made a distinction between these *goets* as 'apocalyptical Pharisees' and the *Sicarii*.

[22] *Bell* 2,264f.

[23] *Bell* 7,438ff. I disagree with Georgi, *op. cit.*, 125, n. 1. and believe that his Palestinian origin was decisive.

Period'[24] that it is no longer possible to accept the widespread opinion that the effects of prophetic charism were only very marginally known in Judaism of that period.[25] In the first place, the evidence in the First Book of the Maccabees that, it has been claimed, points to the cessation of prophecy is no more than an indirect reference to the 'prophet' and high-priest John Hyrcanus.[26] Secondly, the evidence close to the rabbinic tradition which, together with that provided by Josephus and the closed canon, restricts prophecy to the period until the reign of Artaxerxes I,[27] dates significantly from the time following the catastrophe of 70 A.D.

Meyer maintained over against this that 'the great rebellions under Vespasian and Hadrian cannot be understood in the absence of a powerful charismatic element' and that 'early Pharisaism ... itself (made) its own contribution to this ... at the decisive point' because it was at least to some extent closely related to Zealotism.[28]

The following features are characteristic of prophecy in the Hellenistic Roman period:

(1) The Spirit was less effective at that time through direct inspiration.[29] The influence of the Spirit was more frequently felt via the charismatic interpretation of Scripture. The formation of the canon did not necessarily have to result in a cessation of prophecy. On the contrary, only someone who was filled with the Spirit could really adequately interpret the words of Holy Scripture which were inspired by God, but were often very obscure. The prophetic vision of Dan 9.2ff., for example, was brought about by an inability to understand the 'obscure' prophecy of Jeremiah (25.11f.) about the seventy years of the

---

[24] 'Prophecy and Prophets ...', *TD* 6, 812-828; see also his work, *Der Prophet aus Galiläa*, 1940.

[25] For this view, see I. Abrahams, 'Studies in Pharisaism and the Gospels', 2nd. Series, 1924, 120-128; Moore, Judaism, 1, 240f.; *B.-Gr. Rel.* 394f.; W. Foerster, *Palestinian Judaism in New Testament Times*, 4f., 90. For the opposite view, see O. Michel, *Spätjüdisches Prophetentum. Neutestamentliche Studien für R. Bultmann*, 2nd ed. 1957, 60-67; see also R. Leivestad, *NTS* (1972/3), 288-299.

[26] For 1 Macc 4.46; 9.27 and 14.41, see R. Meyer, *TD* 6, 815f.; see also E. Bammel, *ThLZ* 79 (1954), 351ff. R. Leivestad, *op. cit.*, 295f., expresses a different view.

[27] According to Josephus, *Ap* 1,41, the 'precise prophetic succession' ceased after Artaxerxes. The woeful lamentation expressed in SyrBar 85,3 has, as far as the cessation of prophecy is concerned, Lam 2.9 as its model; see also R. Meyer, *op. cit.*, 6, 815f. For the rabbinic views, see Bill. 2, 217f. amd 133f.; E. Sjöberg, 'Endowment with the Spirit in Past, Future and Present', *TD* 6, 385f. and R. Meyer, *op. cit.* 6, 817ff.

[28] *op. cit.* 6, 820; see also 283, n. 4.

[29] Individual cases of direct inspiration can be found, for example, in such persons as the prophet of disaster, Jeshua b. Ananias: *Bell* 6,300ff., and the early Christian prophet, Agabus: Acts 21.10; see also 2 Cor 12.1-4.

destruction of Jerusalem. This passage is interpreted for Daniel after a thorough preparation by repentance, prayer and fasting by the angel Gabriel as 'seventy weeks of years' (9.22). In the case of the teacher of righteousness[30] and the Essenes[31] too, Holy Scripture generally and the prophetic books in particular formed the point of departure for their own charismatic prophecy. This prophetic and charismatic interpretation of Scripture can also be found in early Christianity[32] and the Pauline formula (1 Cor 2.13) can certainly be applied to the whole question: πνευματικοῖς πνευματικὰ συγκρίνοντες. Even Josephus based his prophetic gift among other things on a knowledge of Holy Scripture[33] and R. Akiba took a scriptural text as his point of departure for his prophetic legitimation of Simeon b. Koseba.[34]

(2) As the Spirit was promised as a gift of the time of salvation even in the Old Testament,[35] it is not difficult to understand why those groups of Jews who lived in a state of awareness of the imminence or the arrival of the end of time claimed that they possessed the Spirit. This applies not only to the Essenes,[36] but also to the early Christians.[37] There even seem to have been certain approaches made towards this in early Pharisaism.[38]

[30] See 1QpHab 2,8f. and 7,5ff. A.S. van der Woude, *op. cit.*, believed that the Teacher of Righteousness was the same person as the prophet of 1 QS 9,11 and regarded him as *Moses redivivus*; see also R. Meyer, *op. cit.*, 6, 821.

[31] See *Bell* 2,159. The Essenes' political 'judgement prophecy' (see below, p. 236, n. 39) also seems to have a basis in scriptural exegesis: see, for example, 1 QpHab 9,6; 11,14 and 4QTest (No. 175), 21-30, see DJD V, 58.

[32] See Lk 24.27 and Acts 8.31-35; cf. also the Pauline exegesis, Rom 4.3ff.; 2 Cor 3.4-17; Gal 3.8ff.; 4.21ff. See also O. Michel, *Paulus und sein Bibel*, 1929, 178: 'The πνεῦμα explains the γραφή'.

[33] *Bell* 3,352: Josephus also stresses his priestly origin and his ability to interpret dreams. For Josephus' prophetic gift, see *Bell* 3,399-408, his confession to Vespasian, and *Vita* 208ff., a prophetic dream; see also Suetonius, *Vesp* 5,6 and Dio Cassius 66,1. See W. Weber, *Josephus und Vespasian*, 1921, 44-48.75. J. Hempel, *AO* 38 (1938), 25f., assumed that Josephus took the prophecies of Second Isaiah about Cyrus as his model; see above, p. 101, n. 32. See also M. Hengel, *Judaism and Hellenism*, 202ff. A. Schalit goes into considerable detail in *Aufstieg und Niedergang der Römischen Welt*, II,2, 1975, 208ff.

[34] jTaan 68d,49f. See Bill. 1, 13; for the problem of prophecy on the basis of 'contemplative reflection about Scripture', see R. Meyer, *op. cit.*, 6, 820f.

[35] See W. Bieder, 'πνεῦμα, Spirit in Judaism', *TD* 6, 367; see also Is 32.15; 44.3; Ezek 11.19; 36.26; Joel 3.1f.

[36] See, for example, 1QpHab 2,5; 9,6; CD 4,4; 6,11; 1QSa 1,1 (ed. Barthélémy and Milik, *Qumran Cave I*, 109). According to 1QpHab 2,7f., the interpretation 'of the words of the prophets' took place for the 'last generation'; see also 7,2. The 'secrets of the end of time' were brought to light by study of the Torah: see Fragm 1Q 27 (*Qumran Cave I*, 103, col. 1,3ff.); see also H. Braun, *op. cit.*, 1, 17f.

[37] Acts 2.17ff. (Joel 3.1); 8.15ff.; Rom 5.5; 8; Gal 3.2, etc.

[38] See the Psalms of Solomon and the messianic prophecies in *Ant* 17,43ff. Hillel also promised the whole people that they would possess the Spirit: tPes 4,2 (Z. 162), Bill. 2,

The false prophets mentioned by Josephus can also be seen in this perspective. As men who had been given a prophetic and messianic task by God for the end of time, they believed that they were in possession of the divine Spirit.

(3) As in the Old Testament, these prophecies were also seen by those who believed that they were living under the shadow of the imminent end as relating to a prediction or an interpretation of historical and political events. This is clear both from the apocalyptic description of the time of religious persecution in Daniel and from the praxis of prophecy among the Essenes as reported by Josephus.[39] In early Christianity[40] and in Pharisaism, individual examples of this kind can also be found.[41] In this context — because they were confirmed by the course of history and therefore recorded — predictions of the fall of Jerusalem are particularly numerous.[42]

3. The Zealots' Prophecy as a Charismatic and Eschatological Interpretation of Scripture

It is important at this stage to consider whether the effects of the Zealot 'prophets' were not also determined by the three points: 'a

---

819f., n. 1. For the pouring out of the Spirit at the end of time according to Joel 3.1ff., see Bill. 2, 134.615f.; 4, 915; see also E. Sjöberg, *op. cit.*, 6, 383.

[39] *Bell* 1,78ff. = *Ant* 13,311: the prophecy of the imminent death of the king's brother Antigonus by the Essene Judas. Antigonus had presumably committed a great outrage by his service in the Temple immediately after returning from his campaign (see 1QM 9,8). In *Ant* 15,373, the Essene Menahem prophesies to the young Herod that he will receive the dignity of kingship and therefore that the reign of the Hasmonaeans will end. According to *Bell* 2,112f. = *Ant* 17,346, the Essene Simon's interpretation of a dream dreamed by Archelaus is that the latter's deposition is imminent. All these cases, then, are examples of prophecies of punishment. The Old Testament probably acted as a model here: for *Bell* 1,78ff., see 1 Kings 21.17f. and 2 Kings 1,4f.; for *Ant* 15,373, see 1 Kings 11.29ff. and 19.15f.; 2 Kings 8.10ff. and 9.2f. For *Bell* 2,112f., see Daniel's interpretation of Nebuchadnezzar's dreams; M. Hengel, *Judentum und Hellenismus*, 439.

[40] See Acts 11.28; cf. 1 Kings 17.1 and Acts 21.10f. See also the prophetic parabolic actions in Is 20.2 and Jer 13.1ff. See also Eusebius, *HistEcc* 3,5: the prophetic directive given to the community in Jerusalem to flee to Pella. See also E. Fascher, ΠΟΦΗΤΗΣ, 1927, 161ff., who completely misinterpreted the Essene prophets. Lk 21.20-24 (= Mk 13.14-18) also goes back to a prophetic utterance of this kind.

[41] See *Ant* 14,174ff.: Sameas' prophecy of punishment to Hyrcanus and the Synhedrium; *Ant* 17,43ff.: the Pharisees' messianic 'prophecies' regarding Bagoas; according to tPar 3,8 (Z. 632), Johanan b. Zakkai predicted to a high-priest that his death was imminent and in fact he died promptly; according to Gitt 56a.b., he greeted Vespasian as the future emperor. For Akiba, see below, p. 239. Further examples will be found in R. Meyer, *op. cit.*, 6, 824f.

[42] See Jesus' threatening words in Mk13.2 par., and the ecstatic prophet Jesus b. Ananus, *Bell* 6,300f. For the rabbinic tradition, see Bill. 1, 1045f.: jYom 43d,71,

charismatic interpretation of Scripture', 'an eschatological possession of the Spirit' and 'a historical and political orientation'.

(a) A Messianic Prophecy

Among the main causes of the rebellion, Josephus includes:

'an ambiguous oracular pronouncement, which had also been found in Holy Scripture, that one man from their country would at that time be given command over the world. This they applied to a member of their people and many wise men erred in their interpretation'.[43]

Josephus applied this oracle, by virtue of his own 'prophetic gift', of course, to Vespasian. It was also mentioned later by Tacitus and Suetonius[44] and similarly related to the Roman ruler. This 'ambiguous oracle' would seem to be in accordance with the above-mentioned framework:

(1) It belongs clearly to the type of 'political prophecy'.

(2) The reference to Holy Scripture in Josephus' statement and in Tacitus leads to the conclusion that it was an Old Testament prophecy.

(3) It has an unmistakably eschatological content. It was originally about the eschatological ruler of the world who was to come from Judaea.[45]

(4) The underlying scriptural text could not be immediately understood: it had first to be interpreted by the σοφοί. This presupposes a prophetic charism on the part of the interpreter.

We are therefore bound to ask when this prophecy appeared for the first time and what was the scriptural text behind it. The first question is

---

Johanan b. Zakkai; Bill. 4, 99: Gitt 56a: R. Zadok's fast of forty years; see also Yom 3,11 and the Gemara of the Babylonian Talmud 38a (Goldschmidt, 3, 101).

[43] *Bell* 6,312f.: τὸ δ' ἐπᾶραν αὐτοὺς μάλιστα πρὸς πόλεμον, ἦν χρησμὸς ἀμφίβολος ὁμοίως ἐν τοῖς ἱεροῖς εφρημενος γράμμασιν, ὡς κατὰ υὸν καιρὸν ἐκεῖνον ἀπὸ τῆς χώρας αὐτῶν τις ἄρξει τῆς οἰκουμένης.

[44] Tacitus, *Hist* 5,13: 'pluribus persuasio inerat antiquis sacerdotum litteris contineri, eo ipso tempore fore ut valesceret Oriens profectique Iudea rerum potirentur, quae ambages Vespasianum ac Titum praedixerat, sed vulgus more humanae cupidinis sibi tantam fatorum magnetudinem interpretati ne adversis quidem ad vera mutabantur'. Suetonius, *Vesp* 4,5: 'percrebruerat Oriente toto vetus et constans opinio, esse in fatis ut eo tempore Iudea profecti rerum potirentur. Id de imperatore Romano, quantum postea eventu paruit, praedictum Iudaei ad se trahentes rebellarunt'.

[45] W. Weber, *Josephus und Vespasian*, 1921, 47, n. 1, stressed, in a reference to Philostrates, *Vita Apoll* 5,27, that many such expectations were circulating; see Suetonius, *Nero* 40,2. It is obvious that, in a reference to Vespasian, the original meaning of the prophecy was bound to be lost. See also H. Windisch, *Die Orakel des Hystaspes*, 1929, 65ff.

fundamentally answered by Josephus himself. It is true that E. Norden[46] assumed that this prophecy was 'produced' by the Jewish priesthood 'in order to strengthen men's minds for the final desperate battle', but, according to Josephus, it was this prophecy that caused the rebellion itself to break out.[47] We may therefore conclude from this that it had been widely known even before the war in Zealot circles and that it was disseminated by them among the people in order to gain popular support for the break with Rome. The enormous importance of this 'charismatic interpretation of Scripture' for the Zealots is also clear from this. It provided the members of the new movement with the certainty that their aspirations were 'intended by God'.

The question of the scriptural text that forms the basis of this oracular pronouncement is more difficult to answer. As a rule, the prophecy about the Son of Man in Dan 7.13ff. has been accepted as that basis.[48] In this context, P. Billerbeck stressed the great influence of the Book of Daniel on Palestinian Judaism of the first century A.D. That apocalypse had exerted such influence because of its vision of the four kingdoms of the world and its calculation of the end of time on the basis of the seventy weeks of years:[49]

'The struggle with Rome was accepted because the end of the seventy weeks of years was thought to be approaching and because the Son of Man, 'who would rule the kingdom of the world' (Dan 7.13ff.), that is, the Messiah, was imminently expected'.

There is no doubt that special importance was attached to the Book of Daniel in Zealot circles.[50] Dan 7.13ff. can, however, hardly be regarded

---

[46] E. Norden, 'Josephus und Tacitus über Jesus Christus und eine messianische Prophetie', *NJKA* 31 (1913), 660ff. According to Norden, Tacitus was not dependent on Josephus, but, like Suetonius, went back to an earlier source, possibly the work *de Iudaeis* of the first procurator of Judaea, Antonius Julianus: 664f. W. Weber, *op. cit.*, 102ff.,148, etc., and P. Corssen, *ZNW* 15 (1914), 121, on the other hand, both assumed that all authors were ultimately dependent on the *commentarii* of Vespasian or Titus (ὑπομνήματα; see *Vita* 342.358 and *Ap* 1,56).

[47] τὸ δ'ἐπᾶραν αὐτοὺς μάλιστα πρὸς πόλεμον, see also Suetonius: '. . . praedictum Iudaei ad se trahentes rebellarunt'.

[48] See E. Norden, *op. cit.*; A. Schlatter, *Die Theologie des Judentums nach dem Bericht des Josephus*, 1932, 258, n. 1; R. Meyer, *Der Prophet aus Galiläa*, 1940, 52f.; O. Michel, *Neutestamentliche Studien für R. Bultmann*, 2nd. ed. 1957, 62f. R. Eisler, 2, 706, assumed that a fulfilment of the prophecy in Dan 9.26 could be found in the murder of the high-priest Jonathan (*Bell* 2,256 = *Ant* 20,162ff.). J. Hempel, *AO* 38 (1938), 47f. and W. Weber, *op. cit.*, 42ff. were rightly not in favour of applying this to Dan 7. I. Hahn, *AOH* 14 (1962), 131ff., believed that there was a connection between the prophecy of disaster in *Bell* 6,311 and the oracle in 312 and applied both to Is 10.39.

[49] Bill. 4, 1001ff. (1002); see also A. Schlatter, *GI*, 324.

[50] Josephus also drew attention to the importance of Daniel's prophecies for his own

as having provided the basis for Josephus' 'oracular pronouncement', since the latter speaks of a Jew who is expected as a world ruler, whereas the Son of Man is a heavenly being or was interpreted as the people of Israel and neither can be simply identified with the Messiah.[51] Josephus may perhaps give us an indication here. Although, as a rule, he understandably avoids going into the question of the messianic hope, he cautiously refers to it in at least two places. The first of these is in his discussion of Nebuchadnezzar's vision[52] and the second in that of the fourth prophecy of Balaam.[53] We may therefore assume that both places were of great importance at the time for the further hope of his people. The second prophecy in particular, that of the star that goes up from Jacob (Num 24.17) and first subjugates the peoples surrounding Israel, including Edom (v. 18) in order finally to destroy entirely the powers of the world (v. 24), played a very special part in Palestinian Judaism both before and after the Zealots. It is found, for example, several times in the literature of Qumran[54] and especially in the sects' Messianic Testimonies.[55] It is also found in the work of R. Akiba, who applies them in a play on words to Simeon b. Koseba:

'R. Simeon b. Jochai taught: Akiba, my teacher, publicly proclaimed: "A star went forth from Jacob" — Koseba came forth from Jacob. When my teacher Akiba caught sight of Bar Koseba, he said: "This is the king — the Messiah" '.[56]

---

time; see *Ant* 10,267 and 276. According to this interpretation, Daniel also wrote about the Romans and the devastations caused by them to the Jews.

[51] F. Dornseiff, *ZNW* 46 (1955), 248, going contrary to Josephus, applies the *profecti* of Tacitus and Suetonius collectively to the Jews. This explanation is, however, unconvincing as the Zealots undoubtedly cherished messianic hopes at that time. See below, p. 290ff.

[52] *Ant* 10,210: Josephus has nothing to say about the feet 'partly of potter's clay' of the fourth kingdom, but he lets Daniel speak of the meaning of the 'stone' (Dan 2.45) without handing it on to his readers, since he is only speaking about the past and not about the future; see R. Eisler, 1, 209f. and H. Guttmann, *Die Darstellung der jüdischen Religion bei Flavius Josephus*, 1928, 40.

[53] *Ant* 4,114 and 116f.: The whole earth is to become Israel's dwelling-place for all time (τὴν δ'οἰκουμένην οἰκητήριον δι'αἰῶνος ἴστε προκειμένην ὑμῖν) and their enemies will never again be able to overcome them; for this, see M. Dibelius, *ThBl* 6 (1927), 200, n. 1 and 218, n. 8; see also R. Eisler, *op. cit.*.

[54] CD 7,19; 1QM 11,6f.; TestLev 18,3 and TestJud 24,1.

[55] 4QTest (No. 175), 9-13, see DJD V, 58.

[56] jTaan 68d,49, see Bill. 1, 13: דרך כוכב מיעקב דרך כוכבא מיעקב‎; for this, see R. Meyer, *TD* 6, 824f.: 'From what we know of Akiba's ecstatic states we may assume that this recognition of the true and contemporary meaning of Num 24.17 was based on pneumatic insight.' The star appears on the coins of Bar Koseba as a messianic symbol; see P. Romanoff, *JQR* 33 (1942/43), 2nd. ed., 11.

Would it perhaps not be more true to say that the 'ambiguous oracle' points to a text such as Num 24.17 rather than to Dan 7.13ff.? Josephus' οἰκεῖος would in that case correspond to the 'from Jacob' and it may also be possible to trace the *profecti* (Judaea) that are common to both Tacitus and Suetonius back to the דָּרַךְ of the Old Testament text. The plural form of *profecti* might point to the parallelism of 'star' and 'sceptre' that was applied by the Essenes to both Messiahs — the one from Aaron and the one from Israel.[57] Other interpretations are obviously possible,[58] but it is clear that a high degree of probability can be obtained with Num 24.17.

One of the tasks of the 'Zealot prophets' was to identify both the time of the fulfilment and the person of the Messiah, in other words, to apply the Old Testament prophecies to the present time. As we have seen, R. Akiba did this, referring to Bar Koseba with the help of Num 24.17. Other examples can be found in the New Testament, in which the messianic pretender and the prophet were related to each other.[59] It is therefore possible to raise the question of the Zealot Messiah from this vantage point.

(b) Prophecy and Counter-Prophecy in the Last Battle for the Temple

In his great speech to the insurgents, Josephus repeatedly alludes to the miraculous salvation of Jerusalem from Sennacherib (2 Kings 18.17–19.36). W. R. Farmer was therefore right to insist that the defenders drew special encouragement from the Sennacherib story during their

---

[57] The reading דרך is confirmed in opposition to the conjectural זרח by Akiba's quotation and the messianic Testimonia of Qumran. According to A, Posnanski, *Schiloh. Ein Beitrag zur Geschichte der Messiaslehre*, 1, 1904, 17, K.G. Bretschneider, *Capita theologiae dogmaticae e Fl. Josephi scriptis collecta*, 1812, 37, had already, at the beginning of the nineteenth century, applied Josephus' oracle to Num 24.17ff.

[58] A. Posnanski, *op. cit.*, and R. Eisler, 1, 343, n. 6 and 2, 603ff., both conjecture Gen 49.10; according to Gitt 56b, Johanan b. Zakkai applied Is 10.34 to Vespasian as a text that is connected with Is 11.1; see J.M. Allegro, *JBL* 75 (1956), 179 = DJD V, 13f. N. Bentwich, *Josephus*, 1926, 36, pointed to the prophecy about Cyrus in Is 41.2, whereas Eusebius, *HistEcc* 3,8.11 mentions Ps 2.8.

[59] This relationship between the prophet and the anointed one can also be found in Zech 6.9–14 and Hag 2.20–23; see M. Noth, *Geschichte Israels*, 2nd. ed. 1954, 252. 1QS 9,11; Jn 1.29ff. and Mt 16.16ff. also point to a prophetic and charismatic testimony of the Messiah. The ultimate example would be R. Akiba and Bar Koseba. The Antichrist also has a corresponding relationship with his prophet; see Rev 13.11ff.; 19.20.

[60] *op. cit.*, 96–111; see especially 99: 'Nor do any of the many stories of the victories of Israel's great warriors have such a connection with Jerusalem except . . . the miraculous deliverance of the holy city from the hands of Sennacherib'.

struggle.[60] Josephus uses many arguments in an attempt to show that the
defenders could not interpret this account so that it favoured them.
Sennacherib, he claims, was not defeated by men and weapons, but by
the angel of God.[61] Unlike the Zealots, Hezekiah implored God with
clean hands and the magnanimous Romans did not deserve the
punishment of the perjurious Assyrian king who wanted to burn down
the Temple.[62] The Assyrians were also destroyed, Josephus maintains, on
the first night, when they were encamped outside Jerusalem, and
therefore, were God on their side, he would have taken measures against
Titus at the beginning of the siege.[63] However, Josephus departs from
this scribal argumentation:

> 'I believe therefore that the Deity has fled from his Sanctuary and is on the
> side of those against whom you are fighting'.[64]

He justifies this bold affirmation by claiming that, in fulfilment of an
ancient prophecy, water had begun to flow abundantly from the sources
around Jerusalem that had previously been quite dry.[65] The whole
context can be explained in the following way: The defenders of
Jerusalem were strengthened by the prophets in their firm conviction
that the city was invincible[66] and now Josephus had appeared as the
prophet of the other side and especially of the Flavians[67] and was
'prophesying' the victory of his masters. The result of this was that the
prophets and the counter-prophet stood opposed to each other.

Elsewhere too, Josephus appeals on several occasions to prophecies
predicting the destruction of the Temple. He even asserts that the
Zealots themselves may have known about these threatening prophetic
statements, but that they ridiculed them, thus making themselves

---

[61] *Bell* 5,387f.390; for the significance of the story of Sennacherib, see 1 Macc 7.37ff.
= 2 Macc 15.22ff. and 2 Macc 8.19.

[62] *Bell* 5,403ff.407; this intention on the part of Sennacherib is absent from the biblical
story.

[63] *Bell* 5,408f.

[64] *Bell* 5,412; see also 367f.

[65] *Bell* 5,409; according to Dio Cassius 66,1, the besiegers were running out of water
and had to go a long way to fetch it. W. Weber, *Josephus und Vespasian*, 1921, 75,
assumed that such Old Testament promises as those in Joel 4.18; Zech 14.8 and Ezek
47.1ff. lay behind the miracle of the sources: 'Here an aspect of the ancient mythology
has been transferred to the instrument of God, the Babylonian king and the Roman
Titus, both of whom are punishing Jerusalem'.

[66] See above, p. 221f. The 'rumours' that Jerusalem could not be taken even had an
influence on the besiegers; see Dio Cassius, 66,5 and 6.

[67] See W. Weber, *op. cit.*, 43ff.,75ff.; see also above, p. 11, n. 32.

instruments of their fulfilment.[68] This is another typical case of
'polemical reversal'.

In reality, the defenders of the city — as Josephus himself admits —
continued until the very end, on the basis of such Old Testament
promises interpreted by their prophets as Zech 12.2-6 and 14.2-5, to
hope with unshakable certainty for a miraculous intervention on the
part of God. It is probable that the increasing terror of the war reinforced
their belief that they were living in the three and a half times of Daniel
and when, in the fourth year of the war and after a siege lasting for three
months, the Romans penetrated into the outer court and twelve days
later the Tamid sacrifice was ended on 17 Tammuz,[69] 'many certainly'
seeing in this 'the fulfilment of the prophecy made in Dan 9.27'[70] and
becoming 'convinced ... that the time of decision was now at hand'.[71]

Since the first Temple was destroyed on 10 Ab, when the seventy
weeks of years began,[72] the end of which was now thought to be
imminent, this date was expected with considerable tension. On that
day, the fulfilment of Daniel's seventy weeks of years, a Zealot prophet
prophesied to the population of the city:

> 'God has given the order to go up to the Sanctuary, where they would
> receive the signs of redemption!'[73]

This resulted in the Romans encountering, in the inner forecourts of

---

[68] *Bell* 4,386-388; see also the list of omens in *Bell* 6,288-311.

[69] The siege began on 14 Nisan (*Bell* 5,99); after more than two and a half months, on
4 and 5 Tammuz, the Romans overcame resistance in the Fortress of Antonia and
penetrated into the outer forecourt (6,67f.). On 17 Tammuz, the twice daily sacrifice
was ended (6,93f.; see also Taan 4,6).

[70] 'And he makes the covenant difficult for many for one week and in the middle of the
week he makes the animal sacrifice and meal offering cease and on the wing of an
abomination a desolator, until the predetermined end is poured out on the desolator'.
This translation of Dan 9.27 is based on that by A. Bentzen, *Daniel (HAT)*, 1952, 68.
What are particularly difficult are the text and the content of וְעַל כְּנַף שִׁקּוּצִים מְשֹׁמֵם; see
A. Bentzen, *op. cit.* In 70 A.D., the rebels might have been able to relate this devastation
to the occupation and the burning down of the Temple porticoes by the Romans. The
killing of the 'anointed one' in Dan 9.26 could also have been applied to the murdered
Menahem; see below, p. 293f.

[71] Bill. 4, 1003: my depiction follows Billerbeck; see A. Schlatter, *GI*, 324.

[72] Jer 52.12: On the tenth day of the fifth month; this date is followed by Josephus in
Bell 6,250. 2 Kings 25.8, on the other hand, has the seventh day. The rabbinic tradition
speaks of 9 Ab as the day when the first and second Temples were destroyed; see Schürer,
1, 631, and Bill. 1, 945f. Since the seventy weeks of years in Dan 9.2 and 24 go back to
the seventy years of exile mentioned in Jer 25.11 and Zech 1.12, their beginning and end
would be the date of the destruction of Jerusalem, that is, 10 Ab.

[73] *Bell* 6,285f.; but note the words κατ' ἐκείνην ... τὴν ἡμέραν. See PesR 36,162a =

the Temple, six thousand people waiting there in the expectation of divine intervention, when they stormed the burning Temple on 10 Ab in 70 A.D.[74] According to Dan 7, the heavenly Redeemer was to appear on 'the clouds of heaven'[75] 'until the decreed end is poured out on the desolator'.[76]

It is quite possible that Titus, who had learned about the significance of this day from Josephus and the other Jewish deserters, insisted on storming the Sanctuary on 10 Ab, so that his Jewish opponents would gain the impression that this was a divine judgement.[77]

It is very likely that the Apocalypse of Saint John contains a fragment of this Zealot prophecy. In Rev 11.1f., the visionary is given the order to 'measure the Temple of God and the altar and those who worship there', but 'not to measure the court outside the Temple'. This forecourt and the city were to be 'trampled over' by the pagans for half a week of years. Wellhausen was the first to suggest that these statements might be fragments of an oracle pronounced by Zealot prophets, indicating that it was believed that the Romans could only take possession of the forecourt and the city and were not able to seize the Sanctuary itself. 'Those who clung tenaciously to the Temple were the holy remnant and the seed of the future'.[78]

The typical aspects outlined above are also found in the Zealot prophecy mady during the last battle for the Temple and handed down by Josephus. The first of these points is that it is also based on Old Testament exegesis, in this case, an interpretation of the prophecy of

---

Bill. 1, 151: The Messiah appears on the Temple roof: 'You poor, the time of your redemption is here'.

[74] For the final attack by the Romans on 10 Ab, see *Bell* 6,244ff.250ff.; for the killing of the six thousand, 283ff.

[75] Dan 7.13ff.; according to 4 Ezra 13,35, the place where this revelation took place was the Temple. According to Mk 13.14 and 26 (Mt 24.15 and 30), the 'desolating sacrilege' was set up in the sanctuary and this formed the precondition for the coming of the Son of Man. See also above, p. 223, n. 397.

[76] Dan 9.27; see also 11.45.

[77] See Josephus' argumentation in *Bell* 6,267f.: 'Heimarmene' kept exactly to the time plan and both the first and the second Temple were destroyed on the same day.

[78] See J. Wellhausen, 'Analyse der Offenbarung Johannis', *AGG* (1907), 15; see also *Skizzen und Vorarbeiten*, 6, 1899, 221ff. W. Bousset , *Die Offenbarung Johannis (Meyers Kommentar)*, 6th. ed. 1906, 32f., followed Wellhausen's interpretation. E. Lohmeyer's objections, *Die Offenbarung des Johannes (HNT* 16), 2nd. ed. 1953, 88f., do not seem valid when the author's fundamental prejudice against any contemporary interpretation attempts is taken into account. It goes without saying that the oracle was significantly reshaped by tradition or when it was included in the Johannine Book of Revelation.

Daniel. The second is that it deals with an oracle of eschatological content that is related here to the present time.

4. Summary

From the time of Judas the Galilaean onwards, the prophetic element was, we may assume, actively present in the new sect. It undoubtedly provided the necessary foundation of authority for all those points of Zealot teaching and activity in which no appeal could be made to the tradition that had until that time been valid. These points included especially the message of the 'sole rule' of God, the rejection of the census and co-operation in the eschatological redemption of Israel. Even those measures that were so vehemently condemned by Josephus — the rejection of sacrificial gifts and the election of the high-priest by drawing lots, for example — were probably also at least partly caused by the initiative of Zealot prophets.

A. Schlatter above all pointed clearly to the significance of the prophecy for the Zealots:

'Judah (!) and his band of followers were hardly able to wait in silent, peaceful expectation for the prophecy to be fulfilled. It is more likely that they connected the 'zealous' interpretation of the prophecy with a need for passionate action. Although we have no information about what, for example, Daniel's animal imagery and chronology meant for the members of this circle, the fact is, out of Zealotism grew a prophecy possessed by zeal, with which the Zealots practiced soothsaying and its interpretation. This new form of prophecy inspired by Zealotism continued within the tradition of the ancient prophets and did not strive to describe future events in an all-embracing way. What it did was to give the people directives that aimed to equip them for the coming revelation of God'.[79]

According to Schlatter, the Zealots' exegesis of the Old Testament prophets had lasting significance in that it applied both Daniel's fourth kingdom and the prophecies against Babylon and Edom to Rome[80] and interpreted Is 11.4 as the killing of the Antichrist. It is therefore possible to assume in most cases of Zealot prophecy that the Old Testament formed the point of departure for its 'prophesying' and was applied in an

---

[79] GI, 263; see also 434, n. 239.

[80] Josephus also applies Daniel's 'fourth kingdom' to Rome; see above, p. 238, n. 50 and p. 239, n. 52. This interpretation also emerges clearly in 4 Ezra 12,11f. For the rabbinate, see Bill. 4, 1004ff. See also below, p. 302f. The way had also already been prepared by Herod's rule for the identification of Edom with Rome; see below, p. 303. For the identification of Rome with Babylon, see below, p. 303.

authoritative and charismatic way to concrete situations in the eschatological present. It is not possible to know from Josephus' works to what extent this prophecy took an ecstatic form. It is, however, possible to assume, on the evidence provided by certain contemporary parallels, that the ecstatic form of prophesying was not completely unknown to the Zealots.[81]

There are certain essential differences between the content of the messianic prophecy that flourished before the outbreak of the Jewish War and that of the prophecies that were made during the siege of Jerusalem. These differences were determined by the changed situation. To begin with, that is, before the war, expectation of the Messiah and the establishment of his kingdom formed the central point of the prophecies. Later, however, during the siege — presumably under the influence of the priestly group among the Zealots — interest was increasingly concentrated on the Temple as the place of God's saving revelation at the moment of greatest distress. The prophecies of Daniel accordingly became more and more important over against other messianic prophecies.

B. The Time of Great Anger

1. The Eschatological Woes in Late Judaism

According to the Books of the Maccabees, the religious tribulation of the people was the sign of God's anger, which was then 'turned away' by the zeal of Mattathias and his sons.[82] In the Book of Daniel, that religious distress was interpreted as the final eschatological time of tribulation, as a strictly limited period of destruction (9.26) and as a 'time of trouble (עֵת־צָרָה), such as never has been ...' (12.1).

The intention of this time was to test and purify the people of God before the time of salvation.[83] As a result of this, the expectation of a period of great suffering before the coming of messianic redemption became a firmly established part of Jewish apocalyptic writing both in the Christian and in the rabbinic tradition.[84] The recently discovered

---

[81] See *Bell* 6,300f. It is possible that the constant emphasis placed by Josephus on the Zealots' 'madness' contains a reference to their ecstatic prophesying; see above, p. 16, n. 67.

[82] 1 Macc 3.8, etc. See also above, p. 151f.

[83] Dan 9.24ff.; 11.35; 12.10.

[84] See B.-Gr. Rel. 250f.; Bill. 4, 977ff.; Volz, *Esch*, 147ff. For the Christian tradition,

documents of the Essenes also provide many illuminating examples of this.[85] The concept of 'woes' is, for instance, found for the first time in the Dead Sea texts.[86] In the War Scroll, the time immediately preceding the beginning of the great eschatological war is described, with reference to Dan 12.1, as a 'time of distress for the people of God's redemption' and to this is added the comment that no previous time of distress had even been as great as this one.[87] The period of affliction, however, also had a positive aspect, in that the people of God were to be purified by this test of fire.[88]

The form and content of this time of terror are presented in various ways. It primarily concerns the people of Israel, but it is also extended to cover all nations and ultimately even the order of the cosmos itself. The stars are shaken by it, law and order disappear from human society, the world is filled with war and the shedding of blood, famines and diseases become widespread and most people are killed, only a small remnant being preserved.[89]

For Israel, these terrors consist above all of a final attack by the pagan powers against the Jewish people, their faith and their sanctuary: 'The kingdom of evil in the form of the pagan kingdom of the world increases its evil in the last time to its climax'.[90] It hardly needs to be stressed that the people's experiences during the time of religious distress formed the important example here. Later catastrophes such as the conquest of Jerusalem by Pompey and Sossius or the rebellions following the death

---

see especially the synoptic apocalypse in Mk 13; Mt 24 and Lk 21 and long sections of the Johannine Apocalypse: Rev 8f.; 11; 13; 16–18; for this, see H. Schlier, 'θλῖψις', *TD* 3, 144f. The Christian theology of suffering was also to some extent predetermined by this background; see W. Nauck, *ZNW* 46 (1955), 77f. For the rabbinic traditions, see Bill. 1, 953 and 4, 981ff.; see also J. Klausner, *The Messianic Idea in Israel*, translated by W.F. Stinespring, 1955, 440ff.

[85] The present is the time of God's anger: CD 1,5; see also 1QH 3,28. It is subject to the rule of Belial; see 1QS 1,18.23f.; 2,19; 3,23. This means that life is lived in the 'time of godlessness': 1 QpHab 5,7f.; CD 6,10.14; 12,23, etc.; see also 1 QSa 1,3 (*Qumran Cave I*, 109); 4 QDibHam III, 11ff. = *RB* 68 (1961), 202ff.

[86] 1QH 6,8f.11f.28 (חבלים). In the New Testament, see Mk 13.8; Mt 24.8; in the rabbinate: חֶגְלוֹ שֶׁל מָשִׁיחַ, see Bill. 1, 950.

[87] 1QM 1,11f.; cf. 15,1.

[88] See 4QpPs 37 (No. 171) II, 17ff., see DJD V, 43f. and the fragments of an interpretation of Ps 2 = 4Qflor (No. 174), see DJD V, 53f.; see also 1QS 1,17 and 8,4 and CD 20,27.

[89] See Volz, *Esch*, 155ff. For the triad of war, famine and disease, see Deut 32.24; Ezek 5.17; see also Sib 2,22f.156; in the New Testament: Mk 13.8; Lk 21.10f.; Rev 6.3–8; in the Midrash: SifNum 15,41.115. For the extermination of the majority of people, see Volz, *Esch*, 157; see also Rev 9.15 and Sib 5,103.

[90] Volz, *Esch*, 149.

of Herod only confirmed the conception formed during the time of the Seleucids.

Once again, two fundamental aspects have to be distinguished in this case as well. The kingdom of evil could be given concrete form either as the godless 'eschatological tyrant' who cruelly oppresses God's people and aims to put himself in God's place[91] or in the assault made against Jerusalem by the united pagan nations that is described in Ezek 38.[92]

2. The 'Messianic Woes' and the Zealot Movement

Various movements in Palestinian Judaism from the time of Daniel onwards — the Essenes, the early Christians and even the Pharisaical movement or the rabbinate — were acquainted, then, with the idea of a period of exchatological terror. This idea was also developed within these movements. It is therefore possible to conclude from this fact that the Zealots also shared the same view. I would like to draw attention to five points in this connection:

(1) Because of their insistence that Israel should be ruled by God alone, the Zealots were totally opposed to the political and religious claims of the Roman emperor and the Roman Empire generally. It is therefore reasonable to assume that they identified the Roman rule with the eschatological distress, just as Daniel before them had identified the rule of Antiochus IV Epiphanes with that time of affliction. The continual threat to the sanctuary and the fact that members of their party were constantly being persecuted by the Roman rulers were the external symptoms of these woes. Rome was therefore identified with Daniel's fourth kingdom, with the last 'beast from the sea'. Certain natural events and especially the lasting famine under Claudius with its inevitable consequences[93] reinforced the conviction that the eschatological distress had already begun.

(2) It was possible to distinguish two aspects of this time of terror. Insofar as the Jewish people patiently accepted the rule of the Romans, it was an expression of God's anger about the 'apostasy', but when they refused to obey, under the pressure of increasing distress, their woes were transformed into a period of purification. Their deprivations and

---

[91] This concept was first used by Volz, *Esch*, 282.

[92] See the examples given by Volz, *Esch*, 151f. For evidence in the rabbinate, see Bill. 3, 832ff. and J. Klausner, *op. cit.*, 483ff.

[93] For this, see below, p. 345, n. 72. For the eschatological interpretation of drought and famine, see PsSol 17,18ff.; 4QpPs 37 (No. 171) III, 2f., see DJD V, 44. Other examples will be found in L. Goppelt, 'πεινάω (λιμός)', *TD* 6, 15, n. 25.

sufferings resulting from their struggle against Rome were therefore only a test, proving the value of the remnant that was to be saved.[94]

(3) The period of greatest distress — the desecration of the Sanctuary — was laid down in Daniel as the apocalyptic span of three and a half times or years.[95] The idea is expressed in the little synoptic apocalypse that, because the distress was unbearable, God had 'shortened the days' of tribulation 'for the sake of the elect'.[96] A later rabbinic tradition justified this possible shortening of the time of tribulation with the argument that 'the kingdoms of this world had made the yoke laid on Israel too heavy'. Not only had God adjured the 'kingdoms of the world' not to make that yoke too heavy — he had also adjured the Israelites 'not to rise up against the kingdoms of this world' or 'to bring about the time of the end by force'.[97]

What we have here are fragments of a dispute with the Zealots' view that rising up against the powers of this world, in other words, against Rome, might shorten the time of messianic distress. This is fundamentally no more than a reversal of the idea of 'hastening' the coming of the time of salvation, in other words, that that time could be 'forced' by human activity. If they really succeeded in keeping the sabbath, R. Eliezer b. Hyrcanus promised the Israelites that they would receive salvation from three afflictions: from the 'day of Gog', that is, the assault of the pagan nations, the 'messianic woes' and the 'great day of judgement'.[98] If the typically rabbinic 'keeping of the sabbath' is replaced by the concept 'breaking with foreign rule', we have a genuinely Zealot idea.

(4) Everything, then, depended on the whole of Israel rising up against the enemy of God. As long as the majority of the people

---

[94] The basis of the New Testament conception of 'trials through suffering' (Rom 5.3f.; 2 Cor 8.2f.; 1 Pet 1.6f., etc.) is presumably to be found in an earlier tradition of suffering that goes back to the period of the Maccabees; see W. Nauck, *ZNW* 46 (1955), 79f. The idea of trial by suffering in the eschatological tribulation has its point of departure in Dan 11.35; 12.10f. and can also be found in EthEn 94,5; 96,2f. and in the Essene documents (see above, p. 246, n. 88).

[95] Dan 7.25; see also 9.27 and 12.7; 8.14 and 12.11f., where there is a variation in the numbers. The point of departure is probably 1 Kings 17.2. For the interpretation, see A. Bentzen, *op. cit.*, 67.

[96] Mk 13.20 parr.; for this, see E. Klostermann, *Das Markusevangelium (HNT* 3), 4th. ed. Tübingen 1950, 136: 'As a sign of his special grace, God subsequently reduced the predetermined time somewhat'. See also ApcAbr 29,12; SyrBar 20,1; 4 Ezra 4,26 and Barn 4,3.

[97] See above, p. 124.

[98] MekEx on 16.25 (L. 2, 120).

remained submissive under the pagan yoke, God's anger would continue to rest on them and the end could not be foreseen. If, on the other hand, they united and, following the example of the Zealots, became filled with zeal for God and waged the Holy War against Rome, the distress would end and the time of redemption would begin.

(5) The attitude outlined in sections 3 and 4 above was decisive for the Zealots until the outbreak of the Jewish War. The setbacks that they suffered during the war probably weakened their confidence in their own share in the redemption of Israel, but at the same time it strengthened their hope that God would directly intervene at the moment of greatest distress. That is why the Zealots could not be discouraged in their struggle by any defeats. They kept firmly to the eschatological rule: 'The end will come when there is greatest distress'.[99]

C. THE RETREAT INTO THE DESERT

1. The Retreat into the Desert as a Widespread Phenomenon in Late Judaism

The account of Mattathias' zeal in 1 Macc 2.23ff. ends with these words:

'And he and his sons fled to the hills and left all that they had in the city'.

Many 'who were seeking righteousness and justice' followed them with their families and their cattle.[100] This account is complemented by the statement in 2 Macc 5.27 that Judas Maccabaeus and his companions lived on 'what grew wild, so that they might not share in the defilement'.

Zeal for the law called not only for flight into the desert, but also for the sacrifice of all possessions and indeed for extreme deprivations.[101] This flight into the mountainous region of the desert was in Judaea — as in Egypt — a widespread social phenomenon. With the help of 'anachoresis', it was possible to escape from the clutches of the power of

---

[99] Volz, *Esch*, 158; see Mk 13.19f.24ff.; SyrBar 25,3; Sib 5,106f. and Sanh 97a bar: 'The Son of David will not come until they despair of redemption'.

[100] Later, Jonathan also had to flee into the desert: 9.32ff.

[101] According to 2 Macc 8.14, the Jews who were prepared to fight against Nicanor sold all their possessions: the Holy War required freedom from all personal bonds; see also 1 Macc 3.56. For this, see also below, p. 123ff. For this 'anachoresis', see H. Braunert, *Die Binnenwanderung*. Bonn 1964. Index.

the state. Because of the religious distress, this flight also had a religious aspect. The theme of the retreat into the desert appeared again and again, often assuming new forms. According to PsSol 17,16f., for example, the pious Israelites fled into the desert as a result of the conquest of Jerusalem:

'They wandered around in the desert to save their souls from evil'.

This withdrawal into the desert was also given a particularly emphatic meaning in the literature of the Essene community, the members of which 'separated themselves from the habitation of the men of corruption'. This act of secession was also given an eschatological meaning by the appeal made to Is 40.3.[102] The desert became the place of conversion.[103] The renunciation of personal possessions was also connected with this retreat into the desert. According to the Ascension of Isaiah, the prophet and his disciples withdrew from the godless rule of Manasseh to a mountain in the desert and fed, like Judas, on plants growing in the desert.[104]

According to the War Scroll, the sons of Levi, Judas and Benjamin, those who were 'exiled into the desert' (גלות המדבר) resumed the battle with the neighbouring nations and the 'Kittim of Assyria'. Returning from the 'desert of the nations', they encamped before the great and decisive battle in the 'desert of Jerusalem'.[105]

Taxo, that obscure figure in the Assumption of Moses, called on his sons to withdraw 'into a cave in the field', in other words, into the desert of Judaea, where there were many caves, in order to die there rather than to transgress God's commandments.[106]

John the Baptist appeared 'in the wilderness' in the Jordan district, living there as an ascetic. The text of Is 40.3 is also applied to him in order to emphasize his eschatological significance.[107] Josephus also mentions an ascetic called Bannus who lived in the wilderness and, like John, only ate and clothed himself with what was provided by nature.[108]

Even though Jesus did not call for an exodus into the desert, as R.

---

[102] 1QS 8,13ff.; see also 9,19f.
[103] 4QpPs 37 (No. 171) III, 1, see DJD V, 44: The שבי המדבר were to live for a thousand generations.
[104] AscIs 2,8-12. For this, see D. Flusser, *IEJ* 3 (1953), 30-47.
[105] 1 QM 1,2f.; see also J.M. Allegro. *JBL* 75 (1956), 177, Doc III, Fragm, n. 1. The 'exile in the desert' is identical with the 'exile in the land of Damascus' and refers to the settlement in Qumran: see A.S. van der Woude, *Die messianischen Vorstellungen der Gemeinde von Qumran*, 1957, 53.
[106] AssMos 9,1.6ff.
[107] See Lk 1.80; Mk 1.2ff. parr.; Mt 11.7 = Lk 7.24.
[108] *Vita* 11: κατὰ τὴν ἐρημίαν διατρίβειν.

Eisler believed he did,[109] he certainly withdrew personally into the desert not only at the beginning of his activity, but also on several occasions during his ministry.[110] One element that is clearly present in his case is the demand to be unconditionally prepared to renounce all possessions and security.[111] In the synoptic apocalypse, those who are present at the climax of the eschatological woes — the desecration of the Sanctuary by the Antichrist — are required to flee into the desert, leaving behind all their possessions.[112]

There is probably a relationship here with the apocalyptic vision of the woman — who represented the community — from whom the Messiah was to be born and who was translated into the wilderness. While she was there, she was for a time safe from the snares of the dragon.[113]

The various false prophets who wanted to lead a retreat into the desert have already been cited. The goal towards which they were striving seems, despite their failures to reach it, to have had an effect on the later Haggadah. According to R. Akiba, the Messiah was to have led the people into the desert, where they were to have eaten saltwort and broom (see Job 30.4) for forty years. Historical reminiscences are certainly at the basis of this tradition, which persisted until a much later period.[114]

There are understandably various reasons for this exodus into the

---

[109] 2, 245ff. R. Eisler appeals here among other things to the ideal of ἐκκλησία ἐν ἐρήμῳ, the 'congregation in the wilderness', of Acts 7.38, which Stephen mentions in his address. The way of Jesus clearly led, however, not into the desert, but to Jerusalem.

[110] See Mk1.12 = Mt 4.1ff. = Lk 4.1ff.; Mk 1.35; Lk 4.42; 5.15; Jn 11.54.

[111] See Mk 10.21ff.28f. = Mt 19.2ff.27f.; Mt 8.20 = Lk 9.59. R. Eisler, op. cit. correctly points to the parallel, which is more than simply formal, between Mattathias' call in 1 Macc 2.27 and similar demands made by Jesus; see Mt 10.38 = Lk 14.27 and Mk 8.34 parr. In both cases, what was involved was a following in unconditional obedience to God's will even to the point of dying.

[112] Mk 13.14ff. = Mt 24.15f. = Lk 21.21f.

[113] Rev 12.6,13f. The woman was to stay in the desert for the apocalyptic time of three and a half years and she would be in safety in the desert for the entire period of the 'messianic woes'. J. Wellhausen, Skizzen und Vorarbeiten, 6, 1899, 220, and 'Analyse der Offenbarung Johannis', AGG (1907), 20f., saw in this a prophecy which was originally Pharisaical and was in contrast to Rev 11.1ff. and was intended to justify the flight from Jerusalem in 70 A.D. The Temple and the desert were in this way to a certain extent contrasted with each other as places of God's eschatological help; see below, p. 255.

[114] See Bill. 2, 284; according to Tan עקב (ed. Vienna, 1863) 7b. According to the later tradition found in SongRab 2,9 and Pes 5,8 (Mandelbaum 1, 93), this time of ascesis was to last for forty-five days; see Dan 12.11f. For further variations, see Bill. 1, 6 and 2, 298. See also G. Dalman, Der leidende und der sterbende Messias, 1888, 11 and 25.

desert and the abandonment of house and home that accompanied it:

(1) The flight into the hiding-places of the mountainous region of the desert in the east and south of Judaea may have been caused by the political and religious pressure exercised by the ruling power. The desert had always been a place of refuge, indeed the greatest figures in the history of Israel had to flee to it.[115] Not only the flight of the Maccabees, but also to some extent the secession of the Essenes and similarly the flight into the desert during the messianic woes can all be seen in this perspective.[116]

(2) The desert was also the place of separation (Jer 9.1), ascesis and deprivation. It was at the same time also the place where God was encountered (Deut 32.10). This theme will also have played a certain part in the life of the Essene community. It was certainly essential for ascetics such as John the Baptist and Bannus, as well as for Jesus.

(3) The desert was also the place where Israel was put to the test. According to Deut 8.2, it had this meaning even for ancient Israel. This aspect of the desert also emerges clearly in the account of Jesus' temptations.[117] The desert theme is also connected here with the idea of eschatological distress, which could also be understood as a time of being put to the test.

(4) Certain Old Testament examples providing eschatological motivation to the retreat into the desert on the basis of the equation that 'the beginning of time equals the end of time' were also of critical importance.[118] The fundamental paradigm here was the Exodus from Egypt, when the Israelites were liberated for the first time and led into the desert, where God revealed himself to them. Whereas the reappearance of the miracles of the Exodus were proclaimed in Mic 7.15f., Hosea described the desert as the place where the future salvation of the people would be fulfilled (2.14f.):

---

[115] Moses fled into the desert of the Sinai peninsula: Ex 2.15; David fled into the desert of Judah: see above, p. 27; Elijah also fled into the Sinai desert: 1 Kings 19.3. For flight into the desert generally, see also Ps 55.8; Jer 48.6,28; Job 30.3ff., etc. The same idea is also found in Heb 11.38.

[116] For this (and for what follows), see the unfortunately too brief article by G. Kittel, 'ἔρημος', TD 2, 657-600.

[117] Mk 1.13; see E. Lohmeyer, Das Markusevangelium (Meyers Kommentar), 12th. ed. 1953, 25: The desert has two different aspects: on the one hand, it is the place where God reveals himself and, on the other, it is also the home of demons and dark powers; see Is 13.21; 34.14; Tob 8.3; Mt 12.43 = Lk 11.24f.; see Bill. 1, 652; 4, 516.

[118] See Volz, Esch 370; Bill. 1, 68ff.; 2, 284f.; 4, 55f.783f. J. Jeremias, 'Μωϋσῆς', ThWAT 4, 864ff. See also above, pp. 119,124f.

'Therefore, behold, I will allure her and bring her into the wilderness and speak tenderly to her. And there I will give her her vineyards and make the Valley of Achor a door of hope'.

It was also possible to understand Is 40.3 in a similar sense, if, following the Masoretic text, the words 'in the wilderness' were connected with the phrase 'prepare a way (for) Yahweh' that followed.[119] The withdrawal into the desert was here the presupposition for the revelation of God's salvation. The Exodus and the dawn of the time of salvation were equated in this way in the teaching of the 'false prophets' as described by Josephus and the desert also pointed to the salvation at the end of time in the case of John the Baptist and certain rabbinic traditions.

(5) The desert had two aspects: On the one hand, on the basis of experience that had been confirmed again and again by historical events, it was the place of refuge and deprivation. According to the prophetic promise, on the other hand, it was interpreted as the place where salvation would be revealed at the end of time. These two aspects could be organically combined with each other by means of the eschatological equation: The time of terror equals the preparation of the time of salvation.

2. The Zealots in the Desert

Those who followed the call of Judas the Galilaean and refused to take part in the census had to accept the same consequences as Mattathias and his sons, leaving house and home to flee into the desert. Their possessions would therefore have been confiscated by the Roman authorities.[120]

Unfortunately, Josephus gives us hardly any detailed information about the activity and the tactics of the Zealots in this respect. Like the pious Jews during the period of the Seleucids,[121] and the followers of Bar Koseba later, they presumably had permanent bases[122] in the caves of the

---

[119] See 1QS 8,14. For the rabbinic interpretation, see Bill. 1, 96. See also G. Kittel, *op. cit.*, 2, 656f.

[120] According to *Bell* 2,403, the refusal to pay taxes was equivalent to open rebellion; see also above, p. 133ff. In cases of high treason and lese-majesty, the property of Roman citizens was also confiscated; see T. Mommsen, *Römisches Strafrecht*, 1899, 1006ff. This law must have applied in the first place to provincials. After the Jewish War, the whole of Jewish landed property was included within the Roman *fiscus*: *Bell* 7,216ff.

[121] See 1Macc 1.53; 2.35ff.; 2 Macc 6.11.

[122] See Dio Cassius (Epitome of Xiphilin) 69,12. See T. Reinach, *Textes*, 199: The Jews fortified caves, which were connected to each other by subterranean passages and

Judaean desert and in Acrabatta, which was further north and bordered on Samaria.

Josephus says, for example, of the 'robber captain' Eleazar b. Dinai: 'He stayed for many years in the mountains'. When the Roman army intervened after the attack on the Samaritan villages, he and his followers withdrew again into their 'hiding places' (ἐχυροὺς τόπους).[123] Simon bar Giora enlarged certain caves in a valley in the desert that was probably situated to the north-east of Jerusalem in order to store his booty and his supplies of corn. These caves at the same time formed the permanent quarters for his followers.[124] These conditions can in general be presupposed in the case of the Zealots before the outbreak of the war. The dynasty of Judas the Galilaean was only able to maintain itself for two generations in opposition to the power of Rome by having a number of strongholds and possible ways of evading the Romans.[125] His son Menahem was also active in this district. His storming of the fortress of Masada, situated in the south-east of the desert of Judaea to the west of the Dead Sea — together with the cessation of the sacrifice for the emperor — provided the signal for open rebellion.[126]

The insurrection both began and ended in the desert. After the Romans' conquest and destruction of the sanctuary, Titus called for the last time on the rebels, who were still in command of the upper city, to surrender. The reply that he received from them proved that they formed a religious community bound by oath:

> 'They were unable to accept his conditions of surrender, since they had *sworn* not to do that. They requested free passage with their wives and children, however, because they wanted to withdraw into the desert and leave the city to him'.[127]

After the destruction of the Temple, they suddenly showed no more interest in defending the upper city, despite favourable conditions for defence, but were prepared to hand it over to the enemy because they

---

which they provided with ventilation shafts. The caves that became well known because of the finds at Wadi Murabba'at were probably used by the rebels led by Bar Koseba as strongholds of this kind; see J.T. Milik, *op. cit.*, ch. 1, 89ff. Many examples of extended and adapted caves containing stores of weapons and provisions have been discovered. For the most recent finds, see Y. Yadin, *Bar Kochba*, 1971, 28ff., 32ff., etc.

[123] *Ant* 20,121.124.

[124] *Bell* 4,512f.

[125] See M. Noth, *Geschichte Israels*, 2nd. ed. 1954, 16f.

[126] *Bell* 2,408.433.

[127] *Bell* 6,351.366. See the oath taken by the Essenes in *Bell* 2,139ff.; 1QS 5,7ff. This oath was typical of one taken by a Jewish 'religious party', see also Neh 10.29; Ezra 10.5.

wanted to withdraw into the desert as the false prophets had done before the outbreak of the war. G. Kittel has provided a very concise and correct interpretation of this strange wish: 'The implicit meaning is: there to expect God's long-awaited act of salvation'.[128]

It is, of course, quite possible to interpret the Zealots' stubborn resistance in the mountainous district of the Judaean desert in a completely profane sense, in analogy with so many guerrilla wars, particularly since the desert had always been the ideal territory in which robbers and rebels could operate. Against this, however, is the 'eschatological consciousness' that has to be presupposed in this case and the clear evidence of the religious foundation of the Zealot movement. Because of the very narrow basis provided by the sources, it is hardly possible to provide a detailed answer to the question as to how effective the themes cited above concerning the withdrawal into the desert were in this case. We can, however, assume that the idea of the twofold meaning of the desert — on the one hand, as the premessianic period of distress and being put to the test and, on the other as the place of the revelation of God's salvation — was widespread.

At the same time, a certain opposition arose between the Temple and the desert as two different places with which the promises of God's salvation were associated. The solution was provided by the changing political and religious situation. As long as the 'Zealots' had no prospect of obtaining power over the Sanctuary and this was desecrated by the godless priests, they continued to regard the desert as the most important place of struggle against the Romans and of God's promise. Evidence of this is provided by the false prophets who turned away from Jerusalem and retreated into the desert.[129] After the Zealots had succeeded — contrary to all expectations and after decades of struggling in the desert — in gaining control of the Sanctuary, the whole expectation of salvation understandably became concentrated on that place, especially since the priestly element had become very powerful in their circles. After the Temple had been conquered, desecrated and destroyed by the Romans, however, their attention turned once more to the desert.

---

[128] *TD* 2, 656, l. 42; W.R. Farmer, *op. cit.*, 118f., points to Deut 32.7-14 (10).

[129] See above, p. 229f. It is possible that the *Sicarii* who had withdrawn into the fortress at Masada after the murder of their leader, Menahem, were waiting for a divine revelation of this kind 'in the desert'. They were no longer interested in what might happen in Jerusalem and the Temple and lived in Masada without any sign of outward activity. The only exception was a plundering of Engedi; see *Bell* 4,400ff.

D. READINESS FOR MARTYRDOM

1. Martyrs in Judaism of the Hellenistic and Roman period until the Time of Herod

I do not propose to deal here with the as yet unresolved problem of the origin of the meaning, 'martyr', for the word μάρτυς.[130] In our present context, we must be satisfied with the simple statement that this meaning of the concept was not known at that time in Judaism.[131] The following underlying conception was far more widespread:

'The Jewish religion is a religion of martyrdom. It was born of martyrdom and the suffering of pious Jews during the period of the Maccabees. At the end of our period stands the figure of the martyr R. Akiba, who rejoiced because he fulfilled the commandment: 'You shall love the Lord your God with all your soul' with his death as a martyr'.[132]

Although there were not very many martyrs during the period of religious distress,[133] they certainly left behind an indelible impression in the consciousness of the Jewish people.[134] Even the rabbinate remembered, albeit obscurely, the deaths at that time of their spiritual fathers as martyrs, with which the persecution by Alexander Jannaeus of the new Pharisaical party was associated two generations later.[135]

---

[130] For a discussion of this problem, see E. Günther, 'Zeuge und Märtyrer', ZNW 47 (1956). 145ff. His 'apocalyptical solution' has in any case to be supplemented by the wealth of material containing corresponding concepts found at Qumran.

[131] See H. Strathmann, 'μάρτυς', TD 4, 486ff. Concepts such as תעודה, עדות and the verb העיד occur very frequently in the Qumran texts: 1QS 1,9; 3,10.16; CD 3,15; 20,30f.; 1QH 1,19; 2,37; 6,19, etc. The only corresponding concept that is found in the War Scroll is תעודה: 1QM 2,8; 3,4; 4,5; 11,7f.; 14,4f.13. The twelve members of the sect's counsel are called 'witnesses to the truth concerning the judgement' in 1QS 8,5f., which forms a link with Second Isaiah: Is 43.10,12. In 1QM 11,7f., the prophets are called 'seers of testimonies'. The group of words 'witness-testimony' may well go back to Second Isaiah and places like Is 8.16ff.; see O. Michel, Prophet und Märtyrer (BFChTh 37), 1932, 20ff. H.A. Fischel, 'Martyr and Prophet' JQR 37 (1946/47), has pointed to the close connection between prophecy and martyrdom with an abundance of material.

[132] B.-Gr. Rel. 374; see also H. Strathmann, op. cit., and H.A. Fischel, op. cit., 270.

[133] There is a tendency in the First Book of the Maccabees to increase the number of cases of martyrdom; cf. 1.60 with 2 Macc 6.10. According to 2 Macc, there were, apart from the massacre of the pious Jews who had fled into the caves on the sabbath, only individual cases of martyrdom; 6.11 = 1 Macc 2.32f.

[134] See, for example, the persistence of the story of the steadfast mother with her seven sons, 2 Macc 6 and 7, in 4 Macc, Gitt 57b and LamRab on 1.15; see also Bill. 3, 259.

[135] See the crucifixion of Jose b. Joezer by Jakim (Alcimus, who, according to 1 Macc 7.16, had sixty Hasidim executed) in GenRab 65,22; see Bill. 2, 263f. For the persecution under Jannaeus, see Kidd 66a: 'All the wise men in Israel were killed. The world was laid waste ...'; see also Bell 1,97f. = Ant 13,379ff.

The sufferings of the teachers of righteousness, on the other hand, began at an earlier stage during the period of Jonathan.[136] On the basis of Old Testament examples, martyrdom was extensively ascribed to the early prophets in the pious legends of Judaism.[137]

The Roman rule and the violence of the government led to new waves of martyrdom. These were initiated by those priests 'who placed service of God at a higher level than their own salvation' and were slaughtered at the altar when the Temple was stormed by Pompey.[138] The Hasmonaeans, who were murdered in uninterrupted succession during the decades that followed together with a great number of their adherents, who were also killed, were also regarded — at least in certain circles of the Jewish people — as martyrs who had died for a just cause.

The same applies to the 'robber captain' Hezekiah and his faithful followers. After they had been executed by Herod, their mothers 'implored the king and the people day after day in the Temple' for their death to be avenged.[139] Following the conquest of Jerusalem by Herod and Sossius, many Jews refused to recognize Herod as king even when they were tortured. This refusal was based less on faithfulness to their previous king, as Strabo believed,[140] and far more on the fact that the law did not permit a king 'who, as an Idumaean, was only half a Jew'.[141] This confronts us with our main question, that of the 'Zealot martyrs' who, on the basis of their faith, preferred to be put to death rather than recognize the godless foreign rule and its orders.

2. Martyrdom among the Zealots

(a) Two Cases of Martyrdom under Herod

Although Judas the Galilaean did not found his 'fourth sect' until a decade after Herod had died, there were two cases of martyrdom during the reign of Herod that are worthy of our attention because they point

---

[136] The evil priest and opponent of the Teacher of Righteousness was clearly Jonathan; see G. Jeremias, *Der Lehrer der Gerechtigkeit*, 1963. Whether the Teacher suffered a martyr's death or not is uncertain; see A.S. van der Woude, *op. cit.*, 238ff.

[137] See Ascls 5,2ff.; further examples will be found in the *Vitae Prophetarum*, ed. T. Schermann, *TU* 31.3.R., 1 (1907); see also O. Michel, *op. cit.*, 12ff., etc., and H.A. Fischel, *op. cit.*, 274: 'The whole history of the prophets from Abel on seems to be linked by a chain of genuine and exemplary martyrdoms'. For New Testament examples, see Mt 23.29ff., 37; Lk 11.47ff.,50; 13.33f.; Heb 11.35-37.

[138] *Bell* 1,150 = *Ant* 14,67f.

[139] See below, p. 313f.

[140] *Ant* 15,9.

[141] *Ant* 14,403; see also below, p. 317.

forward to the later development and are reported in detail by Josephus.

Because Herod continued to disregard the law and had pronounced leanings towards Hellenism, ten men eventually conspired against him:

'Since they regarded the breaking down of the inherited laws as a source of great disaster, they saw it as their duty to risk their lives rather than ... to tolerate Herod's introduction by force of a way of life that was not in accordance with the ancient custom, and because although he was, it was true, king according to his title, he behaved in reality as the enemy of the whole people'.[142]

These conspirators armed themselves — as the *Sicarii* did later — with concealed daggers. They were even joined by a blind man, who took part in order to encourage the others by his readiness to suffer, presumably because, from the very beginning, they all anticipated that they would die. They were, however, betrayed before they could attempt assassination and Herod had them brought before him:

'They showed no repentance and did not deny the act. On the contrary, they openly displayed their daggers and freely confessed that the conspiracy was justified and had taken place because of their fear of God (διωμολογήσαντο δὲ καλῶς καὶ σὺν εὐσεβείᾳ τὴν συνωμοσίαν αὐτοῖς γενέσθαι); not because of a desire for gain ... but rather for the sake of the communal customs, which all men had long since regarded as a value which should be retained and for which one is prepared to give up one's life ... After they had confessed their plot so openly (ἐμπαρρησιασάμενοι), they were ... led away and, after they had endured every kind of torture, put to death'.[143]

It is important to draw attention to two points in Josephus' account, which presumably goes back to the Jewish anti-Herodian source. The first is that this attempted assassination is a typical act of 'zeal for the law'. The second is that it displays all the outstanding features of a typical account of martyrdom. These features also appear in the account to which I have already referred, namely that of the two teachers and their disciples who destroyed the eagle in the Temple. Their desire for martyrdom is apparent even in the summons to the act:

'They said: "Even if there were some danger to life, it would still be good to die for the ancient laws. For the souls of those who died would be immortal and would abide in eternal blessedness". Arrested after the destruction of the eagle and brought before the king, they openly confessed their act. Herod first asked them whether they were the ones who had dared to knock down the eagle and they confessed it. To the following question: "On whose

---

[142] *Ant* 15,281ff. Bo Reicke, *Neutestamentliche Zeitgeschichte*, 120, assumes that this was an attack made by a *habhurah* or 'association' of Pharisees.
[143] *Ant* 15,288ff.

order?", they replied: "The law of our fathers!" To the question why they
were so joyful, since they had to expect to die, they replied: "Because we
shall enjoy greater blessedness after death!" '.[144]

In his anger about their unfrightened state, the king forgot his own
sickness. He had the "main guilty ones" condemned to death for desecration
of the Temple; he had them burnt alive and the others, arrested with them,
he beheaded'.[145]

What both accounts have in common is the theme of the defence of
the law, which can call for the sacrifice of one's life. In addition to this,
both contain an open confession to the tyrant, in which the law is once
again the central feature. Another essential element is the absence of any
fear of death. Both accounts also end with a description of the cruel
punishment of the conspirators. The source material available to
Josephus was presumably already fashioned by a Jewish pattern of
reporting cases of martyrdom, in which the central feature was 'zeal' for
the law. We may, however, be permitted to go a step further and assume
that this kind of account of martyrs was already widely known in Zealot
circles.

(b) Zealot Martyrs

Josephus understandably does not provide the detailed, glorified
accounts of the Zealot martyrs as he does with the two cases of
martyrdom under Herod. He does, however, reveal quite clearly the
very important place that martyrdom had for the Zealots in their
desperate struggle.

'They endured quite unusual forms of death and disregarded the death
penalty in the case of relatives and friends, if only they needed to call no man
(their) Lord. Since their stubbornness is universally known and evident, I
shall refrain from reporting it in greater detail. I do not need to fear that what
has been said by me about this may not be believed. On the contrary, I have
rather to be concerned that the words of this account may be too weak to
describe their disregard of the excess of suffering that they have accepted'.[146]

The founder of the new movement presumably suffered a martyr's
death, as his father Hezekiah had done.[147] The same also applies to his

---

[144] *Bell* 1,650.653; see also the detailed speech in *Ant* 17,158ff., which says
fundamentally the same as the impressive and concise presentation in *The Jewish War*.

[145] According to *Ant* 17,167, an eclipse of the moon took place on the night of their
execution. H.A. Fischel, *op. cit.*, 377f., points to the fact that natural and other wonderful
phenomena could be connected with the death of a martyr.

[146] *Ant* 18,23f.

[147] Josephus has nothing to say about this, but this conclusion would seem to be

sons, Jacob and Simon, who were crucified by Tiberius Alexander.[148] Crucifixion was preferred as a form of execution, presumably because it was the most widespread form practised under Roman rule.[149] According to Josephus, Felix, under whom the Zealots were particularly active, had 'countless' robbers crucified.[150] A. Schlatter was right to emphasize that 'everyone who joined them had to be prepared to"carry his cross" '.[151] Also Festus, Felix' successor, is reputed to have taken a great number of robbers prisoner and to have put 'quite a few' to death.[152] The Jewish War brought a new wave of 'blood sacrifices'. Let me give just a few striking examples of this:

'A Galilaean captured at Jotapata "resisted every kind of torture and betrayed nothing about the situation in the town to the enemy, who tried to force this information from him by applying fire. He was finally crucified, although he laughed at death'.[153]

There are numerous examples illustrating the Jews' courageous scorn of death during the Jewish War[154] and their attitude, which was surely unique in the ancient world, seemed like madness (ἀπόνοια) to the Romans.[155]

Even after the ultimate defeat, we find the same uncompromising

---

suggested in Acts 5.37; see above, p. 78f. See also Mommsen, *RG* 5, 515: 'Even though not many men followed his call to arms and he ended on the scaffold a few months later, the holy dead man still represented a greater danger to the unholy victors than the living man had done'.

[148] *Ant* 20,102.

[149] The most striking example is, of course, the crucifixion of Jesus himself, who was executed as one claiming to be the Messiah together with two 'robbers' (Mk 15.27f. parr.); see O. Michel, *ThLZ* 83 (1958), 164. J. Blinzler, *The Trial of Jesus*, 1959, 246ff., and E. Stauffer, *Jerusalem und Rom*, 1957, 123ff. and 160ff., both provide a wealth of examples. Josephus speaks of crucifixions: *Bell* 2,75 = *Ant* 17,295; *Bell* 2,241 = *Ant* 20,129; *Bell* 2,306.308; 4,317; 5,449ff.; 7,202; *Vita* 420. For the legal situation, see above, p. 30ff. See also the discovery of the skeleton of a man crucified at Jerusalem in the first century A.D., N. Haas, *IEJ* 20 (1970), 49ff.

[150] *Bell* 2,253.

[151] *GI*, 264. For the New Testament formula 'carrying one's cross', see Mt 10.38 = Lk 14.27 and Mk 8.34 = Mt 16.24 = Lk 9.23. Although the rabbinic parallels are both late and rare, see Bill. 1, 587 and 3, 324, it is reasonable to assume that Jesus took over a Zealot formula from general linguistic usage; see A. Schlatter, *Der Evangelist Matthäus*, 3rd. ed. 1948, 350ff.

[152] *Bell* 2,271.

[153] *Bell* 3,321: . . . ἀνεσταυρώθη τοῦ θανάτου καταμειδιῶν.

[154] See *Ant* 17,256.258; see also *Bell* 3,9.22.153f.440.475; 4,45.79f.; 5,85.87.315; 6,12f.37.159.277f., etc. See also Tacitus, *Hist* 5,13: 'maior vitae metus quam mortis'.

[155] See above, p. 16, n. 67; see also *Bell* 5,121: Ἰουδαῖοι μὲν, οἷς ἀπόνοια μόνη στρατηγεῖ. According to Tacitus, *Hist* 2,4, the taking of Jerusalem was made more difficult 'ob . . . pervicaciam superstitionis'.

readiness to suffer and die for their conviction among the *Sicarii* who had fled to Egypt:

'There was no one who was not amazed at their steadfastness and — call it what you will — the madness or the strength of mind of these victims.[156] For, although every kind of torture and physical maltreatment had been devised to use against them only for the one purpose, namely to make them confess the emperor as their Lord, not one of them yielded . . .; on the contrary, they all preserved their self-control, which was greater than the compulsion. It seemed as though they accepted the tortures and the fire with unfeeling bodies and almost joyous souls. It was the youthful age of the boys that astonished the spectators most of all, since not one of them let himself be persuaded to call the emperor "Lord". So far did the power of their temerity show itself stronger than the weakness of their bodies'.[157]

There were at least six hundred of these martyrs who had been captured with the help of the Egyptian Jews and in addition many others who had been taken prisoner as individual refugees in various parts of Egypt.[158] Josephus certainly had no reason to exaggerate the steadfastness of the *Sicarii*, but one has the impression that he was so proud of his fellow-countrymen's bravery that he allowed that pride to predominate in this case over the hatred of the rebels that he otherwise usually allowed to prevail.

It is also probable that Epictetus bore witness to the perseverence of the *Sicarii* or 'Galilaeans', as he called them.[159] In Josephus' account, there are two essential points. Firstly, the *Sicarii* appears as a closed and extremely self-disciplined group. Secondly, their steadfastness was not based on some kind of political fanaticism. It was rather deeply religious in its origin and based on an absolute determination to keep to the 'sole rule of God', which for them formed the centre of the law.

The closest parallel to this is undoubtedly the martyrdom of the Essenes in the Jewish War. They also formed a closed order with an iron discipline. They probably also took part — at least in their defence of their settlement — in the battle against the Romans.[160] Like the *Sicarii*, they too

---

[156] . . . ὃς οὐ τὴν καρτερίαν καὶ τὴν εἴτ᾽ ἀπόνοιαν εἴτε τῆς γνώμης ἰσχὺν χρὴ λέγειν οὗ κατεπλάγη.

[157] *Bell* 7,417ff.

[158] *Bell* 7,414ff.

[159] See above, p. 58.

[160] *Bell* 2,152f.; for this, see J. Milik, *Ten Years of Discovery*, 96: The archaeological finds also indicate a violent and sudden destruction, presumably in 68 A.D. by the troops of the Tenth Legion. Milik also assumes that there was a strong Zealot tendency within

'. . . had to undergo all kinds of instruments of torture, to make them either blaspheme the Lawgiver or eat something forbidden by the law'.

But they did not in any way submit to their torturers and showed neither fear nor pain in their presence:

'Smiling in their sufferings and with words showing that they disregarded the torturers, they resigned their souls as cheerfully as though they were expecting to receive them back again'.

It is very likely that the superhuman steadfastness of the captured Jewish insurgents influenced Josephus in his way of presenting the Jews' readiness for sacrifice in his *Contra Apionem* (1,43):

'It has frequently been possible to observe in the past that Jewish prisoners would endure torture and many ways of being put to death rather than utter even a single word against the law and the writings following it.'

3. Religious Suicide as a Special Form of Martyrdom

In Judaism, even suicide could become a special form of dedicating one's life to the law and the people. There were signs of this as early as the Maccabaean period, for example in the heroic self-sacrifice of Mattathias' son Eleazar[161] and in the suicide of Razis, one of the elders of Jerusalem.[162] In the later legend, the steadfast mother of the seven martyrs is reputed to have committed suicide; according to 4 Macc 17.1, 'she threw herself into the flames so that no one might touch her body'.[163] The suicide of Jakim (Alcimus?) as described in the rabbinic tradition is also remarkable. In order to expiate the crucifixion of his uncle Jose b. Joezer, he carried out on himself 'the four death penalties of the court: stoning, burning, sword and strangulation'. This 'self-punishment' gained him immediate access to the Garden of Eden.[164]

---

the sect following the death of Herod: 'The destruction of Qumran is ultimately explained by the Zealot character of the Essene community in this last phase'. According to *Bell* 2,567, a certain 'John the Essene' was among the Jewish leaders at the beginning of the revolt. He fell during the unsuccessful attack against Ascalon; see *Bell* 3,11.19. What we may have here, however, is an erstwhile member who had been excluded from the sect.

[161] 1 Macc 6.44ff.

[162] 2 Macc 14.37–46 (42); see also W.R. Farmer, *op. cit.*, 69f., who speaks of 'religious self-destruction'.

[163] See also Gitt 57b, according to which she threw herself, like Razis, from the roof, at which a Bath Qol sounded. Rab Judah (who died in 299 A.D.) is named as the one who handed down this tradition.

[164] GenRab 65,22. According to Pirke R Eliezer 33 (Bill. 2, 264f.), Samuel advised Saul to commit suicide in order to achieve expiation for all his sins; see also Pseudo-Philo, *AntBib* 64.8 and AZ 18a.

During the clearing of the caves of Arbela in Galilee by Herod, one of the rebels flatly rejected the grace offered by the king and killed first his family and then himself, presumably because he would not transgress the law and recognize Herod as king.[165]

The Jewish War provided numerous examples of this kind of 'religious suicide' on the Jewish side. It is very likely that the long speech in the cistern at Jotapata, which Josephus placed in his own mouth and in which he condemned the suicidal intentions of his companions with a wealth of philosophical and religious arguments is at the same time a polemical attack against a view that was widespread in Jewish and Zealot circles, namely that suicide was, subject to certain conditions, fully in accordance with God's will. His companions certainly saw in the intention to surrender a crime against God and his law, 'since they had for a long time already dedicated themselves to death'.[166]

Suicide as the last way out can also be found in the conquest of Gamala, where entire families threw themselves into the abyss:

'The anger of the Romans seemed more moderate than the fanatic, destructive rage of the defeated people against themselves'.[167]

Similar scenes must also have taken place when the Temple was conquered by the Romans. The defenders actually look for death and many killed themselves:

'They all believed ... that it meant not destruction, but victory, salvation and blessedness if they went down with the Temple'.[168]

The most impressive example, however, is the mass suicide of those occupying Masada immediately before the storming of the fortress by the Romans. They were exhorted to commit this act by the commander Eleazar b. Ari, who was 'the last member of the dynasty of Hezechiah'.[169]

Eleazar's detailed speech is undoubtedly the work of Josephus. Although the Jewish historian presents his own tendentious thesis, namely that the Roman victory was God's will, in this speech, at the same time, however, he also felt obliged, for the sake of historical

---

[165] *Bell* 1,313 = *Ant* 14,429. See also below, p. 316, n. 17.

[166] *Bell* 3,384: ὡς ἂν πάλαι καθοσιώσαντες ἑαυτοὺς τῷ θανάτῳ. The defenders of Jerusalem had sworn a mutual oath not to surrender: *Bell* 6,351. It is possible that such an obligation also existed in Jotapata. For Josephus' speech, see *Bell* 3,362-382.

[167] *Bell* 4,78f.

[168] Dio Cassius 66,6; see above, p. 322f.; see also the suicide of two priests in *Bell* 6,280.

[169] J. Wellhausen, *Israelitische und jüdische Geschichte*, 5th. ed. 1904, 377; see below, p. 332.

atmosphere, to weave certain strands reflecting the Zealots' views into the text, giving it a form that would be understood by Hellenistic readers.[170] For example, he made Eleazar provide a number of reasons for the mass suicide:

'I believe, however, that this grace has been given to us by God, namely to be able to die nobly and freely — a grace that has not been granted to others, who have been unexpectedly overcome'.[171]
    'Only our shared death is able to protect our wives and children from violation and slavery'.[172]

Even hope of eternal life, presented in a form strongly tinted with popular philosophy, is used to encourage his companions. Josephus makes Eleazar declare that death gives the soul eternal freedom and that the soul leaves the body and gains immortality.[173] When he makes him stress explicitly:

'We, who have been brought up at home in this way, should set an example to others in our readiness to die',[174]

this can be regarded as a clear indication that there was a distinct idea of martyrdom and a firm inner readiness for it present in the heart of the Zealot movement that went back to Judas. Eleazar's speech ends with a reference to the law:

'This — suicide — is commanded by our laws. Our wives and children ask for it. God himself has sent us (in other versions: commanded) the necessity for it!'[175]

There were altogether nine hundred and sixty people who killed each other in an order that had been previously arranged. Only two women with five children, who had hidden themselves, escaped with their lives.[176] This horrifying act can be regarded as a sign of the extremely

---

[170] The speech made by Agrippa II and Josephus' two speeches at Jerusalem also have the same tenor; see *Bell* 2,345-404 and 5,362.376-419. At the same time, Eleazar's speech is, in accordance with the custom of ancient historiography, the swan-song of the defeated party; see H. St.J. Thackeray, *Josephus. The Man and Historian*, 1929, 45. V. Nikiprowetzky goes into details in 'La mort d'Eléazar, fils de Jaïre', *Hommages à André Dupont-Sommer, Paris 1971, 461-490*.

[171] *Bell* 7,325f.; see also 334.336.386f.

[172] *Bell* 7,334; see also 380.382.385.

[173] *Bell* 7,344ff.350.353.355f.

[174] *Bell* 7,351: ἔδει μὲν οὖν ἡμᾶς οἴκοθεν πεπαιδευμένους ἄλλοις εἶναι παράδειγμα τῆς πρὸς θάνατον ἑτοιμότητος.

[175] *Bell* 7,387. MS. C reads ἐκέλευσε instead of ἀπέσταλκε. This may have been the original reading, which was changed because it was offensive.

[176] *Bell* 7,389-401. For the interpretation of the mass suicide at Masada, see also E. Stauffer, *Jerusalem und Rom*, 1957, 84.

strict self-discipline that prevailed among the *Sicarii*. A rabbinic anecdote shows that mass suicide was not confined to the *Sicarii*, however, but also took place among Jewish prisoners:

'Four hundred boys and girls were once taken prisoner for a shameful purpose. (The parallel in LamRab 1,16: "Vespasian filled three ships with the great ones of Jerusalem in order to put them into shame"; this is, of course, the brothel.) When they recognized why they were desired, they said: "If we throw ourselves into the sea, shall we enter the future world?" The eldest among them then declared to them: "The Lord says: 'I will bring them back from Bashan, I will bring them back from the depths of the sea' (Ps 68.22) ... When the girls heard these words, they all jumped up and threw themselves into the sea. Then the boys made a decision ... and they also jumped into the sea. Scripture has this to say about them: 'For thy sake we are slain all the day long and accounted as sheep for the slaughter' (Ps 44.22)'.[177]

4. Summary: The Zealots' Understanding of Martyrdom

Like zeal for the law — with which readiness to die as a martyr was very closely connected — the sacrifice of one's own life for the law and the people was a sign of religious devotion, which concerned not only the Zealots, but also all strictly believing Jews.[178] The origins of this attitude can be traced back to the Maccabaean period, since which time the chain of martyrs continued unbroken. An exemplary time for the rabbinate was the period of the martyrs who died during the revolt of Bar Koseba and the following Hadrianic period of religious persecution. The words from Ps 44.22 cited above formed the watchword at that time for the suffering community.[179]

In the period between Herod and the destruction of Jerusalem, by far the greatest number of 'martyrs' came from the Jewish freedom movement, which had, under the influence of Judas the Galilaean, been consolidating itself as the party of the Zealots. All those who fell in the

---

[177] Gitt 57b. The tradition was handed down by Rab Judah (see above, p. 262, n. 163) in the name of (Mar) Shemuel (died 254 A.D., see Strack, *Introduction*, 124, 121). According to other opinions, it went back to R. Ammi (ca. 300 A.D.) and, according to a third view, it is a Baraita. Parallel is LamRab on 1.16; see Bill. 2, 135: according to this parallel text, a Bath Qol of the Holy Spirit followed: 'For these things I weep', Lam 1.16. A parallel from the Christian tradition is mentioned by Eusebius, *HistEcc* 8,12. For this question, see H. Volkmann, *Massenversklavungen (AAWLM)*, 1961, 3, 234f.

[178] See above, p. 182f. This was universally accepted in the Jewish tradition of martyrdom; see E. Stauffer, *New Testament Theology*, 1955, 331ff.

[179] See Bill. 3, 259 for Rom 8.36. For the martyrdoms at the time of Hadrian, see Bill. 1, 223-226.

struggle for the 'sole rule of God' and for the freedom of Israel, whether they died in open fighting or at the hand of the executioner, must have appeared in their eyes as martyrs. Even though they may not have been recognized by members of the leading Jewish circles as such, they were certainly seen by the mass of the people as authentic martyrs. The outbreak of the Jewish War was only possible because the majority of the people, inflamed with the ideas of the Zealots, placed themselves on their side. The examples that I have given of Jotapata, Gamala, the defence of the Temple and the prisoners of war all show that the ordinary people were in many cases as ready to die as their Zealot models, the *Sicarii*, in Masada and in Egypt.

I would like at this stage to summarize the essential points of the Zealots' conception of martyrdom, which had such a deep effect on the whole people.

(1) The growing number of martyrs was undoubtedly the most impressive indication of the fact that this was, for Israel, the eschatological time of great distress, the time of God's anger, when Israel was being put to the test. The martyrdom of the 'wise' can be understood in this sense in the Book of Daniel.[180] The same theme is also found in the Assumption of Moses[181] and above all in the Christian tradition, the gospels and the Apocalypse.[182] It was only because of the certainty of their eschatological meaning that the countless 'blood sacrifices' offered during the fight for freedom were significant. They became the seed of the coming kingdom of God.

(2) This 'eschatological meaning' was primarily found in the fact that the blood of the martyrs was regarded as a call to God to avenge their death[183] and to bring about the salvation of Israel. In the Similitudes of the Ethiopian Enoch for example, the blood of the righteous rises up together with their prayers to the 'Lord of the spirits', while the 'holy ones', in other words, the angels, with a single voice make intercession that the blood and the prayer of the righteous may not be in vain and that justice may not be long delayed. When the books are opened then for justice, the angels rejoice, 'because ... prayer of the righteous had been heard and the blood of righteous had been avenged in the presence of the Lord of the spirits'.[184] Again, in the Assumption of Moses, Taxo is

---

[180] See Dan 11.33,35; see also EthEn 90 and Volz, *Esch*, 149: 'The death of the martyrs becomes a symbol for the time of terror at the end'.

[181] AssMos 8 and 9.

[182] Rev 6.9-11; 7.9-17; 20.4-6.

[183] See Deut 32.43; 2 Kings 9.7; Joel 4.21; see also E. Stauffer, *op. cit.*, 316, No. 25-29.

[184] EthEn 47,1-4; translation based on G. Beer in Kautzsch, *Apokryphen und*

convinced together with his sons that, if they are prepared to die for the law, their blood will be avenged by God.[185] In the Apocalypse (6.9-11), the souls of the martyrs 'under the altar' cry out to God to avenge their blood, which had been shed by 'those who dwell upon the earth'. Finally, there is the ancient Jewish prayer, the *Abinu Malkenu*:

'Our Father, our King, avenge before our eyes the blood of your servants that has been shed!'[186]

It is hardly possible to doubt that this theme, which appears in the apocalyptic, Christian and rabbinic traditions, was also present in Zealot circles, where the greatest number were called to bear witness by their blood. It may be that what was expected there of the many cases of martyrdom was, in accordance with the thesis that the kingdom of God could be 'brought close' by human deeds, a shortening of the messianic time of distress.[187]

(3) The effectiveness of dying a martyr's death went further, however, than simply an admonition with regard to God. It was also believed to have expiatory power or power to bring about God's mercy.[188] This power could be effective for the individual's own sins, but it had above all a representative effect for the whole people. Evidence of this can be found in the Hellenistic Jewish texts about martyrs[189] and in the rabbinic literature.[190] In early Christianity, the whole expiatory

---

Pseudepigraphen, 2, 263; see also 97,5; 99,3 and Lk 18.7, confined here to the prayer.

[185] AssMos 9,7; the revelation of the Kingdom of God follows immediately afterwards.

[186] See W. Staerk, *Altjüdische liturgische Gebete (Lietzmanns Kleine Texte* 58), 1930, 29. The prayer itself can be traced back to the first century A.D.; according to Taan 25b, it is derived from R. Akiba: see I. Elbogen, *Der jüdische Gottesdienst*, 1924, Chapter 24, 11.

[187] The problem of how long the period of waiting would be also appears in EthEn 47,2 and Rev 6.10f. According to Rev 6.11, the coming of the end was dependent on the completion of a certain number of martyrs.

[188] See Moore, *Judaism*, 1, 546f.; H.A. Fischel, *op. cit.*, 372f.

[189] See 2Macc 7.18,37f.; 4 Macc 1.11; 6.29; 9.23f.; 17.22. It is noteworthy that the blood of the martyrs is regarded in 4 Macc as having a directly expiatory effect (see 6.29; 17.22). For this, see also jSanh 30c,28f. (Bill. 2, 279): R. Johanan in the name of R. Simeon b. Jochai: 'Each drop (of blood) that came out of each righteous man (1 Kings 20.37) has expiated the whole of Israel'. See also E. Stauffer, *op. cit.*, 317, No. 42,44,46,47.

[190] Martyrdom is placed here in the wider framework of the expiatory effect of suffering generally; for this, see, apart from Moore and Fischel, Bill. 1, 225f.; 2, 277f.,279f.,281f. Martyrdom was, however, regarded as having the greatest effect, as death was seen as the most powerful means of achieving expiation; see Bill. 1, 169, tYom 5,6ff. (Z. 190). For further examples, see Bill. 4, 1264, Index under '*Sühnemittel*'.

power is concentrated in the sacrificial death of Jesus.[191] Since zeal already had an expiatory effect in the tradition of Phinehas, the expiation of sins must have been all the more fitting to martyrdom as the highest fulfilment of zeal.

(4) In Judaism, the martyr frequently had charismatic aspects (which formed a link between him and the prophet). There were above all the aspects of supernatural and joyous steadfastness and insensitivity to torture on the one hand and prophetic vision at the time of death on the other. This characteristic is reflected in an ideal manner in the martyrdom of Isaiah:

> 'Isaiah neither cried out nor wept when he was being sawn; his mouth kept in conversation with the Holy Spirit until he had been sawn in two'.[192]

There are also charismatic elements present in various cases of Christian martyrdom from the time of Stephen onwards,[193] as well as in such Jewish cases as the martyrdom of Jose b. Joezer,[194] R. Akiba[195] or R. Hanina b. Teradion.[196]

It hardly needs to be stressed that descriptions of prophetic visions in the case of martyred Zealots can hardly be expected from Josephus, who hated the Zealot movement so much. Nonetheless, their extraordinary steadfastness in martyrdom does emerge on several occasions from his texts. He describes, for example, their 'smiling',[197] their 'unfeeling bodies' and 'joyous souls' and their disregard of the pains of torture.[198] This indicates clearly enough that a readiness to die as martyrs was linked in the case of the Zealots — as it was in that of the Essenes — with an ecstatic gift. It is possible that their behaviour towards their Roman executioners was, like the presence in them of prophetic gifts, interpreted as a sign that they were also consciously in possession of the Spirit.

---

[191] It is here that the decisive distinction between the Jewish and the Christian understanding of martyrdom can be found. The suffering of the Christian martyr can only be understood in the perspective of the suffering of his Lord and in itself it has no expiatory power.

[192] c. 5,14 (see also v. 7); translation based on G. Beer in Kautzsch, *Apokryphen und Pseudepigraphen*, 2, 127.

[193] Acts 7.55-60; see also the martyrdom of Perpetua and Felicitas in R. Knopf and G. Krüger, eds., *Ausgewählte Märtyrerakten*, 3rd. ed. 1929, 43, c. 20,3: 'adeo in spiritu et in extasi fuerat'. See also H. Lietzmann, *History of the Early Church*, 1953, 2, 162ff., K. Holl, *Gesammelte Aufsätze*, 2, 70ff., and M. Hengel, *ZThK* 72 (1975), 193f.

[194] GenRab 65,22.

[195] Ber 61b bar, see Bill. 1, 223, where further parallels will be found.

[196] AZ 18a bar, see Bill. 1, 223; for other examples, see Fischel, *op. cit.*, 367ff.

[197] *Bell* 3,321: καταμειδιῶν; among the Essenes, *Bell* 2,153: μειδιῶντες.

[198] See *Bell* 7,418: ἀναισθήτοις σώμασι χαιρούσῃ ... τῇ ψυχῇ. See also *Ant* 18,23.

(5) H. Strathmann was of the opinion that, whereas with the Christian martyrs 'witness is borne to someone', this attitude was not essential in the case of the Jewish martyrs.[199] In reality, however, there was hardly any difference here between the Jewish and the Christian conception of martyrdom. This is clear from the legend of the death of the seven sons with their mother,[200] the martyrdom of Isaiah[201] and the rabbinic tradition of martyrdom.[202]

Even if Josephus was understandably hardly able to describe the 'outspokenness' of the Zealot martyrs — although that characteristic is clearly discernible in the cases of martyrdom among the *Sicarii* and the Essenes[203] — the aspect of confession emerges clearly from his two accounts of martyrdom under Herod. In both cases, the accused men confess to the inviolable validity of the law and fearlessly insist on their readiness to die for it. An outspoken confession of this kind has undoubtedly to be presupposed as a fundamental feature of the Zealots' conception of the martyr and the charismatic theme was probably also contained within it.[204] At the heart of the Zealots' readiness to confess in this way was their clinging to the principle of the 'sole rule of God'.

(6) Hope of resurrection was intimately connected in the Book of Daniel with martyrdom.[205] They were also closely related in Josephus,[206]

---

[199] *TD*, 4,488.

[200] See 2 Macc 6.18-7.42, the Fourth Book of the Maccabees and Gitt 57b. What we have here in each case is a continuous confession of the inviolable validity of the law and the one God. God's judgement is also proclaimed to the tyrant: 2 Macc 7.17,19,34; 4 Macc 9.9,32; 10.11; 12.11, etc. This essential theme also appears in Gitt 57b: the last of the young men pronounces 'woe upon the emperor'. The ruler and his followers cannot avoid the impression that the young men are steadfast: 2 Macc 7.12 and 4 Macc 17.17. See also E. Stauffer, *op. cit.*, 316, No. 25.

[201] c. 5,9f.

[202] Pappus and Julianus in the presence of Trajan: Taan 18b; Jose b. Joezer and R. Hanania b. Teradion even succeed in converting their executioners to faith in God: GenRab 65,22 and AZ 18a; see Bill. 1, 223. R. Akiba taught his disciples even while he was dying a correct understanding of the *Shema*: Ber 61b, see Bill. 1, 224. For other examples, see Fischel, *op. cit.*, 370.

[203] See above, p.260f. The aspect of 'confession' in these cases of martyrdom is indicated by the spectators' astonishment at the behaviour of the young men and the κατειρωνευόμενοι τῶν τὰς βασάνους προσφερόντων among the Essene martyrs.

[204] See above, p. 244f; for the confession of the sole rule of God, see above, p. 90f., *Bell* 7,418. See also the charismatic basis of the confession in the case of Jesus: Mk 13.11; Mt 10.19; Lk 21.15. A parallel Zealot tradition may also exist here.

[205] Dan 12.2; cf. EthEn 90,33 and 2 Macc 7.9,11,14; 12.44f.; 14.46; see also Volz, *Esch*, 231 and E. Stauffer, *op. cit.*, 315, No. 19-23; 316, No. 24. Stauffer, however, makes no distinction between the doctrine of immortality (as in Wisdom and the Fourth Book of the Maccabees) and the hope of resurrection (as in the Palestinian tradition).

[206] *Ap* 2,218f.: '... that God has granted a new existence to those who observe his laws

the Letter to the Hebrews (11.35) and the Apocalypse (20.4–6). The evidence provided by Tacitus is also important in this context, since this goes back to the Roman experiences in the Jewish War:

> 'animosque proelio aut suppliciis peremptorum aeternos putant: hinc gererandi amor et moriendi contemptus.'[207]

It is of no great importance that the immortality of the soul is mentioned by the Roman author rather than the resurrection. This reinterpretation, which is only to be expected in the Hellenistic–Roman world, can also be found to some extent in Josephus.[208] In the presence of Herod, the two teachers base their outspokenness on their hope of immortality. Eleazar b. Ari expressed this hope among his arguments in favour of suicide and it was not difficult, Josephus points out, for the Essenes to accept death, as they believed that they 'received' their souls 'again'.[209]

We may safely assume that the Zealots' hope of resurrection took a similar form to that expressed in Rev 20.4–6. In other words, the martyrs, that is, all those freedom fighters who had been condemned to death by the Romans or who had fallen in battle, would rise again from the dead at the beginning of the time of salvation and would receive special dignities in the messianic kingdom. Their scorn of death was to some extent determined by this hope.

(7) Suicide had a special place in the Jewish and Zealot conception of martyrdom because imprisonment made it to a high degree impossible for Jews to follow the law. There was also the question of consideration for the family. Women were exposed to the danger of being violated and children to that of becoming pagans and serving idols. Many Jews also found the idea of their own bodies being violated unbearable. It was therefore possible for suicide to appear as an act that was necessary for the sake of faithfulness to the law.

(8) To conclude this summary of the Zealots' conception of martyrdom, we may assume that there was in the Zealot movement a distinct tradition of martyrdom, which was at the same time an

---

and who, if it is necessary to die for the law, are ready to give up their life for it and they will receive a better life in the transformation (of all things)'.

[207] Hist 5,5. See also Posidonius on the Celts, FGrHist 87 F 116,28.5f.

[208] Even where Josephus speaks unmistakably about the resurrection, he takes the immortality of the soul as his point of departure; see Bell 2,163 = Ant 18,14 and Bell 3,374.

[209] Bell 2,153; see also 154ff. for their doctrine of immortality. According to Hippolytus, Ref Omn Haer 9,27, GCS ed. P. Wendland, 1916, 1, 260f., the Essenes seem also to have believed in the resurrection of the dead. See M. Hengel, Judaism and Hellenism, 196ff.

expression of the firm discipline that prevailed within the sect. As A. Schlatter has correctly pointed out, they shared with Jesus the demand for unconditional readiness to die a martyr's death.[210] Schlatter is, however, not justified in his conclusion from this that martyrdom was 'for them a hard and inexplicable dispensation of God, confronted with which man had no choice but to submit'. Schlatter is wrong, because their eschatological interpretation enabled the Zealots to understand martyrdom in its positive sense, namely, as the quickest and most certain way to share in the joys of the messianic kingdom.

E. The Holy War

1. In the Old Testament and the Maccabaean Period

The idea of the Holy War was firmly rooted in the Old Testament tradition.[211] For our purposes, however, it is possible to limit ourselves only to those aspects of the Holy War in the Old Testament, including the later tradition, that are concerned with our period.

The warlord in the Holy War was Yahweh himself.[212] Yahweh generally fought his 'battles'[213] 'through a personality who had received charismatic gifts from him'.[214] His warriors, summoned by that personality, assembled as 'volunteers'.[215] 'Neither their armament nor their number' were of decisive importance.[216] Yahweh himself marched at their head and inspired their enemies with fear.[217] Before the battle,

---

[210] *Die Geschichte des Christus*, 1921, 306: 'There was to begin with no group among his (that is, Jesus') listeners who had a better and more willing understanding of such words as "losing one's life" and "carrying one's cross" than the Zealots'.

[211] See F. Schwally, *Semitische Kriegsaltertümer*, 1: *Der Heilige Krieg im alten Israel*, 1901; G. von Rad, *Der Heilige Krieg im Alten Israel*, 1951; O. Bauernfeind, 'πόλεμος', *TD*, 6, 507f. For critical contributions, see M. Weippert, *ZAW* 84 (1972), 460-93; see also F. Stolz, *Jahwes und Israels Kriege*, 1972.

[212] Ex 14.4,14; 15.3; Ps 24.9; Is 42.13; see also G. von Rad, op. cit., 9.

[213] 1 Sam 18.17; 25.28; Num 21.14; see also G. von Rad, *op. cit.*.

[214] O. Bauernfeind, *op. cit.*, 6, 507; G. von Rad, *op. cit.*, 20,23f.,27: 'Any Israelite was recognized as the leader of the army ban whose accession was attested by the Spirit of Yahweh'. See also Judg 3.10; 11.29; etc.

[215] For this call, see Judg 3.27; 6.34; 19.29; 1 Sam 7.5; 11.7. For the volunteers: הַמִּתְנַדְּבִים, see Judg 5.9; cf. 5.2 and 2 Chron 17.16; see also G. von Rad, *op. cit.*, 7 and 37. This concept can also be found in the Qumran texts, see below, p. 277, n. 258.

[216] O. Bauernfeind, *op. cit.*; G. von Rad, *op. cit.*, 9. See also Judg 7.2ff.; 1 Sam 14.6; 17.45,47; Deut 20.1f.

[217] Yahweh marches at the head: Judg 4.14; 2 Sam 5.24; Deut 20.4, etc.; for the fear of Yahweh, see Ex 14.24f.; Deut 11.23; Josh 2.9; see also O. Bauernfeind, *op. cit.*, n. 3, and G. von Rad, *op. cit.*, 12.

the army was exhorted by its charismatic leader or the priests[218] to rely on God's help and cowards or those who were prevented by possessions or family ties were eliminated.[219] In battle, the decision was often made by the intervention on the part of Yahweh himself.[220] The ban formed the climax and the conclusion', but this could have various degrees of intensity.[221] War was 'an extension of the worship service'[222] and, as such, it was like the priestly service in the Sanctuary and subject to a number of ritual obligations.[223]

The religious distress experienced under Antiochus Epiphanes gave a new lease on life to the idea of the Holy War. Because of its 'remarkably secular conception', the charismatic character of the fighting is not given prominence in the First Book of the Maccabees,[224] but this aspect appears with sufficient clarity in the description of the early stages of the fight for freedom. The point of departure, Mattathias' action, was in itself charismatic. The Old Testament model of the Holy War is also unmistakably present, since Judas exhorted his army before the battle with a reference to God's saving acts; following that, he prayed.[225] When the army was being prepared for the attack against Gorgias in the ancient cultic place of Mizpah — there is an unmistakable link here with 1 Sam 7.5-15 — Judas and his brothers fasted and put on sackcloth[226] and consulted Holy Scripture as an oracle, as the Urim and Thummim had been consulted in the past. Judas then divided the army in accordance

---

[218] Josh 8.1; Judg 3.28; 7.5; 1 Sam 7.8ff.; Deut 20.2ff. The rabbinic conception of the one anointed for war is connected with this last passage; see Bill. 4, 174. See also above, p. 160f. See also Phinehas in Num 31.6ff.

[219] Judg 7.3; Deut 20.5-8.

[220] Josh 6.20; 10.10f.; Judg 5.20; 1 Sam 7.10, etc.; see also Deut 9.1ff.

[221] See Num 31.15ff.; Deut 2.34; 20.13ff.,16f.; 1 Sam 15. See also F. Schwally, *op. cit.*, 29.

[222] F. Schwally, *op. cit.*, 63; see also G. von Rad, *op. cit.*, 7.

[223] See the verb קדשׁ pi. and hitp. in relation to war: Josh 3.5; Jer 6.4; Mic 3.5, etc. For the anointing and consecration of weapons, see F. Schwally, *op. cit.*, 49f.; for fasting, *op. cit.*, 50; for sexual abstinence, *op. cit.*, 60ff. According to Num 31.19, a seven day period of purification from the defilement caused by contact with corpses was required at the end of a war; see also Deut 23.13f. These ritual commandments recur later in the War Scroll of the Essenes; see below, p. 278, n. 263,265.

[224] G. von Rad, *op. cit.*, 84. The First Book of the Maccabees, which was probably written between 135 and 104 B.C., that is, during the later period of John Hyrcanus' rule (see O. Eissfeldt, *Old Testament: an Introduction*, 1965, 581), describes the fight for freedom in a predominantly secular manner. This description of the early Maccabaean period has to be supplemented by 2 Macc and Daniel.

[225] 1 Macc 3.18ff.; 4.8ff.,30ff.; 5.32f.; 7.41ff.; see also 2 Macc 8.16ff.,32; 11.6f.; 12.15f.,28ff.; 13.14ff.; 15.8.

[226] 1 Macc 3.46ff.; for the supplication motif, see 11.71; 2 Macc 10.24ff. and 14.5. See also above, p. 153.

with the model of Ex 18.21–26 and, following the precept of Deut 20.5–8, eliminated the fearful and other who were prevented from fighting. According to 2 Macc 8.14, those who were ready to fight sold all their possessions.

The small number of combatants and their poor weapons played no part, for they knew that 'strength comes from God'.[227] God himself was called to join in the battle, as his help was decisive.[228] According to 2 Macc 10.29ff., that help took the form of a miraculous intervention on the part of heavenly warriors.[229] It is, then, clear from all this that the Maccabees' fight for freedom bore all the characteristics — in its initial phase at least — of the Holy War.[230]

2. The Eschatological-Dualistic and the Messianic Interpretation of the Holy War in the Apocalyptic Literature and the War Scroll

(a) The Eschatological-Dualistic Interpretation[231]

The idea of the eschatological war gave way to the conception of the 'Holy War'. The eschatological characteristics are almost completely lacking in the Books of the Maccabees and there is a conscious absence of all references to war in the Book of Daniel. In the Ethipian Enoch, however, it is possible to recognize clearly the conception of eschatological war against Israel's oppressor in the contemporary 'vision of the animal symbols'.[232]

> 'I saw, until a great sword was handed over to the sheep and the sheep marched against all the animals of the field in order to kill them and all the animals and birds of heaven fled from them'.

As this is followed at once by the opening of the judgement, it is clear that the war forms the introduction to the judgement. In the Apocalypse of Weeks, the 'chosen righteous' ones receive a sword in the (eighth)

---

[227] 1 Macc 3.18f.: ἐκ τοῦ οὐρανοῦ ἡ ἰσχύς. See also 4.6ff.; 2 Macc 15.11.

[228] 1 Macc 4.10,32; see 2 Macc 8.23 for the watchword: θεοῦ βοηθείας; see also 2 Macc 11.13 and 15.21.

[229] See also 11.8f. and 15.12–16,23. In EthEn 90,14, Michael helps the 'ram' (that is, Judas Maccabaeus); see also Dan 12.1. The theme also occurs in the War Scroll; see below p. 279, n. 271. It clearly goes back to the Old Testament; see F. Schwally, op. cit., 7f.

[230] See W.R. Farmer, 9th. ed., 17; P. v. d. Osten-Sacken, Gott und Belial, 1969, 62ff.

[231] For what follows, see H. Windisch, Der messianische Krieg und das Urchristentum, 1909, 10ff.: The messianic war in Jewish eschatology.

[232] EthEn 90,19; translation is based on G. Beer's in Kautzsch, Apokryphen und Pseudepigraphen, 2, 296. For the time calculation, see O. Eissfeldt, op. cit., 564f. One of the fragments found among those of 4Q was one of the vision of animals, ca. 87–90 A.D. It is therefore possible for this also to be attributed to the Essene literature; see J.T. Milik, Ten Years of Discovery. 33f.

'week of righteousness', so that they can execute judgement on sinners.[233]

Following the ancient conception of Yahweh as a 'warrior' God, the post-exilic prophets made him intervene as a fighter for the salvation of his people in the conflict with their enemies.[234] This conception had been taken over from the apocalyptic literature, in which God turned not only against the enemies of Israel, but also against the demonic powers acting behind them. The eschatological struggle therefore had a dualistic foundation. The heavenly hosts together with his chosen people Israel are on God's side. This conception, among others, is especially pronounced in the hymns of Qumran:

> The assault of the powers of Belial goes ahead and against them God at a particular moment goes over to the counter-attack: 'God thunders in the fullness of his power and the heavenly host makes its voice resound. The eternal foundations shake and the war of the heroes of heaven sweeps over the earth and does not cease until the time of destruction and eternal decision'.[235]

The same war is, however, also waged with the help of pious Jews:[236]

> The point of departure is once again the attack by chaotic powers, against whose armies the community presents an invicible fortress. The 'wars of godlessness', however, suddenly come to an end and the situation changes completely: 'And then God's sword will hasten to the time of judgement and all the sons of truth will rise up (to destroy the sons) of godlessness.[237] ... Then the hero will draw his bow and open the ring of the siege ... and the eternal gates, so that the implements of war can be taken out ...' Finally, the eschatological ban is imposed on the enemy and they are completely destroyed.

What is essential here is the sudden change from the time of tribulation, which is characterized by Belial's attacks against the community, the so-called 'wars of godlessness', to the victorious eschatological war, by which judgement is executed on the godless and

---

[233] EthEn 91,12; see also 98,12; 99,6.16, the speeches on images 50,2; Jub 24,29; 26,30; Wis 3.7; 1QpHab 5,3f. See also Volz, *Esch*, 316. In the Apocalypse of Weeks we have a fixed eschatological pattern into which the battle for annihilation fought by the elect against the godless is introduced at a decisive point. For the apocalyptic theme of the sword, see Volz, *Esch*, 320.

[234] See Is 59.15-18; 63.1-6; Joel 4.13 and Zech 9.13ff. Glosses on Zech show that the words of the prophet were interpreted as being directed against the Greeks. Israel on the one hand appears as a weapon in God's hand and, on the other, is protected by him.

[235] 1QH 3,34ff. (26ff.); see TestLev 3,1ff.; TestDan 5,10f.; AssMos 10,1-7.

[236] 1QH 6,29ff. (23ff.); see O. Betz, *NT* 2 (1957), 122ff.; M. Mansoor, *JBL* 76 (1957), 145f. and H. Bardtke, *ThLZ* 81 (1956), 600.

[237] Reading with Mansoor, *op. cit.*, ‏[התם בני] רשעה‎L.

the time of salvation is introduced.[238] The whole of God's earthly and heavenly army takes part in this war, which goes far beyond all earthly frontiers.[239]

(b) The Messiah as the Leader in the Eschatological War

The war at the end of time may also be led, on behalf of God himself, by the eschatological anointed one, the Messiah. Among the Essenes, there were two figures who were considered for this role,[240] both of whom were connected with the eschatological war. In the so-called 'Blessings', attention is focused on the high-priestly Messiah with a higher rank[241] and the wish is expressed that he 'may throw down many nations'.[242] The warlike part played by this figure emerges even more distinctly in the War Scroll, in which he has control of the entire spiritual and military leadership of the whole of the estchatological battle. In the Testaments of the Twelve Patriarchs, Levi appears as the warrior who 'wages the war of the Lord'.[243]

The real war Messiah, however, comes from Judah and the line of David.[244] His office is described as 'the prince of the community' (נשיא העדה).[245] To carry out his task 'to establish the kingdom of his people

---

[238] The same pattern is also to be found in the texts quoted from Enoch. It is possible for the annihilation of the enemy in the eschatological war and the beginning of the last judgement to be merged into one another; see Volz, *Esch*, 94, and O. Bauernfeind, *op. cit.*, 6, 511.

[239] See TestReub 6,12: the 'visible' and the 'invisible' wars; Rev 12.7ff.: the war fought by Michael in heaven; 19.1ff.: the victory of Christ coming again on earth.

[240] For the idea of the two Messiahs, see K.G. Kuhn, 'Die beiden Messias Aarons und Israels', *NTS* 1 (1955), 168-179, and A.S. van der Woude, *Die messianischen Vorstellungen der Gemeinde von Qumran*, 1957, *passim*.

[241] For his higher rank, see 1QSa 2,12ff.19, ed. D. Barthélemy and J.T. Milik, *Qumran Cave I*, 1955, 110f.; see also A.S. van der Woude, *op. cit.*, 104ff.

[242] 1QSb 3,18, *Qumran Cave I,*, 124; for this, see the comment by the editor, J.T. Milik: 'This is presumably an allusion to the warlike character of the priestly Messiah'.

[243] 2 TestSim 5,5: οὐ δυνήσονται πρὸς Λευὶ ἀντιστῆναι ὅτι πόλεμον κυρίου πολεμήσει. See also TestReub 6,12, which, in its original form, refers to Levi; see R.H. Charles, *The Greek Version of the Testaments of the Twelve Patriarchs*, 1908.

[244] See the messianic Testimonia of 4Q, edited by J.M. Allegro, *JBL* 75 (1956), 174: the quotation from Gen 49.10; 176: the quotations from 2 Sam 7.11 and Amos 9.11; 180f.: the quotation from Is 11 and *JBL* 77 (1958), 351ff., where both 2 Sam 7.10ff. and Amos 9.11 are quoted and interpreted: all quotations refer to the Davidic Messiah. See DJD V, *Qumran Cave 4*, 1968, No. 174/5, 53ff., and J. Strugnell, *RQ* 7 (1970), 220ff. For the Davidic origin of the Messiah, see G. Dalman, *Words of Jesus*, 1902, 316-324; Volz, *Esch*. 174f.; Moore, *Judaism*, 2, 347ff.; J. Jeremias, *Jerusalem*, 3rd. ed., 1969, 276f.

[245] See 1QSb 5,20, *Qumran Cave I*, 127; see also CD 5,1 and 1QM 5,1. Bar Koseba also gave himself the title of נשיא ישראל. See the letter by him, ed. J.T. Milik, *RB* 60 (1953), 276ff., and his coins, A. Reifenberg, *Jewish Coins*, 64ff. Nos. 190,192f.,199; see also A.S. van der Woude, *op. cit.*, 115f. and 134f. See also below, p. 298f.

into eternity',[246] he has to break the resistance of his opponents:

> So that (you may strike the nations) with the force of your (mouth), lay waste the earth with your sceptre and kill the God(less) with the breath of your lips ... (God) will make for you iron horns and brazen hoofs ..., so that you may toss like a young (bull the nations ...) ... For God has made you the sceptre over the rulers; befo(re you the peoples will all bow down and all na)tions will serve you ...'[247]

In the Damascus Covenant, the 'sceptre from Israel' (Gen 49.9) is applied to the 'prince of the community'[248] and his activity is defined with Num 24.17:

> 'And when he rises up, he will strike down all the sons of Seth'.

In the fragment of a Commentary on Isaiah, a connection is made between the 'prince' and the decisive battle at the end of time.[249] The mention of the 'prince' is followed by a description of the enemy army as it approaches along the traditional way of the plain of Acco[250] to Jerusalem. The decisive battle in which the opponent is destroyed is fought outside the gates of Jerusalem.[251] This is followed by an exegesis of Is 11, in which the Davidic Messiah, who 'will judge nations with his sword', reappears.

J. T. Milik dates this fragment to the middle of the first century A. D. and interprets the Kittim as the Romans.[252] At a time when the activity

---

[246] 1QSb 5,21 (op. cit.). The translation is based on that by A.S. van der Woude, op. cit., 112.

[247] 1QSb 5,24-27 (op. cit.). For the translation and the complete text, see A.S. van der Woude, op. cit., 112ff. For the theme of the sword, see Is 11.4; PsSol 17,24; 2 Thess 2.8 and Rev 19.15,21.

[248] CD 7,20f.; for this, see A.S. van der Woude, op. cit., 57f.,58f.: According to the Jerusalem Targum I, the 'sons of Seth' were Gog's troops.

[249] 4QpIs 10,32 — 11,3 (No. 161) Fragm 8-10; see DJD V, 13; for this, see A.S. van der Woude, op. cit., 179ff.

[250] 4QpIs 10,28ff. Fragm 5,6 l. 11. Acco = Ptolemais was the place where the Roman army assembled for its undertakings against Judaea: Bell 2,67 Varus; 187 Petronius; 501 Cestius Gallus; 3,29 Vespasian.

[251] Unlike the editor, op. cit., 181, I believe, with J.T. Milik, Ten Years of Discovery, 123, and A.S. van der Woude, op. cit., 179f., that this does not refer to the coming of the Messiah, but to the approach of the hostile army. Van der Woude makes the remarkable suggestion that the battlefield outside Jerusalem (see also 1QM 1,3) is identical with the Armageddon of Rev 16.16. He assumes that what are meant are the 'mountains of Migron' (Is 10.28, Μαγέδω and other readings, LXX). For the decisive battle at the end of time outside the gates of Jerusalem, see Volz, Esch, 149; Bill. 3, 836f. for Rev 20.9; the idea probably goes back to Ezek 38.8 or 39.4 or else to the Sennacherib story; see above, pp. 240f. and below, 305f.

[252] op. cit., 111. For the dating of the related War Scroll, see below, p. 278, n. 262, and 279, n. 277.

of the Zealots was becoming more intense throughout the whole country, then, the Essenes seem to have evolved certain ideas about the eschatological war against Rome, which were not so far removed from those of the Zealots.

The Messiah does not figure so prominently as a war hero in the rest of the literature of late Judaism. He appears relatively clearly as such in the Psalms of Solomon (17,22 and 24) and in Rev 19.11–16 (ἐν δικαιοσύνῃ κρίνει καὶ πολεμεῖ) and 19–21, but here too the really warlike aspects are less emphatically presented than the fact of the destruction of Israel's opponents.[253] Philo[254] and Hippolytus[255] also developed a warlike image of the Jewish messianic hope. At a later period, it was above all the popular tradition of the Targums that presented the image of the Messiah as a war hero:

'How fine is the King, the Messiah, who will arise from those of the house of Judah! He girds his loins and goes forth and sets up the ranks of battle against his enemies and kills the kings together with their commanders and no king and commander can stand before him. He reddens the mountains with the blood of their slain and his garments are dipped in blood ...'[256]

In the rabbinic literature, the specifically warlike aspects are transferred to the Messiah b. Ephraim.[257]

(c) The War Scroll

The Essenes were given a military order in the Manual of Discipline, the members of the community calling themselves 'volunteers'.[258] Even in the ideal image of the eschatological community, war against the pagans was presupposed.[259] The War Scroll describes in detail how that was to be waged. What is really astonishing is the 'military realism' of

---

[253] See Volz, *Esch*, 214: 'The eschatological hero annihilates the enemy in a miraculous way'. See 4 Ezra 12, 13; SyrBar 39, 40 and Sib 5,108f.418f. The image of the warrior is merged into that of the judge. For the Messiah as the conqueror of Gog, see Volz, *Esch*, 213 (cf. Num 24.7 LXX),316 and Bill. 3, 833 (a + b).

[254] *Praem* 95 (M 2, 423): ἐξελεύσεται ἄνθρωπος (Num 24.7 LXX) ... καὶ στρατάρχων καὶ πολεμῶν ἔθνη μεγάλα. See also *VitMos* 1, 290 (M 2, 126); for this, see Volz *Esch*, 182.

[255] *Ref Omn Haer* 9,30, GCS ed. P. Wendland, 1916, 7, 264: βασιλέα ἄνδρα πολεμίστην καὶ δυνατόν ... πάντα τὰ ἔθνη πολεμήσας.

[256] Jerusalem Targum I on Gen 49.11, quoted from Bill. 4, 877f., where other places in the Targum will be found; see especially Jerusalem Targum I on Num 24.17, Bill. 3,833.

[257] See below, p. 298f.

[258] 1QS 5,21 on Ex 18.21,25; cf. 1 Macc 3.55; see also CD 13,1; 1QSa 1,14 (*op. cit.*, 110). The celestial armies also have a similar military structure; see EthEn 69,3. For the 'volunteers' (הנדבים), see 1QS 1,7.11; 5,1, etc. See also P. Wernberg-Møller, *The Manual of Discipline*, 1957, 46, n. 13.

[259] 1QSa 1,21 and 26 (*op. cit.*, 110).

this remarkable work.[260] It contains precise military regulations, going into considerable details, which are probably derived from a Hellenistic manual on the art of war.[261]

The earliest version of the War Scroll dates back to the Maccabaean period. The model for later parts of the document may be Herod's army.[262] This does not, however, mean that earlier traditions may not also have been adapted and used, especially in the liturgical passages.

The war described in the Scroll is in every sense a 'Holy War' and is based above all on the presentation of the Holy War in the Books of Numbers and Deuteronomy. Special emphasis is given in the document to the priestly element in those Old Testament books.[263] The leadership in battle is, for example, in the hands of the messianic high-priest.[264] For cultural reasons, the priests do not, it is true, participate directly in the struggle,[265] but they give 'spiritual support' to the combatants, directing the fighting by blowing their trumpets.[266] Corresponding to the time that Israel spent in the desert, the war is calculated as lasting for forty

---

[260] O. Bauernfeind, *TD* 6, 511.

[261] Y. Yadin, מגלת מלחמת בני אור בבני חושך, 1955, 16, assumed that there was a Roman influence: the standards (36ff.) and the arms (106–130) are similar to the Roman equipment under Caesar and during the early imperial period. J.T. Milik agrees with this view, *RB* 64 (1957), 585–593. The equipment and the tactics employed by the Roman army, however, were originated in the Hellenistic period. In its original form, 1QM goes far back into the second century B.C.; see M. Hengel, *Judaism and Hellenism*, 1, 18, n. 101; for note see 2, 13; P. v.d. Osten-Sacken, *Gott und Belial*, 28–115. For the dating, see 29f.

[262] Y. Yadin, *op. cit.*, 22ff. There is, then, a remarkable similarity between the strength of the Herodian army (*Ant* 14,468f.: about thirty thousand men, including six thousand mounted soldiers) and 1QM 9,4f. (twenty-eight thousand men, including six thousand who were mounted); see Y. Yadin, *op. cit.*, 161, nn. 186,165., and K.G. Kuhn, *ThLZ* 81 (1956), 27. The total armed force may therefore have consisted of four legions. The dating of the War Scroll was for a long time disputed; see M. Burrows, *The Dead Sea Scrolls*, 1956, 204ff., but this controversial question seems to have been cleared up by increasing knowledge of the various levels. The assumption that there was a direct Zealot origin is erroneous: B. Katz, for example, assumed that the text was written in Zealot circles at the time of the Caligula episode (see M. Burrows, *op. cit.*, 206). What is much more likely is that the Essenes themselves became radicalized in the direction of Zealotism; see above, p. 276 and below, p. 281f. See also C. Roth, *The Historical Background of the Dead Sea Scrolls*, 1958, 49f., whose conclusions, however, are wrong.

[263] Deut 20.1 = 1QM 10,2ff.; Deut 20.8 = 10,5; Deut 23.10ff. = 7,6f. and 10,1; Num 10.9 = 10,6f.; Num 31.9 = 14,2ff. According to 1QM 7,3ff., women, children and the physically handicapped, in other words, those who were unsuitable for priestly service, were not allowed to enter the camp.

[264] 2,1; 15,4; 16,3; 18,5; 19,2.

[265] 9,7ff.; see also 7,11: for the avoidance of defilement by corpses.

[266] 7,10-15; 8,1ff.; 9,1ff., etc.; see also Num 10.9, quoted in 1QM 10,6.

years. During the sabbath years, there is a period of rest from fighting.[267]

In the hymnic passages,[268] the tradition of war that prevailed in ancient Israel, the Psalms and Isaiah are given greater prominence.[269] God is the warlord,[270] and his angels intervene in the battle,[271] forming with Israel the single community of the children of the light.[272] It is therefore known that victory can be achieved not by the strength of Israel alone, but only with God's help.[273] The War Scroll passes very quickly over Israel's neighbouring tribes, after mentioning them initially as hostile.[274]

The Kittim are named throughout as the principal enemy[275] and it is against them that the greatest and most difficult part of the battle is directed.[276] On the basis of Yadin's dating of the document, these people can be seen as the Romans.[277] In addition to the Kittim, there are also those who had deserted the people of Israel, the 'offenders against the covenant'.[278]

The eschatological struggle also to some extent assumes the features of a judgement against the whole of humanity,[279] at the end of which is

---

[267] 2,8-14, see L. Rost, op. cit., 207; K.G. Kuhn, op. cit., 25f. See also 4QpPs 37 (No. 171), see DJD V, 43f.

[268] 10,1ff.; 14,2ff.; 15,1ff.; 16,15ff.; 18,6ff.

[269] See Y. Yadin, op. cit., 15f.,194ff., see also Index, 378ff.

[270] See the inscriptions on the standards, 4,12; see also the hymnic address, 11,1.4, similarly 15,12.

[271] 12,1ff.7f.; 14,14; 17,6f. and 13,10, where it is Michael who helps Israel. See also Y. Yadin, op. cit., 209ff.

[272] 1,10; see also Y. Yadin, op. cit., 219. For the typically Essene conception of life in community with the angels, see above, p. 143, n. 346.

[273] 11,1f., the example of David and Goliath; see also 11,5f.

[274] 1,1ff.; 2,10-14; for an interpretation, see Y. Yadin, op. cit., 18ff.

[275] The Kittim of Assyria appear frequently: 1,2.6; 18,2; 19,10. The key is provided by 1 QM 11,11, where Assyria is mentioned in a quotation from Is 31.8 in reference to the Kittim. In addition to this, the Kittim are also mentioned individually: 1,9.11; 16,6.9; 17,12.14; 18,4; 19,13 and the 'King of the Kittim' is mentioned in 15,2. They are presumably identical with Japheth: 1,6; 18,2. They are probably identified with Gog, the great eschatological world power, in 1QM 11,16; see A.S. van der Woude, op. cit., 123. In 11,6 the 'sons of Seth' also appear in connection with a quotation from Num 24.17; see above, p. 239, n. 54 and p. 227.

[276] 1,6; Even their power fails in the end: 16,9 = 17,15.

[277] See Y. Yadin, op. cit., 21ff.; see also J.T. Milik, Ten Years of Discovery, 122f. Milik assumes that the document was written in the first half of the first century A.D.

[278] 1,2: they support the 'Kittim of Assyria'. The concept מרשיעי הברית‎ is probably taken from Dan 11.32; see CD 2,7f.12f. and 1 QpPs 37 (No. 171), III, 7f.12f., see DJD V, 44. A.S. van der Woude, op. cit., assumes that 11,7 (= Num 24.19) also refers to the extermination 'of the community of godless priests which is resident in Jerusalem and is hostile to God'.

[279] See 2,7: למש]פט על כול בשר‎ and 15,13: מלחמה לכול ארצות הגויים‎ and the inscription on one of the standards in 4,2f.: מאת אל יד מלחמה בכול בשר עול‎.

'Israel's rule over all flesh'.[280] The 'Holy War' in this way becomes a step on the way to Israel's rule over the world. In this process, the nations are not independent sovereignties. They belong to the kingdom of darkness and behind them are Belial and his angels.[281] Ultimately, the battle is directed against him. The destruction of his power is accomplished by the complete destruction of all enemies.[282]

The entire course of the struggle is strictly ordered and is placed within a firm apocalyptic framework. One finds oneself in the moment of transition between eschatological tribulation and the dawn of the time of salvation. Two contrasting aspects of the 'Holy War' can therefore be distinguished. It is in the first place a 'time of distress': according to Dan 12.1, a 'time of trouble such as never has been before'.[283] In the one place where losses are mentioned, these are therefore interpreted as a putting to the test and a purification enclosed within the mysteries of God.[284] In contrast to Deut 20.8, then, the 'cowards' are challenged to 'turn back', in the sense of repentance.[285] In accordance with the theme of being put to the test, the war community can also be described as a 'remnant'.[286] This dark and negative aspect of the war is, however, completely eclipsed by the second and very positive aspect, that of being present at the dawn of Israel's redemption.[287]

L. Rost was of the opinion that the charismatic element that was so characteristic of the Holy War in ancient Israel was completely absent from Qumran.[288] This impression, which is conditioned by the

---

[280] 17,7f.

[281] Belial 1,1.13.15; 13,4ff.: the curse pronounced against Belial; his angels: 1,15; 13,11f.; 14,10.

[282] 1,5f.10.16; 3,9, etc.; see Y. Yadin, op. cit., 233: the annihilation of all enemies. 1,15f.; 4,1f.; 13,16; 17,4ff.: the annihilation of Belial.

[283] 1,11f.; see also 15,1 and Y. Yadin, op. cit., 261. See also above, p. 245.

[284] 16,11-17.1. The warriors are בחוני מצרף, 'tested in purification', 17,1.

[285] 10,5f.: לשוב כול מסי לבב. Y. Yadin, op. cit., 62f., assumes, in accordance with Deut 20.8, that they were sent home, but I agree here with J.T. Milik, RB 64 (1957), 589, who follows the context and regards it as an admonition to pluck up courage again. The distinction made by Yadin, op. cit., between 'commanded' war and war by 'free choice' (Sot 8,7, etc.), which means that the laws of Deut 20.5-8 can only apply in the second case, lends support to the assumption that the restrictions of Deut 20.5ff. no longer applied in the case of the eschatological struggle at the end of time.

[286] 14,8f.; cf. Jer 31,7; see Y. Yadin, 342, see also 1QH 6,8.

[287] 1,5: עת ישועה; 4,12ff.: The inscriptions on the standards; 11,7ff.; 12,12ff.; 18,10ff.; 19,8.

[288] op. cit.: '... that the prophetic element that appears from time to time in the Chronicle is completely absent here', p. 205.

eschatological content of the War Scroll, is, however, deceptive. After all, if God himself is to take conrol of the course of events at the end of time and impose a firm order on them, there will be no scope for the human, personal initiative of the individual charismatic, rather the whole of the war community will be subject to divine inspiration. This is clear from the communion that it shares with the angels and the war that it wages with incomparable vigour, fighting with a mathematical precision that cannot be seriously disturbed by any counter-effect. It is all 'worship service' and this is probably why, compared with the priests, the Davidic war Messiah only appears peripherally.[289] It is not his 'kingdom' that is the goal, but the kingdom of God and the people.[290]

The War Scroll, then, forms the climax of the tradition of the Holy War. As an eschatological portrait, it on the one hand contains the Old Testament tradition of war in its full dimension and, on the other, it also has a deep dualistic and metaphysical background. Its remarkable blend of military realism and apocalyptic fantasy is an impressive example of the way in which the strictest and most active religious group in late Judaism presented the co-operation between God, his angels and the army of pious believers in the course of the eschatological events. At the same time, religious hope and real political expectations are also inextricably interwoven in the document. No attention was given to the actual political conditions. The only presupposition was that the holy community was ready at the point of time determined by God to commit itself unconditionally. The fundamental tendency of the War Scroll can therefore be seen — despite its Essene origin — as completely 'Zealot'. The fact that so many copies of this work have been discovered, at least in fragmentary form, is sufficient evidence of the importance that was originally attached to it.'[291]

Finally, we should not fail to take into account the possibility that the ideas contained in the War Scroll and similar warlike documents were made available to wider circles among the Jewish people by men like John the Essene. They would undoubtedly have aroused a very positive echo in the minds of the Zealots.[292]

---

[289] 1QM 5,1f.; see A.S. van der Woude, op. cit., 134f.

[290] 19,8: reading with Y. Yadin:‏[והיתה לאדוני למלו]כה וישראל למלכות ע]ו[למים‏; cf. 17,7f.

[291] Four manuscripts in 4Q; see C.H. Hunzinger, RB 63 (1956), 67, cf. also 54.

[292] For John the Essene, see above, p. 261, n. 160; see also J.T. Milik, Ten Years of Discovery, 123, on the War Scroll: 'We should not be surprised to learn that the leaders of the Jewish resistance movement regarded the War Rule as an excellent work of propaganda'.

3. The Holy War and the Zealots

A fairly obvious conclusion to draw from all this is that the Zealots tried, in a way that was similar to that of the Essenes, to provide their struggle against the Roman oppressors with a religious and eschatological basis by means of the idea of the 'Holy War'. There are certain indications pointing in favour of this assumption.

(a) The Period leading up to the Outbreak of the Jewish War

The 'co-operation with God' that was demanded by Judas the Galilaean as a condition for the realization of eschatological redemption formed an essential aspect of the 'Holy War'. It had to be presupposed everywhere where there was a genuine expectation of the coming of the time of salvation, not simply as a heavenly miracle, but as a real war against the powers of this world that were hostile to God. In calling on his compatriots to break with Rome, Judas took no account at all of the temporal power structures, but was exclusively concerned with the total fulfilment of God's will. For him, the inevitable consequence of this obedience to God's commandment was the conducting of a struggle against the Romans which was determined by religion and which was for him at the same time also the beginning of the eschatological war.

The 'ideal' way of conducting a struggle described in the War Scroll was, of course, diametrically opposed to the small scale war waged by the Zealots, but Judas and his followers could draw on several notable examples in the history of Israel who had waged band warfare. Before he became the charismatic leader of Israel in the war against the Ammonites, Jephtah, for instance, had led a band of 'freebooters'. Again, David had for some time had a similar position of leadership in the 'wars of Yahweh'. The Maccabees had also begun their fight for freedom in a similar way.[293]

The situation before the outbreak of the Jewish War was identified with the pre-messianic time of being put to the test, when Israel was to be purified and the eschatological 'remnant' was to be crystalized out. In a certain sense, it was a sign of success that the Romans had not managed, with their far superior military power, to destroy the Zealots' organization completely, together with the dynasty of Judas that was at the head of that organization.

The Zealots' provisional aim in their struggle was to urge the

---

[293] Judg 11.3; 1 Sam 25.28; see also above, p. 151ff.

majority of the Jewish people to take part in the 'Holy War'. It is probable that they expected the great change to take place from the moment that the people as a whole decided to participate in the war against Rome, since thereafter that war could, with God's help, follow a miraculous course similar to the one predicted in the War Scroll. Judas had tried to win the support of the people, but his attempt failed when the high-priest Joazar b. Boethus, whom the people were more disposed to obey, intervened.

A second attempt to involve the people in the struggle against Rome was made after the murder by Samaritans of a Galilaean pilgrim to Jerusalem.[294] The pilgrims who had assembled for the feast left the city to take revenge on the Samaritans, their underlying aim, however, being the break with Rome.[295] They called on Eleazar b. Dinai to be their leader. He was a 'robber captain' of proven value, known in the rabbinic tradition as a man who wanted to hasten the coming of the kingdom of God, 'forcing it' by human effort.[296]

The Procurator Cumanus created such heavy losses among the rebels, however, that they were more inclined to listen to the urgent requests of the distinguished representatives of the peace party. The Zealots' hope of a general uprising on the part of the people was therefore shattered and they had to continue with their small scale war in the desert. The 'Zealots', of course, regarded those upper class Jews who wanted peace as their most dangerous enemies. They were apostates who stood in the way of God's saving acts.[297]

(b) The Jewish War as a 'Holy War'

The maladministration by the procurators made it impossible for the Jewish upper class to prevent a general uprising among the people, with the result that the Zealots were able to achieve the aim that they had pursued for two generations. What was essential for the continued development was that the revolt should take place successfully and according to expectations. The various bands scattered throughout the country were to go to Jerusalem, join the insurgents who were led by the priests and were in control of the Temple and together liberate the holy city from the pagan oppressors.

---

[294] *Bell* 2,232-246 = *Ant* 20,118-136.

[295] *Ant* 20,130; a leading Jew called Doetos was condemned to death in Caesarea together with four other rebels, because 'they had persuaded the people to break with Rome' (πείσειαν τὸν ὄχλον ἐπὶ τῇ 'Ρωμαίων ἀποστάσει).

[296] See above, p. 124.

[297] *Bell* 7,255; see also 2,264 = *Ant* 20,172. They can be equated with the 'offenders against the covenant'; see above, p. 279, n. 278.

Like Eleazar b. Dinai in the past, Menahem now placed himself at the head of the rebellion, presumably as a messianic leader. His murder by the priestly group, however, sounded the first false note and brought about a division in the movement, the original nucleus, the *Sicarii*, grudgingly withdrawing to Masada.[298] This disturbance appears, however, to have been far outweighed by the ensuing successes. It is clear from the Qumran Commentary on Isaiah, 4 QpIs 10,28ff. (DJDJ V, 12 Fragm 5-6), that the Roman army led by Cestius Gallus approached Jerusalem via Acco-Ptolemais. When it was only a few kilometres from the city — on its march back after its unsuccessful undertaking — it was heavily defeated on the ascent of Beth-Horon, a place made famous by earlier Jewish victories.[299]

The importance of this victory can hardly be overestimated. The badly armed Jews, who were for the most part untried in battle, had put the invincible Roman army to flight after it had dared to attack the holy city. Was this not confirmation of the prophetic promises and the messianic expectations that the army of the enemy would suffer an annihilating defeat in its attempt to conquer Jerusalem?[300]

'Cestius' defeat was also a disaster for our whole nation, since those who loved war were encouraged by it and they also hoped, after having conquered the Romans, for a (victorious) consummation'.[301]

It is very likely that the radical groups regarded this as the prelude to the eschatological battle at the end of time. As in the Maccabaean period, Jews entered the holy city laden with booty and singing songs of praise (μετὰ παιάνων)[302] and immediately afterwards went over to the attack against the pagan neighbours. The goal of this attack was Ascalon, but

---

[298] The war had by then ceased to be a Holy War. See *Bell* 2,447; 4,349,504ff. The *Sicarii* confined themselves to lesser undertakings, in other words, to those that were simply aimed at self-preservation.

[299] *Bell* 2,540-555; see also Josh 10.10f.; 1 Sam 14.31; 1 Macc 3.16,24; 7.39. For the place of the battle, see Oelgarte, 'Die Bethhoronstrasse', *PJ* 14 (1919), 73-89, and F.M. Abel, *Les Livres des Maccabées*, 2nd. ed. 1949, 60. It is about 15 km from Jerusalem. The army consisted of about twenty thousand Roman troops and thirty thousand from dependent states: *Bell* 2,499; see also Mommsen, *RG* 5, 532. The Roman losses amounted to five thousand three hundred infantry and four thousand eight hundred cavalry: *Bell* 2,555. See G.F. Brandon, 'The Defeat of Cestius Gallus', *HT* 20 (1970), 38-46.

[300] See above, p. 276, n. 251.

[301] *Vita* 24: ἐπήρθησαν γὰρ ἐπὶ τούτῳ μᾶλλον οἱ τὸν πόλεμον ἀγαπήσαντες καὶ νικήσαντες τοὺς 'Ρωμαίους εἰς τέλος ἤλπισαν. H.St.J. Thackeray, *Josephus, Loeb Classical Library* 1, 10, n. 2, suggests the reading νικήσειν instead of νικήσαντες.

[302] *Bell* 2,554; sf. Ps 118.24; 2 Chron 20.21; 1 Macc 4.24; 2 Macc 15.29.

the advance, which was carried out with an excess of religious enthusiasm, failed lamentably.[303] In accordance with Old Testament examples, God's judgement was probably seen[304] in this defeat and no more great attacks of a similar kind were made against non-Jewish cities. The only leader of the failed attempt who survived was later executed by the Zealots — possibly to expiate for this defeat which had been brought about, it was believed, by God's anger.[305]

The radicals probably regarded this failure as a divine punishment for the laxity of the moderate party. The defeats in Galilee and Peraea did not lead to any counteractions on the part of the Jews. On the contrary, the rebels in the open country tried to reach the protection of the capital. What was presumably expected from that time onwards — in the light of the apocalyptic tradition — was the final great attack by the enemy. According to the Aboth D'R. Nathan, Vespasian and, following him, R. Johánan b. Zakkai, called on the inhabitants of Jerusalem to spare the city and the Temple and to surrender. They received the same reply:

> 'Just as we marched out against the first two before you (Florus and Cestius) and defeated them, so too shall we march out against you and defeat you'.[306]

In the desperate battle against Titus, the defenders were filled with the constant hope that God's intervention was imminent. As the siege continued and reached a climax on 10 Ab, with the storming of the sanctuary, the extent to which the defenders were able to take part themselves in the 'decisive eschatological battle' was reduced and the importance of God's miraculous act of salvation became ever greater. It was at this stage that the example of the defeat of Sennacherib was above all able to encourage the defenders to hold out.[307]

Several details reported by Josephus about his activities in Galilee show that the war against Rome was officially understood to be a 'Holy War'. He attributes the organization of Galilee as a war province to his own initiative, but there are very good reasons for doubting this. He claims to have summoned a council of seventy men from among the

---

[303] *Bell* 3,9-28.

[304] See Num 14.44f.; Josh 7; 1 Sam 4; 2 Chron 24.23ff.; see also 2 Macc 8.36.

[305] *Bell* 4,359f. They probably wanted to meet the enemy's second attack on Jewish territory; see also Josephus' curious observation, *Vita* 78ff., that attacks against the Romans on non-Jewish territory should be avoided. The first even greater failure would have brought such a change in the expectations of the course of the eschatological war.

[306] AbRN 4, ed. Schechter, 22. Cestius Gallus died shortly after his defeat; see Tacitus, *Hist* 5,10: 'qui ubi fato aut taedio occidit'.

[307] See above, p. 240f.

most noteworthy citizens. This institution however was based on the model of the seventy elders of Israel in the wilderness.[308] A similar institution also seems to have been set up by the Zealots in Jerusalem.[309] The division of the army ban into tens, hundreds and thousands was an ancient tradition of the Holy War and went back to the order of Israel in the wilderness.[310] The ethical and religious exhortation of the troops has its model in Deuteronomy and there are also certain echoes in John the Baptist's sermon to the soldiers in Lk 3.14.[311] Whereas Josephus maintains that he trained the Galilaean recruits in the manner of Roman soldiers, this factor can also be found a hundred years before Josephus in the War Scroll. It is probable that these measures were taken by the people's assembly or Synhedrium in Jerusalem, which had already made the necessary arrangements for the 'Holy War' for the whole of Jewish territory.[312] Two notably religious decrees seem also to stem from these measures. In the first place, Josephus had to 'purify' the palace in Tiberias by removing the offensive animal images.[313] In the second place, a legation, which arrived later from Jerusalem, had a general fast proclaimed, linked to a public assembly:

'so that they would bear witness in God's presence to their belief that all weapons would be useless without his help'.[314]

4. Summary

The Old Testament tradition of the 'Holy War' was resumed in the Maccabaean period and given a new eschatological emphasis in the apocalyptic writings. It is therefore not unreasonable to assume that the Zealot movement also developed its own distinctive tradition of holy

---

[308] *Bell* 2,570 (cf., on the other hand, *Vita* 79); see also Ex 24.1; Num 11.16 and Lk 10.1,17.

[309] *Bell* 4,336: The appointment of seventy elders by the Zealots may perhaps indicate a biblicistic correction of the traditonal number seventy-one (seventy-two) members of the Synhedrium handed down by the rabbinate: Sanh 1,6; see Schürer, 2, 249ff. and K.H. Rengstorf, 'ἑπτά', *TD* 2, 634f.

[310] *Bell* 2,578; cf. Ex 18.25.

[311] *Bell* 2,581f.; cf. Deut 20.1ff.; see also above p. 271, n. 218.

[312] Josephus mentions two bodies as authorities: the peoples' assembly, which had been called together in the Temple after the victory over Cestius: *Bell* 2,562, see also *Vita* 65, and the Synhedrium: *Vita* 62.

[313] See above, p. 191f. See also Zech 13.2.

[314] *Vita* 290; for the legation, see 197ff. It is true that Josephus presents Ananias' proclamation as an attack against his person, but his whole presentation of the affair is hardly reliable. For fasting as a preparation for the 'Holy War', see above, p. 272, n. 226.

eschatological war. Even though this tradition cannot be grasped with the same degree of clarity as the corresponding expectations of the Essenes as reported in the War Scroll of Qumran, it should be sufficiently obvious that the struggle conducted against the Romans was conceived in eschatological terms and that it was hoped that an uprising on the part of the whole people would lead, with God's help, to the definitive annihilation of the opponent and the establishment of the messianic kingdom. It is possible to distinguish three different stages of this 'Holy War':

(1) The preparatory stage of small scale war in the desert, which was presumably seen as a time of being put to the test and purification.

(2) The uprising of the whole people of Israel in the struggle against Rome roundabout the year 66 A. D. Because of the initial successes, this period was regarded as the prelude to the ultimate eschatological war of annihilation waged against the Roman Empire.

(3) The passive period, which was introduced by the first setbacks and during which the Jews were subjected to increasing pressure by their opponent and expected the great change to come less as a result of their own success with weapons and more as a result of God's miraculous intervention.

Excursus IV: The Observance of the Sabbath and the Holy War

One criterion applied in Judaism in judging the religious significance of an action was whether it took precedence over the command to keep the sabbath.[315] The evaluation of war could also be considered from this point of view. It would seem at first sight that it was fundamentally impossible for war to be waged on the sabbath and it is valuable to consider a few examples in this context. Ptolemy I, son of Lagus, is reputed to have conquered Jerusalem on a sabbath because the Jews were not permitted to carry arms on that day.[316] At the beginning of the Seleucid period of religious distress, pious Jews would rather be killed than defend themselves on the sabbath. The 'Holy War' waged by the Maccabees restricted the sabbath commandment to such a degree that at least self-defence was permitted,[317] even though it was still forbidden actively to wage war. Judas' army, for

---

[315] See Bill. 1, 620: 'All commandments to perform duties at a particular time take precedence over the sabbath, if it falls on that time'. Service in the Temple, circumcision and the saving of human life came within this category.

[316] 301 (?) B.C., *Ant* 12,4ff. and *Ap* 1,209f.; according to Agatharchides of Knidos.

[317] 1 Macc 2,30-41; 2 Macc 6,11; see also L. Finkelstein, *The Pharisees*, 3rd. ed. 1962, 1, 156f.: The decision to defend oneself on the sabbath was a 'moral revolution'. It was in accordance with the later rabbinic view that human life took precedence over the sanctity of the sabbath; see Bill. 1, 623ff., and Moore, *Judaism*, 1, 156f. See also Josephus' justification, *Ant* 12,276f.

example, ceased to pursue the defeated enemy on the eve of the sabbath and did not share out the booty until the day after the sabbath.[318] John Hyrcanus had to abandon laying siege to his father's murderer, who was at the same time holding his mother and brothers, because a sabbath year was imminent.[319]

Returning from his victory over the Parthians, Antiochus VII Sidetes was forced to arrange a halt in the march on the sabbath out of respect for his Jewish auxiliary troops.[320] The inactivity of the Jews on the sabbath during Pompey's siege of the Temple was disastrous for them, since the Roman leader was able to continue undisturbed with the erection of his siege-works on that day and, on a subsequent sabbath, he stormed the Temple.[321] After having previously conquered the Temple itself, Sossius also apparently conquered the upper city on a sabbath.[322]

Following the Hasidic tradition, the Essenes seem to have fundamentally rejected the practice of waging war on the sabbath. The following commandment is contained, for example, in the Book of Jubilees:

'... and anyone who strikes someone and kills him ... and also whoever fasts and wages *war* on the sabbath: let the person who does anything of this kind on the sabbath day die ...'[323]

It is also explicitly forbidden in the War Scroll to wage war during the sabbath years.[324]

In striking contrast to this, the Zealots commanded the active waging of war on the sabbath. So, for example, they massacred the Roman occupation troops of the Herodium, who had surrendered against the promise of safe conduct, on a sabbath.[325] They also made a successful surprise attack against

---

[318] 2 Macc 8.25ff. The Second Book of the Maccabees appears as a whole to keep more closely to the earlier — Hasidic — tradition concerning the complete sabbath rest. It omits Judas Maccabaeus' statement about self-defence on the sabbath and makes Nicanor express the intention to attack the Jews on a sabbath so that he will defeat them easily: 2 Macc 15.1-6. The Jews who formed part of his army, however, were energetic in their opposition to this.

[319] *Ant* 13,234ff. = *Bell* 1,60.

[320] *Ant* 13,252 (130 B.C.). The halt lasted for two days, since it occurred at the time of the sabbath and the Feast of Weeks.

[321] *Ant* 14,63f. and *Bell* 2,392; see also the detailed descriptions provided by Dio Cassius, 37,164ff. (Reinach, 180f.) and Strabo, 16,2.40 (763). According to Strabo, the conquest took place on a 'day of fasting' (see also Suetonius, *Aug* 76), in other words, on the sabbath. Josephus took this wrong description uncritically from his source: *Ant* 14,66; see Reinach, 104, n. 1; Schürer, 1, 293, n. 23.

[322] Dio Cassius, 69,22.3-6; see Reinach, 186. Here too, Josephus follows Strabo and speaks of a day of fasting: 14,487.

[323] Jub 50,12f., translation based on E. Littmann, in Kautzsch, *Apokryphen und Pseudepigraphen*, 2, 119. The Covenant of Damascus, CD 10,18 (cf. 12,6) forbids the shedding of blood on the sabbath in order to protect one's own property (probably from robbers); see also tErub 4,5 (l. 142).

[324] 1QM 2,8f.

[325] *Bell* 2,456.

the army of Cestius Gallus outside Jerusalem on a sabbath that, moreover, fell during the week of the Feast of Tabernacles:

'But the Jews, when they saw that the war was already approaching the capital, left the Feast, hastened to take up arms and threw themselves courageously, in great numbers, in confusion and with loud shouts into the battle, with no scruples about the seventh day that had been dedicated to rest. In their case, the sabbath was kept holy in a special way. Zeal, however, had thrust their pious attitude into the background and enabled them to gain the upper hand in the battle'.[326]

Although Josephus explicitly points out here that, in other circumstances, the insurgents strictly observed the sabbath, in this case they did not wait — in the Maccabaean tradition — for the enemy to attack, but themelves made a surprise attack against their opponent. Simon b. Giora at the same time seized the enemy's baggage-train and took it into the city.[327] This attitude is also confirmed by the Tosefta:

'When the Goyim march against the cities of Israel, it is permitted to go out armed against them; because of them, it is permitted to profane the sabbath'.[328]

This Halakhah does not seem, however, to have been universally recognized. One of the main arguments of the peace party was that the war against Rome made it impossible to keep the sabbath holy. Josephus therefore made Agrippa II emphasize this point in his peace speech:

'How could you call on God for help when you deliberately neglect the honour that is due to him (that is, keeping the sabbath holy)?'[329]

This was probably a controversial point. H. Graetz has drawn attention to the fact that Shammai and his disciples, who were particularly rigorous in keeping the sabbath commandment,[330] were much more liberal in their attitude towards waging war on the sabbath. A Baraita, in which the beginning of the siege of a non-Jewish city was given the latest date of three days before the sabbath, fundamentally excluded any possible interruption in the siege: 'Thus said Shammai the Elder: "until it falls" (Deut 20.20), even on the sabbath'.[331]

---

[326] *Bell* 2,515.517f.

[327] *Bell* 2,521. See, on the other hand, 2 Macc 8.28. Like the rebels, the Jewish robbers in Mesopotamia, according to *Ant 18,319, struck at the Persian satrap, who wanted to attack them on the sabbath, surprising him by a counter-attack.*

[328] tErub 4,5 (Z. 142); see Bill. 1, 626f. The casuistic restrictions that are joined to this statement are later additions.

[329] *Bell* 2,392ff. (394). Even during the war, there does not seem to have been a totally unified attitude. According to *Vita* 159 = *Bell* 2,634, Josephus sent his soldiers home for the sabbath and was therefore not able to take any action against the rebellion of Tiberias.

[330] 3, 798f.; for the Shammaites' rigorous observation of the sabbath, see tShab 16,21ff. (Z. 136), and bShab 12a; see also Bill. 1, 630.

[331] Shab 19a bar: וכן היה שמאי הזקן אומר עד רדתה אפילו בשבת; see also jShab 4a,72ff./5b: Jericho is supposed to have been conquered on a sabbath. In the parallel text, tErub 4,8 (Z. 142), this statement is attributed to Hillel, but certain important texts (the

Graetz was right to describe this contrast between a rigorous intensification of the sabbath commandment and permitting armed attacks on the sabbath as an aspect of 'political Zealotism'.[332] It is also certainly not by chance that Eliezer b. Hyrcanus, who had once been a Shammaite, was opposed to the explicit prohibition of other teachers and regarded it as permissible for weapons to be carried on the sabbath, 'since these are for him ornamental objects'.

According to the Gemara of the Babylonian Talmud, he also went counter to Is 2.4 and believed that weapons would continue to exist in the messianic kingdom.[333]

Despite the positive evidence quoted above, the waging of offensive war on the sabbath, already clearly regarded as unacceptable by Josephus, continued to be rejected in the rabbinate. This rejection in fact even became more emphatic:

'R. Judah said in the name of Rab: If non-Jews lay siege to Israelite towns, one must not go out in arms against them and the sabbath must not be profaned because of them'.[334]

It is possible to detect a certain aversion to the Zealot point of view in the rabbinate in this judgement of the opposition between the 'Holy War' and the sabbath commandment.

F. Zealot Messianic Pretenders

1. The Presuppositions

Attempts, for the most part based on the proclamation of the sole rule of God made by Judas the Galilaean and his successors, have from time to time been made to deny that the Jewish freedom movement of the first century A.D. had any messianic features.[335] The 'Zealots' can, however, hardly be regarded as anarchists who rejected all political authority,[336]

Vienna manuscript = ב and the first edition of the Venice manuscript of 1521 = ד) read 'Shammai' here. The change can be explained on the basis of the evidence that alleviations were as a rule ascribed to Hillel.

[332] 3,799. For the relationship between the school of Shammai and Zealotism, see above, p. 202f.

[333] Shab 6,4; cf. bShab 63a. See also J. Klausner, *The Messianic Idea*, 502f., n. 3f.

[334] Erub 45a; translation based on Goldschmidt, 2, 135. Rab lived at the beginning of the third century A.D. The severity of the statement was reduced by the principle that permitted saving from mortal danger on the sabbath; see jShab 21d,56ff./22a. For this problem, see M.D. Herr, *Tarb.* 30 (1960/1), 242–56; A.F. Johns, *VT* 13 (1963), 482–486.

[335] *Beginnings*, 1, 423f.: 'There is no reason for connecting the Zealots or even the *Sicarii* with any messianic movement'. See also S. Zeitlin, *Who Crucified Jesus*, 1947, 96ff., and — although in a different context — J. Wellhausen, *Die Pharisäer und die Sadducäer*, 1874, 23: 'The behaviour of the Zealots is strictly speaking a factual negation of the messianic hope'.

[336] This is the view of M.J. Lagrange, *Le Judaïsme avant Jésus Christ*, 3rd. ed. 1931, 214.

since their ideal of theocracy was directed against the pagan foreign rule, while it was perfectly possible for a leader figure authorized by God to be active and effective within their own people. On the one hand, there were very many Old Testament models and promises to support this view and, on the other, the party of the Zealots itself probably always had such a leader or such leaders since the time that it was founded by Judas.[337] It is important to look at individual cases to see whether messianic claims were made by any of these leaders. Before doing this, however, three essential points have to be presupposed:

(1) The fact that the rabbinic sources have nothing to say about the messianic expectations of the Jews before the destruction of Jerusalem should not be taken as evidence that no such expectations existed.[338] On the contrary, this silence can be traced back to an elimination of the earlier messianic tradition at a later period. It is possible that the warlike and political image of the Messiah of that time was no longer acceptable to those handing down the tradition in the second and third centuries A.D. There is evidence of the presence of a strong messianic hope in Pharisaical circles in the Psalms of Solomon, Josephus,[339] the New Testament and the Jewish prayers of the period. It is very likely that the subjection of the Jews by the Romans and the subsequent rule of Herod led to an intensification of the expectation of a political Messiah.

(2) This expectation seems to have been concentrated above all on the ruler from the house of David who could also appear as leader in the eschatological war.

(3) The transition between a prophetic and charismatic self-consciousness and 'messianic claims' was fluid. A leader figure might appear first of all as a prophet and then establish his messianic authority by his actions.

2. Messianic Pretenders in the Jewish Freedom Movement

(a) From the Bandit Leader Hezekiah to Judas the Galilaean

Messianic claims have been ascribed by some to the 'robber captain'

---

[337] The following appeared as such leaders: Judas, the founder of the party (*Ant* 18,23); Eleazar b. Dinai (*Bell* 2,235 = *Ant* 20,121); Menahem (*Bell* 2,434). A considerable number of leaders who were in conflict with each other appeared after the division in the movement; see below, p. 370ff.

[338] See J. Klausner, *The Messianic Idea*, 393ff., who however gives too little attention to the messianic expectation in Pharisaical circles before 70 A.D.

[339] *Ant* 17,43-45; *Ant* 10,210.276; *Bell* 6,312f. Josephus was very familiar with the messianic expectation of his own people. Because his intention was apologetic, however, he rendered it in an extremely distorted form.

Hezekiah, whom the young Herod had executed in Galilee. The apparent rabbinic evidence that is usually brought to the fore in support of this hypothesis can, however, hardly substantiate it.[340]

Messianic ambitions can, however, be assumed with a greater degree of probability in the case of two bandit leaders who appeared during the disturbances that followed Herod's death. Both these men — the slave Simon and the shepherd Athronges — placed the diadem on their own heads and in this way revealed their claims to royalty.[341] Both men were also distinguished by their outstanding bodily strength, a characteristic that was given a messianic significance here in imitation of the Old Testament conceptions of the 'gibbor' as the strong leader in the 'Holy War'.[342] In the case of Athronges, the name itself may possibly be interpreted in a messianic sense[343] and the man originally had the same occupation as the young David.

---

[340] *Bell* 1,204 = *Ant* 14,159. A messianic interpretation of Hezekiah was provided by A. Geiger, *JZWL* 8 (1870), 37f., and later by H. Gressmann, *Der Messias*, 1929, 458f., and especially R. Meyer, *Der Prophet aus Galiläa*, 1940, 73ff. See also A. von Gall, βασιλεία τοῦ θεοῦ, 1926, 375, and R. Eisler, 2, 683, n. 5. According to a tradition dating back to the third century A.D., R. Johanan b. Zakkai is reputed to have said just before he died: 'Clear the court and place a throne in readiness for Hezekiah, the King of Judah!': jSot 24c,29f.; see Bill. 1,30; Volz, *Esch*, 206f. Johanan b. Zakkai, however, can hardly be taken seriously into consideration as a leading witness for the messianic claims of a leader of a band. In the debate that took place relatively late in the third and fourth centuries A.D., what was exclusively discussed was the question as to whether the Old Testament King Hezekiah could be the Messiah; see Bill. 1, 31.75; A. von Gall, *op. cit.*, 397, and M. Zobel, *Gottes Gesalbter*, 1938, 87-90. The idea of Hezekiah as the Messiah can be most satisfactorily explained in the light of 2 Kings 18.5 and the application of the messianic texts from the psalms and Isaiah to Hezekiah that was favoured as an antithesis to Christian teaching; see Justin, *DialTryph* 33,1; 43,8; 67,1, etc. See also M. Zobel, *op. cit.*, 88, and A. von Gall, *op. cit.*, 397, n. 3.

[341] *Bell* 2,57f. = *Ant* 17,273ff.; *Bell* 2,60ff. = *Ant* 17,278ff. Simon is also mentioned by Tacitus, *Hist* 5,9: 'post mortem Herodis . . . Simon quidam regium nomen invaserat'. See also W.R. Farmer, 'Judas, Simon and Athronges', *NTS* 4 (1957/58), 147-155, whose thesis of a Hasmonaean descent, however, is hardly tenable.

[342] See Judg 6.12: Gideon; 1 Sam 16.18: the young David. The concept can be interpreted messianically in Is 9.5; Ps 45.4 and especially Ps 89.19: 'I have set the diadem (reading נֵזֶר) on one who is mighty; I have exalted one chosen from the people'. The text refers to David. For the 'gibbor' in the Holy War at the end of time, see Zech 9.13 and 10.7 on the one hand and 1QM 12,9-11 and 1QH 6,30 on the other. See also Mk 1.7 and Lk 11.23: the 'mightier' one overcomes the 'mighty' one. Simon bar Giora (*Bell* 4,504) and Bar Koseba (jTaan 68d,57ff.; LamRab on 2.2,4; see Bill. 1, 13) were also distinguished by their exceptional physical strength. For the messianic 'gibbor', see also E. Stauffer, *Jerusalem und Rom*, 1957, 91.

[343] According to A. Schlatter, *Die hebräischen Namen bei Josephus (BFChTh* 17), 1913, 115, the name does not occur elsewhere, and probably has as its Hebrew equivalent, אֶתְרוֹנְגָּא, which would seem to point to the אֶתְרוֹג, the citrus fruit that played an

It is not unlikely that Judas the Galilaean emerged with messianic claims. Josephus reports in his *Antiquities* that one Judas, the son of the bandit leader Hezekiah, was already striving to obtain 'royal honour' during the above-mentioned disturbances that occurred after the death of Herod. However, the earlier parallel account in his *Jewish War* is not at all clear about this point,[344] and we must assume that this Judas is the same as Judas the Galilaean (see below p. 331).

All that the account of the founding of the 'fourth philosophy' tells us is that Judas became the leader of this new movement.[345] It has nothing to say about any further ambition that this man may have had. The obvious conclusion to be drawn from Gamaliel's speech as reported in Acts 5.36f., in which the unmistakably messianic early Christian community is equated with the movements originating with Theudas and Judas, is that both these last named groups also had messianic characteristics. What is certainly true is that no clear dividing line can be drawn here between prophetic and enthusiastic proclamation on the one hand and messianic claims on the other. What is more, the fact that a dynasty of bandit leaders originated with Judas and that messianic claims became visible in at least one of those leaders, Menahem, enables us to assume that the so-called 'fourth philosophy' had a messianic basis already with its founder Judas.[346]

(b) Menahem as a Zealot Messiah

In the case of Menahem, Judas' son (or grandson), these messianic claims emerge much more clearly. He introduced the uprising against Rome by taking Masada. He then marched with his retinue of armed followers

'like a king up to Jerusalem, became the leader of the uprising and assumed command of the siege (of Herod's palace)'.[347]

---

important part in the Feast of Tabernacles (see *Ant* 13,372). This *ethrogh* also appears frequently on coins; see A. Reifenberg, *Jewish Coins*, 39 Nos. 4,5 (the Bar Giora bronze shekel, 69 A.D.). For this, see also R. Eisler, 2, 86.

[344] See *Ant* 17,271f. and *Bell* 2,56; see also below, p. 326f. E. Stauffer, *Die Botschaft Jesu damals und heute*, 1959, 112, places Judas the Galilaean parallel with Bar Koseba: 'They regarded themselves . . . as the messianic rulers of a theocratic world kingdom which was to be erected on the ruins of the Roman Empire'.

[345] *Ant* 18,23: ἡγεμών; see also above, p. 84.

[346] According to Origen, *Hom XXV in Luc*, *GCS* 49 (35), ed. Rauer, 150,19ff., Judas the Galilaean was regarded by many people as the Messiah; see A. Strobel, *Kerygma und Apokalyptik*, 1967, 102, n. 3.

[347] *Bell* 2,434: οἷα δὴ βασιλεὺς ἐπάνεισιν εἰς Ἱεροσόλυμα καὶ γενόμενος ἡγεμὼν τῆς στάσεως διέτασσεν τὴν πολιορκίαν.

It is worth looking more closely at the unquestioning way in which Menahem placed himself at the head of the rebels. His ambition to command emerged more and more clearly as time passed and aroused envy among the members of the priestly circle gathered around Eleazar b. Ananias. According to Josephus, he became an 'unbearable tyrant'.[348] He visited the Temple 'adorned with royal clothing and followed by armed Zealots' and was attacked there by Eleazar's followers and, after attempting in vain to flee, was killed.[349]

The murder of a false messianic pretender — by rabbis — is also reported in the Babylonian Talmud.[350] Since Josephus has almost nothing at all to say about the messianic hope of his people,[351] little more can be expected of him regarding a description of any messianic pretenders than a statement about their ambition to achieve royal dignity.

This ambition was present in a very clear way in the case of Menahem. It is important to take into account the situation at the time: the agitation among the people, the enthusiasm about the first successes and the triumph of the Zealots, who believed that they were close to achieving their aims after fighting for sixty years. With this in mind, the conclusion suggests itself that Menahem, scion of the ancient family of freedom fighters, was regarded as the Messiah who was to come, at least within the circle of the Zealots themselves.[352]

The enmity of the priestly group that came about so suddenly can be explained in the following way. The insurgents had originally thought of a dual rule by Menahem as the Messiah from Israel and Eleazar b. Ananias as the priestly Messiah. This dual rule had been in the minds of the Essenes as an eschatological ideal. According to the inscriptions on coins struck at the beginning of the revolt of Bar Koseba, it was also the aim of the revolt, although Bar Koseba quickly seized power for himself as the secular 'prince of Israel'.[353]

---

[348] *Bell* 2,442.

[349] *Bell* 2,444.

[350] According to Sanh 93b, Bar Koseba is reputed to have been killed by the rabbis without a proper trial, since he was not gifted with the special discernment for judgement according to Is 11.3; see M. Zobel, *Gottes Gesalbter*, 1938, 77. It is possible that the recollection of the murder of a messianic pretender was wrongly transferred here to Bar Koseba. See also below, n. 353.

[351] See above, p. 15, n. 65; p. 238f., nn. 50 and 52.

[352] See H. Graetz, 3, 461; A. Schlatter, *GI*, 327, and *The Church in the New Testament Period*, 1955, 269; Klausner, *Hist* 5, 147f.

[353] The possibility of opposition between the the Davidic ruler and the high-priest is indicated in Zechariah (3.8; 4.11ff.; 6.12f.). In Sir 45.31ff., the two powers are

A similar development had clearly been initiated under Menahem, until the priestly group put an end to his struggle for power by their treacherous attack and thus brought about the division in the Zealot movement. Although his temporary stay as a leader in Jerusalem lasted barely four weeks,[354] he seems to have left 'a deep impression'[355] behind on his contemporaries. A Menahem is even named as Messiah in the rabbinic Haggadah:[356]

> 'After that, an Arab informed a Jewish peasant in the field about the destruction of the Temple and at the same time about the birth of the Messiah in Bethlehem. The name of the same was Menahem; his father was called Hezekiah. The peasant, disguised as a merchant, visited the mother of the infant Messiah and heard from her: "His omen is disastrous, because the Temple was destroyed on the day that he was born". He answered her: "We believe that, just as it (the Temple) was destroyed because of him, so too will it be rebuilt because of him".
>
> At a second visit, the mother informed him that the child had been abducted: "Winds and storms came and tore him out of my hands".'

A. Geiger[357] saw in this legend a reference to the Zealot Messiah Menahem (b. Judah) b. Hezekiah and, following H. Gressmann,[358] R. Meyer has provided a plausible explanation. He suggests that underlying this story was an earlier account of the birth of the infant Messiah which

---

juxtaposed. The priest-Messiah had clear precedence in the Essene community. According to 4QpIs (No. 161) Fragm 8-10, 22ff., see DJD V, 14 on Is 11.3, the Messiah was obliged to follow the teaching of the priests. He was also appointed to his office by them. For the Bar Koseba coins, see A. Reifenberg, *Jewish Coins*, 61ff. Nos. 170,189,196,203. In the first and second year of the revolt, we find coins with the sole inscription אלעזר הכהן and, in addition to these, others with the name שמעון on the reverse and finally coins which only have the inscription שמעון נשיא ישראל. From the second or third year of the revolt, only the name of Simeon appears; see also Schürer, 1, 606. These different coinages point to power struggles among the rebels; see also above, p. 116, n. 215.

[354] After the taking of the Fortress of Antonia (on 15 Ab), he came to Jerusalem and was murdered during the period between the conquest of Herod's palace (on 15 Elul) and the capitulation of the cohorts (on 17 Elul, according to MegTaan 14): *Bell* 2,430.433ff.440.448ff.

[355] H. Gressmann, *Der Messias*, 1929, 460.

[356] LamRab on 1.16 = jBer 5a,12ff. See G. Dalman, *Aramäische Dialektproben*, 2nd. ed. 1927, 14f.; Bill. 1, 83; H. Gressmann, *op. cit.*, 449ff.; M. Zobel, *op. cit.*, 135f.; R. Meyer, *Der Prophet aus Galiläa*, 1940, 76f. See also the synchronism between the birth of Alexander and the burning down of the temple of Artemis in Ephesus, Plutarch, *Alex* 3; Cicero, *Div* 1,47; *Nat* 2,69.

[357] *JZWL* 8 (1870), 39; see also H. Graetz, 3, 461, n. 3.

[358] *op. cit.*, 77f.; see H. Gressmann, *ZKG* NS 3 (1922), 189, and *Der Messias*, 1929, 460ff.; see also J. Jeremias, *DTh* 2 (1929), 116f., and *Jerusalem in the Time of Jesus*, 3rd. ed. 1969, 277; R. Eisler, 2, 712, n. 1; C. Roth, *The Historical Background of the Dead Sea Scrolls*, 1958, 17, n. 2.

may possibly go back to the expectation of the Messiah at the time of the destruction of the Temple. After the catastrophe, Meyer believes, this disappointed expectation was changed in such a way that the Messiah was reputed to have come on the day of great misfortune, but only as a little and unknown child, whom God translated again until the day that he would come to rule. This original form was, according to Meyer, adapted by identifying the infant Messiah with a historical figure, that of Menahem (b. Judah) b. Hezekiah.[359]

What is of essential importance in the story is the statement that the Temple was destroyed because of Menahem. We may assume that his followers regarded the murder of their leader in the Temple as such a momentous deed that it could only be expiated by the destruction of the sanctuary.[360] It is also possible that the murder of Menahem was also interpreted by them as a translation.[361]

The objection could be raised against Meyer's attempt to explain this legend that Menahem also appears elsewhere in the rabbinic tradition as the name of a Messiah and that this name can also be traced back, at least to some extent, to Lam 1.16: 'For a comforter ('Menahem') is far from me, one to revive my courage'.[362] or that it can be explained as a re-interpretation of צֶמַח, which has the same numerical value.[363] This symbolical interpretation, however, leaves the question of the origin of his surname, Hezekiah, and the destruction of the Temple 'because of him' open. It is therefore preferable to assume that the various attempts made to interpret the story in the light of biblical texts and by using gematria present us with secondary explanations for a name, the historical origin of which was no longer known.

The name Menahem also appears in another place in an unusual context. There is reference in the Gemara of the Babylonian and the Jerusalem Talmud on Hagigah 2,2 to a teacher Menahem who left the circle of teachers and entered 'royal service' or became an apostate. He was followed by eighty pairs of disciples, who were dressed, according

---

[359] According to NumRab 13,5, the Messiah was born on the day when the Temple was destroyed. See M. Zobel, *op. cit.*, 139; see also the variants of the legend of Menahem mentioned on p. 131ff.

[360] See A. Schlatter, *GI*, 327 and *The Church in the N.T. Period*, 269: 'Because of the guilt which Jerusalem had incurred through the killing of Menahem, a guilt which could not be expiated, his followers put an end to their community with their own people'.

[361] A. Schlatter, *op. cit.*: 'Menahem's followers said of him: "The storm wind has carried him off"'.

[362] Sanh 98b and LamRab on 1.16; see Bill. 1, 66 and 67, and M. Zobel, *op. cit.*, 93f.

[363] jBer 5a,13f.; see Bill. *op. cit.*, and M. Zobel, *op. cit.*, 94f.

to the Babylonian Talmud, in 'silken garments' and, according to the Jerusalem Talmud, in 'golden armour'.[364] A. Geiger applied this Baraita to the Messiah Menahem[365] and he was followed by H. Gressmann, J. Klausner and C. Roth.[366]

(c) Simon bar Giora

Simon bar Giora, who first appeared during the Jewish War,[367] also made claims to messianic dignity. Like Simon the Peraean and Athronges the shepherd, he was also distinguished by exceptional physical strength and daring. Over a period of time, he gathered a large number of followers around him in the open country:

'His army did not consist simply of slaves and robbers. A number of upstanding citizens also obeyed him like a king'.[368]

He was ultimately called to Jerusalem by the opponents of John of Gischala, who wanted him to liberate them from the latter's rule:

'After he had haughtily consented to rule over them, he marched into the city as the liberator from the Zealots and was greeted by the people as their saviour and protector. After he had entered the city with his armed force, however, he (only) thought of strengthening his personal power'.[369]

It is quite possible that the bronze shekels with the inscription 'Year 4' and 'for the redemption of Zion' were struck by Bar Giora and that he felt that he was the bringer of that redemption.[370]

Finally, the remarkable account of his capture must be mentioned. After failing in an attempt to escape through a subterranean passage, he appeared again on the Temple square in white garments, over which he had thrown a purple cloak. According to Josephus, he did this with the aim of striking terror into the hearts of the Temple guards. He may have attributed a celestial effectiveness to his princely robes. He may perhaps also only have wanted to surrender to the Roman military commander displaying the signs of his dignity, since he refused to speak to the guards

---

[364] See Hag 16b and jHag 77d,29ff.; see also Bill. 2, 710f.

[365] *JZWL* 7 (1869), 176ff.

[366] H. Gressmann, *Der Messias*, 1929, 459f.; Klausner, *Hist* 5, 148; C. Roth, *op. cit.* Klausner interpreted the יצא לעבודת המלך of the Babylonian Talmud in the sense of יצא להיות מלך. C. Roth believes that a new interpretation of סיריקון = 'silk' was derived from סיקרין = *Sicarius*. See S. Lieberman, *Greek in Jewish Palestine*, 2nd. ed. 1965, 180f.

[367] For his origin and activity, see below, p. 374, n. 305.

[368] *Bell* 4,510.

[369] *Bell* 4,573ff.;575: σωτὴρ ὑπὸ τοῦ δήμου καὶ κηδεμὼν εὐφημούμενος.

[370] B. Kanael, *BASOR* 129 (1953), 18ff.; for this, see above, p. 117.

and had him called.[371] It is clear that the Romans regarded him and not John of Gischala — who had been in power in Jerusalem for a much longer period of time — as holding an office of higher dignity because, following the triumph of Vespasian and Titus, he was killed in the prison by the Forum, whereas John's punishment was simply life imprisonment.[372] In the light of all these circumstances, Simon can also be considered as a messianic pretender.

3. The Son of David

It is, understandably enough, not possible to learn from Josephus whether the Zealot messianic pretenders also claimed that they were descended from David. According to the rabbinic legend, the Messiah Menahem was born in Bethlehem and identified with the Davidic 'offspring' of the Old Testament, but it is hardly possible to draw any conclusions from this regarding the descent of the historical Menahem. The connection with David was created by the rabbinic tradition. There are, however, several reasons in favour of the thesis that descent from David was at least to some extent claimed by the Zealot messianic pretenders. The four most important reasons can be briefly reviewed here:

(1) In the earlier tradition, Davidic descent was attributed to the war Messiah. It was not until the middle of the second century A.D. that there was a division in the tradition and a 'Messiah b. Joseph' or 'Ephraim' was expected purely as a war hero[373] who would die in

---

[371] *Bell* 7,26-31; for purple and white garments as royal garments, see Mk 15.17ff.; Lk 23.11 and Rev 19.13ff. See also J. Blinzler, *The Trial of Jesus*, 1959, 199,226f. and R. Delbrück's detailed study in *ZNW* 41 (1942), 138ff. I am indebted to Professor J. Jeremias of Göttingen University for pointing this out to me.

[372] *Bell* 6,434 and 7,154f. See also G. Ricciotti, *Flavio Giuseppe*, 3, 327, for 7,154.

[373] For this, see G. Dalman, *Der leidende und der sterbende Messias der Synagoge im ersten nachchristlichen Jahrtausend*, 1888, 1-26; Moore, *Judaism*, 2, 370f.; J. Klausner, *The Messianic Idea in Israel*, translated by W.F. Stinespring, 1955, 401-404 and 483-501; J. Jeremias, 'παῖς θεοῦ', *ThWAT* 5, 685, n. 243, who also provides a concise survey of the recent books and articles published on this subject. Bill. 2, 292-299, and M. Zobel, *op. cit.*, 51ff., provide a very representative selection of the most important rabbinic texts in translation. For the period when this view originated, see J. Klausner, *op. cit.*, 489ff., and Bill. 2, 294. J. Jeremias, *op. cit.*, refers to the Armenian version of the Testament of Benjamin, 3,8, and assumes that there was already a prechristian expectation of a Messiah b. Joseph. In that expectation, however, the people hoped only for a representative expiatory suffering on the part of Joseph. It was, in other words, not a real messianic

battle,[374] after which the real Davidic anointed one would appear. This later development of the messianic hope presumably represents a correction of the earlier views resulting from historical experience. Whereas the eschatological victory over Israel's enemies had until then been expected to come from the 'Son of David' himself, he was at this later stage set free from all warlike obligations and these were transferred to a precursor, who shared the fate of previous messianic pretenders — death at the hands of the enemy.[375]

(2) The importance that is attached in the various New Testament writings to Jesus' descent from David enables us to draw certain conclusions regarding the messianic expectations that were current during the first century A.D. as a whole.[376] A war Messiah who could not in one way or another claim to be descended from David was almost inconceivable.[377]

(3) According to Hegesippus, Vespasian, following the conquest of Jerusalem, is reputed to have ordered all those of David's lineage to be sought out:

---

expectation. In the rabbinic sources, the dying warrior hero and Messiah b. Joseph acquired a certain importance only after the failure of the revolt of Bar Koseba.

[374] In the later Midrashim, the Messiah b. Joseph could directly assume the title, the one 'anointed for war'; see G. Dalman, op. cit., 6f., and Bill. 2, 292. He fell in the battle against Gog; see LekTob Num 24.17; Bill. 2, 298. According to the Jerusalem Targum I on Ex 40.9ff., he was victorious in the battle against Gog; see Bill. 2, 298. The earliest tradition of his death appears in Sukk 52a bar, in the words of R. Dosa (end of the second century A.D.; Strack, Introduction, 116). The Jewish warrior Messiah in Hippolytus (see above, p. 277, n. 255) fell in battle.

[375] J. Klausner, op. cit., 400f.: 'Now after the disaster it became necessary to emphasize the spiritual side of the Messiah. Moreover, the dreadful calamities through which the nation had passed as a result of the work of the slain Messiah (that is, Bar Koseba) cast their gloomy shadows over the messianic conceptions of the depressed and suffering people ... A second Messiah, who is solely a warrior, ... could now play a role in the saddened messianism of the post-Hadrianic generation. So Messiah ben Joseph became a Messiah who dies: he is fated to fall in the war with Gog ... as Bar-Cochba had fallen in his war against Rome'. See also 493f. and H. Gressmann, Der Messias, 1929, 462: 'The tragic end of the political Messiah is expressed in the figure of Ben Joseph'. The scribal argumentation, which was based especially on Deut 33.17 and Zech 12.10 (see G. Dalman, op. cit., 17ff., and Bill. 2, 293f.), was secondary; see J. Klausner, op. cit., 485.

[376] Rom 1.3; Mk 10.47; 12.35ff. For Jesus' family trees, see Mt 1.1ff. and Lk 3.23ff.; Mt 21.9; Lk 1.32; Jn 7.41f.; Acts 15.16; Rev 5.5; 22.16, etc.

[377] Simon bar Giora, whose father was, to judge from his name, a proselyte, is possibly an exception here; see below, p. 374f. It is moreover obvious that the 'Davidic descent' could also be manipulated in various ways; see J. Jeremias, Jerusalem in the Time of Jesus, 287f. A Davidic origin was, for example, later incorrectly attributed to the family of the patriarch of Palestine (which was of the genealogy of Hillel). Another example is Herod who, in order to obliterate his Edomite descent, had his derivation from the first Jews who had returned from exile confirmed; see Ant 14,9.

'so that, among the Jews, none of royal descent would remain alive'.[378]

The same author also reports that the descendants of David were also executed under Domitian and Trajan.[379] The only explanation for this is that those who were descended from David were regarded as politically dangerous after the Jewish War.

(4) The descent of leading personalities was followed with particular interest in late Judaism.[380] In individual cases, unjustified claims were made to descent from David.[381]

With these points in mind, the formation of the dynasty which presumably extended from Hezekiah to Eleazar b. Ari and the messianic ambition that was clearly discernible in that dynasty in at least one case can be explained most satisfactorily by assuming that the claim to Davidic descent was made in that family. It is possible that these Davidic messianic pretensions and the persecution of those who were of Davidic descent by Vespasian are connected with the 'ambiguous oracle' quoted by Josephus and the Roman historians as one of the causes of the war.[382]

4. The Zealots' Messianic Hope and Palestinian Christianity

Justin Martyr, who lived at the time of the Hadrianic revolt, provides the following account of Bar Koseba's persecution of Christians:

'During the recent Jewish War, Bar Cochba, the leader of the revolt of the Jews, had the order issued against Christians that, if they did not deny and defame Jesus Christ, they would be led away to suffer the most severe punishments'.[383]

---

[378] In Eusebius, *HistEcc* 3,12: ὡς μὴ περιλειφθείη τις παρὰ Ἰουδαίοις τῶν ἀπὸ τῆς βασιλικῆς φυλῆς. See Schürer, 1, 528; see also J. Klausner, *op. cit.*, 395.

[379] HistEcc 3,19f. and 3,32.

[380] See Phil 3.5; Lk 2.36; see also J. Jeremias, *op. cit.* The genealogy of Hillel or of the later patriarchs also went back to Benjamin. The Babylonian exilarch, on the other hand, went back to Judah and possibly even to David. Josephus proudly claimed that he was descended from the Hasmonaeans; see *Vita* 1ff.; see also Tob 1.1 and Jdt 8.1.

[381] See J. Jeremias, *op. cit.*, 309ff.: According to Ket 62b, the older R. Hiyya traced his origin back to David. See also above, p. 299, n. 377. For the earlier period between Zerubbabel and the Maccabees, see J.E. Bruns, 'The Davidic Dynasty in Post-Exilic Palestine', *Scrip* 7 (1955), 2ff.

[382] See above, p. 237. J. Jeremias, *op. cit.*, 310, assumes that this claim to Davidic descent was also made by the family of Hezekiah. C. Roth's assumption, *The Historical Background, op. cit.*, 55ff., that the dynasty of Menahem went back to priestly origins contradicts the facts reported by Josephus.

[383] *Apol* 1,31.6 = Eusebius, *HistEcc* 4,8.4.

Bar Koseba persecuted Christians because they did not take part in the general uprising of the people. The reason why they held themselves aloof in this way is obvious: 'Following Bar Cochba would have meant leaving Christ. Here one Messiah was opposed to another Messiah'.[384]

The Jewish Christians of Palestine would also have had the same attitude with regard to the Zealots' expectation of the future and the messianic pretenders resulting from that expectation, even though the sources are silent about the particulars. Traces of this attitude can be found, for example, in the warning against false prophets and messiahs.[385]

In the same way, it is extremely unlikely that Jewish Christians would have participated in the uprising against Rome. They fled as a community from Jerusalem to Pella[386] not only because they feared the threatened siege, but also and at least equally because of the impossibility of combining their own hope for the future with the messianic expectation of the insurgents.[387] To this must also be added Jesus' predictions concerning the fall of Jerusalem.[388] The recent attempt made by S.G.F. Brandon to prove that the flight to Pella was unhistorical[389] and that Palestinian Jewish Christians would almost certainly have participated in the revolt[390] is entirely lacking in credibility.

In Zealotism and early Christianity, two eschatological messianic movements were firmly opposed to each other. Despite certain external parallels, the contrast between them was irreconcilable. The expectation

---

[384] N.N. Glatzer, *Geschichte der talmudischen Zeit*, 1937, 40.

[385] Mk 13.21f. parr.

[386] Eusebius, *HistEcc* 3,5.3. It is significant that this flight from Jerusalem took place on the basis of a prophetic revelation; see above, p. 236, n. 40. Lk 21.20-24 should also be understood in this context.

[387] See A. Schlatter, *The Church in the N.T. Period*, 268–273, and H. Lietzmann, *Geschichte der Alten Kirche*, op. cit., 1, 190.

[388] See Mk 13.1 parr. See above, p. 236 n. 42; see also Eusebius' observation attributed to Josephus, *HistEcc* 2,23.20, that the the later catastrophe followed as a punishment in the wake of the murder of James, the brother of the Lord, by the Jews.

[389] *The Fall of Jerusalem and the Christian Church*, 1951, 167ff.

[390] 179ff.: 'Consequently it would seem to be certain that many of the Jewish Christians of Palestine must have made common cause with their countrymen, taking up arms against the Romans, and thus sharing the common fate either of death in battle or subsequently, as captives, death in the arenas'. Apart from the flight to Pella, however, the fact that the relatives of the Lord were also at the head of the Palestinian community after 70 A.D. is evidence against this view. According to Eusebius, *HistEcc* 3,32, Symeon, son of Clopas, suffered the death of a martyr as the bishop 'of the community in Jerusalem' under Trajan, because 'he was a Christian and descended from David'.

of Jesus as the Son of Man who was to come again[391] and as the judge of the world was bound to contradict all the hopes of the Zealots, which were directed towards such warlike messianic pretenders as Menahem or Simon bar Giora.

G. THE FINAL VICTORY AND ISRAEL'S RULE OF THE WORLD

1. The Annihilation of the Worldly Power that was Hostile to God

(a) The Judgement of Rome

The foundation for the view that became widespread in Judaism, namely that the dawn of the time of salvation would be preceded by a period when Israel was seriously threatened by a superior world power that was hostile to God, had already been laid by Ezekiel, in his prophecy of the attack by Gog (Ezek 38f.), and Daniel, in his visions of the fourth kingdom.[392] At the period with which we are concerned here, this power was obviously identified with the Roman Empire, with the result that Rome, as Israel's eschatological enemy *par excellence*, had to be annihilated as a necessary precondition for the bringing about of the messianic time.[393]

Rome is explicitly called the 'fourth kingdom' in the Fourth Book of Ezra and the Syrian Apocalypse of Baruch,[394] and the Apocalypse of Ezra also speaks of the 'Eagle' that is judged and annihilated by the 'Lion', the Davidic Messiah.[395] What is more, the 'rabbinic scholars without exception believed that Daniel's fourth kingdom was the Roman Empire'.[396]

This idea was presumably significantly earlier, however, and it may perhaps even have been contained in the Assumption of Moses, in which

---

[391] Mk 13.26f. parr; 14.62 parr; Acts 7.56. According to Hegesippus, James, the brother of the Lord, was apparently put to death because of his confession of Jesus as the Son of Man; see Eusebius, *HstEcc* 2,23.13.

[392] Dan 2.40ff. and 7.7f.,23ff.; see above pp. 238 and 246.

[393] See Schechter, *Some Aspects of Rabbinic Theology*, 1909. 99f.; Moore, *Judaism*, 2, 331f.; Volz, *Esch*, 280f. and 310; H. Fuchs, *Der geistige Widerstand gegen Rom*, 1938, 68-73. There is no evidence of any such criticism of Rome continuing in the Greek world after the beginning of the imperial period; see J. Palm, *Rom, Römertum und Inperium in der griechischen Literatur der Kaiserszeit*, Lund 1959.

[394] 4 Ezra 12,10; see also c. 11; SyrBar 36; 39,5ff.; 40,1ff.

[395] 12,31ff.; see also 11,36f. According to its fundamental tendency, 4 Ezra does not deal with a 'fight' on the part of the lion. The lion as an image for the Messiah goes back to Gen 49.9; see also Rev 5.5.

[396] Bill. 4, 1004 (ff.); see the examples provided by Billerbeck on those pages. See also Bill. 4, 1203 (AZ 2a), and S. Krauss, *MonTal* V1, 47 and 83.

it is said that, after God's intervention, Israel 'will mount upon the neck and the wings of the Eagle'.[397] We may assume that this identification determined the entire eschatological expectation of the Jewish people throughout the first century A.D.[398]

In the writings of the Essenes and in the War Scroll especially, the 'Kittim' (in other words, the Romans) appear as the eschatological opponents of the community. In the rabbinate, Rome is virtually the 'evil kingdom'[399] and is given as pseudonyms the names of Israel's ancient and traditional enemies, such as Amalek,[400] Babylon — the power which once destroyed Jerusalem[401] — and above all Esau or Edom. In the last-named case, it is probable that hatred of the Edomite Herod gave support to the application of the concept to Rome.[402] Finally, in addition to the eagle, the unclean pig also appeared as a symbolic beast for Rome.[403]

(b) The Eschatological Tyrant

The ruler of the kingdom that was hostile to God obviously also had to have a corresponding part to play in the eschatological drama. The

---

[397] 10,8: 'Tunc felix eris tu, Istrahel, et ascendes supra ceruices et alas aquilae'. See also the completion of the mutilated text by C. Clemen in Kautzsch, *Apokryphen und Pseudepigraphen*, 2, 327f.: 'et implebuntur (dies aquilae)'. The Assumption of Moses probably originated shortly after 6 A.D.; see C. Clemen, *op. cit.*, 313f.; Schürer 3, 281f; O. Eissfeldt, *Old Testament: an Introduction*, 1965, 624.

[398] The idea of the fourth kingdom can also be found in Josephus and among the rebels during the siege; see above, p. 239, n. 52.

[399] See the Eighteen Benedictions 12 in W. Staerk, ed., *Altjüdische Liturgische Gebete (Lietzmanns Kleine Texte* 58), 2nd. ed. 1930, 13: מַלְכוּת זָדוֹן. The Musaph prayer on Rosh ha-Shanah (*op. cit.*, 23): מֶמְשֶׁלֶת זָדוֹן. For further examples, see Volz, *Esch*, 281. In the rabbinate, בֶּן עוֹלָה is the term that is generally used; see Bill. 3, 818 and 4, 875; see also S. Krauss, *MonTal* V1, Nos. 17,26,29,37a,42,63,79,102,149,336.

[400] MekEx on 17.14ff. (L. 2, 120ff.); see also ExRab 26,1. See also S. Schechter, *op. cit.*, 99,140f.; Volz, *Esch*, 280 and Bill. 1, 179.

[401] 1 Pet 5.13; Rev 14.8; 17.1ff.; 4 Ezra 3,2.31; Sib 5,159f. For the rabbinic interpretation, see Bill. 3, 816.

[402] For rabbinic examples from the Tannaitic period, see Volz, *op. cit.*; see also, for example, SifDeut 11,13.41: 'As long as the Israelites neglect the commandments, Esau will rule over them'. For examples from later periods, see Bill. 1, 175.179.449; 3, 157f.393f.; 4, 861, etc. See also Moore, *Judaism*, 1, 399f. and 2, 371, and Jastrow, *Dictionary*, 1, 16 and 2, 1124. This transference made it possible for Old Testament judgements, such as those expressed in Is 34; 63.1-6; Jer 49.7-22; Ezek 25.12-14; Obad 17-21, to be applied to the hated world power. Even Gen 25.23 acquired a measure of importance in rabbinic exegesis; see Bill. 4, 1281, Index.

[403] In EthEn 89,12, Esau is represented as a black wild boar; see Bill. 1, 449; 3, 393f.; 4, 893, and S. Krauss, *MonTal* V1 Nos. 35,36,75,76. The exegesis of the catalogue of unclean animals in Lev 11.4ff. provided in LevRab 13,5 is particularly instructive in this context; see also below, p. 307f.

great model for this ruler was Antiochus Epiphanes. Later on, the Roman emperor assumed all the characteristics of the eschatological tyrant and this development was encouraged by the cult of the emperor.[404]

The Assumption of Moses provides us with an impressive portrait of the godless ruler of the world at the end of time.[405] He is described as being king over all the kings of the earth. He persecutes the pious and has them crucified. According to the Sybilline Oracles, Belial himself will come on to the earth and persecute faithful Jews.[406] The Christian tradition of the Antichrist probably goes back to this early Jewish conception.[407] This 'devil in human form'[408] might also appear in the ultimate eschatological battle as the opponent of the Messiah. The 'king of the Kittim' also appears once in the War Scroll and, according to the Qumran *pesher* of Isaiah, he probably leads the Roman army against Jerusalem.[409] In the Syrian Apocalypse of Baruch, the last ruler of Rome is finally taken prisoner after the annihilation of his army, judged on Mount Zion and put to death.[410] Finally, one text in the New Testament Apocalypse (Rev 19.19f.) should be also be mentioned in this context. Here the 'beast' is presented with his army gathered to fight against the Christ, but, together with the 'false prophet', is thrown into the lake of fire' and its army is annihilated by the sword of the Christ.

According to A. Schlatter, these views about Rome were most readily able to develop in Zealot circles,[411] because, he believes, they were most fundamentally and irreconcilably opposed to Roman rule. Whereas in the case of the Essenes the conception of God's enemies was applied to members of their own people and in particular to the evil priest-kings in Jerusalem,[412] the Zealots would have projected this idea

---

[404] Dan 7.25; 8.8-14; 11.21-39. For Pompey, see PsSol 2,25; for the cult of the emperor, see above, p. 99ff.; for Caligula, see above, p. 105f.

[405] 8,1ff. The features of the persecution itself are taken partly from the religious distress under Antiochus Epiphanes, but he cannot have been intended as the godless ruler at the end of time. The underlying idea was rather that of an all-embracing world ruler.

[406] Sib 2,167-176; what we have here would seem to be the same theme as in AssMos 8 and 10. See also Sib 3,63ff. and W. Bousset, *Der Antichrist*, 1895, 60.

[407] Mk 13.14; 2 Thess 2.8; Rev 13; Did 16,4; 4 Ezra 5,6.

[408] B.-Gr.Rel. 254.

[409] 1QM 15,2; see A.S. van der Woude, *op. cit.*, 180. See also 4QpIs 10,33f. 10,33f., see DJD V, 13 Fragm 8-10 l. 3ff.

[410] SyrBar 40,1ff. For the killing of the Enemy of God by the Messiah, see also 2 Thess 2.8 and EthEn 62,2.

[411] *GI*, 434, n. 239; see also above, p. 244.

[412] A.S. van der Woude, *op. cit.*, p. 121f. His view seems to be confirmed by the fragment of a messianic florilegium from 4Q 174 published by J.M. Allegro; see DJD V,

on to the Roman emperor, whose claims to rule they were bound to have rejected outright for religious reasons. One of the sources of the idea of the Antichrist can probably be found here.

(c) The Annihilation of the Power of Rome

It was possible for the expectation of the annihilation of the world power that was hostile to God and embodied in Rome to take various forms. One relatively frequent form was an expectation that God would intervene directly.[413] The work of destruction might also be carried out by his angels.[414] There was also some thought of inner self-destruction[415] or of an annihilating attack by the people of the east.[416] Finally, the victory over Rome could be ascribed to the Messiah either with or without the accompaniment of an armed force.[417] It was of course possible to combine these different forms. The Zealots hoped to be able to overcome the power of Rome by the armed force of eschatological Israel under the people's messianic leader, in a situation in which God would send them his supernatural help as he had done when they had been led by Moses and Joshua. They certainly rejected a purely passive hope that God would intervene.

---

53 Fragm 1-12, col. I, 1, where it is confirmed in a quotation from 2 Sam 7.10 that the בן עולה (sing. as opposed to M with LXX) may no longer oppress Israel.

[413] AssMos 10,3ff.; Sib 2,15ff.; MekEx on 17.14 (L. 2, 158f.). See also Volz, Esch 310,315ff.; 'God has waged war with the Pharaoh and with Amalek and with Sisera and with Sennacherib and with Nebuchadnezzar and with Haman and with the kings of the Greeks; but his innermost self will not rest until he has taken revenge on Edom in his own person'. This is followed by quotations from Ps 60.10 and Mal 1.4f.

[414] AssMos 10,2; see also EthEn 10,11.16.20; see also Bill. 4, 858 (y) = 868. See especially ExRab 18,5, where the 'liberator' of Obad 21 is applied to Gabriel and Michael.

[415] See EthEn 99,4f.: 100,1ff.; see also Mk 13.8 parr. For further examples, see Volz, Esch, 157; Bill. 4, 858 (w) = 867f.

[416] See Rev 16.12 and 17.12ff. The 'kings from the rising of the sun' are identified with the ten kings who annihilate the whore of Babylon together with the beast; see W. Bousset, Die Offenbarung Johannis (Meyers Kommentar), 5th. ed. 1906, 397; see also Sib 5,93ff.; the Baraita on Yom 10a and SongRab 8,9.3. The theme of the destruction of Rome by the people of the East is linked to that of self-destruction through civil war in the figure of Nero redivivus that should be presupposed in the Johannine Apocalypse; see Sib 4,119f.138ff.; 5,33f.137-152.217-224.361ff.; B.-Gr. Rel. 255; Volz, Esch, 281.

[417] For the warrior Messiah, see above, p. 275ff. See also Volz, Esch, 212ff.,316. For Rome as the real opponent of the Messiah, see Bill. 4, 873 (h) = 875f. and 878, DeutRab 1,20 in association with Obad 21: 'The Israelites spoke in the presence of God: "Lord of the world, how long shall we be enslaved by his (Esau's = Rome's) hand?" He replied to them: "Until that day comes, of which it is written: 'A star shall come forth out of Jacob' (Num 24.17) ... When that star has come forth from Jacob (that is, the Messiah), he will burn Esau's stubble (see Obad 18) ..." God spoke: "In that hour, I shall make my kingdom shine forth and I shall be king over them" (Obad 21)'.

One probable presupposition for this final battle of annihilation was — as in the War Scroll — a fairly long space of time.[418] Another possible presupposition was the occurrence of certain setbacks. During the later course of the Jewish War, this hope was revised to the effect that what was expected was a miraculous annihilation of the enemy's army outside Jerusalem.[419] It is also possible that, after the murder of Nero, the Jews hoped for civil wars to cause Rome to suffer an inner collapse.[420] In all these cases, the end was the same: the complete annihilation of the 'fourth' kingdom of the world, in other words, the destruction of the Roman Empire, and the establishment of the 'kingdom' or 'rule of God', which was constituted in the world kingdom or rule of Israel

2. The Rule of God and his People

(a) The Rule of God

According to Josephus, the 'ambiguous oracle' proclaimed that the world ruler who was to come would come from Judaea, but was misinterpreted, with the result that it was one of the causes of the outbreak of the Jewish War. It shows clearly, however, that the aim of the radical wing at least of the insurgents was certainly nothing less than the securing of world rule. In his first great speech to the rebels, Josephus suggested as an argument against these hopes that:

'good fortune has been transferred to them (the Romans) from every side and God, who has given rule to the peoples in turn, is now with Italy!' The Jewish ancestors, who were superior to the present generation in strength, courage and resources, would not have submitted to the Romans, 'if they had not known that God was on their side'.[421]

The rebels did not, however, abandon their intense hopes even during the continuing siege. They therefore replied accordingly to Titus when he called on them to put an end to their useless resistance:

'They hurled abuse down from the city wall on the Caesar himself and his father, calling aloud that they despised death, preferring it to slavery. They

---

[418] The War Scroll speaks of forty years of fighting; see above, p. 278f.; see also Bill. 3, 824, Tan עקב (ed. Vienna, 1863) 7b: 'How long will the days of the Messiah last? R. Akiba says: "For forty years; as the Israelites spent forty years in the desert, so too will he (the Messiah) drag them out into the desert and let them eat saltwort and broom" (Job 30.4)'. For this, see also above, p. 251.

[419] See above, p. 276.

[420] See *Bell* 1,4ff.; see also above, p. 305, n. 416.

[421] *Bell* 5,367.

would, however, insofar as it was in their power to do so, inflict harm on the Romans for as long as they could breathe. Those who, as he himself said, were dedicated to death had no need to trouble themselves (about the fate) of the native city, and God had a better Temple than this one, namely the world'.[422]

This proclamation of the world as God's Temple did not signify a devaluation of the Temple in Jerusalem, since the insurgents immediately stressed that God would certainly save his dwelling place. It was rather an expression of God's claim that his rule had to be established throughout the whole world. The Zealots saw in this recognition of the sole rule of God over the whole of the earth the ultimate aim of their struggle. The annihilation of Rome, the cult of the emperor and the service of idols in general formed the essential precondition for the establishment of the true 'kingdom of God'.

This consequence is encountered, for example, in the Assumption of Moses, according to which God himself comes to the fore to punish the pagans and to destroy the images of idols, after which Israel will subjugate the Eagle.[423] In the *Musaph* prayer at the Feast of the New Year, the petition for the destruction of the 'evil kingdom' is followed by the conclusion: 'And may you, Yahweh, rule over all your works'. According to Rev 19.6, the proclamation of the achievement of God's rule will follow the fall of 'Babylon'. In a tradition going back to R. Eliezer b. Hyrcanus[424], the annihilation of Amalek is combined with the eradication of the service of idols; it is only when this has taken place that Yahweh 'will become king over all the earth' (Zech 14.9).

The view that the annihilation of 'Edom' would establish the foundation of the kingdom or rule of God was confirmed above all by Obad 21.[425] In the Targum on this text, for example, we read:

'Liberators will go up to Mount Zion to judge the great city of Esau and the

---

[422] *Bell* 5,458f.: καὶ ναὸν ἀμείνω τούτου τῷ θεῷ τὸν κόσμον εἶναι σωθήσεσθαι ... καὶ τοῦτον ὑπὸ τοῦ κατοικοῦντος. For this, see SyrBar 3,24. The idea itself goes back to 1 Kings 8.27 and Is 66.1. According to *Bell* 5,212, the curtain in front of the Holy of Holies was a symbol of the universe. The Temple as a whole could also be included within this cosmic symbolism: see *Ant* 3,123.180ff. and Philo, *VitMos* 2,76ff. (M 2, 146f.).117 (152f.); see G. Ricciotti, *Flavius Giuseppe*, 3, 153. The Sanctuary was the expression of God's claim to rule over the whole of the world. See M. Hengel, *Judaism and Hellenism*, 1, 170f.

[423] AssMos 10,3ff.7f.; see above, p. 303, n. 397; see also PsSol 17,3.

[424] See above, p. 109.

[425] For the rabbinic exegesis of Obad 21, see Bill. 3, 812. The whole Book of Obadiah is interpreted as being directed against Rome; for v. 1, see Bill. 4, 863: Tan וישלח, 8, ed. Buber 83b, and Tan דברים (ed. Vienna, 1863) 2a, in Bill. 4, 862 (1).

kingdom of Yahweh, his rule over all the inhabitants of the earth, will reveal itself and the kingdom of Yahweh will be for ever'.[426]

R. Samuel b. Nachman provides an original explanation for the name of Rome as 'pig', which possibly goes back to R. Meir:

'And the pig, that is Edom; "and it does not chew the cud", because it will draw no (further) kingdom in its wake. And why is it named "pig" (חזיר)? Because it will give the crown back to their Lord (that is, to God) (מחזירת עטרה). That is what is written: "Liberators will go up ... and the kingdom will be Yahweh's" (Obad 21)'.[427]

It would only be after Rome, the last great world power, had fallen that the way would be made open for the establishment of the unrestricted 'theocracy'. This view was also preserved in the rabbinate,[428] in which it was also possibly further elaborated exegetically. The difference, however, was that attempts were no longer made to bring about God's rule by human actions. The establishment of that rule was left to God's discretion. This also meant that the immediate and imminent expectation and the conviction that one was living at the time when the eschaton was being accomplished receded into the background.

(b) The Rule of Israel

'God's rule' was, however, 'at the same time the rule of the people'.[429] The way had been prepared by Daniel for this equation.[430] It can also be found again and again in the apocryphal and pseudepigraphical writings, in the rabbinate and even in Josephus' *Antiquities*.[431] The same expectation was also expressed by the Essenes.[432]

---

[426] Bill 1, 179.

[427] LevRab 13,5 at the end (on 11.7). According to EcclRab 1,9.1, the play on words goes back to R. Meir (middle of the second century A.D.). For further examples, see Tan תולדות (ed. Vienna, 1863) 33b, in Bill. 4, 863; GenRab 78,14 on 33.14 and DeutRab 1,20 on 2.4 (see above, p. 305, n. 417); EsthRab 1,13 on 1.2, see Bill. 1. 175 (g).

[428] See S. Schechter, *Some Aspects of Rabbinic Theology, op. cit.*, 99ff.: 'Thus the kingdom of heaven stands in opposition to the kingdom of Rome and becomes connected with the kingdom of Israel' (101); see also Bill. 1, 182: the idea of the world mission, which had rededed into the background in rabbinic Judaism, is replaced by the conception of the annihilation of the kingdoms of the world. The idea of the world mission can, however, certainly be combined with that of the annihilation of the power of Rome; see below, p. 309, n. 436.

[429] B.-Gr. *Rel.* 215; *cf.* S. Schechter, *op. cit.*

[430] Cf. Dan 2.44 with 7.27.

[431] See B.-Gr. Rel. 216f.; Volz, *Esch*, 279f.; Bill. 4, 880ff. For Josephus, see also above, p. 239, n. 53 (*Ant* 4,114 and 116f.).

[432] See 1QM 2,7; 11,13; 12,13f.; 17,7f.: 'And the rule of Israel shall be over all flesh';

The Zealots were aware of it in its most acute form, maintaining that Israel's rule over the whole earth at the same time also implied the judgement and punishment of all those who had previously oppressed the people of Israel and all who served idols.[433]

It is possible that the story of Jesus' temptation [434] and above all the third beatitude, which, following Ps 37.11, promises that the 'meek' will 'inherit the earth', contains an authentically anti-Zealot tendency. These words of Jesus were in very sharp contrast to the Zealot teaching and must have struck the Zealots, who called for retributory violence as a response to all injustice, as a form of enthusiasm. On the other hand, the insurgents accepted, in individual cases, pagans into the community if they agreed to be circumcised.[435] There is therefore a distinct possibility that mission formed part of their eschatological programme.[436] The people of the time of salvation would not consist solely of those who had survived the murderous fighting. The full number would be made up by the 'resurrection' of the 'righteous', that

---

4QpPs 37 (No. 171) II, 4, see DJD V, 43 (Ps 37.9b); 4 QpIs (No. 161) Fragm 8-10,20ff., see DJD V, 14 on Is 11.1f.; see also 1QH 6,1f.; CD 2,11f.; 1QSb 3,18f. (see above, p. 275, n. 242); Jub 26,23 and 32,18f.: 'And I shall give the whole earth which (is) below heaven to your seed and they will rule over all nations as they wish and will thereafter possess the whole earth and inherit it in eternity' (translation based on E. Littmann in Kautzsch, 2, 95).

[433] The rabbis who were active during the second century A.D. developed very detailed ideas concerning the extent of the territory that was to be inhabited by the Jews in messianic period. It was to include, for example, Syria, Arabia, Asia (Minor), Thrace and Carthage; see Bill. 4, 899, jSheb 36b and BB 56a bar. See also J. Klausner, *op. cit.*, 505. For the annihilation of Israel's erstwhile enemies, see SyrBar 72,2ff. and Bill. 4, 880 (s). According to Zech 8.23, the other nations should serve Israel: Bill. 4, 895f. (f + g). R. Simeon b. Lakish appealed to Zech 8.23 in his teaching that each Israelite was to have two thousand eight hundred slaves in the messianic kingdom: Shab 32b, see Bill. 3, 149. This interpretation may possibly go back to the second century A.D.; see the statement made by R. Hanina b. Antigonus, SifNum 15,38.115. K.G. Kuhn, *op. cit.*, 344, n. 58, suspects, however, that Resh Lakish embellished this statement. For the elimination of the worship of idols, see Bill. 4, 914f. (uu); see especially R. Eliezer b. Hyrcanus, MekEx 17,14 (L. 2, 158).

[434] Mt 4.8-11; Lk 4.5-9; see also E. Stauffer, *Die Botschaft Jesu damals und heute.* 1959, 112.

[435] See above, p. 143. Non-Jews probably also fought on the Jewish side under Bar Koseba; see Dio Cassius 69,13.2 (Reinach, 199); see also Schürer, 1, 547.

[436] It is possible that the missionary zeal of the Pharisees that is criticized by Jesus in Mt 23.15 had an eschatological foundation. If so, this would be a Jewish parallel to the Christian and especially Pauline understanding of mission. See also Bill. 1, 926ff. A critical attitude towards missionary activity in the messianic period seems, however, to have predominated in the later rabbinate; see Bill. 1 929f.; B.-Gr. Rel. 234, n. 3, and J. Klausner, *op. cit.*, 475ff. There are, however, also positive statements, for example in the Sibylline Oracles; see Volz, *Esch*, 171f. and J. Klausner, *op. cit.*, 481f.; see Ber 57b = Tos 7,2 (Z. 14).

is, by those in particular who had fallen in battle.[437] This explains why the Zealots were so ready to accept martyrdom and death. Here too, the constitution of eschatological Israel was ultimately left to God's miraculous power.

H. SUMMARY

I have tried in this chapter to present in some detail various aspects of the fundamental eschatological mood within the Zealot movement and its ramifications. The following viewpoints can be summarized in conclusion:

(1) The imminent expectation and hope of the time of salvation formed the presupposition and the framework within which Judas the Galilaean and his successors were able to come to the fore with their demand for the sole rule of God. The entire struggle to the bitter end subsequently conducted by the Zealots can also be understood in the light of this presupposition. This party and its whole way of thinking became more and more influential within Palestinian Judaism in the course of the first century A.D. For this reason, it is possible to assume that this imminent expectation was very widespread and prevailed as the fundamental mood in the Jewish population of Palestine at the time.

The so-called 'last things' appear in this context not as dogmatic and speculative truths of faith, but as historical realities which could be experienced and which had already to some extent dawned or cast their shadow over the Jewish world. The Zealots believed that the pre-messianic time of persecution had already begun and that the change heralding the beginning of the time of salvation was imminent. Everything, they thought, depended on whether Israel ultimately acknowledged the sole rule of God. One of the essential differences between the Zealots and the Maccabaean movement was that the Zealots were uncompromising in their certainty of the imminent end.

The Palestinian Jews were no less shattered when the expected time of salvation did not come than the early Christians, who were similarly deeply conditioned by their imminent expectation of the parousia. The development in the direction of the rabbinate ran parallel to the evolution of the formation of the early Catholic Church. Evidence of the rejection of enthusiastic eschatological hopes of the kind cherished by the 'Zealots' can be found in the condemnation of those who wanted

---

[437] 2 Macc 7.9 etc.; see Bill. 4, 1167; EthEn 90,33 and Bill. 4, 1192 (l).

to 'hasten' the approach of the end, the firm denial of all eschatological calculations,[438] the purification of all messianic conceptions,[439] the thesis of the cessation of the prophetic spirit and the development of the conviction that salvation would only be brought about by God without any action on the part of men.

(2) The Zealots' future expectation naturally became dominated to a great extent by the so-called 'national hope' and may also have applied to the eschatological expectation of the majority of the people.[440] The division between a 'national Jewish hope' and a 'transcendent hope of the kingdom of God[441] is in fact a distinction that is based on modern presuppositions. Both hopes were always inseparable from each other in Jewish eschatology. The presuppositions for the 'national' aspects of that hope were fully transcendent, in God's promise and in his election and it could only be fulfilled by means of God's miraculous help. In this sense, then, the Zealots' hope was both 'transcendent' and 'national' at the same time. Their ultimate aim was not the apotheosis of the Jewish people, but the honour of God. The people might, in the distress that would occur at the end of time, be reduced to a small remnant, but what was essential was only that the sole rule of God should be proclaimed and brought about. The real contrast between the Zealots' expectation and that of other Jewish movements — such as moderate Pharisaism — was therefore not to be found in the discrepancy between national and transcendent hope, but in the degree of human activity and in the way in which it was believed that the course of the eschatological events could be influenced. However much man's co-operation was stressed, it was always recognized that God himself would bring about the ultimate redemption by his miraculous power.[442]

(3) The political aspect of the eschatological expectation was unmistakable. For Judaism, political reality and eschatological hope were intimately related to each other, just as the Torah contained the law that was valid for the state, the family, property and work and was at the

---

[438] See Bill. 4, 1013ff.

[439] For the suppression of the tradition of Elijah and Phinehas, see above, p. 168ff. For the division between the Davidic and the Messiah b. Joseph, see above, p. 298f.

[440] Elements of this were preserved even in early Christianity; see Mt 19.28; Lk 22.28; 24.21; Acts 1.6, etc.

[441] See A. von Gall, Βασιλεία τοῦ θεοῦ, 1926, 326ff. and 352ff, see also B.-Gr. Rel. 213ff. For a criticism of the concept 'national' as a description of the Zealots, see above, p. 140f.

[442] See above, p. 123, n. 249. See also above, p. 277ff., for the War Scroll.

same time, as God's unique, unrepeatable and authoritative revelation, the foundation of all religious life.

This close link between politics and religious expectation applied to the Zealots in a very special way. Their fanatical and enthusiastic readiness to give up all their property and life itself was in striking contrast with their ruthless application of all available means to achieve their aims. They also displayed, parallel to an illusory lack of concern with regard to the temporal power structures, a high degree of foresight in political and military calculation.[443]

It is also important not to overlook the social reason underlying their struggle and their hopes. The economic conditions of the country had been thrown into disorder by Herod's maladministration and the position had been made worse by famines. The situation had been interpreted as an expression of the eschatological distress and what was expected of the time of salvation to come was a reordering of property ownership which was in accordance with the original will of God at the time of the taking possession of the land.[444]

(4) The fundamental attitude that was required in view of the imminence of the time of salvation was zeal, in other words, a readiness to commit oneself unconditionally to the honour of God. Even the use of violence was justified to achieve this end. This zeal formed the basis of the Zealots' readiness to accept martyrdom and their decision to give up all possessions and security and withdraw into the desert. Their zeal gave them the certainty of victory over their enemies. They used it to wage the Holy War and it enabled them to hope that they would receive a heavenly reward if they fell in battle.

In this way, zeal played a similar part in the lives of the Zealots as the commandment to study Scripture in the Essene community,[445] the observance of the law in the way of life of the Pharisees[446] and the commandment to love in early Christianity. Even if one must describe the way followed by the 'Zealots' as wrong, it is impossible not to be impressed by the greatness of their fundamental idea and their readiness for self-sacrifice.

---

[443] This contrast is also shown by the War Scroll, which is close to Zealotism in its thinking. Josephus emphasizes that the rebels were masterly in finding devious means and strategems of war: Bell 4,99ff.: 5,109ff.212ff.317ff.469ff.; 6,177ff.

[444] See above, p. 132f.; for the division of the land in the messianic kingdom, see Bill. 4, 900f. (p): BB 122a bar. See also M. Hengel, Property and Riches in the Early Church, 1974.

[445] 1QS 1,1f.; 5,11; 6,7; 8,15; CD 1,10; 6,6ff.17; 7,18; see also P. Wernberg-Møller, The Manual of Discipline, 1957, 44, n. 3.

[446] See B.-Gr. Rel. 392f. and Bill. 3, 160ff.

CHAPTER VI

THE DEVELOPMENT OF THE ZEALOT MOVEMENT

A. The Prehistory until the Banishment of Archelaus

1. The Robber Captain 'Hezekiah' and the Disturbances in Galilee on Herod's Coming to Power

A historical outline of the Jewish freedom movement between the reign of Herod I and 70 A.D. has to begin at the point where Josephus speaks for the first time about Jewish 'robbers', which is the most general term that he uses to include all the groups opposing foreign rule.[1]

We come across these 'robbers' quite abruptly in connection with the sending of the young Herod to Galilee as commander-in-chief:

'Herod, enterprising by nature, quickly found a task to which he could direct his energy. As soon as he learned that the robber captain Hezekiah was active in the territory bordering on Syria with a very large band, he took him prisoner and had him put to death with many of his robbers'.[2]

This action enabled Herod to gain the special favour of the Roman procurator, Sextus Caesar, and of the population of Syria,[3] but his difficulties increased in Jerusalem. The leading Jews complained about him to Hyrcanus II, accusing him of putting Hezekiah illegally to death and claiming that his killing should have taken place only on the basis of judgement by a regular court.[4] Until now Josephus' account is almost the same in both *The Jewish War* and the *Antiquities* — he presumably followed Nicolaus of Damascus' history in both works[5] — but here the second contains an additional tradition:

'The mothers of those murdered by Herod called on the king and the people day after day in the Temple, demanding that Herod should appear before the Synhedrium to answer for what he had done'.

[1] See above, p. 41.
[2] *Bell* 1,204 (= *Ant* 14,159). This act was carried out by the twenty-five year old man at the end of 47 or the beginning of 46 B.C. The governor of Syria, Sextus Caesar, was murdered in 46 B.C.: *Ant* 14,268; Dio Cassius 47,26f.; see Schürer, 1, 248,275f.
[3] *Bell* 1,205 = *Ant* 14,160.
[4] *Bell* 1,209 = *Ant* 14,167.
[5] See above, p. 8, n. 14. In the *Antiquities*, the anti-Jewish tendency of the narrative is significantly toned down; see *Ant* 14,164f.: Antipater's deception and the representation of the 'calumniators', *Ant* 14,165, compared with *Bell* 1,209. See also Schlatter, *GI*, 226 and 429, n. 209.

This continuing accusation from two sides led even the indolent Hyrcanus to take action, namely to summon Herod to Jerusalem to appear before the court. The proceedings before the Synhedrium, which consisted predominantly of Sadducees, produced no result, because the members were too afraid of the accused and his father Antipater to be able to come to a decision. It is clear from the sharp attack made against the assembly by the Pharisee Sameas that Herod had made himself guilty of a serious offence against the law and that the accusation was in no sense based on defamations.[6]

While Josephus' tendentious account in *The Jewish War* (biased in favour of Herod) gives the impression that Hezekiah and his companions were rightly executed as ordinary robbers, there are, however, certain contradictions in the work[7] and the supplemental information in the *Antiquities* probably comes from an anti-Herodian source which would lead one to assume that the true state of affairs did not correspond with the account provided by Nicolaus of Damascus. The following points are worthy of consideration:

(1) A considerable number of the 'robbers' killed were sons of respectable families from Jerusalem. If they had not been, their mothers' accusation would hardly have reached Hyrcanus.[8]

(2) Hezekiah and the members of his party seem to have had a certain importance. If they had been unimportant, the Synhedrium would hardly have been so indignant about their death.[9]

---

[6] *Ant* 14,171-174 and 177. The account of the court session and the episode of the women's accusation probably goes back to an anti-Herodian Jewish source. The session was also preserved in the rabbinic tradition in a distorted form as an anecdote: Instead of Herod we find a 'slave of King Jannaeus', Simeon b. Shetach appears instead of Sameas and King Jannaeus has to vouch himself for his slave. The court, however, because it is afraid, comes to no conclusion, with the result that Simeon, like Sameas, pronounces judgement upon the assembly: Sanh 19a/b; see Derenbourg, 147. For Sameas, see Klausner, *Hist* 3, 254f. and *J of N*, 141. See also A. Schalit, *König Herodes*, 42ff.

[7] See Hyrcanus' completely different attitude toward Herod in *Bell* 1,210 and 211; see also *Ant* 14,168 and 170. In reality, Hyrcanus advised Herod to flee, because he was afraid of Sextus Caesar; see *Ant* 14,170.177. Later, he regretted this decision; see *Ant* 14,178.

[8] S. Klein, *Galiläa von der Makkabäerzeit bis 67 n. Chr. (Palästina-Studien* 4), 1928, 37, was of the opinion that there was a pilgrimage of Galilaean women to Jerusalem. But women from outside the city and rebels' widows would hardly have got through with their petitions. The complaint about the execution of innocent men that was contrary to the law and the demand for satisfaction can also be found after Herod's death: *Bell* 2,5f. = *Ant* 17,206ff.

[9] R. Laqueur, *Der jüdische Historiker Flavius Josephus*, 1920, 180f., was wrong in his claim that the presentation in the *Antiquities* has no historical value. This in fact provides a valuable complement to the one-sided and tendentious representation in the *The Jewish War*. The objection that the king and not the Synhedrium had to decide about capital

(3) Hezekiah was not in open revolt against Hyrcanus. If he had been, Hyrcanus would hardly have tried to bring Herod before the court for killing Hezekiah.

(4) Herod did not succeed in completely annihilating this group of 'robbers'. Galilee continued to be a breeding ground of resistance against foreign rule and, about forty years later, one of Hezekiah's sons emerged as an insurgent.[10]

These λῃσταί, then, were presumably not real robbers.[11] Nor were they the scattered followers of Aristobulus and his family[12], since, in that case, the anger of Hyrcanus II over the annihilation of his most dangerous enemies would be incomprehensible. What is more, it is noteworthy that Josephus never calls the followers of Aristobulus 'robbers'.

It is therefore reasonable to assume that Hezekiah fought in his own cause and that he may have gathered an armed force around him with the approval of the Sadducees in Galilee in order to form a counterbalance to the increasing strength of the Edomite Antipater and his sons. It is unlikely either that Hezekiah appeared as a messianic pretender or that he was regarded as such by his followers.[13] On the other hand, he was a man of rank and influence and he may have belonged to the κληροῦχοι who had been settled in Galilee by Alexander Jannaeus. It is hardly possible to describe him as the founder of the Zealot party.[14] He was at the best a precursor.

Galilee apparently continued as a trouble spot, and stronghold of 'robbers'. After Herod had surprisingly achieved the dignity of kingship

---

offences overlooks the fact that Hyrcanus had lost the dignity of king since the time of Pompey (*Bell* 1,153.155ff. = *Ant* 14,73ff.) and had only been confirmed as high-priest and 'ethnarch' by Caesar (*Ant* 14,191). It is evident that Hyrcanus acted as president in the Synhedrium (for the first time here and previously only γερουσία) and adjourned the session (*Ant* 14,177). The difficulties in the *Antiquities* are the result of the combination of two sources with opposing tendencies.

[10] See below, pp. 327 and 330ff.

[11] See J. Wellhausen, *Israelitisch-Jüdische Geschichte*, 5th. ed. 1904, 319; Klausner, *Hist* 3, 252; K.H. Rengstorf, *TD* 4, 258; G. Ricciotti, *Flavio Giuseppe*, 2, 52f.

[12] H. Graetz, 3, 178: 'A scattered band of Aristobulus' army'; see also J. Wellhausen, *op. cit.*: 'a Hasmonaean freedom fighter' and W. Otto, *Herodes*, 1913, 20. W.R. Farmer's conjecture, *NTS* 4 (1957/58), 151, that a close relative of the Hasmonaean royal house was involved here is probably completely erroneous.

[13] See above, p. 292, n. 340.

[14] This was the opinion of N. Bentwich, *Josephus*, 1926, 22, who believed that Hezekiah was 'the founder of the party of the Zealots'. Klausner, *Hist* 4, 122 and 202, is more cautious: אב־אבות הקנאים. He does, however, express the unjustifiable opinion that the later Zealots went back via Hezekiah to a particular branch of the Hasidim. See also above, p. 68.

in Rome,[15] he tried energetically to gain possession of his new kingdom, in which the Parthians had set up Antigonus, the son of Aristobulus II, as king.

After achieving some initial successes, he went on, in the winter of 39/38 B.C., to clean up Galilee. The principal strongholds of the 'robbers', who controlled the largest part of the country, were in the caves of Arbela and access to these was very difficult. Herod was almost defeated in his first encounter with them and the situation was only saved by his personal valour.

It did not take him long to subjugate the whole of Galilee, with the exception of the caves.[16] These he smoked out one by one, by lowering great chests full of soldiers down the cliff faces. It was here that the 'heroic suicide' of an old 'robber', to which I have already referred, took place. This man killed first his seven sons and his wife and then himself, rejecting Herod's offer of mercy 'because he preferred death to slavery',[17] The Galilaean 'robbers' rose up on a further two occasions against the new king who had been appointed by Rome and each time he had difficulty in overcoming them.[18]

These 'robbers' were not real robbers, nor were they Antigonus' regular troops. They were probably the bellicose inhabitants of the Galilaean countryside who had taken shelter in the almost inaccessible parts of the country, as they did later in the Jewish War. Since there were at that time probably no walled cities in Galilee apart from Sepphoris, they had withdrawn to the natural fortifications. The fine of one hundred talents imposed on the cities of Galilee[19] shows that the majority of the population was involved in the resistance. All that the name λῃσταί means in this context, then, is — at least according to Nicolaus of Damascus — that these were rebels against the legitimate ruler. The word may also indicate that these rebels fought not in closed order, but in small, scattered groups.[20]

What united all these groups was not so much sympathy towards the

---

[15] *Bell* 1,282ff. = *Ant* 14,386; in 40 A.D., see Schürer, 1, 281, and *CAH* 10, 320.
[16] *Bell* 1,304 = *Ant* 14,413-417; for Arbela, see Schürer, 1, 282, n. 6.
[17] *Bell* 1,310-313 = *Ant* 14,420-430; the seven sons point to the Jewish legend: 2 Macc 7; Acts 19.14 and especially AssMos 9: Taxo and his seven sons. K. Kohler, *JE* 12, 640b and *Harkavy-Festschrift*, 14; Klausner, *Hist* 3, 154f. (*J of N*, 143, n. 22) and R. Eisler, 2, 75, n. 3. are in favour of an identification, but this is certainly not permissible. S. Mowinkel, *VT.S* 1, Congress Volume, Copenhagen, 1953, 88-96, points in the right direction for a correct interpretation.
[18] *Bell* 1,314ff. = *Ant* 14,431ff. and *Bell* 1,326 = *Ant* 14,450.
[19] *Bell* 1, 316 = *Ant* 14,433.
[20] See above, p. 42f.

Hasmonaeans[21] as a bitter rejection of Herod, an attitude with its roots in religion, since Herod was an Edomite and had only been formally Jewish since the second or possibly the third generation.[22] According to the royal law, only a real Jew could become king in Israel, certainly not a foreigner.[23] An Edomite only became fully accepted into the Jewish community after the third generation (Deut 23.8f.). If Aristobulus' or Alexander Jannaeus' acceptance of the title of king — a dignity that was reserved for the house of David — had evoked the displeasure of pious Jews and had even led to open civil war,[24] then a king who was no more than 'half a Jew' (ἡμιιουδαῖος) would inevitably be rejected by Jews who were faithful to the law.[25] For Herod, the question of his origin continued to be a sore point and he knew that it was this that made his subjects reluctant to accept him.[26]

A unified aim and firmly established forms of organization are not to be found either in the case of Hezekiah and his band or in that of the later 'robbers' in Galilee. The disturbances were an expression of a deep longing for freedom in Galilee. It cannot, however, be disputed that this quest for freedom had a religious foundation, since the Galilaeans refused to recognize a ruler whose person and rule were not in accordance with the law.

---

[21] The pious Jews were also critical of them; see PsSol 1,2.4.8, etc. and AssMos 6,2ff.

[22] The Edomites' territory had been forcibly Judaized by Hyrcanus I (*Ant* 13,257f. = *Bell* 1,63). This took place some years after the death of Antiochus VII Sidetes in 129 B.C.; see Schürer, 1, 207. Herod himself was born about 84 B.C.; see Schlatter, *GI*, 429, n. 208, following *Bell* 1,647 = *Ant* 17,148.

[23] Deut 17.15; cf. MekEx on 19.6 (L 2, 205): 'I will not have a king set over you chosen from the nations of the world, but (only) from among you'.

[24] See *Ant* 13,301.372ff. = *Bell* 1,70.88ff. See also the rejection of kingship by the Jewish legation sent to Pompey: *Ant* 14,41. For the restriction of the office of king to the house of David, see Sir 47.11 (45.25); PsSol 17,4ff.21.32; MekEx on 12.1 (L 1, 5).

[25] Antigonus had the Roman commandant summoned from the wall (*Ant* 14,403): ὡς παρὰ τὴν αὐτῶν δικαιοσύνην Ἡρώδῃ δώσουσι τὴν βασιλείαν ἰδιώτῃ τε ὄντι καὶ Ἰδουμαίῳ τουτέστιν ἡμιιουδαίῳ. According to Strabo, Jews themselves refused to give Herod the title of king, although they were tortured for it: *Ant* 15,9. There is an obvious parallel here with the *Sicarii*; see above, p. 90ff. According to BB 3b, Herod was a עבדא דבית חשמונאי (see above p. 314, n. 6). He had all rabbis (with the exception of one) killed, because they kept to the teaching of Deut 17.15. According to the Mishnah, Agrippa I burst into tears when he read this text and the people comforted him, saying: 'You are our brother'; Sot 7,8; see also Derenbourg, 151 and 216.

[26] According to *Ant* 14,9, Nicolaus of Damascus traced Antipater's origin back to the first Jews who had come back from Babylonia. According to Strabo 16,2.46 (765), on the other hand, Herod had even attributed a priestly origin to himself; see W. Otto, *op. cit.*, 18 (cf. also AssMos 6,2). In addition to the historically indisputable tradition of Herod's Idumaean origin (*Bell* 1,123 = *Ant* 14,8), there was another tradition, according to which Herod had originated in Ascalon. For this, see W. Otto, *Herodes*, 1913, 2: 'a Christian invention'; see also J. Jeremias, *Jerusalem*, 3rd. ed.

2. Herod's Rule[27]

Herod seems to have succeeded in damping down the flame of rebellion in the people by harsh and skilful methods — at least there are no reports of open revolt during the period of his government. In the first years of his rule, this may have been determined by the fearful losses suffered by the Jews through the vicissitudes of war. Later on, Herod believed that he could make his position to some extent safe by means of terror on the one hand and by making occasional gifts to the people on the other.[28]

His characteristics as a ruler have been recorded by Josephus and in other sources. He was, for example, cruel towards real and imagined opponents.[29] He executed the (probably) predominantly Sadducaean Synhedrium.[30] He also exterminated the last remnants of the Hasmonaean house, including even members of his own family. He was moreover boundlessly avaricious and extravagant.[31] Similar characteristics, however, can also be found in other oriental rulers, including the Hasmonaeans,[32] and it was possible for pious Jews to accept them with resignation as God's punishment for the sinfulness of Israel.[33] But Herod's repeated contempt for the limits set by the law, his causing pagan practice to penetrate into Jewish territory and even into Jerusalem

---

1969,281ff.,331ff.; R. Eisler, 1, 342, nn. 5 and 8, and 352ff.; A. Schalit, *König Herodes*, 4f.678f.

[27] The one-sidedness of the sources makes it especially difficult for us to understand Herod. The main source is provided by Nicolaus of Damascus (exclusively in *The Jewish War*). He was the erstwhile friend of Herod and was so tendentious that even Josephus was critical of this source (*Ant* 16,183). The anti-Herodian texts in the *Antiquities*, which were added by Josephus, who took them from a Jewish source, break the coherence and make the presentation lack homogeneity. See H. Dessau, *Geschichte der römischen Kaiserzeit*, II,2, 1930, 755.

[28] *Ant* 15,326; see also Klausner, *J of N*, 144ff.

[29] *Ant* 15,6 = *Bell* 1,358; *Ant* 15,252.265.290; 16,156, etc.

[30] *Ant* 14,174ff.; cf. 15,4; see also BB 3b and NumRab 14,8: It is possible that this murder of the members of the Synhedrium, likely predominently Sadducees, is identical with the the execution of the forty-five followers of Antigonus (*Ant* 15,6); see J. Wellhausen, *Pharisäer und Sadducäer*, 1874, 105f., and M. Ginsberg, *Rome et la Judée*, Paris 1928, 120.

[31] *Ant* 15,7.330; 16,141.146f.153f., etc.

[32] H. Mosbech, *DTT* 16 (1953), 193ff., may well be right about this point. It is, however, doubtful whether Josephus' criticism of Herod should be described as exaggerated. Like the Hellenistic rulers of his own time, Herod had not the well-being of his country, but his own personal power and honour in mind. An example of Josephus' probably accurate characterization can be found in *Ant* 16,153ff.

[33] See the judgement of the leading Pharisee Sameas, who, together with his teacher, Pollion, advised Jerusalem to surrender to Herod; see *Ant* 14,176: εἰπὼν διὰ τὰς ἁμαρτίας οὐ δύνασθαι διαφυγεῖν αὐτόν (Herod as ruler).

itself under the cloak of Hellenistic culture — that must have seemed to members of religious circles in Jerusalem to be quite unbearable.[34]

His reign as king, which was so contrary to the law, began with his sacrifice to Jupiter Capitolinus in Rome and this contemptuous disregard of Jewish monotheism was later expressed in his having a number of temples erected both inside and outside his territory, especially for Augustus.[35] He also founded Caesarea and Sebaste, having them built on the model of Hellenistic cities with theatres and amphitheatres, and the cities of Jericho and Jerusalem, where he had his residence, were also provided with these gifts of Hellenistic culture.[36]

Personally, he also loved to associate with non-Jews with a Hellenistic education[37] and he had his own sons educated in a Hellenistic manner, even going so far as to have them brought up in a pagan Roman environment.[38] An exclusively Greek text appeared on his coins and the language of his government at the highest level will accordingly also have been Greek.[39]

In administration and legislation, he displayed a sovereign disregard for tradition and the law. An example of this is provided by Josephus, who criticizes him for his tightening up of the penalty for offences against property, according to which thieves were to be sold as slaves outside the country.[40] The Roman practice of throwing criminals to the wild beasts during the games at festivals was also introduced in his reign and gave great offence.[41]

In addition, he made changes in the office of the high-priesthood at

---

[34] See *Ant* 15,266f.281.365; 16,4.158f., etc.

[35] For the sacrifice on the Capitol, see *Ant* 14,388 = *Bell* 1,285. See also A. Momigliano, *CAH* 10, 320. For the emperor's temples, see above, p. 102f.; see also *Ant* 15,326ff.; 16,146ff.; *Bell* 1,407.422.

[36] Caesarea: *Ant* 15,341 = *Bell* 1,415; Sebaste: *Ant* 15,298; see also G.E. Wright, *Biblical Archaeology*, 1962, 219ff.; Jerusalem: *Ant* 15,268; see also G.E. Wright, *op. cit.*, 272ff.; cf. *Bell* 2,44 = *Ant* 17,255; Jericho: *Ant* 17,161.193 = *Bell* 1,666; *Ant* 17,175 = *Bell* 1,659. The corresponding games were also introduced: *Ant* 15,267-275 in Jerusalem; *Ant* 16,136-41 in Caesarea.

[37] See the detailed description of the Hellenization of his court life and his Hellenistic friends in W. Otto, *Herodes*, 1913, 107ff.

[38] When they were being educated in Rome, the sons of Mariamne lived with the Roman Asinius Pollio: *Ant* 15,342; see also W. Otto, *op. cit.*, 106. They were educated by Greeks; see W. Otto, *op. cit.*, 109.

[39] See W. Otto, *op. cit.*, 109f., and A. Reifenberg, *Jewish Coins*, 42ff. See also the comparison between Herod I and Agrippa I, in which Josephus expressed his opinion regarding Herod: Ἕλλησι πλέον ἢ Ἰουδαίοις οἰκείως ἔχειν ὁμολογούμενος (*Ant* 19,329).

[40] *Ant* 16,2ff. It is possible that this represented an attempt to come closer to Roman law; see T. Mommsen, *Römisches Strafrecht*, 1899, 755ff. At the same time, it also meant another source of income.

[41] *Ant* 15,273f.; see also *Ant* 19,328ff.

will — it was changed at least seven times during the period of his rule.[42] There is no doubt that Herod must be held principally responsible for the decline of this supreme religious office in Jerusalem.

He was also quite conscious of the people's attitude towards him. A greatly extended security service,[43] a considerable number of fortified buildings and several military colonies[44] and finally a liberal application of the death penalty provided the safety that he needed. Despite this, however, he lived in constant fear of rebellion:[45]

'He was always concerned with safety in all parts (of the country) and distributed sentries throughout the entire nation so that they would as far as possible not be drawn into the disturbances that could arise at the slightest provocation and so that these disturbances, if they did in fact break out, would not remain hidden from the occupation troops stationed in the neighbourhood, but would be recognized and suppressed'.[46]

The success of this 'home policy' became evident when, after the ruler's death, the first petition, apart from one calling for a reduction in taxes, that was presented by the people to his son Archelaus was to release the 'great number' of prisoners incarcerated 'for a long time' by Herod.[47]

Although this policy followed by Herod was successful in preventing larger disturbances, there were, however, several conspiracies against the

---

[42] The Babylonian Ananel: Ant 15,22f.; Aristobulus, the last Hasmonaean: 15,39ff. After the murder of the latter, Ananel was reappointed. The next change is not reported by Josephus. According to Ant 15,322, the Alexandrian Simon b. Boethus followed Jesus b. Phabes; Matthias b. Theophilus: Ant 17,78; Joazar, his brother-in-law (who is probably identical with the Joazar b. Boethus mentioned in the census, see above, p. 127). According to Ant 20,247, Herod only appointed high-priests from unimportant families. Apart from Aristobulus, all new high-priests were moreover non-Palestinians; see A. Edersheim, The Life and Times of Jesus the Messiah, 1953, 36: 'A keener blow than this could not have been dealt at nationalism'. See also J. Jeremias, Jerusalem, 3rd. ed. 1969, 189f.

[43] Ant 15,285.366ff.369.

[44] The Fortress of Antonia, the royal palace in the west of Jerusalem and the winter palace in Jericho were all reinforced. There were military colonies in Samaria-Sebaste, Gaba in Galilee and Heshbon in Peraea; see 15,292ff. It is also important to consider the complex of Caesarea from the military and political point of view. Herod's aim in founding these Hellenistic cities was to provide a counter-weight to the power of the Jewish population. These places continued to be strongholds of Roman power even later and their inhabitants, who were hostile to the Jews, formed a part of the occupation troops; see below, p. 344, n. 166. The fortress at Masada was set up by Herod as a last place of refuge: Bell 7,300. Very many foreign mercenaries had entered the country: Bell 1,290.397.437.672 and Ant 14,394; 15,217; 17,198; see also A. Schalit, König Herodes, 168f. For the strength of the army, see above, p. 278, n. 262.

[45] Ant 15,231.286.291.365f.424; see also W. Otto, op. cit., 97f.

[46] Ant 15,295.

[47] Ant 17,204.

'enemy of the entire nation'.[48] In the case of the ten conspirators to whom I have already referred above,[49] it was the adornment of the theatre in Jerusalem with images and trophies in honour of Augustus that provided the immediate cause. The fact that the man who had uncovered and denounced the plot was torn to pieces by the people points quite clearly to how they felt.[50] The Pharisees, who had taken up a relatively neutral position during the struggle between Herod and Antigonus, were also driven to oppose the king because of his behaviour. An indication of this change in attitude is provided by the Pharisees' and the Essenes' rejection of the oath of loyalty that Herod made his subjects swear.[51] Most of those who refused to take the oath were 'removed', but the king made an exception in the case of the Pharisees and the Essenes, imposing a fine on the former.

The Pharisees' influence among the people was constantly increasing and they formed the only group of men who were able to offer resistance to Herod's contemptuous disregard of the law and his Hellenizing aspirations:

'They were capable of opposing the king most powerfully, and, cautious in themselves, they boasted that they could also do perceptible damage in open battle'.[52]

Herod's reign of terror seems to have acted as a powerful stimulus to messianic hope. This is clear both from the seventeenth Psalm of Solomon, which probably originated during Herod's rule,[53] and from Josephus' *Antiquities*. According to the latter, messianic ideas were introduced into Herod's family by Pharisees, who had predicted to the wife of the king's brother Pheroras, who had paid their fine for their

---

[48] *Ant* 15,281.

[49] *Ant* 15,272.275ff.282-290; see above, p. 102, n. 135, and p. 258f.

[50] *Ant* 15,289ff.

[51] See *Ant* 15,370f. and 17,42: This was probably a double oath for Herod and Augustus which the people had to swear towards the end of the king's reign; see W. Otto, *op. cit.*, 64f., n., and 98f. The religious Jews' refusal to do this must have considerably devalued the oath of loyalty as a political weapon. The oath seems later to have become an established institution (*Ant* 18,124), but even later the Jews were criticized — by Apion — for refusing to swear oaths; see Juster, 1, 344, and A. Schalit, *König Herodes*. 316-22; P. Herrmann, *Der römische Kaisereid*, 1968.

[52] *Ant* 17,41: βασιλεῖ δυνάμενοι μάλιστα ἀντιπράσσειν προμηθεῖς κἀκ τοῦ προὔπτου εἰς τὸ πολεμεῖν τε καὶ βλάπτειν ἐπηρμένοι. The text is not certain. I am not following Niese's suggestion here, but Schürer's, 2, 383, n. 1, according to the W. and E. manuscripts.

[53] This is the opinion of Schlatter, *GI*. 245ff., and O. Eissfeldt, *Old Testament: an Introduction*, 1965, 612f. The descriptions of the 'foreigner', 17,7, and the 'lawless one', 17,11, would in that case refer to Herod.

rejection of the oath of loyalty, that Herod would be deprived of the right to govern and that her family would rule in his place. They had, again according to Josephus, also even promised a eunuch, Bagoas, that he would be called the 'father and benefactor' of the future king and that he would once again become able to beget a family.[54] Even though this anecdote, which goes back to Nicolaus of Damascus, may be a distorted version of the court tradition, it still shows that messianic hope was very much alive at the time, even penetrating into the royal palace.[55]

The continuous growth of inner opposition to Herod finds its ultimate confirmation in the episode of the eagle in the Temple, to which I have referred several times already. Herod's rebuilding of the Temple was carried out in imitation of the style of Hellenistic architecture. The work followed traditional forms only in the innermost part of the Temple building itself. The king had the name of his Roman friend Agrippa engraved on one of the Temple gates[56] and he had a large golden eagle placed on one of the main portals leading to the inner forecourts, presumably in imitation of other ancient temples and especially the temple of Jupiter Capitolinus in Rome.[57]

Two scribes, who were recognized teachers in Jerusalem, Judas b. Sariphaos and Matthias b. Margelaios,[58] made this eagle the object of their attacks. The king was at that time becoming increasingly ill and, acting on the basis of a rumour that he had died, they urged their disciples and a large number of people to go to the Temple and destroy the offensive image. The king's captain, however, intervened, arresting forty young men together with both the teachers and bringing them before the king. They made an open confession of what they had done and died as martyrs.[59]

---

[54] *Ant* 17,43-45; for this, see J. Wellhausen, *Pharisäer und Sadducäer*, 1874, 25.

[55] See W. Otto, *op. cit.*, 102. Mt 2 also provides a vivid illustration of the effect of the messianic hope in the king's court. R. Eisler's view, 1, 341ff., which he bases on a few patristic texts, has been clearly refuted by the research carried out by H.H. Rowley, *JThS* 41 (1940), 14ff.; see also Klausner, *J of N*, 169f. and 398ff.

[56] *Bell* 1,416. For the Temple building, see Schürer, 2, 57f.

[57] *Bell* 1,648-654 = *Ant* 17,149-167. The account in the *Antiquities* is to a great extent no more than a paraphrase of that in *The Jewish War*. For the place where the eagle was set up, see P. Vincent, *Jérusalem de l'Ancien Testament*, 1956, II,2, 713: the eagle may have been hung over the gate dedicated to Agrippa; for the significance of the eagle, see above, p. 103f.

[58] For the names, see A. Schlatter, 'Die hebräischen Namen bei Josephus, *BFThCh* 17 (1913), 76 and 96: the reading in the *Antiquities* is Σαριφαίου, whereas *The Jewish War* has Σεφωραίου with different variants. In the first case this would indicate a place to the east of the Jordan. In the second case, it would point to Sepphoris in Galilee. This is the view of A. Schalit, *König Herodes*, 638, n. 192.

[59] For the martyrdom of the teachers and their disciples, see above, p. 258f.

The animated complaint about Herod's cruel reign that was made by a Jewish legation to Augustus after the king's death certainly reflected the view held by those at the upper level of Jewish society who were not fundamentally hostile to the Romans . It points to the fearful legacy left by Herod, especially in the country's economy.[60] His boundless extravagance had led to a situation in which his hefty income of about one thousand to one thousand two hundred talents a year was simply not enough.[61] Other 'sources of income' were urgently needed and these were supplied by 'gifts' made by the more prosperous members of the population, including especially the property received in the case of those who had become victims of his arbitrary justice.[62] A great deal of the land seems to have become his personal property in this way,[63] although he made a gift of some of it to his favourites. As a result, most of the population were tenants without property[64] and there was growing economic distress in the country. It is true that, during the fearful famine of 25-23 B.C.,[65] Herod reduced the oppressive burden of taxation by a third.[66] This, however, could only have been a temporary measure, since after his death both the inhabitants of Jerusalem, and the legation to Augustus complained about the intolerably high taxes and customs duties.[67]

It was during the period of Herod's rule in Palestine, then,[68] that the

---

[60] *Bell* 2,84-86 = *Ant* 17,304-310. For this, see A. Schalit, *op. cit.*, 256-298.

[61] This figure is reached from the sum total of the income that was distributed among his descendants by Augustus (*Bell* 2,94-100 = *Ant* 17,317.323): Archelaus received four hundred (2,97) or six hundred talents (*Ant* 17,320); Herod Antipas received two hundred, Philippus one hundred and Salome sixty talents. The returns from the separated Hellenistic towns and cities have to be added to this. Agrippa I drew one thousand two hundred talents from the reduced territory and even this sum was insufficient (*Ant* 19,352); see W. Otto, 91f. and 96f., and J. Jeremias, *Jerusalem*, 3rd. ed. 1969, 91f.; see also M. Hengel, *Judaism and Hellenism*, 1,28f.

[62] *Ant* 15,5ff.; 16,155f.; 17,307.

[63] See *Ant* 16,250; 17,321; *Bell* 1,483; see also F.M. Heichelheim in T. Frank, *An Economic Survey of Ancient Rome*, 1933ff., 5: *Eastern Provinces, Roman Syria*, 161, n. 19; see also W. Otto, *op. cit.*, 92f. His plantations of balsam near Jericho were famous throughout the world; see Strabo 16,2.41 (763), and Horace, *Ep* 2,2.184; see also Schürer, 1, 298, n. 36; H. Dessau, *op. cit.*, II,2, 764. They were extended by Archelaus (*Ant* 17,340) and eventually became imperial property.

[64] For this, see J. Herz, 'Grossgrundbesitz in Palästina im Zeitalter Jesu', *PJ* 24 (1928), 110ff. See also above, p. 131f. and below, p. 335.

[65] *Ant* 15,299-316. Although 'help no longer seemed to him to be possible' (304), he intervened with help. For the length of the famine, see Schürer, 1, 291; W. Otto, *op. cit.* 1, 69f., and J. Jeremias, *Jerusalem*, 3rd. ed. 1969, 141.

[66] This was done above all for 'optical' reasons: *Ant* 15,315. Josephus later mentions a similar reduction in taxation that was restricted to a period of time (*Ant* 16,64).

[67] *Bell* 2,4 = *Ant* 17,204; *Bell* 2,86 = *Ant* 17,310.

[68] My point of departure is the king's attitude towards Palestinian Judaism and its

foundations were laid for the emergence of that radical freedom movement which later came to call itself the Zealot movement. Despite the fragmentary nature of the sources, almost all of which only report events concerning the ruler and not what was happening within the population itself, it is possible to distinguish individual aspects of that development which determined the further course of the history of Judaea:

(1) The king's Hellenizing aspirations gave new life to the ancient hostility, which went back to the Maccabaean period, towards all forms of Hellenistic cultural influences.

(2) The above-mentioned conspiracy against Herod and the example of the two teachers shows how individual groups — because of the king's lawless behaviour — could be so moved by zeal for the law that they fearlessly accepted death as martyrs.

(3) Hatred of the illegitimate ruler and the economic distress that he had caused strengthened the people's longing for the true king and the redemption of Israel. There was an increase in messianic tension and this even had a dynamic effect on the royal court.

(4) Even the Pharisaical party was aroused from its traditional restraint. Individual representatives of the movement at least were moved by zeal for the law to open opposition to the king.[69]

(5) Finally, the increasing poverty of the population formed a favourable breeding ground for the later disturbances. Large sections of the population had nothing but their lives left to lose.

If his reign is seen as a whole, it is clear that Herod did not create any good preconditions for the direct rule of Rome later.[70] The name of 'Esau' or 'Edom' given to the Roman rule of the world may be typical of the transference of the people's hatred of Herod, the Edomite, to his Roman protectors.[71]

---

consequences. The Jews of the Diaspora had a positive relationship with Herod; see *Ant* 16,27-62.160-178; see also A. Momigliano, *CAH* 10, 331f. More particularly, an estimation formed within the widely disseminated Hellenistic culture will have been kinder to Herod. For this, see H. Willrich, *Das Haus des Herodes zwischen Jerusalem und Rom*, 1929. A. Schalit, *op. cit.*, 645-75, is fundamental and balanced.

[69] Both the teachers in the Temple were Pharisees; see H. Graetz, 3, 235.797. Graetz, even on the basis of *Bell* 1,648, claims that they were Shammaites; see also G. Hölscher, 'Josephus', *PW* 9, 1974, and W.O.E. Oesterley, *A History of Israel*, 2, 371.

[70] I do not agree here with Schlatter, *GI*, 235, see A. Edersheim, *op. cit.*, 1, 237, who says: 'This accession of Herod, misnamed the Great, marked a period in the Jewish history which closed with the war of despair against Rome ... It gave rise to the appearance of ... a fourth party that ... of the Nationalists'.

[71] This is the view held by H. Graetz, *op. cit.*, 3, 235; cf. A. Schlatter, *Die Theologie des Judentums nach dem Bericht des Josephus*, 219, n. 1. See also above, p. 303, n. 402.

3. The Disturbances following Herod's Death

Archelaus, whom Herod had designated as his successor, was the son of a Samaritan woman:[72] 'the final insult that the restorer of Sebaste hurled at the Jews'. As little moderation towards and understanding of the Jewish population could be expected from him as from his father. What is more, the situation he had inherited from Herod was strained to the breaking point.

Fear of Herod had led to the postponement of the lamentation for the death of the two teachers and their disciples who had died as martyrs 'for the paternal laws and the Temple' and the first collision occurred when this took place. The Jews who assembled in the forecourt combined it with certain concrete demands. They insisted that Herod's Hellenistic favourites should be punished and that the high-priest Joazar b. Boethus, who had been appointed by the late king, should be dismissed. They claimed that 'they had the right to elect a purer and more God-fearing man'.[73]

All attempts to pacify the crowd proved unsuccessful and a section of soldiers even had to withdraw with losses. In addition to this, even greater numbers of people were entering the city with the approach of the Passover. Archelaus therefore had recourse to a final way out of the problem, summoning all his armed forces, having the Temple hill cordoned off by cavalry and the forecourt itself cleared of people by infantry. The people had already begun to sacrifice their paschal lambs when the ruler's troops initiated a terrible blood-bath. Three thousand people were killed and the rest were scattered.

This bloody act at the beginning of the new ruler's period of government was decisive for its further development. Thousands had been killed in the holy place, the Passover had been violated and the Temple had been desecrated. The people could only regard rulers of this kind as instruments of the devil. According to Josephus, the main impetus for the disturbances in the Temple was provided by a group of Pharisees. The reports in *The Jewish War* and the *Antiquities* are in agreement here, that the crowd was roused to rebellion by teachers of the law (σοφισταί or ἐξηγηταί).[74]

---

[72] *Bell* 1,562; 2,39; *Ant* 17,20.250; see also Derenbourg, 193.

[73] *Bell* 2,7; for the whole episode, see 2,4–13 = *Ant* 17,206–218. In Josephus' account, which is dependent on Nicolaus, those lamenting the martyrs' death are from the beginning called rebels: *Bell* 2,5 = *Ant* 17,206. The possibility of a different presentation is present in the complaint made to Augustus by Salome's son that the Temple had been 'filled with mountains of murdered men': *Bell* 2,30 = *Ant* 17,237.

[74] *Bell* 2,10 = *Ant* 17,216.

After Archelaus' departure for Rome, there was no more peace in the country. Varus, the procurator of Syria, had himself led a legion up to Jerusalem and had left the men there as occupation troops for the period of transition. He was followed by Sabinus, the imperial administrator of Syria's finances.[75] His task was presumably to check Herod's property and the financial capability of the country. For this purpose, he had at his disposal a personal armed staff. The presence of these imperial financial officials, however, led to renewed unrest among the population. They were suspected, probably not without good reason, of having their eyes on the Temple treasure.

A great number of pilgrims entered the city fifty days after the bloody Passover, to celebrate the Feast of Weeks. To protect the Temple, they encamped in three groups, the first to the north and the second to the south of the Sanctuary and the third in the west, in the direction of the royal palace,[76] that is, the legionaries' barracks and the residence of the imperial official.

The legion was ordered by the latter to attack the Temple and to set fire to some of the porticoes in the outer forecourt in an attempt to break the fierce resistance of the Jews. Gaining admission by force in this way, they fell on the Temple treasure with the aim of plundering it.[77] This meant that the Temple had been desecrated twice within the space of fifty days.[78] This evil action stimulated the Jews even more to fight and even Herod's Jewish troops — undoubtedly because of the violation of the Temple — also went over to their own countrymen.[79]

It soon became clear, however, that this rebellion had not resulted from a long period of preparation and that it was not supported by an organized movement. When Varus approached the city with two legions and a corps of auxiliary troops, he was offered no resistance worthy of the name. On the contrary, the population of the city received him with fervent assurances of their innocence. Varus confined

---

[75] *Bell* 2,16: ἐπίτροπος Συρίας = *Ant* 17,221: καίσαρος ἐπίτροπος, that is, a *procurator Caesaris*, an official who was directly responsible for the management of the imperial finances and was independent with regard to the governor. Freedmen and even the emperor's slaves were for the most part employed in this office; see *Bell* 2,228 = *Ant* 20,113. See also H. Dessau, *op. cit.*, 1, 191ff.: 'The procurators formed a kind of parallel government, on which the emperor was able to rely more than he could rely on his soldiers'.

[76] See *Bell* 2,44. It emerges even more clearly in the *Antiquities* (17,255) that the Temple was to be defended.

[77] *Bell* 2,49f. = *Ant* 17,261ff.

[78] The Romans constantly threatened the Temple; see above, p. 206ff.

[79] *Bell* 2,52 = *Ant* 17,266. Agrippa II's troops behaved in a similar way at the beginning of the Jewish War: *Bell* 2,437 and *Vita* 407.

himself to tracking down the 'principal culprits' in the country and had two thousand of them crucified around Jerusalem.[80] The memory of this catastrophe was preserved for a long time in Judaism.[81]

Before Varus' intervention, complete chaos had prevailed in the predominantly Jewish parts of the country.[82] In Idumaea, Herod's cousin Achiab was harassed by two thousand of the king's veterans.[83] In Sepphoris, Judas, the son of the 'robber captain' Hezekiah who had been killed by Herod, had gathered a considerable band of followers around him and had seized hold of the royal armoury. In *The Jewish War*, Josephus is not clear about his aims,[84] but, in his *Antiquities*, he speaks about his enormous ambition and says that his zeal was even directed towards the status of kingship.[85] His armed forces were so powerful that, during his march to Jerusalem, Varus had to send quite a large detachment of his army against him from Ptolemais. These troops broke all resistance in Galilee, conquered Sepphoris and destroyed the city, selling the entire population into slavery.[86]

Judas was presumably still able to save his life and go into hiding. In the meantime, Simon, who had once been one of Herod's slaves and was a man of exceptional physical strength,[87] revolted in Peraea, directing his attacks against royal property. He, for example, burnt down the king's palace in Jericho and, in addition, destroyed many valuable country houses. He soon came into conflict, however, with the Sebastenes and the Trachonite cavalry — Herod's elite troops, who had not gone over

---

[80] *Bell* 2,73ff. = *Ant* 17,293ff.; see also AssMos 6,8f.: 'In par(t)es eorum (coh)ort(e)s venient et occidenti(s rex potens, qui) expugnabit eos et ducent captiuos et partem aedis eorum igni incendit, alios crucifigit circa coloniam eorum'.

[81] It is called 'Varus' polemos' in the Seder Olam Rabbah 30, ed. A.D. Neubauer, *Medieval Jewish Chronicles*, 1895, 2, 66. See H. Graetz, 3, 176; Derenbourg, 194; Schürer, 1, 332f., n. 9: 'in *Seder Olam* ... it is said that "from the war of Asveros to the war of Vespasian there were eighty years"'. Either אורוס or ורוס should be read here instead of אסורוס ('Asveros'); see the parallel in *Ap* 1,34. The Proto-Gospel of James, 25, also points to the disturbances following the death of Herod; see Hennecke-Schneemelcher, *New Testament Apocrypha*, 1963, 1, 388.

[82] For what follows, see *Bell* 2,55-70 = *Ant* 17,269-285.

[83] *Bell* 2,55 = *Ant* 17,270f. Judaea appears — erroneously — in the *Antiquities*; cf. *Bell* 2,76ff.

[84] *Bell* 2,56: τοῖς τὴν δυναστείαν ζηλοῦσιν ἐπεχείρει. The question arises here as to who was attacked: the Herodians, the Romans or the rival leaders of bands. In other contexts, Josephus only reports cases of fighting between insurgents in his description of the civil war in Jerusalem.

[85] *Ant* 17,272: ἐπιθυμίᾳ μειζόνων πραγμάτων καὶ ζηλώσει βασιλείου τιμῆς.

[86] *Bell* 2,69 = *Ant* 17,288f. The inhabitants of the rebuilt city were from that time onwards totally opposed to attempts at insurrection and, during the Jewish War, were firmly on the side of the Romans.

[87] *Bell* 2,57f. = *Ant* 17,273ff.

to the Jews — by whom he was killed and his band was decimated. Herod's palace in Beth-haram[88] was set on fire by a second group of Peraean rebels.

The most remarkable figure among these leaders of bands was undoubtedly the shepherd Athronges. Like Simon, he placed the royal diadem on his own head and, again like Simon, was also distinguished by great physical strength. Both Simon and Athronges were probably messianic pretenders.[89] Athronges' four brothers supported him, each leading armed groups as 'generals', while he, as the 'king', was in supreme command of the force. Despite the enemy's superiority, he and his brothers were able to continue for some time. Among other things, they made a surprise attack near Emmaus against a Roman transport of weapons and corn that was protected by a cohort, killing its leader and forty of his men. The harassed cohort was only saved by the intervention of the Sebastenes.[90]

After the return of Archelaus, the brothers continued their struggle. It was only when two of them had fallen and a third had been taken prisoner that the fourth surrendered to Archelaus on the basis of an agreement.[91] This fighting company of brothers (or close relatives) has striking parallels. It can also be found in the case of David (1 Sam 22.1; 1 Chron 2.16f.), the Maccabees and later the sons of Judas the Galilaean.

A number of points that are typical of this later period also emerge from a consideration of the disturbances following the death of Herod. I would list them as follows:

(1) The immediate cause of the general revolt was the desecration of the Sanctuary by Archelaus and later by the Roman troops. This desecration touched one of the most sensitive areas in the faith of the Jewish people.

(2) A clear distinction can be made between what happened in Jerusalem and what took place in the country. Even in the city, the armed revolt was above all the work of the pilgrims who had poured in from the country for the feast, whereas the city dwellers, who were

---

[88] This is according to the Old Testament description (Josh 13.27). The text in *The Jewish War* is corrupt. The place that was later known as Julias or Livias was extended by Herod Antipas; see H.W. Hoehner, *Herod Antipas*, 1972, 87ff.

[89] *Bell* 2,60-64 = *Ant* 17,278-284. For their messianic claims, see above, p. 291ff.

[90] In revenge for this attack, Varus razed Emmaus to the ground: *Bell* 2,71 = *Ant* 17,291.

[91] See *Ant* 17,284; according to *Bell* 2,64, three brothers were taken prisoner.

more disposed towards peace, submitted at once, as soon as the Roman army approached.[92]

(3) The 'robber war' in the country[93] was waged with special energy in the frontier provinces of Idumaea, Galilee and Peraea, which had not been acquired again until the reign of the Hasmonaeans. This phenomenon was later repeated at the beginning of the Jewish War.

(4) The rebels' anger was directed not only against the Roman oppressors and their Herodian supporters,[94] but also against the Hellenistic luxury buildings erected by the lawless ruler himself. This aspect was also to become apparent again in 66 A.D.

(5) The disturbances also had a clear social undertone. It was above all the dispossessed, such as discharged soldiers, slaves and shepherds, who were disposed to rebellion.

(6) The tension brought about by an imminent messianic expectation was also increased to breaking point. It is probable that the distress experienced during Herod's reign had been interpreted as 'messianic woes' and, after the tyrant's death, those who were claiming the Messiah's throne began to sprout as quickly as mushrooms in damp soil. Wealth and position were not essential preconditions for that dignity. A man who was daring enough and had an ecstatic gift could establish the authority that he claimed for himself.[95]

(7) What typified all the attempts made in Palestine to achieve freedom since the end of the Hasmonaean dynasty was that they were fragmented and lacked unity. They lacked the single essential religious idea that might have formed the basis for a successful attempt. Such an idea, central to the Jewish faith and able to combine into a single unified whole all the other conceptions, such as those of the law, the Temple, the imminent expectation of a Messiah and the messianic rule, at the same time making it clear to the Jewish people that it was the holy will of God to break with Rome — that effective idea was not present at that time. In

---

[92] See the apology offered to Varus by the inhabitants of Jerusalem: *Bell* 2,73 (*Ant* 17,293): They would rather have been besieged by the Romans than have fought together with the rebels. Even at the beginning of the Jewish War, the population of Jerusalem adopted a moderate attitude.

[93] *Bell* 2,65 (*Ant* 17,285): τότε δὲ ληστρικοῦ πολέμου τὴν Ἰουδαίαν πᾶσαν ἐνεπίμπλασαν.

[94] See *Bell* 2,62 = *Ant* 17,281.

[95] See above, p. 244: There was a close connection between a pseudo-messiah and a pseudo-prophet, A remarkable parallel with the messianic pretenders of the post-Herodian period is provided by the Syrian slave Eunus in Sicily, who, appealing to a revelation made by the Dea Syria, made himself king and initiated a slaves' revolt which caused great difficulties for the Romans in 135-132 B.C. See Mommsen, *RG* 2, 77-79, and R. Eisler, 2, 722ff.

contrast to the Maccabaean period, the foundation of the Jewish faith —
monotheism, the law and the service of the Temple — was not at that
time — despite all encroachments — seriously threatened by the Roman
rulers. It was still possible for most Jews, as the example of the Diaspora
shows, to find a *modus vivendi* within the special laws provided by the
Romans.[96]

B. FROM THE FOUNDING OF THE FOURTH SECT TO THE DEATH OF AGRIPPA I

1. The Founding of the New Movement by Judas the Galilaean

That effective idea was in fact given to the Jewish freedom movement
by Judas the Galilaean, who at the same time also created an organization
that persisted for two generations and was eventually successful in
drawing almost the whole Jewish population of Palestine into open
revolt against Rome.

This did not, however, happen until ten years after the death of Herod
I. Archelaus had been banished to Gaul in 6 A.D. because of his
maladministration and his territory was from then onwards
administered as an 'annexe' of the province of Syria by an imperial
procurator of equestrian rank who possessed the necessary military,
judicial and financial powers.[97] Closely related to this change by which
Judaea became an imperial province was the census on which its taxation
was based. This was carried out by the new legate of Syria, P. Sulpicius
Quirinius, presumably because he had a trained staff at his disposal and
greater experience, and not by the first procurator, Coponius, who had
been sent at the same time.[98] Such an assessment of fortune and estate was
linked to a population count and a registration of landed property. It was
therefore firmly rejected by the people as an offence against the law and
it was only with difficulty that the high-priest Joazar b. Boethus was able
to persuade them to let the census take place. He made himself so
unpopular, however, by favouring the interests of the Romans in this
way that, after the census, Quirinius sacrificed him to the people's anger
and removed him from office.[99]

---

[96] For the Romans' special laws and their protective legislation concerning the Jewish
religion, see Schürer, 2, 97-103, and Juster, 1, 160-172.224ff.357ff., etc.

[97] *Bell* 2,111.117 = *Ant* 17,342ff.355; 18,2; cf. Dio Cassius 55,27.6. For this, see also
Schürer, 1, 360f., who, however, underestimates the superiority of the Syrian legate. He
was probably the permanent superior over the procurator; see G. Ricciotti, *Flavio
Giuseppe*, 2, 207, for *Bell* 2,117 and H. Braunert, *Hist* 6 (1957), 209.

[98] For the question of the census, see above, pp. 127-138.

[99] *Ant* 18,3.26; see also above, p. 138.

It was at this time that Judas, who was named 'the Galilaean' and came from Gamala in Gaulanitis, made his appearance.[100] He can probably be identified with the Judas who had lit the flame of revolt ten years before in Sepphoris, the capital of Galilee.[101] The solution to this long disputed question is probably to be found in the observation that underlying Josephus' account of the revolt of Judas b. Hezekiah was the work of Nicolaus of Damascus, whereas the author had to go back to other sources for the later period and he neglected to bring the various sources into harmony with each other.[102]

The claim that Judas b. Hezekiah and Judas the Galilaean are identical is strengthened by the existence of points of departure in both cases for the formation of a dynasty. These are not present in the case of other leaders of the Jewish movement of revolt, although there are parallels in the dynasty of Hillel and in the position of the relatives of the Lord in the Palestinian community.[103]

It is highly probable that Menahem, the Galilaean's son, made

---

[100] In *Ant* 18,4, Judas is called Γαυλανίτης ἀνὴρ ἐκ πόλεως ὄνομα Γάμαλα; elsewhere, he often has the nickname ὁ Γαλιλαῖος; see *Ant* 18,23; 20,102; *Bell* 2,118.433; see also Acts 5.37. S. Klein, *Neue Beiträge zur Geschichte und Geographie Galiläas (Palästina-Studien* 1), 1923, 36, believed that this was an error on Josephus' part in *Ant* 18,4 and insisted that Judas' homeland was in Gamala in upper Galilee. See also G. Dalman, *Sacred Sites and Ways*, 1935, 9, n. 2. This view was accepted by Klausner, *J of N*, 162. It is, however, quite possible that Judas — assuming that he was identical with the son of Hezekiah — after the death of his father, grew up in Gamala, which was to the east of the Sea of Gennesaret and, being almost inaccessible, was therefore remote from Herod's power, and that he later returned to Galilee; see J. Spencer Kennard, 'Judas of Galilee and his Clan', *JQR* 36 (1945/46), 281-286. M. Stern, *JRS* 52 (1962), 259, believes that 'Gamala was sometimes described loosely as a part of Jewish Galilee'.

[101] For the view that the two figures were identical, see H. Graetz, 3, 250.258; J. Wellhausen, *Israelitische und Jüdische Geschichte*, 5th. ed. 1904, 353; O. Holtzmann, 2nd. ed. 1906, 55; G. Hölscher, *Geschichte der israelitisch-jüdischen Religion*, 1922, 227; *ibid.*, 'Josephus', *PRE* 9, 1944; Schlatter, *GI*, 260f.; R. Eisler, 2, 69, n. 3; J. Jeremias, *Jerusalem*, 3rd. ed. 1969, 277; W.O.E. Oesterley, *op. cit.*, 366; Klausner, *Hist* 4, 200; G. Ricciotti, *op. cit.*, for *Bell* 2,118; F.M. Abel, *Histoire de la Palestine*, 1952, 1, 423; H. Braunert, *op. cit.*, 213, and Schürer, 1, 351f. For the opposite view, that is, that they were different persons, see G. Dalman, *Words of Jesus*, 1902, 137f.; Foakes Jackson and K. Lake, *The Beginnings of Christianity*, 1920ff., 2, 424 (cf. Foakes Jackson, *Josephus and the Jews*, 1930, 265, n. 1); E. Meyer, *Ursprünge und Anfänge des Christentums*, 1921, 2, 403, n. 1; M.J. Lagrange, *Le Judaïsme avant Jésus-Christ*, 3rd. ed. 1931, 213, n. 1; R.H. Pfeiffer, *History of New Testament Times*, 1949, 35.

[102] Josephus is relatively frequently imprecise in this way: see above, p. 13, n. 51 and p. 15, n. 61: he has, for example, 'feast day' instead of 'sabbath'; in *Ant* 17,339, the deposition of Joazar b. Boethus by Archelaus, in *Ant* 18,26, by Coponius. Schlatter, *GI*, 260, has pointed to this and J. Spencer Kennard, *JQR* 36 (1945/46), 281ff., has established the identity in detail.

[103] For the dynasty of Hillel, see J. Jeremias, *Jerusalem*, 3rd. ed. 1969, 287ff.; see also A. Schlatter, *Die Theologie des Judentums*, 1932, 82, n. 2.

messianic claims and it is also possible that he appears in the rabbinic tradition as Menahem b. Hezekiah. The dynasty that began with Hezekiah the 'robber captain' can be outlined in the following way:

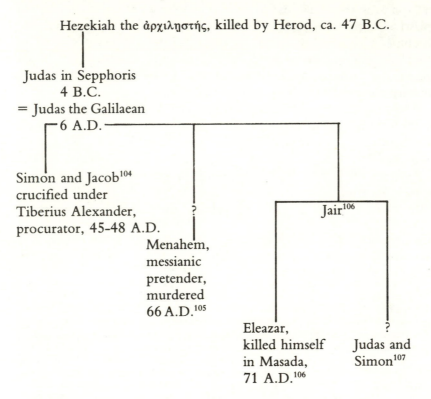

Hezekiah the ἀρχιληστής, killed by Herod, ca. 47 B.C.

Judas in Sepphoris
4 B.C.
= Judas the Galilaean
6 A.D.

Simon and Jacob[104]
crucified under
Tiberius Alexander,   ?   Jair[106]
procurator, 45-48 A.D.
                    Menahem,
                    messianic
                    pretender,
                    murdered
                    66 A.D.[105]
                              Eleazar,   ?
                              killed himself   Judas and
                              in Masada,   Simon[107]
                              71 A.D.[106]

Josephus also calls Judas, as he called the two teachers who were responsible for the destruction of the golden eagle in the Temple, a

---

[104] *Ant* 20,102.

[105] See below, p. 358ff.; Menahem is described as Judas' son in *Bell* 2,433. Because of the intervening space of time of about sixty years, it is possible to assume that he was a grandson; see the long intervals of time in Josephus' own family tree, *Vita* 3ff., in which there are also certain gaps. For this, see J. Spencer Kennard, *op. cit.*, 284.

[106] See *Bell* 7,253. Eleazar's father was called Jair: Ἰείρου, *Bell* 2,447 = יָאִיר, see A. Schlatter, *Die hebräischen Namen* (BFChTh 17), 1937, 53. Eleazar himself is described in *Bell* 7,253 as 'Judas' descendant' and in *Bell* 2,447 as a relative of Menahem; see J. Wellhausen, *op. cit.*, 377: 'the last member of the dynasty of Ezechias and Judas the Galilaean'.

[107] Two brothers, Judas and Simon, the sons of Ari = Jair, distinguished themselves particularly among the Zealots in the defence of the Temple: *Bell* 5,250; 6, 92.148. Judas, leading a group of refugees, fell in the forest of Jardes, *Bell* 7,215. In this case, however, descent from Judas is extremely questionable.

σοφιστής, even adding the epithet δεινότατος in his case.[108] This indicates that Judas was not merely a leader of a band, but also at the same time a teacher of the law. The concept can best be represented as a 'scribe who leads the people astray'. Even in the rabbinic tradition, Judas may perhaps be mentioned as a pious man (חָסִיד) and a 'son' or disciple of the Torah (בֶּן־תּוֹרָה):

'R. Zeira (ca. 300 A.D.) said: How many pious men and sons of the Torah would have been worthy of being ordained (לימנות), like, for example, Judah the son of R. Hezekiah (יהודה ב״ר חזקיה). About such men Scripture (Eccles 1.11) says: "And also of later things ... (there will be no remembrance)". But, in the (messianic future), the Holy One, may he be praised, will ordain an association and have its members sit down beside him in the great community'.[109]

The interpretation of this passage has been disputed.[110] The fact that the text makes good sense without being changed speaks in favour of its referring to Judas. The term of honour, 'Hasid', probably points to a pious man from the distant past and the statement leads us to assume that this Judah b. Hezekiah was refused ordination during his lifetime and was therefore not recognized by most teachers of the law. It is also remarkable that there is no other mention in the rabbinic sources of this Judah b. Hezekiah. Certainty is, in any case, not possible.

Judas also appeared with a Pharisee called Saddok. Attempts have been made to identify this Saddok with a historical person living at that time, but with little success.[111] From his co-operation with Judas,

---

[108] Menahem is also described as such in *Bell* 2,118.433; 2,445. In *The Jewish War*, the term is ambiguous. The two teachers in the Temple are also called this in *Bell* 1,648. According to *Ant* 17,149 (cf. 216), they are, however, described as 'interpreters of the traditional laws' and it is only later (152.155) that they are called σοφισταί. It is probable that Nicolaus of Damascus applied this concept to the two teachers. In *Ap* 2,236, Josephus calls two Greek authors σοφισταί and men who lead young men astray. Philo also uses the word in a negative sense. See also R. Eisler, 1, 53f., and A. Schlatter, *Die Theologie des Judentums nach dem Bericht des Josephus*, 1932, 280.

[109] EcclRab on 1.11; see Derenbourg, 161, n. 3; K. Kohler, *JE* 12, 641; Klausner, *J of N* 203; *Hist* 5, 149, n. 37; S. Applebaum, *JRS* 61 (1971), 160.

[110] According to one assumption, based on a reference to the commentator, R. David b. Luria, for example, 'Judah and Hezekiah' should be read instead of 'Judah b. Hezekiah', with the result that the sons of R. Hiyya (ca. 200) were meant here; see W. Bacher, *Aggada der palästinischen Amoräer*. 1899, 3, 31; Bill. 2, 651; Klausner, *op. cit.*. Since the sons of R. Hiyya were recognized teachers (see W. Bacher, *op. cit.*, 1892, 1, 48ff.; Strack, *Introduction*, 119), this statement can hardly be applied to them.

[111] Derenbourg, 195, n. 2; H. Graetz, 2nd. ed. 1863, 3, 208.485, who was much more cautious in the fifth edition of his work, 1905, 3, 798, and K. Kohler, *JE* 12, 642a, and *Harkavy-Festschrift* 15, suspected that he was the priest R. Zadok, who is mentioned in tYom 1,12 (Z. 181); bYom 23a; Yeb 15b; Gitt 56a, etc. and who was, according to Yeb 15b, a Shammaite. This R. Zadok must, however, have lived at a much later period. According to tYomTob 2,13.16 (Z. 204), he was, together with his son, still friend and

however, it is possible to conclude that the radical Pharisaical wing was at least quite closely connected with Judas' teaching. Judas himself may have been a *Haber* and Josephus may have remained silent about this, not wanting to bring this party, to which he, on his own testimony, belonged, into further disrepute.[112]

There are various indications which lend support to H. Graetz' supposition that the school of Shammai showed some tendency to move in the direction of the Zealot party founded by Judas.[113] It is perhaps here that we should look for the cause of the later development of both schools. In the period preceding 70 A.D., the Shammaites, because of the high value that was placed on 'zeal' within Pharisaism, were in the ascendancy. Following the catastrophe, however, they surprisingly enough receded completely into the background and the Hillelites assumed the leadership of the people, the presidency of the school at Jabneh being taken over by the descendants of the master, who at a later period also held the office of Patriarch of Palestine.[114]

The sect founded by Judas, then, may have first appeared as a radical Pharisaical splinter group. Quite soon, however, because of its activity in its own right, it developed into an independent party. It is, however, very likely that good relationships were maintained with the Shammaite wing of the Pharisees.[115]

---

house-mate of R. Gamliel II, in Jabneh; see A. Geiger, *JZWL* 5 (1867), 268. R. Meyer, *TD* 7, 42, n. 46, points to the references in the Clementine literature (Ps-Clem, *Recogn* 1,53f.) and Syrus Ephraem to the separation of the 'Sadducees' at the time of John the Baptist.

[112] See *Ant* 18,4.23 and *Vita* 12.

[113] For the eighteen Halakoth of the school of Shammai, see above, p. 200ff.; for the question of waging war on the sabbath, see above, p. 288f. See also H. Graetz, 3, 256f.,472f. and n. 24: 767ff., n. 26: 805ff., n. 29: 820ff; see also Derenbourg, 272ff.; A. Edersheim, *The Life and Times of Jesus the Messiah*, 2nd. unabbreviated ed. 1953, 1, 239; K. Kohler, *JE* 12, 641b; E. Stauffer, *Jerusalem und Rom*, 1957, 70.

[114] L. Finkelstein, *The Pharisees*, 3rd. ed. 1962, 619f., traces the contrast between Hillel and Shammai back to the period following Herod's conquest of Jerusalem: The patriotic and conservative population of the country turned more towards Shammai, whereas the city-dwellers were more inclined towards Hillel. For the predominance of the Shammaites before 70 A.D., see Moore, *Judaism*, 1, 81: 'The Shammaites were the more numerous, as well as the more aggressive, and it was perhaps only after the fall of Jerusalem that the Hillelites gained the ascendancy'. See also Schlatter, *GI*, 352: The decision in favour of Hillel in Jabneh is supposed to have been made when a voice spoke from heaven, in other words, as the result of God's direct judgement; see jBer 3b,67ff. bar parr.; see also Bill. 1, 128.

[115] A fundamental conflict between Zealotism and Pharisaism, to which A. Schlatter, *GI*, 262,264; *Die Theologie des Judentums nach dem Bericht des Josephus*, 215; *The Church in the New Testament Period*, 1955, 199f., repeatedly draws attention, was probably not present. The conflict existed within Pharisaism itself. For the different attitudes of individual Pharisees at the beginning of the Jewish War, see below, p. 370, n. 283.

The new movement also had quite a number of social aspects. Herod had been able to gain possession of a great deal of land, distributing some of it among his favourites. After the banishment of Archelaus, it became the property of the emperor and much of it was either sold or leased to interested parties,[116] but the large land-holdings administered by tenant farmers continued predominant. These tenants were obliged to hand over a considerable portion of the harvest yielded on their land to their landlords and, in addition, they had to pay taxes and religious levies. They also had to bear the risk of failed harvests: a long drought could result in the loss of all their goods and chattels and even of their freedom and family.[117]

The economic superiority of the great landowners also threatened the small peasant farmers who still existed. The land and poll tax levied by the Roman administration could have a similar effect on them as the payment of rent could have on the tenant farmers. They easily got into debt and lost the land that they had inherited.[118] It was from these empoverished circles that the Zealots continued to gain new followers.[119] It was also here that Josephus' criticism that the main characteristic of the Zealot movement was its greed had its origin.[120] Like the Essenes and the early Christians, they may have regarded the name 'poor' as an honorary religious title.[121] During the Jewish civil war

---

[116] *Ant* 18.2. Individual estates, such as, for example, the balsam plantations in Jericho (see above, p. 323, n. 63), continued to be imperial property. According to Pliny the Elder, *HistNat* 12,113, the Jews tried to destroy these estates during the Jewish War, but were prevented from doing so by the Romans. For the Roman landed property, see F.M. Heichelheim in T. Frank, *An Economic Survey of Ancient Rome* 4 (1953), 145, n. 19. S. Applebaum, *JRS* 61 (1971), 158, n. 27a, suspects farming out here.

[117] See M. Rostovtzeff, *Social and Economic History of the Roman Empire*, 1957, p. 516, n. 24: 'It is evident that large estates remained the outstanding feature of the economic life of the Empire throughout the first century.' The system of tax collection employed meant that great landowners and government officials promoted each others' interests. If they were to pay their taxes, small farmers had constantly to take out loans until they reached the point where their whole property was mortgaged.

[118] The Gospels also refer to these conditions; see, for example, Mk 12.1ff. parr.; Mt 18.23; Lk 16.1ff., etc. See also J. Herz, 'Großgrundbesitz in Palästina im Zeitalter Jesu Christi', *PJ* 24 (1928), 99: 'The small farmer was at the mercy of two classes of men, whom he regarded as his worst enemies: the judge and the rich man'. See also the detailed description in Klausner, *J of N*. 187ff.

[119] See *Bell* 2,265 = *Ant* 20,187; the destruction of the archive with the record of debts: *Bell* 2,427; *Vita* 66; *Bell* 4,414; 7,412.438. See also E. Meyer, *Ursprung und Anfänge des Christentums*, 1921ff., 2, 74, n. 2: The Jews' struggle with Rome 'was, despite its religious character, more like a social revolution and a civil war than a national uprising...'; see also R. Eisler, 2, 711, n. 1; Schlatter, *GI*, 324; J. Jeremias, *Jerusalem*, 3rd. ed. 1969, 120f.; S.G.F. Brandon, *op. cit.*, 155f.

[120] See above, p. 441f.

[121] See 1QpHab 12,3.6.10; 1QM 11,9.13; 1QH 2,32; 3,25; 18,14, etc.; 4QpPs 37

that took place between 67 and 70 A.D., Simon bar Giora had 'proclaimed' the release of all Jewish slaves (προκηρύξας δούλοις ... ἐλευθερίαν). A. Strobel correctly saw in this a reference to Is 61.1.[122]

Josephus has nothing at all to say about the further immediate fate of the new sect. All that he tells us is that, in the proclamation of his message, Judas was acclaimed with joy and that his movement grew very quickly. Young men in particular were attracted by it.[123] As a secret society that represented a danger to the state, it was always threatened by the power of Rome and, for this reason, it had to be skilfully led and tightly organized, to prevent it from being crushed within a short time. It would seem that Judas was able to provide the new movement with both these requirements. It is also probable that the region where the new sect was most effective was not primarily Galilee, since the census had presumably not been carried out there, in the sovereign territory of Herod Antipas. Moreover, Judas' nickname — the 'Galilaean' — could have originated anywhere except in Galilee itself.[124]

The fact that Judas and his followers waged a small-scale war against the Romans, as his sons did later, is suggested by Josephus and the Acts of the Apostles.[125] Their way of fighting was similar to that of the young David, the early Maccabaeans, Athronges and his followers and finally those who took part in the revolt of Bar Koseba. From the caves and their other hiding-places on the eastern edge of the Judaean hills, they made surprise attacks against small detachments of Roman troops and

---

(No. 171) II, 8f. and III, 10, see DJD V, 43 and 44; 1 QSb 5,22 (Qumran Cave I, 127); see also PsSol 5,2; 10,6; 15,2. For the New Testament, see Lk 6.20; Mt 5.3; Lk 4.18; 7.22; Mt 11.5; Rom 15.26; Gal 2.10. The terms אביונים and ענוים are also to be found with a positive meaning in the Psalms. It was only in late Judaism that they became honorary titles for particular communities. For the Jewish Christian Ebonites, see O. Cullmann, *RGG* 3rd. ed. 1958, 2, 297f. See also E. Bammel, 'πτωχός', *TD* 6, 891ff., 895: the elimination of poverty at the end of time; 896f.: the significance of the concept in Qumran.

[122] *Bell* 4,508.510; see also A. Strobel, *Kerygma und Apokalyptik*, 1967, 11, n. 2. For the whole question, see also H. Kreissig, *Die sozialen Zusammenhänge des jüdischen Krieges*, 1970.

[123] *Ant* 18,6; see also Acts 5.35. For the effect on young men, see *Ant* 18,10.315; *Bell* 2,225.346; 4,128; *Vita* 185; see aso Klausner, *Hist* 4,202.

[124] See F.J. Foakes Jackson, *Josephus and the Jews*, 1930, 264. Judas may have been nicknamed 'the Gaulanite' (*Ant* 18,4) when he was active in Galilee after Herod's death and 'the Galilaean' because of his Galilaean period when he was opposing the census outside Galilee itself.

[125] *Ant* 18,4: ἠπείγετο ἐπὶ ἀποστάσει; Acts 5.37: ἀπέστησεν λαὸν ὀπίσω αὐτοῦ. It is hardly imaginable that 'defection' would have been brought about without the use of weapons. The editors of *The Beginnings of Christianity*, 1, 422, believe that the effects of the 'fourth sect' were confined to the spread of an 'intellectual attitude'; see also F.J. Foakes Jackson, *op. cit.*. 265. who assumes that Judas was purely a teacher.

officials and high-ranking persons who were travelling and incursions into the estates of rich Jews and into non-Jewish territory.[126] As far as possible, however, they spared the ordinary Jewish rural population, on whose goodwill they depended.[127] In the larger centres, they may well have had men whom they trusted, who supplied them with information and through whom they were able to negotiate with the most diverse groups, including even the Roman authorities.[128]

We cannot be sure whether Judas himself, as the leader of the insurrectionists, made messianic claims. We may, however, assume that, like other men of his period who initiated a popular movement, he appeared as a charismatic provided with prophetic gifts. It is also impossible to answer the question: Did he give his sect the honorary title of 'Zealots'? In the same way, we cannot solve the problem of his later fate. According to Acts 5.37, his attempted rebellion failed, he himself died and his followers were scattered. We do not, however, know when and under what circumstances this is supposed to have happened. According to the historical development of the following fifty years, the new party continued to grow in strength. Judas' family must therefore have survived the catastrophe.

2. The Zealot Movement in the Time of Jesus

Tacitus' *sub Tiberio quies* is hardly likely to have included the small-scale war in the desert.[129] We cannot be sure about the extent to which Sejanus' hostility towards the Jews, to which E. Stauffer has drawn attention, had an influence on Palestine.[130] The Samaritans' and Pilate's encroachments on the Temple constituted a confirmation of the Zealots' view that it was impossible to combine a recognition of imperial rule

---

[126] For their surprise attacks against troops, see above, p. 328; see also Dio Cassius, 66,4 and 5, where the author speaks of attacks made against individual Roman soldiers during the siege of Jerusalem (Reinach, 191f.). For onslaughts against Roman officials, see above, p. 37f. and below, p. 346f.; attacks on peaceful and rich people, see *Bell* 2,264f.; *Ant* 20,172; *Bell* 7,254; raids into non-Jewish territory, see *Ant* 20,2.5.121f.; *Bell* 2,234f.; *Vita* 105.

[127] See *Bell* 2,253; see also *Bell* 2,229 = *Ant* 20,114.

[128] See *Ant* 20,161.163.209.255; see also *Vita* 66.

[129] *Hist* 5,9; see also E. Stauffer, *Jerusalem und Rom*, 1957, 16: 'It was a graveyard calm, but the Zealot movement continued to operate underground'. J.W. Lightley's assumption, in *Jewish Sects and Parties in the Time of Jesus*, 1925, 388, that the Zealots were inactive is without foundation.

[130] *op. cit.*, 16ff., see also 134, nn.5 and 6; according to Philo, *LegGai* 159ff., Sejanus' attacks against the Jews were confined to Italy, The text in Eusebius' chronicle, *GCS*, Eusebius 7, ed. Helm, 1956, 176, is based on an exaggerated version of Philo's data. For Pilate, see H. Volkmann, *Gym* 75 (1968), 124-135.

with the holiness of the Jewish faith. They probably at least partly contributed to strengthening the new party.[131]

The New Testament contains certain traces of the activity of the fourth sect of Judas the Galilaean. Simon 'the Zealot', one of Jesus' twelve disciples, is, for example, the first evidence that we have of the party name 'Zealots'. The new party, then, also obtained a foothold in Galilee, where the census had probably not been carried out. It is not known whether other disciples of Jesus had previously been close to the Zealot movement. Little precise information can be derived from their nicknames.[132]

According to Lk 13.1, certain Galilaeans were murdered by Pilate, but it cannot be proved that they were Zealots,[133] since the report is so concise that it is no longer possible to reconstruct the event and what lies behind it. All that can be determined with some degree of certainty are the place and time of the event.[134]

The much discussed passage about the 'storming' of the kingdom[135] also does not refer to the Zealots. To interpret it as applying to the latter is to go counter not only to the whole context, but also to the dating 'from the days of John the Baptist until now'[136] and the fact that it is hardly possible to interpret βιάζεσθαι and ἁρπάζειν in the sense of 'forcing' or 'hastening' the coming of the kingdom. Following G. Dalman, A. Schlatter and M. Dibelius, O. Betz pointed in the right direction in his interpretation.[137]

---

[131] See *Ant* 18,29ff.; *Bell* 2,169-177 = *Ant* 18,55-62.

[132] For Simon Barjona, see above, p. 55; for Judas Iscariot, see above, p. 47, n. 192. Both R. Harris, *The Twelve Apostles*, 1927, 34, n. 1, and, more recently, S.G.F. Brandon, *The Fall of Jerusalem and the Christian Church*, 1951, 106, are especially in favour of the widest possible Zealot interpretation of the names of Jesus' disciples. See also M. Hengel, 'War Jesus Revolutionär?', *CH* 110 (1970); 'Gewalt und Gewaltlosigkeit', *CH* 118 (1971), 38ff. On the other hand, S.G.F. Brandon has greatly overestimated the part played by the Zealots in his book *Jesus and the Zealots*, 1967.

[133] For this, see above, p. 59, nn. 277 and 278. F. Scheidweiler, *ZNW* 43 (1950), 173, believed that Jesus' partners in dialogue were Zealots who 'wanted to win [Jesus] over for their aims'. This claim, however, is also without foundation.

[134] O. Michel, *ThLZ* 83 (1958), 164: 'The narrative . . . presupposes an incident in the forecourt of the Temple at the time of the Passover, not a Zealot revolt . . .' For the place and time of this action, see J. Jeremias, *Jerusalem*, 3rd. ed. 1969, 77f. See also J. Blinzler, *NT* 2 (1957), 24-49.

[135] Mt 11.12 (Lk 16.16). H. Windisch, *Der messianische Krieg und das Urchristentum*, 1909, 35f.; A. von Gall, Βασιλεία τοῦ θεοῦ, 1926, 393; Klausner, *J of N*, 206f.; R. Eisler, 2, 88; S.G.F. Brandon, *op. cit.*, n. 1, and O. Cullmann, *The State in the New Testament*, 2nd. ed. 1963, 20f. are all in favour of a Zealot interpretation.

[136] Unless R. Eisler's chronology, which is based on the Slavonic Josephus, is followed, *op. cit.*, n. 5; see also F. Scheidweiler, *op. cit.*, 171ff.

[137] See G. Dalman, *Words of Jesus*, 1902, 139-143; A. Schlatter, *Der Evangelist*

The parable of the shepherd in Jn 10.1ff. and its interpretation should be understood in connection with the polemic against the false prophets and the messianic pretenders who were appearing as leaders of the people at that time.[138] In this sense, the Zealot movement and its leaders were also included within this category. A direct application of the word λῃστής in verses 1 and 8 to the Zealots is, however, made impossible by the whole context.

What is remarkable, however, is that, just as he does not directly refer to the Essenes, Jesus also never openly refers to the Zealots. On the other hand, his proclamation of the kingdom of God and his guidance about behaviour, as outlined, for example, in the Sermon on the Mount, contains enough to show quite clearly how very sharply his message differs from the ideas of the Zealots.[139] What we may possibly have here, then, is a rule of the game, frequently seen in Judaism, which avoids openly naming the opponent.[140]

A clear indication of the views that originated with Judas the Galilaean can be found in the question of the payment of tribute-money to Caesar, which probably has a close inner connection with the messianic acclamation of the pilgrims in Jerusalem when Jesus entered the city and with the cleansing of the Temple.[141] Those who questioned Jesus suspected that, as the new prophet and a possible messianic

---

Matthäus, 3rd. unabridged ed. 1948, 368; M. Dibelius, *Jesus*, 2nd. ed. 1949, 63; O. Betz, *NT* 2 (1957), 125ff.: 'The βιασταί in Mt 11.12 are both hostile spiritual powers and worldly rulers, ... Behind all these opponents is Belial and it is not an everyday, but an eschatological attack'. G. Braumann, *ZNW* 52 (1961), 123ff., regards them as the persecutors of the community.

[138] For the parabolic character of Jn 10.1-4(5), see R. Bultmann, *The Gospel of John*, 1971, 370, n. 4. For the New Testament polemic against prophetic and messianic leaders, see above, p. 231f.

[139] See above, p.181, n. 180. The view that Jesus and his disciples were close to Zealotism has been expressed again and again since H.S. Reimarus first suggested it in the eighteenth century (see A. Schweitzer, *Geschichte der Leben-Jesu-Forschung*, 5th. ed. 1933, 17ff.). More recently, it has been taken up again in particular by R. Eisler and S.G.F. Brandon. It is, however, untenable. In the same way, it would also be wrong, however, to leave the political theme in the Gospels entirely out of account, as A. Schweitzer, *op. cit.*, 24, 392ff., and E. Meyer, *op. cit.*, 1, 330, do. For this question, see H.G. Wood, 'Interpreting this Time', *NTS* 4 (1956), 262-266.

[140] This rule applies among others to the rabbinic writings, in which Christians are deliberately hardly mentioned. S.G.F. Brandon, *op. cit.*, 105, explains Jesus' silence by claiming that all positive attitudes with regard to the Zealot movement were suppressed in the later tradition. This, however, is a distortion of the true state of affairs.

[141] W.R. Farmer, *Zealots*, viif., and E. Stauffer, *Jesus*, 1957, 91, are correct in maintaining that the palm branches in Jesus' entry into Jerusalem were a sign of his dignity and victory; see also P. Romanoff, *JQR* 34 (1943/44), 438. For the cleansing of the Temple, see above, p. 215f.

pretender, he was close to Judas' movement. They therefore asked him the question which would make a true 'Zealot' confess his Zealot conviction if he did not want to deny it. They wanted, in other words, to prove that he was a political revolutionary.[142]

Jesus' arrest took place in the same way:

'Have you come out as against a robber (ὡς ἐπὶ λῃστήν) with swords and clubs to capture me? Day after day I was with you in the Temple teaching and you did not seize me'.[143]

The word λῃστής can possibly be interpreted here as 'Zealot'. Unlike the members of the Zealot 'underground movement', Jesus never failed to make his proclamation public. The charge that he was a rebel against the state order is rebutted by these words. His enemies, however, had him condemned before Pilate as a messianic pretender who endangered the state[144] and, together with two 'robbers',[145] who may have been real Zealots, he suffered the same death as so many members of the Jewish freedom movement before and after him.

One figure who played a part in Jesus' trial probably also belonged to the Zealot movement:

'And among the rebels in prison, who had committed murder in the insurrection, there was a man called Barabbas ...'[146]

According to this text, an insurrection, during which at least one murder

---

[142] For the payment of tribute-money, see above, p. 193f. E.E. Jensen, 'The First-Century Controversy over Jesus as a Revolutionary Figure', *JBL* 60 (1941), 261-272, regards Jesus as a revolutionary. This is quite possible, but Jesus' attack was directed not against the Roman rulers, but against the religious and political ruling class in Judaism itself, the Sadducaean priests and the Pharisees. It was they and not, as the Zealots believed, the Romans who stood in the way of the dawn of the kingdom of God. See also J. Blinzler, *The Trial of Jesus*, 1959, 52: 'Jesus was the enemy ... of everything that was part of the ruling class in the country'.

[143] Mk 14.48 parr.; see also Jn 18.20. For this question, see A. Schlatter, *Der Evangelist Matthäus*, 756, and K. Rengstorf, *TD* 4, 261f., as opposed to J. Blinzler, *op. cit.*, 72, n. 57.

[144] This is established beyond all doubt by Pilate's question, which is handed down in all four Gospels (Mk 15.2; cf. Mt 27.11; Lk 23.2f.; Jn 18.33) and by the inscription on the cross. See also O. Michel, *op. cit.*: 'Above all the historical fact should be admitted that Jesus was condemned and crucified as a Jewish messianic pretender'. The uncertainty of contemporary research into Jesus on this point is evident in the case of G. Bornkamm, *Jesus of Nazareth*, 1960, in the astonishing contradiction, whereby the author allows the historicity of the inscription on the cross (165), while fundamentally disputing Jesus' messianic claim (177f.).

[145] Mk 15.27 parr.; Jn 19.18.

[146] Mk 15.7: ἦν δὲ ὁ λεγόμενος Βαραββᾶς μετὰ τῶν στασιαστῶν δεδεμένος, οἵτινες ἐν τῇ στάσει φόνον πεποιήκεισαν; cf. Mt 27.16: δέσμιον ἐπίσημον. According to Lk 23.19, the murder took place in Jerusalem.

had occurred, had apparently taken place a short time previously in or near Jerusalem and the guilty parties had been taken prisoner with their leader, Barabbas, as the result of intervention on the part of the occupying power. This man was, it would seem, not unknown to the inhabitants of Jerusalem and he would not have been an ordinary murderer or they would not have asked for him to be released in place of Jesus.

All this would suggest that Barabbas was a member of the Jewish freedom movement, towards which the people were to some extent sympathetic. Political murder was frequently committed by the Zealots,[147] who are also repeatedly mentioned as causing disturbances.[148] The author of the Fourth Gospel characterizes Barabbas simply as a λῃστής (Jn 18.40), in so doing using the name that was so often employed by Josephus for the Zealots and with the same meaning.[149] We have as little cause to doubt the historicity of Barabbas as we have his release. It is also reported that the procurator Albinus released captured Zealots.[150]

3. From Pilate until the Death of Herod Agrippa I

Josephus is also silent about the activity of the Zealots in this period. Yet it was at this time, a few years after the death of Jesus, that it was made very clear to the Jewish people by the actions of Caligula that the emperor's rule, taken together with the religious claims that were made in connection with it, constituted a constant threat to the Jewish faith. The deep and long-lasting agitation experienced by the Jewish people may have strengthened the position of the Zealots. Instead of carrying out the customary spring cultivation of the fields, the rural population prepared for the threatening war with Rome.[151] A legation of eminent

---

[147] See *Ant* 18,7; *Bell* 2,256ff.269; Acts 23.13ff.

[148] See *Bell* 2,225.267.286.295 (see also 2,5).

[149] See A. Schlatter, *Der Evangelist Johannes*, 2nd. unabridged ed. 1948, 342; R. Bultmann, *op. cit.*, 657, n. 5.

[150] For this discussion, see J. Blinzler, *op. cit.*, 205ff., and Excursus X, 218ff. The objections to the episode, which are based above all on the absence of sufficient ancient reports about the legal basis of amnesty, are unconvincing, especially since it is not possible to provide a satisfactory explanation for the subsequent emergence of this account. The hypothesis suggested by H.A. Rigg Jnr., *JBL* 64 (1945), 435ff., that Jesus and Barabbas were originally identical is fantastic. Even if we have no precise knowledge about the legal foundation of amnesty, there are numerous parallels; see E. Lohmeyer, *Das Evangelium des Markus* (Meyers Kommentar), 12th. ed. 1953, 336f.

[151] *Bell* 2,200 = *Ant* 18,272. Whereas Josephus is silent about the threat of war in *The Jewish War*, that threat is stressed in the *Antiquities* and by both Philo and Tacitus; see above, p. 217.

Jews described the situation in Judaea before Petronius in the following way:

> '[He ought to] write to Gaius, telling him that the acceptance of the statue is intolerable for them, that they have neglected to cultivate their fields and have prepared to resist, that they do not want to wage war, but that they would rather die than transgress their laws and that the scourge of robbers would of necessity follow their neglect to sow seed, because the payment of taxes would be impossible'.[152]

The murder of Caligula on 24 January 41 put an end to the fate that threatened the Jews, but, in their historical tradition, they preserved a memory of the shattering experience.[153]

During the short reign of Agrippa I, the Jewish people were able to breathe again.[154] Unlike his grandfather, Herod I, Agrippa relied above all on the Jews among his subjects and tried to consolidate the political and military power of the people.[155] The building of Jerusalem's northern wall, which, according to Josephus, would have made the city almost impregnable, was initiated by him, but, on the order of the emperor, he had to leave it unfinished; but later the rebels tried, as far as possible, to finish building it.[156]

The aim of the assembly of client-kings at Tiberias convened by him and broken up by the intervention of the Roman governor of Syria, Vibius Marsus, may have been to consolidate independence with regard to Rome.[157] Since Agrippa regarded it as important to appear as a Jew who was faithful to the law and was also energetically committed to furthering the interests of the Jewish religion,[158] the Zealots had little opportunity during his reign to be active in promoting their aims.

---

[152] Ant 18,274.

[153] See above, p. 110, nn. 158 and 159. For the dating of this incident, see E.M. Smallwood, Philonis Alexandrini legatio ad Gaium, 2nd. ed. 1969, 47ff.; Schürer, 1, 397: from the winter of 39/40 until the beginning of 41.

[154] See H. Graetz, 3, 353: 'A friendly twilight before the coming of a fearful night'.

[155] Ant 18,274. Agrippa may possibly have appointed a Shammaite as commander of the Antonia. According to Orl 2,12, the Shammaite Joezer had the title of איש הבירה; see Schlatter, GI 1, 435, n. 243; J. Jeremias, Jerusalem, 3rd. ed. 1969, 211f. According to AZ 55a, Agrippa, as commander of the troops, is reputed to have directed questions to R. Gamliel the Elder; see H. Graetz, 3, 347, n. 3.

[156] According to Bell 2,218, the building of the wall was interrupted by the death of Agrippa I and, according to Ant 19,326 and Bell 5,152f., this was done, after an accusation made by Vibius Marsus, at the emperor's command. See Tacitus, Hist 5,12: 'Atque per avaritiam Claudianorum temporum, empto iure muniendi, struxere muros in pace tanquam ad bellum'. For the completion by the rebels, see Bell 2,648; 5,155.

[157] Ant 19,338ff.; for this, see M.S. Ginsberg, Rome et la Judée, 1928, 116f., and M.P. Charlesworth, CAH 10, 680f.

[158] See Ant 19,293ff.328ff.331; Acts 12.1ff. For the rabbinic witnesses, see Derenbourg, 217f.; Schlatter, GI 271 and 435, n. 243.

Although he gave rise to criticism in some circles of strictly pious Jews,[159] he was a generally popular and appreciated king, whose rule led to a diminution of the Zealots' influence on the people. The most convincing proof of the Jews' appreciation of him, however, is the hatred of him that emerged among the Hellenistic population after his death.[160]

C. THE SPREAD OF THE ZEALOT MOVEMENT AFTER THE DEATH OF AGRIPPA I UNTIL THE OUTBREAK OF THE JEWISH WAR

1. The Development from Cuspius Fadus until the Deposition of Cumanus

The Roman decision to appoint Herod I as king of Judaea was the first mistake with grave consequences that they made in their policy with regard to the Jews. The second was to change Judaea back into an imperial province after the death of Agrippa I.[161] According to Josephus, the historical development during the two decades that followed showed a steady gravitation in the direction of an insurrection of the Jewish people in 66 A.D. The revival of the 'scourge of robbers' was one clear sign of increasing dissatisfaction on the part of the Jews. On the eastern frontier, there was even open fighting between the ordinary Jewish population — without the consent of the more respectable citizens, as Josephus hastens to state quite explicitly — and the inhabitants of Philadelphia, the Jews initiating the attack.[162]

One of the first tasks confronting the new procurator, Cuspius Fadus, was to try to settle this dispute. He arrested three of the leaders of the Jews and had one of them, 'Αννίβας,[163] executed and the other two, Eleazar and Amram,[164] banished. A 'robber captain', Tholomaeus, who

---

[159] See *Ant* 19,332ff.; for the doubts about the purity of his descent, see also Sot 7,8b and the sharp criticism of R. Nathan, tSot 7,16 (Z. 308) = bSot 41b. Acts 12.20ff. may also go back to a Jewish tradition that was hostile to Agrippa; see *Ant* 19,343ff.

[160] *Ant* 19,356f.365f. Agrippa died in the spring of 44 B.C.; see Schürer, 1, 452f.; see also Haenchen, *The Acts of the Apostles*, 1971, 61.

[161] See M.P. Charlesworth, *CAH* 10, 681: 'The decision was unfortunate; even so, direct Roman rule over a sensitive race might have been mitigated by good rulers, but the procurators sent out were little credit to the imperial administration ...'

[162] *Ant* 20,2f. The object of the conflict was the district around a village (M Μία, Conj. Ζιᾶ; see Niese, 4, 276 on l. 19); see F.M. Abel, *Histoire de la Palestine*, 1952, 1, 455.

[163] The form and the origin of the name are both uncertain. The Latin has *antibam*. Derenbourg, 237, n. 1, has suggested Hanniboschet and H. Graetz, 3, 361, Hannibal, but both are very unlikely. A. Schlatter, *Die hebräischen Namen*, *op. cit.*, 121, and A. Schalit think that it is an erroneous writing of 'Αντίπας; Klausner, *Hist* 5, 11, nn. 1 and 16, basing his hypothesis on Kel 5,10, has suggested 'Akhnai' (עכנאי = snake), who is named together with 'Ben Dinai' as the builder of an oven; see also BM 59b, above.

[164] This Amram is perhaps the man who is mentioned in SongRab 2,7 together with

had ravaged the frontier territory of the Arabs and the Nabataeans, was also taken prisoner and condemned to death by him.[165]

There were two decisions taken by the Roman administration which were to have a very unfavourable effect on the future. Among other things, Cuspius Fadus was also charged with the punishment of the inhabitants of Caesarea and Sebaste for their riots after the death of Agrippa I. Above all, the cavalry detachment, which consisted predominantly of citizens of these towns, and the five auxiliary cohorts that had taken part in the disturbances were to be transferred for punitive reasons to the Pontus. These troops — mustered by Herod I for the purpose of keeping his Jewish subjects down — had since time immemorial been bitterly hostile towards the Jews.[166] Through an embassy to Claudius, they were able to avoid this penalty. In the two decades that followed, they continued to attack the Jews and, because they did not hesitate to offend in the religious sphere, they frequently touched the most sensitive area for the Jewish population.[167] In Caesarea, their garrison town, they played a particularly unwholesome part, contributing directly towards the outbreak of the Jewish War. The memory of this seems to have been preserved even in the rabbinic tradition.[168]

A second serious psychological mistake was the order given by the

---

Eleazar b. Dinai and Bar Koseba as one of those who wanted to hasten the coming of the end; see above p. 124, n. 252.

[165] *Ant* 20,5; Derenbourg, 237, points to the deceiver, תַּלְמִיּוֹן in LevRab 6,3. The name occurred relatively frequently at that time and was probably used as a borrowing from the Greek Πτολεμαῖος; see A. Schlatter, *op. cit.*, 114; Bill. 1, 536 on Mt 10.3, and Jastrow, *Dictionary*, 2, 1673.

[166] See *Ant* 19,365f. The troops consisted of about three thousand men. These formed the nucleus of the Roman occupation force in Palestine; see Schürer, 1, 362ff. For its establishment, see *Ant* 15,295f. During the disturbances during Herod's reign, these troops remained faithful to the Roman cause (*Bell* 2,52 = *Ant* 17,266; see also *Bell* 2,58.63.74). It is probable that they were then taken over by Agrippa and once again entered the service of the Romans. See also T.R.S Broughton in *The Beginnings of Christianity*, 5, 427ff., and C.H. Kraeling, *HTR* 35 (1942), 266ff. The σπεῖρα Σεβαστή may also have belonged to these Sebastene cohorts; see Schürer, 1, 364; *Beginnings*, 5, 443.

[167] See *Bell* 2,224f. = *Ant* 20,108f.: The lewd gesture made by a guard in the Temple porticoes; 2,229ff. = *Ant* 20,114ff.: The burning of the scroll of the Torah; see also *Bell* 2,298ff.305ff.326ff.332.

[168] See *Bell* 2,268ff. = *Ant* 20,176ff.; *Bell* 2,291f.; see EsthRab 1,19 on 1.3 (S. Krauss, *MonTal* V1, No. 346; see also H. Graetz, 3, 359f., n. 3): 'R. Yitzhak said: The Decumani (דְּיקוּמָנִי) and the Augustiani (אֲוּוּסְטִיאָנֵי), were they who gave Nebuchadnezzar advice, so that he went up and destroyed the Sanctuary, with the result that the Holy One — may he be praised! — let their tribe be exterminated'. Graetz believes that the reference to the Decumani was an allusion to the tenth legion, which took part in the conquest of Jerusalem and later occupied Judaea, and that the Augustiani were the Sebastenes. See also GenRab 94,9.

procurator to the priesthood to deposit the high-priestly garment that had been handed over by Vitellius, the procurator of Syria, once again in the Antonia, in charge of the Romans. After their experiences in the past, this must have seemed to the Jews to be a profanation of the holy cultic vestment. The Roman demand was supported by the presence of a considerable armed force. The immediate result was a renewal of great agitation in the country. The Jews finally obtained permission, by giving hostages, to send a legation to Rome, where Claudius, acting on the basis of the intercession of Agrippa II, decided against the procurator in their favour.[169]

From that time onwards, it seems, there was no end to the number of complaints that the Jews made to the higher authority — a sign that their relationship with the procurator in power became increasingly tense.[170] Theudas, the first false prophet in Judaea, who is mentioned by Josephus, appeared during the procuratorship of Cuspius Fadus. This can also be interpreted as a sign of the great internal unrest that had spread among the Jews. The procurator acted quickly to put the situation right by armed violence. This later became the usual way of dealing with such situations.

Fadus was followed by Tiberius Alexander, a Jewish renegade and the son of the alabarch in Alexandria.[171] It was probably during his period as procurator that the 'great famine' mentioned in the New Testament began, with all its momentous social and economic consequences.[172] This catastrophe, which threatened wide circles of the empoverished

---

[169] *Ant* 15,403f.; 18,90.92ff. In *Ant* 20,8-14, Josephus retained the imperial commitment to the Jews in the original.

[170] See *Ant* 20,132ff. = *Bell* 2,242ff.: the complaints made in Rome under Cumanus; *Vita* 13ff. and *Ant* 20,182ff.: under Felix; *Ant* 20,193: under Festus; *Bell* 2,280ff.: under Gessius Florus. See also *Bell* 2,270.284ff.: the conflict about citizenship in Caesarea. See Schlatter, *GI*, 282: 'The continuing weakening of the power of the state encouraged the outbreak of the war'.

[171] *Ant* 20,100: for his personality and his apostacy from Judaism, see V. Burr, *Tiberius Julius Alexander* (*Antiquitas RI* 1), 1955; *PIR*, 2nd. ed., 1, 139.

[172] *Ant* 3,320f.; 20,51f.101; Acts 11.28; see also Suetonius, *Claudius* 18, according to whom the famine seems to have lasted longer and have affected far more parts of the Roman Empire. For this, see the collection of various ancient reports in Schürer, 1, 567, n. 8; E. Meyer, *op. cit.*, 3, 166ff.; *Beginnings*, 5, 452ff. J. Jeremias, *Jerusalem*, 3rd. ed. 1969, 141ff., dates the famine to the years between 44 and 48 A.D. It was possibly accentuated by the fact that there was a sabbath year between 47 and 48 A.D.; see J. Jeremias, *ZNW* 27 (1928), 100. E. Haenchen, *The Acts of the Apostles*, 1971, 62f., defines the period even more precisely, dating it at 46-49 A.D. For the rabbinic witnesses, see Derenbourg, 226; H. Graetz, 3, 406.787, and J. Jeremias, *Jerusalem*, 3rd. ed. 1969, 143. The inhabitants were liberally supported in their distress by the royal house in Adiabene. Apart from Josephus' witnesses, there is also BB 11a bar. The early Christian community also received help from the communities outside Palestine; see Acts 11.29. It is possible that

inhabitants of both the rural districts and the towns with starvation, was probably also accompanied by increased apocalyptic speculation. Josephus explicitly stresses that it also prepared the way for Zealotism.[173] Many people presumably preferred flight into the desert to dying of starvation or serfdom as a result of unpaid debts. Tiberius achieved, however, one notable success with regard to the Zealots: he took Jacob and Simon, the sons of Judas the Galilaean, prisoner and had them both crucified.[174] This brief note shows clearly that, forty years after the foundation of the Zealotism, the movement was still continuing to fight underground against the Romans under the leadership of members of the founder's family.

Ventidius Cumanus[175] succeeded Tiberius Alexander. During his period, an imperial slave — probably an official of the *fiscus Caesaris* — was attacked and robbed by 'robbers' on the main highway from Caesarea to Jerusalem, near the ascent of Beth-Horon.[176] Cumanus' reaction to this was to have the neighbouring villages plundered by soldiers and the village elders brought to him in chains. He probably did this not so much because — as Josephus argues in *The Jewish War*, in an attempt to exonerate the Jewish population — they had not pursued and captured the robbers after their attack, but because the inhabitants were suspected of having supported the 'bandits'.[177] This was clearly a particularly unpleasant case of Zealot activity, since the emperor would inevitably have learned of such a bold attack against one of his slaves and Cumanus' procuratorship would have been open to the charge of general lack of stability.

The Zealots finally felt powerful enough to risk an attempt to draw the whole population into fighting against the Roman rule. The cause was provided by the murder of a Galilaean pilgrim, who was on his way to the Feast of Tabernacles in Jerusalem, in Ginaea, a place on the frontier between Galilee and Samaria.[178] Because Cumanus refused to accept

---

Paul's collections in Rom 15.26; 1 Cor 16.1ff. and 2 Cor 8 and 9 should be understood in the light of the consequences of this time of famine.

[173] *Ant* 18,8: λιμός τε εἰς ὑστάτην ἀνακείμενος ἀναισχυντίαν.

[174] *Ant* 20,102; for this, see Klausner, *Hist* 5, 13: דור שלישי לקנאים, in opposition to the editors of *Beginnings*, 1, 289.421ff.

[175] 48–52 A.D.; see Schürer, 1, 458ff. For the name, see Tacitus, *Ann* 12,54.

[176] *Bell* 2,228 = *Ant* 20,113: one hundred stages before Jerusalem. Josephus explicitly emphasizes the fact that the attack took place on the 'public highway'.

[177] In *Bell* 2,229, Josephus only speaks generally of the inhabitants; in *Ant* 20,114, he speaks of τὰς πλησίον κώμας. No further reason is given for the plundering. The accusation of lack of pursuit may well conceal the fact that the Jewish population of the country made common cause with the 'robbers'; see also *Bell* 2,253.

[178] *Bell* 2,232–246 = *Ant* 20,118–136. The place is modern Jenin. For the correct

responsibility for punishing the guilty parties, the great number of people who had come to Jerusalem from the whole country decided on their own account to take revenge on the Samaritans and attacked the border territory of Samaria in the south-east from the direction of Akrabatene. Eleazar b. Dinai, the leader of a band of guerillas, and a man named Alexander put themselves, with their 'robbers', at the head of this undertaking.

Cumanus, however, took very effective counter-measures. He sent his cavalry, the 'Sebastenes' and four cohorts to support the Samaritans and quickly extinguished the Jews' aggressive mood. At the same time, he also made them more inclined to listen to the insistent remonstrations of the people's leaders, who had hastened from Jerusalem to the scene and who, dressed in sackcloth and with ashes on their heads, called on them to desist from their senseless plan. The Jews scattered and the robbers also withdrew to their hiding-places, as soon as they recognized that there was no hope of a general uprising against Rome on the part of the people.[179]

All the same, this attempt seems to have strengthened their ranks considerably:

> 'Many (of the Jews), however, turned to brigandage, because they had no fear of punishment (from that quarter) and predatory raids took place throughout the whole country, together with revolts on the part of audacious people'.[180]

Peace was probably not restored as quickly as Josephus would have us believe. The governor of Syria, Ummidius Quadratus, was invited to act as umpire. As a deterrent, when the Jews showed themselves again inclined to insurrection, he had those who had been taken prisoner by Cumanus crucified. He even executed a leading Jew, Doetos, together with several companions, because they had allegedly 'persuaded the people to break with the Romans'.[181] Together with a large number of

---

reading Γίν(ν)αια, see Cumanus and Hegesippus in *Bell* 3,48 (Niese, 6, 280 on l. 18); see also *Ant* 20,118. See also A. Schlatter, *Die hebräischen Namen, op. cit.*, 86. The whole event took place in the autumn of 51 A.D. According to the *Antiquities*, several Jews were killed, but this is probably an apologetic correction.

[179] *Ant* 20,121ff. = *Bell* 2,235ff. Eleazar b. Dinai had already spent many years in the mountains. An otherwise unknown Alexander is also mentioned in addition to him in *The Jewish War*. H. Graetz, 3, 747, identifies him with the Techina b. Perisha mentioned together with Eleazar in Sot 9,9; see, however, below, p. 349, n. 189.

[180] *Bell* 2,238 = *Ant* 20,124: 'From then onwards, the whole of Judaea was filled with robber bands'.

[181] *Ant* 20,129f.: Quadratus had Jewish prisoners crucified in Samaria. From there he went to Lydda and had Doetos executed together with four other main perpetrators.

prominent Jews and Samaritans, the high-priest Ananias b. Nebedai and the Captain of the Temple, Ananus,[182] were sent in chains to Rome to answer for themselves. Even Cumanus himself and one of his officers had to make the journey to Rome and appear before the judgement seat of Claudius. Once again acting on the basis of the intercession of Agrippa II, the emperor decided for a second time in favour of the Jews. The Samaritans were executed and Cumanus was banished and replaced by Felix. The tribune Celer — the commander of a cohort — was taken to Jerusalem and, after having been dragged publicly through the city, was decapitated. This gave complete satisfaction to the Jews and the danger of a general uprising was once again averted.[183]

2. The Increasing Deterioration of the Situation from Felix until Albinus

Antonius Felix, a freedman and the brother of the emperor's favourite, Pallas, was sent to Judaea to replace Cumanus.[184] The success[185] that he achieved during his term of office, which presumably lasted eight years, is in keeping with his character. He played an essential

---

According to *Bell* 2,241f., the mass crucifixion took place in Caesarea, while he had another eighteen Jews decapitated in Lydda. The statement in the *Antiquities*, that Quadratus had become convinced of the Samaritans' guilt, is correctly described by E. Haenchen, *op. cit.*, 10th. German ed. 1956, 66, n. 1, as a 'tendentious travesty'. The text of the *Antiquities* also seems to be corrupt here.

[182] *Ant* 20,131; according to *Bell* 2,243, the high-priest Jonathan (b. Ananus), who had already represented the Jews in the presence of Quadratus, was sent to Rome. J. Blinzler, *The Trial of Jesus*, 1959, 62, n. 30, assumes that the Temple guard also fought on the Jewish side, since the commander was also sent in chains to Rome. The journey was made before the Passover in 52 A.D; see E. Haenchen, *op. cit.*, 1971, 70.

[183] In *Ann* 12,54, Tacitus provides a description of the Galilaean and Samaritan disturbances which cannot be reconciled with that provided by Josephus. According to the Roman author, the disturbances came about as a result of the conflict between the procurators of the two parts of the country, Cumanus and Felix. Together with other scholars, however, I would give preference to Josephus' account; see Schürer, 1, 459f., n. 15; E. Meyer, *op. cit.*, 3, 46ff.; E, Haenchen, *op. cit.*, 68f. H. Graetz, 3, 425.728f., does not take this view. A. Momigliano, *CAH* 10,853, tries to compromise. It should be noted, however, that Tacitus also says of the flourishing scourge of bands: 'Igitur raptare inter se, inmittere latronum globos, componere insidias et aliquando proeliis congredi . . .'

[184] *Ant* 20,137ff. = *Bell* 2,247; his period of office was probably between 52 and 60 A.D.; see Schürer, 1,460, 465f.; see also E. Meyer, *op. cit.*, 3, 53f.; W.O.E.Oesterley, *A History of Israel*, 1932, 438; F.M. Abel, *Histoire de la Palestine*, 1952, 1, 466. The objections raised by E. Haenchen, *op. cit.*, 70f., to the date of his recall had already long since been refuted by Schürer. Josephus' reasons for the journey to Rome also presuppose a fairly long term of office on Felix' part; cf. *Vita* 13ff.

[185] Suetonius, *Claudius* 28. See also Tacitus, *Hist* 5,9: 'Per omnem saevitiam ac libidinem ius regium servili ingenio exercuit'; *Ann* 12,54: 'Cuncta malefacta sibi impune ratus tanta potentia subnixo'.

part in the ruin of Roman rule in Palestine. According to Josephus,

> 'relationships continued to deteriorate, since the country was once again filled with robbers and deceivers who led the people astray'.[186]

It cannot be denied that Felix at first made energetic attempts to put an end to these activities:

> 'The number of robbers who were crucified by him and of common people who were found guilty of having community (with them) and whom he had punished could not be counted'.[187]

It is clear, however, from what Josephus says here that this movement had already gained a great deal of support among the people and that it could no longer be rooted out simply by police actions. At the same time, Felix achieved at least one considerable success without the use of armed violence. By breaking his word and by cunning, he succeeded in taking Eleazar b. Dinai prisoner.

This leader of a band had been able to hold out against the Romans for twenty years in the hill country of Judaea and had played an important part in the Samaritan disturbances.[188] It is possible that, after the crucifixion of Simon and Jacob, the two sons of Judas the Galilaean, Eleazar assumed leadership within the Zealot movement, a position that was later taken over by Menahem. Something is also said about him in the rabbinic tradition. The increase in the general lack of stability led, for example, to the repeal of the law defined in Deut 21.1:

> 'Since murderers had become so numerous, the breaking of the neck of a calf was abolished, (that is), since the appearance of Eleazar b. Dinai and Techina (b. Perisha). Ben Perisha he was called — later he was called the son of the murderer'.[189]

---

[186] *Ant* 20,160.

[187] *Bell* 2,253: τῶν δ' ἀνασταυρωθέντων ὑπ' αὐτοῦ λῃστῶν καὶ τῶν ἐπὶ κοινωνίᾳ φωραθέντων δημωτῶν, οὓς ἐκόλασεν, ἄπειρόν τι πλῆθος ἦν.

[188] *Ant* 20,161; *Bell* 2,253; see above, p. 346f. Nothing is said in *The Jewish War* about Felix' breaking of his word.

[189] משרבו הרוצחנין בטלה עגלה ערפה משבא אלעזר בן דיני ותחינה בן פרישה (בן פרישה) היה נקרא חזרו לקרותו בן הרוצחן. (Sot 9,9a). The Tosefta, 16,1 (Z. 320), takes the Halacha back to R. Johanan b. Zakkai, with the significant comment: 'but now murder is committed publicly'. For the text, see H. Bietenhard, *Sota, Die Mischna*, III, 6, 1956, 152 and 154f. n. 6: The first Ben Perisha is absent from the majority of manuscripts (NJBM). An interpretation therefore becomes much more difficult, because it is no longer clear whether Techina b. Perisha was merely a pseudonym for Ben Dinai or whether a person who was different from him was involved. The Gemara of the Jerusalem Talmud 24a,23 explains the בן הרוצחן by בירה קטולה, which, according to Derenbourg, 279, n. 3, is a reference to the Idumaean

The name of Eleazar b. Dinai probably appears in this context as the representative of the Zealots as a whole. 'Ben Dinai's oven' is mentioned in the Mishnah and his wife is mentioned in the Babylonian Talmud.[190] It is also significant that he is named alongside Ben Koseba in the Midrash among those who wanted to 'hasten' the approach of the end. This shows clearly that his struggle had an eschatological orientation which was in accordance with one of the fundamental themes of Judas the Galilaean.[191] The fact that he was popular is also revealed by his being named in a lamentation on the 9 Ab composed by the poet Eleazar Kalir, who was writing in the seventh and eighth centuries: 'My people called in the days of Ben Dinai: Yahweh is righteous! (Ps 11.7)'.[192] Felix, then, succeeded in enticing the leader of the Zealots to come to Caesarea by promising him that he would not be punished, but, breaking his word, he took him prisoner and sent him in chains to Rome.[193]

The Zealots adopted fresh tactics to combat the Felix' activity in the

---

leader Simeon b. Kathla, although it is only an Aramaic interpretation: 'his son, (who is) a murderer'. See H. Bietenhard, op. cit., 155. Graetz, 3, 747, and Bill. 1, 717, believe that there are two different persons in Sot 9,9. K. Kohler, *JE* 12, 641, believes that the 'Annibas' of *Ant* 20,4 is to be found in Techina b. Perisha; see above, p. 343, n. 163. In the *Harkavyfestschrift* 16, he interprets the surname 'Perisha' as 'Pharisee' and identifies 'Techina b. Perisha' with the 'Abba Tachina the Hasid' named in EcclRab 9,7. L. Goldschmidt, 6, 171, thinks that there was only one person. Klausner, *Hist* 5, 15, thinks the same and regards the second name as a pseudonym for Eleazar b. Dinai, which he used to conceal his identity from the Romans. Appealing to SifDeut 21,1.205, he also stresses that Eleazar was called 'Rabbi'. See also the detailed position adopted by H. Bietenhard, op. cit., 152-155, who assumes either — with A. Büchler — that Ben Perisha was Ben Dinai's successor or that he was his companion in arms, Alexander (*Bell* 2,235). We may conclude, then, that it is hardly possible to find a satisfactory solution to this problem.

[190] Kel 5,10; Ket 27a (according to the Mishnah, 2,9: A woman imprisoned for a crime is forbidden to associate with her husband): 'Rab said: "For example, the wives of thieves". Levi, his disciple, said: "For example, the wife of Ben Dinai" '.

[191] SongRab 2,7.1; see above, p. 122ff.

[192] See G. Dalman, *Sacred Sites and Ways*, 1935, 57ff.: צָעַק עַמִּי בִּימֵי בֶּן־דְּנַאי צַדִּיק הוּא יְהֹוָה. Dalman assumes that 'the tragedy that he caused for many people' was 'regarded as a just judgement'. It is more probable, however, that the just judgement of God on the enemies of the people was seen in the twenty years during which Ben Dinai was fighting; see also H. Bietenhard, op. cit., 154. It is significant that this tradition concerning Ben Dinai was linked with Nazareth.

[193] *Ant* 20,161. R. Meyer, *Der Prophet aus Galiläa*, 1940, 152, believes that he also had messianic characteristics; see also the judgement expressed by Schlatter, *GI*, 322: 'Eleazar, the son of Dinai, stayed for twenty years in northern Judaea as the leader of a band fighting the Romans ... This would not have happened if he had been simply regarded by the Jews as a robber and a murderer; they regarded him as a saint because of his banditry and therefore did not allow their judgement to be shaken by the rabbinate's rejection of him'.

open countryside. This new approach made it possible for them also to be effective in Jerusalem and even in the Temple precincts. They hid short daggers under their garments and used them to attack their victims without being recognized even in dense crowds of people. Transferring the fight for freedom in this way to Jerusalem itself must have greatly reinforced their power and increased the fears of the peace-loving city-dwellers. These new tactics also led to the Zealots being given a new name, that of *Sicarii*. This name probably first became current among the Roman authorities and soldiers and was later taken over by the native population.[194]

It is typical of Felix that he himself should have made use of these new tactics employed by the Zealots for his own ends through the mediation of a citizen of Jerusalem. With the help of Zealot murderers, he had the erstwhile high-priest Jonathan b. Ananus, who was out of favour with him, removed. The Zealots would hardly have objected to an act such as this, since they hated the priestly nobility, as men who exploited the people and desecrated the Sanctuary, as much as they hated the Romans.[195] The conspiracy of forty men, who planned to murder the 'apostate' Paul and offered their services to the Synhedrium, shows there were certain links between members of the influential circles in the capital and the *Sicarii*.[196] The relatively strong guard that accompanied Paul when he was taken to Caesarea can perhaps be regarded as an indication that the power of the Zealot movement lay behind this plot.

Despite all countermeasures, then, the Zealots' power continued to spread. In the same way, more and more enthusiastic prophets and demagogues appeared and Felix was obliged to use armed force against them as well.[197] Josephus is much more detailed in his accounts of the activity of the freedom movement from this point onwards, saying that, in league with the 'deceivers', the *Sicarii* increasingly urged the people to rebel against Rome and threatened to kill those who were disposed towards peace. He also reports that they were scattered over the country in bands and made raids on the property of the rich, killing the owners and plundering their possessions.[198]

---

[194] *Bell* 2,254ff. = *Ant* 20,165ff.186ff.

[195] In *Bell* 2,256, Josephus only provides an account of the murder of the high-priest by the *Sicarii*; according to *Ant* 20,162f., it was Felix who initiated the murder, persuading a 'friend' of Jonathan, a man called Doras, to call on the *Sicarii* to intervene. For the person of Jonathan, see Schürer, 2, 230, No. 15.

[196] Acts 23,12ff.; for the Zealots' vehmic justice, see above, p. 351. For the possibility of a Zealot attack, see A. Schlatter, *The Church in the New Testament Period*, 1955, 84f.

[197] For the false prophets, see above, p. 229ff.

[198] *Bell* 2,264f.; *Ant* 20,185ff.

To this extent it is possible to believe what Josephus tells us. What he says about the senseless thirst of the *Sicarii* for blood, however, can be ascribed to his tendentious presentation of the members of the Jewish freedom party as criminals in every respect.[199] It hardly needs to be stressed that, after a struggle lasting for two generations and resulting in many victims, the Zealots displayed a certain tendency to disorder. This was caused above all by the increase within the movement, as its power extended and the economic distress grew, of those who were motivated not by religion but, above all, by a desire for booty.

They would, however, never have been able to win over wide sections of the population and persuade them to wage war against Rome if they had been, as Josephus claimed, merely criminals. Towards the end of his period of office, Felix seems to have become very much less committed to the task of fighting against the Zealots. There was also a general tendency to disorder. This is clear both from the unrest which broke out again and again in Caesarea, which Felix eventually tried to suppress by sending his troops against the Jewish population,[200] as well as from the leading families of the priestly and city nobility in Jerusalem, many of whom gathered bands around themselves to protect their own interests. These also engaged, in part at least, in public armed encounters and harassed the population.[201] The leading priestly generations used their power above all to enrich themselves at the expense of the ordinary priests, thus threatening the very foundation of the latters' existence, with the result that many of them probably turned to Zealotism. A further consequence of this misuse of power was the emergence of the deep gulf between the priestly nobility and the ordinary clergy that later contributed to the outbreak of the Jewish War.[202]

Felix was followed by Porcius Festus, who took up the fight against the Zealots with renewed vigour. According to Josephus, 'he took a very great number of robbers prisoner and killed several'.[203] While he was procurator, a bitter confrontation developed between the priestly nobility and King Agrippa II. The king had persuaded Festus to order the wall, which the priesthood had erected in the Sanctuary in order to protect the interior of the Temple from being seen from the royal palace

---

[199] See *Bell* 2,257; 7,256ff.; *Ant* 20,165.

[200] *Bell* 2,266ff. = *Ant* 20,173ff.

[201] *Ant* 20,179ff.205ff.213f.

[202] See J. Jeremias, *Jerusalem*, 3rd. ed. 1969, 181, 206f.

[203] *Bell* 2,271. Festus assumed office in 60/61 A.D; see Schürer, 1, 467; E. Meyer, *op. cit.*, 3, 54. He died in 62 A.D.: *Ant* 20,197.

in the upper city, to be pulled down. For the priests, the integrity of the Sanctuary played a vital part in their confession of their faith, 'since they could not bear to go on living if part of the Temple was pulled down'.[204]

The matter was taken to Nero, who acted on the basis of the intercession of his wife Poppaea and decided in favour of the priesthood. The two Jews who played a leading part in this question, the high-priest Ishmael b. Phiabi and the treasurer Helkias, were, however, held as hostages. The honour afforded Ishmael in the Tannaitic tradition points to the fact that his courageous commitment to the cause of the Temple was recognized in pious Jewish circles:

Of the four calls that were made from the forecourt of the Temple, the third was: 'Lift up your heads, you gates, that Ishmael b. Phiabi, the disciple of Phinehas, may enter and rule over the high-priesthood'.[205] The Mishnah also confirms the singular esteem in which this man is held: 'The lustre of the priesthood ended with the death of R. Ishmael b. Phiabi'.[206] He may possibly have been banished to Cyrene by the Romans and later executed there.[207]

Agrippa II took his revenge by opposing the will of the priesthood and granting special privileges to the levitical singers in the Temple.[208] These episodes show that there was not only a deep gulf between the Zealots and the members of the priestly nobility, who had up till that time claimed leadership of the people, but also bitter hostility between the priestly nobility and the Herodians, who were closest to Rome. This may perhaps explain why it was possible for some of the later members of the high-priestly nobility to go over to the war party.

Albinus, the successor of Festus, who died in office, seems to have accepted relatively quickly the continuing activity of the Zealots with resignation, since Josephus observes that 'subsequently, the arrogance of those longing for rebellion in Jerusalem increased'.[209] The abduction by

---

[204] *Ant* 20,189-196 (193); the Jews wanted to conceal holy cultic activity from profane eyes. For their sensitivity regarding any changes in the structure of the Sanctuary building, see 1 Macc 9.54f. and *Ant* 12,413.

[205] Pes 57a bar; for the context, see above, p. 212, n. 347.

[206] Sot 9,15. His family is also mentioned in the great woe directed against the priestly families in tMen 13,21 (l. 533). This is not, however, necessarily directed against the person of the high-priest, who was living in exile. For his personality, see Klausner, *Hist* 5, 26, and J. Jeremias, *op. cit.*, 97, 142f., 196. The analysis made by H. Bietenhard. *op. cit.*, 196, is too one-sided.

[207] See *Bell* 6,114; for this, see H. Graetz, 3, 554, n. 2, and Klausner, *Hist* 5, 26.

[208] *Ant* 20,218; see also J. Jeremias, *op. cit.*, 213.

[209] *Bell* 2,274; As opposed to what he says in *The Jewish War*, Josephus maintains in the *Antiquities* that Albinus was primarily concerned with restoring peace in the country; see

the *Sicarii* of the scribe of Eleazar, the captain of the Temple, during a feast is an example of this 'increasing arrogance'. Eleazar was himself a son of the high-priest Ananias, who had by his wealth and influence made himself the most powerful man in Jerusalem.[210] The abducted scribe was used as an object to be exchanged for ten *Sicarii* who had been imprisoned by Albinus and whose release was brought about by Ananias.

The *Sicarii* seem to have used this method successfully on the family of Ananias several times. We may therefore conclude from this and similar events that the Zealots were the masters who were really in control in the open country and that the Romans' power was to a great extent limited to Hellenistic territory and to fairly large cities where they had occupation troops. The Zealots' probable aim was above all to gain control of Jerusalem and its entire population, which was quite considerable in terms of the ancient world.[211]

The fate of the whole nation turned on the attitude of the inhabitants of Jerusalem. In the city itself, however, the various bands belonging to the individual leading families seem to have been in control. Apart from the members of the priestly nobility, among whom Ananias was the most powerful man, the Herodians also had personal bodyguards operating in bands.[212] Albinus was not able to do much in opposition to this development. His activity was confined in fact to accepting bribes

---

Ant 20,204. This zeal, however, seems to have cooled very quickly. According to *Bell* 6,300ff., Albinus came to Jerusalem before the Feast of Tabernacles in 62 A.D.

[210] *Ant* 20,208ff.; see also 204f. The man involved here was the high-priest Ananias b. Nedebai, who was appointed in about 47 A.D. by Herod of Chalcis; see *Ant* 20,103. He was sent to Rome by Quadratus and seems to have held the office of high-priest towards the end of Felix' term of office (Acts 23.2). His removal from office is not reported by Josephus. For his murder by the Zealots, see below, p. 364, n. 255. For his person, see Schürer, 2, 231; see also above, p. 212f.

[211] J. Jeremias, *op. cit.*, 96 of German ed., estimated 55 000 inhabitants, but reduced this number in his essay on 'Die Einwohnerzahl Jerusalems zur Zeit Jesu', *ZDPV* 66 (1943), 24ff., to 25-30 000, a figure that is probably too low. See also, Jeremias, *op. cit.*, 77-84 of English translation. The initial successes of the Jews during the revolt in 66 A.D. would, if Jeremias is correct, be inexplicable. We cannot, in any case, take the present-day population density as our point of departure. The estimate of the population provided by S. Baron, *A Social and Religious History of the Jews*, 1937, 1, 131, was 100 000 and that given by I. Finkelstein, *The Pharisees*, 3rd. ed. 1946, was about 75 000. We can perhaps reckon with about 40 000 people living in the city at the outbreak of the Jewish War. According to *Ant* 20,219, there were 18 000 men working on the Temple; the number of those defending the city was 23 000 according to *Bell* 5,248ff. and the number of prisoners taken during the whole of the war was, according to *Bell* 6,420, 97 000, and here too a fair number would have come from the population of Jerusalem.

[212] *Ant* 20,207.213f.; see also *Bell* 2,275.

from the different parties.[213] He even accepted such gifts from the Zealots — at least after he had received news of his recall — and released a great number of prisoners in return. According to Josephus, 'the prison was thus cleared of prisoners, but the countryside was filled with robbers'.[214]

3. The Final Escalation of the Situation under Gessius Florus

Josephus believed that Gessius Florus was one of those responsible for the outbreak of the Jewish War, but this is probably an exaggeration.[215] What is certain, however, is that, on his appointment to office in 64 A.D., he found the country in a chaotic state. Like his predecessor Albinus, he too seems to have accepted the Zealots with resignation from the beginning. Certainly Josephus does not mention any measures taken by Gessius Florus against the Zealots. He does, however, accuse the new procurator of being in alliance with them and of leaving them unmolested so long as they gave him a share of their booty.[216]

It should not, however, be forgotten, in any attempt to account for Florus' lack of achievement, that he inherited a policy that had been failing for decades when he came to office and that this policy confronted him with tasks to which he was not equal either from the point of view of his personal character or because of the relatively limited means of power at his disposal.[217] Relying on his good relationships with the imperial family,[218] he therefore tried to gain as much as possible for

---

[213] *Ant* 20,205.209; see also *Bell* 2,274.

[214] *Ant* 20,215. According to *Bell* 2,273, they were imprisoned by the local authorities; see V. Tcherikover, *IEJ* 14 (1964), 69.

[215] For his accession to office, see *Ant* 20,257 and Schürer, 1, 470. The outbreak of war in Artemesius in 66 A.D. (May/June), took place in the second year of his period of office. This must therefore have commenced at the end of 64 A.D. For Josephus' accusations, see *Bell* 2, 277f.282f.332.420. He made the highly improbable accusation that Florus was working directly towards a war. According to *Bell* 2,531, he bribed Cestius Gallus' officers so that they would persuade the governor not to make an attack against Jerusalem; see also *Ant* 18,25 and 20,257. Josephus probably wanted in this way to exonerate his people as a whole and therefore overemphasized the importance of the part played by Gessius Florus in the outbreak of the war. The fact that the critical point in a development towards which the way had been prepared for a long time was reached with Gessius Florus is more clearly expressed in Tacitus, *Hist* 5,10: 'Duravit tamen patientia Judaeis usque Gessium Florum procuratorem: sub eo bellum ortum'. See H. Drexler, *Klio* 19 (1925), 283, and H. Willrich, *Das Haus des Herodes*, 1929, 159.

[216] *Bell* 2,278 = *Ant* 20,258.

[217] The Roman occupation troops in Palestina were relatively weak in numbers. There were little more than three thousand men; see Schlatter, *GI*, 277. See also above, p. 344, n. 166.

[218] *Ant* 20,252: His wife Cleopatra was a friend of Poppaea, Nero's wife. This explains

himself from the restless province that was living under the constant threat of rebellion and made no attempt to reduce the chaotic situation there to order. Finally, it is worth noting that his attitude towards the Jews in the cities who were still subject to his influence was dominated by mistrust and uncertainty. This accounts both for his unpredictable cruelty on the one hand and his timorous leniency on the other.[219]

From his time onwards, events in Judaea followed a rapid and inevitable course. The people and their leaders asked Cestius Gallus, the governor of Syria, who had come to Jerusalem for the feast of the Passover,[220] for an improvement in the Roman administration, but their request was unsuccessful. The city was full of people during this feast, which may perhaps also have been regarded as a political demonstration and during which a curious population count, which is recorded in the rabbinic tradition,[221] took place. Among other things, Josephus also mentions the procurator's insatiable greed for money and his repeated practice of extorting it both from prosperous citizens and from the cities themselves. This should probably not be traced back to his own private shortage of money, but to the fact that he was trying in this way to achieve a balance in Judaea's constantly diminishing income from taxation. The Jews consequently expected that the Romans would make inroads into the Temple treasury and therefore avoided accumulating large capital sums there.[222]

This was followed by fresh disturbances in Caesarea, during which the religious feelings of the Jews were seriously hurt and Florus provoked the Jewish section of the population in an incomprehensible manner.[223] Finally, presumably in an attempt to balance the country's tax deficit, he withdrew seventeen talents from the Temple treasury, an

---

why Agrippa II steadfastly refused to recommend that a legate of Jews should be sent to Nero to complain: *Bell* 2,342f.

[219] The last aspect is easily overlooked, but it should nonetheless be borne in mind: *Bell* 2,331f.420f.

[220] This is usually dated at 65 A.D. It is, however, open to question whether the Jews had as much reason to complain at this point in time as Josephus claims. In addition, there would then be more than a year between *Bell* 2,280ff. and 284. The proceedings against the Jews can be satisfactorily explained on the basis of Florus' attitude, as set out in *Bell* 2,282f. The Passover in question would then have occurred in 66 A.D; see also F.M. Abel, *op. cit.*, 1, 478.

[221] *Bell* 2,280ff., cf. 6,422ff; see also H. Graetz, Note 28, 3, 815–820, who regards this as the 'Passover of oppression' mentioned in tPes 4,3 (Z. 163). See also J. Jeremias, *Jerusalem*, 77ff.

[222] *Ant* 20,219f.

[223] *Bell* 2,284–292. There was an 'insurrection synagogue' in Caesarea in the third century; see Bill. 4, 117 = 118e.

act causing a tumultuous reaction in Jerusalem.[224] Florus hastened with a cohort and some cavalry to the capital in order to restore his threatened authority. Although the leading personalities, to whom preserving peace was very important, showed themselves to be extremely compliant, Florus behaved with unusual harshness and had the 'upper market' in the upper part of the city plundered and a great number of citizens crucified. He achieved, however, the very opposite to the deterrent effect that he had hoped for.

There was an open encounter between two further cohorts that had been brought in haste from Caesarea and the people, who, reacting to Florus' demand and the earnest pleading of their leaders, had gone out to greet the troops. The latter drove them back into the suburb Bezetha and — probably acting on the procurator's order — tried to force their way to the Temple. The cohort in Herod's palace also moved in the direction of the Fortress of Antonia. When the inhabitants of Jerusalem saw that the Sanctuary was threatened from two sides, they barred the troops' way in the narrow streets of the city and attacked them with missiles from the houses and roof-tops. The porticoes linking the Temple to the Antonia were also set on fire with the aim of making it impossible to approach and occupy the Sanctuary from the direction of the fortress. The Roman troops, surprised by this sudden resistance, withdrew into the royal palace. Florus, who had thrown almost his entire armed force into the encounter,[225] was afraid that he would no longer be equal to the situation and, leaving one cohort behind, set off for Caesarea.[226]

With this encounter with the Roman troops, the population of Jerusalem had declared themselves to be fundamentally in favour of the Zealots' cause.[227] But, as previously, in the struggle with the Samaritans under Cumanus, when there had also been armed encounters, the peace party did not abandon their cause and still hoped that political sense would have the victory. The one essential difference between this situation and the previous one was that Cumanus had remained victorious, whereas Florus had quit the field. Both Florus and the leaders in Jerusalem appealed to Cestius Gallus, whose officers advised him to

---

[224] For what follows, see *Bell* 2,293-332. Josephus speaks in *Bell* 2,296 of an 'army', which was in reality only a reinforced cohort (332).

[225] With the city cohort (see Schürer, 1, 366), he had more than four cohorts and a detachment of cavalry at his command, in other words, the overwhelming majority of the occupation troops in Palestine as a whole.

[226] *Bell* 2,331f.

[227] See the request made to Florus by the peoples' leader, *Bell* 2,304: εἰ προνοεῖ τῆς κατὰ τὸ ἔθνος εἰρήνης καὶ βούλεται Ῥωμαίοις περισώζειν τὴν πόλιν. See also H. Drexler, *op. cit.*, 283: 'Jerusalem was at that time not in any sense as peaceful as it appears to have been in Josephus' writings ...'

appear with an army outside Jerusalem and measure the citizens' loyalty to the Romans with this tried and tested means of support. But, instead of following Varus' example, he merely sent an officer, who appeared with Agrippa II in Jerusalem, which, outwardly at least, appeared peaceful to him.[228] Despite the insistence of those who sought a peaceful solution, Agrippa II was unable to decide in favour of supporting a legation of the people that would bring the Jews' complaints about Florus to the attention of Nero and his speech to the inhabitants of Jerusalem also had no effect.

What had, in other words, been taking place for some time was a gradual movement towards revolt against the Romans. Their taxes had remained unpaid,[229] their troops had been prevented by force from entering the Temple and the porticoes connecting their fortress to the Temple had been destroyed. Negotiations between Agrippa II and the population of the city continued for a short time, but, as he unwaveringly refused to undertake any measures against Florus, he was eventually officially banished from the city.[230]

D. THE COLLAPSE OF THE ZEALOT MOVEMENT IN THE JEWISH WAR AND ITS END

1. Eleazar and Menahem

It was only when Jerusalem had decided to support the cause of revolt that the Zealots openly attacked the strongholds of the Roman occupation. They made a surprise attack against Masada on the Dead Sea. This fortress had been built by Herod and was almost impregnable, but the Zealots overcame the Roman occupying forces, seized control of it and occupied it themselves with their own people.[231] The weapons and equipment that they found there were divided by their leader, Menahem, the son of Judas the Galilaean,[232] among his followers and the

---

[228] *Bell* 2,333-341.

[229] The speech made by Agrippa II in *Bell* 2,345-401 was composed by Josephus. Its purpose was, among other things, to bring the power of the Romans to the attention of the Jews in the East. According to 403f. and 405f., it was successful insofar as taxes were collected again and the porticoes that had been destroyed were rebuilt. Quite apart from the fact that there is a distinct contrast between 405 and 407, this readiness seems soon to have changed into the opposite reaction. For an analysis, see H. Lindner, *Die Geschichtsauffassung des Flavius Josephus* (AGSU 12), 1972, 21-25.

[230] *Bell* 2,406.

[231] *Bell* 2,408ff. It is probable that the same is said again in 433f. According to this, Menahem was the leader in the undertaking. For the history and the significance of Masada, see M. Avi-Yonah, N. Avigad et al., 'The Archaeological Survey of Masada, 1955-1956', *IEJ* 7 (1957), 1-8; Y. Yadin, *Masada*, 1966.

[232] For his descent and personality, see above, p. 330ff.

population of the country. At the same time, on the instruction of Eleazar b. Ananias, the captain of the Temple, the twice daily sacrifice offered for the emperor was ended.[233]

It is very likely that this decision was connected with the Shammaite decision made at about that time no longer to accept 'gifts' from non-Jews.[234] It is open to question whether Eleazar the *sagan* is identical with (Eleazar b.) Hanania b. Hezekiah b. Garon, who is connected in the rabbinic tradition with this prohibition and the so-called eighteen Halakoth.[235] Be this as it may, he was able, with the support of the majority of the ordinary priesthood and the Levites, to end the sacrifice made for the emperor despite the protests in the people's assembly of the priestly nobility and the 'most notable Pharisees' — who were presumably members of the school of Hillel. The main argument of the peace party, the contradiction to the hitherto accepted tradition no longer made any impression on the priests and the people: Where God's holy will was at stake, even the argument of ancient tradition had to lose its meaning.

Josephus has nothing to tell us about the reasons that led Eleazar, the captain of the Temple, to break with the Sadducaean tradition of his own family and to go over to their most bitter opponents.[236] During the procuratorship of Albinus, he had even been the victim of a Zealot

---

[233] *Bell* 2,409; see also above, p. 107, n. 162, and p. 205. This custom had been practised since the time of the Persians; see K. Galling, *ZDPV* 68 (1951), 134-142. See also, however, the criticism in tSot 14,10 (Z. 321).

[234] See above, p. 200ff.; H. Graetz' date for the eighteen Halakoth is 9 Adar 67 A.D. (3, 809), but the very late account that he takes as his point of departure has hardly any historical value. It is more likely that the eighteen Halakoth formed the basis for the important decision to terminate the sacrifice made for the emperor.

[235] H. Graetz, 3, 810ff., has more than any other made a detailed case for this identity. He took as his point of departure the fact that Eleazar b. Hanania b. Hitzkiyya b. Garon appears as a name instead of Hanania b. Hitzkiyya b. Garon: MekEx on 20.8 (L 2, 252f.); SifDeut 23,14.294, etc.; see also W. Bacher, *Die Aggada der Tannaiten*. 2nd. ed. 1903, 19, n. 1. Since the absence of the name from the existing accumulation of names is easier to explain than an addition, preference should be given to the former form of the name. Graetz may well be quite correct in this (3, 813). At the same time, however, insoluble difficulties are encountered in any attempt to identify the Shammaite (Eleazar b.) Hanania ... with the son of the high-priest Eleazar. In the first case, the grandfather is called Hitzkiyya and in the second he is called Nedebai; see above, p. 354, n. 210; see Pes 57a bar: בֶּן־נְדְבַּאי. The fact that Ananias' brother was called Hezekiah (*Bell* 2,441) is no proof that his father also had this name; see Derenbourg, 479. Those who have followed Graetz in supporting this thesis have passed over this point too lightly; see, for example, J.Z. Lauterbach, *JE* 8, 427f.; A. Edersheim, *The Life and Times of Jesus the Messiah*, unabridged ed. 1953, 1, 239; S. Zeitlin, *Megillat Taanit*, 1922, 3; H. Lichtenstein, *HUCA* 8/9 (1931/32), 257; R. Meyer, *Hellenistisches in der rabbinischen Anthropologie*, 1937, 137.

[236] He calls it simply a νεανίας θρασύτατος (*Bell* 2,409), a fundamentally 'misleading

plot.[237] Now, contrary to all expectations, he took the cause of the freedom party to the final, victorious decision. It is possible that he was encouraged to take this bold step because he knew that the members of the priestly nobility, who were friendly towards the Romans, were becoming less and less influential, whereas the Zealots' influence among the mass of the people was growing irresistibly. In addition to this, the leading priestly families were no longer safe from encroachments from the Roman rulers during the recent years.[238]

There are two further questions in this context. The first is whether Eleazar was a scribe who was also influenced by a Pharisaism with a Shammaite emphasis. This is closely connected with the attempts made by Graetz to identify him[239] and therefore cannot be answered with any certainty. The second is whether he exercised high-priestly functions. There is also no unambiguous answer to this question.[240] Josephus only informs us about his office as captain of the Temple. As such he was in command of a small, tightly-knit armed force, the Temple guard, which he could employ at any time for his own purposes.[241]

By his change of fronts, Eleazar probably gave increased validity to a view that had been widespread for a long time among the ordinary priests. The point of departure here was the central, radical group of 'Zealots', the members of which later came to the fore as a separate party under the leadership of the priests Eleazar b. Simon and Zechariah b. Amphicalleus and whom Josephus as a rule called οἱ ζηλωταί.

Zechariah also appears under the name זכריה בן אבקולס in the rabbinic legend. According to this, he rejected the sacrifical animal sent, on the basis of the denunciation made by one Qamza bar Qamza,[242] to

---

description"; see H. Drexler, *Klio* 19 (1925), 278. For his father Ananias, see above, p. 354, n. 210.

[237] *Ant* 20,208; see also above, p. 354f. Eleazar must have held this influential position for quite a long period, at least since the time of Albinus.

[238] See *Ant* 20,131f.163f.193-196.202f.216ff.

[239] This is the view held by Klausner, *Hist* 5, 145: תלמיד חכם וסְגָן הכהנים.

[240] This is the view held by Schlatter, *GI*, 450f., n. 372, who believes that the high-priest Eleazar b. Harsum who is mentioned in the rabbinic tradition because of his wealth and his death as a martyr was the Eleazar who was the Captain of the Temple and who, he presumes, acted as high-priest on the Day of Atonement in 66 A.D. Graetz, 3, 724ff., on the other hand, identifies that high-priest with Ananias, Eleazar's father. What is more likely is that there is a connection between that rabbi and high-priest Eleazar b. Harsum and the 'priest Eleazar' on the coins of Bar Koseba; see A. Reifenberg, *Jewish Coins*, 61, Nos. 169,170. This is suggested above all by the connection in LamRab on 2.2,4; see also J. Jeremias, *Jerusalem*, 97, n. 33.

[241] For the office of the captain of the Temple or 'sagan', see Schürer, 2, 277ff., and J. Jeremias, *op. cit.*, 160ff., 197f. For the Temple guard, see *op. cit.*, 63f.; see also p. 30, n. 56.

[242] In *Vita* 33, Josephus includes among the friends of the Romans in Tiberias one

Jerusalem by the emperor with the aim of testing the Jews' loyalty to him. What is more, the animal was rejected by the priest because of a slight imperfection that Bar Qamza had himself deliberately introduced. According to the rabbinic source, it was this rejection that led to the outbreak of the war and the destruction of Jerusalem.[243] On the other hand, according to the Tosefta,[244] the Temple was destroyed because of the 'leniency' of Zechariah b. Abkulus. In the same context, the Tosefta also emphasizes that Zechariah was even more rigorous than the Shammaites in the question of the Sabbath. We may assume that it was this Zechariah who played an important part in ending the sacrifice for the emperor.

This rupture in the traditional service of the Temple signalled the Jewish cult's official break with Roman rule. It could therefore be claimed that the war against Rome began in the Temple,[245] a fact that gives emphasis to the religious character of the uprising. From the military point of view too, the Temple was the point of departure for the rebellion in Jerusalem. In the knowledge that nothing more could be gained by persuasion, the peace party had entreated both the procurator, Florus, and King Agrippa II to send troops to Jerusalem. Florus, who did not want to sacrifice his small armed force in such a hazardous undertaking, gave no reply to the envoys. Agrippa II, on the other hand, sent two thousand cavalry from Batanaea and Trachonitis.[246] Supported by these troops and the Roman city cohort, the leading priests and the citizens, including above all the Herodians, attempted to hold the upper city, while those who, led by Eleazar, had decided in favour of war, occupied the Temple.

The fighting continued undecided for seven days until the 'Feast of 'Wood-offering'. All who were faithful to the Romans, irrespective of their origin and dignity, were excluded from the ceremony marking this feast.[247] In addition to this, the *Sicarii* also provided a powerful reinforcement for the rebels at the time of the feast by attacking the royal troops with renewed vigour and, on the same day, driving them out of

---

Compsus son of Compsus. Derenbourg, 267; Graetz, 3, 822, and Klausner, *Hist* 5, 146, also think that it was the same person.

[243] Gitt 56a; a more recent and more detailed version appears also in LamRab on 4.2,3; see Graetz, 3, 820–822; Derenbourg, *op. cit.*; K. Kohler, *JE* 12, 642b; Klausner, *op. cit.*.

[244] tShab 16,7 (Z. 135); see also bTal 143a. Josephus mentions him in *Bell* 4,225.

[245] *Bell* 2,417; see above, p. 219, n. 377. See also C. Roth, *HThR* 53 (1960), 93–97.

[246] *Bell* 2,418ff.

[247] *Bell* 2,425ff. According to Taan 4,5, the wood was supplied by privileged families on nine different days of the year, the most important of which was 15 Ab. According to Josephus, the date fell on 14 Ab; see *Bell* 2,430; see also J. Jeremias, *Jerusalem*, 226f.

the upper city into the royal palace on the western edge of the city. The insurgents set the house of the high-priest Ananias and the palaces of Agrippa II on fire. Finally, they also burned the city archives. The social reason for the revolt also emerges clearly from the following text from Josephus' *Jewish War*, namely that the Zealots' programme probably included a new distribution of landed property that conformed to the will of God:

> 'They hastened to destroy the money-lenders' debentures and to make the collection of debts impossible, so that they could win over the mass of debtors and incite the poor to rise up against the rich without fear of punishment'.[248]

The Zealots, who were tested in battle, had strengthened the position of the insurgents within the city and this guaranteed that the struggle would be energetically pursued. On the next day, 15 Ab,[249] they attacked the Antonia and, after laying siege to it for two days, took it by storm. The Roman occupying troops were killed and the fortress itself was burnt down. They then went on to attack the extraordinarily well fortified royal palace, into which Agrippa's troops, together with individual Roman sympathizers, had withdrawn, and besieged it from four sides.[250]

It was at this time that the Zealot leader Menahem came from Masada with an armed body of supporters and, entering Jerusalem 'like a king', was at once made 'leader of the revolt' and 'led the siege' of the palace. This son of Judas the Galilaean is one of the key figures in any attempt to understand the Zealot movement. His entry into the city and his later appearance point strongly to the fact that he made messianic claims and had both special authority and a position of power.[251] He was probably not only the leader of one of the many 'robber bands' that were in control of the open country, but also the head of the Zealot movement in the whole of the country. His authority was based on his descent from the founder of the sect, Judas, on his own military power, which he had increased by his successful attack against Masada, and, last but not least, on his personal experience in battle and his own forceful personality. He may perhaps also have been — like his father Judas — a scribe, since Josephus describes him as a σοφιστής.[252]

---

[248] *Bell* 2,427; for this, see above, pp. 131ff. and 335.

[249] *Bell* 2,430; for the first time since *Bell* 2,315 (the looting in Jerusalem by Florus on 16 Artemisus = Iyyar), Josephus gives a precise date here. The disturbances in Caesarea therefore took place about three months previously. For the destruction of the Antonia, see above, p. 219 and below, p. 398f.

[250] For the fortification of the royal palace, see *Bell* 5,161-183 and *Ant* 15,292.318f.

[251] *Bell* 2,433ff.; see also above, p. 293ff.

[252] *Bell* 2,445; see also Klausner, *Hist* 5, 148. See also above, p. 333, n. 108.

It is only if these presuppositions are taken into account that his immediate assumption of the leadership of the struggle after his 'royal entry' into Jerusalem can be satisfactorily explained. One may well ask whether the Zealots did not proceed under his leadership according to a prearranged plan. The disturbances in Caesarea and the procurator's intention to indemnify himself against a tax deficit by withdrawing money from the Temple treasury led them to provoke unrest among the population of Jerusalem. Florus' failed attempt at pacification must have stirred up the flames of rebellion.

The citizens who were loyal to the government asked the Roman authorities to send troops to the city. At the same time, the Zealots had demonstrated their military strength by their successful surprise attack against Masada. Either simultaneously or immediately afterwards, by virtue of his influential position and with the support of the Zealot majority of the lower clergy, Eleazar, the *sagan* who had come over to their side, managed to win the struggle for the Temple. However, the battle for Jerusalem was not decided until the *Sicarii*, who were tested in battle and were Menahem's elite troops, had intervened. The entry of their lord into the city followed their initial successes. This was the sign that the revolution had really succeeded. The Zealots had worked for two generations towards and had now achieved their aim. Almost the entire population had joined in the Holy War against Rome.

Menahem continued to besiege Herod's palace both energetically and cautiously. Although they had no knowledge of siege techniques and lacked the necessary equipment, the insurgents succeeded in undermining one of the towers and making it fall. It is true that those who were besieged had erected a second provisionary wall behind the collapsed rampart, but they recognized the futility of continued resistance and, offering to surrender, they entered into negotiations with Menahem. This offer made by the royal troops, who were themselves Jews, was accepted, while the remnants of the Roman cohort fled into the other three towers of the palace.[253] Pursued by Menahem, it was only with difficulty that the Jewish commander of the fortress, Philippus b. Jakim, was able to remain alive for a time. Later, in Tyre, he was accused of having betrayed the Roman occupation troops to his Jewish compatriots.[254]

---

[253] The Herodium was taken on 6 Gorpaios = Elul; see *Bell* 2,435–440.

[254] *Vita* 46.407f. Vespasian sent him later to Rome to account for himself. Many of Agrippa II's troops later fought on the Jewish side: *Bell* 2,520; *Vita* 220.397. According to *Vita* 50, Varus, Agrippa II's official adviser, made the accusation that there had been an agreement with the rebels. The obscurity in which a figure such as Philippus appears is an

The high-priest Ananias (b. Nedebai) and his brother Hezekiah, who had sought refuge in the king's palace, were killed by the 'robbers'.[255] It is very probable that the murder of his father gave Eleazar, the sagan and leader of the rebellious priesthood, his outward opportunity to break with Menahem, but there were undoubtedly deeper underlying reasons for this rupture. On the one hand, there was the traditional opposition between the city and the country.[256] On the other hand, there was the deep gulf between the priesthood and the laity, in other words, between the priestly and the royal claims to rule. This gulf had opened again and again in Jewish history.

It is possible that Eleazar and Menahem may originally have thought of a priestly and royal dual rule of the kind that was practised by the Essenes and is suggested later during the period of Bar Koseba. Menahem's military successes, however, point with increasing clarity to his attempt to achieve unrestricted total rule for himself. The Temple was the centre of resistance to him. Although the Temple priests to a great extent probably shared his religious views — the eponym of the movement was at the same time the ancestor of the first generation of priests — they were not prepared to abandon their claims to leadership, which were based on the 'nobility of their birth', to a leader of free-booters from the hill country. Josephus, who had recently returned from Rome and was under suspicion because of his tendency towards friendship with the Romans, was concealed in the Temple to protect him from Menahem. This is a sign that the solidarity among the priests was superior to the enthusiasm of the Zealots.[257] There was probably a conspiracy and the Temple was chosen as the safest place for the elimination of the messianic pretender who had become unacceptable to them. He was attacked by Eleazar's followers when he entered the

---

example of the impenetrable nature of the relationships generally at the beginning of the revolt. See also H. Drexler, op. cit., 309.

[255] Bell 2,441; this took place one day later, on 7 Elul. For Ananias, see above, p. 354, n. 210.

[256] This opposition was already present in the Old Testament; see 2 Kings 11.18-20; 14.21. It also appeared in the period of the Maccabees, during the disturbances following the death of Herod (see above, p. 328f.). It was also prominent on several occasions as the Jewish War continued: Bell 4,138ff.151.158ff.; the attitude of the Idumaeans, 233ff.; the opposition between the 'Zealots' in Jerusalem and Simon bar Giora, 514ff.533ff. It is also essential for a true understanding of the passion of Jesus.

[257] For the unique position of the priestly class, see J. Jeremias, Jerusalem, 147ff., 97ff. etc.: the high-priest 'formed . . . the holy summit of the people as ordained by God'. Far too low a value is placed on the significance of the priesthood in B.-Gr. Rel. 114ff. Eleazar's party explicitly emphasizes in Bell 2,443 that Menahem is far below them in rank; for this, see H. Drexler, op. cit., 289: The Jews could not find a leader, as they had done in the Maccabaean period, because the way was blocked by the aristocracy.

Sanctuary in 'royal finery' and accompanied by the 'Zealots' to take part in the worship and a crowd of people who had been specially prepared threw stones at him. Those who were with him resisted for a short time, but soon had to leave the Sanctuary under the pressure of the priests' superiority and seek safety in flight. Most of them, however, including Menahem himself, who had hidden in the Ophel on the southern side of the Temple,[258] were captured and killed. Only a few, Eleazar b. Ari among them, suceeded in reaching Masada. This surprising murder or banishment of Menahem and his followers was possible both because the population of the city had predominantly sided with the priesthood and because the troops of Agrippa II, who had gone over to the besiegers, had probably provided the priests and citizens of Jerusalem with a certain military reinforcement.

This whole sequence of events led to a division in the ranks of the Zealot movement precisely at the moment when a consolidation of all its forces under a single leadership was required. It is probable that Menahem, the son of Judas, the founder of the sect, was the only man possessing the necessary authority and experience to organize a lasting resistance to the Romans based on the Zealot movement throughout the whole country. This assumption would certainly seem to be suggested by the example of Bar Koseba, who lacked the support of a strongly fortified Jerusalem, but whose military achievements with insignificant resources and a population that had been decimated by the catastrophes that had occurred in the preceding ten or so years were very much greater than those of the rebels after 66 A.D. The consequences of this act of violence were of critical importance for the entire further development of the struggle for freedom. I would single out the following:

(1) Menahem's most faithful followers and especially the tribe of the Galilaean Judas withdrew to Masada and took no further part in the subsequent course of the war, even though it is clear from recent finds of coins that the external link with Jerusalem was at least partly preserved. These men believed that the Temple had been desecrated by this bloody act and was therefore doomed to destruction. They remained faithful to their earlier views, however, and continued to follow Eleazar b. Ari, a grandson of Judas, as their leader until their mass suicide immediately before the conquest of the Fortress of Masada by the Romans in April 73 A.D.[259]

[258] *Bell* 2,442–448. For the Ophel, see *Bell* 5,145.254; see also above, p. 293f.
[259] *Bell* 7,275–406; see above, p. 262ff.; see also *Bell* 4,399–405.505ff. For this question, see also Y. Yadin, *Masada*, 1966; V. Nikiprowetzky, *Hommages à André Dupont-Sommer*, Paris 1971, 461–490.

(2) The groups of Zealots in the various parts of the territories settled by the Jews lost their common leader and therefore the bond that held them together. They consequently operated without any sensible plan and were deeply distrustful of the authorities in Jerusalem.[260]

(3) The leading men in Jerusalem, who were drawn predominantly from priestly circles, could only make a little headway in the open country, which was still controlled by the Zealot bands. Therefore neither were they in a position to continue fighting against the Roman armed forces in a planned way and under a central leadership. The individual territories under the command of local leaders continued to be dependent on self-help.[261]

(4) Menahem's death had weakened the Zealots. Their weakness inevitably resulted in a strengthening in Jerusalem of the moderate forces inclined towards a compromise with Rome. There was therefore bound to be a renewed, intensified confrontation with the radical wing, which had been reinforced by the refugees from the frontier territories. The radicals, however, lacked leaders with universally recognized authority, with the result that there were struggles for power. These undermined the strength of the Jewish resistance.[262]

The consideration of the Zealots as a solidly united party ends therefore with the murder of Menahem. It is true that Zealot ideas still persisted until the destruction of the city and even later, until the revolt of Bar Koseba. The ultimate aim of the sect, the 'eschatological' struggle of the entire people against Rome which had begun so promisingly, was, however, condemned to failure from the very beginning. The division of the movement into different groups at war with each other enabled Rome to achieve a victory even before the Holy War itself had properly commenced.

2. The Further Course of the Jewish War until the Defeat of Cestius Gallus

To begin with, the murder of Menahem did not change the generally warlike mood in any way — at least externally.[263] The siege of the

---

[260] See *Vita* 28f.; *Bell* 2,563f.; 4,132-137.406ff.509ff.538ff. Josephus' effectivity in Galilee can also only be understood in the light of this critical attitude towards Jerusalem.

[261] Neither Galilee nor Peraea and Idumaea received any support from Jerusalem when they were attacked by the Romans: see *Bell* 3,135ff.; 4,410-449 and 550-555.

[262] For the part played by the refugees, see *Bell* 2,588; 4,121ff.135ff.138.413f.

[263] In *Bell* 2,445.449, Josephus does, however, report, in an attempt to exonerate the Jewish people, that the population of Jerusalem had hoped for a restoration of peace after

Roman cohort in the three towers was continued and Eleazar replaced the murdered Menahem as supreme commander. The Roman commander finally offered to surrender in exchange for unarmed safe conduct and the besiegers apparently agreed to this offer, but then killed the unarmed Romans, Josephus stressing the fact that they did this on a sabbath. Only their leader, Metilius, who accepted circumcision, escaped with his life.[264]

One figure who was prominent in the negotiations with the occupying force is Ananias Zadduki.[265] He is probably the same Ananias as the Pharisee who later participated in the legation to Galilee that was directed against Josephus.[266] The Pharisees — or at least some of them — were also firmly on the side of the war party. In addition to this Ananias, Josephus also names a Gorion, the son of Nicomedes. This man may perhaps — under a changed name — be identified with a member of the council called Nakdimon b. Gorion, who is mentioned several times because of his extraordinary wealth and who is reputed, among other things, to have gathered, together with two other rich men, great supplies of food for the siege, which were then burnt by the Zealots in the civil war.[267]

The rebels also achieved military successes outside Jerusalem. In the neighbourhood of Jericho, they overcame the dominant fortress of Cypros, where the occupying troops were, like those in Jerusalem, killed and the fortress itself was destroyed. In Machaerus, on the other hand, the Jews took possession of the fortress by promising safe conduct for the Roman garrison. The Herodium also probably fell into the hands of the rebels during this period.[268]

---

the murder of the 'tyrant', but this is hardly likely. The victory over Cestius was only possible because the majority of the population was ready to fight the Romans.

[264] *Bell* 2,450-456. According to the Scroll of Fasting, MegTaan 14, the murder of the Romans took place on 17 Elul, ten days after the conquest of the royal palace. The murder of Menahem occurred between these two events.

[265] *Bell* 2,451; for the name, see A. Schlatter, *Die hebräischen Namen*, 93. Zadduki is, however, not the name of a party here, but a patronymic; see Klausner, *Hist* 5, 149: חנניה בן צדוק.

[266] See *Bell* 2,628; *Vita* 197.290.316.332.

[267] EcclRab 7,12; LamRab on 1.5,31; in a different form also in Gitt 56a and AbRN, c. 6, ed. Schechter (1887), 31f.; see also Derenbourg, 281, n. 1; Graetz, 3, 528f., n. 4; Klausner, *op. cit.*. For the destruction of the supplies, see *Bell* 5,24 and Tacitus, *Hist* 5,12. Changes of name of this kind often appear in Josephus' work; see, for example, *Bell* 2,563 and 4,159.

[268] *Bell* 2,484-486. The Herodium is mentioned first in 4,518ff. and 555 and was at that time in the rebels' hands. According to V. Corbo, *RB* 71 (1964), 260, a furnace for the making of arrowheads, dating back to the time of the revolt, has been found.

In the Syrian towns, the inhabitants responded to the Jewish uprisings with pogroms against Jews, since they felt threatened by the Jewish minorities within their own walls.[269] The Zealots probably also hoped for a general uprising in the Diaspora at the beginning of the struggles; such an insurrection among the very numerous Jews of the Diaspora might have been a real danger to the Romans.[270] They showed little inclination, however, to join in the risky undertaking of their Palestinian brethren and the rebels were only given fairly strong support in the Parthian territories of the east and Adiabene.[271] The first influx of refugees into the home territory of the Jews came with the Jewish persecutions and this was reinforced a year later by Vespasian's military successes. As a radical group, these refugees had, in the period that followed, an important influence on the further course of the Jewish War.

In the meantime, Cestius Gallus had responded too slowly and too late and moved up an army against the rebellious Jews on the traditional path along the Phoenician coast via Acco-Ptolemais. The Galilaean insurgents first succeeded in defeating the rearguard of the Syrian auxiliary troops that Cestius had left behind in Ptolemais[272] A little later, however, after a fierce encounter, they suffered a heavy defeat at a mountain called Asamon at the hands of a strong detachment of Romans led by Caesennius Gallus, the commander of the Twelfth Legion.[273]

All these vanguard encounters, including the sacking and burning of Narbatene and the destruction of Joppa,[274] were overshadowed by the surprising conquest by the Jews of the territory before Jerusalem and especially their victory over the retreating Roman army on the Beth-

---

[269] *Bell* 2,457ff.487ff.559ff.; 7,361ff.; see above all 2,461: 'The Syrians were admittedly no less active in killing Jews, . . . not only, as in the past, out of hatred, but also in order to forestall the danger that threatened them'. W. Weber, *Josephus und Vespasian*, 1921, 19 and 33, concluded from this that the Jews living in the Syrian Diaspora were planning an insurrection at a certain time and that the Syrians anticipated this.

[270] According to Dio Cassius 66,4.3 (Reinach, 190), the Jews also received some support from the Diaspora of the Roman Empire. The strength of the Jews in certain parts of the Diaspora can be measured by the violence of the revolts in Cyprus and Cyrenaica under Trajan. See also Juster, 1, 210, and H. Drexler, *Klio* 19 (1925), 312. For the general attitude of rejection of the western Diaspora, see *Bell* 7,361-367.

[271] See *Bell* 1,5 and the criticism of Titus in *Bell* 6,343. A few Babylonian Jews are named explicitly, including the members of the royal house of Adiabene; *Bell* 2,520; 5,473; 6,356. See also the allusions of Agrippa II in *Bell* 2,388f. and Dio Cassius, *op. cit.*.

[272] *Bell* 2,506; two thousand Syrians are reputed to have died.

[273] *Bell* 2,510-512; for the site of the battle, see S. Klein, *MGWJ* 59 (1915), 163f.; G. Dalman, *Sacred Sites and Ways*, 1935, 75, n. 1; Klausner, *Hist* 5,159.

[274] *Bell* 2,507-509.

Horon road.[275] Even though it would be wrong to place too high a value on the purely military success achieved against Syrian legions, which were notorious for their lack of discipline,[276] the Jewish victory was nonetheless of decisive importance for the continuation of the fight for freedom. It led to even moderate groups of Jews either going over to the side of the war party or else leaving the city.[277] The radicals saw in this victory God's confirmation of their cause and the beginning of the Holy War of annihilation against Rome. Typically enough, two of the new leaders who were, with their groups, to determine the fate of Jerusalem in the years ahead emerged for the first time during these battles before Jerusalem. The leader of a band, Simon bar Giora, seized hold of the Roman baggage-train on the Ascent of Beth-Horon and took it to Jerusalem, while a certain Eleazar b. Simon appeared as the leader of the radical and probably predominantly priestly 'Zealots'. To judge from the latter's large share in the booty, he had played a leading part in the battle itself.[278]

3. The Political Change following the Jewish Victory over Cestius, the Civil War resulting from this and the End of the Insurrectionary Movement

It is very remarkable that, in the people's assembly that followed, the radical party lost its decisive influence in the leadership of the war. Annas, the erstwhile high-priest who was descended from the powerful family of the New Testament high-priest of the same name[279] and a certain Joseph b. Gorion assumed supreme leadership. The leader of the 'Zealots', Eleazar b. Simon, was indeed very influential, but he held no office. The initiator of the revolt in the Temple, Eleazar b. Ananias, who had held such a central position three months previously, was sent off to Idumaea.[280] All this points to the fact that internal changes were taking

---

[275] *Bell* 2,517-555; the unfortunate operations carried out by Cestius Gallus at Jerusalem lasted from the middle of Tishri — according to *Bell* 2,515, the Feast of Tabernacles of 15-22 Tishri had just begun — until the definitive victory of the Jews on 8 Marshesvan (555). For the battle itself and its after-effects, see above, p. 283ff.

[276] See Mommsen *RG* 5, 383; H. Dessau, II,1, 347. The twelfth legion had already suffered a serious defeat at the hands of the Parthians in 62 A.D; see Mommsen, *RG* 5, 390, and J.G.C. Anderson, *CAH* 10, 768ff.

[277] *Bell* 2,556; it was above all the important Herodians who belonged to this party.

[278] *Bell* 2,564. For his priestly origin, see *Bell* 4,225. As the leader of the probably predominantly priestly party, to which Josephus gave the name of 'Zealots', he appears in *Bell* 2,564ff.; 5,5ff.21.250. For this question, see also above, p. 360.

[279] *Bell* 2,563: Ananus b. Ananus; see Schürer, 2, 232, No. 24. He had been high-priest for only a short time and was deposed by Albinus because of the execution of James, the brother of the Lord: *Ant* 20,199-203.

[280] *Bell* 2,566. The text is not without ambiguity: according to the majority of

place in Jerusalem, the causes of which can only be partly understood. I would draw attention to three:

(1) Another division had probably occurred within the war party, which was influenced by the priests, after the death of Menahem and the old opposition between the priestly nobility and the ordinary priesthood may perhaps have broken out again. In any case, Eleazar, the son of the high-priest, retreated into the background — Josephus does not mention him again after saying that he had been sent to Idumaea — and Eleazar b. Simon, an ordinary priest, emerged as leader of the 'Zealots'.

(2) The moderates had skilfully adapted themselves to the changed circumstances and had decided — at least outwardly — to support the cause of the war. The weakening of the radicals' position by the murder of Menahem and the internal disunity gave them the opportunity to regain their influence on the population of the city. Energetic members of the old families and parties were able once again to take over positions of leadership in Jerusalem. Jesus b. Gamala, a leading Sadducaean and erstwhile high-priest,[281] and the leader of the moderate Pharisaical wing, Simon b. Gamaliel, a grandson (or great-grandson) of Hillel,[282] appear alongside the high-priest Ananus b. Ananus (in other words, Annas). In addition to this, the priestly element predominated in the leadership of the city, Pharisees appearing above all alongside these priests.[283]

(3) This success of the moderates achieved by the inhabitants of Jerusalem, however, increased the danger both that the city would become completely isolated and at the same time encouraged the fragmentation of the Jewish insurgents outside Jerusalem. The bands and groups of Zealots in the different parts of the country were bound to regard the new leaders in Jerusalem with greater distrust than had previously been the case.

---

witnesses, the reading is Νέου, Codex C ναίου; the name is completely omitted in the Latin and in Hegesippus. Originally it probably read 'Ανανίου; see Niese, 6, 256, on l. 17.

[281] See *Bell* 4,238ff.283; for his death: 316-325. He was a friend of Josephus' family; see *Vita* 192.204. He was high-priest from 63-65 A.D.; see *Ant* 20,213.223; see also Schürer, 2, 232, No. 26. He is mentioned several times in the rabbinic tradition, especially as the spouse of a rich woman, Martha, of the house of Boethus; see Derenbourg, 248f.; Klausner, *Hist* 5, 22f. According to BB 21a, he is reputed to have introduced compulsory school attendance into Judaea.

[282] *Bell* 4,59f.; *Vita* 189ff.216.309; for the reference to him in the rabbinic tradition, see Derenbourg, 270ff.; Bill. Introduction, 121; J. Jeremias, *Jerusalem*, 33,237,244,255. He probably became a war victim.

[283] See the combination of the different legations in *Bell* 2,566ff.; *Vita* 29.197; see also the triad of Ananus b. Ananus, Jesus b. Gamala (who had both been former high-priests) and the Pharisee Simon b. Gamaliel in *Vita* 191ff. Gorion the son of Joseph, a member of the lay nobility of Jerusalem, also appears in *Bell* 4,159 (see also 2,563). For his murder by the Zealots, see *Bell* 4,358.

This probably was the reason why legations were sent to various parts of the country.[284] They had the task of reducing the influence of the radical forces or of directing it along the right paths and of strengthening or of retying the bonds with Jerusalem that had been endangered or already broken. The enthusiasm for war that the victory over Cestius had inspired gave the legates the support that they needed. That the legates were empowered to make certain religious resolutions and to take charge of the preparations for war is a sign that the new authorities were committed to the cause of the Holy War.[285]

It was for this purpose that Josephus was sent to Galilee together with two other priests. The fact that he, recently returned from Rome and suspected of being friendly towards the Romans, a member of the priestly nobility and a friend of the Sadducee Jesus b. Gamala,[286] could have been given this task is clear evidence of the deep change that had taken place in Jerusalem. He skilfully outmanoeuvred his less able fellow-legates in Galilee and was above all concerned with the formation of his own domestic force. He succeeded in winning over the various bands of Zealots at least partly by a regular award of pay.[287] On the other hand, however, he was equally concerned to have good relations with the opposing side.[288] This double game must have earned for him the hostility of such radical party leaders as Jesus b. Sapphia[289] and John of Gischala, who regarded him as an undesirable power-seeker. At the same time, it must also have aroused the suspicion of those in Jerusalem who had given him the task, with the result that they sent a

---

[284] The 'generals' of the individual provinces (*Bell* 2,566ff.) are probably based on a falsification by Josephus, who wanted in this way to obtain a certain military rank. In reality, they were probably members of the legations that were sent into the various districts; see *Vita* 28ff.

[285] For this question, see above, p. 285f.

[286] *Vita* 204; see also 17-23, a confession that throws light on the divided attitude of the moderate leaders of the people in Jerusalem. Josephus' opponent in Galilee, John of Gischala, appears as the close friend of the Pharisaical leader Simon b. Gamaliel in *Vita* 190ff. It is therefore possible to ask whether Josephus was at that time already a Pharisee, as he himself says that he was (*Vita* 12), and whether he was not, as a member of the priestly nobility and a friend of the head of the Sadducean party, Jesus b. Gamala, very close to Sadduceism. It is quite understandable that he should later join the only surviving party, that of the Pharisees. See also the resistance of the members of religious circles in Galilee, *Vita* 134f.149f., and of Ananias the Pharisee, 197.290 etc.

[287] *Vita* 77. Josephus is silent about this embarrassing fact in *The Jewish War*, in which he is only in command of 'regular' soldiers, *Bell* 2,577ff.

[288] *Vita* 112f.128ff.149ff.; see also *Bell* 3,346ff.

[289] *Vita* 66f.134 (unlike *Bell* 2,599, here, only Jesus is named). 271.278ff.294ff. 300ff. He is probably identical with the Jesus b. Tupha who is named several times in *Bell* 3,450-498; see Niese's note, 6, 333, on l. 13.

legation — which was in any case unsuccessful — to Galilee to remove him.[290]

Seen as a whole, Josephus' devious activity and obscure manoeuvring in Galilee provide us with a clear example for the collapse of the Jewish resistance before the war had begun in earnest. This is why the radicals — probably rightly so — repeatedly made the charge that the leaders of the moderates were secretly concerned to reach a negotiated peace with the Romans.[291] The repeated defeats — at Ascalon as well as in Galilee, Peraea and Idumaea — must have reinforced this opinion. In addition, the same defeats could be interpreted as signs of God's anger over the ruling heads in Jerusalem. At the same time, refugees were once again beginning to pour into Jerusalem and this too would have considerably strengthened the radical party.

The radicals finally felt that they were strong enough to choose a new high-priest by lot from the Zadokite generation.[292] The attempt made by the energetic high-priest Ananus, supported by the conservative majority of the citizens of Jerusalem, to break the growing power of the 'Zealots', who were led by priests and concentrated in the Temple, was frustrated by the intervention of the Idumaeans.[293] This resulted in the destruction of the moderate party, the ultimate and definitive victory of the radicals and the brutal murder of Ananus b. Ananus and his colleague Jesus b. Gamala. According to a rabbinic text, the shops belonging to the sons of Hanan were destroyed three years before the catastrophe (67 A.D.), because their fruits had not been tithed.[294]

The majority of the Idumaeans, however, separated themselves again from the probably too radical 'Zealots', left Jerusalem with two thousand citizens and returned home, while the refugees from the city joined Simon bar Giora.[295] The old antagonism between the population

---

[290] See the accusation made by John of Gischala against Josephus in Jerusalem, *Vita* 189ff., and the lengthy negotiations with the legation which was sent from Jerusalem to oppose Josephus and was eventually sent back by Josephus to Jerusalem accompanied by an armed escort, *Vita* 196-332.

[291] See *Bell* 4,216.226f.228.245ff.320f. This charge was also made against Josephus; see *Vita* 132. It is clear from *Vita* 17-23 that it was well founded. For this question, see Schlatter, *GI*, 328; S. Zeitlin, *JQR* 34 (1943/44), 352ff., and M. Gelzer, 'Die Vita des Josephus', *Hermes* 80 (1952), 73.

[292] *Bell* 4,155ff.; see also above, p. 220.

[293] *Bell* 4,158-325. John of Gischala went to Jerusalem at the beginning of November 67 A.D.

[294] *Bell* 4,314-322; Bill. 2, 571, for SifDeut 14,22.105.

[295] See *Bell* 4,353, according to which all the Idumaeans left the city after having liberated two thousand of its citizens. This to some extent contradicts what is said in *Bell* 4,566ff. In this passage, Josephus tells us that the Idumaean group from John of Gischala's army rose up at a later point of time against John or against the Zealots and, acting

of the city and the inhabitants of the country — who had fled to Jerusalem — continued. In the city itself, the priestly 'Zealots' were soon outmanoeuvred by John of Gischala, who, supported by the refugees, seized absolute power for himself.[296]

The murder of Nero on 9 June 68 A.D. and the Roman civil war that followed the emperor's death led to a postponement of the attack against the city that the Romans were threatening to make.[297] The insurgents, however, took hardly any advantage of this delay. While John was in control of Jerusalem, Simon bar Giora was terrorizing the open country. He brought Idumaea especially under his control and was eventually, in Nisan 69 A.D., allowed to enter Jerusalem by the citizens and the Idumaeans so that he could liberate them from John's tyranny.[298] An indecisive civil war was fought during the following year between John, who had occupied the Temple hill, and Simon, who had occupied the upper city, and this continued until Titus began the siege of Jerusalem on 14 Nisan 70 A.D.[299]

These parties and their struggles were only indirectly connected with the movement founded by Judas the Galilaean. Judas' true descendants, the *Sicarii*, remained almost totally uninvolved in their fortress of Masada and the priestly group of 'Zealots', who could claim that they belonged to an earlier tradition that went back to the period before the war,[300] had practically no influence on the further course of the conflict. Their leader, Eleazar b. Simon, failed in his attempt to escape from the enforced alliance with John of Gischala. The priestly 'Zealots' were able to control the Sanctuary itself for a short time, but John succeeded relatively quickly in reconquering it.[301] They numbered only two thousand four hundred men and were therefore the smallest of the four rival groups in Jerusalem.[302]

---

together with certain leading citizens, let Simon bar Giora enter Jerusalem. It is possible that only a number of Idumaeans had previously left the city.

[296] *Bell* 4,389ff.

[297] *Bell* 4,491ff.; see also above, p. 306, n. 420.

[298] *Bell* 4,503-544.570-584. Simon entered the city in Nisan 69 A.D. (577). It is peculiar that the Idumaeans, whom Simon had reputedly treated so badly, came over as a whole to his side; see *Bell* 4,521-529.534-537.

[299] *Bell* 5,71ff.

[300] See above, p. 360. This group may perhaps go back to Judas the Galilaean's erstwhile supporters in the Temple. Their gradual isolation would then be the result of an overweening self-importance of the priestly nobility, which did not allow them to form an integral part of Judas' predominantly lay movement.

[301] See *Bell* 5,5ff.98ff.

[302] For the strength of this group, see *Bell* 5,250. Zechariah b. Amphicalleus, whom I have already mentioned above (see p. 360, n. 242), appeared as leader (see *Bell* 4,225)

The two leaders of the rebels during the siege also did not come from the original Zealot movement. At the beginning of the war, John was an opponent of the war party. His close friendship with Simon b. Gamaliel indicates that he may possibly have belonged to the school of Hillel.[303] It was only when Gischala had been destroyed by the inhabitants of Tyre and Gadara that his attitude changed. After that event, he gathered a band of four hundred refugees around him and became Josephus' most dangerous adversary in Galilee. After his flight to Jerusalem, he first allied himself with the party of the high-priest Ananus, but it was not long before he went over to the 'Zealots'.[304] He played an important part in the victory over Ananus' moderate party. His influence continued to increase, with the result that he was finally able to set the old priestly leaders of the 'Zealots' aside and win over the μοναρχία, which led him into conflict with Simon first in the open country and later also in Jerusalem itself. During the civil war that followed, he could also continue to defend himself with his six thousand men against Simon's ten thousand because of his favourable position on the Temple hill.[305]

As his name indicates, Simon bar Giora was the son of a proselyte.[306] He came originally not from the Jewish motherland, but from Gerasa in the Hellenistic Decapolis. This was a town which had dealt with its Jewish inhabitants not by killing them, but by simply expelling them from its territory.[307] We do not know when Simon left his home town. Josephus first mentions him in connection with the battles against

---

and, in the later fighting, the two brothers Simon and Judas, the sons of Ari: *Bell* 5,250; 6,92.148. The second fell in the forest of Jardes as the leader of a group of fugitives, *Bell* 7,215.

[303] See *Vita* 43f. (as opposed to *Bell* 2,587, where he is described from the beginning as a 'robber'), and *Vita* 192.

[304] *Bell* 4,126f.208. In his edition of *The Jewish War*, 2nd. reprint ed. 1957, 3, 62f., H. St.J. Thackeray draws attention to the fact that Josephus' description of John has certain affinities with Sallust's description of Catiline. It was presumably the work of Josephus' Greek stylist.

[305] *Bell* 4,389ff.393; see also 558.566ff. For the relationship between the strength of the two groups, see *Bell* 5,250.

[306] From the Aramaic גִּיוֹרָא = Hebrew גֵּר, see Derenbourg, 265; Schürer, 1, 499, n. 73, and G. Kittel, *Forschungen zur Judenfrage* 2 (1937), 44f. 'Bargiora' is found as a form of the name in Dio Cassius 66,7.1 and Tacitus, *Hist* 5,12, where it is, however, wrongly linked with the name of John. For his person, see O. Michel, *NTS* 14 (1967/8), 402-408.

[307] For his origin, see *Bell* 4,503ff. For the behaviour of the Gerasenes, see *Bell* 2,480. In contrast to this, Josephus reports in *Bell* 4,487ff. that Gerasa was stormed by the Romans; see also *Bell* 2,458. M. Stern, *JRS* 52 (1962), 258f., regards this as a misinterpretation. It may perhaps point to a second place for this name (*Bell* 4,487, according to A. Schalit, *Namenwörterbuch*, 34) in Samaria (nowadays known as Jerash).

Cestius Gallus.[308] Later he seems to have led a band in Akrabatene, but, confronted with an armed force sent out by Ananus, he was forced to retreat to Masada, the territory protected by the *Sicarii*. After Ananus' fall, he quickly became much more active than his hosts, with the result that he was soon able to extend his power until it covered the whole of Judaea and Idumaea.[309]

What is particularly striking in this context is Simon's social-mindedness. He set the Jewish slaves free and his armed force was composed of these emancipated slaves and peasants. His successes, which reached a peak with his entry into Jerusalem, probably led him to attribute messianic dignity to himself.[310] In Jerusalem, he was in control of the whole city apart from the Temple hill and, together with the Idumaeans, who were his allies, he had by far the greatest armed force under his command.[311] Despite his undistinguished origin and the fact that he had previously been the leader of a band, he was later executed in Rome as the foremost leader of the insurgents.[312]

Simon, then, stands at the end of a tragic development. Jerusalem rejected a leader such as Menahem, who could, after all, look back on an honourable family tradition, at the beginning of the revolt because of his efforts to become the ruling strong man. Then, after years of internal fighting and open civil war, the same city ultimately became the victim of Simon, who was no more than a man of violence.

There are also certain significant differences to be found in the end of the various groups and their leaders. There is little glory to be found in the capture of John of Gischala and Simon bar Giora and their fate as prisoners,[313] but the desperate act of the *Sicarii* in Masada and the heroic suffering of those who fled to Egypt appears in quite a different light. The priestly 'Zealots' too seem to have fallen fighting steadfastly in the blazing Temple. There is in any case no mention of their leaders after this event.[314]

Despite the fragmentation of the Zealot movement after the death of Menahem, we may make certain assumptions. Both the fundamental

---

[308] *Bell* 2,521; see also above, p. 369.

[309] *Bell* 2,652ff.; 4,503-544.

[310] *Bell* 4,508.510; see also above, pp. 297f. and 336.

[311] *Bell* 5,250. Ten thousand men were directly under his command; there were also six thousand Idumaeans.

[312] For an estimate of the number of proselytes, see J. Jeremias, *Jerusalem*, 320ff. For his death, see above, p. 298; see also Dio Cassius 66,7.1.

[313] See *Bell* 6,433; 7,26ff.153ff. For religious suicide, see above, p. 262ff. For the death of the *Sicarii* as martyrs in Egypt, see also above, p. 261.

[314] See Dio Cassius 66,6; see also above, p. 222f. The only exception was Judas b. Ari, who fell while fleeing in the forest of Jardes; see above, p. 332, n. 107.

religious end stressed by Judas, with its characteristic emphasis on the sole rule of God and on zeal, and eschatological consciousness were preserved in the various radical groups. Both in the conflict between Menahem and Eleazar and in that between John of Gischala and Simon bar Giora, these fundamental religious views were hardly disputed — on the contrary, they were recognized by both sides. What was at stake was the question of power in the coming Jewish 'nation under God'. It is not purely fortuitous that a movement, which began with the idea of a political realization of unrestricted theocracy,[315] should later — even before any decisive encounter with the opponent had taken place — founder on the fundamental human problem of the division of power.

---

[315] The term θεοκρατία is the most suitable one to apply to the aim of the Zealot freedom movement. Josephus uses this concept in *Ap* 2,165 to describe the πολίτευμα of the Jews established by Moses: θεῷ τὴν ἀρχὴν καὶ τὸ κράτος ἀναθείς.

A SURVEY OF THE WHOLE AND AN INDICATION OF THE QUESTIONS POSED BY THE NEW TESTAMENT

The history of the Jewish freedom movement during the period studied in this book falls clearly into three stages: (1) The preparatory phase until the appearance of Judas the Galilaean during the census of 6 A.D.; (2) The period of activity of the party founded by him until the murder of Menahem at the beginning of the Jewish War in 66 A.D.; (3) The period of the decline of the freedom movement during the course of the Jewish War itself.

The party founded by Judas came originally from the radical wing of the Pharisees and continued to have close links with the Shammaites. It formed a well organized secret society with a permanent leader. Its fundamental doctrine consisted of a demand for the sole rule of God and this led to a radical break with the claim to rule made by the Roman emperor. This demand was connected with the expectation that the eschatological liberation of Israel would be initiated by a struggle against the Roman oppressor.

Essential aspects of this new movement were charismatic prophecy, an unconditional readiness to fight against all the internal and external enemies of God and of Israel and therefore a readiness to die as a martyr, as well as a rigorous concept of the law, which aimed above all at Israel's total separation from its pagan Hellenistic environment and the integrity of the Sanctuary. The zeal of Phinehas and Elijah likely formed the great example and it is probable that the new movement derived its honorary title of 'Zealots' from them. Its spiritual roots went back to before the beginning of the Roman rule, to the Maccabaean revolt. The party of Judas the Galilaean, however, had much sharper and more radical views than the Maccabees.

The new movement also had certain affinities with the Essenes, whose views, like those of the Pharisees of the period, had clearly rigoristic and Zealot characteristics. From its very inception, it also had a considerable influence on the Jewish people. That influence increased noticeably after the death of Agrippa I, to such a degree that the Zealots eventually succeeded in impelling the overwhelming majority of the people to wage open war against Rome in a struggle to which an eschatological significance was probably ascribed. This success was underpinned by the strong social element that was present in the Zealots' fight for freedom.

377

If this struggle is viewed as a whole, it can be regarded as a first attempt to establish by violent means an unrestricted theocracy in the earthly and political sphere. Repeated efforts have been made to do this in later periods of history.[1] Failure to achieve this goal forced rabbinic Judaism later to move in many ways in a fundamentally new direction.

A detailed investigation into the relationships between Zealotism and the New Testament would go beyond the scope of my present study. Throughout the book, however, I have indicated various points of contact.[2] For this reason, it is relevant to mention in broad outline a few points of departure for further research:

(1) Jesus' proclamation likely contains certain statements which, even though the Zealots are not named explicitly, are undoubtedly directed against views that were widespread in Zealot circles. His anti-Pharisaical polemic was probably — at least in part — directed against the Zealots as the most radical representatives of the left wing of the Pharisees.

(2) In the proclamation of his message, Jesus touched on certain ideas that may perhaps have been made familiar by the activity of the Zealots.[3]

(3) Jesus himself was handed over to the Romans by the leaders of the Jewish people as alleged Zealot messianic pretender and condemned and executed as such.

(4) The conflict within early Church about the Christian attitude towards the Roman state has to be seen against the background of the Zealots' struggle against Rome. The discrepancy between Rom 13 and Rev 13 points to certain antitheses that early Christianity had inherited from Judaism.

(5) The question of the eschatological time, that is, the question of the beginning of the period of salvation and of the possibility of a human

---

[1] One is reminded here of Islam in its early period, of the Crusades and certain enthusiastic and chiliastic movements at the time of the Reformation. Any attempt to defend or to extend the rule of God with weapons is bound to lead to similar consequences to those found in Zealotism.

[2] See, for example, Mt 5.5,9,21ff.,38ff. (Lk 6.29f.), 43ff. (Lk 6.27f.,32ff.); Mt 8.11ff. (Lk 13.27ff.); 9.13 = 12.7; 11.28; 26.52; Lk 10.33ff.; 12.58ff.; 17.20f. In the anti-Pharisaical polemic, the words about 'tax-collectors and sinners' are also at the same time directed against the attitude of the Zealots; see Mk 2.14ff.; Lk 18.1-8, etc. See also above, pp. 180f., 226f.

[3] The following should also be seen in this light: Jesus' social preaching, see Lk 6.21,25; 16.19ff., etc.; the relativization of family ties with regard to the call of the kingdom of God, see Mk 3.31ff.; Mt 10.37 parr and Lk 14.26 (for this, see Deut 33.9 and *Ant* 18,23b); the demand for unconditional obedience and readiness to die a martyr's death, see Mt 5.10 (Lk 6.22); 10.19,26ff. parr; 10.34,38f. parr; 16.24f., etc.; see also above, p. 260, n. 151. For this, see also M. Hengel, *Nachfolge und Charisma* (*BZNW* 34), 1968 and *ibid.*, *Property and Riches in the Early Church*, 1974, 23ff.

influence on it — for example, in the eschatological interpretation of the mission by Paul or the idea of the full measure of eschatological suffering[4] — may also have had certain examples in Zealotism.

(6) The significance of the unconditional commandment to love as the foundation of early Christian ethics is placed in absolute contrast to the idea of 'zeal for God' in the violent sense, which appears only marginally in the New Testament.[5]

(7) The 'antipolitical tendency' of the Fourth Gospel, which reaches a climax in Jesus' reply to Pilate in Jn 18.37, contains an ultimate rejection of the Jewish and Zealot ideal of theocracy.

In conclusion, then, it is possible to say that, despite certain points of contact, the proclamation of Jesus and the early Christian Church represented the real overcoming of the Zealots' attempt to bring about God's rule on earth by violence.

---

[4] See Rom 11.26 in connection with 15.19,23f. and Mk 13.10. For Rev 6.11, see above, p. 266. See also M. Hengel, 'Die Ursprünge der christlichen Mission', *NTS* 18 (1971/2), 17ff.

[5] For this, see above, p. 179f., and M. Hengel, *War Jesus Revolutionär?* (*CH* 118), 1971; W. Klassen, 'Jesus and the Zealot Option', *CJT* 16 (1970), 12-21.

APPENDIX

ZEALOTS AND SICARII
The Question of the Unity and Diversity of the Jewish
Freedom Movement in 6–74 A.D.[1]

The most difficult problem confronting the scholar specializing in ancient history is the limited, fortuitous and tendentious nature of the sources. Jewish history, which is, at the beginning of the Christian era, particularly instructive for the biblical scholar, is certainly no exception to this general rule. On the contrary, it is an almost classic example.

Our main source is, of course, Josephus and our knowledge would be unimaginably reduced if his work had not been preserved. The historical framework of the New Testament would lose its clear outlines and dissipate into a mere shadow, making it difficult if not impossible to classify early Christianity historically.

Josephus' work is and will always be the most important ancient 'commentary' on the New Testament. The scattered and often purely fortuitous reports by non-Jewish ancient authors on Jewish history of the first century A.D.[2] raise even more questions than they answer and the same also applies to the scattered references and legends in the Talmudic literature. J. Neusner has drawn our attention to the historical problems surrounding this tradition.[3] A correct interpretation of the astonishing finds made at Qumran would also be quite impossible without Josephus.

When contradictory statements are found in the principal source — which, in our case, is Josephus — historical problems often become tied up in an inextricable knot. One of the most serious of the historical puzzles with which Josephus confronts us is that of the unity or diversity of the 'Jewish freedom movement' between the death of Herod in 4

---

[1] This appendix first appeared in a shorter version in *Josephus-Studien. Festschrift O. Michel zum 70. Geburtstag*, Göttingen 1974, 175-196. I am indebted to my colleague K.H. Rengstorf for material from his concordance on Josephus.

[2] T. Reinach's collection of these reports, *Textes d'auteurs grecs et romains relatifs au Judaïsme*, Paris 1895, reprinted Hildesheim 1963, is unfortunately very incomplete. See also, however, the new edition of the texts prepared by Menahem Stern, *Greek and Latin Authors on Jews and Judaism*, 1, 1974. The second volume, which includes Tacitus and Dio Cassius, is to be published soon.

[3] J. Neusner, *Development of a Legend. Studies on the Traditions concerning Yohanan ben Zakkai*, Leiden 1970; *ibid.*, *The Rabbinic Traditions about the Pharisees before 70*, 1-3, Leiden 1971.

B.C. or Quirinius' census of 6 A.D. and the Jewish War of 66-74 A.D., a movement which made a deep mark on this period. The first of the two important landmarks at this time is the unrest following Herod's death, during which Judas, the son of the 'robber captain' Hezekiah, appeared with 'royal ambitions' and plundered the Herodian arsenal in Sepphoris.[4] It is not unreasonable to assume that this Judas was identical with the Galilaean of the same name, who, ten years later, urged in his preaching a rejection of the census and revolt against Rome.[5] The second of these landmarks is the mass suicide of the defenders of the fortress at Masada under the leadership of Eleazar, the son of Jair, a grandson of that Judas,[6] and the annihilation of the last of the *Sicarii*, who had fled to Egypt.[7]

Between these two landmarks is the real *puzzle* of the development of

[4] *Bell* 2,56 is ambiguous here, but *Ant* 17,272 is clear: ἐπιθυμίᾳ μειζόνων πραγμάτων καὶ ζηλώσει βασιλείου τιμῆς. For this, see above p. 326f. In the case of these radical groups, the claim to 'royal dignity' must be interpreted as having messianic ambitions; see above, p. 291ff. and V.A. Tcherikover, *CPJ* 1, 90, n. 82. M. Black, *Josephus-Studien, op. cit.*, 45-54, suspects a relationship with the royal Hasmonaean family here. M. de Jonge expresses a different opinion in *NT* 8 (1966), 145f.; *TD* 9, 511ff. Josephus admittedly does not avoid employing the term *christos* simply because, apart from the case of the 'personal name' in *Ant* 20,200, he never uses the word. As one who was firmly opposed to the Zealots' expectation and who acted as the apologist of Judaism for the Romans, he was silent about the Jewish hope for the future (see below, p. 384f.). For this problem, see also M. de Jonge, *Josephus-Studien, op. cit.*, 205-219, and E. Bammel, *op. cit.*, 9-22.

[5] See above, p. 330ff.; see also K. Schubert, 'Die jüdischen Religionsparteien in neutestamentlicher Zeit', *SBS* 43 (1973, 67; S. Applebaum, 'The Zealots: The Case for Re-evaluation', *JRS* 61 (1971), 129f., and M. Black, *Josephus-Studien, op. cit.*, 45-54. A different view is expressed by H. Kreissig, *Die sozialen Zusammenhänge des jüdischen Krieges*, Berlin 1970, 114ff., and M. de Jonge, *Josephus-Studien, op. cit.*, 217. The solution to the historical enigma of a rebel called Judas being named twice is perhaps that the first reference, which occurs in connection with Sepphoris in Galilee, comes from the source of Nicolaus of Damascus, whereas the reference to the Galilaean Judas comes from Josephus himself (see below, p. 382, n. 8).

[6] *Bell* 7,275-406. For the dating of the taking of the fortress in April 74 A.D., see W. Eck, 'Die Eroberung von Masada und eine neue Inschrift des L. Flavius Silva Nonius Bassus', *ZNW* 60 (1969), 282-289, and *Senatoren von Vespasian bis Hadrian*, 1970, 93-111, for L. Flavius Silva as governor in Judaea (73/4-81 A.D.). For the defeat of the *Sicarii* and Eleazar's speech, see V. Nikiprowetzky, 'La mort d'Eléazar', *Hommages à André Dupont-Sommer*, Paris 1971, 461-490; S.B. Hoenig, 'The *Sicarii* in Masada — Glory or Infamy?', *Trad.* 11 (1970), 5-30; S. Spero, 'In Defence of the Defenders of Masada', *Trad.* 11, *op. cit.*, 31-43, who gives further bibliographical details in n. 1 on p. 29 and in nn. 1 and 2 on p. 41 of this article. See also H. Lindner, *Die Geschichtsauffassung des Josephus im Bellum Judaicum*, Leiden 1972, 33-40, and O. Michel and O. Bauernfeind, eds., *Flavius Josephus, De Bello Judaico*, II,2, 276ff.

[7] *Bell* 7,409ff.; see also V.A. Tcherikover, *CPJ* 1, 79f. We may perhaps assume that the seed scattered by the *Sicarii* in Egypt continued to have an effect and contributed to the catastrophe of 116/117 A.D. See Schürer, 1, 529ff.

the 'liberation movement' itself, which — on the basis of Josephus's very limited information — we can first trace more precisely in the final third part of this period, following the death of Agrippa I and the change of Judaea back into a Roman province in 44 A.D. It is here that the first point of controversy occurs: Is it possible to speak of a 'Jewish freedom movement' or is it simply a question, in the case of the insurgents to whom Josephus as a rule gives the stereotyped name of 'robbers' (ληϲταί)[8] or 'rebels' (ϲταϲιαϲταί)[9], of scattered groups of bands that were completely independent of each other and basically had nothing to do with one another?

The second argument seems to be supported by the fact that Josephus himself describes the situation in Judaea after the outbreak of the Jewish War and up to the beginning of Titus' siege as a state of chaos with a multiplicity of groups fighting one another among changing constellations, in which he gives, in various lists,[10] prominence to five groups in particular:

(1) The so-called *Sicarii*, who go back to Judas the Galilaean, but who had withdrawn, after the murder of their leader Menahem in the Temple at the beginning of the war, to the fortress at Masada;

(2) the Galilaean John of Gischala and his followers, who at the end defended the Temple hill;

---

[8] What is particularly striking here is that, with one exception in *Ant* 9,183, Josephus only uses this term for those who were revolting against the Roman rule. The first reference to 'robbers' (ληϲταί) begins with a reference to the killing of the 'robber captain Hezekiah' — who was presumably the father of Judas the Galilaean — by the young Herod in *Bell* 1,204 = *Ant* 14,159. Josephus probably took this linguistic usage over from his anti-Jewish and pro-Herodian source, the historical work of Nicolaus of Damascus. The term is in accordance with Roman legal thinking, according to which all rebels, who were not able to declare war officially against Rome or who were not considered by Rome to be worthy of a declaration of war, were regarded not as *hostes*, but as *latrones*. See above, pp. 24-32; R. MacMullen, *Enemies of the Roman Order*, Cambridge Mass. 1966, 255ff. See also Ilona Opelt, *Die lateinischen Schimpfwörter*, 1965, Index, 247 under *latro*, and B.S. Jackson, *Theft in Early Jewish Law*, 1972, 23ff.33ff.162.183f.

[9] Josephus employs the concept for the first time in his historical account of the war (*Bell* 1,180) for the 'rebellious followers of Aristobulus'. Later in the same work, in 2,9, he also uses it for the rebels who opposed Archelaus in the Temple and, in 2,267.289f., for the Jewish rebels in Caesarea. Finally, he employs it with great regularity, in 2,406.411.424.432.441, for those who initiated the revolt in Jerusalem. The term is therefore used synonymously with ληϲταί. The word 'rebels' also occurs frequently in Books 5 and 6, that is, in the description of the siege laid by Titus. ϲταϲιαϲτής, on the other hand, rarely appears in the *Antiquities*. It is applied to Antipater, Herod's father, in 14,8 — a clear sign of Josephus' anti-Herodian change — and to Antigonus in 14,382. Its use in *Ant* 17, 214 corresponds to that in *Bell* 2,9 and, in *Ant* 20,227, it describes the radicals who appointed the last high-priest Phinehas.

[10] *Bell* 4,224ff.235; 5,248ff.358; 6,92.148 and the great final reckoning in 7,253-274; for this, see O. Michel and O. Bauernfeind, eds., *op. cit.*, II,2, 266ff.

(3) Simon bar Giora and the members of his party, who were the last to have penetrated into Jerusalem, but who possessed the most powerful armed force and bore the main burden of the defence of the city;

(4) the Idumaeans, who, after changing constellations, ultimately fought on the side of Simon bar Giora, and finally

(5) the so-called 'Zealots', whose stronghold was in the Temple itself and who defended the Temple hill together with John of Gischala.[11]

The first thing that strikes one about these different groups is their diversity. Two of them are linked with definite and named leaders. One clearly has the character of an association of compatriots. Only the first and the last have the names of parties — Sicarii and 'Zealots' — and these names had, on the basis of their origin, completely different meanings. Josephus, however, uses non-specific names for all the combatant groups together, e.g., the derogatory, 'robbers' (see above, p. 382, n. 8), also 'rebels' (see above, p. 382, n. 9), 'tyrants' or simply 'Jews'.[12]

Admittedly, this 'atomizing' way of looking at the situation has its special difficulties. Above all, it makes it impossible to understand the development leading to the Jewish War, its preparation, its sudden outbreak and its early successes, including the liberation of the Temple and the city of Jerusalem and the victory over Cestius Gallus.[13] For here there must have been — in opposition to the delaying resistance of the people's leaders and of a large section of the population of Jerusalem — a *solidified will* on the part of the members of the radical 'liberation movement', *whose aim was an open 'people's war' with the Roman oppressors.*

Josephus stresses explicitly that the radicals had been moving in the direction of this goal since the time of the census and the attempted revolt under Judas the Galilaean. He also points out that there were several occasions when it seemed almost possible to achieve that aim. The first notable example of this was when Caligula wanted to have his image erected in the Temple in Jerusalem (in 40/41 A.D.).[14] The second

---

[11] *Bell* 4,151ff.162ff.196-207. 298ff.570-584; 5,7ff.98ff.358.562ff.

[12] See above, p. 43f. στασιασταί and Ἰουδαῖοι are used by Josephus above all in his description of the siege itself. This may perhaps go back to his Roman sources. For τύραννος, see *Bell* 4,164.178; see also 278.398; 5,439, etc.

[13] *Bell* 2,408-555. These surprising initial successes would hardly have been possible if those who had decided in favour of war against Rome had not acted together at the beginning. The first — and most serious — break came with the murder of Menahem; see below, p. 399.

[14] *Bell* 2,184-203 = *Ant* 18,261-309; see also above, pp. 105f., 208, 341f. For this, see also E.M. Smallwood, *Philonis Alexandrini Legatio ad Gaium*, 2nd. ed. Leiden 1969, 197, and 'The Chronology of Gaius' Attempt to Desecrate the Temple', *Latomus* 16 (1957), 3-17. In his interpretation, H. Kreissig, *op. cit.*, 124, completely fails to understand the

was the act of revenge undertaken against the Samaritans after the murder near Ginae-Jenin of a Galilaean pilgrim on his way to the Feast of Tabernacles in Jerusalem under the procurator Cumanus (in 51/52 A.D.).[15] If we are looking for something more than H. Kreissig's completely one-sided profane-political and socio-economic explanation of the Jewish War and its prehistory, then we are bound to consider the *connecting religious and political 'ideology'* underlying the efforts shared by all the radical groups, against all political reason, to impel the Jewish people into a war to the bitter end against the omnipotence of Rome. Despite the hostility that they felt for each other, these groups had all sworn an oath to go on to the end and not to surrender. The compatriot group of Idumaeans was the only one that broke this understanding.[16]

To judge from all that we know about Jewish history from the time of the Maccabaean revolt onwards, this kind of suicidal persistence could only have a *religious motivation*. This impression is confirmed by such impartial witnesses as Tacitus, Suetonius and Dio Cassius.[17] Religion and politics were inseparably fused together in ancient Judaism. It is, however, very understandable that Josephus, who was receiving a pension from the victorious Flavian imperial house, cannot remain completely silent about these religious motives and does everything in his power to displace them by a moral (or amoral) political motivation.[18] He wanted, after all, to remain faithful in his new environment to his own people and to the faith of the patriarchs and therefore attempted in

---

effect that Caligula's attempt had on the entire Jewish population and not simply on the upper stratum. His lack of understanding, which has its origin in a vulgar Marxist interpretation of history, results again and again in his making wrong judgements.

[15] For the disturbances under Cumanus, see *Bell* 2,232-246 = *Ant* 20,118-1ɔ0; see also above, pp. 283f., 346ff.

[16] *Bell* 6,351.366.378ff.; cf. 7,323. For this, see O. Michel and O. Bauernfeind, eds., *op. cit.*, II,2, 202, n. 190. See also above, p. 158f.

[17] See Tacitus, *Hist* 5,5, on the religion of the Jews and especially 3: 'animosque proelio aut suppliciis peremptorum aeternos putant: hinc generandi amor et moriendi contemptus'. See also the description of the conquest of the Temple in Dio Cassius, 65,6.2f. The account of an 'ambiguous oracle' that led to the Jewish War (*Bell* 6,312f.; Tacitus, *Hist* 5,13, and Suetonius, *Vesp* 4,5) and the prophecies of salvation shortly before the conquest of the Temple (*Bell* 6,285f.) confirm the eschatological background to the Jewish uprising. Num 24.17 also lies behind this. H. Kreissig, *op. cit.*, 129f., consistently sets these statements aside as unimportant. I. Hahn's derivation of this prophecy from a conscious misinterpretation of Dan 9.22 in Qumran circles, which can be found in H. Bardtke, ed., *Qumran-Probleme* (*SSA* 42), Berlin 1963, 171f.,180, is quite fantastic. For the whole question, see above, pp. 237-244; H. Windisch, *Das Orakel des Hystaspes* (*VNAW*, NS 28), 3, 1929, 65ff.; H. Lindner, *op. cit.*, 69ff.

[18] For the political 'tendency' and 'polemical reversal' in Josephus, see above, pp. 6-16, 183ff. See also M. de Jonge, *Josephus-Studien, op. cit.*, 218f.

this way to exonerate and defend his people and their religion as a whole.

He believed that — in addition to the incompetence of the later Roman procurators — it was the work of individual criminal persons and groups that had led to the fateful development. He also felt bound, as an apologist for Judaism, not to state openly in an environment that was largely hostile to Judaism that the cause of the catastrophe was to be found in certain fundamental Jewish religious themes such as the ideal of 'theocracy', 'zeal for the law' and the people's messianic expectation.

Doubts have time and again been expressed as to whether the Jewish freedom movement had an essentially eschatological foundation, since Josephus has nothing to say about this.[19] These doubts have, however, to a great extent arisen because of a complete failure to recognize that, in his position, he was bound to remain silent about the Jewish future expectation. At the same time, however, his work contains numerous indications which show clearly enough that he knew much more than he cared to say.[20] He proclaimed in clear terms to his Roman and Jewish readers that God had given the Romans the task of ruling the world *now*,[21] while remaining silent about the future: *sapienti sat*.

It should be clear from this, then, that Josephus had no interest at all in explaining to his readers the real background facts of the Jewish War and its prehistory. It was sufficient for him to brand certain individuals as criminals and to present the majority of his people as innocent and unfortunate, in an attempt to arouse sympathy for those who had been struck down by fate or punished by God for the sins committed by a minority. As far as our particular problem is concerned, this means in the first place that it is essential to check Josephus' accounts of the 'Jewish freedom movement' during the Jewish War and its prehistory critically and to compare them with other — for example, rabbinic and Christian — accounts. In the second place, it also means that the freedom fighters had a far greater religious motivation than the Jewish historian wanted to admit.

Two factors indicate clearly that the Jewish rebels can be understood not only from their chaotic state of internal division (Josephus'

---

[19] See, for example, K. Wegenast, 'Zeloten', *PW*, Series 2, 9, 1967, 2483; see also H. Kreissig, *op. cit.*, 15,102ff.,113-148: 'Expectation of the Messiah undoubtedly also played a part in the activities of the Judaean and Galilaean ληϲταί. It was, however, not able to become the unifying force leading to insurrection, since, by nature, it hindered rather than encouraged the idea of "self-help". Judas of Galilee knew this, but his demand that God's help should be brought about by one's own activity was a contradiction it itself' (147f.).

[20] See *Ant* 4,114.116f. (Balaam's prophecy, Num 24.17); 10,210 (Dan 2); cf. also 10,267.276; see also above, p. 239 and M. de Jonge, *Josephus-Studien, op. cit.*, p. 211f.

[21] For this, see H. Lindner's detailed treatment, *op. cit.*, 21ff.,49ff.,69ff.,142ff.

perspective), but also — at least as a working hypothesis — from the standpoint of a relative 'ideological unity'. The first of these is the heroic shared struggle to the bitter end. The second is the fact that a 'theocratic ideology of the fight for freedom' was there at the very beginning, when the provincial census was carried out in 6 A.D.

Stimulated by the translation of Josephus made by Professors O. Michel and O. Bauernfeind, who died at the end of 1972, and in which I participated as an assistant twenty years ago, I began to investigate these ideological foundations of the Jewish freedom movement in 1955. This study formed the basis of my dissertation, which was completed in 1959. The point of departure for this difficult undertaking was an analysis of the various names given by Josephus to the insurgents: robbers, *Sicarii*, Zealots and so on.[22] I went on from this to attempt to gain an insight from various points of view into the religious background of the Jewish struggle against foreign rule.

The obvious approach to an understanding of this problem was via the teaching of the rebel preacher Judas the Galilaean, who, according to Josephus, had, together with the Pharisee Saddok, introduced a new doctrine that had 'never yet been heard' and, with it, had founded a 'fourth philosophy' in Palestinian Judaism (*Ant* 18,9). He had, in other words, created a new Jewish 'party'. His fundamental religious demand was for the 'sole rule of God', in other words, that, apart from God, no one should be recognized as Lord and king. Almost seventy years later, at the end of the tragedy involving the *Sicarii* who had fled to Egypt and who let themselves be tortured to death rather than venerate the emperor as 'Kyrios' and 'Basileus' (*Bell* 7,417ff.), this demand is found again. The question that confronted me, then, was: Can one so understand Josephus as to conclude that this Judas had laid the decisive spiritual foundations for the unceasing disturbances which followed and which only came to an end in the general conflagration of the Jewish War — a conflagration which Judas himself had tried, admittedly at first without success, to ignite with his insurrectionary preaching?[23]

The second complex was concerned with the 'zeal' that was oriented

---

[22] See above, p. 24-75.

[23] See Josephus' detailed description of the ominous part played by the *Sicarii* founded by Judas in *Bell* 7,253-274; note especially the τότε in 254. See also O. Michel and O. Bauernfeind, eds., *op. cit.*, II,2, 267: 'In 7,254.324, the *Sicarii* are seen as continuing the tradition of insurrection that can be traced back to the time of Judas'. A similar view is expressed by M. Black, *Josephus-Studien, op. cit.*, 51: '*fons et origo* . . .' See also the text of *Ant* 18,6ff.25, which Josephus wrote almost twenty years later: 'The madness which had come from there (that is, from Judas and Saddok) began to infect the people under Gessius Florus . . .'

on Phinehas' bloody deed in Num 25.10ff., an action that earned the
hero the unique epithet of the 'Zealot'[24] which then formed the basis for
the honorary title of the party: the 'Zealots'. This is, as we have seen, the
only specifically Jewish name for the group that constituted the Jewish
'freedom movement' which has been handed down to us by Josephus,
the Talmud and Christian sources. What underlies this concept is zeal for
— in a xenophobic sense — an even more stringent Torah.[25] The third
complex was connected with the question of the charismatic-
eschatological consciousness of the Jewish insurrectionary groups.[26]

It is indisputable that a distinction has to be made between the various
bands and groups, but it is equally certain that they all had the same aim:
the liberation of the people of God from the Roman yoke and the
purification of the Holy Land from all trangressors of the law and all
traitors. This can be inferred from certain fundamental tendencies that
they all had in common. The emphasis that Josephus places on the
disastrous consequences of the activity of Judas the Galilaean leaves us in
no doubt that both he and his teaching had decisive effects. Were I to
undertake today the work that I began twenty years ago, I would still
regard my attempt to understand the Jewish 'freedom movement'
between 6 and 70 A.D. in the light of certain fundamental and unified
religious themes as fully justified. I would, however, admittedly
supplement this approach by placing more emphasis now than at that
time[27] on the social factors involved in the struggle for freedom. I would

---

[24] See above, p. 156ff. and below, p. 393, n. 43. See also L. Ginzberg, *The Legends of the
Jews*, 3, 383ff.; 6, 137f.; 7, 37; C. Colpe, *ZDPV* 85 (1969), 168ff.

[25] See Chapter IV on 'Zeal' above, pp. 146–228.

[26] See Chapter V on 'The Zealots as an Eschatological Movement' above, pp. 229–
312.

[27] See above, pp. 134ff., 323f., 335f.; G. Baumbach, 'Das Freiheitsverständnis in der
zelotischen Bewegung', *Das ferne und nahe Wort. Festschrift für L. Rost* (*BZAW* 105),
1967, 11–19; M. Hengel, 'Das Gleichnis von den Weingärtnern', *ZNW* 59 (1968),
11ff.,19ff.; O. Michel, 'Simon bar Giora', *Fourth World Congress of Jewish Studies*, Papers
1, 1967, 77–80; see also H. Kreissig, *op. cit.*, who has abundant material, but is far too
one-sided in his method. It is clear, however, that there were by no means sufficient social
reasons to motivate the development between 6 and 74 (or 135) A.D. from the fact that
there was no such bitter fight for freedom against the Romans conducted in other
territories in the East, Syria, Asia Minor or even Egypt, even though there was no less
exploitation in those places than there was in Judaea. The struggles in Germania and parts
of Gaul, or in Illyria and Pannonia also cannot be compared with those in Judaea. Those
districts were inhabited by barbaric tribes that had only recently been made Roman
subjects and had hardly been brought to peace. For this question, see S.L. Dyson, 'Native
Revolts in the Roman Empire', *Hist* 20 (1971), 239–274. Despite their geographically
better position, even the Nabataeans offered no resistance that is worth mentioning to
Trajan's annnexation of their kigdom in 105 A.D.; see G.W. Bowerstock, 'The

do this especially in view of the inseparable link in ancient Judaism between justice in the social order and religious hope in the light of prophetic preaching and the teaching of Deuteronomy.

Criticism of my book has been concerned with one point above all, a point which is fundamentally a special problem of the question of the unity or disparity of the Jewish 'freedom movement' itself. It is my use of the party names 'Zealots' and *Sicarii*.

Kirsopp Lake pointed out in the early nineteen-twenties that — in contrast to the language usually employed by scholars in this field — Josephus made a clear distinction between *Sicarii* and 'Zealots':

> 'It is somewhat of a shock to discover from Josephus that, if his evidence be correct, the use of the name Zealot to describe a Jewish sect or party cannot be earlier that A.D. 66'.

This observation is quite correct, but it is unfortunately given a wrong basis:

> 'The first use of the word 'Zealot' in Josephus as the name of a party in Jerusalem is in *Bellum Judaicum* IV.3.9. After this he uses it frequently, and always in the same sense. It is the name arrogated to themselves by the followers of the famous John of Gischala ...'[28]

In reality, the name οἱ ζηλωταί appears three times in the second book of *The Jewish War*. According to the context of *Bell* 2,651, the word refers unambiguously to the *party of the Zealots* long before the emergence of John of Gischala. Josephus describes the divided situation in the city after the victory over Cestius Gallus and the efforts of the high-priest Ananus to suppress the enthusiasm for war:

> 'Ananus' intention was admittedly gradually to put an end to arming for war and to put down the rebels and suppress the madness of the so-called 'Zealots' (καὶ τὴν τῶν κληθέντων ζηλωτῶν ἀφροσύνην) for the common good. He succumbed, however, to their violence'.[29]

My sharpest critic, Morton Smith, assumed that Josephus was

Annexation and Initial Garrison of Arabia', *ZPE* 5 (1970), 37-47. For the special situation in Judaea, see also M. Hengel, 'War Jesus Revolutionär?', *CH* 110 (1970); 'Gewalt und Gewaltlosigkeit', *CH* 118, 30,59f., nn. 71,72, and *Property and Riches in the Early Church*, 1974, 15ff. A. Ben-David has made a fundamental study of the economic situation in Palestine in his *Talmudische Ökonomie*, 1974, 41ff.,58ff.,291ff.,313ff.

[28] *The Beginnings of Christianity*, I, *The Acts*, 1, *Prologomena*, London 1920, 421,423. For a criticism of this study, see above, p. 65, n. 324. See also G. Baumbach. *ThLZ* 90 (1965), 735; H.P. Kingdon, *NTS* 17 (1970/71), 69ff., and 19 (1972/73), 74; see also M. Black, *Josephus-Studien, op. cit.*, 51.

[29] The addition of κληθέντων points to a group resembling a party; see *Bell* 2,254; 4,400; *Ant* 20,186 for the *Sicarii* and *Bell* 4,161 and 7,268 for the Zealots.

referring here, not to the party of the Zealots, but to 'many individual zealots in the city'. This assumption is, however, quite without foundation.[30] Josephus either knows nothing of or intentionally ignores the 'ideal of "the zealot"' as a private individual, imitating Phineas and Elijah'. In addition to this, the existence of such a 'private ideal' leading to individuals being named 'the Zealot' is also extremely questionable (see below, p. 393). The realization of Phinehas' exemplary action, that is, the eradication of transgressors of the law and the pagans who had led them astray, called, under Roman rule, for a well organized group. Political terrorism can — if it aims to have lasting and successful results, as it did in Palestine — not be accomplished by individual desperados, but only by permanent and organized groups. That applies to present-day Ireland as much as it applied to Palestine at the beginning of the Christian era.

In Josephus' next reference to the 'Zealots' (*Bell* 4,160f.), the narrative thread that had been broken in 2,651 is clearly taken up again:

> 'The most highly regarded of the high-priests, Jesus, the son of Gamala, and Ananus, the son of Ananus, rebuked the people severely at the assemblies for their inertia and stirred them up against the 'Zealots'. That is what these men called themselves, as though they were striving to achieve noble aims and not to perform the worst actions in which they surpassed each other'.[31]

Josephus is not giving a new meaning to the name οἱ ζηλωταί here. In both cases, he is unambiguously referring to the *party of the Zealots in Jerusalem*. The other two texts in the second book (*Bell* 2,564 and 444) have therefore to be interpreted in the light of this linguistic usage:

One of the leaders of the radical war party in Jerusalem, Eleazar, the son of Simon, is mentioned for the first time in *Bell* 2,564. Although he had acquired a large share of the Roman booty and public treasure after the victory over Cestius Gallus, he received no public office in the people's assembly that followed the victory. This was because, according to *Bell* 2,564,

> 'they knew his tyrannical nature and the 'Zealots', who were devoted to him behaved like bodyguards towards him'.

The words τοὺς ὑπ' αὐτῷ ζηλωτάς that are used in this text should not be

---

[30] HThR 64 (1971), 16; cf. 6.

[31] What we have here is the only case known to us of the name 'Zealots' as given by the members of the Jewish freedom movement to themselves; see O. Michel and O. Bauernfeind, eds., *op. cit.*, II,1, 213, n. 45. See also the similar derivation of the name in *Bell* 7,269. In reality, Josephus hellenizes and conceals the origin of the term. This is comparable to his failure to mention the concept 'zeal' in his reference to the act performed by Phinehas in Num 25.10ff.; see *Ant* 4,131-150. For this, see above, p. 155.

translated as 'followers' or, as Thackeray has rendered them, as 'admirers'. It is also wrong to interpret them as 'individual zealots'. They clearly point to a permanent and organized group.[32] This is obvious from the fact that this Eleazar b. Simon appears later as the real leader of this party of the 'Zealots'. Josephus says that 'at the beginning (of the uprising)' he 'separated the "Zealots" from the population of the city and took them into the precincts of the Temple' (*Bell* 5,5) and that 'the Zealots' attack against the population of the city led to the conquest of the city' (5,3).

Josephus sometimes calls the members of this group, after their separation from John of Gischala, simply 'Eleazar's followers'.[33] Later, after a successful attack against the Temple, the 'Zealots' again joined John of Gischala, but even then Eleazar continued to be their leader (*Bell* 5,98.104.250). When this group of the 'Zealots' began as a 'party' remains an open question. Eleazar would also seem not to have been the founder of that party. Josephus presupposes the existence of such a party in his first reference to Eleazar, but he also mentions other leaders in addition to him. These include Zechariah b. Amphicalleus, who, like Eleazar, was of priestly descent (*Bell* 4,225) and whose strict adherence to the law led, at least according to the Talmudic legend, to the outbreak of the war against Rome.[34]

The first mention of οἱ ζηλωταί in *Bell* 2,444 is undoubtedly the most difficult and the most disputed text.[35] The 'Zealots' are linked here not with the priest Eleazar b. Simon, but with Menahem, the son (or grandson) of Judas the Galilaean, in other words, with the members of that group whom Josephus, on the basis of their murderous tactics, also from time to time calls the *Sicarii*.[36] According to this text, Menahem entered, after the city had been liberated, into the Temple

'full of pride and in the finery of royal garments' καὶ τούς ζηλωτὰς ἐνόπλους ἐφελκόμενος.

Following Thackeray, Morton Smith prefers the translation 'his fanatical followers' for here. In support of this, he appeals to the Latin translations of later antiquity.[37] This translation, however, is in

---

[32] See M. Stern, 'Zealots', *EJ Yearbook*, 1973, 141.

[33] *Bell* 5,10,21.99: οἱ περὶ τὸν Ἐλεάζαρον; 5,12: οἱ ἀμφὶ τὸν Ἐλεάζαρον.

[34] tShab 16,7; Gitt 56a; LamRab on 4,2.3; see also above, p. 360f. and *EJ* 19, 959.

[35] For this, see C. Roth, 'The Zealots of the War of 66-73', *JSSt* 4 (1959), 334; see also above, p. 64f.; G. Baumbach, *ThLZ* 90 (1965), 733f.; H.P. Kingdon, *op. cit.*; O. Michel and O. Bauernfeind, eds., *op. cit.*, I, 271: 'when a band of armed Zealots followed him'.

[36] *Bell* 2,254.425; 4,400; 7,253-274; *Ant* 20,186.

[37] *HThR* 64 (1971), 7f. The reference to the ancient Latin translations is indeed

contradiction both to the contemporary Greek linguistic usage and to Josephus' own usage. In Greek literature up to the second century A.D. (Plutarch and Lucian, for example), ζηλωτής only appears in the sense of 'follower' or 'emulator'. It is never used in the absolute sense, but is always governed by an attribute in the genitive, that is, by a thing or a person or at least by a possessive pronoun, which is absent from the text that we are considering here. I had already drawn attention to this in 'Die Zeloten', but Morton Smith unfortunately failed to take this fact into consideration.[38]

On the other hand, Josephus uses the term ζηλωτής fifty-five times altogether in his *Jewish War*, in fifty-three of these cases in the absolute sense as οἱ ζηλωταί, in other words, as the name of a party. The disputed first mention in *Bell* 2,444 is no exception to this! The concept does not appear at all in *The Jewish War* in the sense of 'followers of a person', but it is — in two cases only — used to refer to the Roman soldiers, who are praised as ζηλωταὶ τῆς ἀνδρείας (*Bell* 5,314 and 6,59). We may therefore almost assume that, in the sense of the polemical reversal that Josephus valued so highly (see above, p. 384, n. 18), these Roman 'emulators of courage' are contrasted with the criminal Jewish 'Zealots'.[39]

The situation is quite different in Josephus' other writings, in all of

---

misleading. Hegesippus 2,10.6 (*CSEL* 61, 161) — 'regressusque in Hierosolyma stipatoribus tamquam regio more comitantibus immane insoleuerat' — refers not, as Morton Smith claims, to *Bell* 2,444, but to Menahem's entry into Jerusalem in 2,434, with a transition to 442. The Latin translation attributed to Rufinus ('studiosos armatos secum trahens') quite naively follows the customary linguistic usage of the period (the second half of the fourth century A.D.), in which the absolute ζηλωτής could also be employed in isolated cases in the sense of disciples; see the examples above, p. 62, n. 298: Iamblichus, *VitaPyth* (VI) 29: ἐν... Κρότωνι... προτρεψάμενος πολλοὺς ἔσχε ζηλωτάς as the object in the accusative without the article, and Marinus, *VitaProcl* 38, ed. Boissonade. There is, as far as I can see, no evidence of this linguistic usage at an earlier period.

[38] See above, p. 59ff. It is not at all difficult to add to the data assembled on those pages. See Aeschines, *Orat* 2,166 (Reiske, 50,26); Philodemus, *Piet* 125,18f. (T. Gomperz, *Herc. Stud.* 2, Leipzig 1866): (ὁ δὲ ἀ)δελφὸς α(ὐτ)οῦ (κ)αὶ ζηλωτής; cf. Plutarch, *Cato Minor* 781 F: ἑταῖρος αὐτοῦ καὶ ζηλωτής; Lucian, *Scyth* 4; Plutarch, *Cicero* 878 A and 882 E: ζηλωταὶ τοῦ Κικέρωνος; *Themistocles*, 112 D; *Pelopidas* 292 A; *Phocion* 743C; Epictetus according to Arrian, *Diss* 1,19.6; 3,24.40: ζηλωτὰ τῆς ἀληθείας καὶ Σωκράτους καὶ Διογένους. The meaning of the only exception that I have been able to find is notably obscure; see T. Gomperz, 'Die Überreste eines Buches von Epikur', *WSt* 1 (1879), 30. It is also striking that what we have here is preponderantly a literary concept that appears in individual inscriptions; see W. Dittenberger, *SIG*, 3rd. ed. 1915ff., 675,27f.; 717,33; *OGIS* 339,90; 352,46; *SEG* 7, 62,19; 19, 834,23f. It does not, however, occur in the Egyptian papyri.

[39] See also J.-A. Morin, *RB* 80 (1973), 334, n. 13.

which the term occurs only four times. In *Ant* 12,271, the priest Mattathias calls on his fellow-countrymen with the words: 'If anyone is zealous for our country's laws and worship of God, let him follow me!' (εἴ τις ζηλωτής ἐστιν τῶν πατρίων ἐθῶν ...). This is, in fact, a more precise definition of the statement made in 1 Macc 2.27: Πᾶς ὁ ζηλῶν τῷ νόμῳ καὶ ἱστῶν διαθήκην ἐξελθέτω ὀπίσω μου.

In *Ant* 20,47, the mother of King Izates of Adiabene and his Jewish teacher Ananias are afraid that the king might lose the throne because his subjects would not tolerate a ruler over them who was a τῶν παρ' ἑτέροις ζηλωτὴς ἐθῶν. In *Ap* 1,162, the author follows a traditional thesis in Jewish apologetics claiming that Pythagoras was a ζηλωτής of Jewish laws. Finally *Vita* 11 provides us with the only case in which the term is applied to a person, Josephus saying of himself that he was a pupil of the ascete Bannus. The concept is not applied, however, without a governing genitive in any of these three works to a group of Jewish insurgents; rather the usage is very closely in accordance with the customary Greek usage of the period.

Also in view of the alleged linguistic usage of ὁ ζηλωτής as an honorary religious title for certain pious Jews postulated by Kirsopp Lake and taken up again by Morton Smith, I can only state emphatically that there is, with the exception of one special case, no unambiguous evidence in support of this claim. It is true that the concept 'zealot for the law' is found in the New Testament (Acts 21.20; 22.3; Gal 1.14) and here and there in Hellenistic Jewish writings (2 Macc 4.2; Phil, *SpecLeg* 2,253; see also *Ant* 12,271), but this concept is not frequent in the extant Hellenistic Jewish texts. The genitive combination 'zealot for the law' or 'for God' is completely within the framework of the customary Greek use of the word. There are, to my knowledge, only two examples of the absolute use of ὁ ζηλωτής. These are:

(1)The disciple Simon ὁ ζηλωτής, who was one of the Twelve (Lk 6.15; Acts 1.13 = ὁ Καναναῖος Mk 3.18; Mt 10.4). In this case, the question as to whether what we have here is the name of a Palestinian party must be left open. If this is so, the 'Zealot' Simon would have been an erstwhile 'Zealot' who was comparable to the erstwhile 'Essene' John (*Bell* 2,567; 3,11.19).[40]

---

[40] See above, p. 69f.; H.P. Rüger, *ZNW* 59 (1968), 118. For linguistic reasons, I find the interpretation suggested by J.-A. Morin, *op. cit.*, 332-349, unconvincing. M. Borg's interpretation, *JThS* 22 (1971), 507f., is similar to Morin's. S.G.F. Brandon's speculations, *Jesus and the Zealots*, Manchester 1967, see Index, under 'Simon the Zealot', are therefore even less justified. If Brandon were right, it would be equally justified to conclude, on the basis of texts on the tax collectors in the Gospels and the statement in Mt 10.3 that Matthew was a tax-collector, that Jesus was a friend of the Romans. H.

(2)Phinehas, who is described as ὁ ζηλωτής in 4 Macc 18.12, in which text the father is said to have told his seven sons about 'the Zealot Phinehas'. What we have here is not simply any pious 'zealot', but a unique name establishing the emergence of this linguistic usage and throwing light on the religious background to the name of the party.[41] There is no need to discuss in this context the name of God as θεὸς ζηλωτής in the Septuagint as a translation of *El qanna'* and the negative Christian linguistic usage in the sense of 'jealous'.[42]

The fact that the name 'Zealot' in the singular (*qanna'i* or *qan'an* as an adjective acting as a noun) is applied in the rabbinic literature to one figure only — Phinehas — seems to me to be of decisive importance. According to the rabbinic tradition, God himself gave Phinehas that name.[43] I have found no evidence at all of the application of the honorary

---

Kreissig, *op. cit.* 120f., appealing to Sanh 43a, claims, for example, that 'Jesus was close to the government'. It is possible to prove anything in this way! For Brandon, see my review in *JSS* 14 (1969), 231-240.

[41] See above, p. 159f. Morton Smith's criticism and interpretation, *HThR* 64 (1971), 11, miss the point entirely.

[42] See above, p. 60f.; see also the apologist Aristides 7,3; 8,2; 10,7; 11,2: It is always a question here of demarcating the one God from the angry and jealous gods of the pagans. For the θεὸς ζηλωτής, see the following note.

[43] There is astonishingly little evidence and I have cited the most important data on pp. 156f. and 159f. above. I am indebted to Benjamin Kossovsky for supplying me with four texts from the Babylonian Talmud. The relevant volume of his concordance has not yet been published. The word appears once only in the singular in Sanh 82b: The serving angels wanted to thrust Phinehas aside, but God prevented them: 'Leave him! He is a Zealot, the son of a Zealot, a turner away of anger, the son of a turner away of anger'. The words 'son of a turner away of anger' are probably an allusion to his ancestor Levi; see above, p. 159, n. 78; see also NumRab 21,3; TanPinehas, 3, ed. Buber 76a; Pirke R. Elieser 47 (112b): Levi was the first to be zealous in his opposition to unchastity. He is, however, only given the title *qanna'i* in the immediate context of the veneration of his descendant Phinehas. See the Jerusalem Targum I on Num 25.11: 'Phinehas the Zealot (*qanna'ah*), the son of of Eleazar bar Aharon, the priest who turned away the anger of the children of Israel'. In the Targum Neofiti and the Targum Onkelos, the addition of 'the Zealot' is missing. The original version can be found in SifNum 25,1 (Horovitz, 173): 'Phinehas, the priest, the son of a priest, the Zealot, the son of a Zealot (*qanna'i ben qanna'i*)'. See also LevRab 33,4 (Margulies, 4, 752); PesK 13,12 (Mandelbaum, 236); YalShim on Num 25.11. 771 (535). One has the impression that Phinehas' title 'the Zealot' has from time to time been to some extent suppressed. As far as I can see, the concept is absent, for example, from jSanh and NumRab. What we presumably have here is an ancient memory which later became offensive, like the act itself performed by Phinehas. It is clear from the fact that the hero in 4 Macc 18.12 is described as ὁ ζηλωτής that this name goes back to the first century A.D. (see above, p. 392 and n. 41). What is of decisive importance here is that it is God himself who gives this special honorary title to Phinehas; see above, p. 159f. We may assume, but only as a hypothesis, that what lies behind it is the idea of imitating God, since the *El qanna'* of the Old Testament is translated in the LXX by θεὸς ζηλωτής. The term *qanna'i* — *qanna'* — *qan'an* = jealous

title of 'Zealot' to individual pious Jews that has been postulated by Kirsopp Lake, Morton Smith and others, just as I have found none in the case of *saddiq* or *hasid*. There are, however, two traditions in which the 'Zealots' (*qanna'im* or 'Kannaim') appear in the plural:

(1) The tradition of the 'Zealots' in Version A of the Aboth D'R. Nathan. These Zealots set fire to the supplies of corn in Jerusalem during the disturbances in the city. It is clear that this account refers to the party of the 'Zealots'. What is indeed striking, however, is that the parallel tradition in Version B ascribes this act twice to the *Sicarii* (*siqarim*). The remark by Morton Smith that this is the result of 'confusions of medieval copyists', is only evidence of his own lack of knowledge of the period and the history of the tradition of this historically particularly valuable rabbinic writing and its versions.[44]

(2) The enigmatic Mishnah Sanh 9,6:

'Whoever steals the sacrificial bowl and whoever curses with kosem and whoever cohabits with an Aramaean woman (= a non-Jewess) — Zealots may descend on him (קנאין פוגעין בו)'.

---

is, moreover, used only in the negative sense in the Targums. See, for example, with reference to Abraham, YalShim on Gen 14.13. 72 (38) *qanna'i* = GenRab 41 (42),8 (Theodor/Albeck, 1, 413) *qunyon*, revengeful. We may therefore conclude that 'Zealot' in the singular is — apart from the established tradition of Phinehas — certainly not a positive name indicating piety.

[44] See Morton Smith, *HThR* 64 (1971), 11. For this, see AbRN, ed. Schechter, Vs A c. 6, 32: 'When Emperor Vespasian came to destroy Jerusalem, 'Zealots' (*qanna'im*) tried to burn all the property (= supplies) with fire'. See also Vs B c. 13, 31: 'The *siqarin* burned the supplies in Jerusalem' and Vs B c. 7, 20: 'When Vespasian came and surrounded Jerusalem (with a rampart), he pitched camp in the east. All the *siqarin* rose up and burned the supplies that were in Jerusalem'. A parallel tradition in EcclRab on 7.12 (20a) speaks of 'Ben Battiach', the nephew of Johanan b. Zakkai, as the 'leader of the *Sicarii* (*ro'sh sqrin* = *siqarin*), gave the order to burn the supplies. For the historicity of this tradition, see *Bell* 5,24 and Tacitus, *Hist* 5,12; see also above, 50f.,66f. It is apparently a question here of two parallel but independent traditions. What is particularly striking is that the rabbis — as opposed to Josephus — were also able to describe the defenders of Jerusalem as *Sicarii*. Further examples of this will be found below, p. 401, n. 57. In his translation of *PW*, London 1916, 5f., G. Friedländer also includes the text on the burning of the supplies in this case by the *Zealots*. This passage is absent from the generally accepted edition of the text (Warsaw 1852). What we may have here is a special tradition of the Vienna manuscript (Epstein) which was used by Friedländer and which has since been lost. For the age and the quality of the tradition of the AbRN, see the introduction to Schechter's edition of the text, xxf.; J. Finkelstein, *JBL* 57 (1938), 13-50; *ibid., Mabo le-Massektot Abot ve-Abot d'Rabbi Natan*, New York 1950; J. Goldin, *HUCA* 19 (1945/6), 97-120; *ibid., The Fathers according to Rabbi Nathan*, New Haven 1955, xviiff. According to Goldin, the AbRN was edited between the seventh and the ninth centuries, but contains only Tannaitic tradition. The language and style of the text are in accordance with those of the Tannaitic period. See J. Neusner, *Development of a Legend*, Leiden 1970, 113, who is in agreement with this view. M.

S. Krauss has pointed out in his commentary[45] that the valuable Munich manuscript of the Talmud and the Gemara of the Palestinian Talmud (jSanh 9,11; 27b.31) have the reading *haqqana'im* (or *haqqana'in*) rather than *qanna'in*. He has drawn a conclusion from this that is worth mentioning here, namely that 'all the more must one think in this context of definite zealots, indeed, of the well-known Zealots themselves'. B. Salamonsen had serious doubts about this interpretation and appealed to another rabbinic text in which the 'court of the Hasmonaeans' is supposed to have forbidden intercourse with a pagan woman (Sanh 82a; AZ 36b). He came to the conclusion that 'the *qanna'im* were private persons acting on behalf of the community during the age of the Hasmonaeans'.[46]

In reality, we have no evidence of any kind of the activity of 'Zealots' under Hasmonaean rule. The regulation points rather to an act of unofficial vehmic justice that was carried out in accordance with the exemplary action performed by Phinehas, since there was no official penalty for this. This fits less easily into the Hasmonaean period, when the Jews had unrestricted penal jurisdiction, than into the period between 6 and 66 A.D., when — apart from the short time when Agrippa I was ruling, that is, between 41 and 44 A.D. — the Jews were deprived of the right to execute.[47]

Lynch justice of this kind was also not the work of individual 'pious' Jews. This is evident from the plural form. The fact that Phinehas' action is dealt with in the Gemara of the Palestinian and the Babylonian Talmud on Sanh 9,6 in each case in the typically graphic language of the rabbis is not the product of secondary scriptural scholarship,[48] but a clear indication that Phinehas was, on the basis of his action, the eponymous

---

Stern's judgement, *op. cit.*, 137, that the word was used 'more flexibly' in the rabbinic sources 'than in Josephus' is quite correct.

[45] See his volumes, IV,4 and 5, *Sanhedrin-Makkot*, in the Giessen edition of the Mishnah, 1933, 262; see also above, 69ff., 186ff.

[46] *NTS* 12 (1965/66), 175; see also *DTT* 27 (1964), 149-162. He is followed in this by M. Borg, *JThS* 22 (1971), 506f. See also Morton Smith's criticism, *op. cit.*, 9, n. 48.

[47] See above, p. 68. For the Jewish law of execution, see J. Blinzler, *The Trial of Jesus*, 1959, 160ff. For the question of the Jewish 'self-help justice' and its criticism of this, see Boaz Cohen, *RIDA* 2 (1955), 116f. = *Jewish and Roman Law*, New York 1966, 2, 633f. See also above, p. 214.

[48] This was Salomonsen's opinion, *op. cit.*, 174. The connection between the *qanna'im* and the only *qanna'i* mentioned in the rabbinic sources by name, Phinehas, is not a fortuitous secondary connection, but an original one. The rabbinic tradition makes a connection between the 'Zealot' Phinehas and the 'Zealots' of Sanh 9,6 by reporting that Phinehas 'remembered' the Mishnah in his extreme need and then killed the transgressor of the law and his pagan temptress: Sanh 82a; jSanh 27b,30f.; NumRab 20,25. In reality, the *qanna'im* derived their name from the *qanna'i* Phinehas.

hero of the *qanna'im*. The few Greek and rabbinic examples of the absolute use of ὁ ζηλωτής = *[haq]qanna'i* outside Josephus' *Jewish War* allow the possibility, indeed probability, that already before the outbreak of the Jewish War, there were fanatical groups of Jews calling themselves 'Zealots' and trying to imitate the 'zeal' of Phinehas. The rabbis' later criticism of Phinehas' zealous action cannot therefore be purely fortuitous.[49] According to the evidence of the extant sources, *qanna'i* — *qan'an* — ζηλωτής was certainly not a generally widespread honorary religious title like *saddiq* or *hasid*.

What exactly was the relationship between these 'Zealots' and the 'fourth philosophy' founded by Judas the Galilaean on the one hand and the later *Sicarii* who were the product of it on the other? This must remain an open question. Josephus does not even give a name to the 'fourth Jewish sect'.

It is instructive in this context to consider his use of the word σικάριος. The concept is a loan-word from the Latin *sicarius*, which, according to the ancient glossarists means, 'murderer' and especially 'assassin', but can also mean an armed robber intent on murder. The Latin word is derived from *sica*, a dagger. In the exigencies of the Roman civil war, it was a popular term of abuse, used to defame the opposite party.[50] What is interesting in this context is that this loan-word occurs only in Josephus, once in Luke (Acts 21.38) and in the Church Fathers who were dependent on them and finally, in isolated cases, in the rabbinic literature. It does not appear at all in any other Greek literary sources, nor does it occur in the Egyptian papyri.[51] It was apparently introduced

---

[49] See above, p. 168ff. See also Boaz Cohen, *op. cit.*, 117 (= 2, 634). According to a Baraita, the Zealot's act was 'not in accordance with the will of the wise': jSanh 27b,36.

[50] See I. Opelt, *Die lateinischen Schimpfwörter, op. cit.*, 133,135,209; R. Till, *Hist* 11 (1962), 322, n. 14. See also the various interpretations of *sicarius* in the ancient glossaries in G. Löwe, G. Götz and F. Schöll, eds., *Corpus Glossariorum Latinorum*, Leipzig 1888-1924: 2, 183,32 σφάκτης ἀνδροφόνος σφαγεὺς λῃστής; 2, 378,13: ξιφηφόρος *sicarius ensifer*; 2, 472,45: φονεὺς *homicida iugulator necator caesor sicarius*; 3, 336,21; 374,60, etc.: φονεύς; 4, 171,14: *latro*; 5, 149,40: *homicida percussor*; 5, 557,53, etc.: *gladiator*. See also above, p. 46f.; O. Betz, *TD* 7, 278f. A *sicarius* was in the first place an assassin and secondarily in the figurative sense an armed robber. The *lex Cornelia de sicariis*, which originated at the time of Sulla, was, according to *Inst* 4,18.5, directed against 'homicidas ... vel eos, qui hominis occidendi causa cum telo ambulant'. This also accounts for the etymology: 'sicarii autem appellantur a sica, quod significat ferreum cultrum'. In Roman criminal trials at the time of Cicero, cases of murder were dealt with under the key-words *de sicariis* or *inter sicarios*; see Cicero, *Orat* 2,105; *Fin* 2,54; *Off* 3,73; *Inv* 2,60; *MarcAntPhil* 2,1(8), etc. For some of these examples of the use of *sicarius*, I have consulted the *Thesaurus Linguae Latinae* in Munich.

[51] See above, p. 46, n. 184. It is only in the Oxyrhynchus papyrus, X, 1294,8 (second

by the Romans on the basis of the special situation of revolt in Palestine, which may even have been peculiar to the east of the Roman Empire, and was then taken over by the Jews themselves: 'It is clear that such a pejorative name was first given by their Roman opponents'.[52]

Josephus mentions the *Sicarii* for the first time when dealing with the period of the procurator Felix:

> 'The country had hardly been purified when a new kind of robber appeared, the so-called *Sicarii*. In broad daylight and in the centre of the city, they murdered people and especially during feasts they mingled among the crowd and stabbed their opponents with little daggers which they had hidden under their clothes' (*Bell* 2,254f.)

The reference to the *Sicarii* in Acts 21.38, also points to the same period. In the Lucan text, the tribune in command of the Fortress of Antonia asks Paul:

> 'Are you not the Egyptian, then, who recently stirred up a revolt and led the four thousand men of the Assassins (ἄνδρας τῶν σικαρίων) out into the wilderness?'

In the first, historically more original account, the name is derived from the new tactics employed by the Jewish freedom movement, which had, employing terrorist methods, entered the city from the plain and had, by murdering individuals, made the whole population insecure. Luke, on the other hand, uses the name simply a synonym for fanatical Jewish insurgents in Palestine. According to him, the commandant of the Antonia at first suspected that Paul was a dangerous rebel, but was quickly disabused by the apostle's Greek education. We may therefore conclude that the Romans called certain particularly active groups *sicarii* on the basis of these new tactics and that this term was then taken over by the Jews and generalized, with the result that it could also be applied to insurgents as a whole. Not only Luke, but also the rabbinic use of *siqarim* and Hippolytus' identification of ζηλωταί with σικάριοι in the *Philosophumena* point to this.[53]

---

or third century A.D.) that σικάριον is used for dagger as a loan-word from Latin. L.Y. Rahmani, *Atiqot* 2 (1959), xxiv, Fig. 4, cf. 188f., has published an illustration of an ossuary, which shows, between two rosettes, such a dagger, with the tip of its blade pointing upwards. The artist seems to have chosen this theme because he was influenced by the spirit of his age.

[52] M. Stern, *op. cit.*, 173.

[53] 9,26.2, *GCS*, ed. P. Wendland, 26, 260: (concerning the Essenes, who were divided into four groups) ὅθεν ἐκ τοῦ συμβαίνοντος τὸ ὄνομα προσέλαβον, Ζηλωταὶ καλούμενοι, ὑπό τινων δὲ Σικάριοι. For the tradition of the text, see C. Burchard, *Josephus-Studien*, 78ff. For an assessment and a historical classification of the whole of this datum, which is not found in Josephus' account, see above, pp. 70ff., 190ff., 197ff. The additional

Although Josephus mentions the *Sicarii* and their new tactics only once in *The Jewish War*, he speaks about them several times in his *Antiquities*. In the earlier work, he says that they first appeared when Felix was procurator (52-59/60 A.D.), in connection with the murder of the high-priest Jonathan (*Ant* 20,164). According to the *Antiquities*, however, the *Sicarii* came to the fore under Festus (60?-62 A.D.):

> 'When Festus arrived in Judaea, the country was being laid waste and all the villages were being burnt down and plundered by robbers. The so-called *Sicarii*, however — the word means 'robbers' - were particularly numerous at that time. They used daggers which were similar in size to the Persian *akenakai*, but in their curved blade similar to the Roman *sicae*. It is from this word that the robbers' name was derived and they murdered many men' (*Ant* 20,186)

Albinus attempted to eradicate them (*Ant* 20,204), but failed. They abducted the secretary of Eleazar, the son of Ananias and the captain of the Temple, who, a few years later, put an end to the sacrifice made for the emperor and had in this way officially opened the war. This enabled them to secure the release of ten of their followers who had been imprisoned (*Ant* 20,208ff.). This extortionary manoeuvre was one that they repeated again and again:

> 'As soon as they had reached a considerable number they acquired greater courage and terrorized the whole country'.

Here, then, the name *Sicarii* is applied to that group within the insurrectionary movement which, by virtue of its bold undertakings, began to exert the greatest influence and the greatest power in the open country even before the outbreak of the war itself. In *The Jewish War*, on the other hand, they appear quite abruptly at the beginning of the war. At the same time (ἅμα), since the captain of the Temple, Eleazar, the son of the high-priest Ananias, had persuaded the priesthood to cease offering the sacrifice for the emperor, a 'band particularly inclined towards war' (τινὲς τῶν μάλιστα κινούντων τὸν πόλεμον) conquered the fortress at Masada by cunning' (*Bell* 2,408).

---

information about the rigorous keeping of the prohibition of images and compulsory circumcision also undoubtedly has a historical background. G.R. Driver's supposition, *The Judaean Scrolls*, Oxford 1965, 120 and 248f., that the *Sicarii* or Zealots came, for these and other reasons, from the Essenes, is fantastic. G. Baumbach, *ThLZ* 90 (1965), 737, and *ibid., Jesus von Nazareth im Lichte der jüdischen Gruppenbildung*, 1971, 22, has assumed, on the basis of the text in Hippolytus, that there was a close connection between the 'Saddokite' Essenes and the priestly Zealots. There is no support for this in the sources available to us. I. Hahn, *AOH* 14 (1962), 135, thought, on the other hand, that, according to *Bell* 2,142 and CD 12,6ff., the Essenes had dissociated themselves from 'the individual terrorist methods of the *Sicarii*' (138).

This coincidence certainly came about not fortuitously, but by arrangement. There were struggles in Jerusalem itself between the rebels who had occupied the Temple and those who were for peace and who, supported by Agrippa's troops and the Roman cohorts, were in control of the upper city and the Antonia. This fighting lasted for days but remained undecided, moving first in favour of one side, then in favour of the other. Eventually, the rebels were reinforced by 'a great number of *Sicarii*, who had infiltrated into the Temple with the defenceless people' (*Bell* 2,425).

In other words, the insurgents in Jerusalem received help from the successful freedom fighters outside the city. This help decided the outcome of the struggle. The upper city and the Fortress of Antonia were conquered and only the royal palace in the west of the city continued to resist for a short time. The social aspects of the struggle can also be seen in the burning of the city archives with the debentures (*Bell* 2,427).[54]

At the same time, Menahem, the son of Judas the Galilaean and the conqueror of Masada, 'returned like a king to Jerusalem, became the leader of the revolt and assumed supreme command in the siege of the royal palace' (γενόμενος ἡγεμὼν τῆς στάσεως διέτασσεν τὴν πολιορκίαν; 2,433f.; see also 437). With the exception of the the three royal towers, the palace was soon taken and the high-priest Ananias, Eleazar's father was killed together with his brother Ezekias. Menahem wanted to wrest all power to himself: '. . . since he believed that he had no (longer any) opponent who could contest his rule, he became an insufferable tyrant' (2,442). A short time after this, when he was about to enter the Temple 'in the finery of royal garments and followed by armed Zealots' (see above, p. 390), he was attacked by the followers of Eleazar, the son of Ananias and the captain of the Temple, and killed after attempting, without success, to flee. There are many possible reasons for this violent act, which opened the door to the civil war that followed:

(1) the long-standing opposition between the priestly nobility and the laity,

(2) the equally deep opposition between the inhabitants of the city and the rural population,

(3) the blood-feud for the murder of the father and the uncle or

(4) Menahem's claims to power, which were probably of a messianic kind and which seemed to the captain of the Temple, who was

---

[54] See M. Stern, *op. cit.*, 138 and 150, n. 12, who points to a parallel from the Peloponnesus in 115 B.C.

descended from the highest ranks of the priestly nobility, to be intolerable.

On the other hand, however, the *Sicarii*, who controlled — or rather, who terrorized — the open countryside, and large sections of the priestly nobility must have been in close contact with each other even before the outbreak of the war. The conquest of Masada and the cessation of the sacrifice for the emperor clearly combined to form a signal for the beginning of a general insurrection and there was also excellent and successful military co-operation during the first few weeks of hostilities. There was a common aim — the rejection of foreign rule and the 'purification' of the Temple and the Holy City — and there was no reluctance to accept the enormous risk of war against the power of Rome. The outbreak of open insurrection was only possible because of this successful co-operation.

Finally, it is worth noting that, in this context, Josephus uses the two terms οἱ σικάριοι (2,425) and οἱ ζηλωταί (2,444) and is evidently referring in both cases to the same group following Menahem. This corresponds to the two versions of the Aboth D'R. Nathan and Hippolytus' *Philosophumena* (see above, p. 397). According to the account of the rallying in *Bell* 7,254, the *Sicarii* had already assembled to oppose Rome under Judas' leadership at the time of the census (τότε γὰρ οἱ σικάριοι συνέστησαν). The word *Sicarii* was, moreover, originally certainly not a name that they gave to themselves as a *Jewish insurrectionary group*, but a secondary name used by their opponents and describing their tactics as guerrilla fighters. The characteristically Jewish religious name 'Zealot', on the other hand, could undoubtedly be applied to themselves by various groups of Jewish insurgents, such as Menahem's followers and later the predominantly priestly 'party' led by Eleazar b. Simon.

It is also noticeable that Josephus differentiates between the two terms in the course of his *Jewish War* and that he limits his use of the name *Sicarii* to those of Menahem's followers who were left and who, under Eleazar b. Ari's leadership, fled to Masada (*Bell* 4,400.516; 7,253-274), while for the most part calling only Eleazar b. Simon's faction 'Zealots'. This may, however, simply be connected with the fact that he employed *certain terms with the aim of defining various groups more precisely*. We may assume that both groups considered themselves 'Zealots', but the model of Phinehas was more applicable to the 'assassins' with 'daggers hidden under their clothes' than to the priestly 'Zealots' who were concentrated in the Sanctuary.

At the same time, however, Josephus does not keep strictly to the distinction that he makes between the two concepts. He is able, for example, to describe the followers of John of Gischala for some time as 'Zealots'.[55] It is also clear that the *Sicarii* who fled to Egypt were not those who occupied Masada, since the latter committed suicide, but came from other groups.[56] ·Finally, the *Sicarii* in Cyrenaica (*Bell* 7,437.444) were an indigenous movement. Unlike Josephus, the Talmudic sources speak consistently of the *siqarim* as the *insurgents in Jerusalem*.[57]

It is interesting to observe in this context how those who claim that there was a complete disparity within the Jewish freedom movement both prior to and during the Jewish War provide completely different descriptions of the individual groups. Baumbach regards the *Sicarii* as a strongly socially defined Galilaean (!) movement. Morton Smith, on the other hand, rightly emphasizes the fact that, as his name so clearly shows, Judas the Galilaean must have appeared in Judaea when he protested against the census and that his sons and followers must have operated there later.[58] In addition to this, Baumbach regards the Zealots as a decidedly priestly party that was in close contact with the Saddokitic Essenes (see above, p. 397, n. 53). In reality, it is only possible to speak with certainty, on the basis of the finds made at Masada, of contacts between the Essenes of Qumran and the *Sicarii* in the fortress at Masada.[59] On the other hand, there would seem to have been continuing

---

[55] This gave rise to Kirsopp Lake's error; see above, p. 388, n. 28. See *Bell* 4,389ff.490.514.566ff.: John fighting as the leader of the 'Zealots' against Simon bar Giora; 5,5ff.: the secession of the priestly 'Zealots' from John of Gischala; 5,96ff.: the taking of the Temple and the restoration of unity.

[56] *Bell* 7,410ff. Josephus only speaks of those ἐκ τῆς στάσεως τῶν σικαρίων, who were able to flee to Egypt. He has nothing to say about their origin. The translation 'insurrection/revolt' or 'party' is disputed; see O. Michel and O. Bauernfeind, eds., *op. cit.*, II,2, 149,281, n. 190. See also *Bell* 7,210ff.: the fugitives from Jerusalem and Machaerus, who were killed in the forest of Jardes. The activity of the *Sicarii* in Egypt is difficult to reconcile with the passivity of those at Masada. M. Stern, *op. cit.*, 138, has suggested that they were followers of Simon bar Giora and came from Jerusalem.

[57] See above, p. 50ff.: Maksh 1,6; LamRab on 4.4, 7 (according to the reading of S. Buber, Wilna 1899); Gitt 56a: 'Abba Sikera, the head of the bandits in Jerusalem', a further development of earlier traditions; for this, see p. 394, n. 44.

[58] G. Baumbach, *ThLZ* 90 (1965), 735; *Jesus von Nazareth*, 18ff. Baumbach goes quite contrary to Josephus in making a connection between the Galilaean John of Gischala and the *Sicarii*. Morton Smith's conclusion, *HThR* 64 (1971), 15, is correct here. See also my statement above, p. 336: in 6 A.D., 'the census had presumably not been carried out there, in the (Galilaean) sovereign territory of Herod Antipas. It was, after all, possible for Judas' nickname — the 'Galilaean' — to arise anywhere except in Galilee itself'. A similar view was expressed by F.J. Foakes Jackson in *Josephus and the Jews*, 1930, 264.

[59] See the finds of fragments of scrolls from Qumran made at Masada: Y. Yadin, *Masada*, 1966, 172ff. In addition to the liturgy of the sabbath sacrifice, the Ben Sirach fragments and the remnants of the Jubilees may have originated in Qumran.

connections between Masada and Jerusalem, since the coins struck in Jerusalem to mark the revolt were used at Masada and the priestly tithes and taxes were levied there. The fact that the *Sicarii* at Masada were close to Pharisaism is clear from the ritual bath or *miqweh* and the synagogue discovered there. This is also a confirmation of the truth of Josephus' clear statement that the 'fourth philosophy' was deeply influenced by Pharisaism, as against the presuppositions of G. Baumbach and K. Schubert.[60]

There is also the interesting rabbinic statement, unearthed by S. Lieberman, which speaks of the 'Idumaeans' who were 'at that time disciples of the house of Shammai' and of the 'dissensions' between 'Menahem and Hillel', leading to Menahem's departure 'with eight hundred students ... dressed in golden scale armor'. This is followed in the rabbinic text by a reference to the murder of the high-priest Ananias (Hanin) by Judas, a brother of Menahem, and to the later murder of Ananus by Eleazar b. Simon. The last-named is said to have driven the Romans out of Jerusalem. The account concludes with the words: 'Dissensions and quarrels broke out (at that time) in Jerusalem'.[61]

This account describes the bloodshed that took place at the outbreak of the Jewish War apparently anachronistically as a dispute between rabbinic schools. It is possible, however, that some historical truth is concealed behind it. Josephus also uses the word teacher (σοφιστής, *Bell* 2,118.433) to describe Judas and Menahem. For his part, Morton Smith disputes the predominance of priests among the 'Zealots' and believes that they gained recruits from among the inhabitants of the country who had penetrated into the city. What remains unexplained thereby is why they continued to occupy the Temple and to maintain their defenses after they had separated from John of Gischala, in the courts of the

---

[60] For the finds of coins, see Y. Yadin, *op. cit.*, 108,168; for the priestly tithes and the taxes, see 96f.; for the ritual bath, see 164ff.; for the synagogue, see 181ff. For doubt as to whether there was a link between the Pharisees and the insurrectionary movement, see G. Baumbach, *BiLi* 41 (1968), 6f.; *Jesus von Nazareth*, 13ff.,21f. Baumbach complicates the whole issue by combining the 'Pharisee Saddok' (*Ant* 18,4.9) with Ps-Clem 1,53f. and forming a link with the Saddokite priestly Zealots. This throws the door wide open to speculation. For K. Schubert, see his review of my book *WZKM* 58 (1962), 259, and *SBS* 43 (1970), 67ff. The possibility of a split in the Pharisaical movement is not even considered. A correct view is suggested by R. Meyer, *TD* 9, 26ff.

[61] S. Lieberman, *Greek in Jewish Palestine*, 1965, 179-184. This indirectly reconfirms the earlier supposition of H. Graetz, who believed that the school of Shammai was closely connected with the Jewish insurrectionary movement, whereas the school of Hillel, the most important representative of which was Johanan b. Zakkai, was opposed to it. See above, pp. 86ff., 200ff., for the question of the eighteen Halakoth. See above, p. 296f., for Menahem's leaving of the circle of teachers; cf. Lieberman, *op. cit.*, 180f. See also M. Stern, *op. cit.*, 144.

Sanctuary[62] and above all in those to which only priests had access.

They also met their end in the defence of the Temple. The Jewish people from the country were, on the other hand, for the most part on the side of their bitter enemy Simon bar Giora, while John of Gischala was above all able to rely on his Galilaean fugitives. The Idumaeans first joined the Zealots, then some of them went over to John of Gischala, although they left him and were later to be found on the side of Simon bar Giora. The unfortunate inhabitants of the city of Jerusalem were crushed between all these groups.

During the civil war and the siege of the city, then, there were various and to some extent changing constellations of power. These were not so much determined by a specific ideology as by the various claims to power made by their leaders and by individual associations of compatriots and with certain social groupings. In the case of those radicals who pressed forward under the banner of an unconditional battle against foreign rule and who preferred to die rather than to surrender the city, however, a certain fundamental and unified religious view of the struggle, which, in my opinion, had been decisively marked by the imprint of the first 'ideologist' of the revolt, Judas the Galilaean, would seem to have predominated. Only this can account for the fanatical detemination to fight against Rome which prepared the way so purposefully for the Jewish War and only this can explain the no less fanatical eschatological struggle. The inscriptions on the Jewish coins of the revolt speak for themselves here.[63]

If today we give these groups, including the *Sicarii*, the name of 'Zealots', it is certainly a correct name, since they were all orientated towards Phinehas' paradigmatic act. On the other hand, it cannot be denied that the problem of the 'party names' raises certain questions on the basis of the language used by our main source, Josephus.[64]

[62] *HThR* 64 (1971), 15ff. The assumption that 'the roots of that party were mainly in the Judaean peasantry' has no foundation at all in the sources. That 'peasant piety' might lay behind their behaviour (17) is equally arbitrary. The core of the group, with Eleazar b. Simon at its centre since the beginning of the war (see above, p. 390, n. 33), was unambiguously priestly. That is why they later became the smallest faction. In addition to this, they were also supported by the first fugitives from the frontier territories, Galilee, Peraea and the coastal plain, who had been the first to flee to Jerusalem. See M. Stern's criticism, *op. cit.*, 151, n. 27.

[63] See above, p. 116ff. See also I. Kadman, *The Coins of the Jewish War*, Jerusalem 1960; B. Kanael, *BA* 26 (1963), 57ff.; Y. Meshorer, *Jewish Coins of the Second Temple Period*, Tel-Aviv 1967, 88ff.,154ff. Great numbers of coins were found even in Masada; see above, p. 402, n. 60.

[64] M. Stern, *op. cit.*, 144, also speaks, in his very considered examination of this problem, in favour of 'a certain connection between the Zealots and the Fourth Philosophy'. He is right to stress the common Pharisaical and that is Shammaite basis.

A modern example may perhaps clarify this problem. Not every
socialist is necessarily a Marxist or a communist, nor does every Marxist
regard himself as a communist. On the other hand, every communist
would claim to be a true Marxist and socialist. I would not care to speak
in this context of Leninists, Stalinists, Titoists, Maoists, Trotskyists,
Neo-Marxists, Austromarxists and revisionists, except to say that they
are all in one way or another connected with Karl Marx and are all
striving to achieve 'socialism'. Any historian working at a later period
will not have an easy task here!

If, then, relationships in modern parties and ideologies are so
complex, how is it possible for us to venture boldly into a detailed
elucidation of the often obscure and imprecise statements that Josephus
makes about the Jewish 'freedom movement'? All that we can really do
is to ask which hypotheses are supported by a *conspectus of all the sources*
and at the same time by the more convincing arguments.

It is for this reason and because I am supported here by many historical
arguments that I believe that the Jewish freedom movement between 6
and 70 A.D. had a certain unified ideological foundation. It was close to
the direction followed by Pharisaical piety and bore a strongly
eschatological imprint. Its special model was the zealous action
performed by Phinehas, who was, for the members of the freedom
movement, the first true 'Zealot', and it was deeply influenced by the
revolutionary theses of Judas the Galilaean. This does not mean,
however, that it was not organized, especially after 66 A.D., in different
groups, which were to some extent in competition with each other and
which, after the outbreak of the war, even tore each other to pieces in
their struggle for power. The words spoken in Georg Büchner's play
Danton's Death can certainly be applied to them: 'Revolution is like
Saturn — it eats its own children'.

ABBREVIATIONS

a) Josephus

Ant   = Flavius Josephus, Antiquitates Judaicae.
Bell = Flavius Josephus, De Bello Judaico.
Ap   = Flavius Josephus, Contra Apionem.

b) Old Testament and Apocrypha:

Am	= Amos	Lev	= Leviticus
Bar	= Baruch	Macc	= Maccabees
Chron	= Chronicles	Mal	= Malachi
Dan	= Daniel	Mic	= Micah
Deut	= Deuteronomy	Nah	= Nahum
Eccles	= Ecclesiastes	Neh	= Nehemiah
Ex	= Exodus	Num	= Numbers
Ezek	= Ezekiel	Obad	= Obadiah
Gen	= Genesis	Prov	= Proverbs
Hab	= Habakkuk	Ps	= Psalms
Hag	= Haggai	Sam	= Samuel
Hos	= Hosea	Sir	= Sirach (Ecclesiasticus)
Is	= Isaiah	Song	= Song of Songs
Jer	= Jeremiah	Tob	= Tobit
Josh	= Joshua	Wis	= Wisdom of Solomon
Judg	= Judges	Zech	= Zechariah
Lam	= Lamentations	Zeph	= Zephaniah

c) Pseudepigrapha and Hellenistic Jewish literature:

ApcAbr	= Apocalypse of Abraham	Sib	= Sibylline Oracles
Arist	= Epistle of Aristeas	TestReub	= Testament of Reuben
AscIs	= Ascension of Isaiah	TestSim	= Testament of Simeon
AssMos	= Assumption of Moses	TestLev	= Testament of Levi
SyrBar	= Syrian Apocalypse of Baruch		
CD	= Damascus document	TestJud	= Testament of Judah
4 Ezra	= Apocalypse of Ezra	TestDan	= Testament of Dan
EthEn	= Ethiopic Enoch	TestNaph	= Testament of Naphtali
SlavE	= Slavic Enoch	TestGad	= Testament of Gad
Jub	= Jubilees	TestAsh	= Testament of Asher
PsSol	= Psalms of Solomon	TestJos	= Testament of Joseph
AntBib	= Pseudo-Philos liber antiquitatum biblicarum	TestBen	= Testament of Benjamin

d) Qumran texts: see also the List of Abbreviations in D. Barthélemy and J. T. Milik, Qumran Cave I, Oxford 1955, 46ff:

IQH	= Psalms of Thanksgiving	IQS	= Manual of Discipline (Community Rule)
IQpHab	= Commentary on Habakkuk	IQSa	= The Messianic Rule s. Barthélemy and Milik 109f
IQM	= War Scroll	IQSb	= Blessings, op. cit. 120ff.

e) Rabbinic texts:

Tractates of the Mishnah:

Ab	= (Pirke) Aboth	Ned	= Nedarim
AZ	= Abodah Zarah	Naz	= Nazir
Arak	= Arakhin	Ohal	= Oholoth
BB	= Baba Bathra	Pes	= Pesachim
BK	= Baba Kamma	Qidd	= Qiddushim
BM	= Baba Mezia	RH	= Rosh haschana
Ber	= Berakoth	Sanh	= Sanhedrin
Bikk	= Bikkurim	Shab	= Shabbath
Erub	= Erubin	Shebi	= Shebiith
Gitt	= Gittin	Shebu	= Shebuoth
Hag	= Hagiga	Shek	= Shekalim
Hor	= Horayoth	Sot	= Sotah
Kel	= Kelim	Sukk	= Sukkah
Ker	= Kerithoth	Taan	= Taanith
Ket	= Kethuboth	Tam	= Tamid
Kidd	= Kiddushin	Ter	= Terumoth
Makk	= Makkoth	Yad	= Yadaim
Maksh	= Makshirin	Yeb	= Yebamoth
Meg	= Megilla	Yom	= Yoma
Men	= Menachoth	Zeb	= Zebahim
MK	= Moed Katan		

Further abbreviations:

ARN	= Aboth de R. Nathan
b	= Babylonian Talmud
bar	= Baraita
DeutRab	= Deuteronomy Rabba
EcclRab	= Ecclesiastes (Koheleth) Rabba
EsthRab	= Esther Rabba
ExRab	= Exodus Rabba
GenRab	= Genesis Rabba
j	= Jerusalem (Palestinian) Talmud
LamRab	= Lamentations Rabba
LevRab	= Leviticus Rabba
MegTaan	= Megillath Taanith
MekEx	= Mekilta on Exodus (ed. Lauterbach = L.)
MTeh	= Midrash Tehillim
PesR	= Pesiqta Rabbati

SifDeut	= Sifre on Deuteronomy
SifLev	= Sifra on Leviticus
SifNum	= Sifre on Numbers
SongRab	= Canticum (Song of Songs) Rabba
Tanch	= Midrasch Tanchuma
t	= Tosephta (ed. Zuckermandel = Z.)
Tg jer I	= Jerusalem Targum I

f) New Testament and Apostolic Fathers:

Acts	= Acts of the Apostles	Joh	= Gospel acc. to John
Barn	= Epistle of Barnabas	Lk	= Luke
Clem	= Epistles of Clement	Mk	= Mark
Cor	= Epistles to Corinthians	Mart Pol	= Martyrdom of Polycarp
Did	= Didache	Pet	= Epistle of Peter
Gal	= Galatians	Phil	= Philippians
Hbr	= Hebrews	EpPol	= Epistle of Polycarp
Ja	= James	Rev	= Revelation of John the Divine
Ro	= Romans	Tim	= 1 + 2 Timothy
Thess	= 1 + 2 Thessalonians	Tit	= Titus

g) Other abbreviations:

Abbreviations for journals and compilations not shown here have been taken from the List of Abbreviations of Die Religion in Geschichte und Gegenwart, 3rd edn. 1957, pp. xvii ff.

B.-Gr., Rel.	= W. Bousset, Die Religion des Judentums im späthellenistischen Zeitalter, 3rd edn. ed. by H. Gressmann, Tübingen 1926
Beginnings	= The Beginnings of Christianity, Part I The Acts of the Apostles, ed. by F. J. Foakes Jackson and Kirsopp Lake, 4 vols., London 1920ff.
Bill.	= H. Strack and P. Billerbeck, Kommentar zum Neuen Testament aus Talmud und Midrasch, 4 vols., München 1922–1928
CAH	= Cambridge Ancient History
CPJ	= V. A. Tcherikover and A. Fuks, Corpus Papyrorum Judaicarum I, Cambridge Mass. 1957 (see Bibliography I.h.)
Derenbourg	= J. Derenbourg, Histoire de la Palestine depuis Cyrus jusqu'à Adrien, Paris 1867.
dig.	= Digesten, s. Corpus juris civilis vol. I (see Bibliography I.h.)
R. Eisler	= ΙΗΣΟΥΣ … 2 vols. Heidelberg 1929ff.
W. R. Farmer	= Maccabees, Zealots, and Josephus, N.Y. 1957
H. Graetz	= Geschichte der Juden, vol. 3, 3rd edn. revised by Braum, Leipzig 1905
HistEcc	= Eusebius' Ecclesiastical History (see Bibliography I.f.)
I.G.	= Inscriptiones Graecae (see Bibliography I.h.)

Jastrow, Dict.	= M. Jastrow, A Dictionary of the Targumim, the Talmud babli and yerushalmi and the Midrashic Literature, 2 vols., N.Y. 1950
JE	= Jewish Encyclopaedia
J. Jeremias, Jerusalem	= Jerusalem in the Time of Jesus, 3rd edn. London 1969.
inst.	= Institutiones, s. Corpus juris civilis vol. I (see Bibliography I.h.)
Istrin	= La Prise de Jérusalem de Josèphe le Juïf, texte vieux-russe publié par V. Istrin et. al., 2 vols., Paris 1934, 38.
Juster	= J. Juster, Les Juifs dans l'Empire Romain, 2 vols., Paris 1914
J. Klausner, Hist.	= היסטריה של הבית השני, 5 vols., 4th edn. Jerusalem 1952
J. Klausner, JvN	= Jesus von Nazareth, 3rd edn. Jerusalem 1952
S. Krauß, MonTal	= Monumenta Talmudica, vol. V, 1 Wien/Leipzig 1914.
Liddell-Scott	= H. G. Liddell and R. Scott, A Greek-English Lexicon, A New Edition revised and augmented throughout by H. S. Jones and R. McKenzie, 12th edn. (reprint of the 9th edn. of 1940), Oxford 1953
Mommsen, R. G.	= Th. Mommsen, Römische Geschichte Vols. I–III and V., 14th edn., Berlin 1933
Moore, Judaism	= G. F. Moore, Judaism in the First Centuries of the Christian Era, 3 vols. Cambridge Mass. 1927–1930
PIR²	= Prosopographia Imperii Romani
A. Reifenberg Jew Coins	= Ancient Jewish Coins, 2nd edn. Jerusalem 1947
Th. Reinach	= Textes d'auteurs Grecs et Romains relatifs au Judaisme, réunis, traduits et annotés par ... , Publications de la Société des Etudes Juives, Paris 1895
G. Ricciotti, Flav. Gius.	= Flavio Giuseppe tradotto e commentato, Vols. I–III 2nd edn., 1949
A. Schlatter, G. I.	= Geschichte Israels von Alexander d. Gr. bis Hadrian, 3rd edn. Stuttgart 1925
Schürer	= E. Schürer, The History of the Jewish People in the Age of Jesus Christ. A new English version revised and edited by G. Vermes & F. Millar, 3 vols. Edinburgh 1973–87.
Volz, Esch.	= P. Volz, Die Eschatologie der jüdischen Gemeinde im neutestamentlichen Zeitalter, 2nd edn. Tübingen 1934

Journals and Series

AGG	= Abhandlungen der Königlichen Gesellschaft der Wissenschaften zu Göttingen.
AO	= Der alte Orient.
AThANT	= Abhandlungen zur Theologie des Alten und Neuen Testaments.
BASOR	= Bulletin of the American Schools of Oriental Research.
BHTh	= Beiträge zur historischen Theologie.
BFChTh	= Beiträge zur Förderung christlicher Theologie.
BJRL	= Bulletin of the John Rylands Library.
BWANT	= Beiträge zur Wissenschaft vom Alten und Neuen Testament.

BZAW	=	Beihefte zur Zeitschrift für die alttestamentliche Wissenschaft.
DLZ	=	Deutsche Literaturzeitung.
DTh	=	Deutsche Theologie.
FRLANT	=	Forschungen zur Religion und Literatur des Alten und Neuen Testaments.
GCS	=	Die Griechischen Christlichen Schriftsteller der ersten drei Jahrhunderte.
HThR	=	Harvard Theological Review.
HUCA	=	Hebrew Union College Annual.
IEJ	=	Israel Exploration Journal.
JJS	=	Journal of Jewish Studies.
JQR	=	Jewish Quarterly Review.
JRomS	=	Journal of Roman Studies.
JSS	=	Journal of Semitic Studies.
JThS	=	Journal of Theological Studies.
MGWJ	=	Monatschrift für Geschichte und Wissenschaft des Judentums.
Nov Test	=	Novum Testamentum.
NTS	=	New Testament Studies.
PEQ	=	Palestinian Exploration Quarterly.
PJ	=	Palästina-Jahrbuch.
RAC	=	Reallexikon für Antike und Christentum.
RB	=	Revue Biblique.
RdQ	=	Revue de Qumran.
REJ	=	Revue des Études Juives.
RHR	=	Revue de l'Histoire des Religions.
SAH	=	Sitzungsberichte der Heidelberger Akademie der Wissenschaften.
SUNT	=	Studien zur Umwelt des Neuen Testaments.
ThBl	=	Theologische Blätter.
ThLZ	=	Theologische Literaturzeitung.
TU	=	Texte und Untersuchungen.
VT	=	Vetus Testamentum.
WMANT	=	Wissenschaftliche Monographien zum Alten und Neuen Testament.
WZKM	=	Wiener Zeitschrift für die Kunde des Morgenlandes.
ZAW	=	Zeitschrift für die alttestamentliche Wissenschaft.
ZDPV	=	Zeitschrift des deutschen Palaestina-Vereins.
ZKG	=	Zeitschrift für Kirchengeschichte.
ZNW	=	Zeitschrift für Neutestamentliche Wissenschaft.
ZPapEp	=	Zeitschrift für Papyrologie und Epigraphik.
ZRGG	=	Zeitschrift für Religions- und Geistesgeschichte.

BIBLIOGRAPHY

I. Sources

a) *Josephus*:

Flavii Iosephi opera ed. at apparatu critico instruxit Benedictus Niese:
  Vol. I–IV: Antiquitatum Iudaicarum libri I–XX et Vita;
  Vol. V: Contra Apionem libri II;
  Vol. VI: De bello Iudaico libros VII edd. I. A. Destinon et B. Niese;
  Vol. VII: Index; 2nd edn. Berlin 1955.
Josephus, with an English Translation by H. St. J. Thackeray, in the Loeb Classical Library:
  Vol. I: The Life, and Against Apion, 2nd edn., London 1956.
  Vols. II–III: The Jewish War, 2nd edn., London 1956–7.
Flavius Josephus, Geschichte des Jüdischen Krieges. Übersetzt und mit Einleitung und Anmerkungen versehen v. Heinrich Clementz, Halle a.d. S. 1900.
Des Flavius Josephus Jüdische Altertümer. Übersetzt ... v. Heinrich Clementz, 2 Bde. Berlin/Wien, 1923.
Flavio Giuseppe tradotto e commentato, Bol. II–III, La Guerra Giudaica, a cura di Giuseppe Ricciotti, 2ª ed., Torino etc., 1949.
Flavius Josephus, Vom Jüdischen Kriege I–IV, nach der slawischen Übersetzung, deutsch herausgegeben und mit dem griechischen Text verglichen v. A. Berendts u. K. Graß, Dorpat 1924.
La Prise de Jérusalem de Josèphe le Juif, Texte vieux-russe publié par V. Istrin, A. Vaillant, P. Pascal, Textes publiés par l'Institut d'Etudes slaves Nº 2, 2 vols., Paris 1934 u. 38.

b) *Old Testament and Apocrypha*:

Biblia Hebraica, ed. R. Kittel and P. Kahle, 3rd edn. Stuttgart 1937.
Septuaginta, ed. A. Rahlfs, 2 vols. Stuttgart 1935.
The Wisdom of Jesus the Son of Sirach in R. H. Charles ed., *Apocrypha and Pseudepigrapha of the OT*, Vol. 1, pp. 268–517, tr. G. H. Box and W. E. Oesterley.
H. L. Strack, Die Sprüche Jesu, des Sohnes Sirachs. Der jüngst gefundene hebräische Text mit Anmerkungen und Wörterbuch, Leipzig 1903.

c) *Pseudepigrapha and Hellenistic Jewish literature*:

R. H. Charles, The Apocrypha and Pseudepigrapha of the Old Testament, 2 vols. Oxford 1913.
J. H. Charlesworth ed., The Old Testament Pseudepigrapha, 2 vols. London, 1983 and 85. (The following texts are taken from this work)
Pseudo-Philo's Biblical Antiquities, tr. D. J. Harrington, in vol. 2, pp. 297–377.
The Sibylline Oracles, tr. J. J. Collins, in vol. 1, pp. 317–472.
The Testaments of the Twelve Patriarchs, tr. H. C. Kee, in vol. 1, pp. 775–828.
P. Rießler, Altjüdisches Schrifttum außerhalb der Bibel, üs. u. erklärt v. ..., Augsburg 1928.
The Testament of Moses [formerly known as The Assumption of Moses], tr. J. Priest, in Charlesworth, vol. 1, pp. 919–34.
The Syriac Apocalypse of Baruch, tr. A. F. J. Klijn, in vol. 1, pp. 615–52.

410

The Lives of the Prophets, tr. D. R. A. Hare, in vol. 2, pp. 379–99.

See also The Biblical Antiquities of Philo, tr. M. R. James, rev. edn. by L. H. Feldman, New York, 1971.

The complete works of Philo of Alexandria, Loeb Classical Library, 10 vols., tr. F. H. Colson and G. H. Whittaker, London 1929–62.

d) *Qumran-Texts*

The Dead Sea Scrolls of St. Mark's Monastery, Vol. I: The Isaiah Manuscript and the Habakuk Commentary, ed. M. Burrows, New Haven 1950.

The Dead Sea Scrolls of St. Mark's Monastery, Vol. II: The Manual of Discipline, New Haven 1951.

The Dead Sea Scrolls of the Hebrew University, ed. E. L. Sukenik, Jerusalem 1955 (= War Scroll and Psalms of Thanksgiving).

A Genesis Apocryphon, A Scroll from the Wilderness of Judaea, ed. N. Avigad and Y. Yadin, Jerusalem 1956.

Qumran Cave I, Discoveries in the Judaean Desert I, ed. D. Barthélemy and J. T. Milik, Oxford 1955.

J. M. Allegro, A newly discovered Fragment of a Commentary on Psalm XXXVII from Qumrân, PEQ 86 (1954), 69–75.

——, Further Light on the History of the Qumrân Sect, JBL 75 (1956), 89–94 (4QpNahum and 4QpPs 37).

——, Further messianic References in Qumran Literature, JBL 75 (1956), 174–187 (4QTestimonia and 4QpJes).

——, Fragments of a Qumran Scroll of eschatological Midrashim, JBL 77 (1958), 350–354.

H. Bardtke, Die Kriegsrolle v. Qumran übersetzt, ThLZ 80 (1955) 401–402.

——, Die Loblieder von Qumran I–IV, ThLZ 81 (1956) 149–154; 589–604; 715–724; ThLZ 82 (1957) 339–348.

Th. H. Gaster, The Scriptures of the Dead Sea Sect in English Translation, London 1957.

P. Wernberg-Møller, The Manual of Discipline, translated and annotated, in Studies on the Texts of the Desert of Judah, Vol. I, Leiden 1957.

e) *Rabbinic Texts*:

The Aboth de Rabbi Nathan, in The Minor Tractates of the Talmud, ed. A. Cohen, The Soncino Press, 1965, vol. 1, pp. 1–210. (See also *The Fathers according to Rabbi Nathan*, tr. J. Goldin, New Haven 1955.)

Yalqut Shim'oni, 2 vols., Jerusalem 1952.

A. Jellinek, Beth ha-midrasch, Sammlung kleinerer Midraschim u. vermischter Abhandlungen aus der älteren jüdischen Literatur, Bd. 1–4, Leipzig 1853ff.

Mekilta de Rabbi Ishmael, ed. J. Z. Lauterbach (with translation), 3 vols., Philadelphia 1949.

Midrash ha-gadol forming a collection of ancient Rabbinic homilies to the Pentateuch ... Genesis, ed. S. Schechter, Cambridge 1902.

Midrash Rabbah, ed. H. Freedman and M. Simon, 10 vols., London and Bournemouth, 1951.

Midrash Tanchuma, ed. S. Buber, 2 vols., New York 1946.

Die Mischna, Text, Übersetzung und ausführliche Erklärung, hrsg. v. G. Beer, O. Holtzmann, S. Krauß, ...:

I,1 Berakot, Text, Übersetzung u. Erklärung v. O. Holtzmann, Gießen 1912;

I,11 Bikkurim, ... v. K. Albrecht, Gießen 1922;

II,1 Schabbat, ... v. W. Nowack, Gießen 1926;

III,6 Sota, ... v. H. Bietenhard, Berlin 1956;

IV,4.5 Sanhedrin-Makkot, ... v. S. Krauß, Gießen 1933;

IV,9 Abôt, ... v. K. Marti u. G. Beer, Gießen 1927;

VI,11 Jadajim, ... v. G. Lisowsky, Berlin 1956.

Mischna: H. Danby, Tractate Sanhedrin, Mischnah and Tosefta, in Translations of early Documents, Series III, London 1919.

S. A. Wertheimer, Batte Midraschoth, Kleinere Midraschim Heft 4, Jerusalem 1897.

H. Danby, The Mishnah, translated from the Hebrew with introduction and brief explanatory notes, London 1933.

A. D. Neubauer, Medieval Jewish Chronicles and Chronological Notes ed. from printed books and manuscripts, vol. II (Anecdota Oxoniensia, Semitic Series vol. I, part VI), Oxford 1895 = Seder Olam Rabba.

Siddur Sᶜphath ämäth, Edition B, Frankfurt-Rödelheim 1927.

Sifra on Leviticus (Torath Kohanim), ed. J. H. Weiß, Wien 1862.

Sifre zu Numeri: Siphre d'be Rab, Corpus Tannaiticum III, 3. Fasciculus primus: Siphre ad Numeros adjecto Siphre zutta ed. H. S. Horovitz, Leipzig 1917.

Sifre zu Numeri, Tannaitische Midraschim Bd. III (II), üs. u. erklärt v. K. G. Kuhn, Stuttgart 1954–1959.

Midrash: Sifre on Numbers, tr. P. P. Levertoff, London 1926. (This is not a complete ET)

Sifre on Deuteronomy, translated by L. Finkelstein, New York 1969.

W. Staert, Altjüdische liturgische Gebete hrsg. v. ..., Lietzmanns k. Texte 58, Berlin 1930.

The Babylonian Talmud, ed. I. Epstein, London 1938–52. (Also includes translations of the Mishnah.) Talmud babli, Hilna 1895–1908, 12 Bde.

Talmud jeruschalmi, Reprint of the Krotoschin edition, New York 1949.

The Palestinian (Jerusalem) Talmud, vol. 1 only, Berakhoth, in M. Schwab, *The Talmud of Jerusalem*, New York 1969 (orig. 1886). (Not a recommended ET; and the rest of the Jerusalem Talmud is untranslated.)

Le Thalmud de Jérusalem traduit pour la première fois par Moïse Schwab, 11 vols., Paris 1878–1889.

Targum jeruschalmi I: Targum Pseudojonathan (Targum Jonathan b. Uzziel zum Pentateuch). hrsg. v. M. Ginsburger, Berlin 1903.

The Jerusalem Targum, in J. W. Etheridge, *The Targums of Onkelos and Jonathan ben Uzziel on the Pentateuch with the Fragments of the Jerusalem Targum 1–11*, 2 vols., 1862–65, reissued as 2 vols. in 1, New York 1968. Targum Pseudojonathan is vol. 1, pp. 157–344, 443–580, vol. 2, pp. 149–240, 340–471, 557–685.

Monumenta Talmudica, Bd. V Geschichte, Teil 1, Griechen und Römer, bearbeitet v. S. Krauß, Wien and Leipzig 1914.

H. Strack and P. Billerbeck, Kommentar zum Neuen Testament aus Talmud und Midrasch Bd. I–IV München 1922–1928, Bd. V. (Rabbinischer Index) 1956.

M. Zobel, Gottes Gesalbter, Der Messias und die messianische Zeit in Talmud und Midrasch, Schocken-Bücherei 90–91, Berlin 1938.

Tosephta nach den Erfurter und Wiener Handschriften ed. M. S. Zuckermandel, Pasewalk 1881.

The Tosephta, in H. Danby, *Translations of Early Documents: Tractate Sanhedrin, Mishnah and Tosephta*, London 1919. (Only a partial ET of the Tosephta is included.)

(Readers may also wish to consult H. Strack, *Introduction to the Talmud and Midrash*, Philadelphia 1945. Also further details of English editions of rabbinic texts and available ETs are in J. Bowker, *The Targums and Rabbinic Literature*, Cambridge 1969.)

f) *Christian Sources*:

Novum Testamentum Graece cum apparatu critico curaverunt Eberhard et Erwin
Nestle, 20. A. 1950.

Aphraates, ed. J. Parisot, Patrologia Syriaca, Vol. I, Paris 1894.

Aphraates, 8 Homilies, in Nicene and Post-Nicene Christian Fathers, tr. J. Gwynn,
Oxford 1890–1900; a selection of others in J. Neusner, *Aphrahat and Judaism*,
Leiden 1971. (These do not amount to a complete ET.)

Apostolische Konstitutionen: Didascalia et Constitutiones Apostolorum ed. F. X. Funk,
2 Bde, Paderborn 1905.

Die Apostolischen Väter, Neubearbeitung der Funkschen Ausgabe v. K. Bihlmeyer, 1.
Teil, Sammlung ausgew. kirchen- und dogmengeschichtl. Quellenschriften II, 1,
Tübingen 1924.

Epistula Apostolorum, in C. Schmidt u. J. Wajnberg, Gespräche Jesu mit seinen Jüngern
..., hrsg. übersetzt u. untersucht. TU Bd. 43 (3. Reihe 13. Bd.) Leipzig 1919.

H. I. Bell and T. C. Skeat, eds. Fragments of an unknown Gospel and other early
Christian Papyri, London 1935.

Justin Martyr in E. J. Goodspeed, Die ältesten Apologeten, Texte mit kurzen
Einleitungen, Göttingen 1914.

R. Knopf, Ausgewählte Märtyrerakten hrsg. v. ..., 3. A. bearb. v. G. Krüger,
Sammlung ausgewählter kirchen- u. dogmengeschichtl. Quellenschriften, N.F.,
Tübingen 1929.

—, Lactantius De mortibus persecutorum, CSEL 27, 2 ed. G. Laubmann, Wien 1897.

—, Minucius, Felix Octarious, CSEL 2 ed. C. Halm, Wien 1867.

Origen Der Johanneskommentar, GCS 10 ed, E, Preuschen, Leipzig 1903.

—, gegen Celsus, GCS 2 u. 3 ed. P. Koetschau, Leipzig 1899.

Sulpicius Severus, Chronica, CSEL 1 ed. C. Halm, Wien 1866.

Tertullian, Apologeticum, Florilegium Patristicum ed. G. Rauschen, fasc. VI, 2. A.
1902.

E. Hennecke, New Testament Apocrypha, tr. and ed. R. McL. Wilson, 2 vols., London
1963.

Eusebius Demonstratio evangelica, GCS 23 ed. I. A. Heikel, Leipzig 1913.

—, Kirchengeschichte, ed. E. Schwartz, Kleine Ausgabe, 5. A. (unv. Nachdruck d. 2.
A.) Berlin/Leipzig 1952.

—, Kirchengeschichte üs. v. P. Hauser, Bibliothek d. Kirchenväter, 2. R. 1. Bd.,
München 1932.

Hippolytus, Refutatio omnium haeresium (Philosophumena), GCS 26 ed. P.
Wendland, Leipzig 1916.

—, Widerlegung aller Häresien, üs. v. Graf K. Preysing, Bibliothek d. Kirchenväter,
München 1922.

g) *Latin and Greek Secular Authors*:

Achilles Tatius: Scriptores erotici graeci, rec. R. Hercher Bd. I, Leipzig 1858.

Aeschines, Orationes rec. F. Blaß, 2. A. 1908.

Ammonius, De differentia adfinium vocabulorum, ed. Valckenaer, Leipzig 1822.

Appian, Historia Romana, rec. 1. Bekker, Leipzig 1852.

Apuleius, Metamorphosen oder der Goldene Esel, lateinisch u. deutsch v. R. Helm,
Berlin/Darmstadt 1956.

Cicero, Scripta quae manserunt omnia, edd. Marx, Strobel u.a., Bibliotheca
Teubneriana, Leipzig 1914ff.

Dio Cassius, Historia Romana, rec. L. Dindorf, 5 Bde, Leipzig 1863–1865.

Dio Chrysostom, Orationes, rec. G. de Budé, 2 Bde, Leipzig 1916.
Diodorus Siculus, bibl. historica, rec. F. Vogel u. C. T. Fischer, 5 Bde. 3. A. Leipzig 1888ff.
Diogenes Laertius, rec. H. G. Huebner, 2 Bde., Leipzig 1828.
Epicurus, De rerum natura, ed. T. Gomperz, Wiener Studien 1 (1879), 27–31.
Epitetus, The discourses as reported by Arrian, the Manual, and fragments with an English translation by W. A. Oldfather, 2 vols., London/Cambridge Mass. 1952 (Loeb's Classical Library).
Galen, opera ed. C. G. Kühn, Bd. 2, Leipzig 1823.
Heliodorus, Aethiopica, rec. I. Bekker, Leipzig 1855.
Herodian, Ab excessu divi Marci, rec. I. Bekker, Leipzig 1855.
Horace, Epistulae, für den Schulgebrauch erklärt v. G. T. A. Krüger, Teil II, 2. 13. A. Leipzig 1894.
Isocrates, Orationes, rec. G. E. Benseler, 2. A. ed. F. Blaß Leipzig 1913.
Iamblichus, De vita Pythagorica, ed. T. Kiessling, Leipzig 1815.
Justinus M. Junianus, Epitoma Pompei Trogi Historicae Philippicae ed. O. Seel, Leipzig 1933.
Juvenal, Saturae, ed. C. F. Herrmann, Leipzig 1926.
Livy, Ab urbe condita, rec. M. Hertz, 4 Bde., Leipzig 1863; epit. s. Bd. 4: periochae librorum CXXVII–CXXXII.
Lucian of Samosata, rec. C. Jacobitz, 3 Bde. 1871–74.
Marinus, Vita Procli, ed. I. F. Boissonade, Leipzig 1814.
Martial, ed. L. Friedländer, Leipzig 1886.
Musonius, ed. O. Hense, Leipzig 1905.
Paulus: Pauli libri quinque sententiarum, in: Collectio librorum iuris anteiustiniani, ed. P. Krüger u. Th. Mommsen, Bd. 2, Berlin 1878.
Pausanias, Descriptio Graeciae, rec. F. Spiro, 3 Bde., Leipzig 1903.
Petronius, Saturae, rec. F. Büchler (6. A. cur. W. Haeraeus), Berlin 1922.
Philodemus, Rhetorica, rec. S. Sudhaus, 2 Bde., Leipzig 1896.
Plato, Protagoras, ed. J. Burnett, script. class. biblioth. Oxoniensis Bd. 3, Oxford, o. J.
Pliny the Elder, Historia naturalis, rec. L. Jan u. K. Mayhoff, 5 Bde., Leipzig 1892ff.
Pliny the Younger, Epistulae, rec. H. Keil, Leipzig 1896.
Plutarch, Moralia, ed. C. Hubert u. W. Nachstädt u.a., Leipzig 1925.
—, Vitae parallelae, ed. C. Lindskog u. K. Ziegler, 4 Bde. in 8, Leipzig 1914ff.
Quintilian, Declamationes, ed. C. Ritter, Leipzig 1884.
Th. Reinach, Textes d'auteurs Grecs et Romains relatifs au Judaisme, réunis traduits et annotés par …, Publications de la Société des Etudes Juives, Paris 1895.
Sallust, de coniur. Cat. u. de bell. Jugurth., ed. R. Dietsch, 4. A., Leipzig 1874.
Scriptores historiae Augustae, rec. H. Jordan u. F. Eisenhard, Berlin 1864.
Seneca, Opera quae supersunt, rec. F. Haase, 4 Bde., Leipzig 1887.
Stobaeus, Anthologium, ed. C. Wachsmuth u. O. Hense, Berlin 1909.
Strabo, Geographica, 3 Bde., rec. A. Meineke, Leipzig 1864.
Suetonius, Vita Caesarum, with an English translation by J. C. Rolfe, London/Cambridge Mass. 1913f, (Loeb's Class. Library).
Tacitus, Annalen (ab excessu divi Augusti), erklärt v. K. Nipperdey, 10. verbesserte A. besorgt v. G. Andresen, 2 Bde., Berlin 1904.
—, Histories, with introduction and notes by A. D. Godley, London 1887–90, (Macmillan Classical Series).
Thucydides, hist., ed. C. Hude, Bd. I, 2. A. Leipzig 1930.
Varro, De lingua Latina, rec. C. O. Müller, Leipzig 1833.
—, De re rustica, ed. G. Goetz u. F. Schoell, Leipzig 1910.

h) *Epigraphic, papyrological, numismatic and similar compilations*:

R. Cagnat-Lafaye, Inscriptiones Graecae ad res Romanas pertinentes, 3 vols., Paris 1911–1927.

Corpus Inscriptionum Graecarum, ed. A. Böckh, Royal Prussian Academy of Science, Berlin 1825–59.

Corpus Inscriptionum Latinarum, Royal Prussian Academy of Science, Berlin 1869ff, vol. 2, Spanien ed. E. Hübner 1869; vol. 3 die Donauprovinzen u. d. Osten ed. Th. Mommsen et. al. 1873.

Corpus iuris civilis, vol. I (Institutionen u. Digesten), ed. P. Krüger and Th. Mommsen, 15th edn. Berlin 1928.

W. Dittenberger, Orientis Graeci Inscriptiones selectae, 2 vols., Leipzig 1903–1905.

——, Sylloge Inscriptionum Graecarum, 4 vols., 3rd edn. Leipzig 1915–1924.

J. B. Frey, Corpus Inscriptionum Judaicarum, Recueil des inscriptions juives qui vont du IIIᵉ siècle avant Jésus-Christ au VIIᵉ siècle de notre ère. Vol. 2: Asie-Afrique, Rom 1958.

G. F. Hill, Catalogue of the Greek Coins of Palestine, A Catalogue of the Greek Coins in the British Museum 27, London 1914.

Inscriptiones Graecae, Royal Prussian Academy of Science, Berlin 1873ff; vol. VII ed. W. Dittenberger 1892.

The Oxyrhynchus Papyri, ed. v. Grenfell, Hunt, Bell et. al., vols. I and X, London 1898 and 1914.

A. Reifenberg, Ancient Jewish Coins, 2nd edn. Jerusalem, 1947.

V. A. Tcherikover and A. Fuks, Corpus Papyrorum Judaicarum I, Cambridge Mass. 1957.

II. STUDY RESOURCES (Dictionaries, Indices, Reference Works):

W. F. Arndt and F. W. Gingrich, A Greek-English Lexicon of the N.T. and other early Christian Literature, Cambridge 1957.

W. Bauer, Griechisch-Deutsches Wörterbuch zu den Schriften des Neuen Testaments und der übrigen urchristlichen Literatur, 7th edn. 1971.

C. Brockelmann, Lexicon Syriacum, 2nd edn. Halle 1928.

G. Dalman, Aramäisch-Neuhebräisches Handwörterbuch, 3rd edn. Göttingen 1938.

A. Forcellinus, Lexicon totius Latinitatis, 4 vols., Schneeberg 1831ff. (See also *The Oxford Latin Dictionary*, ed. P. G. W. Glare, Oxford 1982.)

E. Hatch and H. A. Redpath, A Concordance to the Septuagint and the other Greek versions of the Old Testament ..., 3 vols. in 2, 2nd impression (Reprint of the 1st edn. of 1897), Graz 1954.

M. Jastrow, A Dictionary of the Targumim, the Talmud babli and yerushalmi and the Midrashic Literature, 2 vols., New York 1950.

L. Köhler and W. Baumgartner, Lexicon in Veteris Testamenti Libros, Leiden 1953. (See also W. L. Holladay, *A Concise Hebrew and Aramaic Lexicon of the O.T.*, Leiden 1971.)

J. Leisegang, Philonis Alexandrini opera quae supersunt, vol. VII, 1 u. 2, Indices, Berlin 1928.

J. Levy, Neuhebräisches und Chaldäisches Wörterbuch über die Talmudim und Midraschim, 4 vols., 2nd edn. Leipzig 1876–89.

H. G. Liddell and R. Scott, A Greek-English Lexicon, a New Edition revised and augmented throughout by H. S. Jones and R. McKenzie, 12th edn. (reprint of the 9th edn. of 1940), Oxford 1953.

G. Lisowsky, Konkordanz zum Hebräischen Alten Testament nach dem von P. Kahle in der Biblia Hebraica ed. R. Kittel besorgten masoretischen Text ..., Stuttgart 1957/58. (See also B. Davidson, *A Concordance of the Hebrew and Chaldee Scriptures*, London 1876.)

The Oxford Classical Dictionary, 2nd edition, ed. N. G. L. Hammond and H. H. Scullard, Oxford 1970.

F. Passow, Handwörterbuch der Griechischen Sprache, 4 vols., 5th edn. Leipzig 1841ff.

H. St. J. Thackeray and R. Marcus, A Lexicon to Josephus, Paris 1930ff.

Thesaurus Graecae linguae ab Henrico Stephano constructus ..., tertio edd. B. Hase, G. Dindorf and L. Dindorf, Paris 1842–1842.

D. Wyttenbach, Lexicon Plutarcheum, 2 vols., Leipzig 1843.

III. SECONDARY LITERATURE

F. M. Abel, Les Livres des Maccabées, Études Bibliques, 2nd edn. Paris 1949.

——, Histoire de la Palestine depuis la conquête d'Alexandre jusqu'à l'invasion Arabe, 2 vols., Etudes Bibliques, Paris 1952.

J. Abrahams, Studies in Pharisaism and the Gospels, 2 vols., London, vol. I 1917, vol. II 1924.

V. Aptowitzer, Die Parteipolitik der Hasmonäer im Rabbinischen und Pseudepigraphischen Schrifttum, Kohout-Foundation V, Wien/Leipzig 1927.

M. Avi-Yonah, M. Avigad etc., The Archaeological Survey of Masada 1955–56, IEJ 7 (1957), 1–60.

——, Review of W. R. Farmer, Maccabees, Zealots ..., IEJ 8 (1958), 202–204.

W. Bacher, Die Aggada der Tannaiten, 2 vols., 1st vol. 2nd edn. Straßburg 1903, 2nd vol. 1890.

——, Die Aggada der Palästinensischen Amoräer, 3 vols., Straßburg 1892–1899.

——, The supposed Inscription upon 'Joshua the robber'. JQR 3 (1891), 354–357.

E. Bammel, Die Bruderfolge im Hohenpriestertum der herodianisch-römischen Zeit, ZDPV 70 (1954), 147–153.

——, ἀρχιερεὺς προφητεύων ThLZ 79 (1954), Sp. 351–356.

——, Art. πτωχός, sections B and C, in Theological Dictionary of the New Testament [hereafter cited as TD], ed. G. Bromiley, vol. 6, 1968, pp. 888–902.

H. Bardtke, Die Handschriftenfunde am Toten Meer, Berlin 1953.

S. Baron, A Social and Religious History of the Jews, 8 vols., Philadelphia 1937.

W. W. Graf Baudissin, Kyrios als Gottesname im Judentum und seine Stelle in der Religionsgeschichte, edited by O. Eißfeldt, 3 parts, Giessen 1929.

W. Bauer, Art. Essener, PW Supplement IV, 1924, 386ff.

——, Rezension von Rudolf Eislers Werk, ThLZ 55 (1930), 557–563.

O. Bauernfeind, Die Apostelgeschichte, ThHKzNT, Leipzig 1939.

——, Art. πόλεμος, TD vol. 6, 1968, pp. 502–15.

A. Baumstark, Art. Bild I, RAC 2.287–302, 1954.

The Beginnings of Christianity, Part I The Acts of the Apostles, ed. by F. J. Foakes Jackson and Kirsopp Lake, 4 vols., London 1920ff.

H. Bentwich, Josephus, Philadelphia 1926.

A. Bentzen, Daniel, HBzAT, 2nd edn., Tübingen 1952.

A. Berendts, Die Zeugnisse vom Christentum im Slavischen 'De bello Judaico' des Josephus, TU Neue Folge XIV, 4, Leipzig 1906.

O. Betz, Jesu Heiliger Krieg, NovTest 2 (1957), 116–137.

E. Bickermann, Die Römische Kaiserapotheose, ARN 27 (1929), 1–34.

——, Sur la version vieux-russe de Flavius-Josèphe, Mélanges Franz Cumont, Annuaire de l'Institut de Philologie et d'Histoire orientales et slaves IV, Bruxelles 1936.

——, The God of the Maccabees: Studies on the Meaning and Origin of the Maccabaean Revolt, tr. H. R. Moehring, Leiden 1979.

——, The Date of IV Maccabees, Louis Ginzberg Jubilee Vol. English Section, 105–112, New York 1945.

——, The Warning-Inscriptions of Herod's Temple, JQR 37 (1946/47), 387–405.

W. Bieder, Art. πνεῦμα, section C, TD vol. 6, 1968, pp. 367–89.

M. Black, The Account of the Essenes in Hippolytus and Josephus, Studies in Honour of C. H. Dodd, The Background of NT and its Eschatology, 172–175, Cambridge 1956.

G. Bornkamm, Jesus of Nazareth, tr. I. and F. McLuskey and J. M. Robinson, London 1960.

W. Bousset, Kommentar zur Apokalypse, Meyers krit-exeget. Kommentar über d. N. T., 6th edn. Göttingen 1906.

——, Eine jüdische Gebetssammlung im 7. Buch der Apostolischen Constitutionen, NAG phil. hist. Kl., Göttingen 1915, 435–489.

——, Die Religion des Judentums im späthellenistischen Zeitalter, in 3rd edn., ed. H. Greßmann, HBzNT 21, Tübingen 1926.

S. G. F. Brandon, The Fall of Jerusalem and the Christian Church, London 1951.

H. Braun, Spätjüdisch-häretischer und frühchristlicher Radikalismus, vol. 1: Das Spätjudentum, vol. 2: Die Synoptiker, BHTh 24, Tübingen 1957.

H. Braunert, Der Römische Provinzialcensus und der Schätzungsbericht des Lukas-Evangeliums, Historia 6 (1957), 192–214.

K. G. Bretschneider, Capita Theologiae Judaeorum dogmaticae e Flavii Josephi scriptis collecta …, Leipzig 1812.

J. E. Bruns, The Davidic Dynasty in post-exilic Palestine, Scripture 7 (1955), 2–5.

A. Büchler, Studies in Jewish History, London 1956.

R. Bultmann, The Gospel of John, tr. G. R. Beasley-Murray, Oxford 1971.

F. C. Burkitt, The Syriac Forms of New Testament proper Names, Proceedings of the British Academy, vol. V, London 1912.

V. Burr, Tiberius Julius Alexander, (= Antiquitas, R.I. Vol. 1), Bonn 1955.

The Cambridge Ancient History, vol. X, 44 B.C.-A.D. 70, ed. S. A. Cook, F. E. Adcock, M. P. Charlesworth, 2nd edn. Cambridge 1952.

M. P. Charlesworth, Trade-routes and Commerce of the Roman Empire, Cambridge 1924.

C. Clermont-Ganneau, Une stèle du Temple de Jérusalem, Revue Archéologique 23 (1872), 214–234, 290–296.

T. Corbishley, Quirinius and the Census: A Restudy of the Evidence, Klio 29 (1936) 81–93.

P. Corssen, Die Zeugnisse des Tacitus und Pseudo-Josephus über Christus, ZNW 15 (1914), 114–140.

J. M. Creed, The Slavonic Version of Josephus' History of the Jewish war, HTR 25 (1932), 276–319.

O. Cullmann, The State in the New Testament, 2nd edn., London 1963.

——, Art. Ebioniten, RGG, 3rd edn., 2,297f, Tübingen 1958.

F. Cumont, L'aigle funéraire d'Hierapolis et l'apothéose des empereurs, Etudes Syriennes, 2,35ff., Paris 1917.

G. Dalman, Der leidende und sterbende Messias der Synagoge im ersten nach-christlichen Jahrtausend, Schriften des Institutum Iudaicum in Berlin 1888.

——, Aramäische Dialektproben, Leipzig 1896.

——, The Words of Jesus considered in the Light of post-Biblical Jewish Writings and the Aramaic language, Edinburgh 1902.

——, Grammatik des jüdisch-palästinischen Aramäisch, 2nd edn., Leipzig 1905.

——, Jesus-Jeshua: Studies in the Gospels, London 1929.

——, Sacred Sites and Ways, tr. P. P. Levertoff, London 1935.

——, Jerusalem und sein Gelände, BFChTh, 2nd series, vol. 19, Gütersloh 1930.

J. C. Dancy, A Commentary on I Maccabees, Oxford 1954.

A. Deissmann, Light from the Ancient East, tr. L. R. M. Strachan, London 1927.

H. E. del Medico, Deux Manuscrits hébreux de la Mer Morte, Paris 1951.

——, The Riddle of the Scrolls, tr. H. Garner, London 1958.

R. Delbrück, Antiquarisches zu den Verspottungen Jesu, ZNW 41 (1942), 124–145.

G. Delling, Art. μάγος, TD vol. 4, 1967, pp. 356–9.

——, ΜΟΝΟΣ ΘΕΟΣ, ThLZ 77 (1952), Sp. 468–476.

J. Derenbourg, Essai sur l'Histoire et la Géographie de la Palestine d'après les Thalmuds et les autres sources Rabbiniques. Première Partie: Histoire de la Palestine dépuis Cyrus jusqu'à Adrien, Paris 1867.

H. Dessau, Geschichte der Römischen Kaiserzeit, vols. I–II,2 Berlin 1924–1930.

——, Urchristliche Geoschichte und Weltgeschichte, ThBL 6 (1927), 214–224.

M. Dibelius, Jesus, tr. C. B. Hedrick and F. C. Grant, 2nd edn., London 1949.

M. Dibelius, Studies in the Acts of the Apostles, London 1956.

F. Dornseiff, Zum Testimonium Flavianum, ZNW 46 (1955), 245–250.

H. Drexler, Untersuchungen zu Josephus und zur Geschichte des Jüdischen Aufstandes, Klio 19 (1925), 277–312.

S. Dubnow, Weltgeschichte des Jüdischen Volkes, Orientalische Periode, vol. 2: Alte Geschichte, trans. from the Russian by A. Steinberg, Berlin 1925ff.

A. Edersheim, The Life and Times of Jesus the Messiah, 2 vols. Grand Rapids/Michigan 1953.

W. Eichrodt, Theology of the Old Testament, tr. J. A. Baker, London 1961/7.

Eisler, ΙΗΣΟΥΣ ΒΑΣΙΛΕΥΣ ΟΥ ΒΑΣΙΛΕΥΣΑΣ. Die messianische Unabh ängigkeitsbewegung vom Auftreten Joh. d. Täufers bis zum Untergang Jakobus d. Gerechten nach der neuerschlossenen Eroberung von Jerusalem des Flavius Josephus und den christlichen Quellen dargestellt, 2 vols. Heidelberg 1929f.

O. Eissfeldt, The Old Testament: an Introduction, tr. P. R. Ackroyd, New York 1965.

I. Elbogen, Der Jüdische Gottesdienst in seiner geschichtlichen Entwicklung, Frankfurt/a. M. 1924.

——, סיקריקון, eine Studie, MGWJ 69, NF 33 (1925), 249–257.

W. Eltester, Schöpfungsoffenbarung und natürliche Theologie im frühen Christentum, NTS 3 (1957), 93–114.

W. R. Farmer, The Patriarch Phineas, AThR 34 (1952), 26–30.

——, Maccabees, Zealots, and Josephus, An Inquiry into Jewish Nationalism in the Greco-Roman Period. New York 1957.

——, Judas, Simon and Athronges, NTS 4 (1958), 146–155.

E. Fascher, ΠΡΟΦΗΤΗΣ, eine sprach-und religionsgeschichtliche Untersuchung, Gießen 1927.

S. Feist, Zur Ethymologie von סיקריקון, MGWJ 71 (1927), 138–141.

L. I. Finkelstein, The Pharisees, the sociological background of their faith, 2 vols., 3rd edn., Philadelphia 1946.

H. A. Fischel, Martyr and Prophet, a study in Jewish Literature, JQR 37 (1946/47), 265–280; 363–386.

D. Flusser, The Apocryphal Book of the Ascensio Jesajae and the Dead Sea Sect, IEJ 3 (1953), 30–47.

W. Foerster, Art. κύριος, section D, TD vol. 3, 1965, pp. 1081–5. See also Lord, tr. H. P. Kingdon, London, 1958.

——, Art. ὄρος, sections B and C, TD vol. 5, 1967, pp. 479–85.

——, Herr ist Jesus, Herkunft und Bedeutung des urchristlichen Kyrios-Bekenntnisses, Neutestamentliche Forschungen, Gütersloh 1954.

——, Palestinian Judaism in New Testament Times, tr. G. E. Harris, Edinburgh 1964.

T. Frank, An Economic Survey of Ancient Rome, vol. IV: Eastern Provinces, Roman Syria, pp. 123–257 by F. M. Heichelheim, Baltimore 1940.

——, Dominium in 'solo provinciali' and 'ager publicus', JRomS 17 (1922), 141–161.

J. B. Frey, La question des images chez les Juifs à la lumière des récentes découvertes, Biblica 15 (1934), 265–300.

L. Friedländer, Darstellungen aus der Sittengeschichte Roms in der Zeit von Augustus bis zum Ausgang der Antoninen, 10th edn. rev. by G. Wissowa, vols. I–IV, Leipzig 1922ff.

——, Roman Life and Manners under the Early Empire, tr. J. H. Freese and L. A. Magnus, London, 1928.

H. Fuchs, Der geistige Widerstand gegen Rom, Berlin 1938.

A. Frhr. v. Gall, ΒΑΣΙΛΕΙΑ ΤΟΥ ΘΕΟΥ. Eine religionsgeschichtliche Untersuchung zur vorkirchlichen Eschatologie, Heidelberg 1926.

A. Geiger, Jüdische Zeitschrift für Wissenschaft u. Leben, vol. 2 (1863); 5 (1867); 7 (1869); 8 (1870).

——, Urschrift und Übersetzungen der Bibel, Reprint of the 1857 edition, Frankfurt a/M 1928.

M. Gelzer, Die Vita des Josephus, Hermes, 80 (1952), 67–90.

M. S. Ginsburg, Rome et la Judée, Contribution à l'histoire de leurs relations politiques, Diss. Paris 1928.

L. Ginzberg, The Legends of the Jews, Philadelphia, vol. 3 (1911), vol. 6 (1916).

N. N. Glatzer, Geschichte der talmudischen Zeit, Schockenbücherei, Berlin 1937.

L. Goldschmid, Les impôts et droits de douane en Judée sous les Romains, REJ 34 (1897), 192–217.

E. R. Goodenough, Jewish Symbols in the Greco-Roman Period, vol. 4, Part 5, New York 1954. vol. 8, 1958, Bollingen Series XXXVII.

L. Goppelt, Art. πεινάω, TD vol. 6, 1968, pp. 12–22.

H. Graetz, Das Sikarikongesetz, Jahrbuch des jüdisch-theologischen Seminars Breslau 1892.

——, History of the Jews, Philadelphia 1893.

H. Greßmann, Das religionsgeschichtliche Problem des Ursprungs der hellenistischen Erlösungsreligionen I, ZKG NF 3 (1922), 178–191.

——, Der Messias, FRLANT NF 26, Göttingen 1926.

W. Grundmann, Art. δύναμις, TD vol. 2, 1964, pp. 284–317.

E. Günther, Zeuge und Märtyrer, ZNW 47 (1956), 145–161.

C. Guignebert, The Jewish World in the Time of Jesus, tr. S. H. Hooke, New York 1959.

A. Gulak, סיקריקון, Tarbiz 5 (1933/1934), 23–27.

H. Guttmann, Die Darstellung der jüdischen Religion bei Flavius Josephus, Breslau 1928.

E. Haenchen, The Acts of the Apostles, Oxford 1971.

J. Hänel, Die Religion der Heiligkeit, 1931.

A. v. Harnack, Judentum und Judenchristentum in Justins Dialog mit Trypho, TU 39 (NF III, 9), Leipzig 1913.

——, Geschichte der altchristlichen Literatur bis Euseb,
Part I: Die Überlieferung und der Bestand,
Part II: Die Chronologie, 2 vols., Leipzig 1893 u. 1897–1904.

420 BIBLIOGRAPHY

——, The Mission and Expansion of Christianity in the First Three Centuries, 2nd ed., London, 1908.

H. Heinen, Zur Begründung des römischen Kaiserkults von 48 v. bis 14 n. Chr., Klio 11 (1911).

R. Helm, Review of R. Laqueur, Der jüd. Historiker Flavius Josephus, Phil. Wochenschrift, 41 (1921), 481–493 u. 505–516.

J. Hempel, Politische Absichten und politische Wirkung im biblischen Schrifttum, AO 38 (1938).

D. J. Herz, Großgrundbesitz in Palästina im Zeitalter Jesu, PJ 24 (1928), 98–126.

G. Herzog-Hauser, Art. Kaiserkult, PW Suppl. IV, 806–852, 1924.

A. Hilgenfeld, Die Ketzergeschichte des Urchristentums, Leipzig 1884.

E. G. Hirsch, Art. Galilee, JewEnc 5, 554ff.

H. Hitzig, Art. crux, PW IV, 1728–31, 1901.

G. Hölscher, Art. Josephus, PW IX, 1934–2000, 1916.

——, Geschichte der Israelitisch-Jüdischen Religion, Gießen 1922.

——, Die Hohenpriesterliste bei Josephus und die evangelische Chronologie, SAH, phil. hist. Kl., 3. Abhandlung, Jg. 1939/40, Heidelberg 1940.

G. Hoennicke, Das Judenchristentum, Berlin 1908.

O. Holtzmann, Neutestamentliche Zeitgeschichte, Tübingen, 1st edn. 1895 and 2nd edn. 1906.

G. Humbert, Art. latrocinium, Daremberg-Saglio, Dictionnaire des Antiquités grecques et romaines, 2, 991f, 3rd edn. Paris 1881ff.

C. H. Hunzinger, in: Le travail d'édition des Manuscrits de Qumrân, RB 63 (1956), 67.

J. W. Jack, The historic Christ, An examination of Dr. Eisler's theory according to the Slavonic version of Josephus, London 1933.

F. J. Foakes Jackson, Josephus and the Jews, The Religion and History of the Jews as explained by Flavius Josephus, London 1930.

E. E. Jensen, The first century controversy over Jesus as a revolutionary figure, JBL 60 (1941), 261–272.

J. Jeremias, Jerusalem in the Time of Jesus: an Investigation into Economic and Social Conditions during the New Testament Period, tr. F. H. and C. H. Cave, 3rd edn., London, 1969.

——, Sabbathjahr und neutestamentliche Chronologie, ZNW 27 (1928), 98–103.

——, Erlöser und Erlösung im Spätjudentum und Urchristentum, DTh vol. 2: Der Erlösungsgedanke, Bericht über den 2. deutschen Theologentag in Frankfurt a./M (Herbst 1928), Göttingen 1929.

——, Art. Ἠλ(ε)ίας, TD vol. 2, 1964, pp. 328–41.

——, Art. Μωϋσῆς, TD vol. 4, 1967, pp. 848–73.

——, Die Einwohnerzahl Jerusalems zur Zeit Jesu, ZDPV 66 (1943), 24–31.

——, Art. παῖς θεοῦ, section C, TD vol. 5, 1967, pp. 677–700.

H. U. Instinsky, Begab es sich in jenen Tagen, Hochland 49 (1956/57), 97–108.

J. M. Jost, Geschichte des Judentums und seiner Secten, vol. 1, Leipzig 1857.

J. Juster, Les Juifs dans l'Empire Romain, leur condition juridique, économique et sociale, 2 vols., Paris 1914.

L. Kadman, A Coin Find at Masada, IEJ 7 (1957), 61–65.

B. Kanael, The historical background of the coins 'Year four of the redemption of Zion.' BASOR Nr. 129, February 1953.

H. Karpp, Art. Christennamen, RAC 2, 1114–1138, 1954.

J. S. Kennard, Politique et religion chez les Juifs au temps de Jésus et dans l'Eglise primitive, Diss. Paris 1927.

——, Judas of Galilee and his clan, JQR 36 (1945), 281–286.

A. Kindler, More Dates on the Coins of the Procurators, IEJ, 6 (1956), 54–57.

G. Kittel, Das Konnubium mit den Nichtchristen im Antiken Judentum, Forschungen zur Judenfrage II, Hamburg 1937.

——, Die Probleme des palästinischen Spätjudentums und des Urchristentums, Stuttgart 1926.

——, Art. ἔρημος, TD vol. 2, 1964, pp. 657–60.

J. Klausner, Jesus of Nazareth, tr. W. F. Stinespring, New York, 1925.

——, היסטוריה של הבית השני, 5 vols., 4th edn. Jerusalem 5714 = 1954.

——, The Messianic Idea in Israel, from its Beginning to the Completion of the Mishnah, trans. from the 3rd Hebrew edn. by W. F. Stinespring, New York 1955.

S. Klein, Neue Beiträge zur Geschichte und Geographie Galiläas, Palästina-Studien, Heft I, Wien 1923.

——, Galiläa von der Makkabäerzeit bis 67 A.D. Palästina-Studien, Vol. IV, Wien 1928.

——, Der Berg Asamon, Bell. Jud. II, 11, MGWJ 71 NF 35 (1927), 264–267.

Kleinfeller, Art. sicarius, PW 2. Series 2, 2185–2186, 1923.

E. Klostermann, Das Markusevangelium, HBzNT 3, 4th edn. Tübingen 1950.

L. Köhler, Old Testament Theology, tr. A. S. Todd, London 1957.

K. Kohler, Art. Zealots, JewEnc 12, 639–643, 1906.

——, Wer waren die Zeloten oder Kannaim, eine Studie, Festschrift zu Ehren des Dr. A. Harkavy, ed. Baron D. v. Günzburg and I. Markon, St. Petersburg 1908.

E. Kornemann, Zur Geschichte der antiken Herrscherkulte, Klio 1 (1901), 51–146.

C. H. Kraeling, The Episode of the Roman Standards at Jerusalem, HTR 35 (1942), 263–289.

S. Krauß, The Jews in the Works of the Church-Fathers, JQR 5 (1893), 122–157.

——, Zur griechischen und lateinischen Bibliographie, ByZ 2 (1893), 511ff.

——, Griechische und Lateinische Lehnwörter in Talmud, Midrasch und Targum, 2 vols., Berlin 1898/99.

——, Talmudische Archäologie, 3 vols., Leipzig 1910/1912.

M. Krenkel, Josephus und Lucas, der schriftstellerische Einfluß des jüdischen Geschichtsschreibers auf den christlichen, Leipzig 1894.

W. Kubitschek, Art. Census, PW 3, 1914–1920, 1899.

F. Küchler, Der Gedanke des Eifers Jahwes im Alten Testament, ZAW 28 (1908), 42ff.

K. G. Kuhn, Art. Βαλαάμ, TD vol. 1, 1964, pp. 524–5.

——, Art. βασιλεύς, section C, ibid. pp. 571–4.

——, Die beiden Messias Aarons und Israels, NTS 1 (1954/55), 168–179.

M. J. Lagrange, Le Judaisme avant Jésus-Christ, 3rd edn. Paris 1931.

R. Laqueur, Der jüdische Historiker Flavius Josephus, Giessen 1920.

——, Review of W. Weber, Josephus u. Vespasian in der Philolog. Wochenschrift 41 (1921), Sp. 1105–1114.

——, Review of R. Eisler, I.B., HZ 148 (1933), 326–328.

J. Z. Lauterbach, Art. Megillat Taanit, JE 8, 427f, 1904.

H. Levy, Review of R. Eisler, I.B., DLZ 51 (1930), Sp. 481–494.

H. Lichtenstein, Die Fastenrolle: Eine Untersuchung zur jüdisch-hellenistischen Geschichte, HUCA VIII/IX (1931/32), 257–351.

S. Lieberman, Hellenism in Jewish Palestine, Texts and Studies of the Jew. Theol. Sem. of America XVIII, New York 1950.

——, The Discipline in the socalled Dead Sea Manual of Discipline, JBL 71 (1952), 199–206.

H. Lietzmann, An die Galater, HBzNT 10, 3rd edn. Tübingen 1932.

——, A History of the Early Church, tr. B. L. Woolf, 4 vols., London 1953.

J. W. Lightley, Jewish Sects and Parties in the Time of Jesus, London 1925.

E. Lohmeyer, Das Evangelium des Markus, Meyers krit. exeget. Komm., 12th edn. Göttingen 1953.

——, Die Offenbarung des Johannes, HBzNT 16, 2nd edn. Tübingen 1953.

H. Luther, Josephus und Justus von Tiberias, Diss. Halle 1910.

M. Mansoor, Studies in the Hodayot IV, JBL 76 (1957), 139–148.

A. Marmorstein, The old Rabbinic Doctrine of God, I The Names and Attributes of God, Jew's College Publications N° 10, London 1927.

S. Mendner, Die Tempelreinigung, ZNW 47 (1957), 93–112.

E. Meyer, Ursprung und Anfänge des Christentums, 3 vols., Berlin 1921 ff.

R. Meyer, Der Prophet aus Galiläa. Studie zum Jesusbild der drei ersten Evangelien, Leipzig 1940.

R. Meyer, Art. περιτέμνειν, TD vol. 6, 1968, pp. 72–84.

——, Art. προφήτης, ibid., pp. 812–28.

——, Art. προφήτης Abschnitt C, ThWB 6, 813–828, 1958.

——, Hellenistisches in der rabbinischen Anthropologie, BWANT IV, 22, Stuttgart 1937.

O. Michel, Paulus und seine Bibel, BFChTh 2nd Series, vol. 18, Gütersloh 1929.

——, Prophet und Märtyrer, BFChTh 37 (1932).

——, Der Brief an die Römer, Meyers krit. ex. Komm., 10th edn. Göttingen 1955.

——, Der Brief an die Hebräer, Meyers krit. ex. Komm., 10th edn. Göttingen 1957.

——, Spätjüdisches Prophetentum, Neutestamentliche Studien f. Rudolf Bultmann, 2nd edn. Tübingen 1957, 60–67.

——, Das Problem des Staates in neutestamentlicher Sicht, Review Essay on O. Cullman, Der Staat im Neuen Testament, ThLZ 83 (1958), 161–166.

J. T. Milik, Ten Years of Discovery in the Wilderness of Judaea, tr. J. Strugnell, London 1959.

——, Une lettre de Siméon Bar Kokheba, RB 60 (1953), 276–294.

——, Review of Y. Yadin, Megillat milhemet bene'or bivne hosek, RB 64 (1957), 585–593.

L. Mitteis and U. Wilcken, Grundzüge u. Chrestomathie der Papyruskunde, 4 vols. Leipzig/Berlin 1912 ff.

Th. Mommsen, Römisches Strafrecht, Systemat. Handbuch d. deutschen Rechtswiss., Leipzig 1899.

——, Römische Geschichte, vols. I–III and V, 14th impression Berlin 1933.

G. F. Moore, Judaism in the First Centuries of the Christian Era, 3 vols. Cambridge Mass. 1927–1930.

H. Mosbech, Herodes den Store, DTT 16 (1953), 193–202.

S. Mowinkel, The Hebrew Equivalent of Taxo in Assumptio Mosis IX, Congress Volume, Copenhagen 1953, VT Suppl. I, London 1953, 88–96.

N. Müller-N. Bees, Die Inschriften der jüdischen Katakombe am Monteverde zu Rom, Leipzig 1919.

W. Nauck, Freude im Leiden, ZNW 46 (1955), 68–80.

B. Niese, Der jüdische Historiker Josephus, HZ 76 (1896), 193–237.

——, Josephus, in ed. J. Hastings, Encyclopaedia of Religion and Ethics, vol. 7, 1914, pp. 569–79.

M. P. Nilsson, Geschichte der Griechischen Religion, Vol. II: Die hellenistische u. römische Zeit, HAW V, 2, 2, München, 2nd edn. 1961.

——, A History of Greek Religion, tr. F. J. Fielden. New York, 1925, rev edn. 1964.

E. Norden, Josephus und Tacitus über Jesus Christus und eine messianische Profetie,

Neue Jahrbücher f. d. klass. Altertum, Gesch. u. dt. Lit. 31 (1913), 637–666.

M. Noth, The History of Israel, tr. S. Godman, London 1958.

Oder, Art. Adler, PW 1, 371–375, 1894.

W. O. E. Oesterley, A History of Israel, vol. II: From the Fall of Jerusalem 589 B.C. to the Bar-Kokhba Revolt A.D. 135, 6th impression of the 1932 edition, Oxford 1951.

Th. Oelgarte, Die Beth-Horon-Straße, PJ 14 (1919), 73–89.

W. Otto, Herodes, Beiträge zur Geschichte des letzten jüdischen Königshauses, Stuttgart 1913.

E. Peterson, Der Monotheismus als politisches Problem, ein Beitrag zur Geschichte der politischen Theologie im Imperium Romanum, Leipzig 1935.

Pfaff, Art. latrocinium, PW 12, 978–980.

R. H. Pfeiffer, History of New Testament Times, New York 1949.

A. Posnanski, Schiloh, ein Beitrag zur Geschichte der Messiaslehre, Part I, die Auslegung von Gen. 49, 10 im Altertum bis zum Ende des Mittelalters, Leipzig 1904.

H. Preisker, Neutestamentliche Zeitgeschichte, Berlin 1937.

G. Quell, Art. κύριος, section C, TD vol. 3, pp. 1058–81.

G. v. Rad, Art. βασιλεύς, section B, TD vol. 1, pp. 565–71.

——, Der Heilige Krieg im alten Israel, AThANT, Zürich 1951.

——, Old Testament Theology, vol. 1: The Theology of Israel's Historical Traditions, tr. D. M. G. Stalker, London and Edinburgh 1962.

H. Rasp, Flavius Josephus und die jüdischen Religionsparteien, ZNW 23 (1924), 27–47.

Bo Reicke, Diakonie, Festfreude und Zelos in Verbindung mit der altchristlichen Agapenfeier, UUA 5 (1951), Uppsala/Wiesbaden 1952.

——, Der geschichtliche Hintergrund des Apostelkonzils und der Antiochia-Episode Gal. 2, 1–14, Studia Paulina, (Festschrift f. J. de Zwaan) 172–187, Haarlem 1953.

S. Reinach, Jean Baptiste et Jésus suivant Josèphe, REJ 87 (1929), 113–131.

K. H. Rengstorf, Art. δεσπότης, TD vol. 2, pp. 44–49.

——, Art. ἑπτά, ibid. pp. 627–35.

——, Art. λῃστής, TD vol. 4, 1967, pp. 257–62.

Revue Biblique, 64 (1957), 218–261: Chronique Archéologique (o. Verf.).

G. Ricciotti, Flavio Giuseppe tradoto e commentato Vol. I, Introduzione: Flavio Giuseppe lo storico Giudeo-romano, 2ª, ed. Turin et. al. 1949.

——, The History of Israel, tr. C. della Penta and R. T. A. Murphy, 2 vols., Milwaukee 1955.

H. A. Rigg, Barrabas, JBL 64 (1945), 417–456.

P. Romanoff, Jewish Symbols on Ancient Jewish Coins, JQR 33 (1942/43), 1–14; 34 (1943/44), 161–177; 299–312; 425–440.

F. Rosenthal, Das Sikarikongesetz, MGWJ 37, NF 1 (1893), 1–6; 57–63; 105–110.

L. Rost, Zum 'Buch der Kriege der Söhne des Lichts gegen die Söhne der Finsternis', ThLZ 80 (1955), 205–208.

M. Rostofftzeff, Social and Economic History of the Hellenistic World, 3 vols., Oxford 1941.

——, Social and Economic History of the Roman Empire, rev, by P. M. Fraser, Oxford 1926.

C. Roth, An Ordinance against Images in Jerusalem, HThR 49 (1956), 169–177.

——, Messianic Symbols in Palestinian Archeology, PEQ 87 (1955), 151–164.

——, The Historical Background of the Dead Sea Scrolls, Oxford 1958.

H. H. Rowley, The Herodians in the Gospels, JThS 41 (1940), 14–28.

——, Qumran, the Essenes, and the Zealots, in 'Von Ugarit nach Qumran'. Btr. z. atl. u.

altoriental. Forschung, O. Eissfeldt … dargebracht, ed. J. Hempel and L. Rost, Berlin 1958.

S. Safrai, Sikarikon, Zion 17 (1952), 56–64.

A. Schalit, Josephus und Justus, Studien zur vita des Josephus, Klio 26 (1933), 66–95.

S. Schechter, Some Aspects of Rabbinic Theology, London 1909.

F. Scheidweiler, Sind die Interpolationen im altrussischen Josephus wertlos? ZNW 43 (1950/51), 155–178.

A. Schlatter, Jochanan b. Zakkai, BFChTh 10 (1906).

——, Wie sprach Josephus von Gott, BFChTh 14 (1910).

——, Die hebräischen Namen bei Josephus, BFChTh 17 (1913).

——, Die Geschichte des Christus, Stuttgart 1921.

——, Geschichte Israels von Alexander d. Großen bis Hadrian, 3rd edn. Stuttgart 1925.

——, The Church in the New Testament Period, tr. P. P. Levertoff, London 1955.

——, Die Theologie des Judentums nach dem Bericht des Josephus, BFChTh 2nd Series, vol. 26, Gütersloh 1932.

——, Der Evangelist Matthäus, 3rd impression, Stuttgart 1948.

——, Der Evangelist Johannes, 2nd impression, Stuttgart 1948.

H. Schlier, Art. ἐλευθερία, TD vol. 2, pp. 487–502.

——, Art. θλῖψις, TD vol. 3, pp. 139–48.

——, Der Brief an die Galater, Meyers krit. exeget. Komm., 11th edn. Göttingen 1951.

T. Schneider, Art. Adler, RAC 1, 87–94, 1950.

H. J. Schoeps, Aus frühchristlicher Zeit, religionsgeschichtliche Untersuchungen, Tübingen 1950.

——, Die Opposition gegen die Hasmonäer, ThLZ 81 (1956), 663–670.

F. Schultheß, Das Problem der Sprache Jesu, Zürich 1917.

——, Zur Sprache der Evangelien, ZNW 21 (1922), 216–236; 241–258.

E. Schürer, The History of the Jewish people in the Age of Jesus Christ, ed. G. Vermes, F. Millar, M. Black, 3 vols., Edinburgh 1973–86.

——, Review essay on A. Berendts, Die Zeugnisse vom Christentum im slawischen de bello judaico, TU NF 14, 4 (1906), ThLZ 31 (1906), 262–266.

F. Schwally, Semitische Kriegsaltertümer, Book 1: Der Heilige Krieg im alten Israel, Leipzig 1901.

A. Schweitzer, Geschichte der Leben-Jesu-Forschung, 5th impression of the 2nd edition, 1913, Tübingen 1933.

H. Seesemann and G. Bertram, Art. πατέω ThWB, 5, 940–946, 1954.

E. Sjöberg, Art. πνεῦμα, section C, TD vol. 6, pp. 367–89.

A. Spiro, The Ascension of Phineas, Proceedings of the Am. Acad. for Jew. Research 22 (1953), New York 1953.

——, Samaritans, Tobiads, and Judahites in Pseudo-Philo, Proceedings of the Am. Academy for Jew. Research 20 (1951), New York 1951.

E. Stauffer, New Testament Theology, tr. J. Marsh, London 1955.

——, Christ and the Caesars, tr. K. and R. Gregor Smith, London 1955.

——, Jerusalem und Rom im Zeitalter Jesu Christi, Dalp-Taschenbücher 331, Bern 1957.

——, Jesus and His Story, tr. R. and C. Winston, New York 1960.

——, Die Botschaft Jesu, Dalp-Taschenbücher 333, Bern 1959.

H. L. Strack, Jesus, die Häretiker und die Christen nach den ältesten jüdischen Angaben, Schriften des Institutum Judaicum in Berlin Nr. 37, Leipzig 1910.

——, Einleitung in Talmud und Midraš, 5th edn. München 1921.

——, Der Kampf um Beth-Ter, PJ 23 (1927), 92–123.

H. Strathmann, Art. μάρτυς, TD vol. 4, pp. 474–514.

A. Stumpf, Art. ζῆλος, TD vol. 2, 1964, pp. 877–888.

L. R. Taylor, Quirinius and the Census of Syria, American Journal of Philology, 54 (1933), 161ff.

H. S. J. Thackeray, Josephus, the man and historian, New York 1929.

L. E. Toombs, Barcosiba and Qumran, NTS 4 (1957/58), 65–71.

P. L. H. Vincent, Jérusalem de l'Ancien Testament, Recherches d'archéologie et d'histoire, Parts 2 and 3 in one vol., Paris 1956.

P. Volz, Die Eschatologie der jüdischen Gemeinde im neutestamentlichen Zeitalter, 2nd edn. Tübingen 1934.

W. Weber, Josephus und Vespasian, Untersuchungen zu dem Jüdischen Krieg des Flavius Josephus, Stuttgart/Leipzig 1921.

H. Weller, Art. Postliminium, PW 22, 863–873.

J. Wellhausen, Einleitung in den drei ersten Evangelien. 2nd edn. 1911.

——, Skizzen und Vorarbeiten VI (1899), 215–234. (See also *Sketch of the History of Israel and Judah*, London and Edinburgh 1891.)

——, Analyse der Offenbarung Johannis, AGG 1907, 1–34.

——, Israelitische und jüdische Geschichte, 5th edn. Berlin 1904.

——, Die Pharisäer und Sadducäer, Greifswald 1874.

H. H. Wendt, Die Apostelgeschichte, Meyers krit. exeget. Komm., 8th edn. Göttingen 1913.

N. Wieder, The Law-Interpreter of the Sect of the D.S.S.: The Second Moses, JJS 4 (1953), 158–175.

H. Willrich, Das Haus des Herodes zwischen Jerusalem und Rom, Heidelberg 1929.

W. Windfuhr, Review essay on R. Eisler, I.B., Philolog. Wochenschrift 50 (1930), 1421–1427.

H. Windisch, Der messianische Krieg und das Urchristentum, Tübingen 1909.

——, Unser Wissen um Jesus, Neue Jahrbücher f. Wiss. u. Jugendbildung 7 (1931), 289–307.

P. Winter, Simeon d. Gerechte und Gaius Caligula, ZRGG 6 (1954), 72ff.

H. G. Wood, Interpreting this Time, NTS 4 (1956), 262–266.

A. S. v. d. Woude, Die Messianischen Vorstellungen der Gemeinde von Qumran, Studia Semitica Neederlandica vol. 3, Assen/Neukirchen 1957.

G. E. Wright, Biblical Archaeology, Philadelphia 1957, revd. 1962 (English original).

Y. Yadin, מגלת מלחמת בני אור בבני חושך, 2nd edn. Jerusalem 1957.

S. Zeitlin, Megillat Taanit as a source for Jewish Chronology and History in the Hellenistic and Roman Times, Philadelphia 1922.

——, Josephus on Jesus with particular reference to the Slavonic Josephus and the Hebrew Josippon, Philadelphia 1931.

——, Who crucified Jesus, 2nd edn. New York/London 1947.

——, Judaism as a Religion, JQR 34 (1943/44), 1–40; 207–241; 321–364.

J. Ziegler, Die Königsgleichnisse des Midrasch beleuchtet durch die römische Kaiserzeit, Breslau 1903.

SUPPLEMENTARY BIBLIOGRAPHY (to 1974)

S. Applebaum, The Zealots: The Case for Revaluation. JRS 61 (1971) 155–170.

M. Avi-Yonah, Geschichte der Juden im Zeitalter des Talmud, Berlin 1962.

M. Baillet, Un recueil liturgique de Qumrân, Grotte 4: 'Les paroles des Luminaires', RB 68 (1971) 195–250.

G. Baumbach, Jesus von Nazareth im Lichte der jüdischen Gruppenbildung, Berlin 1971.

——, Die Zeloten — ihre geschichtliche und religionspolitische Bedeutung. Bibel und Liturgie 41 (1968) 1–25.

——. The Significance of the Zealots (abridged version of art.) in *Theology Digest*, vol. 17, 1969, pp. 241–6.

——, Zeloten und Sikarier. ThLZ 90 (1965) Sp. 727–740.

A. Ben-David, Jerusalem und Tyros. Ein Beitrag zur palästinensischen Münz-und Wirtschaftsgeschichte (126 B.C.–57 A.D.), Tübingen 1969.

——, Talmudische Ökonomie, Hildesheim 1974.

H. Bengtson, Grundriß der römischen Geschichte, München 1967.

H. D. Betz, Nachfolge und Nachahmung Jesu Christi im Neuen Testament, BHTh 37, Tübingen 1967.

O. Betz, Art. σικάριος, TD vol. 7, pp. 278–82.

M. Black, Judas of Galilee and Josephus's 'Fourth Philosophy', in: Josephus-Studien, Festschrift O. Michel zum 70. Geburtstag, Göttingen 1974, 45–54.

——, The Patristic Accounts of Jewish Sectarianism. BJRL 41 (1958) 285–303.

J. Blinzler, Die Niedermetzelung von Galiläern durch Pilatus. NovTest 2 (1957) 24–49.

M. Borg, The Currency of the Term Zealot. JThSt NS 22 (1971) 504–512.

G. W. Bowersock, The Annexation and Initial Garrison of Arabia. ZPapEp 5 (1970) 37–47.

S. G. F. Brandon, The Defeat of Cestius Gallus. History To-day 20 (1970) 38–46.

——, Jesus and the Zealots, Manchester 1967.

G. Braumann, Das Mittel der Zeit. ZNW 52 (1971) 117–145.

H. Braunert, Die Binnenwanderung, Bonn 1964.

G. W. Buchanan, An Additional Note to 'Mark 11.15–19: Brigands in the Temple'. HUCA 31 (1960) 103–105.

——, Mark 11.15–19: Brigands in the Temple. HUCA 30 (1959) 169–177.

C. Burchard, Zur Nebenüberlieferung von Josephus' Bericht über die Essener Bell, 2,119–161 bei Hippolyt, Porphyrius, Josippus, Niketas Choniates und anderen, in: Josephus-Studien, Festschrift for the 70th birthday of O. Michel, Göttingen 1974, 78–96.

P. Bureth, Les titulatures imperiales dans le papyrus, les ostraca et les inscriptions d'Egypte (30 B.C.-284-A.D.) Brüssel 1964.

B. Cohen, Jewish and Roman Law, Vol. II, New York 1966.

C. Colpe, Das Samaritanische Pinehas-Grab in Awerta und die Beziehungen zwischen Hadir- und Georgslegende. ZDPV 85 (1969) 163–196.

V. Corbo, Chronique Archéologique. Gebel Furcidis. RB 71 (1964) 258–263.

O. Cullmann, Jesus and the Revolutionaries, tr. G. Putnam, New York, 1970.

G. R. Driver, The Judean Scrolls, Oxford 1965.

——, Review of M. Hengel, Die Zeloten. JThS 14 (1963) 130–133.

S. L. Dyson, Native Revolts in the Roman Empire. Historia 20 (1971) 239–274.

W. Eck, Die Eroberung von Masada und eine neue Inschrift des L. Flavius Silva Nonius Bassus. ZNW 60 (1969) 282–289.

——, Senatoren von Vespasian bis Hadrian. Prosopographische Untersuchungen mit Einschluß der Jahres- und Provinzialfasten der Stratthalter, Vestigia 13, München 1970.

Th. Frankfort, La date de l'autobiographie de Flavius Josèphe et des oeuvres de Justus de Tibériade. Revue Belge de philologie et d'histoire 39 (1961) 52–58.

K. Galling, Königliche und nichtkönigliche Stifter beim Tempel von Jerusalem. ZDPV 68 (1951) 134–142.

D. Georgi, Die Gegner des Paulus im 2. Korintherbrief, WMANT 11, Neukirchen 1964.

M. Goguel, Les Théories de M. Robert Eisler. RHR 10 (1930) 177–190.
J. Goldin, The Fathers According to Rabbi Nathan, New Haven 1955.
——, The Two Versions of Abot de Rabbi Nathan. HUCA 19 (1945/46) 97–120.
E. R. Goodenough, The Rabbis and Jewish Art in the Greco-Roman Period. HUCA 32 (1961) 269–279.
J. Gutmann, The "Second Commandment" and the Image in Judaism. HUCA 32 (1961) 161–174.
N. Haas, Anthropological Observations on the Skeletal Remains from Giv'at ha-Mivtar. IEJ 20 (1970) 38–59.
I. Hahn, Zwei dunkle Stellen bei Josephus (Bellum Judaicum VI, § 311 und II, § 112). Acta Orientalia Academiae Scientarum Hungaricae 14 (1962) 131–138.
N. Q. Hamilton, Temple Cleansing and Temple Bank. JBL 83 (1964) 365–372.
R. Harris, The Twelve Apostles, Cambridge 1927.
J. Heinemann, The Formula melekh hà-'olam. JJS 11 (1960) 177–179.
O. Hirschfeld, Kleine Schriften, Berlin 1913.
A. Heitmann, Imitatio Dei, Rom 1940.
M. Hengel, Eigentum und Reichtum in der frühen Kirche, Stuttgart 1973.
——, Judentum und Hellenismus, WUNT 10, Tübingen 2.Aufl, 1973.
——, Nachfolge und Charisma, BZNW 34, Berlin 1968.
——, Rez S. G. F. Brandon, Jesus and the Zealots, JSS 14 (1969) 231–240.
——, Between Jesus and Paul, tr. J. Bowden, London 1983.
——, Victory over Violence, tr. D. Green, Philadelphia 1973.
——, War Jesus Revolutionär?, CH 110, Stuttgart 1970.
M. D. Herr, The Problem of War on the Sabbath in the Second Temple and the Talmudic Periods (hebr.). Tarbiz 30 (1960/61) 242–256.
P. Herrmann, Der römische Kaisereid, Göttingen 1968.
H. W. Hoehner, Herod Antipas, Cambridge 1972.
S. B. Hoenig, Oil and Pagan Defilement. JQR 61 (1970/71) 63–75.
——, The Sicarii in Masada—Glory or Infamy? Tradition 11 (1970) 5–30.
K. Holl, Die Vorstellung vom Märtyrer und die Märtyrerakte in ihrer geschichtlichen Entwicklung, Ges. Aufsätze Vol. 2, Tübingen 1928, 68–102.
B. S. Jackson, Theft in Early Jewish Law, Oxford 1972.
G. Jeremias, Der Lehrer der Gerechtigkeit, Göttingen 1963.
A. F. Johns, The Military Strategy of Sabbath Attacks on the Jews. VT 13 (1963) 482–486.
A. H. M. Jones, The Herods of Judaea, Oxford 1938.
M. de Jonge, Josephus und die Zukunftserwartungen seines Volkes, in: Josephus-Studien, Festschrift O. Michel zum 70. Geburtstag, Göttingen 1974, 205–219.
L. Kadman, The Coins of the Jewish War of 66–73, Jerusalem 1960.
H. P. Kingdon, Who Were the Zealots and Their Leaders in A.D. 66? NTS 17 (1970/71) 68–72.
W. Klassen, Jesus and the Zealot Option. Canadian Journal of Theology 16 (1970) 12–21.
H. Kreissig, Die sozialen Zusammenhänge des jüdischen Kriegs, Berlin 1970.
G. W. H. Lampe, A Greek Patristic Lexicon, Oxford 1969.
R. Leivestad, Das Dogma von der prophetenlosen Zeit. NTS 19 (1972/73) 288–299.
H. J. Leon, The Jews in Ancient Rome, Philadelphia 1960.
S. Lieberman, Greek in Jewish Palestine, New York 2nd edn. 1965.
H. Lindner, Die Geschichtsauffassung des Flavius Josephus im Bellum Judaicum, AGAJU 12, Leiden 1972.
Y. Meshorer, Jewish Coins of the Second Temple Period, Tel-Aviv 1967.

R. Meyer/H. F. Weiss, Art. Φαρισαῖος TD vol. 9, pp. 11–48.

O. Michel, Studien zu Josephus. Simon bar Giora. NTS 14 (1967/68) 402–408.

O. Michel/O. Bauernfeind (Eds.), Flavius Josephus, De Bello Judaico, vols. I–III, München 1959–69.

J. A. Morin, Les deux derniers des Douze: Simon le Zélote ed Judas Ishkarioth R 8 (1975) 332–358.

J. Nedava, Who Were the 'Biryoni'. JQR 63 (1972/73) 317–322.

J. Neusner, Development of a Legend. Studies on the Tradition concerning Yohanan ben Zakkai, Leiden 1970.

——, The Rabbinic Tradition about the Pharisees before 70, vols. I–III, Leiden 1971.

V. Nikiprowetzky, La mort d'Éléazar fils de Jaïre ..., in: Hommages à André Dupont-Sommer, Paris 1971, 461–490.

C.-O. Nordström, Rabbinica in frühchristlichen und rabbinischen Illustrationen zum 4.Mose, in: Idea and Form, Stockholm 1959, 38–47.

I. Opelt, Die lateinischen Schimpfwörter, Heidelberg 1965.

P. v. d. Osten-Sacken, Gott und Belial, SUNT 6, Göttingen 1969.

J. Palm, Rom, Römertum und Imperium in der griechischen Literatur der Kaiserzeit. Acta reg. soc. hum. Lit. Lund LVII, Lund 1959.

L. Y. Rahmani, The Tomb of Jason. Atiqot 4 (1964).

Bo Reicke, The New Testament Era, tr. D. E. Green, London 1968.

J. Reiling, The Use of ΨΕΥΔΟΠΡΟΦΗΤΗΣ in the Septuagint, Philo and Josephus. NovTest 13 (1971) 146–156.

K. H. Rengstorf, A Complete Concordance to Flavius Josephus, Vol. I, Leiden 1973.

K. H. Rengstorf ed., A Complete Concordance to Flavius Josephus, Supplement I, Leiden, 1968.

C. Roth, The Debate on the Royal Sacrifices A.D. 66. HThR 53 (1960) 93–97.

——, The Historical Implications of the Jewish Coinage of the First Revolt. IEJ 12 (1962) 33–46.

——, Melekh ha-'olam: Zealot influence in the Liturgy. JJS 11 (1960) 173–175.

——, The Zealots in the War of 66–75. JSS 4 (1959) 332–355.

H. P. Rüger, Zum Problem der Sprache Jesu. ZNW 59 (1968) 113–122.

B. Salomonsen, Nogle synspunkter fra den nyere debat omkring zeloterne. DTT 27 (1964) 149–162.

——, Some Remarks on the Zealots with Special Regard to the Term 'Qannaim' in Rabbinic Literature. NTS 12 (1964/65) 164–176.

A. Schalit, König Herodes, Der Mann und sein Werk, Studia Judaica 4, Berlin 1969.

——, see Rengstorf, *supra*.

W. H. Schmidt, Königtum Gottes in Ugarit und Israel, BZAW 80, Berlin 2nd edn. 1966.

K. Schubert, Die jüdischen Religionsparteien in neutestamentlicher Zeit, SBS 43, Stuttgart 1970.

——, Review of M. Hengel, Die Zeloten. WZKM 58 (1962) 258–260.

E. Schuerer, see p. 431, *supra*.

A. N. Sherwin-White, Roman Society and Roman Law in the New Testament, Oxford 3rd edn. 1969.

E. M. Smallwood, The Chronology of Gaius' attempt to Desecrate the Temple. Latomus 16 (1957) 3–17.

——, Philonis Alexandrini legatio ad Gaium, Leiden 2nd edn. 1969.

M. Smith, The Description of the Essenes in Josephus and the Philosophumena. HUCA 29 (1958) 273–313.

——, Zealots and Sicarii. Their Origin and Relation. HThR 64 (1971) 1–19.

S. Spero, In Defence of the Defenders of Masada. Tradition 11 (1970) 31–43.

M. Stern, Review of M. Hengel, Die Zeloten. JRS 52 (1962) 258f.

——, Art. Zealots, EJud Year Book 1973, 135–152.

F. Stolz, Jahwes und Israels Kriege, Zürich 1972.

A. Strobel, Kerygma und Apokalyptik, Göttingen 1967.

——, Untersuchungen zum eschatologischen Verzögerungsproblem, Leiden 1961.

J. Strugnell, Notes en marge du Volume V des 'Discoveries in the Judean Desert of Jordan'. RdQ 7 (26/1970) 163–276.

R. Syme, Tacitus, Oxford 1958.

F. Taeger, Charisma, vol. 2, Stuttgart 1960.

V. Tcherikover, Hellenistic Civilization and the Jews, Philadelphia/Jerusalem 1961.

——, Syntaxis and Laographia. Jour. Jur. Pap. 4 (1950) 179–307.

——, The Third Book of Maccabees as a Historical Source of Augustus' Time. Script Hieros 7 (1961) 1–26.

——, Was Jerusalem a Polis? IEJ 14 (1964) 61–78.

C. Thoma, Auswirkungen des jüdischen Krieges gegen Rom (A.D. 66–70/73) auf des rabbinische Judentum. BZ NF 12 (1968) 30–54. 186–210.

R. Till, Ciceros Bewerbung ums Konsulat. Historia 11 (1962) 315–338.

E. Trocmé, L'expulsion des marchands du Temple. NTS 15 (1968/69) 1–22.

R. de Vaux, Essenes or Zealots? NTS 13 (1966/67) 89–104.

H. Volkmann, Die Massenversklavungen der Einwohner eroberten Städte in der hellenistisch-römischen Zeit, AAMz 1961 Nr. 3, Wiesbaden 1961.

——, Die Pilatusinschrift von Caesarea Marittima. Gymnasium 75 (1968) 124–135.

B. Z. Wacholder, Nicolaus of Damascus, Berkeley 1962.

K. Wegenast, Art. Zeloten, PW 2nd Series, vol. XVIII 1967, Sp. 2474–99.

I. Weiler, Titus und die Zerstörung des Tempels von Jerusalem — Absicht oder Zufall? Klio 50 (1968) 139–158.

M. Weippert, 'Heiliger Krieg' in Israel und Assyrien. ZAW 84 (1972) 460–493.

H. Windisch, Die Orakel des Hystaspes. Verhandelingen der Koninklijke Akademie van Wetenschappen te Amsterdam. Afd. Letterkunde N.R. 28, 3, Amsterdam 1929.

Y. Yadin, Bar Kochba, Hamburg 1971.

——, Masada, tr. M. Pearlman, London 1966.

The Scroll of the War of The Sons of Light against the Sons of Darkness, tr. B. & C. Rabin, Oxford 1962.

S. Zeitlin, The Dead Sea Scrolls: Fantasies and Mistranslations. JQR 48 (1958) 71–85.

——, Zealots and Sicarii. JBL 81 (1962) 395–398.

SUPPLEMENTARY BIBLIOGRAPHY (UP TO 1987)

M. Aberbach, The Roman-Jewish War (66–70 A.D.): Its Origin and Consequences. London 1966.

S. Appelbaum, Judaea as a Roman Province; the Countryside as a Political and Economic Factor. ANRW II.8, 355–386.

H. Arenhoevel, Der 'Eifer' der Makkabäer. BiKi 37 (1982), 78–82.

J. R. Armenti, On the Use of the Term 'Galileans' in the Writings of Josephus Flavius: A Brief Note. JQR 72 (1981), 45–49.

D. E. Aune, The Use of ΠΡΟΦΗΤΗΣ in Josephus. JBL 101 (1982), 419–421.

M. Avi-Yonah/E. Stern (ed.), Encyclopedia of Archaeological Excavations in the Holy Land. Four Vols. Jerusalem/London 1975–1978.

M. Avi-Yonah/Z. Baras/A. Peli (ed.), The World History of the Jewish People. First Series: Ancient Times. Vol. 7: The Herodian Period. Jersualem 1975.

Y. Baer, Jerusalem in the Times of the Great Revolt (hebr.). Zion 36 (1971), 127–190.

D. L. Balch, Two Apologetic Encomia: Dionysius on Rome and Josephus on the Jews. JSJ 13 (1982), 102–122.

E. Bammel, Die Blutgerichtsbarkeit in der römischen Provinz Judäa vor dem ersten jüdischen Aufstand. JJS 25 (1974), 35–49.

——, Joasar. ZDPV 90 (1974), 61–68.

——, Sadduzäer und Sadokiden. EThL 55 (1979), 107–115.

E. Bammel/C. F. D. Moule (eds.) Jesus and the Politics of His Day. Cambridge 1984.

B. Bar-Kochva, Notes on the Fortresses of Josephus in Galilee. IEJ 24 (1974), 108–116.

——, Seron and Cestius Gallus at Beith Horon. PEQ 108 (1976), 13–21.

P. W. Barnett, The Jewish Sign Prophets A.D. 40–70 – Their Intentions and Origin. NTS 27 (1981), 679–697.

——, 'Under Tiberius all was Quiet'. NTS 21 (1975), 564–571.

G. Baumbach, Einheit und Vielfalt der jüdischen Freiheitsbewegung im 1. Jahrhundert A.D. EvTh 45 (1985), 93–107.

A. Baumgarten, Josephus and Hippolytus on the Pharisees. HUCA 55 (1984), 1–25.

——, The Name of the Pharisees. JBL 102 (1983), 411–28.

H. Bengtson, Die Flavier: Vespasian. Titus. Domitian. Geschichte eines römischen Kaiserhauses (Beck'sche Sonderausgaben). München 1979.

H. H. Ben-Sasson (ed.), Geschichte des jüdischen Volkes. Vol. 1: Von den Anfängen bis zum 7. Jahrhundert. Von A. Malamat, H. Tadmor, M. Stern, S. Safrai. München 1978.

O. Betz, Jesus, der Messias Israels (WUNT 4). Tübingen 1987.

E. Bickerman, Studies in Jewish and Christian History. Part I–III (AGJU, IX, 1–3). Leiden 1976–1986.

P. Bilde, The Causes of the Jewish War According to Josephus. JSJ 10 (1979), 179–202.

——, Josephus som historieskriver En undersøgelse of Josefus Fremstilling of Gaius Caligulas konflikt med jøderne i Palaestina med soerligt henblik på forfatterens tendens og historiske pålidelighed (Bibel og historie 1) Copenhagen 1983.

——, The Roman Emperor Gaius (Caligula)'s Attempt to Erect his Statue in the Temple of Jerusalem. StTh 32 (1978), 67–93.

J. Blenkinsopp, Prophecy and Priesthood in Josephus. JJS 25 (1974), 239–262.

D. Blosser, The Sabbath Year Cycle in Josephus. HUCA 52 (1981), 129–139.

D. Braund, Four Notes on the Herods. CQ N.S. 33 (1983), 239–242.

M. Broshi, The Credibility of Josephus. JJS 33 (1982), 379–384.

M. Broshi, La population de l'ancienne Jérusalem. RB 82 (1975), 5–14.

P. A. Brunt, Josephus on Social Conflicts in Roman Judaea. Klio 59 (1977), 149–153.

A. Byatt, Josephus and Population Numbers in First Century Palestine. PEQ 105 (1973), 51–60.

R. J. Cassidy, Jesus, Politics and Society. A Study of Luke's Gospel. Maryknoll/New York 1978.

M. Cohen, Quelques observations au sujet de la personnalité et du rôle historique de RYBZ. RHR 187 (1975), 27–55.

S. J. D. Cohen, Josephus in Galilee and Rome. His Vita and Development as a Historian (Columbia Studies in the Classical Tradition 8). Leiden 1979.

——, Masada: Literary Tradition, Archaeological Remains, and the Credibility of Josephus. JJS 33 (1982), 385–405.

D. Daube, Typologie im Werk des Flavius Josephus (Bayerische Akademie der Wissenschaften. Philosophisch-historische Klasse. Sitzungsberichte Jahrgang 1977 Heft 6). München 1977.

F. Dexinger, Die Sektenproblematik im Judentum. Kairos 21 (1979), 273–287.

O. Edwards, Herodian Chronology. PEQ 114 (1982), 29–42.

R. Egger, Josephus Flavius und die Samaritaner. Eine terminologische Untersuchung zur Identitätsklärung der Samaritaner (Novum Testamentum et Orbis Antiquus 4). Göttingen 1986.

R. Eisenman, Maccabees, Zadokites, Christians and Qumran. A new Hypothesis of Qumran Origins (StPB 34). Leiden 1983.

L. H. Feldman, Flavius Josephus Revisisted: the Man, His Writings, and His Significance. ANRW II.21.2, 763–862.

——, Josephus and Modern Scholarship (1937–1980). Berlin/New York 1984.

——, Masada: A Critique of Recent Scholarship. In: J. Neusner (ed.), Christianity, Judaism and Other Greco-Roman Cults. Studies for Morton Smith at Sixty. Part 3: Judaism before 70 (Studies in Judaism in Late Antiquity 12, 3). Leiden 1975, 218–248.

——, The Term 'Galileans' in Josephus. JQR 72 (1981/82), 50–52.

S. Freyne, The Galileans in the Light of Josephus' Vita. NTS 26 (1980), 397–413.

——, Galilee from Alexander the Great to Hadrian. 323 B.C.E. to 135 C.E. A Study of Second Temple Judaism (University of Notre Dame. Center for the Study of Judaism and Christianity in Antiquity 5). Wilmington 1980.

G. Fuks, Again on the Episode of the Gilded Roman Shields at Jerusalem. HThR 75 (1982), 503–507.

R. Furneaux, The Roman Seige of Jerusalem. London 1973.

J. Genot-Bismuth, Pacifisme pharisien et sublimation de l'idée de guerre aux origines du rabbinisme. ETR 56 (1981), 73–89.

J. Giblet, Un mouvement de résistance armée au temps de Jésus? RTL 5 (1974), 409–426.

M. Gichon, Cestius Gallus's Campaign in Judaea. PEQ 113 (1981), 39–62.

——, Cestius Gallus's March on Jerusalem, 66 C.E. (hebr.). In: A. Oppenheimer, U. Rappaport, M. Stern (ed.), Jerusalem in the Second Temple Period. Abraham Schalit Memorial Volume. Jerusalem 1980, 283–319.

D. Goldenberg, Josephus Flavius or Joseph ben Mattithiah. JQR 70 (1979/80), 178–182.

M. Goodman, The First Jewish Revolt: Social Conflict and the Problem of Debt. JJS 33 (1982), 417–427.

H. Guevara, La resistencia judía contra Roma en la epoca de Jesús. Meitingen 1981.

M. Hadas-Lebel, L'évolution de l'image de Rome auprès des juifs en deux siècles de relations judéo-romaines 164 B.C.–A.D. 66. ANRW II.20.2, 715–856.

G. Hata, Is the Greek Version of Josephus' Jewish War a Translation or a Rewriting of the First Version? JQR 66 (1975/76), 89–108.

M. Hengel, Messianische Hoffnung und politischer 'Radikalismus' in der 'jüdisch-hellenistischen Diaspora'. Zur Frage der Voraussetzungen des jüdischen Aufstandes unter Trajan A.D. 115–117. In: Apocalypticism in the Mediterranean World and the Near East. Proceedings of the International Colloquium on Apocalypticism. Uppsala, August 12–17, 1979. Ed. by D. Hellholm, Tübingen 1983, 655–686.

——, Rabbinische Legende und frühpharisäische Geschichte. Schimeon b. Schetach und die achtzig Hexen von Askalon (AHAW. PH 1984, 2nd Essay, Heidelberg 1984).

——, review of L. Mildenberg. The Coinage of the Bar-Kochba War. Aarau, Frankfurt-am-Main/Salzburg, 1984. In: Gnomon 58 (1986), 326–331.

E. J. Hobsbawm, Bandits. Rev. edn., New York 1981.

——, Primitive Rebels, New York 1959.

R. A. Horsley, Ancient Jewish Banditry and the Revolt against Rome, A.D. 66–70 CBQ 43 (1981), 409–432.

——, High Priests and the Politics of Roman Palestine. A Contextual Analysis of the Evidence in Josephus. JSJ 17 (1986), 23–55.

——, Josephus and the Bandits. JSJ 10 (1979), 37–63.

——, The Sicarii: Ancient Jewish 'Terrorists'. JR 59 (1979), 435–458.

——, The Zealots. Their Origin, Relationship and Importance in the Jewish Revolt. NT 28 (1986), 159–192.

——, The Ruling Class of Judaea. The Origins of the Jewish Revolt against Rome A.D. 66–70, Cambridge 1987.

S. R. Isenberg, Millenarism in Greco-Roman Palestine. Religion 4 (1974), 26–46.

I. Jacobs, Eleazar ben Jair's Sanction for Martyrdom. JSJ 13 (1982), 183–186.

G. Jossa, Chi sono i Galilei nella Vita di Flavio Giuseppe? Riv Bib 31 (1983), 329–339.

D. C. Kallander, The Defense of Jerusalem in the Roman Siege of 70 C.E.: A Study of First Century Apocalyptic Ideas. Diss AB A 41 No. 11 (1981), 4797.

A. Kasher, The Circumstances of Claudius Caesar's Edict and of his Letter to the Alexandrians (hebr.). Zion 39 (1974), 1–7.

A. Kasher, The Jews in Hellenistic and Roman Egypt. The Struggle for Equal Rights. (Texte und Shidien zum antiken Judentum 7). Tübingen 1985.

H. P. Kingdon, The Origins of the Zealots. NTS 19 (1972/73), 74–81.

D. J. Ladouceur, Masada: A Consideration of the Literary Evidence. GRBS 21 (1980), 245–260.

D. J. Ladouceur, The Language of Josephus. JSJ 14 (1983), 18–38.

N. R. M. deLange, Jewish Attitudes to the Roman Empire. In: P. D. A. Garnsey/C. R. Whittaker (ed.), Imperialism in the Ancient World. Cambridge Classical Studies. Cambridge 1978, 255–281, 354–357.

J.-P. Lémonon, Pilate et le gouvernement de la Judée. Textes et monuments (Etudes Bibliques). Paris 1981.

B. Levick, Tiberius the Politician (Aspects of Greek and Roman Life), London, 1976.

L. I. Levine, The Jewish-Greek Conflict in First Century Caesarea. JJS 25 (1974), 381–397.

B. Lifschitz, Jérusalem sous la domination romaine. Historie de la ville depuis la conquête de Pompée jusqu' à Constantin (63 B.C.–A.D. 325) ANRW II.8, 444–489.

F. Loftus, The Anti-Roman Revolts of the Jews and the Galileans. JQR 68 (1977/78), 78–98.

M. Luz, Eleazar's Second Speech on Masada and its Literary Precedents. RMP N.S. 126 (1983), 25–43.

R. MacMullen, Enemies of the Roman Order. Treason, Unrest, and the Alienation in the Empire. Cambridge (Mass.) 1966.

J. Maier, Die alttestamentlich-jüdischen Voraussetzungen der Zelotenbewegungen. BiKi 37 (1982), 82–89.

F. X. Malinowski, Galilean Judaism in the Writings of Flavius Josephus. DissAb A 34 No. 9 (1974), 6099.

O. Michel, Die Rettung Israels und die Rolle Roms nach den Reden im 'Bellum Iudaicum'. Analysen und Perspektiven. ANRW II.21.2, 945–976.

H. R. Moehring, Joseph ben Matthia and Flavius Josephus: the Jewish Prophet and Roman Historian. ANRW II.21.2, 864–944.

C. Möller/G. Schmitt, Siedlungen Palästinas nach Flavius Josephus. Beihefte zum Tübinger Atlas des Vorderen Orients. Series B., Geisteswissenschaften Nr. 14. Wiesbaden 1976.

J. Murphy-O'Connor, The Essenes and their History. RB 81 (1974), 215–244.

J. Neusner, A Life of Yohanan ben Zakkai A.D. 1–80. 2nd edn., completely revised (StPB 6) Leiden 1970.

V. Nikiprowetzky, Sicaires et Zélotes – une réconsidération Semitica 23 (1973), 51–64.

A. M. Rabello, The Legal Condition of the Jews in the Roman Empire. ANRW II.13, 662–762.

T. Rajak, Josephus and the 'Archaeology' of the Jews. JJS 33 (1982), 465–477.

——, Josephus. The Historian and His Society. London 1983.

——, Justus of Tiberias. CQ N.S. 23 (1973), 345–368.

U. Rappaport, John of Gischala: From Galilee to Jerusalem. JJS 33 (1982), 479–493.

——, The Relations Between Jews and Non-Jews and the Great War against Rome (hebr.). Tarbiz 47 (1978), 1–14.

K. H. Rengstorf, A Complete Concordance to Flavius Josephus. Vol. II–IV. Leiden 1975–1983.

D. M. Rhoads, Israel in Revolution: 6–74 C.E. A Political History Based on the Writings of Josephus. Philadelphia 1976.

——, Some Jewish Revolutionaries in Palestine from 6 A.D. to 73 A.D. According to Josephus. DissAb A 34 No. 9 (1974), 6100 s..

E. Rivkin, A Hidden Revolution. The Pharisees' Search for the Kingdom Within. Nashville 1978.

C. Roth, The Constitution of the Jewish Republic of 66–70. JSSt 9 (1964), 295–319.

——, The Pharisees of the Jewish Revolution of 66–73. JSSt 7 (1962), 63–80.

D. R. Runnalls, Hebrew and Greek Sources in the Speeches of Josephus' Jewish War. DissAb A 33 No. 2 (1972), 684 s..

S. Safrai/M. Stern et al (eds), The Jewish People in the First Century Historical Geography, Political History, Social, Cultural and Religious Life and Institutions. 2 Vols. (Compendia Rerum Iudaicarum ad Novum Testamentum I, 1.2) Assen/Amsterdam 1974/1976.

S. Safrai, Vespasian's Campaign of Conquest in Judea (hebr.). In: A. Oppenheimer, U. Rappaport, M. Stern (eds), Jerusalem in the Second Temple Period, Abraham Schalit Memorial Volume. Jerusalem 1980, 320–339.

C. Saulnier, Lois romaines sur les Juifs selon Flavius Josephe. RB 88 (1981), 161–198.

P. Schäfer, Die Flucht Johanan b. Zakkais aus Jerusalem und die Gründung des 'Lehrhauses' in Jabne. ANRW II.19.2, 43–101.

A. Schalit, Die Erhebung Vespasians nach Flavius Josephus, Talmud und Midrasch. Zur Geschichte einer messianischen Prophetie. ANRW II.2, 208–327.

G. Schmitt, Zur Chronologie des Jüdischen Krieges. Theokratia (Jahrbuch des Institutum Judaicum Delitzschianum) III (1973–75). Leiden 1979, 224–231.

——, Topographische Probleme bei Josephus. ZDPV 91 (1975), 50–68.

H. Schreckenberg, Rezeptionsgeschichtliche und textkritische Untersuchungen zu Flavius Josephus (ALGHL 10). Leiden 1977.

E. Schürer, The History of the Jewish People in the Age of Jesus Christ (175 B.C.–A.D. 135). A new English Version revised and edited by G. Vermes and F. Millar, Vol. II, III.1.2, Edinburgh 1979–87.

D. R. Schwartz, Kata touton ton kairon: Josephus' Source on Agrippa II. JQR 72 (1981/82), 241–268.

——, Pontius Pilate's Appointment to Office and the Chronology of Josephus' Jewish Antiquities Books XVIII–XX (hebr.). Zion 48 (1983), 325–345.

R. Seager, Tiberius. London 1972.

E. M. Smallwood, The Jews under Roman Rule. From Pompey to Diocletian (Studies in Judaism in Late Antiquity 20). Leiden 1976.

D. Sperber, Social Legislation in Jerusalem During the Latter Part of the Second Temple Period. JSJ 6 (1975), 86–95.

G. Stemberger, Die Beurteilung Roms in der rabbinischen Literatur. ANRW II.19.2, 338–396.

——, Die römische Herrschaft im Urteil der Juden (Erträge der Forschung 195). Darmstadt 1983.

W. Stenger, Bemerkungen zum Begriff 'Räuber' im Neuen Testament und bei Flavius Josephus. BiKi 37 (1982), 89–97.

M. Stern (ed.), Greek and Latin Authors on Jews and Judaism. Edited with Introductions, Translations and Commentary. 3 Volumes (Fontes ad res judaicas spectantes). Jerusalem 1974–1984.

——, The Suicide of Eleazar ben Jair and his Men at Masada, and the 'Fourth Philosophy' (hebr.). Zion 47 (1982), 367–397.

G. H. Stevenson, Roman Provincial Administration till the Age of the Antonines. Second impression. Oxford 1949.

M. E. Stone, Reactions to Destructions of the Second Temple. Theology, Perception and Conversion. JSJ 12 (1981), 195–204.

—— (ed.), Jewish Writings of the Second Temple Period. Apocrypha, Pseudepigrapha, Qumran Sectarian Writings, Philo, Josephus (Compendia Rerum Iudaicarum ad Novum Testamentum II). Assen/Philadelphia 1984.

H. L. Strack/G. Stemberger, Einleitung in Talmud und Midrasch. 7., completely revised new edition. München 1982.

R. D. Sullivan, The Dynasty of Judaea in the First Century. ANRW II.8, 262–294.

W. C. van Unnik, Flavius Josephus als historischer Schriftsteller (Franz Delitzsch Lectures, new series. Ed. K. H. Rengstorf). Heidelberg 1978.

P. Vejnberg, Probleme der sozialökonomischen Struktur Judäas vom 6. Jh. v.u.Z. bis zum 1. Jh.u.Z. Zu einigen wirtschaftshistorischen Untersuchungen von Heinz Kreißig. Jahrbuch für Wirtschaftsgeschichte 1973, I, 237–251.

P. Villalba i Varueda, The Historical Method of Flavius Josephus (ALGHL 19). Leiden 1986.

Z. Yavetz, Reflections on Titus and Josephus. GRBS 16 (1975), 411–432.

J. H. Yoder, The Politics of Jesus. 3rd impression, Grand Rapids, 1975.

S. Zeitlin, Who Were the Galileans? New Light on Josephus' Activities in Galilee. JQR 64 (1973/74), 189–203.

——, The Rise and Fall of the Judaean State. A Political, Social and Religious History of the Second Commonwealth. 3 Vols. Philadelphia 1962–1978.

——, Studies in the Early History of Judaism. 4 Vols. New York 1973–1978.

INDEX OF PASSAGES CITED

Preliminary note: The arrangement of Part III (Apocrypha, Pseudepigraphica and related literature) is based on W. G. Kümmel (ed.) *Jüdische Schriften aus hellenistisch-römischer Zeit*, Gütersloh 1973ff.

The arrangement of Part VIII (Rabbinic Literature) is in accordance with that found in Bill. V (Rabbinic Index).

I. OLD TESTAMENT

Genesis		20.4	195	Numbers	
8.22	199	20.5	62, 146, 182	1.2ff	129
14.13	182	22.19	107	1.3	119
15.2	94	24.1	286	4.7	67
15.5	129	26.1	191	5	146
15.8	94	26.31	191	5.14	179
16.12	28	30.12ff	129	5.30	179
17.4	197	32	160, 179, 202	10.9	278
22.17	129	32.16	116, 120, 122	11.16	286
24.14	146	32.26–29	148	14.44f	285
25.23	303	34	146	21.14	271
32.12	129	34.14	62, 146	22.7	67
34	160, 178–9, 187,	38.25ff	129	23.21	92
	188			23.23	67
37.11	146			24.7 (LXX)	277
49.9	276, 302	Leviticus		24.17	239, 240, 276,
49.10	240, 275	11.4ff	303		279, 305, 384, 385
49.11	116	16.8ff	220	24.18	239
49.17	28	18.6–22	186	24.19	279
49.19	28	18.27	186	24.24	239
49.27	28	19–26	186	25	147–8, 153, 158,
		19.2	186		163, 168–9, 170,
Exodus		19.4	191, 196		174–7, 179, 188
2.15	252	19.20	114, 116	25.1–6	147
3.17	199	19.26ff	186	25.1	147
4.24ff	197	19.29	186	25.4	147
5.2	57	19.31	186	25.5–13	67
6.6	117	20.6	186	25.5ff	174
6.25	156–7, 167	20.7	186	25.6	147
12.44	197	20.10–21	186	25.7–18	147, 149
12.48	197	20.10ff	186	25.7ff	67
13.18ff	230	20.21	189	25.7	151
14.4	271	20.26	186	25.8f	147
14.14	271	20.27	186	25.10ff	387, 389
14.24f	271	21.9	186, 188	25.11–13	147–8
15.3	271	22.3	215	25.11	146, 163
15.13	117	25	133	25.12f	162, 167
15.18	91, 109	25.17f	133	25.12	159, 162, 167
18.21–26	273	25.23	132	25.13	157
18.21	277	25.25ff	133	25.15	147
18.25	277, 286	25.35ff	133	25.17	147
20	146	26.1	191	26.35	124
20.4ff	191				

II. NEW TESTAMENT

III. APOCRYPHA, PSEUDEPIGRAPHA AND RELATED LITERATURE

IV. QUMRAN WRITINGS

V. PHILO

VI. JOSEPHUS

VII. EARLY CHRISTIAN LITERATURE

VIII. RABBINIC LITERATURE

IX. GREEK AND ROMAN PROFANE AUTHORS

X. COLLECTED WORKS (INSCRIPTIONS, PAPYRI, ETC.)

INDEX OF GREEK, HEBREW AND LATIN WORDS DISCUSSED

GREEK WORDS

HEBREW WORDS

LATIN WORDS

INDEX OF MODERN AUTHORS

GENERAL INDEX

'fourth kingdom' 239, 244, 247, 302, 303, 306
'fourth philosophy' 64, 73, 74, 76–8, 79–99, 144–5, 293, 396, 402
   doctrines 81–3, 86, 90–9, 104, 107–18, 121, 122–3, 139–45
   newness 87, 89
   organization 86
freedom 81, 110–23, 136, 145
freedom movement, Jewish 313–17, 320–5, 326–30
   and priestly nobility 211
   continuity of 79, 83
   divisions within 42, 43, 44, 48–9, 51, 62–5, 74, 82–5, 374
   Josephus' views on 14, 16, 73, 77
   names for 24–5, 32, 40–75, 88–9
   self-descriptions 74–5
   need for religious basis 329–30
   organization 326, 329, 352
   social factors 387–8
   support for 324
   see also 'fourth philosophy' and Zealots

Gabriel (archangel) 235
Galen 32
Galilaeans and freedom movement 317
'Galilaeans' as description of freedom movement 56–9, 74
Galilee 56, 74, 316
Gamala 263, 266, 331
Gamaliel 78, 233, 293
games 319
Gamliel I, R. 342
Gamliel II, R. 182, 334
Gaul 387
genealogy 298–300
Gerasenes 374
Germania 387
Gessius Florus 14, 34, 85, 137, 208, 285, 345, 355–8, 361, 363
'gibbor' 292
gifts from non-Jews, prohibition against 205, 206
Gischala 374
God
   and the desert 252, 253
   anger 245
   as warlord 271–2, 273, 274
   co-operation with see under last times (hastening of)
   doctrine of sole rule see under Zealots (doctrine)
   jealousy see his zeal

Kingdom of 91–4, 104
   see also eschatology and last times
names of 67, 94–8
   writing 57
philosophers' ideas of 61
zeal/jealousy 62, 146–7, 149, 177, 182–3, 393–4
Goets see Deceivers
Gog 248, 277, 299, 302
Gorgias 272
Gorion 367
Gorion b. Joseph 370
Greeks 274
   culture see Hellenistic culture
   language 201, 203–5, 206–7, 319
guerrilla warfare 41, 43, 255, 336–7
guilt 296
   see also expiation

Haberim 140, 334
Hadrian 49, 52
Halakoth, the eighteen 189–90, 193, 200–6 passim, 359
Haman 305
Hanania b. Hezekiah b. Garon 359
handicaps, people with 278
Hanina b. Antigonus, R. 309
Hanina b. Gamliel II, R. 219
Hanina b. Hama, R. 161
Hanina b. Teradion, R. 268, 269
Hanania, R. 203
Hannas see Ananus b. Ananus
Hannibal/Hanniboschet see Annibas
Hanukkah (Chanukah), feast of 207
Hasidim 68, 152, 153, 187, 210, 224, 350
Hasmonaeans 68, 167, 172, 188, 192, 257, 315
   and high-priesthood 153–4
   Essenes and 82, 211
   Herod and 41, 189, 318
   Josephus and 6, 8, 154, 300
   opposition to 211
   prophecy about 236
   'robbers' and 317
   see also Maccabees
Hazael 148
Hebrew 204–5, 206
'Heimarmene' 243
Helbo, R. 124
Helkias 353
Hellenistic culture/Hellenization 45, 192, 204, 318–19, 322, 324
   see also ruler (cult of)
Herod I 29, 41, 101, 102, 191, 193, 257–9, 292, 313–25, 358